REFORMATION FROM BELOW:
Looking at Münster Anabaptism Anew
Through Korean Minjung Theology

Youjin Chung

Foreword by Dion A. Forster

WIPF & STOCK · Eugene, Oregon

Wipf and Stock Publishers
199 W 8th Ave, Suite 3
Eugene, OR 97401

Reformation From Below
Looking at Münster Anabaptism Anew Through Korean Minjung Theology
By Chung, Youjin and Foster, Dion A.
Copyright © 2021 APTS Press All rights reserved.
Softcover ISBN-13: 978-1-6667-3488-1
Hardcover ISBN-13: 978-1-6667-9136-5
eBook ISBN-13: 978-1-6667-9137-2
Publication date 9/13/2021
Previously published by APTS Press, 2021

This edition is a scanned facsimile of the original edition published in 2021.

TABLE OF CONTENTS

Endorsement   v

Foreword   ix

Introduction   1

PART 1   37
Re-Reading the Reformation from Below
- Chapter 1 - The Radical Reformation   38
- Chapter 2 - Re-Reading Anabaptism from the Radical Reformation   73

PART 2   95
Re-Reading the Radical Reformers as Being-in-the-Common People
- Chapter 3 – Profiles of the Radical Reformers   96
- Chapter 4 – Profiles of the Radical Reformers   135
- Chapter 5 – Profiles of the Radical Reformers   161

PART 3   197
Re-Reading Korean Minjung Theology as Being-in-the-Korean-Minjung
- Chapter 6 – Korean Minjung Theology as the Keyhole to the Radical Reformation   198
- Chapter 7 – Contextualization of Korean Minjung Theology   231
- Chapter 8 – Profiles of Four Key Korean Minjung Theologians   273
- Chapter 9 – Profiles of Four Key Korean Minjung Theologians   307

PART 4   335
Re-Reading Münster Anabaptism from Korean
Minjung Theology
    Chapter 10 – Another Look at the Anabaptist   336
        Kingdom of Münster
    Chapter 11 - Profiles of the Münster Reformers   347
    Chapter 12 – Profiles of the Münster Minjung: 379
        Beyond the Radical, Reactionary, and Eclectic

PART 5 – Conclusion   401
    Chapter 13 - Re-Reading Münster Anabaptism as the   402
    Minjung-Messiah Interplay

Bibliography   409

ENDORSEMENT

A critical, creative, and constructive work that bridges the history and theology of the Radical Reformation with the Korean Minjung Theology. This book revisits the concept of minjung or ordinary people as the subjects of history from the perspectives of history from below, mission from the margins, and the underside of Reformation. For these reasons, I highly recommend this book, which provides excellent insights into the reformation of Christianity and the transformation of society today.

Rev. Dr Jooseop Keum
Distinguished Professor of World Christianity
Presbyterian University and Theological Seminary
Seoul, South Korea

In this book, Youjin Chung, creatively reconstructs the 16th century Radical Anabaptist theological history from the lens of the Korean Minjung Theology of solidarity and suffering. He attempts to generate a counter-history of the tragic Münster Anabaptism through a responsible hermeneutical lens. In the process, the book tries to give voice to both the powerful and less powerful, the victors and victims. It is a history that seeks to empower common people engaged in the struggle for justice not only in the Korean but other contexts as well. I heartly recommend this book to the wider public.

Professor Henry Mbaya
Faculty of Theology
University of Stellenbosch, South Africa

In *Reformation from Below: Looking at Münster Anabaptism Anew Through Korean Minjung Theology,* Youjin Chung offers a creative interpretation of the 16th century Radical Reformation, and particularly, Münster Anabaptism, by looking at these related movements through the lens of 20th century Korean Minjung theology. Chung's skillfully written and informed attempt to do "history from below" by highlighting the contributions of common people rather than the elite offers the reader rich insights into the both the Radical Reformation and Minjung Theology. Through careful analysis of the key figures that helped shaped these seemingly disparate movements, Chung is able to present more positive assessments of Thomas Münster and Münster Anabaptism than most previous scholars have allowed. Although Chung does not develop the implications of his study for Pentecostalism, this book might stimulate Pentecostal responses to his descriptions of Münster Anabaptism and Minjung theology. Additionally, Chung's book could encourage Pentecostals, not many of whom have been considered "wise" or "powerful" by "worldly standards" (1 Cor. 1:26), to write "history from below" as they produce their own histories.

Robert Menzies
Director of the
Asian Center of Pentecostal Theology
Kunming, China

Dr. Chung's book is highly recommended for anybody interested in the history of Anabaptism. By looking at the grassroots of the Radical Reformation, one which takes into consideration the socio- political, economic and religious experiences of the 'common' folk people and peasants, Chung not only does an excellent job in showing the complex interplay of the 1525 Peasants War, the rise of Anabaptism and the Radical Reformation in its totality, but also in turning the focus away from mainstream historical accounts of the Reformation that have predominantly focused on figures like Luther, Calvin or Zwingli. His addition of Korean Minjung theology as a means of re-reading Münster

Anabaptism as a harmonious movement between the 'common people' and their representatives is particularly intriguing and helps to bring a larger overview of how the Church, as a history of the faithful, unfolds throughout time and within various cultures.

Prof. Dr. Peter De Mey
Vice-Dean for International Relations Research Unit Systematic Theology and the Study of Religions Centre for Ecumenical Research
Faculty of Theology and Religious Studies
Leuven, Belgium

In this fine and in-depth study, Youjin Chung provides a fresh perspective – through the lens of Korean Minjung theology – on the 16th century Radical Reformation, and in particular Münster Anabaptism. Drawing on a methodological level on the emphasis on "a history from below" or "a people's history of Christianity," this book offers a rich contribution that will enhance future discussions on the topic.

Münster and Minjung combines a historical and constructive approach in an informative and creative way, and as such serves the project of a critical re-reading of Reformation historiography well. Highly recommended!

Robert Vosloo
Professor in the Department of Systematic Theology and Ecclesiology
Stellenbosch University, South Africa

We are thankful to Dr. Chung for challenging us to think differently and pointing out some of the weaknesses of the inherited history, and helping us to understand "people's history of Christianity." I hope we will be profoundly challenged by Dr. Chung's creative imaginations and thoughts. I am sure readers will be provoked and gained new insights for the construction of a better common future.

Prof. Wati Longchar
Dean, Program for Theology and Cultures in Asia (PTCA)

My friend and colleague, Dr. Youjin Chung has crafted a wonderful work that will challenge the elitist versions of church history, which are often trapped by standard Western narratives. The involvement of traditional Korean cultural worldviews and Minjung versions of church history in this re-reading of key events in the Reformation period of the church will encourage fresh voices from the margins. The successful publication of this work will embolden other scholars from the Global South to remain grounded in their own cultural environment while contributing to the continuing global theological dialogue.

Tham Wan Yee
President, Asia Pacific Theological Seminary

FOREWORD

The writing of any history is a complex task. Whose stories get told? What sources are used to construct a particular historical narrative? What are the power relationships that contributed towards the construction of particular historical narratives instead of others? Why are some narratives given a higher qualitative value than others?

In contemporary historical scholarship there is an important focus upon unearthing and telling "people's histories". Such projects are predicated upon an ideological commitment to "re-read" the events and historical sources of historical narratives, and of course to include new perspectives and new sources, to tell a different story or focus on a different element in the telling of the story. In church history, and the history of Christianity, such approaches are described variously as liberative, de-colonial, contextual, or social histories (among others). The re-telling of history from differing perspectives invites the reader to adopt a different vantage point in her or his understanding of persons and events that constitute the narrative. This has the possibility to unlock new meaning, to ask deeper and more critical questions, and to gain a greater appreciation for the complexity of the task of the historian. Of course, it can also create space for silenced persons to speak, and marginalised communities to be seen.

Dr. Youjin Chung invites us into such a process as he seeks to "re-read" the histories of the Anabaptist Münster traditions through the hermeneutic lens of Korean Minjung Theology. He is uniquely qualified to undertake this task given his own theological tradition, his cultural heritage, and his academic training. All of these elements serve to enrich his scholarly contribution in this text.

This book poses some important methodological questions for scholars in the field of church history. A primary question is, "To what extent should Christian history give the ordinary people their voice?"

His contention is that it is the responsibility of the academic Church historian to seek to identify, listen to, and present the voices of the "ordinary faithful" in their research.

Of course, such a task is not without some challenges. It is laden with power—the power of the academic historian, the power of the analytical tools, and the power of the present and absent sources that construct the narratives. If such a task is not undertaken with care, self-awareness, and scholarly rigour it could unknowingly present a distorted view of the persons and events under consideration. One way in which the academic historian can guard against such a mistake is by presenting their commitments, presuppositions, and intentions with transparency and clarity. In this case, Dr. Chung has chosen to adopt a 'Minjung optic' for his task. By doing so he acknowledges that all histories are written by persons within their own social, cultural, and ideological settings. Consequently, what they write stems from both known and unknown premises. Each of these elements play a role in shaping what is read, or not read, who is included, and who is excluded, and the value that is attached to sources that are present, or not present in the research journey. By adopting a 'Minjung optic' Dr. Chung is signalling to his readers that he is making some important choices related to his research methodology and the analysis that results from his engagement with historical sources. In this case, he undertakes to revisit interpretations of the Radical Reformation and Anabaptist histories from the perspectives of the 'ordinary faithful'. There are many fine histories that focus on major figures in these historical narratives. Their thoughts, words and actions were recorded (because they were prominent persons), and in the centuries since they have been engaged and presented in varying forms by numerous historians for various purposes. Dr. Chung, however, aims to ask what a reading 'from below' might add to the dominant narratives of Radical Reformation and Anabaptist histories.

One of the more creative elements that emerges in Dr. Chung's project is the notion of the "guru-avatar" dialectic. In this study the guru-avatar metaphorically represents the notion of "reinterpretation" and "double transformation" that a history from below introduces. One possibility that he highlights is that in the dialectical interchange of reinterpretation, a history from below can reconfigure both what we regard as history, and so how history is re-told. As you will see, he argues that this has both narrative and methodological implications for future historians in this field.

I found it fascinating to read Dr. Chung's manuscript. It invited me to revisit both my understanding of the histories of Anabaptist traditions, and my understanding of how church historical research is undertaken. I commend his commitment to focus upon the 'ordinary faithful' in the re-telling of important historical events. I do so, first, because it has the possibility of treating history with a measure of ethical responsibility. History is made up of individuals and communities who lived and acted within various contexts. Some are remembered, and some are not. Some are remembered in ways that celebrate their lives and contributions, while others are ignored, misrecognized, or even vilified. An approach to history that asks honest and important questions about these choices in credible and rigorous ways ultimately serves historical scholarship. Second, I commend his approach to you since Dr. Chung's doctoral supervisor, the late Professor Mary-Anne Plaatjies van Huffel, encouraged her students to ask difficult and critical questions about historians and the constructions of histories. Prof. Plaatjies van Huffel, who passed away very suddenly in the 19th of May 2020, was well known for her use of Foucauldian post-structuralist approaches to church history. I am certain that Mary-Anne would have endorsed Dr. Chung's project enthusiastically! Hence, I am grateful to do so on her behalf. I celebrate Dr. Chung's scholarly contribution and recognise the important work that is represented in this text. I appreciate his commitment to echoing the voices and perspectives the 'ordinary faithful' in his engagement with history, and thank him for the way in which his academic progress honours the work and guidance of our late colleague Prof. Mary-Anne Plaatjies van Huffel.

Prof. Dr. Dion A. Forster
Head of Department, Systematic Theology and Ecclesiology
Director, Beyers Naudé Centre for Public Theology,
University of Stellenbosch, South Africa

Introduction

Background of Research

Recently, many church historians[1] have preferred to define church not as "the hierarchical-institutional-bureaucratic corporation," but rather as "the laity and the ordinary faithful people" (Janz 2007: xiii). Nonetheless, it seems evident that church history (or the history of Christianity) has for too long given greater concern to one small segment of "the great deeds of great men" than to the vast majority of the simple folk (Janz 2007: xiii). Despite its need and worth for studying, this has restricted the study of church history almost exclusively to the religion of 'elites', whether spiritual, intellectual, or power elites. Its result is the prevalence of a one-sided approach to theology, dogma, and institution centered on a few great men. What has always been left out of it is the mass of 'ordinary faithful'.

There is an increasing call for reflection about this conventional pattern of church history. The elitism of historical investigation has been greeted with an increase in scholarly questioning and criticism, especially in terms of a balanced history of Christianity. And it even requires a new approach—the so-called 'history from below' or 'grassroots history' that aims at "rescuing the [ordinary] Christian people from their historic anonymity" (Janz 2007:xv). This new quest has become the great challenge to the sixteenth-century Reformation historiography in particular, where the great men like Martin Luther, Huldrych Zwingli, and John Calvin had played important roles as the champions of the times.

The crucial point here is whether this new approach (i.e., a people's history of Christianity) can offer something decidedly different from the

---

[1] Among them are R. Horsley, V. Burrus, D. Krueger, D.E. Bornstein, P. Matheson, A. Porterfield, and M.F. Bednarowski, whose works are well represented in the seven volume series, "A People's History of Christianity."

old one and thus shift its center of gravity from the great men to the common folk. Indeed, if the commoner's role can be relocated at the center stage and not merely playing second fiddle to the great men, this may lead to a new and more balanced version of the history of Christianity—one that provides a more adequate and healthy perspective that is redressing an unnecessary imbalance.

In one sense, a people's history of Christianity raises a critical question among many church historians—"Whose Reformation was it?" (Matheson 2007:2). This is followed by another one—"Does not a balanced perspective require that the Reformation could have stirred the blood of the ordinary people as well as the great men?" Thus, it seems no longer as convincing to think that the majority simple folks just sat down passively when the vast religious upheaval was dawning before their very eyes. Rather, it is plausible that, they must have felt a sense of urgency to ride the wave of such new changes—the Reformation—for their own rights and freedom. However, the questions still remain: "What part, then, did the ordinary people have in shaping the Reformation?" and "Did they really dare to blaze a new trail in the course of the Reformation?" (Matheson 2007:4-5). In this light, a way of looking at Christianity's past from the vantage point of the ordinary folk may alert one to a different path—that the common people themselves actively participated in and even contributed to the Reformation as one of the leading agents of the history.

In another sense, this approach of history from below opens a new portrayal of "the troublemakers, the excluded, and the heretics, those defined by conventional history as the losers" (Janz 2007: xiv-xv). This notion, in fact, throws new light on the left wing of the Reformation in general and the Anabaptists in particular, who had been bitterly persecuted and discriminated against by those of the official (or magisterial) Reformers. On the surface, it seems contradictory that a people's history of Christianity would deal with this small number of mavericks, rather than the majority of ordinary people. Indeed, the radicals of the Reformation were actually a minority group, despite their wide variety of clusters. It was rather the official Reformers who held a majority in the whole course of the Reformation. What then has the small army of radicals to do with the Christian masses?

Their close connection with the Peasants' War of 1525 could be a hint as to this question. It is hard to deny that there was the dynamic interplay between the majority of the simple folk (peasants) and the minority of the radicals in the sixteenth-century Reformation. Both had a great impact on each other, being advised, counseled, and encouraged by each other when they protested the existing religious as well as political authority. To them, this protest was about justice under the name of "pure Gospel," which required a complete change (Blickle 1992:159). By seeing "Christ as their captain, as the Christ of the poor, they denounced the oppressive princes, bishops, and magistrates" as nothing but the anti-Christ (Matheson 2007:7). This convinced both of them to see their protest as a "religiously legitimated revolt" (Snyder 2006:554). From it a new interpretation came into being—one that viewed the Peasants' War as the culmination of the Communal Reformation[2] between the simple folk and the radicals. The implicitation was that one can understand the Reformation best by seeing not only from the centers, but also from the margins; not only from the Magisterial Reformers, but also from the radicals (Matheson 2007:11).

The new scholarly approach, then, has greeted the results even to the extent of linking the Peasants' War to the "Radical Reformation"[3] as a form of the Communal Reformation (Stayer 1991:7). Thanks to such scholarly works, the importance of what the common folk thought and believed is beginning to be virtually recognized. Alongside its religious

---

[2]This term, "the Communal Reformation" is coined by Peter Blickle, who interprets the Peasants' War of 1525 as a revolution of the common men. He rightly sees that there was a close connection between the early Reformation and the German Peasants' War of 1525. By acknowledging the common men as both the lower and upper middle classes in towns (burghers) and the peasants in the countryside, Blickle prefers to call the early Reformation as the "Communal Reformation" in its dialectical unification between the rural peasants (laborers) and urban burghers (artisans) to promote Christianization of the social and political order if need be by means of a revolution (Blickle 1981:183-85).

[3]Within Christian history, there have been scholarly debates as to how to categorize and name the sixteenth-century radical wings of the Reformation, centering particularly in Anabaptism. Among them, G.H. Williams has proposed the Radical Reformation as "a collective designation for all those groups of religious innovators who remained in neither the Roman Catholic nor mainline Protestant churches in the sixteenth-century Reformation context" (Williams and Mergal 1957:19-38). Roland H. Bainton, on the other hand, has preferred calling it a tendency—"It was so amorphous, varied and vague that it can better be described as a tendency than as a movement" (Bainton 1965:123), Timothy George has considered it as a tremendous movement of spiritual and ecclesial renewal that "posed a thoroughgoing critique of the *corpus christianum* in both its mainline Protestant and Tridentine Catholic mutations" (George 1988:252).

appeal, this new approach saw the concept of divine justice as a focal point for the peasants' aspirations, which not only inspired and informed, but also motivated and legitimated their revolts (Stayer 1991:95).

To the simple peasants, it was absurd to separate social justice from divine justice for they are two sides of the same coin (Matheson 2007:9, Stayer 2007:191). Furthermore, the sermons and tracts of the Radical Reformers made these ordinary peasants wise enough to become conscientized to their oppressive reality, so that they committed themselves to change the unjust status quo with the awareness of the necessary struggles (Matheson 2007:260-61). This radical awareness, which was mingled with the dynamics of apocalyptic thought of the times, soon turned into the divine justice, which brought with them new hope for the establishment of a New Jerusalem wherein they would be liberated from current oppression and corruption (Matheson 2007:260). The more they had struggled for a better church and society, the more they had been convinced that, if the Christian gospel would mirror God's will for justice, then it must go together with concrete socioeconomic and political issues (Blickle 1992:100, 153, Stayer 2007:202-203).

Given this approach, the *Twelve Articles*,[4] the most widespread and popular statement during the Peasants' War, best preserved the peasant's demands and aspirations (Blickle 1981:195-96). For the basis of all these articles was "to hear the Gospel and live accordingly" (Blickle 1992:100, Scott and Scribner 1991:253). Their struggle for justice, in this sense, negated the conventional interpretations in at least two ways. First, it freed the peasants from the problematic image as being the crusading rebels who were only interested in social outcomes without passionately engaging with faith in God—that is, the underpinning of the historical-materialist analysis of the Marxists (Stayer 1991:60). Second, it no longer regarded the ordinary peasants as the passive recipients of orders from on high; but rather it gave equal emphasis to how these simple folks had

---

[4]The Articles, as the manifesto of the Peasants' War of 1525, presented "a rejection of serfdom, an affirmation of the traditional common property of villagers and a criticism of paying tithes and rents" (Scott and Scribner 1991:252). In this way, it gave the peasants justification for their revolt, following the divine law. Its authorship is attributed to Lotzer from Memmingen (Blickle 1998:59-60).

actively reshaped the new order as the willing participants in the (radical) Reformation (Matheson 2007:274-76).

Notably, these struggles for divine justice by the ordinary peasants ended in failure and this changed the whole course of the Reformation. First, in the wake of their defeat in the Peasants' War, the center of gravity had been rapidly moving from the simple peasants to the princes and theologians (Scott 1989:114, Stayer 2007:192). Second, as a result, characteristics of the post-Peasants' War became explicitly favorable toward the powerful elites over the powerless peasants (Blickle 1981:185). As such, this led to the so-called "Babylonian Captivity of the Reformation by the powerful," while the ordinary people began to lose their vital role and were completely excluded from its course. It eventually quickened the birth of the "Magisterial Reformation,"[5] the Reformation from above, which primarily served the needs and priorities of the powerful elites (Stayer 2007:192). However, this new scholarship does not consider it the end of the Reformation from below. According to it, the bottom-up struggle for divine justice had continued to express itself in the radicals of the Reformation and nowhere was this clearer than among the Anabaptists, who just began to appear after the Peasants' War of 1525 (Stayer 1991:91). Since it was the Anabaptists who had rekindled its flickering anti-elitist notion of divine justice, and were closely linked to the "Radical Reformation" against the "Magisterial Reformation," and since they were "the troublemakers, the excluded, the heretics, and the losers," this approach rather calls for the need to look critically at the Reformation from below—that is, a people's history of Christianity.

By acknowledging the need for history from below, this book sets out to reestablish key figures and events in the sixteenth-century "Radical Reformation," with the Peasants' War of 1525 as central in the rising of the Anabaptist movement, which was an open challenge to both the

---

[5] Here, "the Magisterial Reformation" is a technical term that represents the sixteenth-century Reformation by the official or major Reformers, including Martin Luther, John Calvin, and Huldrych Zwingli, who believed that any kind of reforming works must be done either under the direction of or with the approval of secular rulers or civil authorities. Thus, it stood as a diametrical opposite of the Radical Reformers, such as Thomas Müntzer, Andreas Karlstadt, and the Anabaptists, whose concerns were directed to immediate and radical changes of the Church, emphasizing the complete separation of Church and State.

ruling elites and the so-called Reformers of the "Magisterial Reformation."

Research Questions

The main concern here is how traditions might have influenced one another over time both critically and creatively. Especially, this book enquires as to what extent the twentieth-century Korean Minjung Theology[6] stands in the tradition of the sixteenth-century Radical Reformation rather than the Magisterial Reformation. In order to answer this question, this book attends to the following sub-questions:

- To what extent should Christian history give the ordinary people their voice?
- Just who are 'the ordinary faithful'? Is the term applicable to the radicals of the Reformation whom the Magisterial Reformers condemned as mavericks, dissidents, outsiders and rebels, and even to the "minjung"[7] in the twentieth-century theological movement in Korea?
- Can a perspective from below become a catalyst to set the Anabaptists free from the yoke of the violent *Schwärmer* (enthusiasts)?

---

[6]Minjung (民衆) Theology is a Korean contextual theology born in the 1970s under the military dictatorship of General Park. It is a theology of the *minjung* (common people) whose identity grew out of Christian experiences in the political struggle for justice and human rights. Thus, Minjung Theology has primarily attended to a political hermeneutics of the Gospel based on the Korean reality and tried to provide a relevant theology in the Korean context. More details on it, including the meaning of *minjung* and its unique characteristics, will be discussed in later parts of this book.

[7]Minjung (民衆) is a Korean word composed of two Chinese characters. As "min (民)" means 'people' and "jung (衆)," means 'mass,' combining the two can simply be translated into English as "the mass of people" (Moon 1985:1). Yet, Minjung theologians reject any such simple definition. Rather they prefer to see the *minjung* as a living reality in which their stories and their biographies can only be an effective way of expression (Kim 1981:185). Here the term *'minjung'* is used as the equivalent of 'ordinary, common people' or 'simple folk', but it carries with it thick descriptions in its dynamic and contextual nature. More details on its significance and meanings will be discussed in later parts of this book.

- Is Münster Anabaptism[8] a unique phenomenon, or is it a paradigm for the common people (*minjung*) and their reformation?
- Is Münster Anabaptism a tombstone *(han)*, or is it a birth place *(dan)* for the common people (*minjung*) and their movement?[9]
- How does a people's history of Christianity offer a comprehensive and responsible alternative to the sixteenth-century Radical Reformation and the twentieth-century theological movement in Korea?
- Can such a people's history of Christianity enable one to express and find a more dynamic and balanced version of Christianity from the sixteenth-century Radical Reformation and the twentieth-century theological movement in Korea?

The answers to these questions may vary, but it may well be the impending task for a more dynamic and balanced interpretation of the sixteenth-century Radical Reformation and the twentieth-century theological movement in Korean Christianity. Significance is best clarified by showing how these answers complement each other in altering and rehabilitating—without destroying—the one-sided picture of the sixteenth-century Radical Reformation, and particularly the Anabaptist Kingdom of Münster, which had long been taken for granted as a mutated aberration of the Reformation in its historiography.

---

[8]Here Münster Anabaptism represents the Anabaptist rule at the city of Münster in 1534-1535, which is notorious for its violent and militant activities. In this book, the problem and controversy on this historical event serves as the keyhole to look at the sixteenth-century Radical Reformation afresh as part of people's history of Christianity.

[9]*Han* and *dan* are Korean words which have thick meanings. Simply speaking, *han* is an accumulated bitterness of the Korean *minjung* (common people), while *dan* is the way of cutting off this bitterness, namely the resolution of *han*. The significance of such concepts will be dealt with carefully in later parts of this book.

Justification

Revisionist Interpretations of the Radical Reformation and Anabaptism

The growing scholarly willingness to discuss the mutual influence of revolutionaries and the non-resistant in the sixteenth-century Radical Reformation reveals that the Swiss origins of Anabaptism, which have been widely believed in Anabaptist historiography, need to be reexamined. It shifts attention to the heterogeneity in Anabaptism, emphasizing that there is not a mono-genesis but a poly-genesis of Anabaptism, including the Swiss, the South-German and the Dutch (Stayer, Packull and Depperman 1975:83-121). Focusing on this plurality of Anabaptism, this scholarship, called "the revisionist view," casts new light on the Peasants' War of 1525 as a pivotal event, leading to the political as well as religious reform (Stayer 2007:191-211). It elevates the close connection between the Reformation, the Peasants' War, and Anabaptism, holding communal, anticlerical, and radical aspects as the common denominators. This, therefore, merits special attention to the revisionist view on Anabaptism presented particularly by Peter Blickle, Hans-Jürgen Goertz, James M. Stayer, and Karl-Heinz Kirchhoff. Following is a brief discussion of the view that each one espoused.

First, Peter Blickle challenges the traditional view of the Reformation in terms of its absolutizing the role of the elite groups, who held most of the ecclesiastical and political power already. He has drawn needed attention to the crucial role played by 'the common men', the neglected agent of the Reformation (Blickle 1992:184). In his view, the religious beliefs of the leading Reformers, especially Martin Luther, were certainly a factor in the Reformation, but a growing awareness of natural law and communal rights were even stronger forces for the rise of Protestantism (Blickle 1992:153). Thus, he asserts that, in its most original and undistorted form, the Reformation was a communal event in which the common men of both urban and rural areas turned the theological ideas of a few Reformers into a vast social movement (Blickle 1992: xiv). He calls this authentic Reformation of the commoners the Communal Reformation, a term that provides him a keyhole insight into the whole process of the Reformation (Blickle 1998:147). By demonstrating the principle of communalism as an ideological and political reality for both city and countryside, Blickle has unfolded his idea on how the Peasants' War of 1525 transformed into the revolution of the common men as the kernel of the Communal Reformation (Blickle 1992:184).

Second, it is Hans-Jürgen Goertz who poses a critical question as to whether a purely theological reading satisfactorily captures all aspects in the Reformation and the Anabaptist movement in particular. By observing a great gap separating theology from everyday life, Goertz argues that the primary animator of what became the Reformation was "anticlericalism" (Goertz 1994:499-520). From this, he begins to connect the Reformation anticlericalism to the apparent diversity of Anabaptism as the important social and religious nexus. Goertz claims that, from its inception, Anabaptism participated in and contributed to this anticlericalism (Goertz 1996:36-67). The term "anticlericalism" has a special meaning for Goertz, just as the term Communal Reformation has for Blickle. It serves him as an essential touchstone for Anabaptist interpretation. From it Goertz derives his three-fold revisionist outlook on Anabaptism, which is antithetical to the previous dominant interpretation. He refuses any notion of (1) Anabaptist single origins, (2) its universal characteristic of non-violence; and (3) its unified leadership, program, or theology (Goertz 1996:10-11). Instead, he draws much attention to variations and diversity in Anabaptism, while maintaining a social-protest penchant as its underlying commonality among them (Goertz 1979:186, 1982:15). In his emphasis on anticlericalism as a major motivational force that fueled the early Anabaptist protest, Goertz turns a pure normative model of Anabaptism on its head.

Third, James M. Stayer also counters the prevailing Anabaptist historiography with this challenging question—"Was there a unified, pacifist non-resistance among the sixteenth-century Anabaptists?" (Stayer 1996:118). His significant contribution on this topic lies in his demonstration of the degree of disagreement over the use of the sword. Starting with the early Protestant teaching on 'the sword', Stayer uncovers the variety of Anabaptist responses to it, based on these four different positions—(1) the "crusader" (Müntzer, Hut, and the

Melchiorites),[10] (2) the "real-politician" (Zwingli and Hubmaier), (3) the "apolitical moderate" (Luther and Sattler), and (4) the "apolitical radical" (the Swiss Brethren and Anabaptism as a whole) (Stayer 1972:25-90). This typology comes with his clear recognition of the great diversity of thought on the sword in early Anabaptism (Stayer 1972:335). Thus, his conclusion is that there was no uniform doctrine on the sword among the early Anabaptists, even though they all eventually "arrived at the same kind of radical apoliticism" (Stayer 1972:34).

Although this encompasses the fact that there were both non-resistant and violent Anabaptists, Stayer's view is more concerned with the latter case. Here, he shows that even the Swiss Brethren were not firmly committed to non-resistance until "Schleitheim" settled the matter (Stayer 1972:91-132) and that Hans Hut's view of the sword was an interim ethic, a temporal non-resistance presupposing the use of the sword on the Day of Judgment (Stayer 1972:189-202). In Münster Anabaptism, readiness to participate in violence was widespread to the extent that "the revolutionary group was in the majority, while the non-resistant were the dissenters" (Stayer 1972:227-282). In this attempt, Stayer makes corrections in the direction of the essential qualities of the early Anabaptist teaching on the sword by an explicit recognition of the diverse and sophisticated spectrum from apoliticism to radicalism, from non-resistance to violence (Stayer 1972).

Without doubt, Blickle's, Goertz's, and Stayer's revisionist outlooks on Anabaptism have established the critical overview of the previous interpretations on the sixteenth-century Radical Reformation and particularly Anabaptism. This opens the mind to new and fruitful perspectives that Anabaptist research must pursue in a particular fashion. It can hardly be history of theological ideas as propounded by a few eminent leaders; rather it needs to be social history or social biography of the ordinary faithful people. Thus is created a new perspective to look at the Peasants' War and Anabaptism from a lens of the common people (Stayer 1988:99-135, Goertz 1996:10-11). Here, Anabaptism is seen as a continuation of the revolution of the common men for political, social, economic, and lastly military goals, sanctioned

---

[10] The term "Melchiorites" refers to the followers of Melchior Hoffman, one of the leading figures in the sixteenth-century Radical Reformation.

and consolidated after 1525 by adherents of believer's baptism (Snyder 2006:553-54). In this light, sixteenth-century Anabaptism (seen from the revisionist views) demands a different approach, one that entails the exposition of the life and faith not only of the leaders, but also of the common folk, who have rendered the Reformation communal, anticlerical, and radical as a whole.

These revisionist views on Anabaptism, perhaps apart from its original plan, sketch a new and impressive picture of the Anabaptist Kingdom in Münster. In fact, the Anabaptist theocracy that arose in Münster in 1534 and 1535 exhibits many of these characteristics. In its brief description, Münster had initiated a typical form of local reformation; burghers and evangelical preachers had combined traditions of urban communalism with anticlerical sentiments, and the demand for a biblically based religion in which the common people could play an active role (Moller 1972:90-103, Ozment 1980).

Münster's reformation was greeted with radical religious ideas, promoted by the immigrant Dutch Melchiorites, who primarily belonged to the suffering lower classes (Mellink 1953:1-19 quoted by Stayer 1975:115). Under the spell of the apocalyptic excitement, the Anabaptist political takeover of Münster in 1534 spurred them to undertake radical changes to both the city's political order and religious life (Deppermann 1975:115). In this process, the militant Melchiorite influence in Münster became strengthened and even legitimized, although such revolutionary mood threw Anabaptism into the most dangerous crisis of its history (Bakker 1986:111). At any rate, the revisionist views give the impression that the Anabaptist Kingdom of Münster was a vast melting pot where the communal, anticlerical, and radical Anabaptism were intermingled as a separate-but-integrated whole.

Fourth, Karl-Heinz Kirchhoff provides yet another interesting interpretation. He regards Münster Anabaptism not as "the Protestantism of the poor" but as a broad popular movement of all classes (Kirchhoff 1973:93-226 quoted by Stayer 1986:281). This significant revision comes from his systematic study of the records of Anabaptist property, which was confiscated following the Bishop's conquest of the city (Kirchhoff 1973:2-13 quoted by Stayer 1986:282). Thus, Kirchhoff's perspective stands closer to that of W. J. Kuhler than to that of Karel Vos and of A. F. Mellink. Kuhler sees the Melchiorites as the apocalyptic enthusiasts, not as the social revolutionaries, so as to assume the existence of peaceful Anabaptists in Münster Anabaptism (Kuhler 1932:97-101, Grosheide 1938:75-81 both quoted by Deppermann 1975:115); whereas Vos and Mellink regard them as the suffering lower classes from outside, so that Münster Anabaptism owes nothing to an earlier peaceful Anabaptism (Vos 1980:85-91, Mellink 1953:327 quoted by Stayer 1986:263). By analyzing the social structure of the native residents in Münster who had participated in Münster Anabaptism, Kirchhoff proposes that there was a peaceful Anabaptist congregation before, during, and after the Münster revolt (Kirchhoff 1970:357-70, 1973:42 quoted by Deppermann 1975:116).

This careful study even leads Kirchhoff to a more sympathetic view to Münster Anabaptists and their leaders. To him, Anabaptist rule in Münster is seen as an *ad hoc* response to the emergency conditions of a defensive war and thereby its violence as a self-defense to protect themselves against the violent prince-bishop's troops (Kirchhoff 1962:77-170, 1970:360).[11] Kirchhoff's view is a direct challenge to the standard polemical history of Münster Anabaptism, which started from Hermann von Kerssenbrock, who was a partial eyewitness to the Anabaptist takeover of Münster (Kirchhoff 1970:358). As a result, it weakens the larger assumptions about the violent nature of Münster Anabaptism and thus helps to rehabilitate the portrait of Münster Anabaptists from diabolical monsters to simply ordinary sixteenth-century men and women who found themselves in extraordinarily dangerous circumstances (Kirchhoff 1962:77-170, Stupperich 1958:12).

The above four revisionist views on Anabaptism are not without significance. In one sense, they have rendered the very concept of revolution richly ambiguous in terms of illuminating the religious and socio-political dynamics of Münster in the 1530s. Also, they put Melchior Hoffman in an ambiguous light as a source of both peaceful and revolutionary Anabaptism (Packull 1985:146). But in another sense, these views are helpful in re-orienting overall stories of Münster

---

[11]This view, which considers the Münster' resistance as an act of self-defense, had actually been suggested by Robert Stupperich before Kirchhoff presented. It was Stupperich who had already acknowledged and elaborated this line of interpretation in advance (Stupperich 1958:12).

Anabaptism together with the political and military battles around it. Its subsequent effect has been to reduce a lurid light on Münster Anabaptism and begin to see it as part of the history of Anabaptism and of the Reformation. This even gives rise to the intriguing question of whether Münster Anabaptism can be seen as an extensive and subtle version of the popular Reformation, including both the revolutionary and the peaceful, the upper and the lower, and the native and the immigrant.

Several scholars, however, have taken issue with these revisionist views on Anabaptism, arguing that they seem to stretch or overstep the bounds of critical scholarship. These critics maintain that the first three revisionists simply overstate the importance of the Communal Reformation in Blickle's case (Scribner 1994), anticlericalism in Goertz's (Voolstra 1997), and radical apoliticism in Stayer's (Strübind 2004), as if they may find the single key to unlock the Reformation and Anabaptism proper. To critics, this one-size-fits-all solution is fundamentally flawed. They also argue that these overriding concerns lead into overgeneralization or oversimplification of the case. Thus, they criticized Blickle for magnifying the Swiss and South German example in his hasty generalization (Scribner 1994:199-207). Similarly, Goertz is blamed for overly reducing theology to sociology; in his strict socio-historical approach (according to them), he disintegrates the poly-thematic Anabaptist interpretation into mono-thematic factors, despite the fact that he succeeds in propagating a poly-genesis of Anabaptism (Voolstra 1997). And Stayer's typology on the sword (they contend) falls into the fallacy of the un-connectedness of many Anabaptist sects, giving a far more favourable portrait of the violent Anabaptists (Strübind 2004:297-313).

In a similar vein, Kirchhoff's revisionist view has come under criticism from other scholars. They attribute a main weakness of Kirchhoff's work to its simplicity of scope, that his study has conceived too exclusively a piece of local history of Münster (Oltmer and Schindling 1990:481 quoted by Haude 2000:3). Thus, Kirchhoff's presentation of the continuing importance of social hierarchy among Anabaptists in post-Anabaptist Münster receives little attention from other scholarship (Haude 1993:14). To critics, Kirchhoff's revision is just considered another key beside the existing ones, which are the

Communal Reformation of Blickle, anticlericalism of Goertz, and radical apoliticism of Stayer.

All in all, critics insist that these revisionist views on Anabaptism are not shared by them due to the revisionists' biased perspectives. In their eyes, the sieve that the revisionists chose to use is too small and narrow to appreciate Anabaptist dynamics. What these critics really wish, therefore, is to revise the revisionists' views (Snyder 2006:501).

Ironically, such growing criticisms against the revisionist view on Anabaptism necessitate its self-renewing. In other words, the challenge by critics becomes a salutary reminder for the need for the revisionist views to open to change—as *ecclesia semper reformanda*, so *ecclesia interpretationae semper reformanda*. In fact, those views on Anabaptism may overlook the potential problems of a one-sided socio-political interpretation, which eclipses its religious aspect, and vice versa. For example, each view too easily pushes its concern to resort to the idea of the Communal Reformation, anticlericalism, and radical apoliticism respectively under the pretext of building a more appropriate social history interpretation. Or, conversely this may shift its focus on an exclusively religious reading of the Radical Reformation, the very one it has undermined. Then the cycle of either/or distinction can be perpetuated through the operation of the charged anomaly of religion and science, of theology and social theory in general, and of the reformers and radicals, peasants and princes in particular.

In this sense, Korean Minjung Theology becomes a welcome collaboration to bridge the gap. In particular, the idea of the dialectic of *han* and *dan* in Korean Minjung Theology[12] may serve as a connecting link between the Magisterial and the Radical Reformation, the great and the common men, the legitimate and the bastard *(sic)* line of the Reformers, and the peaceful and revolutionary Anabaptists, holding both of them as the perpetrators as well as the victims of *han*. Here, *han* represents an accumulative feeling of suffering of the victims caused primarily by injustice and oppression, while *dan* signifies its resolution, namely the cutting-off of *han* (Suh 1983:65).

---

[12]The idea of *han* and *dan* is decisive to understand the nature of Korean Minjung Theology, so that this will be discussed separately in later parts of this book with more details.

In Korean Minjung Theology, the dialectic of *han* and *dan* has two dimensions. In one sense, *han* serves as a productive force of the victims, producing a righteous indignation against the perpetrators (Suh 1983:59). But in another sense, if left unchecked, once power is taken by the oppressed, *han* can also be used to oppress others so as to give rise to another *han*. Thus, they no longer are merely the victims acted upon, but rather are the perpetrators who repeat an unhealthy cycle of oppression of *han* (Suh 1981:64-5). This is why *dan* (cutting-off) is necessary, for it holds *han* in check so that *han* of the victims does not fall short of *han* of the perpetrators (Suh 1981:61, Lee 1994:154). In this light, the idea of the dialectic of *han* and *dan* in Korean Minjung Theology may bring positive contribution to the revisionist views on Anabaptism.

When applied to Anabaptism, this alerts one to the need for a shift of angle from either/or dualism to both/and chiasm, in which each party—the victims and the perpetrators—are inseparably joined together. For both stand in a direct connection not as contradictory but as complementary. Instead of seeing them in a binary fashion, the dialectic of *han* and *dan* opens the possibility in impossibility. That is, both parties have their own particularly distinctive contributions to play in transforming of self, community, and society as a whole.

Here, Korean Minjung Theology revisits the revisionist views on Anabaptism to 'revise' itself by embracing the idea of the dialectic of *han* and *dan*, which includes inner dynamics between the elites and the common men, the peaceful and the radical, and the sinners and "the sinned-against."[13] This is a critical and creative synthesis in order to reinterpret the sixteenth-century Radical Reformation from the perspective of the twentieth-century Korean Minjung Theology. In this collaboration, the sixteenth-century Radical Reformation and Anabaptist ethos of Christianity are not lost but rather honoured and explicitly incorporated. Thus, the revisionist views on Anabaptism (as seen from Korean Minjung Theology) can serve as the point of departure for looking anew at the sixteenth-century Radical Reformation—especially Münster Anabaptism.

---

[13] The term "sinned-against" is found in the works of Raymond Fung (1980:162-69, 1989:18-9), a Baptist Christian leader of Hong Kong. Fung once mentioned that the poor are not only sinners, but they are also the sinned-against—i.e., the victims of injustice and oppression (1989:162-69).

Anabaptist Kingdom of Münster and Korean Minjung Theology

Münster Anabaptism in 1534-1535 represents one of the worst violent and destructive scandals of the sixteenth-century Reformation (Mackay 2007:1). Why, then, should we take such the bizarre event into consideration? There are at least two reasons. One is ironically attributed to the impact of Anabaptist terror in Münster. From its inception, Anabaptism was not a welcomed guest to mainline Christianity. There was no place for Anabaptists, people considering them as "neither Catholics nor Protestants" (Klaassen 1981). And the Anabaptist Münster uprising 1534-1535 made their position even more precarious, giving them the 'scarlet letter' of fanatics and thereby giving their opponents a cause for action. The Anabaptist Münster Kingdom then met a tragic end under the banner of 'retributive justice'. In short, the Kingdom of Münster ended up as the Kingdom of Monster, where the violent 're-baptizers'[14] were perishing in their own karma.

But in another sense, the Anabaptist Münster event, despite (and perhaps because of) its fiasco, leaves open the possibility that it can be seen as a microcosm of the dialectic of *han* and *dan*. In Münster, there was a kaleidoscope of *han* (suffering) and *dan* (healing) between the common people and the radicals. Thus, it is too naive to attribute everything in the Anabaptist takeover of Münster to the so-called "bastard line *(sic)* of Radical Reformers," such as Thomas Müntzer, Hans Hut, Melchior Hoffman, and John Bockelson (Stayer 1972). To be sure, the picture was not merely one-sided. The real portrait of Münster Anabaptism was quite varied and dynamic, even to the extent of holding to the Communal Reformation, where both the common men and the radicals played a leading role in their dynamic correlation (Blickle 1998:178-88). This, then, includes the necessity for the critical and creative interplay between the two to be the key for reinterpreting Münster Anabaptism, embracing the idea of the dialectic of *han* and *dan*.

However, it would be equally inadequate to deny the central role of this bastard line *(sic)* of Radical Reformers. Although the way of their reforming activities is questionable, their significant impacts on the

---

[14] Anabaptists mean 're-baptizers' and this nickname was given them by the opponents in the pejorative sense.

common people in Münster (both practically and theologically), is undeniable. Furthermore, being simultaneously sinners (perpetrators) and the sinned-against (victims), these radicals were involved in this "Communal Reformation" as one of its leading agents. In this way, they left an indelible imprint on the Anabaptist Kingdom of Münster (both positively and negatively). This implies that, in Münster, they played the roles of the reactionaries as well as the radicals, the common men as well as the great men, and the sinned-against as well as the sinners who strove to bring *dan* into the *han*-ridden city. Here, Münster Anabaptism is a good case in point. Seen from Korean Minjung Theology, it is stressed as the microcosm of the Communal Reformation, which is dynamically interacting with the whole relational matrix with its rich diversity.

Methodology

Historical and Constructive Theological Approach

This book is a historical and constructive theological research. Its aim is to bring the two historical events—the sixteenth-century Radical Reformation and the twentieth century theological movement in Korea—in conversation with each other. In this sense, it differs from a historical analysis, which places two historical movements in comparative perspectives. Rather, it is interdisciplinary in its approach in terms of creating a positive connection between the two. To be more specific, there is a focus in it on specifying the historical interpretation as conceived from a theological vantage point. By shifting the emphasis from product to process (or conclusion to conversation), this approach is intended to offer a new way of talking about history with theology. It is about constructing an alternative history, or counter-history.[15] Or putting it differently, a historical and constructive theological approach endeavours to replace an either/or (i.e., either history or

---

[15]The term "counter-history" is from David Biale. According to him, "Counter-history is a type of revisionist historiography, but where the revisionist proposes a new theory or finds new facts, the counter-historian transvalues old ones." He does not deny that his predecessors' interpretation of history is correct as does the revisionist, but he rejects the completeness of that interpretation" (Biale 1982:7).

theology/product or process) with a both/and perspective through the critical and creative conversation between history and theology.

As such, a historical and constructive theological approach allows for no completeness and no essence in its favour of counter-history, a history being constructive. Yet this book as a historical research is concerned primarily with the complete and the essential. How then does such an approach sit within the historical research? From it emerges the need for constructive theology that is both self-critical and self-renewing in its conversation with history. In other words, counter-history presupposes constructive theology as its source, and vice versa. In this connection, constructive theology offers a promising direction for reconstructing history. Here, the recognition that constructive theology is a prelude to constructive history requires a close look at the genesis of constructive theology.

Constructive theology was born in 1975 at Vanderbilt University in the United States by a number of groups of theologians (Wyman 2017:312-3).[16] Calling themselves the "Workgroup in Constructive Christian Theology," they have committed to constructive theology as being the best pedagogical approach to today's Christian leaders and readers (Wyman 2017:313-4). In general, the history of constructive theology can be divided into three periods of development, roughly based on four textbooks written by the Workgroup (Wyman 2017:322) through which they also propagated this theology. Period 1—*Christian Today* and *Readings in Christian Theology* (published in 1982 and 1984, respectively) are critically liberal; Period 2—*Reconstructing Christian Theology* (in 1994) offers a more postmodern and contextual perspective, with particular attention to the liberation theology; and Period 3—*Constructive Theology* (in 2005) affirms the Workgroup's continued liberal/liberationist agenda, holding to critique of the tradition (Wyman 2017:322-23).

Despite their diverse responses to the shift, the main thrust of the Workgroup's consecutive generations is that "constructive theology is permanently in the mode of agenda-setting" (Wyman 2017:316). To them, constructive Christian theology "acknowledges the constructive

---

[16] They are particularly Walter Harrelson, Sallie McFague, Peter C. Hodgson, Rober H. King, Walter Lowe, Julian Hartt, Schubert Ogden, and Gordon Kaufman (Wyman 2017:313).

discursive role theologians play in constructive Christianity, rather than supposing that theology describes an objective, external religious reality" (Wyman 2017:312). The most important contribution is the notion of theology being constructive—i.e., theology is to be a work in progress, a composition in the making (Wyman 2017:316). In this light, the Workgroup accepts "the essential diversity of theological claims and opinion as strength rather than as a fatal flaw or heresy" (Wyman 2017:324). This results in making constructive theology thoroughly steeped in its openness to "contemporary relevance, interdisciplinarity, and practical application" (Wyman 2017:323). It affirms then that "ultimate theology is a constructive, discourse-building discipline with real-life ramifications for people living in the present" (Wyman 2017:324).

Here, constructive theology is to harbor a critical impulse—the impulse to do historical research differently. Although a historical research purports to construe historical reality from an observer's point of view, there is nonetheless a demand to let particulars be themselves. Hence, a historical research is situated in constructive theology. In this light, a historical and constructive theological approach embraces the fullness of historical research while using the diversity of constructive theology to free historical interpretations from domination by one voice—i.e., a refusal to let one voice have a monopoly on its historical interpretation. It rather engages actively in constructive thought and conversation by using the method of constructive theology; and thereby it refuses any pretense that suggests historical research is to describe exclusively an objective, external historical truth. What becomes clear in this approach, then, is that the historical research as propositional logic is often not the best (and certainly not the only) reading of history.

History as product mostly (if not always) comes with historical writings, its nature being essentially interpretive. A primary form of this interpretation is narration (White 1990:21). In this sense, history is never dead and, in fact, not even past but has power that interprets the present as well. However, at issue here is, "Who has the power to claim history?" For "a historical narrative is not a transparent representation or copy of a sequence of past events. Narration irreducibly entails selecting the events to be included in its exposition as well as filling in links that are not available in the evidential record. The historian does not find or discover her narrative; she constructs it. This process of construction involves distortion" (Carroll 1990:134). In light of this understanding, history is not neutral; rather, history in the dissertative mode involves a "paradigm choice . . . the choice of an ideological perspective" (White 1978:51-80). This proves that history is not objective; instead, it is inevitably dominated by the choice of a particular interpretation which is inherently being constructive as a process. Thus, history can be seen as both product and process. Here, a responsible engagement with historical research may not avoid this essential dimension. Whether this dialectic of product-process leads to genuine historical reality remains as another interpretation—one that is constructive.

Yet such a history-being-constructive does not mean that historical research, which offers objective and universal events, cannot be a truthful product. Rather it shows that historical research is to be understood as perpetually an ongoing process; in fact, it is essentially an interpretation in progress. Each process is affected by and seeks to affect the historical event (product). In this connection, interpreting history as process stands together with interpreting history as product. There is a correspondence (although never a perfect one) between the two. By connecting them together, a historical and constructive theological approach generates an alternative history or a counter-history to prevent one from advocating too firmly any single interpretation as an ultimate historical reality. Instead, it provides a way to move from a tradition's account of reality toward reality itself constructed by a plethora of perspectives.

Here, a historical and constructive theological approach, understood as a counter-history, can better challenge both the variety of latent professional and ecclesial assumptions in which historical interpretations are somehow neutral and the arguments designed to ensure that history remains untainted even if dominated by those who know how to play the game of power. This approach stimulates the need to apply such method to the two historical movements—namely, the sixteenth-century Münster Anabaptism and the twentieth-century Korean Minjung Theology—in order to gain a more dynamic and balanced historical reality, a history being constructive in the dialectic of process and product.

As such, by acknowledging the product-process interplay in history, this book attempts to set up a constructive dialogue *en route* to a more responsible and balanced historical hermeneutics for Münster Anabaptism through Korean Minjung Theology. Methodologically, the book therefore forgoes *magnum opus*, but rather opts for an "open-ended, fallible, revisable imaginative construction" as an effort to bring about the critical and creative discussion (Wyman 2017:313, 316). From this vantage point, it purposefully challenges an objectivistic interpretation that pretends to be complete and authoritative. Instead, it gives more attention to a discursive construction that "values the collage of different faces, voices, styles, questions, and constructs" (Chopp and Taylor 1994:4). Put another way, inviting the twentieth-century Korean Minjung Theology as a conversation partner, this book revisits the sixteenth-century Münster Anabaptism. This not only is intended to see how the traditional interpretations are challenged and transformed under this methodology, but also proposes how a historical reality of Münster Anabaptism can be renewed and reconstructed as a process as well as a product in light of a historical and constructive theological approach.

In this way, a historical and constructive theological approach can courageously and creatively engage in a people's history of Christianity, a history from below. By emphasizing imaginative dynamics, which primarily come from the common people (the *minjung*), this approaches Münster Anabaptism "from below, from the perspective of the outcast, the suspects, the maltreated, the powerless, the oppressed, the reviled—in short, from the perspective of those who suffer" (Bonhoeffer 1972:17). Here, Korean Minjung Theology is plugged into it in a cooperative fashion. Following the idea of dialectic of *han* and *dan*, this attempts not only to delve into a deep and wide variety in Münster Anabaptism as the praxis of *han*, but also to re-read its history "as hope-filled responses to 'crises' of suffering" of the *minjung* as the praxis of *dan* (Chopp and Taylor 1994: ix).[17] This helps one to reconstruct Münster Anabaptism

---

[17]This strongly suggests the reason for the rediscovery of the *minjung* (common people) as the continuing task of the Church. In this sense, Vischer's insight is noteworthy—"The history of the Church is the Gospel actually experienced. The experience of poor and oppressed people is especially important. Since it was to them that Jesus himself turned especially, we have here in a real sense the key to the correct interpretation of church history. The task of the historian is to trace out the history of the Gospel in relation to the poor and oppressed" (Vischer 1981:107).

from below, from the perspective of the *minjung*, while creating a new and distinctive portrait of Münster Anabaptism in the concept of 'hybridity',[18] where both the great men and the common men, the victimizers and the victims, and the sinners and the sinned-against are inexorably intertwined with each other.

From such a vantage point, this book suggests the possibility of a critical and creative rendezvous between Korean Minjung Theology and Münster Anabaptism. This includes a two-fold outlook—(1) the Radical Reformation as the Communal Reformation between the common men and the Radical Reformers; and (2) Münster Anabaptism as the place of hybridity, which holds the inner dynamics (including tensions and contradictions) not as a complete story, but as an open-ended conversation between the great men and the common men, the victimizers and the victims, and the sinners and the sinned-against. This rendezvous can then engage Münster Anabaptism in a distinctively historical and constructive theological way. Via such connection, the history of Münster Anabaptism is to be reinterpreted and reconstructed as counter-history, a history being constructive.

Blickle's Communal Reformation

This book is primarily in line with Peter Blickle's thoughtful and stimulating interpretation of the Reformation and the Peasants' War of 1525. Blickle argues that the key to the Reformation's early success was adoption of the pure Gospel by the common men in both towns and rural areas (Blickle 1992: xiv). Here, he unfolds his revisionist view, calling the Peasants' War of 1525 a revolution of the common men (Blickle 1981). This is the main thesis of his book, *Die Revolution von 1525*, published in 1977. (It was translated into English by Thomas A. Brady, Jr. and H. C. Erik Midelfort in 1981 and titled *The Revolution of 1525: The German*

---

[18]The term "hybridity," originating from biology, provides a nuanced understanding of the nature of ambiguity. Yet Considine's definition especially deserves attention. Referring to Homi Bhabha and Wonhee Ann Joh, Considine approvingly describes hybridity as "an indeterminate space, created by the asymmetrical and ambiguous coalescence, collision, and confrontation of diverse discourses of knowledge. This indeterminate space then has a destabilizing effect on set power structures as something new emerges" (Considine 2014:49-73, esp. p. 68, note 9).

Peasants' War from a New Perspective, with a broadened and bibliographically extended edition coming out in 2004.[19] It is this 1981 translated version which was utilized in this book.)

Blickle's revisionist assessment of the Peasants' War of 1525 is a major historical work, which has provoked extensive scholarly discussion. However, it is important to say that his work does not go without contestation. For example, regarding economic grievances of the peasants as the most significant factor to cause the Peasants' War, Blickle is charged with overlooking the religious nature of the uprisings, so that the Reformation and the Peasants' War of 1525 eventually remain as two separate phenomena.

Yet, the notion of "Communal Reformation"[20] developed by Blickle is an effort to put the relation of the Gospel to society into practice. Here, the Gospel serves as a source for the peasants' demands and rebellions with a doctrine of "godly law" (Blickle 1981:9). This even leads him to define the Peasants' War of 1525 as an "unfolding of the Reformation itself," motivated by the communal thought and religious propaganda under the collaboration of townsmen and villagers (Blickle 1992:179). In his perception, both the rural peasants and the urban burghers contributed to making the uprising in 1525 into a revolution of the common men.

---

[19]Other major works also published by Blickle are: "Economic, Social and Political Background of the Twelve Articles of the Swabian Peasants of 1525" (1976); "Peasant Revolts in the German Empire in the late Middle Ages" (1979); *Religion, Politics, and Social Protest: Three Studies on Early Modern Germany* (1984); "The Criminalization of Peasant Resistance in the Holy Roman Empire: Toward a History of the Emergence of High Treason in Germany" (1986); "Communalism, Parliamentarism, Republicanism: Parliaments, Estates, and Representation" (1986); "Communal Reformation and Peasant Piety: The Peasant Reformation and Its Late Medieval Origins" (1987); *Communal Reformation: The Quest for Salvation in Sixteenth-Century Germany* (1992); "The Popular Reformation" (1995); *Obedient Germans? A Rebuttal: A New View of German History* (1997); "Resistance, Representation, and Community" (1997); *From the Communal Reformation to the Revolution of the Common Man* (1998); "Heimat: A Critical Theory of the German Idea of Homeland" (2002); and "Communal Reformation: Zwingli, Luther, and the South of the Holy Roman Empire" (2008).

[20]The term "Communal Reformation" *(Gemeindeformation)* has a special meaning for Blickle. In his work, he delineates this concept more specifically—"Theologically and ethically, communal reformation was the demand to hear the pure Gospel preached and to live accordingly; organizationally it was the desire to establish the church on the basis of the community; politically it was the wish to link the legitimacy of authority to the gospel and the community" (Blickle 1992:100).

To Blickle, the defeat of the peasants in 1525 was, therefore, fatal to the Communal Reformation. In its wake, the compromise between the state and religion was strengthened and substantiated. Furthermore, the Reformers (especially Luther) began to advocate reform 'from above' as the only answer and to reject any violent radicalism 'from below'. Herein communalism is effectively lost with confessional Christianity taking its place. Its ultimate result is a princely takeover of the Communal Reformation. After 1525, the Reformation takes an entirely different direction—a "folk-reformation" being superseded by a "princes-reformation" (Blickle 1998:149-61). From then on, the Reformation is forced to abandon its community basis and to hide itself in separatist Anabaptist conventicles (Stayer 1988:99-139).

Blickle's revisionist interpretation offers two significant contributions to this book. One is re-adoption of the concept of the Communal Reformation into the Radical Reformation in general and Münster Anabaptism in particular; the other is rediscovery of the common men as the historical co-agent of these two events: the Peasants' War of 1525 and the (radical) Reformation. In one sense, Blickle regards the concept of the Communal Reformation as the most significant factor in producing the revolution of the common men (Blickle 1992: xiv). Although he does not deny the role of mainline Reformers such as Zwingli and Luther as the catalysts for the remarkable changes in church and society, a more decisive one to him is a new concern for communal rights, stimulated primarily by the common men in both town and countryside. It makes the leap from the Peasant's War of 1525 as a kind of Peasants' Reformation to the revolution of the common men as a kind of Communal Reformation (Blickle 1981:10, 1992:48-49).

This book uses Blickle's bold theory of the Communal Reformation as an entry point to Münster Anabaptism, where the different social classes and groups (i.e., the immigrant radical prophets and the native reactionary reformers) are closely intertwined, both being independent of yet interdependent with each other as the dynamic corpus. In this sense, his idea of the Communal Reformation gives Münster Anabaptism a new dignity as a "silent revolution."[21] It was a 'revolution'

---

[21]The idea of a "silent revolution" is borrowed from Tine De Moor and her writing (2008:179-212).

in the sense that it started from below and proved to have been as important to the ultimate course of the Radical Reformation as any other revolution. It was also 'silent' in that it was at first based primarily on "tacit agreements" between the Radical Reformers and the common men and then became explicit only after a time (Moor 2008:179). In light of this understanding, this book attempts to look at Münster Anabaptism anew as a silent revolution, based primarily on Blickle's idea of the Communal Reformation.

In another sense, Blickle provides a creative and challenging image of the common men. He views them as the most significant group of "potential recipients of reformation ideas" (Blickle 1992:11). To him, it was such a wide range of common people who actually introduced the Reformation by translating the Reformers' theology into a communal movement (Blickle 1992:184). The commoners found in their radical interpretation of the Gospel the necessity of applying godly law in not only the religious but also the secular realm. A godly law was to be forged into a natural law, even if it challenged the institution, such as serfdom and the lord-vassal relationship (Blickle 1992:48-9). In this way, they contributed to and modified the Reformation in a way that the mainline Reformers did not. Thus, a shift of perspective occurred from the great theologians and reformers, to whom are attributed the most important roles in the Reformation, to the common people, who embraced the radical interpretation of the Gospel both theologically and practically.

This, then, overturns the two-fold offensive stereotype of the common men (attached particularly to the peasants) as not only passive and servile subjects but also rude and reckless daredevils. Blickle rather proposes a liberating view of these commoners, who played a creative and critical role in the Reformation. They were able not merely to voice grievances but to translate those grievances into legislation—or more precisely, to transform the Reformation theology into a political theology (Blickle 1992:184). Here, Blickle's perspective spurs this book to see Münster Anabaptism from a different angle. It helps to redefine the portrait of the common men in Münster as the subjects of the movement who had shaped and sharpened the Reformation in their radical interpretation of the Gospel.

However, this book recognizes that the main thrust of Blickle's interpretation is not without limitation. For instance, his insistence on the Communal Reformation is subject to the Swiss and South German example only. Also, his elevation of the common men is prone to romanticizing them to the extent that his emphasis on the Peasants' War of 1525 and defeat of the peasants is overrated (Scribner 1994:199-207).

However, these signs of partiality aside, the main weakness in Blickle's view is that he simply sees the Anabaptist movement as "the dialectical reversal of the Communal Reformation," without offering its dynamic interconnection (Blickle 1992:104). This leads him to regard the transition of the Communal Reformation into Anabaptism in a somewhat negative sense, seeing the rise of Anabaptism as merely the downgraded version of the Communal Reformation (Blickle 1992:104). This is why Blickle's terms—the Communal Reformation and the common men—deliver a provocative but provisional balance on an issue of this book, in this case, representing the distinctive character of radical Anabaptism in Münster.

Furthermore, Blickle is not all that successful in discussing the relationship between the common men and the great men. In his view, the great men (i.e., the mainline Reformers) have played an ambiguous role both as the catalyst and the determent. Despite this, the Reformers made their theological messages popular by unconsciously appealing to an already existing communal movement (Blickle 1992:184). Thus, they are ultimately disposable—even a hindrance—for this movement (Blickle 1992:199), whereas the common men are "more creative and courageous" as an impetus to this Reformation (Blickle 1992:108).

Consequently, there is a considerable gap between the common men and the mainline Reformers in Blickle's interpretation. This calls for a revisit to Korean Minjung Theology as a new 'connecting thread' to this gap. In its emphasis on the dialectical unification of theology and practice, Korean Minjung Theology helps reinterpret Münster Anabaptism as a continuation of the Communal Reformation, which holds a dynamic correlation between the common men and the great men, the immigrant radicals and the native reformers, the violent and the non-resistant Anabaptists as a coherent whole.

Korean Minjung Theology

By recognizing some dubious factors in Blickle's views, such as a *völkisch* aspect (a glorification of the simple folk), this book gives credit to a collaboration of the common men with the Radical Reformers for looking anew at the Radical Reformation, particularly Münster Anabaptism. At this point, this book invites Korean Minjung Theology as a new 'keyhole'. Minjung Theology is a Korean contextual theology emerging from the struggles for social and political justice in the nation. It began in the 1970s against the backdrop of political oppression and developed during the political dictatorship of the 1980s (Kim 2015:188-201). Korean Minjung Theology defines *minjung* as the socially, politically, and economically suffering people (or simply, the underdogs) as opposed to the rich and powerful (Kim 1987:252). By showing infinite affection toward *minjung*, this Korean-style contextual theology has committed itself to doing theology from the perspective of *minjung*. Yet its most important contribution is the rediscovery of *minjung* as the real subject and motivating force of history (Suh 1983:183). In Minjung Theology, *a priori* is to see God as the God of *minjung*, and *a posteriori* is to interpret his salvation history in the present situation of the suffering *minjung* (Suh 1981:18).

In this light, *han* has a special meaning for Minjung Theology. By defining *han* as "a deep resentment against unjustifiable suffering" (Lee 1994:99), Minjung theologians hold that it is the main task of Minjung Theology to resolve the vicious cycle of the *minjung's han*. *Dan*, defined as "cutting-off," is the answer that Minjung Theology has found as a remedy for *han* (Suh 1983:65). This leads to the development of many distinctive and different methodologies used by Minjung theologians for bringing the theological response and witness to the *han*-ridden reality of *minjung* (Park 1984:1-11).

One key concept in Minjung Theology is found in the idea of solidarity and connectivity between Jesus and the *ochlos-minjung* (Ahn

1983:138-54).²² This is intended to ensure a non-dual relationship—or a radical sense of interdependence and interpenetration—between the two. In Minjung Theology, such an understanding is too strong even to the extent of identifying Jesus with the *ochlos-minjung* (Ahn 1983:138-54). Here, Jesus' incarnation is caught up in the *ochlos-minjung*'s deification,²³ so that he and *minjung* are in a reciprocal relation (Ahn 2004:138). By taking this mutual interaction as a reference, Minjung theologians find in their theology a direct continuity with *minjung*. Inspired by the theology of solidarity in suffering (Kim 2009:21-22), Minjung theologians and *minjung* exist reciprocally, with one standing upon the other. Implicit in that is a certain kind of dynamic interplay between *minjung* and Minjung theologians which transcends Blickle's *völkisch*-prone aspect.

This, then, offers a special contribution to reinterpreting the nature of Münster Anabaptism. By looking at the radical Anabaptism in Münster through this theology of solidarity with the suffering *minjung*, a history of solidarity between the common men and the Radical Reformers is recognized as being constructive. Here, the Radical Reformers have consciously involved themselves in common men's life and destiny, while the common men are more sensitive in encouraging the Radical Reformers to participate actively in Münster Anabaptism. In this mutual solidarity, the enduring stigma of Münster Anabaptism as "the Protestantism of the poor" (Kirchhoff 1973) can be disintegrated into a place of hybridity (or a silent revolution) wherein both great men and the common men, the radicals and the reactionaries, the victimizers and the victims, the sinners and the sinned-against have co-existed and co-participated together and apart in their commitment to the Communal Reformation.

---

²²In his studies of the Gospel of Mark, Ahn Byung-mu, one of the founders of Korean Minjung Theology, finds that the word *ochlos* is used to refer to the crowd around Jesus, those who were religiously forsaken, economically alienated, and politically oppressed (Ahn 1983:138-54). Ahn, in the end, identifies this biblical term *ochlos* with the Korean word *minjung*.

²³The idea of deification, or *theosis*, is common in the East as another concept of salvation. It generally refers to an ongoing process of transformation into the likeness of Jesus Christ. Since *theosis* intends to "begin here and now in the present life" in a cooperation between God and the human beings, the latter's voluntary participation is inseparable from the former's saving action (Ware 1993:236, 1996:34).

Taking a cue from this dynamic interplay of both sides, this book attempts to re-invite the bastard line (*sic*) of Radical Reformers in relation to Münster Anabaptism, that line being Thomas Müntzer, Hans Hut, Melchior Hoffman, and John Bockelson. In applying the principle of dynamic interdependence to each of them, it is intended to re-read a history of Münster Anabaptism in an alternative way—i.e., how it is shaped and reshaped by a series of symbioses between the Radical Reformers and the common men who were inspired by a theology of solidarity in suffering. This implies, then, that the real portrait of this bastard line (*sic*) of radicals can be conceived of only in their relationship with the common men and vice versa. In their mutual correlations, both are no longer bound to the dualistic principle. The Radical Reformers and the common men are not two; however, neither are they one. In this way, this book draws a two-fold re-reading; it attends to Korean Minjung Theology, (1) not only for applying the idea of non-dual relationship between Jesus and *minjung* to *minjung* and Minjung theologians, (2) but also for reapplying it to the Radical Reformers and the common men in Münster Anabaptism for the sake of a counter-history, a history being constructive.

Dialectic of Guru-Avatar

The idea of the dialectic of *guru-avatar* is used as another methodology in this book. For this concept is also instructive, especially for reinterpreting Münster Anabaptism as a counter-history. It is based on a specific theological notion—namely, double transformation. The term connotes the double-edged process that, when a concept is employed in theological translation, its meaning always undergoes transformation (Brinkman 2007:1). To be more specific, just as the Hindu concept of *guru-avatar* is to be changed in some crucial aspects when applied to the Christian frame of reference, so also it is to be changed in a substantial way when applied to the relationship of the Radical Reformers and the common men in Münster Anabaptism. This presupposes then that the *guru-avatar* interplay "becomes a principle that animates, directs and unifies [*the Reformers-Commoners interplay*], transforming and remaking it so as to bring about a new [*dynamic interrelationship*]" (Shorter 1988:11, *italics are mine*).

Furthermore, if the *gurus* (despite their plural meanings[24]) must by definition be religious teachers (Aravamudan 2006) and their messages tailor-made to particular times and circumstances so as to develop a following of disciples (Forsthoefel and Humes 2005:7), then no one is more suitable than the bastard line (*sic*) of radicals in Münster Anabaptism. For they had taken an active and influential leadership role not only in shaping their timely messages, but also in expanding their ardent disciples—the common men—to challenge new situations. Indeed, their fundamental Reformation concept of freedom and the justice of God highlighted the existing injustice and thereby provided the common men a rationale for abolishing the current inequality and oppression in church and society (Oberman 1976:110).

Yet what is unique about these Radical Reformers is to be seen not in their *guru*-ship but in their *avatar*-hood—that is, the incarnation of themselves into the common men. As the Reformers who not only ministered to the common men (particularly the poor) on a day-to-day basis, but also eye-witnessed the oppressive conditions of their lives, they could not neatly separate the religious reform from the secular one (Matheson 2007:4). Instead, they engaged radically the lived reality with the need for reform by becoming the *avatars* themselves in solidarity with the common men.

Moreover, the double transformation is based on the premise that any alteration in this process does not take place only in one direction (Brinkman 2007:1), but rather brings forth new meaning in both. Thus, the common men are also changed by the Radical Reformers in a significant and innovative way, "becoming visible," or "wising up" (Matheson 2007:260). This mutual encounter empowers the common men, enabling them to articulate their own concerns and even boldly challenge the existing contradictions (Matheson 2007:264-66). In this way, the common men come to the forefront in the Reformation and are, in Blickle's term, the actual protagonists who have introduced the Reformation to the Radical Reformers (Blickle 1992:184). This means, in another sense, the common men have critically and creatively accommodated themselves to the Reformation as the *gurus* of the Radical

---

[24]The term "*guru*" has multifarious meanings—a Hindu spiritual teacher, each of the first ten leaders of the Sikh religion, and an influential teacher or expert and so on (Copeman and Ikegame 2012:1).

Reformers. (In this light, the word *avatar* is viewed in a new way). This requires a more proactive and dynamic interpretation of the *guru-avatar* interplay in Münster Anabaptism. Whereas the term *avatar* in its original meaning is manifestative, instrumental, and thus ultimately the functional relationships in *guru*, here the dynamic relationship between the Radical Reformers and the common men in Münster Anabaptism transcends such a purely functional aspect. It even dismisses the term *avatar* as being passive and subordinate in respect to its nature and relationship with *guru*.

For better understanding, this *guru-avatar* interplay in Münster Anabaptism is in contact with an inclusive *yin-yang* thinking;[25] denying dualistic logic of the excluded middle, or either/or distinction, it involves the organic and relational view of both/and—that is, of non-duality[26] (Lee 1979:3-9). Here, the idea of dialectic of *guru-avatars* includes contradictions and opposites, but both also correspond and are interconnected with each other as a coherent whole. Put differently, like the Möbius strip,[27] both *guru* and *avatar* are not juxtaposed nor is the one absorbed by the other, but rather they remain in a reciprocal and dynamic correlation. In this sense, the Radical Reformers as the *avatars* of the common men are inseparable from the common men as the *gurus* of the Radical Reformers in Münster Anabaptism. Therefore, depicting the Radical Reformers as the *avatars* of the common men does not diminish their theological *guru*-ship, nor does characterizing the common men as the *gurus* of the Radical Reformers dispense with their potential *avatar*-hood. Rather, the dialectic of *guru-avatar* underlines

---

[25]In Chinese thought, the two poles of cosmic energy are *yang* (positive) and *yin* (negative). The key to the relationship between *yin* and *yang* is mutual arising or inseparability; there can be no *yang* without *yin* and vice versa. In *the yin-yang* view, therefore, everything and everybody are in mutual sequence, which is in opposition to western dualistic thinking (Lee 1979, 1980).

[26]The term "non-duality" (literally "not two") is equivalent to the Hindu notion of *advaita*. In this way of thinking, all things are in non-dual relation, including the world and even God. Panikkar, a Spanish Roman Catholic priest and scholar, tries to apply this *advaitic* principle to the Christian doctrine of the Trinity (Panikkar 1973).

[27]The Möbius strip is originally a mathematical term. It "is a one-sided non-orientable surface obtained by cutting a closed band into a single strip, giving one of the two ends thus produced a half twist, and then reattaching the two ends" (Gray 1997:322-23). Here this term is intended to represent a paradoxical and dynamic correlation between the common men and the Radical Reformers in Münster Anabaptism as both *guru* and *avatar*.

the mutual interdependence and interpenetration of two agents who must paradoxically be regarded together as the focal point in Münster Anabaptism.

This implies that the Radical Reformers in Münster Anabaptism—Thomas Müntzer, Hans Hut, Melchior Hoffman, and John Bockelson (John of Leiden)—are a whole, which (to put it in a simplistic way) consists of both a *guru*-ship and an *avatar*-hood element. Although seeming to be opposite and even contradictory, they are actually interdependent and complementary, like a relation of *yin-yang* and the Möbius strip. This represents a paradoxical co-relation or a co-existence between the Radical Reformers and the common men in Münster Anabaptism as both *guru* and *avatar*.

It is, however, to be noted that despite the introduction of the dialectic of *avatar-guru* as a helpful methodology in developing the dynamic correlationship between the common men and the Radical Reformers in Münster Anabaptism, this book gives special attention to the *avatar*-hood of the bastard line *(sic)* of Radical Reformers—i.e., they are more than *gurus* of the common men; they are also the *avatars* of the common men.

Delimitations

This book is delimited in its findings in the following ways. First, it recognizes the limitation of resources in light of language issues. The main research materials about the sixteenth-century Reformation are primarily German, Dutch, and Latin sources, and the most relevant primary materials utilized in this book are from the texts written in English. According to the library index of the University of Stellenbosch, only a German version of Blickle's *Die Revolution von 1525* is available. Neither the original nor the English versions of other revisionist works are fully accessible at the Stellenbosch library. Thus, it was the texts translated into English that the researcher used to construct the historical realities of the sixteenth-century Reformation and Anabaptist movement.²⁸

The research opportunity in Katholieke Universiteit Leuven (KU Leuven) in Belgium is in this sense beneficial for the researcher to offset such limitations (significantly, if not completely) with considerable reflections and insights, which encourage him to further thinking on the related topics. During the research period, he utilized KU Leuven's specialized library (including inter-library loan), attended some conferences, and established new research contacts with professors from the Evangelical Theological Faculty in Leuven and a professor from the Protestant Theological Faculty of the University of Münster, Germany. This helps compensate considerably for the limitation of getting important and authentic sources, even though most of them are translations of the original texts.

Special contributions are made by such readings of the relevant historical works concerning the Radical Reformation in general and Münster Anabaptism in particular, the original authorship of which is attributed mainly to European writers. However, the researcher is willing to state that these revisionist perspectives do not go without contestation. There are some weak links in the chain of their arguments, as mentioned earlier. Nonetheless, many revisionists and their translated works on the

---

²⁸In particular, source documents on the Anabaptist movement are mainly written in German. The literary analysis in this book is based primarily on academic works that deal with translations of the original German texts. This book amplifies literature on the Anabaptist movement available for English readers, for example Peter Blickle's magisterial work, *The Revolution of 1525: The German Peasants War from a New Perspective* (1981); T.A. Brady's *Ruling Class, Regime and Reformation at Strasbourg 1520-1555* (1978); L.H. Zuck's *Christianity and Revolution: Radical Christian Testimonies, 1520-1650* (1975); J.K. Zeman's *The Anabaptists and the Czech Brethren in Moravia 1526-1628* (1969); J.H. Yoder's *The Hermeneutics of the Anabaptists* (1966); E.R. Wolf's *Peasant Wars of the Twentieth Century* (1969); G.H. Williams and M. M. Angel's *Spiritual and Anabaptist Writers: Documents Illustrative of the Radical Reformation* (1957); K. Von Greyerz's *Religion and Society in Early Modern Europe, 1500-1800* (1984); H.J. Hillerbrand's *The Reformation and the German Peasants War* (1972); W. Klaassen's *Anabaptism in Outline: Selected Primary Sources* (1981); C.P. Clasen's *Anabaptism: A Social History, 1525-1618* (1972); H.J. Goertz's *Karlstadt, Müntzer and the Reformation of the Commoners, 1521-1525* (2006); D.J. Grieser's *Seducers of the Simple Folk: the Polemical War against Anabaptism 1525-1540* (1993); L. Harder's *Sources of Swiss Anabaptism* (1985), and F. Engels, *The German Revolutions: The Peasant War in Germany, and Germany: Revolution and Counter-Revolution* (1967), etc.

Reformation and Münster Anabaptism are utilized in this book as useful sources for developing the research topic.

<u>Second</u>, this book is conducted under a specific methodology—the *avatar-guru* interplay and the double-mirror reading. These are designed and selected to enrich and elaborate the dynamic relationship between *minjung* (common people) and the Radical Reformers on the one hand and *minjung* and Messiah (Jesus) on the other. These methodological hypotheses, which depend heavily on "a logical supposition, a reasonable guess, and an educated conjecture" (Leedy 2015:5), attempt to contribute to a critical and creative synthesis by looking anew at the sixteenth-century Radical Reformation and Münster Anabaptism through the lens of the twentieth-century Korean Minjung Theology. But this aims primarily at a theological fusion of horizons rather than a direct historical linkage between the two movements. This presupposes, then, that there are in effect more theological than historical affinities and parallels in this approach.

<u>Third</u>, this book is attentive to the common men's perspective on history rather than the great men. This is based on the assumption that, if the history is written by one with particular power, it often involves the attempt to manage and even govern history on its behalf. The danger of this historical interpretation is that it too often and too quickly becomes ideological. If the other side cannot gain proper recognition but just is silenced more by force than by will, its historical judgment must remain open to the possibility of revision.

With that in mind, this book approaches the sixteenth-century Radical Reformation and Münster Anabaptism from below. Yet it does not mean a perspective from below is chosen for the final cut while a perspective from above is abandoned. Instead, this pinpoints that the former is chosen to show the way for the latter to the final cut. In other words, this is intended to remain the portrayal of the common men (and the radicals) in Münster Anabaptism ambiguous both as objects and subjects, victims and victimizers, and sinner and sinned-against, including contradictions and conflicts from within. Indeed, this is an attempt to reinterpret the sixteenth-century Münster Anabaptism as seen from the twentieth-century Korean Minjung Theology in order to create an open-ended people's history of Christianity rather than to make an exclusive and final conclusion on it.

Fourth, this book has some limitations as to Korean Minjung Theology. It deliberately sifts through a great deal of its contents and perspectives with just one guild of Minjung theologians in mind. This means the researcher traces and analyzes the line and direction from the first generation of Minjung theologians, particularly Suh Nam-dong, Anh Byung-mu, Kim Yong-bok, and Hyun Young-hak. It does not mean that the research has not acknowledged the development of its own scholarship or ignored the creative works of a new generation of Minjung theologians. Rather, the researcher is in agreement that Korean Minjung Theology has constantly "drunk from its own wells." This contextual theology of *minjung* has continued to carry out its own scholarship in ever-changing contexts without losing its theological significance. In so doing, it has brought Korean voices back into the international conversation.

Nevertheless, for the purpose of this study, this book will focus on gathering the early harvest of the first generation of Minjung Theology in the 1970s. This is partly because of their stress on a combination of Jesus and *ochlos-minjung* in favour of Christian social responsibility. The first generation of Minjung theologians had evidently advocated a theology of witness, identifying themselves with *minjung* by participating in their sufferings. In this solidarity with the suffering *minjung*, they too became the suffering *minjung*. This led Minjung Theology to a legitimate place in the life of the Korean *minjung* (Back 1984:13-28). By connecting such self-giving identity to the concept of dialectic *guru-avatar* and *double transformation*, this book is intended to engage the characteristics of the first generation of minjung theologians in significance.

Potential Impact

This book approaches the history of the sixteenth-century Radical Reformation and Münster Anabaptism from below. This is a people's history of Christianity built on, first and foremost, the ordinary simple folk whose names are largely lost to history. From this perspective, the central focus is common people, and the impending task is to rehabilitate them as another leading protagonist of Christian history. Even if quite suggestive, this bold approach remains not so much a history 'of' the common men but a history 'for' them. Putting too much a premium on the common men, this approach seems to overlook that there are at all times cases in which one falls victim to oneself. The sad irony is that such a history rewritten from below is readily caught up in the dialectical reversal of history written from above. It unwittingly sidesteps the impending problem of *völkisch*—a self-glorification of the simple folk, which could be used to suppress others, especially the previous victors.

In this sense, a re-reading of Münster Anabaptism from below (from the *minjung* hermeneutics) may offer a significant contribution to recast this bizarre event into a silent revolution or hybridity that holds potential for healing, liberation, and salvation on both sides, based on the dynamic interplay of the great men and the common men, the victimizers and the victims, the sinners and the sinned-against being in the dialectic of *guru-avatar* and *han-dan*. This shift in focus helps to see that it is the rank-and-file *minjung* (common men) as well as the Radical Reformers who have played important roles in the history of Münster Anabaptism as the extensive Communal Reformation.

Nonetheless, it is significant to remind ourselves that the strategy of this re-reading is like that of a jigsaw puzzle in which each piece, incomplete in itself, contributes to the design of the whole. This effort is a preliminary sketch, which, if successful, can only produce a profile, not a complete portrait. However, seen from a long-term perspective, the total of these relatively small, dim, and seemingly insignificant pictures takes shape as part of broader historical trends. Further in-depth studies are thus welcomed in many areas to make a more dynamic and balanced assessment on this matter as part of reconstructing a counter-history, a history being constructive.

Part 1

RE-READING THE REFORMATION FROM BELOW

Chapter 1

The Radical Reformation

A Brief History of the Anabaptist Kingdom of Münster

The sixteenth-century Anabaptists, who emerged as the group of radicals after Martin Luther and Thomas Müntzer chronologically, had shared a negative worldview in general and thus the need for reformation (Oberman 1989:41). They were not satisfied to merely point out socio-political and religious discontents but were determined to work toward the pursuit of radical social alternatives (Brady 1988:30). This led to widespread persecution by both Catholic and Protestant authorities who were alert to the resurgence of the Peasants' War (Lindberg 1996). But that persecution produced an apocalyptic fervor within the Anabaptist movement (Cohn 1961). Their calls to construct an alternative society began to be associated with chiliastic thought, especially in areas influenced by Hans Hut in South Germany (Oyer 1960:219-48, 1961:5-37, Goertz 1996:17) and by Melchior Hoffman in North Germany, Flanders, and the Netherlands (Verheyden 1961:15, Finger 2004:35-6).

Münster's tolerance of and level of accommodation to religious dissenters attracted a large number of chiliastically-minded Anabaptists to the city in 1532-1533 (Eichler 1981:46). The fierce anticlerical sermons of native Münster preacher Bernhard Rothmann became a catalyst for switching the city's allegiance from Catholicism to Lutheranism (Klotzer 2007:226). Coupled with the prolonged political unrest and economic inflation within Münster, his appearance inspired many of the lower-class citizens (Bax 1903:119). Soon, this led to new evangelical reforms in the city of Münster centering on this young preacher, Rothmann (Hsia 1984:3).

Yet Münster's religious developments took a more radical turn when Rothmann aligned himself with Anabaptism, openly questioning a number of Lutheran beliefs, including infant baptism and the Eucharist (Baaker 2009:99-100). His espousal of Anabaptism led to significant popular support. In addition, through conversion and mass immigration, the number of Anabaptists in Münster had grown enough to bring about an Anabaptist council in 1534 (Haude 2000:4, 46-47). The radical Protestants quickly used this favourable circumstance as a chance to formally seize power. Toward the end of 1533, former baker John Matthjisson, who had recently replaced Melchior Hofmann's leadership among Dutch Anabaptists, sent out apostles to Münster to proclaim the city as "New Jerusalem" (Stayer 1995:269). The reaction was immediate and heated. Within a week about 1,400 of Münster's citizens were rebaptized and thousands of Dutch Anabaptists from neighbouring towns sought to immigrate to the city (Estep 1975:155-56, Littell 1958:30-1).

By declaring himself the prophet Enoch, Matthjisson assumed the real leadership in Münster, superseding the formal authority structure with its city council and elected mayors (Williamson 2000:29-9). All evangelicals and Catholics there were forced either to leave or to accept rebaptism (Klotze 2007:234). The Anabaptist political as well as religious takeover alarmed the Prince-Bishop of Münster, Franz von Waldeck, to the extent that he threatened to initiate a blockade (Eichler 1981:46)—a threat that rather bound the Münsterites together under Matthjisson's leadership. However, Matthjisson's exercise of unchecked power was brief. After a little over a month, he was killed while (under 'divine revelation') leading only a few men in a failed sortie against the Prince-Bishop's besieging army (Goertz 1984:30-1).

Matthjisson's death gave Anabaptist Münster new leadership under John Bockelson, a second-in-command (Eichler 1981:47). Taking a cue from his predecessor's failure, Bockelson established strict rules of conduct and behaviour in the city in order to cement his authority (Klotze 2007:241-42). At his behest, the Münster city council and guilds were superseded by a body of 12 elders; polygamy and a forceful form of community of goods were instituted; and a coronation was ordered to have Bockelson crowned king of the whole world (Haude 2000:13, Snyder 1995:219). But all his collective efforts ended in failure. As both the Prince-Bishop increased pressure on the city and famine intensified, the Anabaptist 'kingdom' was betrayed by its own (Klotze 2007:243,

Haude 2000:15). The bishop's forces entered the city and its citizens were too weak to fight. Thus, in 1535, the city fell, and Bockelson along with his lieutenants were executed (Haude 2000:16, Snyder 1995:221), their bodies put on permanent display as a warning regarding future rebellion (Cameron 1991:324-25). This short-lived Anabaptist reign in Münster (23 February 1534 to 24 June 1535) then became a byword for total aberration of the Reformation. John Bockelson was portrayed as *Führer* (tyrannical leader), intended as an opprobrious epithet, who led his followers into a disastrous political-religious adventure.

Even as sixteenth-century Anabaptism had begun to shake off the stigma of being a "stepchildren of the Reformation,"[1] the enduring dark image was far from disappearing (Bender 1944:8). For indeed, the 1534-35 Anabaptist rule in Münster had made a significant contribution to this opprobrious attention. To be sure, the short-lived Anabaptist takeover had displayed the worst example of the Radical Reformation in the sixteenth-century (Haude 2000:20). Thus, the tragic episode of Münster Anabaptism is still a curse on the Anabaptists in general and the radicals in particular (Baring-Gould 1891, Hudson-Reed 1989:89).

This is the strain of interpretation that the scholarship today is repeating. Like the myth of Pandora's Box, out from Anabaptist Münster flew every trouble and problem, such as a reign of terror and totalitarianism, cruel and fanatical violence, introduction of forceful communism, and sexual deviance—polygamy. This makes Münster a monster whose task is to release all the evils upon the world (Rowland 2004:1-18). Therefore, the Anabaptist madness in Münster deserved its bloody repression like Sodom and Gomorrah (Kerssenbrock 2007:181). From this viewpoint, "a long line of polemical histories of Anabaptist rule appeared" (Driedger 2016). The mainline scholarship has placed a taboo on any attempt to rehabilitate the depravity of Münster Anabaptism. Yet the question now arises as to whether Anabaptism in Münster really opened the lid of Pandora's Box, which contained a

---

[1]This term was coined by Leonard Vurduin, especially in his book, *Reformers and Their Stepchildren* (1964).

source of trouble—i.e., odious deviations from the Reformation—so that its demise was the natural outcome of false and rebellious enthusiasm.[2]

History from the Great Men and the Common Men

Recently, those historians whose perspectives are critical to the official history have challenged the dominant religious history, which has been mainly inspired by the great men. In linking interpretations of events and ideas with the imprint of the interpreter, these challengers argue that history can be tailor-made to the taste of those in power. Hence the problem. If the history was written by one with the power, it often attempts to manage and govern history on its behalf, the result being that history is produced depending upon the vote of one party— the more powerful and/or more prevalent voice. This immediately provokes skepticism in its ideological fashion. If the other side cannot gain proper recognition and is silenced more by force than by will, its historical judgment deserves to be reconsidered. For in history, to be victorious is not necessarily to be righteous. Thus, it calls for the perpetual revision of history—"Every generation must rewrite the history in its own way" (Collingwood 1946:248) in order to stop promoting justice backed by the powerful alone.

Regarding Christendom, ecclesiastical history has not found it difficult to take a similar course. Many historians in the past have tended to focus on the doctrines and religious concepts of elites and intellectuals by regarding them as the privileged, if not exclusive, objects of historical interpretation. Thus, among the consequences is the exclusion from history of voices of the ordinary faithful; or if they are admitted at all,

---

[2]Two of the most significant of Münster Anabaptist histories were composed by Hermann von Kerssenbrock and Heinreich Gresbeck respectively, both eyewitnesses to the event. The former wrote of the Anabaptist takeover of Münster with a vivid and long historical account. The sources were narrated several decades after the demise of the Anabaptist Kingdom, but first published in 1730. Within it, as a Catholic, von Kerssenbrock showed a highly anti-Anabaptist viewpoint. The latter, as one of the Anabaptist soldiers who betrayed, described the event, in less detailed accounts than the former. Gresbeck was rather particularly interested in the Prince-Bishop's forces and the condition after the fall of the Anabaptist Kingdom. Most recently, Christopher Mackay has translated both primary sources into English under the titles, *Narrative of the Anabaptist Madness: The Overthrow of Münster, the Famous Metropolis of Westphalia* (2007) and *False Prophets and Preachers: Henry Gresbeck's Account of the Anabaptist Kingdom of Münster* (2016), respectively.

they are relegated to secondary status. An even more deleterious corollary is the simplistic association of religious or political dissenters, who have been sensitive to the power, with bad Christians. Therefore, the task of these historians is to get them right in service of the intellectual elite and powerful class.

These blind generalizations, which force every deviator from the larger Christian community into being a despised heretic, would surely impoverish Christian history.[3] For it may serve as an act of self-defense on one hand but also as an act of self-destruction on the other. If the origins of Christianity are rooted in a movement of oppressed people, the original message of salvation for the oppressed was interrupted when Christianity became a religion solely suitable to the interests of the ruling powers—"Christianity brooked no rivals in religion, just as state power tolerated no rivals in politics" (Frey 1984:22). As a result, such a totalitarian inner coherence allows no room for heterodoxy, while the memories of its oppositional origins remained alive only in heretical movements (Vogler 1984:178-79). This does not mean that there cannot be any heresy, but that word immediately conveys the vision of a flaming stake, invented and ignited by the leaders of the church (Klaassen 1981:290).[4] Be that as it may, this is obviously a value judgment based on theological penchant and thus constitutes a red flag—"To burn heretics

---

[3] Walter Bauer's claim (1971) calls for special attention, despite his not being strange to controversy. As against the classical view that heresy was originally an offshoot from orthodoxy, Bauer has set out to establish the principle of the coexistence of heresy with orthodoxy. To him, there was no clear-cut division between the two; both arising simultaneously within the Church itself. This is epitomized by his two principal theses of defining the relationship between orthodoxy and heresy in the first two Christian centuries. Bauer agrees in stressing the diversity and the fluidity of early Christian thought. According to him, Christianity from the outset was a congeries of different groups having profoundly different interpretations of Jesus. This explains that the heresies were not illegitimate deviations from an originally unified and orthodox mainstream like orthodox writers as Eusebius would have insisted. This leads Bauer to conclude that, as formal orthodoxy began as a splinter or minority movement under episcopal leadership and only slowly reached a dominant influence in the life of the Church, heresies even attained a greater degree of importance for a longer period than did orthodoxy in such places as Edessa, Egypt, and Asia Minor until the orthodox victory became decisive and nearly universal in the course of the third century. Bauer's giving credence to the Church of Rome as hero is another distinction in this regard.

[4] Some scholars even propose that heresy is a product of the inner dynamics of orthodoxy, which is systematically produced by great "axial religions" (Eisenstadt 1999, Gauchet 1997).

is to recognize Christ in appearance, but to deny him in reality" (Hubmaier 1524 quoted by Klaassen 1981:30-33).

A warning bell must ring when the singular orthodoxy has held the ideological monopoly in interpreting entire church history. Therefore, one is to be more careful that there might be much truth in the dictum, "One generation's heresy is frequently the next generation's orthodoxy" (Kurtz 1986:5). Indeed, Jesus was condemned as a heretic to contemporary people. As only few beliefs have been held "always and everywhere and by all," the other side of Christian history needs to receive new light.[5] That light encourages Christians to see in every ecclesiastical battle that there is another side and that sometimes there are more people on the other side. Of course, it does not necessarily mean one should glorify or absolutize the outsiders, for they suffer under their historical predicaments. It should be remembered that, in traditional historical and theological terms, they might also be under sin and in a state of sin.

What would emerge is rather the reworking of history's plot with the common men as the central narrative or, put simply, the re-reading of history from below—from those who "have never had a say; have always played a minor role; have left no records" (Mollat 1986:29). Thus, at issue here are the questions of whose experiences and whose interpretations, both of which challenge the customary views of granting the religion of great men and the monopoly of being objects of historical interpretation. Yet this new path is not without limitation. Even though a guild of historians have made efforts to include studies of the conditions and reactions of the poor and/or the oppressed, to a large degree, the primary focus has been on perspectives of the non-poor toward the poor, the oppressor toward the oppressed, and the great men toward the common

---

[5] There had been some early Christian theologians and church leaders who were rejected and questioned by Christian orthodoxy because of their different teachings in regard to heresy. Origen (185-254 CE) puts it like this; "All heretics at first are believers; then later they swerve from the rule of faith (Commentary on the Song of Songs, 3); Tertullian (155-240 CE), a father of Latin Christianity, speaks similarly at the end of *Prescription Against Heretics 36* through his analogy of the wild live tree (heresy), which springs from a cultivated seed (orthodox doctrine) (quoted from Bauer 1971: xxiii). One of the recurrent devices in the struggle against heresy is seen as frustrated ambition; it drives the one in question out of the church and causes him/her to become a heresiarch. Tertullian already says this of Valentinus *(Against Valentinus* 4; cf. *Prescription Against Heretics* 30). Epiphanius (310-320-403 CE) also reports a similar story about Marcion *(Her.* 42.1).

men. Conversely, this affirms the necessity of the re-reading of history from below, not the optimistic, evolutionary history of the victors, but the forgotten history of the victims (Metz 1999:95).

In short, history should not be used to belittle the sources available, which are mostly stemming from the great men. This is necessary and useful; and it may produce a real, important, and true history despite the fact that it is conditioned by the preferences and proclivities of the powerful voice. But by itself, it is important to make all voices heard seriously, whether learned or unlearned, academic or popular, high or low. No voice is granted a special status merely because of its privileged position and affiliation. Therefore, this suggests the "impossible possibility" of two-fold reading of history. Reading history from below and reading history from above are not opposite; the former serves as the condition for the latter, and vice versa. To be more specific, reading history from below would no longer be the opposite of reading history from above but, on the contrary, it would be what truly enables reading history from above, and vice versa.[6] It therefore urges us to think on the "impossible possibility" of reading history both from below and from above not as contradictory but as complementary.

Reformation from the Great and the Common Men

The re-reading of history from below includes the necessity of re-reading the Reformation from below. Was there ever a Reformation for the common people? It is quite obvious that experts in Reformation history have concentrated on what is familiar to them—i.e., the formation, growth, and functioning of the leadership office, centering on Martin Luther, John Calvin, and other major Reformers. Therefore, history of the Reformation becomes a tale of heroic figures, the history of great men. The problem is not in this approach itself, for there is always a need for an account of institutional reform from above. Rather, the problem is its willful ignorance regarding the majority—the simple folk. In it, such a vast number of people are considered merely a silent

---

[6]This idea is drawn from Jacques Derrida's understanding of the possible and the impossible (Derrida 2001:98).

background to the Reformation, they being simply swept along by the leading without any contribution to it.

Thus, the re-reading of the Reformation from below intends to challenge this customary practice of reading it on the assumption that all previous presuppositions based on the saga of the great Reformers remain open to revision. It recognizes that the history of the common people *(der gemeine Mann)*—their "stories of joy and suffering, hope and despair, love and hatred, freedom and oppression, stories not recorded in history books written by victors but kept alive in the 'dangerous memory' of the 'underside of history'"—become the primary resources of the Reformation (Phan 2006:16). This encourages one to see not only how the Reformation affected the common people, but also how they themselves contributed to and even modified it. Thus, this queries the nature of the Reformation to rediscover the role the common people played, not as bad Christians but as radical believers.[7]

On this basis, a group of historians began to propose that the sixteenth century Reformation from its inception was radical and plural or polycentral (Stayer 1993:39-47, Goertz 2002:29-42). Others have claimed a long age of Reformation (over three centuries, from the 1300s to the 1600s)[8] on the premise that there was not a single Reformation, but a variety of Reformations (Lindberg 1996, Payton 2010).[9] From that emerges the term 'second Reformation'. One group of historians tends

---

[7]It is interesting to note that Luther's ideas were, in a sense, not original but were essentially the republication of older heresies—namely, the bad Christians. Luther was a Hussite in his theology of contrition, a Wycliffite in his doctrine of confession, and a Manichaean in his theology of grace and free will. Here, "the Reformation represented a reappearance of older heresies" (McGrath 1987:29).

[8]Here the researcher agrees with recent historiographical tendencies which have especially placed its emphasis on the blurring of traditional dividing lines between the later Middle Ages and the Reformation. Under this outlook, the idea of the Reformation as a violent interruption in the Middle Ages is no longer compelling. Rather this views the Reformation as one long and interrelated "era of reforms" that lasted between the 14th and 16th centuries (Schilling 1975:5-31, quoted by Wriedt 1996:182-3).

[9]On this matter, a general consensus among scholars and historians is that there might be no one monolithic experience of Reformation in Europe during the long period. The 150 years between the 14th and 16th centuries can be divided into at least three distinctive parts—(1) a series of radical challenges to the established church throughout the close of the Middle Ages; (2) a successful evangelical assault in about the second quarter of the 16th century; and (3) a later phase of what used to be called the Second or Counter-Reformation, which is more generally referred to as Lutheran, Calvinist, or Catholic confessionalization (Kumin 1996:3). These confessional churches, albeit with marked variations in degrees, allied with the states and thus became state-churches, *vis-à-vis* smaller but numerous rival sects.

to distinguish between two Reformations in the sixteenth-century, the first being the minor one by Luther and Calvin and the second being the major Reformation of late humanism (Gelder 1961)—or in other words, the first as "Reformation by the princes," the second as "Reformation by people" (Dickens 1976).

Others, especially Czech church historians, have called the fifteenth-century Hussite movement the first Reformation, while Lutheranism was the second Reformation (Molnar 1980:322 quoted by Klueting 2004:41). According to them, although the second Reformation "partially joined and continued the struggles" of the first, its heavy emphasis on the Pauline epistles—not under law but under grace—diluted the message of the law of God, including the ethical demands of the Gospel in both church and society, and thus reduced its reforming activity to purely the spiritual and internal realm (Zeman 1969:41-5, Enns and Seiling 2015:439). Furthermore, while the first Reformation was closely related to the multitude of poor and simple folks, the second was largely connected to the middle stratum and, therefore, was more conservative (Enns and Seiling 2015:439). This leads to a growing scholarly concern for the relation between the first Reformation and the Radical Reformation, centering on the commoners, both urban inhabitants and rural peasants.

It is now very old news that even in the time of the sixteenth-century Reformation, there was not one Reformation but many, such as the humanist, the Catholic, the communal, the Zwinglian, the Calvinist, and the radical (Matheson 2007:8). This idea of multifaceted Reformations (Wiesner-Hanks 1998:111-12) indicates that there was the obvious "wild profusion" in the "Long Age of Reformations" (Watt 2006). Therefore, diversity and heterogeneity were the key elements in the early years of the Reformation.[10] Yet such context of great religious (also social, political, and intellectual) struggles of the time had spared no middle-ground as it went through. This means one could not avoid

---

[10]Thus it is noteworthy to quote that "Conventional social theory errs in supposing that historical change is caused by changes in basic social, economic, and political conditions alone. There is, in fact, no such thing as social, economic, and political conditions (or forces) alone; they are always part of a context of perception and feeling. Nor are there values, ideas, and beliefs alone; as a social matter, they are always interconnected with 'material interests.' Power is also an idea; justice is also a force. Neither causes the other in the physical-science sense of that world" (Berman 1983:403).

taking a stand for or against the Reformations or the Reformers. As a result, contending solutions came to the forefront, some being irenic, others belligerent. Soon, what had been a juxtaposition of views became a tension; diversity turned into opposition. As this disagreement heightened, a group of so-called Radical Reformers[11] had boldly and often confrontationally confessed their criticism against the major Reformers, including Martin Luther (1483-1546), Huldrych Zwingli (1484-1531), and John Calvin (1509-1564).

There were at least three major disputes between the radical and the major Reformers—the completion of reform, the scope of reform, and the subject of reform. <u>First</u>, the radical Reformers sought to reform Christian life and the church in a way which constituted an alternative to the existing Christendom. Therefore, the reform should be continued to the extent of going beyond the status quo. Yet as far as they were concerned, the completion of reform had stalled and suffered major setbacks due to the Magisterial Reformers' complacency and compliance with the *Obrigkeit* (the political authorities). <u>Second</u>, against the major Reformers, who were simply inclined to confine their reform to the ecclesiastical realm, the radical Reformers strove to extend its scope into political and social change by taking the common people's context seriously. <u>Third</u>, one of the major flash points between the radical and the official Reformers was whether political power was necessary for religious reform. The former disregarded it as the resurgence of the

---

[11] For the complex typology of the Radical Reformers, G. H. Williams' tripartite classification seems to be most helpful, which is (1) the Anabaptists, (2) the Spiritualists, and (3) the Evangelical Rationalists (Williams 2000: xxix). But this is also to be considered with caution in that such a line of demarcation is, to a greater measure, not clear and fine but rather fluid and even chaotic from its early stage.

Constantinian compromise,[12] which is "an expansion of secular authorities at the expense of ecclesiastical autonomy" (Hsia 1994:731-2). Thus, they eschewed it as an unholy alliance or a sort of cartel justified by its cheerful advocacy of developing political power. The latter, on the contrary, considered this church-state coalition as positive and espoused it as a new propaganda.[13]

---

[12] The concept of a fallen or corrupted Christendom had been a recurrent theme among the radicals, including Anabaptists. Yet its perspective varied considerably even among themselves regarding when this fall occurred. For example, from Polish Anabaptism came the record of the dating of the fall of Christendom "with the death of Simeon, the last of the grand old men who had known Jesus and the Twelve," in A.D. 111 on the basis of Eusebius (Eusebius 32, quoted by Littell 1955:62). However, Sebastian Franck wrote in 1531 concerning an alteration of "the outward church of Christ," which occurred "right after the death of the apostles," or 1,400 years before— i.e., A.D. 131 (Williams 1957:149). Franck's view seems to have influenced John Campanus; and through Campanus, it seems to have been transmitted even to the Wassenberger preachers and Bernhard Rothmann of Münster (Littell 1955:40, 73). Thomas Müntzer, one of the leading Radical Reformers, affirmed that the Christian church "did not remain a virgin any longer than up to the time of the death of the disciples of the apostles and soon thereafter became an adulteress" (Williams 1957:51). Nonetheless, more common among radical writers is the dating of the fall of the true church in the 4th century, in which the union of church and state began to be forged by Constantine and concluded by Theodosius. This interpretation occurs in one passage in the Hutterite Chronicle, according to which "the cross was conquered and forged to the sword . . . through the slyness of the Old Serpent" (Littell 1955:63). Michael Servetus (1511-1553) also dated the fall of true Christianity in the 4th century at the Council of Nicea (325) with its dogmatic formulation of Trinitarian doctrine (Bainton 1951:77). Menno Simons (1496-1561) held that the fall was a process beginning in early Christian times, increasing under Constantine, and culminating in Innocent I's edict enforcing infant baptism in 407 (Krahn 1936:136, quoted in Littell 1955:63). Interestingly enough, Martin Luther also shared this view with the Radical Reformers but with a different date. He had pinpointed the fall of the church in the 8th century, when the bishops of Rome became great temporal rulers after the Donation of Pepin in 55. For this line of interpretation, this book is largely indebted to Garret's article (1958:111-27).

[13] Here, a basic distinction between the "Reformer" and the "Radical" is beneficial. The "Reformer" is one who sees the system as fundamentally sound and only in need of being made workable. Its presuppositions are still valid but have been overgrown with secondary developments and needs to be pruned back to the essentials. On the contrary, for the "Radicals," the system is false and needs to be overthrown and replaced by a new system founded on fundamentally different presuppositions. The same is true of the 16th century Reformers and Radicals in this regard. On one hand, the former (from Luther to Calvin) accepted key presuppositions in common, especially about the necessity of an established church, binding on all citizens as the sole church body recognized by the state and the territorial parish as the local unit of this civic church. Thus, they believed that a certain renewal of theology, a certain naturalization, a certain amount of structural reorganization would be sufficient to renew the church and reveal the lineaments of its original meaning. On the other hand, there were the Radicals, including Anabaptists, who were convinced that the very concept of a church as a social body allied with the political order was fundamentally incorrect and represented the betrayal of the authentic nature of the Christian community. Hence there could be no talk of reform but only of a rebirth of

Given these circumstances, the radical Reformers first threw the gauntlet down to the official Reformers. The former refused every attempt to cooperate and compromise with the secular authorities by criticizing them as those who once had supported the simple folks' demands but now turned against them to secure their own interests and status. These radical hard-liners accused the major Reformers of following in the footsteps of the Constantinian framework,[14] which had turned Christianity from being a religion of the oppressed into a religion of the oppressors, of the common men into the great men. Although the radical Reformers' resistance was not a decisive blow to the major Reformers, the former did become a thorn in the side of the latter.

The German Peasants' War of 1525 played against the radical Reformers, with the major Reformers using this revolution of the common people as a pretext for muzzling their rivals, who had sided with the violent peasants. In the long run, what the Peasants' War produced was a winner and a loser. The major Reformers received the 'halo of righteousness' (the good Christians), while the radical Reformers had the stigma of heresy (the bad Christians). As the head of victors, Luther and his followers stridently denounced all who disagreed with them.[15]

---

the church as a counter-community representing a new humanity into which one can enter only by departing from the fallen society of "the world" (Ruether 1969:271-72).

[14]In this Constantinian framework, H.-J. Goertz finds the logic of the Radical Reformation as anti-clericalism. By attending to Thomas Müntzer's life and theology, Goertz traces the "radicalization of the logic of anti-clericalism from the common Reformation rejection of the mediatory role of Roman priests to denunciation of the similarly elitist claims of humanist biblical scholars, to thundering against Wittenberg theologians, and finally to the rulers who extended them protection." According to him, this in its final stage leads to rejection of the world and transformation of the world with its utopian theme (Goertz 1993 quoted by Stayer 1997:147). Furthermore, under the Reformation context, anti-clericalism and apocalypticism went together and provided a breeding ground for the Radical Reformation (Lindberg 2000:265).

[15]It is little known that, prior to the Peasants' War of 1525, Luther was concerned about reform in society as well as in the church, or that he did sympathize with the aspirations and goals propounded by the simple folk. Yet later, he clearly appealed to those in authority rather than the common people to accomplish it (Hillerbrand 1972:106-36).

The upshot was the immediate condemnation of the radical Reformers as the *Schwarmers*,[16] the heretical, schismatic, and seditious dissenters.[17] From then onward, continuity and unity had outweighed change and diversity. When the major Reformers chose the path of negotiation and compromise with the *Obrigkeit*, the Reformation was doomed to keep the status quo (Blickle 1992).[18] Soon, the hierarchical concentration of power directed the whole process of reform as an effective tool for enlarging, solidifying, and perpetuating their dominion (Strauss 1978:25 8).[19] As a result, more power began to concentrate on

---

[16]This is Luther's preferred term against the radicals, which "brings to mind the uncontrollable buzzing of bees around a hive, and which the German Reformers, following him, applied indiscriminately to a wide host of adversaries" (George 1988:257). At that time, the Anabaptists were a general designation used for all religious dissenters and cultists, so being condemned as the first *Schwarmers*. Interestingly enough, Luther declared that both the papists and the *Schwarmers* erred on "the left side and the right" by ironically reversing the modern positioning, placing the Catholics on the left and the radicals on the right (George 1988:257). Gordon Rupp once translated this term as "too many bees chasing too few bonnets" (Rupp 1957:147).

[17]With regard to this, much of the condemnation was particularly laid at the head of Anabaptists (namely, "re-baptizers") who advocated for believers' baptism and attacked infant baptism. "Since infant baptism typically served as the cornerstone of the church-state Christendom amalgam, whereby the child was enrolled in the census and granted citizenship, marriage privileges, and inheritance rights, most magistrates [and the Magisterial Reformers] found the abolition of this practice quite threatening to civil [and ecclesiastical] stability and wished to punish re-baptizers." For both the magistrates and the Magisterial Reformers, there was the high affinity between re-baptism and treason (MacGregor 2006:144). For more details on this relation, see also Cairns' book (1996).

[18]This reminds one of Lewis A. Coser's classical theory that conflict with an opposing force can strengthen internal cohesion and increase centralization, make members more conscious of their group bonds, increase their participation, and reaffirm the group's value system (1956:87-90). The victory of the major Reformers over against radicals probably accelerated this process more easily and more effectively.

[19]It is quite certain that none of major Reformers withdrew their hostile stance against the radicals and the common men in a substantial way. Since they believed that what the gospel demanded was the preservation of the religious and political status quo, it was of the devil when the radicals and their following masses had arbitrarily used the gospel for their own sake. Therefore, they stuck to their initial position— "As theologians the [official] Reformers did not stoop to joining [radicals and the simple folks] when it came to interpreting the gospel . . . As intellectuals, the [official] Reformers did not stoop to the political aspirations of the radicals and the simple folks" (Blickle 1992:199).

fewer elites, and a more politically centralized body cemented a more ecclesiastically conservative and moderate Reformation.[20]

However, once set up, this political and religious uniformity was never moderate and tolerable. In dealing with outsiders, the major Reformers and the political authorities showed no mercy. Whereas they formed an alliance to oust the radical Reformers and the common people, who had sided with them (Strauss 1978:30), the major Reformers especially came out firing on all cylinders, smashing their rival party to prevent any attempt which could advocate for the social and political new order[21] under the banner of "pure gospel"[22] (the main slogan of the common people). This aggressive attack toward outsiders ended in the monopoly of the gospel by those who were already blessed and privileged.

In short, the Reformation, seen as history from below, became good news to the powerful but bad news to the powerless. To be sure, the right of Reformation *(ius reformandi)* was reduced for the common people to the political and religious bigwigs in general and to the city fathers in Zwingli's case and the territorial princes in Luther's case (Yoder 1984:23, Brady 2008:24). This *volte-face* of the Reformation had culminated in the

---

[20]Many—if not all—scholars have agreed that there was the fundamental change of attitude in Luther in this regard. This transition of his stance itself is an interesting topic but the following examples would suffice to show how Luther changed his viewpoint on the impending issue. It can be traced against his view of political authority, against his later pamphlets, directed against insurrection or rebellion, against his attitude in the Peasants' War of 1525, and against his later approval for establishment of the *Landeskirchen* (territorial church) (Krey 1983:1-69).

[21]Yet, some historians insist that it is much the oppression of the gospel from above that triggered radical resistance from below. In this sense, Luther's sharp criticism of the rebellious peasants can be heard as self-accusation. He argued that "the Christian name, the Christian name, I say, leave it alone and do not abuse it as a cover for your impatient, un-peaceful, unchristian understanding; I do not want to allow or accept it, but tear it all from you, by words and writings, to the best of my ability, as long as there is one vein in my body." Here, Luther insisted that whoever told the peasants to draw secular conclusions from the gospel was a "false prophet," even a "murderous prophet" (quoted by Blickle 1998:67).

[22]In fact, the term "pure gospel" has a special meaning for the common people. From their perspective, the Reformation was always a voluntary movement to implement the pure gospel, without any addition of human doctrine. In this sense, all demands of the commoners were based on the aspiration "to hear the gospel and live accordingly." Since the gospel mirrors God's will for justice, the Reformation should take both religio-theological and socio-political factors seriously, both of which were closely intermingled with their concrete life situation (Blickle 1992:100, 153). In this light, the common people saw that the Reformation was stalled and suffered both religio-ecclesiastically and socio-politically when the major Reformers began taking the lead.

dictum of *cuius regio eius religio*.[23] From a lens of history from below, the princely takeover reduced the Reformation to re-formation of the powerful, who tamed its original vigor, and its pure message was diluted so as not to materialize the hoped-for Reformation from below. Yet this does not mean that a bottom-up Reformation inspired by the common men was totally replaced by a top-down Reformation sponsored by the great men. Rather, it marks a "caesura" for the coming of the new history of the Radical Reformation (Reinhard 2001:313-20 quoted by Blickle 2008:76), which now will be looked at more closely.

The Characteristics of the Radical Reformation

From Theology to History

The concept of the sixteenth-century Radical Reformation has constantly evolved toward better redefinition since it was introduced by George Huntston Williams in 1962. From then onward, it has served as an attractive alternative to Anabaptists, the amorphous mass organized under the banner of believer's baptism (Stayer 1995:249). Williams prefers to put the Radical Reformation under a more theological category, consisting of "theological belief of believer's baptism, the sleep of the soul pending the resurrection, the separation of church and state, a commitment to missions," and insistence on free will against predestination (Stayer 1995:249). However, this has come under harsh criticism because not a single one of these beliefs was actually held by all radicals of the Reformation. Lutheran church historians and theologians have also argued that, if theological innovation is an important criterion for the Radical Reformation, then Luther is to be hailed as a champion of the Radical Reformation due to his rupture with the medieval traditions (Lindberg 1976). More problematic is that Williams' Radical Reformation rather stands closer to the right wing of the Reformation than to the left, in its close affinity with the traditions (Stayer 1995:249).

---

[23]This literally denotes "whose realm, his religion," meaning that the religion of the ruler was to dictate the religion of those ruled. This was the principle of the Augsburg Imperial Diet of 1555.

Aware of such controversy, the current scholarship is reconsidering the substance of the Radical Reformation as the social and historical movement that was closely associated with the expectation of a fundamental change in church and society against the moderate Reformation undertaken by the established Protestant churches (Goertz 1987). This leads to a significant turn of scholarly concern from the intellectual and theological rupture of the immediate past to social and historical break with the society of the present (Goertz 1982:21, Laube 1988:9-23). At issue here is the subject of the Radical Reformation in all its facets—social, economic, political, religious—not just its intellectual content (Laube 1988:9-23). Here, the core of the Radical Reformation has begun to be seen "as history, as an event of the distant past, and as a complex network of historical relationships" (Moeller 1972:7).

As such, there have been emerging voices attempting to achieve a historical rehabilitation of the once-rejected figures of the sixteenth-century Reformation. Attention has been particularly paid to the radicals of the Reformation who changed themselves from co-workers of the major Reformers to critics of a "stalled" Reformation (Goertz 1982:9)—i.e., those individuals who not only were ostracized by the world of their own day, but also were condemned by the world of the future. A group of scholars encouraged by this interpretation begin to regard these despised and rejected figures as the forerunners of the early Reformation. Some examples for this new trend have to suffice.

Following the pioneering works of Leopold von Ranke (1795-1886), who explored a broad spectrum of these untamable figures from Thomas Müntzer (1489-1525) through the Anabaptists to Paracelsus (1493-1541), Ludwig Keller (1849-1915) tried to trace the origins of the Anabaptists back to the primitive church by way of the Waldensians; Carl Adolf Cornelius (1819-1903) worked for a source-based presentation of the Anabaptist Kingdom of Münster; and Karl Kautsky (1854-1938) searched for the forerunners of modern socialism among the sixteenth-century radicals of the Reformation.

The studies of Max Weber (1864-1920) and Ernst Troeltsch (1865-1923) in the area of the sociology of religion marked an important new departure. Troeltsch especially separated the peaceful Anabaptists from the revolutionary Müntzer and established the gifted Spiritualists as a distinct group (Troeltsch 1931:691706). From it emerged the several types of radicals as the objects of increasingly scholarly research. Yet the most important expression of research appeared in George H. Williams' concept of the Radical Reformation as an entity set over against the official Magisterial Reformation, its most striking characteristic being the separation between church and temporal power (Williams 1962: xxiv).

Encouraged by Williams' introduction of the Radical Reformation, some progressive historians have developed more impressive detailed studies of the various personalities and movements in the sixteenth-century Reformation context. This new scholarship has suggested that the lines between all the groups of the sixteenth-century Reformation were extremely fluid and chaotic (Packull, Stayer and Deppermann 1975:83-121). Furthermore, it has recognized that the term 'radical' is itself an ambiguous and relative notion (Laube 1988:15). In its various and fluctuating standards, the term must always specify as to what context someone or something is radical. For example, Luther was radical in 1517-18, as was Zwingli a bit later. Ten years later, both were still radical in relation to Catholic thought; but now there were other Reformers who had broken with both of them and therefore were radical, while Luther and Zwingli were not in relation to these radicals at all. Here, the term 'radical' no longer can be defined as merely the antithetical counterpart of mainline or magisterial reform of the Protestant theologians, obscuring its own links to the radical reforming movements of various kinds.

The ambiguities in the word 'radical' require the necessary condition for radicalness that it must never lose its connection with the social context (Goertz 1982:20). By this standard, any idea or action would be radical to the degree that it may shake the foundations of society. Seen in this way, "Radicalness cannot simply be measured by the criterion of a rupture with the intellectual tradition of the immediate past, but only by the break with the society of the present" (Goertz 1982:21). This leads the new scholarship to redefine the radicals of the Reformation as those who undertook to alter the existing societal order on the basis of Scripture. The key element here is neither the attempt to alter society without an explicit theological point of reference nor the mere opposition to the existing social order (Hillerbrand 1986:29-30). Instead, according to the new scholarship, the determining factor to make the radicals of the Reformation really radical was nothing but the will to change the societal order on the religious ground, particularly the pure gospel.[24]

This helps one draw the line between the radical and moderate Reformers in the sixteenth-century Reformation. The former stood with the Reformation model in which ecclesiastical and secular institutions should be reformed as a whole, while the latter strove to keep religious and worldly reforms strictly separate. In this new scholarship, the Reformation is no longer considered as originally moderate and then subjected to radicalization, rather its reverse is true (Goertz 2004:70-85). It was Luther who made the Reformation not only radical through his rupture with tradition, but also moderate in his mixture with secular authority (Stayer 1995:250). Here, "Luther once broke the pope's pitcher but still kept the pieces in his hands" (Zieglschmid 1943:43 quoted by Hillerbrand 1986:36). The original radical impulse was therefore kept alive not by the moderate Reformers, but by the Radical Reformers.

All such developed research makes it possible to bring the sixteenth-century radicals into clearer focus, they being the neglected agents who had played a decisive role in initiating and maintaining the Reformation from the beginning. Thus, it integrates both the radicals and their reforming activities into part of the history of the Reformation. However, this is not the whole point that the re-reading of the Reformation from below would like to address. It must go further even to rediscover the common folk who were at the core of the demands for change and thus became the patrons of the Reformation (Schmidt 1986:332 quoted by Blickle 2008:79). Here the conventional reading of Magisterial Reformation served as a lesson for the Radical Reformation—"In becoming an encyclopedia of certain types of religious and theological phenomena, it loses all sense of unified narratives" (Stayer 1995:250). Just as the Reformation should not be simply defined by ideas or theology of the major Reformers, so must the Radical Reformation not be defined by those of the radicals. Rather, it must be seen as a complex of social, political, economic, and religious processes that necessarily

---

[24]Through the *Twelve Articles*, the peasants affirmed that all of society must be changed on the basis of Scripture. To them, religious change was seen as prerequisite for fundamental social reform (Scott and Scribner 1991:252).

include the ideas, aspirations, and actions of the common people (Scribner 1994:5).

In this light, the restored picture of the sixteenth-century radicals must be a mirror that reflects another picture behind them—namely, the common people. Thus, the objects to be investigated include the history of their struggle, life, reality, freedom, and solidarity. This presupposes that the common people are primarily agents or doers—both as history-making and history-telling—within the continuum of past, present, and future (Phan 2006:14). Such then calls for the re-reading of the sixteenth-century Radical Reformation from theology to history or, more specifically, from the theology of Reformers to the history of the radicals on one hand, and from the history of the radicals to the history of the common people on the other.

From the Reformers to the Radicals

The fluid and plural character of the early Reformation indicates that the radicals are to be seen not as a difference in kind but as a difference in degree from the major Reformers. Indeed, the sixteenth-century Reformation was a theologically divided house, characterized by a diversity of points of view so as to produce "a breadth of ideas and a precarious lack of coherence" (Hillerbrand 2012:171). Implicit is that the distinction between the Radical and Magisterial Reformation did not go back into the process by which schisms developed in the Reformation camp. Rather it took shape only gradually, sharper and clearer in some instances than in others. This further suggests that the division between a Reformation authorized by the magistracy and one free from the magistracy cannot be the immediate cause of schism between the two. Thus, the question as to what made them go their separate ways needs to be given special attention on its own merit.

Lutheran background

It was October 1517 when Augustinian friar Martin Luther launched the so-called Protestant Reformation by circulating his famous 95 Theses (Hendrix 2008:3). This posed a serious challenge to "the logical underpinnings of the universal church of the Middle Ages" (Mackay

2007:4). Luther's major objection was manifested in the notion of human's total depravity—i.e., a human's inability to justify himself by his own actions without the grace of God through Jesus Christ. This elevated 'faith' that Jesus had redeemed him through his (Jesus') death by crucifixion, while at the same time relegating the role of the church, which could secure the soul's release from purgatory through the institution of indulgences (Hendrix 2008:3). Luther's rejection, therefore, logically denied "the medieval church's general claim that there were meritorious acts that could earn the believer 'credit' in heaven and that the control of these works rested with the church" (Mackay 2007:4).

Luther was rather naive as to the consequences of his action. He simply expected this positive outcome—that his rejection of indulgences would enable the pope and church hierarchy to recognize their errors and, as a result, abandon the practice (Hendrix 2008:4). Yet, it did not take long for Luther to understand the severity of the situation. For Luther's rejection of indulgences actually included urging the Church to reconstruct "the entire edifice of what was taken at the time to be the traditional practice of the universal church" (Mackay 2007:5). This pushed Luther and the church hierarchy into a serious touch-and-go situation. His resilience in adversity was legendary; he had a narrow escape from being burned alive as an unrepentant heretic (Hendrix 2008:13). Such hardships simply made Luther stand firm by "[turning] his rejection of indulgences into a repudiation of papal authority" (Mackay 2007:5). Eventually, Luther found a staunch defender—Frederick III, the electoral duke of Saxony, whose protection allowed him to disseminate his views effectively (Mackay 2007:5).

Luther's attack on the traditional church was two-fold. The first was the idea of *solafideism* (faith-alone-ism), and the second was *sola scriptura* (Scripture alone) (Mackay 2007:6). The former represented Luther's rejection of the traditional idea on good works and the validity of the papal authority in terms of salvation, while the latter exposed his emphasis on the authority of the Scriptures as the sole criteria for the faith and practice of the Christian (Mackay 2007:6), which thereby spurred his translation of it into the vernacular languages for further propagation of his evangelical message. Here for Luther, theology was to be the language of the Reformation (Stayer 1995:251) and that theological position was not taken to serve ulterior purposes. However, he would find later that some were willing to extend his ideas much further than he was. Among those 'some' were the so-called radicals of the Reformation.

Infant baptism vs. believer's baptism

Luther's two major arsenals—*solafideism* and *sola scriptura*—sometimes backfired. Despite that his notion concerning *solafideism* was in itself extremely radical (to the extent of scandalizing the traditional ideas about good works and the entire papal hierarchy), Luther found himself in a rather conservative position which seemed to conform to various medieval dogmas and practices, but conflict with his advocacy of *sola scriptura* (Mackay 2007:6-7). For example, he not only rejected iconoclasm (biblical destruction of religious images), but also aggressively suppressed it when it happened in Wittenberg under the leadership of Andreas Karlstadt (1486-1541), his university colleague (Mackay 2007:7). Also, he accepted a real physical presence of Christ in the Eucharist with the bread and wine. And as for baptism, he followed the traditional practice of infant baptism (Mackay 2007:7).[25]

All these strange entanglements became reasons for Luther's more radical followers to doubt and even oppose him (Mackay 2007:7). To their eyes, in his early stage, he was radical in his entirety; but as he moderated his views, his initial impulses were essentially put aside. This made them challenge their theological predecessor, which lost him the original impetus of the Reformation. During such a state of tension, the encounter between Luther and the so-called Zwickau Prophets[26] at

---

[25] Luther maintained that some infants do possess faith by noting that "Faith, so to speak, is imputed to the infant in baptism even though he is not aware of it. This is all the more a confirmation of God's gratuitous mercy since the infant is helpless to effect his own baptism" (George 1988:94-95).

[26] Their leader was Nicholas Storch (pre-1500-1536), a layman and weaver; and with him were Mark Stubner, a former student of Melanchthon at Wittenberg, and Thomas Drechsel, a descendent of a priestly family (Rupp 1969:166). Characteristics of the Prophets' preaching were radical Biblicism, the spiritualistic interpretation of the Scriptures, emphasis on the inner illumination of the Spirit, abandonment of infant baptism, and belief in the Millennium (Oyer 1953:19-20). All were getting on Luther's nerves, particularly in connection with their emphasis on the freedom of the Spirit, as opposed to Luther's *solafideism* (faith-alone-ism).

Wittenberg in 1521-22 hinted at being a prelude to the birth of the Radical Reformation, which turned the character and direction of the moderate Reformation on its head (Preus 1974).

Soon, Luther and his radical ex-followers stood in stark contrast over the nature of baptism. Luther and other major Reformers had advocated the traditional position of infant baptism, or pedobaptism (from the Greek *pais,* meaning child) as counterpart to circumcision in the Old Testament.[27] However, his radical followers held to believers' baptism or credobaptism (from the Latin *credo,* meaning I believe) as the act of a knowing adult who personally confessed faith in Jesus, of which an infant was literally incapable (Mackay 2007:7). Since there is a lack of biblical evidence for the practice of infant baptism, it is hard to explain why Luther had strictly adhered to it from his theological conviction only (Mackay 2007:7). In fact, the issue of infant baptism was more complicated, for it "involved the most serious implications for the entire relationship between Church and state, a matter that was of the greatest concern in the attempt of the Magisterial Reformers to set up an institutional framework for their new understanding of the Church" (Mackay 2007:7).

At any rate, to Luther and the major Reformers, this close relationship of ecclesiastical and secular authority had important implications for the nature of the church (MacGregor 2006:144). They rejected papal suzerainty; but just as in the medieval conception, they held to the sacral assumption that the universal church contained both the secular and spiritual authority. This gave them the legitimacy to practice infant baptism. Under that sacral assumption, every citizen of the state necessarily belonged to the new reformed church, and infant baptism was seen as a way to signify that each society member was a member of the universal church (Mackay 2007:8-9). Indeed, infant baptism marked the infant as a citizen of the nation and a loyal subject of the reigning political order because it marked the infant as a Christian. All in all, while Luther and other mainstream Reformers once "rejected papal tradition and the Roman hierarchy, now they rejected neither parish organization and infant baptism nor all ecclesiastical hierarchy"

---

[27]Luther had actually been quite positive in defense of infant baptism so as to marshal biblical, theological, and historical arguments to cement his belief (Zietlow 1994:147-71).

(Driedger 2007:512).

To be sure, the major Reformers saw infant baptism as a way to incorporate newborn babies into the secular community so as to cement the link between church and state (White 1982:443). It was Luther's and the major Reformers' conviction that civic order required cultic unity or uniformity since there was held to be a close connection between religion and government (Peachey 1977:11). A rejection of the latter constituted a repudiation of the former (Clasen 1972:179-80). This might have been the main reason why Luther and the major Reformers clung to the theologically doubtful instruments of infant baptism, which had its root in the medieval *Corpus Christianum*, referring to unity of church and state, mediated by baptism (Deppermann 1984:96). Thus, the radicals' strong rejection of infant baptism became a serious threat to them, enabling them to see believers' baptism as subversive of all order and thereby justifying the persecution of the radicals. In short, the *Corpus Christianum* was determinative for the major Reformers positively and for the radicals negatively (Peachey 1977:11).

Relationship between church and state, and magisterial reformation

Medieval ecclesiology taught that church and state were one as a sacral society, the very concept of *Corpus Christianum*; "the Church determined the correct interpretation of God's ordinance for human behavior and the secular state implemented this" (Mackay 2007:8). Luther was no exception to this position. He continued to assume the sacral assumptions of medieval society, seeing the church as one great body of Christ that had in it both church and state. But since hierocracy, the ruling body composed of priests, was given supreme priority to pope over emperor, the question arose as to which was supreme. In this light, Luther was exceptional. He instead subjected the church to the German nobility, so that his reforms were only from above—i.e., the princes who were in league with his religious movement (Holborn 1959:183-91). By strengthening cooperation with ecclesial and secular authorities, Luther, one-time Radical Reformer, successfully established new kinds of relationship between state and church, paving the way to the moderate or Magisterial Reformation (Mackay 2007:8).

The Peasant's War of 1525, the radical expression of the peasants whose economic grievances were intermingled with demands for religious reform, provided an ample fodder for the alliance of secular and religious power (Blickle 1981). Luther was especially allergic to this uprising, in part because he saw it as a serious threat to his reforming work. Also, Luther vowed to harden his heart when his radical religious opponents, especially Thomas Müntzer, actively supported this revolt (Mackay 2007:8). However, although the Peasants' War of 1525 failed, it was the watershed event which divided the Reformation into two: the Reformation from above, *in behalf of,* and *for* the common men; and the Reformation from below, *by* and *of* the common men.

From the Radicals to the Common People

The German Peasants' War and the Reformation

The contemporary scholarly consensus is that the German Peasants' War of 1525 represents both the last great medieval peasant revolt and the first modern revolution (Scribner and Benecke 1979:1),[28] "which extended across all of Europe, from Italy to the Low Countries and from southern France to Bohemia" (Oberman 1979:39). Yet among many historians, it has always been the subject of controversy. A more recent debate has been between Marxist and non-Marxist interpretations. While the former, first developed by Friedrich Engels, saw the German Peasants' War of 1525 as an "early bourgeois revolution" based on socio-economic conflict (Engels 1967, Steinmetz 1965:9-10 quoted by Blickle 2008:89), the latter, embodied by Gunther Franz's argument, regarded it as a political movement that sought to revive the older principle of right and just (Buszello 1969 quoted by Scott 1979:694, Oberman 1979:39-51). Succinctly, where Marxists saw the revolt of 1525 as a revolutionary

---

[28]Contemporary historians unanimously agree that in its scope, on one hand, the Peasants' War of 1525 was comparable to the medieval peasant rebellions in Italy (1304-7), Flanders (1323-8), France (1356), England (1381), Northern Spain (1437), Hungary (1514), and the Hussite movement in Bohemia (1419-34), which involved a highly developed but simplified commodity production within the framework of the feudal order. On the other hand, it was a component of the early bourgeois revolution, its characteristics dependent on development of manufacturing capitalism, especially the rise of mining production (Lindberg 1996:158-59, Engels 1933).

movement, non-Marxists viewed it as a conservative, even reactionary one (Scribner and Benecke 1979:4).[29]

However, recently there have been some stimulating attempts not only to bridge the gap between political and socio-economic interpretations, but also to consider it as a many-sided affair in which religious, economic, social, and political factors determined causes as much as effects (Blickle 1981). Here the German Peasants' War of 1525 began to be seen as a people's movement, motivated by a mix of religious zeal and social and economic grievances (Stayer 1992:60, Packull 1986:51-67).

These new and revisionist interpretations enable contemporary scholarship to further recognize a fundamental link between the Peasants' War of 1525 and the Reformation (Cohn 1979:3-31). Taking a cue from the new Peasants' War historiography,[30] the new revisionists elaborated the characteristic of the peasants' revolt in 1525 as a popular movement economically and socially motivated; the peasants were being tyrannized and that called for resistance. However, it was also supported (even provoked) by the rhetoric of the Reformation "to hear the Gospel and to live accordingly" (Blickle 1992:100, Scott and Scribner 1991:253). This view was well supported in the peasants' demands in their rebellion, which are the *Twelve Articles*. In it, they "demanded justice, relief, freedom from oppression by landlords, the right to choose their pastor, and the restoration to the village of the land once common" (Chadwick 1964).

---

[29]In fact, the conservative fear of Ranke and revolutionary disappointment of Engels both found expression in their treatment of the Peasants' War. Since these two saw the spectacle of the Peasants' War more or less as an exaggerated threat to the old and promise of a new social order respectively, the shadow of such views lies heavily over present interpretations (Stalnaker 1979:24-5).

[30]According to this interpretation, the term 'Peasants' War' cannot do justice to the phenomenon as a whole. Its reason was at least twofold. First, the conflict opposed not only peasants and lords, but also subjects and rulers in general. In other words, from the social structure of the movement, it was supported by peasants, burghers, and miners as the whole body of subjects (Blickle 1998:117). Second, from the beginning, it was not the war but the brutal massacre. The peasants were at a disadvantage because of (1) their little or no military training; (2) their poor coordination, which prevented them from properly communicating with other revolting groups in order to form one cohesive group; and (3) their conventional weapons, which consisted of scythes, axes, flails, and other farming tools. On the other hand, the princes' armies had advanced weapons, including cannons and armed horsemen. Hence, such a one-sided game resulted in a holocaust, killing about 100,000 peasants and sympathizers (Blickle 1981).

The deep-rooted hatred against the nobility and clergy, under whom the rural population suffered particularly, was stirred further by Reformation sermons that depicted the monks who collected the small tithe as socially worthless and un-Christian (Stayer 1977:89-99). Here, the Reformation served as a motivating force to express the peasants' grievances and thus provided some strength to their arguments (Scott 1986:234). In fact, those arguments came from an economic and social beginning but were bound up in the rhetoric of Reformation and appealed to Scripture as a useful tool of authority (MacCulluch 2003).

In their efforts to seek justification in Scripture, the peasants could both universalize their appeal and radicalize their demands. They found in the Bible evidence that they were freemen (Rothkrug 1984:33). They also saw in the doctrines of the Reformation an opportunity to improve their own legal and economic position against the temporal secular authority (Blickle 1981:275-80). For example, the principle of the priesthood of all believers proved to be the view that Christ had shed his blood for "the lowliest shepherd as well as the greatest lords" (Cohn 1979:15). Implicit in that is that the aim of the poor common men was not to do away with the old order but to reconstruct it on the basis of the holy gospel (Blickle 1992:42). Therefore, the revolt had a definite aim, which was to harmonize economic, social, and political demands with the divine Word (Blickle 1979:142). Thus, the way was clear for recognizing that the Peasants' War of 1525 was the expression of the common people's fight for their Reformation (Stayer 1991:6). In this light, the revolt of 1525 was a prelude to the Reformation of the common men, whose aim was to construct a just and egalitarian society—the invocation of Christian commonweal and brotherly love (Scott 1979:710).

However, it must be noted that the peasants were not mere rebels who utilized violence as a sole means to express their grievances. Rather, more plausible was that the inner conflict between militancy and non-resistance had its prehistory among the resisting commoners of 1525 (Stayer 1972). Worth observing in this regard was the existence of the half-political status of the rural armies that could win commoners, peasants, and unprivileged townsmen (Blickle 2008:81). Similar to the parliaments, "Autonomous village and urban communes were bound together in armies, which became political rather than chiefly military bodies" (Blickle 1981:189). Other significant conclusions to be made are that there were elements of legal resistance, carnival mockery, and strike among the rebels of 1525 (Stayer 1991:21) and that the bloody war actually came not from the commoners but from the mercenary armies of the princes (Waas 1938:473-91 quoted by Stayer 1991:21).

At any rate, there was evidently close connection between the Peasants' War of 1525 and the Reformation, the latter certainly being a catalyst for the former. However, we need to discern what role the Reformation may have played in that Peasants' War. This question has at least two different answers. First, the common men's appeal to the Reformation was entirely sincere, and the Reformation provided them new faith that they were able to change society, not without or against God but following divine and scriptural justice (Spillmann 1965:43 quoted by Broadhead 1984:171). Second, the Reformers, both the radicals and the moderates, could be seen as having had an effect on the common men, giving them a medium for their grievances and shining new light on old problems via the Reformation. The life as well as the ideas of both groups of Reformers certainly influenced the way the common men called for change.

But in the end, it proved to be the fact that their roles became quite the opposite. While the radicals supported the revolution of the common men as sharing their lot, the major Reformers aided in crushing this movement once they joined their voice with the secular authorities (Blickle 1981:185). In the long run, the princes' and major Reformers' victory subjugated the common men and radicals. Yet the failure of the Peasants' War of 1525 does not mean the failure of the revolution of the common men. In the immediate aftermath of that war, many of the radical remnants joined the new covenant of Anabaptism and complicated its character at its beginning.[31]

---

[31] It is to be reminded that Anabaptism was neither a religion of the poor peasants only nor its movement an exclusive version of the revolt from below. Rather, the recent studies indicate that the majority of Swiss and South German Anabaptists came from small towns, villages, and farms—at least 60 percent at the start and eleven out of twelve at the end of the 16th century. The most characteristic Swiss and South German Anabaptist leader was the village craftsman (Classen 1972:305-34, Stayer 1991:5). Yet in North Germany and the Netherlands, where the movement was more numerous, it centred in the towns and attracted a greater following of notables and persons of wealth (the same as to the Anabaptist Kingdom of Münster) than in the south. Commoners were assuredly more prominent in the Radical Reformation than in institutional Protestantism, but their

The German Peasants' War and Anabaptism

This revisionist outlook alerts many scholars to the relation of the German Peasants' War of 1525 and Anabaptism, even if the connection between the two movements still remains a matter of dispute. Among them are John Oyer (1964), Walter Klaassen (1978), Gottfried Seebass (1980:158-63), Arnold Snyder (1984), Hans-Jürgen Goertz (1996), Martin Haas (1975:50-78), Werner Packull (1977) and James Stayer (1977:83-102, 1985:62-82), to name a few (Stayer 1988:100). The traditionally dominant positions render this link much more tenuous. For in Franz Gunther's view, the participants of the Peasants' War of 1525 were primarily rural and militant, so their objectives were closely related to social, economic and political issues (Stayer 1991:5); whereas Clasen's Anabaptists were largely urban and non-resistant, so their goals echoed the religious tenet toward withdrawal from society (Clasen 1972).

However, as the new Peasants' War historiography of the 1970s and the 1980s began to provide a possible point of contact between the two, the Peasants' War of 1525 received new light as a popular movement beyond the social limits of the peasantry (Blickle 1995:161-92). According to this viewpoint, what occurred in 1525 was no mere Peasants' War. Rather, it was a revolution of the common men, with both urban burghers and rural peasants spearheading the massive shifts in the structure of the economy and society on the basis of the gospel (Scott 1979:966). Here, the bearers of the movement were common men from both city and countryside and not exclusively peasants.[32] Only the authorities had indiscriminately used the term 'peasants' to disparage their opponents.

In a similar vein, recent historical research has pointed out that, from the beginning, Anabaptism was also a movement not limited to any

---

predominance was not absolute. In this sense, the concept of "Communal Reformation" (coined by Peter Blickle) once again appears to have some meaningful ground.

[32] It seems evident that a great deal of the uprising occurred in cities rather than in the countryside. This suggests then that the term 'peasant' is to be employed in the relatively broad sense of encompassing the various kinds of occupants, including peasants, miners, craftsmen, local preachers, citizens of territorial towns, and the politically disenfranchised from imperial cities (Fabian 1962 quoted by Hillerbrand 1972:126, note 4).

single region and group but engaged in all social classes.[33] Implicit in that, the early Anabaptists were nearer to a "chaotic masses of group" whose characteristics were in its fluid and flexible dynamics, like that of the Peasants' War of 1525 (Hillerbrand 1962:168, Packull, Stayer and Deppermann 1975:83-121). Furthermore, the princely officials regarded the Anabaptists as direct descendants of the peasants' resistance of 1525, even though most of its participants were not involved in the believer's baptism, a trademark of Anabaptists (Stayer 1991:6). Of course, the Peasants' War was a much broader historical phenomenom than Anabaptism, but this new revisionist view proposes that Anabaptism can be seen as the extension of the revolution of the common men of 1525,[34]

---

[33] Evidently, Anabaptism was a movement supported and welcomed greatly by the peasantry and craftsmen. Yet this does not preclude the possibility for representing other elements in the population. In fact, some of the outstanding leaders came from prominent intellectual circles. For example, in the Swiss Brethren, Conrad Grebel (1498-1526) was a member of a wealthy, patrician family in Zurich and educated at universities in Basel; Felix Manz (1498-1527) was also well-educated; Melchior Rink (1493-1561/63) was trained at universities in Leipzig and Erfurt; Balthasar Hubmaier (1480-1528) was a trained theologian; Ludwig Haezter (1500-1529) and Hans Denck (1500-1527) had gained high education with academic proficiency. Many others of them were found in the ranks of the clergy—Michael Sattler (1490-1527), Georg Blaurock (1491-1529), Johannes Brotli (1494-1528), Menno Simons (1496-1561), Dirk Philips (1504-1568) and Adam Pastor (d.1560) from the regular secular clergy. Some of the Anabaptists were apparently descended from prominent families or were themselves noted officials in their communities—Pilgram Marpeck (d.1556) being both a mining magistrate in Tirol and in the council of Rattenberg before his conversion to Anabaptism; Eitelhans Langenmantel (d.1528) born into a leading patrician family in Augsburg; Lord Leonhard (1482-1534) of Liechtenstein acquainted with Anabaptist teaching as a member of the nobility. At any rate, in the urban centres, the movement attracted a large number of artisans, teachers, book-sellers, weavers, furriers, millers, bakers, hatters, cartwrights, as well as simply wage-earners. In the rural areas, Anabaptists were popular among the farmers. Historical evidence based on court records showed a wide diversity of occupations among the Anabaptists. From it, the notion that Anabaptism was the haven of the discontented, destitute, and disinherited in hope of getting easy material gain pales into insignificance (Klassen 1964:83-97).

[34] However, Claus-Peter Clasen has raised the question of whether Anabaptism may realistically be described as a Radical Reformation, which implied that large numbers of people were involved and thus had the same impact as the counterforce of the Magisterial Reformation, held by George H. Williams. According to Clasen's investigations, Anabaptism may have spread to a very large number of communities; but for the most part, it appealed to an extremely small number of persons in a given community. Therefore, from a quantitative point of view, Clasen concluded that Anabaptism was no more than a small separatist movement. In fact, on the basis of his figures, he calculated that there were only about 3,000 converts in ten years, which meant their proportion of the population was just 0.1%. In his view, the history of early Anabaptism was little more than a dramatic footnote to Reformation history (Clasen 1972:15-29). However, that conclusion has been challenged by other scholars, especially Goertz and Stayer.

or "a religious aftereffect of the Peasants' War" (Blickle 1981:185, Stayer 1991:4), its nature originally radical, anticlerical and communal (Stayer 1977:83).[35]

In this viewpoint, the Anabaptists were merely the remnants of the peasants' revolt with a goal of communalizing the church and thus sacralizing the Christian community (Blickle 2008:81). Therefore, it is not coincident that the movement became a significant force after 1524, centering on Thomas Müntzer's heirs. For example, in 1525, there were 43 Anabaptist communities; by 1529, that number had risen to 500 under the twin persecution of the Catholic and the Protestant authorities (Blickle 1992:105). Nor is it questionable that failure to enforce the gospel as the pillar of Christian life and conduct against secular power galvanized the committed re-baptizers into withdrawal from the social and political order. Despite diverse origins, "Among their shared positions was their rejection of Luther, who had tied his gospel to the princes. The linking of theology to established authority became in their eyes a dreaded vision of a renewed authoritarian and official church, something they had to escape" (Blickle 1992:105). In short, in this revisionist view, it is quite evident that there is close connection between Anabaptism and the Peasants' War of 1525.

Anabaptism

Before Anabaptism was born, there were radicals of the Reformation who had already broken with the major Reformers over whether infants or adults should be baptized. These opponents of infant baptism pointed out that the New Testament did not describe instances of infant baptism. Rather, all baptisms recorded in the New Testament involved adults who had conscious, deliberate faith in Jesus Christ (Mark 1:4, 16:16). Therefore, it was hard for them to accept that an infant could believe and repent. They argued that baptism must be seen as including confession of faith by an adult—i.e., believer's baptism (Mackay 2007:9).

---

[35]From this viewpoint, James Stayer came to the conclusion that Swiss Anabaptism was originally a revolutionary movement. For him, Anabaptism of Brotli in Zollikon and Reublin in Witikon, in terms of the opposition to the tithe with its religious and economic connotation, were not separated from the turbulent and revolutionary currents of the day, especially the rampant peasants' movement (Stayer 1977:83-102).

However, this view was barely tolerable in the context of the sixteenth-century, making their position even more precarious; and soon, persecutions became their fate. Their persecutors (both Protestant and Catholic) named them Anabaptist, referring to the practice of "re-baptizing"[36] when one converted, even if one had been baptized as an infant. Thus, since adherents of believer's baptism rejected the validity of the initial infant baptism because it was not part of Scripture, there could be no rebaptism for them; and the term 'Anabaptist' was in origin nothing but one of hostility (Mackay 2007:9).

On the baptism issue, Huldrych Zwingli (1484-1531), a leading Reformer in Zurich, followed Luther's footsteps by accepting the practice of infant baptism under the pretext of establishing a new reformed church as a form of "state-sponsored" religion (Mackay 2007:8, 10, Stephens 1986:206-16). This brought the increasing tension between Zwingli and his followers who advocated more radical reforms (Mackay 2007:10). In 1523 an official disputation between the two ended in the victory of Zwingli. Against it, several radicals, following the leadership of Conrad Grebel (1498-1526) and Felix Manz (1498-1527), began to prepare for an independent church of believers (Mackay 2007:10).

In January 1525, Zwingli was trying to push ahead by suppressing the objections of his detractors. An official decree was passed stating that all who continued to refuse baptizing their infants should be expelled from Zurich unless they had them baptized within one week (Mackay 2007:10). Against it, sixteen of the radicals met on Saturday evening, January 21, 1525, and Conrad Grebel baptized George Blaurock (1491-1529); in turn, the two baptized the assembly of all members.[37] This marked the formal birth of Swiss Anabaptism (Ruth 1975, Mackay 2007:10).

---

[36]The term 're-baptizer' appeared for the first time in a report of Hans Brenwald, pastor of Hinwil, to the Zurich town council on November 13, 1525 (Muralt and Schmid 1952:129 quoted by Clasen 1972:439-40, note 13).

[37]Zwingli was later to write that he and his followers had wondered at first why the radicals were so insistent on the question of baptism; but subsequently they realized that, if infant baptism was rejected, it would be necessary for the radicals to baptize conscientious believers, thus establishing a new church. In other words, Zwingli regarded establishment of a separate church of Christian purists as the radicals' essential concern (Clasen 1972:5).

But the fate of Anabaptism was marked by bitter experiences. Both Catholics and Protestants considered it a threat to society and thus persecuted the Anabaptists, resorting to torture and execution in attempts to curb the growth of the "neo-Donatist" movement (Mackay 2007:10). Nonetheless, the movement gained adherents across an expanse of territory stretching from Switzerland through southern Germany into Austria. Even though the movement was never organized into a unitary hierarchical institution, it was spread by a number of charismatic leaders (Mackay 2007:10). Notable was a parallel development of the role of Anabaptist congregations, which began to commission their leaders. These congregations chose their leaders that had not been appointed by either ecclesiastical superiors or the government (Littell 1958:92-3). In a historical twist of fate, the demand for popular election, which was made by the peasants in the uprising of 1525, was fully carried out by future Anabaptists (Clasen 1972:52-3).

To some extent, the Anabaptist worldview became the road to withdrawal from the world. It arose from a conflicting reading between two biblical passages—Romans 13:1 and Acts 5:29 (Mackay 2007:11). The Catholics and the Magisterial Reformers found the validity of the Christian loyalty to the state in Paul's assertions in Romans, while the Anabaptists rejected the state's pretensions, arguing that it was necessary to obey God rather than human beings as Peter declared in Acts (Mackay 2007:11-12). Thus, for both Catholic and Protestant authorities, who conceived of *Corpus Christianum*—the coexistence between a civil society and the established religious community—it was not simply the rejection of infant baptism that distinguished the Anabaptists from their neighbours (Mackay 2007:11-12).

It was rather the worldview of the Anabaptists which brought direct and serious threat to the ruling authorities, including refusal to pay taxes, swear oaths, or perform military service (Mackay 2007:12). To be sure, the decision to baptize adults seriously undermined the claim to universal inclusiveness that was the foundation of both ecclesiastical and secular order (Driedger 2007:515). Therefore, Anabaptist resistance came as a shock to them, recalling the peasant revolt in 1525, which proved a subversive potential of revolution from below. The proof of this was the bloody history of Anabaptism as a whole, with persecution by both Catholic and Protestant authorities (Blickle 1981:185).

In summation, in the new Anabaptist historiography, the Peasants' War of 1525, Anabaptism and the Reformation are all intimately intertwined with one another and at the centre of these movements are the common men, called sometimes peasants, or Anabaptists and other times radicals. Reshaping the Peasants' War of 1525 and the Anabaptist movement into the context of the Reformation, therefore, includes a shift of focus from great men's thoughts and deeds to those of the common men, while not denying the importance of the former. In it, the Peasants' War of 1525 is no longer just the socially and economically driven rebellion by the peasants. Rather, both urban and rural common men are the most ardent participants and supporters of this revolution from below. Hence, it is to be seen as a revolution of the common men for their freedom and communal autonomy that is motivated by a mix of religious zeal and social and economic grievances.

This communal form of revolution is, then, infused by the rhetoric of the Reformation—"to hear the Gospel and to live accordingly" and the support of the early Reformation by the common men is best explained by the fact that both city and village communities had conspicuously attempted to communalize the church through their communal action. This approach also gives Anabaptism new dignity. Appearing as a 'religious aftereffect' of the Peasants' War of 1525, this movement had sought another more radical form of Reformation, embracing all social classes beyond the intellectual and the laity.

In light of this framework, all three movements converge on two major characteristics: radical and communal. On one hand, all are "radical" not only religiously and morally, but also as to socio-economic and political reforms. All aim at bringing about not merely the restoration to its original state, but the total restitution, the act of restoration, which is open to an alternative and even a new state. On the other hand, all are "communal" in that both urban burghers and rural peasants made the same demands of the church and society—namely, the invocation of communal Christianity without the entire hierarchical structure of both church and society.

In short, all three movements—the Peasant's War of 1525, Anabaptism, and the Reformation—can be characterized as radically communal and communally radical and the pillar of them are the common people. By contrast, in this approach, the major Reformers and their Reformation are conservative and even reactionary in opposition to the peasants' revolt and Anabaptism from magisterially sanctioned reform. This new interpretation, then, urges us to re-read all three movements differently as both the Radical and the Communal Reformation from below—i.e., the Radical Reformation to the common men—for a more nuanced and balanced interpretation of the sixteenth-century Reformation.

Chapter 2

Re-Reading Anabaptism from the Radical Reformation

Anabaptism and the Radical Reformation

Blueprints of the sixteenth-century Magisterial Reformation—the Reformation from above—were relentlessly vetoed by all radical participants, including those Anabaptists who were significantly connected with the Peasants' War of 1525. Their allegiance to believer's baptism made them the heretical descendants of the ancient Donatists (Shelley 1995:248), and their link to the peasants' revolt aggravated the already negative images held by many as being subversive and violent dissenters (Friesen 1974:46-7)

In one sense, it becomes evident that there is a close connection between the radical Anabaptism and the Peasants' War of 1525 (Stayer 1988:99-135, Goertz 1996:10-11). To be sure, those places that experienced a more violent version of the revolt (e.g., Franconia, Thuringia, South Tyrol) became mostly Anabaptist (Stayer 1988:99-135). But in another sense, neither were all peasants radical Anabaptists nor did all of them participate in the Peasants' War of 1525. Nonetheless, the term "Anabaptist" was often used interchangeably with the militant radicals by their opponents (Shelley 1995:248). Whether some of the leaders of the revolt were really Anabaptists or not, it is hard to deny that there is a significant link between the early Anabaptist leadership and the Radical Reformers, such as Thomas Müntzer, Andreas Karlstadt, and Caspar Schwenckfeld, and this relationship added fuel to the defamation of the "radical rebaptizers" (Haude 2002:241). This proves a close affinity between Anabaptists and radicals once again; for both were similar in their characteristics, even to the extent that they could not be distinguished from each other by their opponents (Williams and Mergal 1957:25).

The rich diversity in Anabaptism[1] lends significant insights to the relationship of the Radical Reformation and Anabaptism. On one hand, within Anabaptism, there were divergent groups. At one end of the spectrum were the Swiss Brethren, a biblical group that shared the idea of *sola scriptura* with the mainline Reformers, who considered the Sermon on the Mount a binding law (Williams 1962:853). At the other end, there were the spiritualist groups who disregarded all Christian norms in the name of the freedom of the Spirit (Oyer 1953:88, Williams 1962:854). Some, like Michael Sattler, pledged themselves to strict pacifism in the "Schleitheim Articles,"[2] while others, like Melchior Hoffman and Münster Anabaptists, proclaimed the annihilation of the godless by the sword (Williams 1962:207, 855). In relation to this, one believed in the possibility of a Christian government, while the other considered that impossible, especially after the experiences of the Peasants' War of 1525 (Matheson 1988:188-224). To be sure, in Anabaptism, all divergent groups had developed their own beliefs and practices, both regionally and doctrinally.

At point here is that such diversity in Anabaptism was transformed into unity with the arrival of the Magisterial Reformation (Williams and Mergal 1957:29). Despite a wide spectrum of doctrinal and disciplinary traits, the divergent Anabaptist groups became one unified force in opposition of the Magisterial Reformation (Williams 2000:1305). Here, their diversity paled into insignificance against the seriousness of the

---

[1] Already in 1531, Sebastian Franck was writing of the perplexing diversity in the Anabaptist doctrines, mentioning few groups by name; in 1538, Kaspar Heido presented a list of thirteen groups; in 1544, Johannes Gast listed seven; and in 1566, Wendel Arzt also listed seven (Clasen 1972:30). Recently, G.H. Williams has clarified Anabaptism into seven regional groupings, they being (1) Swiss Brethren; (2) South German and Austrian Anabaptists; (3) Hutterites; (4) Melchiorite Lower German, Netherlandish, English, and Prussian Anabaptists; (5) the revolutionary Münsterites; (6) anti-Nicene North Italian Anabaptists; and (7) anti-Nicene Polish and Lithuanian Brethren (Williams 1962:853).

[2] However, the recent scholarship suggests that, contrary to what is usually believed, the early congregation of the Swiss Brethren was affected by the eschatological mania. For example, in June 1525, groups of the brethren of Zollikon came to Zurich shouting in the streets for the day of impending judgment. At St. Gallen, two prophets claimed that the Lord would come at Christmas 1525. In May 1527, Michael Settler also declared that the Lord would soon appear, followed by similar predictions (Clasen 1972:119).

Reformation from above. To the Anabaptists, the Reformation became moderate and lukewarm when it relied solely on the authority of the civil magistrates under the church-state nexus of *Corpus Christianum* (Christian society)[3] (Ricca 2017:27). This made these diverse groups unhappy and united them in opposition to the state-sponsored Reformation (Williams 2000:1289).

In this sense, Anabaptists were not a separate one-plus-one, but rather an organic multi-dimensional unity in spite of their heterogeneity. The common denominator in all their diversity was the inherent rejection of the propagation of the Magisterial Reformation repeating the mistake of the "Constantinian captivity" (Ricca 2017:27). This then drew much attention to the nature and beginnings of Anabaptism as the spearhead of the sixteenth-century Radical Reformation—the Reformation from below.

Anabaptist Historiography

The question of Anabaptism proper has long been an ambiguous one. In fact, many theologians and church historians have often held different (even opposing) interpretations of the nature of Anabaptists, a sixteenth-century diverse group. However, the tangled debates converged on two major propositions, one exclusive and the other inclusive in regard to the Reformation.

Adherents of the exclusive position tend to place Anabaptists outside the orbit of the Reformation so as to define them as "heirs of the Old Evangelical," "the successors of the Spiritual Franciscans," "medieval sectarians" or "mystics," and even "existential Erasmine humanists" (Hillerbrand 1960:405). In this view, Anabaptists had not so much radicalized themselves as the new driving forces for change, but rather simply held their own position without resorting to the influence of the Reformation (Friedmann 1950:10, Dillenberger and Welch 1958:63). The heavy reliance on medieval spiritual mysticism even considers

---

[3] "It [*Corpus Christianum*] is a phrase more frequently connected with the name of emperor Constantine the Great and is more specifically used to describe the position, influence, and status of the post-Constantine church throughout the Middle Ages in relation to the totality of life (especially public life) in all its facets…In short, the original meaning of the *Corpus Christianum* was the ecclesialising of society to such an extent and in such a way that it was termed ecclesiocracy" (Engelbrecht 1979:11-2).

Thomas Müntzer as the originator of Anabaptism. At any rate, under this perspective, Anabaptism is another parody of Roman Catholicism (Coggins 1986:191-93, Hillerbrand 1960:404-24).

In contrast, exponents of the inclusive view see in the Anabaptist movement the culmination of the Reformation (Bender 1944:3-24). This group of scholars insists that Anabaptism must be understood as an integrated part of the whole of the Reformation (Bender 1950, Littell 1958, Yoder 1968). Accordingly, Anabaptists have basically concurred with the mainline Reformers in all essential doctrines. However, their great disappointment in the sluggishness of the Lutheran Reformation made them the radical dissenters (Yoder 1958:128-40, Walton 1968:45-56). Hence, their uncompromising stance against the mainline Reformers was nothing but enthusiasm for the fulfillment of the original vision of Luther and Zwingli (Estep 1975:143).[4] Seen in this way, the view elevates the Anabaptists as the true Reformers, while relegating the major Reformers as merely the "prince-hireling" (Hillerbrand 1960:405, 418). Thus, in this outlook, Anabaptism is to be understood as the counter-revolt within the Reformation camps against the compromise (Stayer 1991:123). Here, Anabaptism is seen as a direct heir, not as an offshoot, of Protestantism (Bender 1944).[5]

These scholarly debates led the quest for Anabaptism proper to quite a new stream of research (Hillerbrand 1960:404-23), with the scholars beginning to see Anabaptism from a different perspective—i.e., neither Catholic nor Protestant (Klaassen 1981). But the aim of this double negation is to alert one to the *sui generis* characterization of Anabaptism that is both inclusive and exclusive. In its inclusive concern, it entails the necessity of interpreting Anabaptism proper as a *centrifugal* force,

---

[4]Interestingly enough, this position was already found in the 19th century by a Reformed scholar. "Historically seen, the Anabaptist movement is the extension and development of the church reformation in the entire area of the ethical and the secular—even the political . . . It represented *the more fundamental, more decisive, more complete and more powerful Reformation*, which was given up by Luther after 1522 and by Zwingli after 1524" (Goebel 1849:137-38 quoted by Durnbaugh 1986:97-118).

[5]This line of view is not without criticism. For example, Hans J. Hillerbrand posed a critical question, "Was there a Reformation in the sixteenth century?" in terms of a radical break with the past of religion and theology (2003:525-52). Therefore, some scholars continue to propose that the Protestant Reformation had its roots in the medieval past and that the Reformation in the 16th century was an essentially medieval phenomenon (Mullett 1980:55).

functioning as a "middle way between Protestantism and Roman Catholicism" (Bender 1953:2, Wenger 1946:252) and thus regulating both Catholic and Protestant manifestations in a harmonious way (Coggins 1986:192).

Instead, in its exclusive concern, Anabaptism proper is seen as a *centripetal* force, emerging as a third alternative that opposes both Catholic and Protestant. It depicts the Anabaptists as the radicals who took a firm stand against the church's entanglement with the state, which the major Reformers took over from the Catholics (Williams 1964, Clasen 1972, Mullet 1980:105). This new approach even complicates the search for Anabaptism proper with the question "Who were the Anabaptists in the sixteenth-century context?"

Protestant View on Anabaptism

From its beginning, the Protestant view of Anabaptism had a long academic tradition of discrimination. The derogatory term 'Anabaptism' was coined by the exponents of this view; literally, the Greek *"ana"* is a prefix meaning "again," thus the word 'Anabaptist' means "one who re-baptized" (Littell, 1958: xv). The sixteenth-century Protestants, who believed in a single, universal church and thereby classified anyone not belonging to it as a heretic, had intentionally linked Anabaptism to the fourth-century Donatist heresy (Sunshine 2005:67). In the eyes of mainline Reformers like Bullinger, Melanchthon, and Luther, Anabaptism was nothing but a repetition of this ancient heresy in disguise and, as such, posed a major threat to the current religious and political order (Oyer 1964:174). Therefore, the reinstatement of the ancient Justinian Code was seen as the best answer to these neo-Donatists—drowning as a capital punishment for the Anabaptists (Williams 1962: xxiii).

Especially, Martin Luther was quite aggressive in attacking the Anabaptists. Indeed, his harsh condemnation of Anabaptism contributed to widespread persecution of Anabaptists by Protestants. Luther denounced the Anabaptists as the *Schwarmer* or "dangerous fanatics," so that Anabaptism was simply "the *Schwarmer's* religion" (Oyer 1953:30). This sweeping generalization was directly handed over to Luther's followers, thus contributing to a deep antipathy toward anything associated with the Anabaptists (Packull 1979:313). Thus, these followers created blind prejudices against Anabaptism, with every Anabaptist falling into one of two categories—either the *Schwärmer* or the would-be *Schwärmer* (Oyer 1964:248).

This prejudgment was reinforced by the Anabaptist militant takeover of Münster in 1534-35. The major Reformers considered it as counter evidence to unveil the true colors of the Anabaptists as arrogant and bellicose (Elton 1963:103, Oyer 1953:30). The debacle of Münster thus added fuel to the Protestants' condemnation of the Anabaptists. Soon, Anabaptism became synonymous with *Schwärmer* and Thomas Müntzer, a ringleader of the *Schwärmer*, with all the pejorative overtones (Williams and Mergal 1957:26). In short, the Protestant view undervalued Anabaptism as the first *Schwärmer* and closely related to Thomas Müntzer, which was the stigma of the sixteenth-century Reformation.

Marxist View on Anabaptism

Marxist historians of the Reformation embarked upon criticism of the Protestant interpretations of Anabaptism. Taking a cue from their economic interpretation of history, they placed the movement into the Marxist perspective (Friesen 1970:17). In that perspective, the Anabaptist lower strata of social matrix, which is determined by the historical-social conditions, provided the significant clue to the movement. From their vantage point, Marxist historians (starting from Wilhelm Zimmermann and Friedrich Engels) have tended to define Anabaptism as a revolution of the oppressed against the oppressor (Friesen 1970:18). Rendering the movement as a "class struggle for a classless society" (Friesen 1974:140-45),[6] they focused on the hatred of the exploited lower classes against the ruling authorities lurking behind every Anabaptist revolutionary tenet (Haude 2002:240, Friesen 1970:30-

---

[6]Engels in particular illustrated this point in the selection from his letters to Starkenberg on January 25, 1894—"The political, juridical, literary, artistic, and other developments rest upon the economic. But they all react upon each other and upon the economic basis. It is not that the economic situation is the only active cause and all the rest passive reaction. But it is an interchange on the basis of economic necessity, which in the long run finally always prevails" (Engels 1955:622).

31).

As a result, the Marxist historians put the external social conditions as the central issue of Anabaptism rather than the inner religious conflicts. In this frame of reference, Anabaptism was seen as the seed of the original proletarian revolution and the Anabaptists as the proto-Marxists (Kautsky 1894, Bax 1903, Friesen 1974:203). The Marxist historians argued that this social revolutionary aspect of Anabaptism was rooted in the Peasants' War of 1525 and that, after the debacle of the revolt of 1525, the peasants' struggle against the feudal hierarchy had rubbed off on the Anabaptists, who were the sixteenth-century proletariats (Coggins 1986:185). Thus, the task for freedom from socio-economic suppression was also given to them, which could characterize Anabaptism as the advocacy of violent revolution from below, originating in Saxony with Thomas Müntzer, hero of the Peasants' War (Friesen 1974:140-42, Haude 2002:240).

At this point, the Marxist view of Anabaptism did not differ greatly from the Protestant view, both of which regarded Thomas Müntzer as the father of Anabaptism (Coggins 1986:185, Friesen 1974:206). Yet there was a striking contrast between the two. The Protestants rendered Müntzer's influence on Anabaptism as negative, while the Marxists deemed it as positive (Coggins 1986:185). In fact, in the Marxist camp, Müntzer as a ringleader of the *Schwärmer* was insignificant beside Müntzer as a hero of the *Völk* (Smirin 1952 quoted by Friesen 1974:182-86, Goertz 1976:83). Thus, it's no surprise that the Marxists regarded the Anabaptists as the heirs of Müntzer, they being drawn mostly from the impoverished of the time (Friesen 1974:140-45). The transfer of Müntzer's revolutionary potential into the Anabaptists was, therefore, a logical consequence—"Anabaptism stiffened the determination of the peasants to revolt against their rulers and where the peasants had not yet risen, [they] incited them to revolt" (Friesen 1970:21). In that light, Marxists saw the Anabaptist movement as the social protest from below and within the orbit of Müntzer's influence (Friesen 1970:25). This gave the Marxist historians a great tolerance for the Anabaptists' use of violence as the rational revolution against socio-economic injustice (Zimmerman 1856:168-199 quoted by Friesen 1965:307).

However, this interpretation of oppressor-oppressed binary has been made suspect. Indeed, maximization of the socio-political sphere of

Anabaptism (or minimization of its religious-spiritual sphere) came into question even within the Marxist camp. This view emerged as the so-called new Marxist interpretation. What was new was a shift of emphasis to the religious character in Anabaptism (Zschabitz 1958:19 quoted by Friesen 1965:317). These Marxist revisionists proposed that, for both Müntzer and Anabaptism, the religious and social concerns were inextricably interwoven during the Peasants' War (Coggins 1986:185). In their perspective, "Müntzer was primarily a theologian and Anabaptism was primarily a religious refuge for ex-revolutionaries" (Coggins 1986:185, 197).

Also from that viewpoint, Thomas Müntzer was neither a mere forerunner of the social revolution (Kautsky 1894:42 quoted by Friesen 1974:174, Bax 1903:86) nor were the Anabaptists Müntzer's secret agents who simply incited the disillusioned peasants to a violent revolt (Kautsky 1894:129 quoted by Friesen 1974:177). Rather, giving equal emphasis to religious and social dimensions, the new Marxist interpretation began to grant both of them a dual character (Stayer 1988:132). It depicted Müntzer as a mystical-religious theologian as well as a social revolutionary (Bax 1968:86, Friesen 1974:179) and Anabaptism as a religious movement as well as a socio-political counter-revolution to the existing hierarchical order (Zschabitz 1958:160, quoted by Friesen 1974:206).

Nonetheless, this attempt to link Müntzer and Anabaptism to both religious and social movements was self-contradictory in the logic of Marxist thinking. For even in the new Marxist interpretation, the role of religion was doubtful (if not hateful), though not as much dubious as "an opium of the oppressed" (Marx and Engels 1975). This view was ambivalent toward religion and its effect on the masses as a motivating factor for change. Religion encouraged the socially disoriented to revolt against current conflicts and contradictions while at the same time discouraging them to be silent against them. Yet the new Marxist interpretation heavily weighted its concern toward the latter so that religion was nearer to a negative than a positive catalyst for change (Friesen 1965:307). Thus, religion proved to be the major obstacle to the ultimate goal for which Müntzer and the Anabaptists had really hoped (Friesen 1974:238-39). In this viewpoint, Müntzer, though he was "the great leader of the downtrodden masses," was defeated because of the religious errors of his time, and the Anabaptists were condemned by the religious prejudice of church dignitaries (Smirin 1952:59 quoted by Friesen 1965:314).

On the other hand, this further elaborated the interpretation of the Peasants' War of 1525 in a more subtle way. Unlike the older Marxists, the new Marxists began to see the Peasants' War of 1525 as an early bourgeois revolution in which the proletariat (Müntzer and the Anabaptists) cooperated with the bourgeoisie (Coggins 1986:185, Bloch 1960:51 quoted by Friesen 1965:313). In it, the proletariat receded into the wings and took on supporting roles. Supplanting them at centre stage was the bourgeoisie (the upper middle-class). Alone, the bourgeoisie lacked power to overturn the princes (the high-ranking class), so they tried to make an ally of the peasants (the lowest class), who were most active in their opposition to the ruling classes (Brady 1978:199).

In the new Marxist interpretation, this link between bourgeois and proletariat was fragile from the outset. Just as the religious adoption eventually mitigated the act of social protest from Müntzer and the Anabaptists, so the fiasco of the Peasants' War of 1525 was already expected when the peasants were working hand-in-glove with the bourgeoisie (Friesen 1970:32). It proved to be true that the bourgeoisie used this alliance not to close but to continue the exploitation of the peasants under the princely power (Moeller 1972:25). Given those circumstances, it was a foregone conclusion that the Peasants' War of 1525 would end in failure (Musel 1952:13 quoted by Friesen 1970:27). For although allied, the two groups had different goals—the bourgeoisie not ready to give up their privileges and the peasants urging the wealthier classes to take genuine action (Friesen 1970:32).

Furthermore, when the demands of the peasants were combined into the general interests of the bourgeoisie, the peasants began to become subordinate to the bourgeoisie as a whole, the upshot being the emasculation of the peasants in the Peasants' War (Friesen 1970:32-33). The bourgeoisie were overrepresented in that war since they provided the overwhelming majority of its leadership. In this "'early', still immature form of bourgeois revolution", the mass of peasants were brought under the sway of their new masters (Vogler 1969:704 quoted by Bak 1976:98). Thus, the epilogue of the Peasants' War became the epilogue of the revolution from below (Tschistoswon 1965:409 quoted by Friesen 1970:33). From that point on, the revolutionary tendencies of the grassroots were forced underground and quickly transferred into the hands of the petite bourgeoisie, whose aims were fundamentally different from those of the Anabaptists, the sixteenth-century proletariats (Friesen 1974:208-9, 228).

In short, unlike the older Marxist view, the new interpretation admitted the diversity and complexity of the Peasants' War of 1525 and Anabaptism. In it, neither of the movements was a proletarian revolution nor were the participants drawn chiefly from the lower classes. Rather, both were seen as a dynamic mixture of religious and social factors in which the proletariat cooperated with the bourgeoisie (Coggins 1986:185). However, this did not mean that the new Marxist interpretation broke entirely with the older view. Instead, much of the new is still in tune with the original one, both depicting the Peasants' War of 1525 and Anabaptism as a class struggle in religious garb (Friesen 1965:307). In this sense, the new Marxist interpretation reiterated the older Marxist theme but in perhaps a more elaborate way. However, both understood the Peasants' War of 1525 and Anabaptism as an abortive social revolution through an uneasy combination between proletariat and bourgeoisie, whose goals were quite different (Coggins 1986:185).

American Mennonite (Benderite) View on Anabaptism

This polarity between the Protestant and Marxist interpretations provoked the advent of the so-called "normative-typological view of Anabaptism" (Strubind 2003:22, quoted by Stayer 2004:297). Presuming both interpretations presented a prejudiced perspective of Anabaptism, a group of Anabaptist scholars, mostly American Mennonites, began to reinterpret the sixteenth-century Christian radicalism from a different point of view. Deeply indebted to Troeltsch's idea of Anabaptism as the sect-type,[7] they devoted their energies to restoration of the Anabaptist

---

[7]Ernst Troeltsch (1865-1923), a religious sociologist, described the Anabaptists as a "sect-type" in a three-part religious typology, consisting of churches, sects, and mystical groups. Furthermore, he made a major contribution to the Anabaptist interpretation by distinguishing individual radicals (Spirituals) from the radical congregations (Anabaptists). He recognized the distinct nature of the Anabaptists far more distant from the teaching and practice of the major Reformers. In his statement, Troeltsch placed the genesis of Anabaptism in Zurich rather than Wittenberg (1931:742-43).

name, which had suffered a fall from grace. The centre of gravity of this vibrant scholarship was Harold S. Bender, the American Mennonite historian who believed Anabaptism was "consistent evangelical Protestantism" (Bender 1944:13). Basing his opinion on the first-hand Anabaptist writings as source materials, he tried to rehabilitate the battered and bruised Anabaptists not as a byword for rebellious heretics or the violent proletariats, but rather as the sixteenth-century epitome of peaceful and evangelical Christians (Hillerbrand 2003:533).

Bender seemed to view himself as the herald of a third wave of Anabaptist historiography. With an in-group perspective, he began casting a critical eye on the established outlooks of both Protestants and Marxists, which gave Anabaptism a negative image, while at the same time broadening his views of this subject. As a result, he proposed the three-fold reconstruction of Anabaptism—its Zurich priority over Zwickau, its religious over socio-political aspect, and its non-resistance over violent revolution (Bender 1944:11). In his view, Thomas Müntzer and his revolutionary circles were insignificant (Bender 1953:2). Rather, the idea of a suffering church with Conrad Grebel and his peaceful successors should receive more spotlight as Anabaptism proper (Bender 1944:13). To Bender, the genuine heirs of the Reformation were the Swiss Brethren, who strove to recreate the original New Testament church, while Luther and Zwingli failed to fully implement their reform ideals (Bender 1944:13).

This recognition of religious sincerity of the Grebel circle enabled Bender to put the socio-economic element in Anabaptism asunder. Not surprisingly, he concluded that the Anabaptists were a religious, not a socio-political, group whose characteristics were in their discipleship through believer's baptism (Bender 1944:20). It was the logical consequence, then, that Bender tried to keep the Anabaptist movement separate from the violent revolution, particularly from the Peasants' War of 1525, Müntzer's apocalyptic crusade, and Münster Anabaptism. By putting the peaceful Anabaptists in the spotlight, this American Mennonite historian established a new identity of "evangelical Anabaptism"—one in which all revolutionary elements were eliminated (Bender 1950:25, Packull 1979:313).

Under the Benderite umbrella, only three branches were genuine Anabaptists—the Swiss Brethren in Switzerland and South Germany, the

Hutterites in Moravia, and the Mennonites in the Netherlands (Coggins 1986:187). For Bender, Anabaptism's non-resistance took precedence over its violent revolution (Bender 1950:25-32) and its theology of martyrdom over its theology of revolution (Bender 1944:27-8, Stauffer 1945:179-214).

In summary, fundamental to Bender's normative vision was a reworking of the sixteenth-century Anabaptists. This began with his veto of the Protestant and Marxist outlooks. He made any radical heritage (especially from Müntzer and Münster) extraneous to the origin, source, and essence of sixteenth-century Anabaptism. Instead, he constituted the triangle norm in the Anabaptist interpretation—first, the elevation of the Swiss Brethren and Zurich as its origin; second, the elevation of evangelical Protestantism as its source; and third, the elevation of the peaceful New Testament ecclesiology as its essence. In doing so, Bender transformed Anabaptism from "the left wing of the Reformation" to "the culmination and fulfillment of the original intention of the reformers" (Packull 1979:313) and the Anabaptists from the revolutionary *Schwärmer* (fanatics) to non-resistant evangelical Protestants (Bender 1950:76-88).

New Mennonite View on Anabaptism

The Benderite view has come under criticism, however.[8] In the 1960s, a guild of North American scholars began to challenge Bender's normative interpretation, saying that Bender's vision was too sectarian and ideal to be acceptable. They soon yielded a new school, labeling it the "new Mennonites," in part, due to their lingering debt to Bender (Coggins 1986:189). Yet it was George H. Williams who left an indelible mark on this new scholarship. Indeed, it is no exaggeration to say that these new Mennonites were Williams' protégés (Coggins 1986:189-90). What particularly attracted them was his new outline of the sixteenth-century Christian grouping. Williams incorporated three previous groups—Catholic, Protestant, and the left wing (including Anabaptists)—into two—Catholic and Reformation (Williams and Mergal 1957), while dividing the Reformation into three—Lutheran,

---

[8]For a helpful introduction to this debate, see John Roth (2002:525-35).

Reformed and Anglican, and radical (including Anabaptists) (Coggins 1986:189). This reshuffling gave the Radical Reformation a new identity that competed not only with Catholics, but also with Protestants (Coggins 1986:189), the subsequent effect of which was to make the Radical Reformation more dynamic and polyphonic.

Going beyond that, Williams divided the Radical Reformation into three groups—Anabaptists, Spiritualists, and Rationalists—on the basis of their different roots of faith, those roots being the New Testament church, the Spirit, and reason, respectively. Then he subdivided each of these groups even further—Anabaptists into evangelical, spiritual, and revolutionary branches; Spiritualists into evangelical, revolutionary, and rational; and Rationalists into either evangelical Catholics or free spirits (Williams and Mergal 1957).

Significantly, this somewhat meticulous categorization led to a significant shift of scholarly concern (Coggins 1986:190). By recognizing the Radical Reformers as more diverse via their being divided into dynamic groups, scholars began to do away with the previous monolithic image of this left wing of the Reformation. They instead looked at it anew as a multi-pronged movement which, from its first stage, possessed inner dynamics, including tensions and contradictions (Coggins 1986:189). The new Mennonites did not hesitate to draw fresh water from Williams' well to remove the straitjacket of Bender's evangelical Anabaptism (Coggins 1986:190) and in so doing turned Benderite interpretation of Anabaptism on its head.

The new Mennonites challenged Bender's primacy of the New Testament church as the essence of Anabaptism. They argued that the church was not the central issue to Anabaptists, but rather the question of salvation (Oyer 1964:228). The new Mennonites discovered that, in the sixteenth-century context, behind every conflict between Anabaptists and Protestants stood soteriology (Oyer 1964:234, Hillerbrand 1960:411). To them, it became evident that both groups had struggled primarily on different concepts of grace (Peachey 1977:1026). Protestantism held fast to predestination and original sin, while Anabaptism to human free will; Protestantism was predicated upon justification by faith alone, while Anabaptism constituted discipleship as its replacement (Hillerbrand 1960:415). Here, the new Mennonites urged the Benderite view to attend to soteriology, not ecclesiology, as the essence of Anabaptism.

Also, the new Mennonites' stress on soteriology overturned Bender's assertion that Anabaptism had its source in Protestantism. Thus, the question had to be asked, "Was Anabaptism Protestant or Catholic?" In one sense, the Anabaptists seemed closer to Roman Catholicism in their advocacy of free will (Hillerbrand 1960:406-7, 418); but in another, they seemed to belong to Protestantism in their belief in the priesthood of all the believers and in the Scripture (Coggins 1986:192). This *sui generis* characterization of Anabaptism, then, required the reinterpretation of the Anabaptist sources.

Scholars offered three different positions. The first was best found in Walter Klaassen's work, which tended to see Anabaptism as a third alternative that was distinct from mainline Christianity, thus being "neither Catholic nor Protestant" (Klaassen 1973). Yet this implied that the reverse could also be true—i.e., Anabaptism could be seen as both Catholic and Protestant (Bender 1970:2). In this double connotation, on one hand, Anabaptism represented radicalism which was an opposing force against Roman Catholicism and the Magisterial Reformation (Williams 1962); whereas, on the other hand, it also signified universalism, thus standing midway between Protestantism and Roman Catholicism (Hillerbrand 1967). At any rate, this outlook gave the Anabaptists an identity beyond both Protestant and Catholic (Coggins 1986:192).

The second position was championed by Kenneth R. Davis. In his book, *Anabaptism and Asceticism*, he described Anabaptism as a repetition of a medieval theme, especially stressing its close proximity to medieval Catholic asceticism in the pursuit of holiness and discipleship (Davis 1974:26-31). That theory was indebted to Davis' two predecessors—Albrecht Ritschl (1822-1889) and Walther Kohler (1870-1946). In one sense, he revived Albrecht Ritschl's thesis that Anabaptists were the successors of the spiritual Franciscans (Ritschl 1880:22-36 quoted by Williams and Mergal 1957:27, Davis 1974:35). In another sense, he followed Walther Kohler, who singled out Erasmus as the spiritual father of Anabaptism (Liehhard 1997:91 quoted by Williamson 2005:1). In addition, Davis gave great importance to the *Devotio*

Moderna[9] as a nexus of humanism and Anabaptism (Davis 1974:266-348). In this way, he proposed a new Anabaptist lineage, starting from the *Devotio Moderna* to Erasmine humanism and finally to Anabaptism, as a continuation of medieval ascetic reform (Coggins 1986:193). Yet Davis' elaborate theory of transmission had an Achilles' heel in presenting the close link between the three. The distinct character of each pales into insignificance beside his loose definitions of concepts. In the long run, this tenuous connection confused the issue of whether Anabaptism derived from spiritual Franciscanism, Erasmine humanism, or Protestantism, making his theory less popular among scholars (Coggins 1986:193).

The third position attributed the Anabaptist source to the heritage of late medieval mysticism. This may be the most widespread view since Karl Holl's unequivocal statement that "[T]here is no Anabaptism that did not lean upon mysticism" (Holl 1923:424 quoted by Zeman 1976:260). Indeed, there is a growing scholarly consensus on a vital link between Anabaptism and medieval mysticism. This even became a historical pedigree that mysticism was clearly mediated to Anabaptism (especially German Anabaptism) through two outstanding forerunners—Thomas Müntzer and Hans Denck (Coggins 1986:193). There is an undercurrent of doubt towards the Swiss origin of Anabaptism in this theory, thus helping Müntzer's revolutionary and Denck's spiritualistic tendencies to once again gain momentum.

The new Mennonites immediately responded to this challenge with a two-fold strategy. In one sense, they reiterated the Benderite presupposition. Against Müntzer's primacy, they insisted on the importance of the Swiss Brethren in Zurich. Even though Müntzer's heritages were clearly detectable in early Anabaptism, particularly in connection with Hut's discipleship (Klaassen 1962:209-27, Loewen 1974:70-9) and the Zurich Anabaptists' soteriology (Hillerbrand 1962:152-80, Klaassen 1967:258) that did not necessarily mean

---

[9]*Devotio Moderna*, meaning 'new devotion', is best understood as a religious reform movement within Catholicism established by Gert Groote from Deventer (1340-1384), spanning from the end of 14th century to the 16th century. It aimed for personal, inward oriented piety, both practical and individualistic. As such it was a contemplative middle way between the church and the world, functioning as a reaction against both the extreme scholastic methodology and violent revolution. The "Brethren of Common Life" represents this movement within the church.

Anabaptists were merely Müntzer's emissaries (Loewen 1974:70-9). Rather, in their view, Anabaptism was originated by the Swiss Brethren in Zurich, who incorporated Müntzerite discipleship and Zwinglian Biblicism into a new ethic of non-resistance—"the concept of following the example of the suffering Christ" (Coggins 1986:194).

However, in another sense, the new Mennonites turned against Bender's ignorance of spiritualism. They came to recognize that the Anabaptist continuum had many shades between biblical literalists and spiritualists—i.e., between emphasis on Scripture as the outer word and on the Holy Spirit as the inner word (Zeman 1976:261). Thus to them, the conventional distinction between the Spiritualists and the Anabaptists was inexcusable (Packull 1975:100-11), for such spiritual elements remained intact even after the inauguration of evangelical Anabaptism. This enabled them to embrace many of the so-called charismatic Anabaptists into the Anabaptist main camp (Klaassen 1967:254-59, Yoder 1967:104). Here, the new Mennonites began to see the Anabaptists more inclusively—both evangelical and charismatic re-baptizers as the witness of the Spirit as well as Scripture (Armour 1966:135-37, Yoder 1967:104).

All in all, the new Mennonite interpretation of Anabaptism reshuffled the Benderite normative categories in subtle ways. Such a viewpoint both preserved and modified the older Benderite presuppositions. The essence of Anabaptism was basically discipleship soteriology; its sources were medieval mysticism (for discipleship soteriology) and Protestantism (for Biblicism and the priesthood of all believers); and its origins were the Swiss Brethren in Zurich, who incorporated Müntzer's radical apocalypticism and Denck's spiritualism into a critical and creative new ethic of love and non-resistant pacifism (Coggins 1986:195).

Syncretist (Revisionist) View on Anabaptism

By the late 1960s, the quest for Anabaptist historiography had entered a new phase. This appeared as the radical change of the centre of gravity in Anabaptist studies from American scholars to Canadian (James M. Stayer, Werner O. Packull, and C. Arnold Snyder) and European (Hans Jürgen Goertz, Klaus Deppermann, and Gottfried

Seebass) ones. They were called both "secularists" for their advocacy of methodological atheism in history (Goertz 1979:186) and "syncretists" or "revisionists" for their attempt to reconcile the (new) Mennonite and Marxist interpretations of Anabaptism (Goertz 1982:15). From their viewpoint, Anabaptism is to be seen as a dialectical synthesis between theological ideas, as elucidated by the new Mennonites, and the socio-economic context, as described by the Marxists (Goertz 1982:21).[10] In other words, they put the intrinsic link between ideas and context as a key for of interpreting Anabaptist history. This combination of theology and socio-economic context, then, began to break the mold. The syncretists argued that both Mennonite and Marxist views erred in defining Anabaptism proper by giving more priority to either theological or sociological factors (Goertz 1982:21). Thus they adopted the holistic approach to Anabaptism as an alternative, which enabled them to approach Anabaptist historiography differently—from the Mennonite-Marxist debate to the Mennonite-Marxist interplay (Goertz 1982:15).

As such, the syncretists' dialectical relationship between ideas and actions (or between the Mennonite and Marxist interpretations) challenged the scholarship to rethink about the nature of Anabaptism. Since the syncretists regarded the nucleus of Anabaptism as flexible and fluid dynamics rather than fixed and flat rigidity (Stayer 1982:111), chaos-in-order and vice versa came to the forefront as the main thread of Anabaptist characteristics. To them, there had been considerable confusion and diffusion among the early Anabaptists as an amorphous mass until they sorted themselves out in a specific way or until after the Schleitheim Confession of 1527 (Coggins 1986:197-98).). It was only later that the practice of believers' baptism (re-baptism) became the trademark of Anabaptism (Packull 1979:315). Before that, this formlessness served as a boundary marker of early Anabaptism.

The syncretists even argued that this state of fluidity was the common denominator not only in Anabaptism, but also in the Radical Reformation as a whole (Coggins 1986:197). According to them, the Radical Reformation was nearer to a "chaotic mass of groups" whose

---

[10]This alerts one to the danger of extreme interpretations, emphasizing strongly either purely socio-economic or purely pious motive as a root cause of the Anabaptist movement (Cameron 1991:3). Rather, it suggests a consideration of social, political, and religious factors as equally important in principle (Schilling 1992:247-301).

characteristics were varied and even conflicting with each other (Hillerbrand 1962:168, Goertz 1982). The implications of this view are two-fold. First, in this chaotic state, the boundaries between the Anabaptists and the radicals became blurred, evincing a flux of character between the two. Second, at the outset, there were only the radicals of the Reformation with no discernible boundary markers, and then gradually emerging from them distinct groups such as revolutionaries, Anabaptists, and spiritualists (Packull 1977:112-13, Coggins 1986:198).

Taking a cue from this viewpoint, the syncretists proposed that the Anabaptists were a varied group of radicals that consisted of not only evangelical, but also spiritual and even revolutionary groups of people (Packull 1975:5767). To them, the concrete boundary marks of Anabaptism were ironically attributed to its confused, chaotic, and oscillating elements. This significantly paled Bender's normative vision of Anabaptism as being just the non-resistant Swiss Brethren (Packull 1973:327-38). In the syncretists' view, there was no longer a single Anabaptism but many consisting of inner dynamics (including tensions and even contradictions).

From such a vantage point, the syncretists built their own interpretation of Anabaptism. The first element was its multiple origins, at least three distinct ones—Swiss, German, and Dutch (Packull, Deppermann, and Stayer 1975:83-121). They remained separate from each other without assimilating (Clasen 1972, Stayer 1978:193). The second element was its sources in the social experience of sixteenth-century upheavals, the Peasants' War of 1525 in particular. In their view, Anabaptism drew chiefly from the lower class, especially the downtrodden peasants (Clasen 1972) and thus was revolutionary, the main aim being to "shake the foundation of society" (Goertz 1982:20, Packull 1975:57-67). The third element was its chaotic nature. Anabaptism was in this state of flux within the Radical Reformation, being distinguished only by its practice of believer's baptism (Packull 1979:315).

Because of these interpretive factors, the syncretists began to recognize the importance of Anabaptism's spiritual and revolutionary aspects, which enabled them to confidently stress Thomas Müntzer's influence on early Anabaptism (Coggins 1986:200).

Chapter Summary

Because Anabaptist historiography has developed with its historical controversies and disputed points, a number of unexplored areas remain. Nonetheless, the emerging consensus is that there was a Christian radicalism in the sixteenth-century (neither Catholic nor Protestant) now called the Radical Reformation. Even within this Radical Reformation, various groups existed, such as the revolutionaries, the spiritualists, and the Anabaptists. Yet contemporary scholarship holds that such separate categories were not clearly identified in its early stage.

Regarding the *origins* of Anabaptism, both the new Mennonite and the Marxist views considered Thomas Müntzer as the key protagonist; whereas the Benderites gave more emphasis to the Swiss Brethren, a peaceful Biblicist group as the genuine progenitor. The syncretists added a third—the Dutch under the influence of Melchior Hoffman, although Müntzer was also given some prominence.

Regarding the *sources* of Anabaptism, the Old Protestant ideas of medieval heresy contrasted with the Benderite suggestions of Protestantism. Although both acknowledge Thomas Müntzer as being the man behind the scenes, one overvalued him as a 'kernel' of the *Schwärmer's* religion, whereas the other undervalued him as a 'husk' of evangelical Anabaptism. That controversy became more subtle when the Marxist historians hailed Müntzer as a hero and began to separate the Protestant revolutionary Müntzer from the Benderite religious Müntzer position.

By contrast, the new Mennonites saw the spiritual Müntzer in medieval mysticism as a primary source in connection with its discipleship soteriology, whereas the syncretists insisted on the great influence of the Peasants' War of 1525 and thus stressed Müntzer the revolutionary rather than Müntzer the theologian, who left a crucial mark on Anabaptism. According to them, the idea of peaceful, pacifist, and separatist Anabaptism was not shared by the majority of Anabaptists until at least 1535. This only came after they had suffered two catastrophes—the Peasants' War of 1525 and the Anabaptist Kingdom of Münster of 1534-1535 (Stayer 1972, Deppermann 1984:101).

Regarding the *essence* of Anabaptism, the nominalist definition that Anabaptists were all those who re-baptized is no longer satisfactory because that definition excludes the radical opponents of infant baptism, who never took the further step of instituting adult baptism. Thus, Thomas Müntzer, the Zwickau Prophets, and Andreas Karlstadt were not Anabaptists despite their strong objection to infant baptism.[11] While the radical Anabaptists were nevertheless Anabaptists, the followers of Müntzer and the defenders of the Anabaptist regime in Münster in 1534-35 were not peaceful persons, even though they were upholders of the baptism of adults. This means that both the Peasants' War of 1525 and the Münster event of 1534-35 are to be part of genuine Anabaptist history (Snyder 2007:478).

Most historians seem to be in agreement that believers' baptism is not the essence of Anabaptism but rather a sign of something else. The Benderites saw it as a sign of the New Testament ecclesiology, with its emphasis on pacifism against the onslaught of revolutionary tenets that thrived in both the Protestant and the Marxist camps; the new Mennonites argued that it was a sign of discipleship soteriology; and the syncretists laid emphasis on its chaotic nature within the Radical Reformation. However, despite all the differing explanations, the answer to the question of essence still remains, which reiterates the point that "Anabaptism was probably too dynamic a movement to be reduced to one simple definition" (Peachey 1957:330). Figuratively speaking, Anabaptism refuses to be laid on a Procrustean bed, an arbitrary standard in which exact conformity is forced.

Nonetheless, in the new Anabaptist historiography, it seems evident that there was a close relationship between the Radical Reformation and early Anabaptism, deeply anchored by the social experience of the German Peasants' War of 1525, the revolution of the common men. Indeed, the radicals anticipated the socio-economic demands of the peasants, while Anabaptism reacted as a religious aftereffect of the revolt of 1525 (Stayer 1988:113). To be sure, the Peasants' War of 1525 expressed the common men's ambitions to put Luther's Reformation ideas into practice, and despite its fiasco, it channeled the flourishing of

---

[11]In 1523 and 1524, the Zwickau Prophets and Thomas Müntzer had rejected infant baptism and demanded the baptism of believers, but there is no evidence that they baptized adults or were baptized by others (Bender 1953:266).

the Anabaptist movement in new and radical ways.[12] While it is certainly true that not all the common men were radicals and not all peasants became Anabaptists, it is also true that the Anabaptism of 1525 was radical enough and not in a purely religious sense (Stayer 1977:102). The idea of true Anabaptism as evangelical, peace-loving, and tolerant was in no sense common to the whole movement.

Therefore, this calls for a re-reading of the Anabaptism from the perspective of the Radical Reformers who played a decisive role in initiating and (re)shaping the history of Anabaptism as part of the revolution of the common men. Those 'radicals' included Thomas Müntzer (1489-1525), Hans Hut (1490-1527), Melchior Hoffman (1495-1543), and John Bockelson (John of Leiden) (1509-1536).

---

[12] It is noteworthy then that after the suppression of the revolt of 1525, only the Anabaptists of the southern Germanic territories connected the defeated rebels' efforts to the concrete social commands of the divine justice (Stayer 1991:3).

Part 2

RE-READING THE RADICAL REFORMERS AS BEING-IN-THE-COMMON-PEOPLE

Chapter 3
Profiles of the Radical Reformers

The profiles of four Radical Reformers are discussed in this chapter and the following two chapters. These four reformers were the so-called bastard line *(sic)* of radicals whose revolutionary ideas were interwoven with the history of Anabaptism in general and Münster Anabaptism in particular.

Chapter 3: Thomas Müntzer, "the mystic with the hammer" (Goertz 1976), had unfurled the revolution of the common men of 1525 and shared his lot with them.

Chapter 4: After the debacle of the Peasants' War of 1525, Thomas Müntzer's comrade-in-arms in the Frankenhausen battle, Hans Hut, continued to fan the flame of revolution by transforming the agent from the peasants to the Anabaptists, who had once joined the peasants' revolt.

Chapter 5: Melchior Hoffman encountered Hans Denck, a baptizer of Hans Hut (Depermann, Packull and Stayer 1975:86). Hoffman's movement continued to grow and found expression in the Anabaptist communitarianism and the apocalyptic regime that was established in the city of Münster in 1534-35, whose king was John Bockelson, the Dutch disciple of Melchior Hoffman.

This chain of connections reached its climax in the apocalyptic messianic hope that was commonly held by all. Starting from Thomas Müntzer's prediction to the people of Prague in 1522 that, if they refused to be the apocalyptic elect under his leadership, "God will let you be struck down by the Turk," Hans Hut reset the Last Day for Pentecost to be 1528, three and a half years after the Peasants' War of 1525 (Seebass 1980:154-63). Supported by some of Hans Hut's prophetic followers in Strasbourg, Melchior Hoffman also foretold that the Lord would return in 1533 (Deppermann 1987). This then passed down to Hoffman's two Dutch disciples—John Matthjisson and John Bockelson. As the first Melchiorite prophetic overlord of Münster, Matthjisson adjusted the end-time to Easter 1534 and died in a battle on that day when his prophecy failed (Stayer 1991:123-38). Then John Bockelson (John of Leiden), the new tailor king of Münster, gave a new prediction of *parousia* before Easter 1535, and it too ended in failure.

All this stresses the intensity and creativity of the apocalyptic conviction of these radicals. In fact, the radicals of this bastard line were intimately connected to one another in their (in)direct engagement in an apocalyptic struggle, especially its last stage coming down to the city of Münster (the New Jerusalem). Here Thomas Müntzer acted as a point of contact between the peasants and the Anabaptists, Hans Hut between the remnants of the Müntzerites and of the Anabaptists, Melchior Hoffman between the native Anabaptists and the immigrant Melchiorites, and John Bockelson between the radical Melchiorites and the peaceful Münsterites, which hints at the close link between the radicals and the common people. This further suggests that all of them were being-in-the-common-people through being-in-the-messianic-hope or, said another way, being-in-the-*avatar*-hood for the common people through being-in-the-*guru*-ship of the common people. In this intriguing connection, the four remained loyal to each other, shaping and reshaping the revolution of the common people in general and Münster Anabaptism in particular. Let's take a closer look at them, starting with Thomas Müntzer.

Thomas Müntzer (1489-1525)

Müntzeriana: a Historiographical Overview of Interpretation of Thomas Müntzer

It is well known that Martin Luther always overreacted to anything associated with Müntzer's name. Indeed, Thomas Müntzer and his radical enthusiasm had long been a thorn in the side of Martin Luther. Even in his last sermon on February 15, 1546 (21 years after Müntzer's death), Luther referred to him as "Master Wiseacre" who impeded the gospel's course by trying to dominate it with his own satanic wisdom.

This contributed to the stereotypical view of Müntzer as a "symbol of dissent and heresy" (Gritsch 2006:120). Furthermore, to Luther's disciples (particularly Heinrich Bullinger), both Müntzer and Anabaptists were intrinsically inseparable, the former being the beginner of the latter "down there in Saxony" (Bullinger 1560 quoted by Friedmann 1957:79). The Anabaptist takeover of Münster in 1534-35 even urged both Protestant and Catholic princes to join their crusade against them. When the revolt proved abortive and most of its participants were annihilated in 1535, this served to legitimize Protestant orthodoxy's belief that the spirit which drove the Anabaptists was satanic, having its root in Thomas Müntzer, their fanatic father (Gritsch 2006:120).

While the Protestant view of the Müntzer legend attempted to disassociate him from Luther, the Roman Catholic view portrayed him as the embodiment of radicalized Lutheranism (Lindberg 1990:195). Many Catholic historians sought to downplay Luther's influence upon the Reformation by promoting the idea that conditions in Germany at that time were already ripe for reformation. For there was an intense anti-papal and anti-clerical movement held by the majority of the population, which merely needed a leader—and Luther was the prime beneficiary of the time (Lortz 1968). This alerted the population to many vital figures to whom we owe the Reformation, such as Ulrich Zwingli, Andreas Karlstadt, and Thomas Müntzer, apart from Martin Luther.

Also, Luther's role in the Peasants' War of 1525 was under controversy. Indeed, he compared the peasants to a mad dog that must be destroyed (Franz 1968:414-15 quoted by Bainton 1982:12-3) and this provided the ruling authorities with a rationale for the ruthless crackdown on them. But at the same time Luther was to blame for causing the revolt of 1525 for his messages stirred up the peasants to riot by reminding them of divine justice based on the pure gospel (Spillmann 1965:43 quoted by Broadhead 1982:171). Therefore, in this view, Luther was a facilitator of the revolt by the peasants in 1525 and Luther's "associates" had simply carried out what he had preached, whereas Thomas Müntzer, as the leader of the revolt, did what Luther had advocated in his earliest years (Lortz 1968:356, Oyer 1964:34).

The research on Thomas Müntzer entered a new phase with the Marxist historians, who regarded him as a theologian of liberation from social and political oppression (Lindberg 1990:195-96, Mjaaland 2016:167). Taking a cue from Frederick Engels's interpretation, the early Marxist scholars adopted Müntzer as a forerunner of their cause. They incorporated the Reformation into "the early bourgeois revolution" in religious guise (Scribner and Beneke 1979:9-18) and characterized the Peasants' War of 1525 as its violent culmination (Engels 1920:54). Thus pride of place stood not with Martin Luther who had betrayed the common men, but with Thomas Müntzer, who championed the masses, even declaring that "Power shall be given to the common men" (Baylor 1993:193, 197).[1] According to these scholars, Müntzer's aim was to establish the Kingdom of God on earth—namely, the classless society (Engels 1967:65). His political doctrine extended far beyond social conditions, but it failed because the historical conditions were not yet ripe for a realization of his ideals (Engels 1920:105-6).

However, later Marxist historians tended to give more weight to the theological cast of Müntzer. Acknowledging that his revolutionary activities have been somewhat overrated (Kautsky 1897, Bloch 1962:108), they nonetheless put his chiliasm in the spotlight (Bloch 1960:25, quoted by Loewen 1977:160). The importance of Müntzer, then, lay in his ability to inspire the oppressed with his chiliastic vision (Bloch 1962:108). But this required a significant caveat. Even if they admitted that he was largely motivated by religious factors, it was seen as merely a catalyst to bring about the revolution (Zschabitz 1958, quoted by Loewen 1977:162). To them, despite Müntzer's religion being external and active, he was the great revolutionary hero of the suffering masses (Smirin 1952:83 quoted by Loewen 1977:161).

Indeed, in the sixteenth-century context, there was no way for Müntzer except to use religious ideas, for religion was the only language that the common people could understand (Smirin 1952:87 quoted by Loewen 1977:161). In this way, these later Marxists depicted him as the founder of the sixteenth century "people's reformation" (*Völksreformation*) which, in contrast to "Luther's party" (*Luthers Partei*), advocated a socio-political revolution that would begin with the

---

[1] It was Wilhelm Zimmermann who first identified Thomas Müntzer as a revolutionary figure. Zimmermann's radical interpretation had indeed deeply influenced Frederick Engels to see Müntzer as a precursor of all later revolutionaries (Mjaaland 2016:167).

Peasants' War of 1525 (Meusel 1952:178 quoted by Loewen 1977:162, Smirin 1956:646, 648).

At any rate, the Marxist interpretation gave Müntzer a new dignity, despite some overstatement of the case and thus became a stimulus for a new, more sophisticated Lutheran analysis of Müntzer. It was Karl Holl, the founder of modern Luther research, who offered a critical assessment of him (Holl 1928-32:425). For Holl, Müntzer's theology was derivative of Luther's. But since its elements were filled with medieval mysticism, it brought a tension into his socio-political activism (Holl 1932 quoted by McLaughlin 2008:88). In a way, Holl was "yes" to the Marxist interpretation when it argued that Müntzer's revolutionary activities were not based on theology, but he was "no" to its attribution of Müntzer's theology to social consequences (McLaughlin 2008:88). This led Holl to place Müntzer into the context of a broad interpretation of the sixteenth century Radical Reformation (Holl 1923:425 quoted by Gritsch 2006:123).

Against Holl's interpretation, Heinrich Böhmer, another Lutheran, proposed that Müntzer's theology had its root not in mysticism but in apocalypticism derived from Taborite chiliasm (Böhmer 1927:187-222, quoted by McLaughlin 2008:89). In Böhmer's view, Müntzer was not a social revolutionary who led the Peasants' War of 1525, but an apocalyptic *Mordprophet* (murderous prophet) who proclaimed the renewed Kingdom of God (Böhmer 1927:187-222 quoted by McLaughlin 2008:88-9). Finally it was Ernst Troeltsch, characterizing Müntzer the first "sect type" opponent over the Protestant church type (Troeltsch 1931:754).

All in all, from such various and dynamic interpretations, Müntzer created the templates for the rest of the century—"the mystic, the apocalyptic, and the revolutionary" (McLaughlin 2008:89, Goertz 1993).

Müntzer and Luther

The downward spiral of the relationship between Thomas Müntzer and Martin Luther was attractive to many scholars. Indeed, an assessment of Müntzer's link to Luther has remained controversial. He went his own way despite the fact that "he may have been in Luther's orbit during his early career" (Gritsch 2006:125). Walter Elliger's summary of Müntzer's relationship to Luther underscored its complexity. Müntzer was Luther's disciple "who, to be sure, already came to Wittenberg with the bias of an independent and personal formulation of questions... Luther made the radical break, not Müntzer, even though it was he [Müntzer] who had already separated himself from him [Luther]" (Elliger 1975:7 quoted by Gritsch 2006:125-26). From this ambiguity, he was even called an ally "who admired and supported Luther without, however, ever having become dependent on him" (Bensing 1989:30 quoted by Gritsch 2006:126).

Hayo Gerdes's study in this regard was equally inconclusive. He saw Müntzer's dependence on Luther in the one sense but also his distance from Luther when he began to preach about the imminent end of the world (Gerdes 1955:152-63, quoted Gritsch 1988:57). Carl Hinrichs, who compared the two men's views of political authority and the individual's right to resist, concluded that they were classic opponents having virtually nothing in common—Luther demanded submission to authority, while Müntzer faced official opposition (Hinrichs 1952 quoted by Gritsch 1988:58). Thomas Nipperdey agreed regarding Müntzer's dependence on Luther but contended that "he turned Luther's theology upside-down, focusing on the subjective experiencing of the Holy Spirit" (Nipperdey 1963:140, 147, 183-84, quoted Gritsch 2006:126).

However, Bernhard Lohse reached a different conclusion. Because Müntzer was heavily influenced by late medieval German mysticism, he could no longer be viewed as a disciple of Luther but instead must be seen as an independent thinker who unfurled spirit-revolution over against Luther's Bible faith (Lohse 1974:12-32, quoted by Gritsch 1988:60). Ulrich Bubenheimer also called attention to Müntzer's independence from Luther, having found its root in Müntzer's anti-Roman Catholic stance (Gritsch 2006:126). He was already a "persecutor of injustice," his theological critique of indulgences in Braunschweig preceding Luther's 95 Theses in 1517 (Bubenheimer 1983:6-7 quoted by Gritsch 2006:126). This proved that Müntzer developed his theology without the influence of Luther (Bubenheimer 1983:36-7 quoted by Gritsch 2006:126).

Max Steinmetz also raised the question of Müntzer's independence of Luther. Contending that the womb of Müntzer's thought was in the class struggles of 1521 to 1525 rather than in Luther's influence,

Steinmetz tried to make a clear distinction between the two (Steinmetz 1979:9-22). He then elaborated the basic components of Müntzer's theology formulated in his struggle against Luther's social and political passivity—that struggle involving the doctrine of the Holy Spirit over against the authority of the Bible; the doctrine of the Cross manifested in spiritual suffering and in purification for the sake of true faith, and the doctrine of the Sword, which included the right to resist godless authority and bring justice to the poor and oppressed (Steinmetz 1975:665-85 quoted by Gritsch 1988:60-1).

In addition to the Luther-Müntzer relationship issue, there has also been discussion regarding Müntzer's spirituality (Gritsch 1963:172-94). Recent research works tend to ascribe more significance to the influence of mysticism on Müntzer than any decisive impact that Luther may have had on him (Goertz 1967 quoted by McLaughlin 2008:90). In 1967, Hans-Jürgen Goertz in particular depicted Müntzer as a revolutionary in a mystical spirit, the roots of which linked not to Luther but to Tauler (Goertz 1967:25-8 quoted by McLaughlin 2008:90). Goertz argued that Müntzer joined in Luther's early reformation activity, but he had done so on the basis of a mystical spirituality. He used this mystical thought to form a dialectic of internal and external order and thus the link between theology and revolution (Goertz 1967 quoted by Gritsch 1988:59).

Heiko A. Oberman suggested an interesting connection between mysticism and political history in Müntzer's theology (Oberman 1986:205-14 quoted Gritsch 1988:59). According to him, Müntzer related the young Luther's notion of faith (described in terms of bride-mysticism) to his own interest in predestination, arguing for "the great sorting out"—first microcosmically in heart and soul then macrocosmically in world and history (Gritsch 1988:59). However, Reinhard Schwarz was reluctant to agree that Müntzer was decisively influenced by medieval mysticism. Instead, he tried to link his theology to Taborite eschatology (Schwarz 1977:125-26 quoted by Gritsch 1988:59-70). In Schwarz's view, Müntzer's theology and activities were the products of a "peculiar fusion" that played against each other, between the influence of Luther, of mysticism, and of the chiliastic Taborite tradition within an acute apocalyptic framework (Schwarz 1977:8, 62-64, quoted by Petersen 1993:59-70).

M. M. Smirin likewise tried to portray Müntzer as a mystic who was dependent on Joachimite-Taborite eschatology but linked its radical nature with his People's Reformation (Smirin 1952 quoted by Friesen 1974:182-86). However, Stephen E. Ozment took a more cautious stance to this kind of popular sovereignty to Müntzer. Apart from Smirin's paradigm, Ozment held that "Müntzer's theology of heart became a revolutionary ideology when applied to society, but that there is much controversy on this relationship" (Ozment 1973:91).[2]

Siegfried Brauer and Helmar Junghans also included and acknowledged the contribution of medieval mysticism to Müntzer's thought (Brauer and Junghans 1989 quoted by McLaughlin 2008:90). According to them, the beginning of his theology of revolution can be traced back to "grade of tradition" in medieval mysticism, to the apocalyptic milieu created by Joachimite eschatological speculations plus Taborite (Hussite) millennialism, and to the early writings of Luther "in the way Müntzer understood them" (Brauer and Junghans 1989 quoted by Gritsch 1988:57). Both of them, however, explained that, since Müntzer's thoughts were "erratic" and "associative," the motives behind his actions were not always clear (McLaughlin 2008:91).

In summation, much remains unclear about Thomas Müntzer's early life, about his relationship to Luther, and about his affinity to or dependence on medieval thought. Thus, such a labyrinth of research and controversy about Thomas Müntzer shows that a good assessment of his identity is still in process and needs to be put in the widest possible contexts—i.e., that his aims and achievements (whether theological and social or political) must be related to those of all the other varieties of reform. Nonetheless, it's clear that he cannot be understood at all apart from his relationship with the common people, so that it calls our special attention to his biographical sketch.

---

[2]Hillerbrand, in particular, argued that Müntzer's concern was not practical and thus political and social considerations were secondary for him. Therefore, when he talked about the "poor," he meant the poor in spirit, the "people" were the elect, and the "rulers" were the godless. To Hillerbrand, since Müntzer was a man of words rather than deeds, his involvement with the peasants was seen as a nightmare—a terrible involvement made possible by his theological dualism (Hillerbrand 1967:22-30).

Biographical Sketch

Thomas Müntzer was born around 1489 in Stolberg (not far from Eisleben, where Martin Luther was born) and spent his childhood in Quedlinburg.[3] Contrary to widely held assumptions, he was born, not to poverty, but to modest comfort (Cohn 1961:251, Hillerbrand 1967:3).[4] Although there is little information on personal records about Müntzer, we do know that he began the basic university curriculum at Leipzig in 1506 and appeared six years later at the University of Frankfurt on the Oder (Gritsch 2006:3). Young Müntzer sought new knowledge voraciously, even to the point of being a bibliomaniac—i.e., one who was unable to see a book without buying it (Gritsch 2006:14). Once he ordered 75 books at one time and was tardy in payment (Hillerbrand 1967:3-4). In 1514, he accepted a benefice in Braunschweig and became a priest of the Halberstadt diocese (Goertz 2007:21).

Around 1518, Müntzer stayed in Wittenberg, travelled to Franconia, and probably attended the famous Leipzig disputation of 1519,[5] where Karlstadt, Luther, and Eck debated the teaching authority of the popes and councils (Seidemann 1842:4 quoted by Hillerbrand 1967:4, Scott 1989:10). On Easter 1519, Müntzer preached against the Franciscans at Juterbog, where he had a reputation as being a Lutheran. Next, he became a father confessor for Cistercian nuns at Beuditz near Weißenfels (Goertz 2007:21). There, he read some historians of the ancient church and the records of the Council of Constance, the German mystics, and tracts and pamphlets on humanism (Friesen 1990:33-52, Gritsch 1967:13).

It was the economically important city of Zwickau where Müntzer caught the public eye to begin his official career in May 1520 (Wappler 1966:19-20 quoted Ozment 1973:61). Luther recommended that

---

[3]Unfortunately, only a few facts are known about Müntzer's childhood and youth. Not even the year of his birth is quite certain.

[4]It was Ulrich Bubenheimer who came upon an important result for Müntzer's early life and education. According to his research, Müntzer's family was related to the goldsmith trade, which implies that he was not a man of the lower classes (Bubenheimer 1989 quoted by McLaughlin 2008:90).

[5]In his later treatise, Müntzer charged Luther: "You were doing all right at Leipzig, held a bouquet of carnations in your hand while departing through the city gate and you drank good wine with Melchior Lother." This suggests a firsthand acquaintance with the event (Hinrichs 1952:97 quoted by Hillerbrand 1967:4).

Müntzer fill a vacancy in St. Mary's church, with the intention of influencing the local church situation in the direction of the Reformation (Gritsch 1967:18). However, he soon moved to a permanent position at St. Catherine's church, one that brought him closer to the lower class (Klaassen 1992:35). During his time there, Müntzer's involvements were nothing extraordinary, certainly far from a decision to carry out his own People's Reformation. He had simply joined in the usual anti-clericalism, which was often entangled with economic discontent and social protest (Hillerbrand 1967:4).

At Zwickau, Müntzer experienced the effect of mystical piety and theology in the anticlerical struggle under the initiative of an uneducated but spiritually gifted apocalyptic visionary, Nicolaus Storch (Klaassen 1962:209).[6] Anti-clericalism had encouraged Müntzer to begin thinking about and working for the Reformation on one hand, while the mystical tradition provided him with theological arguments on the other (Goertz 1982:33). His entanglement with Storch and his circle, however, polarized public opinion in Zwickau, resulting in the council being urged to dismiss him (Klaassen 1962:209). So he left Zwickau for Bohemia in April 1521, going first to Saaz then to Prague.[7]

Müntzer's theology, quickened by his experiences at Zwickau, began to take shape more clearly in his November 1521 composition of the

---

[6]He was known as a weaver and radical lay-preacher in the town of Zwickau. Little is known about his life and theology. However, in the history of Marcus Wagner (Erfurt, 1597), there are reports not only of Storch's support of polygamy, communism, revolt against established political authority, and denial of infant baptism, but also of his insistence on the direct presence of the Spirit as God's singular means of grace (Ozment 1973:64). Furthermore, it was a well-known fact that Storch worked closely with Thomas Müntzer. In fact, from the pulpit, Müntzer not only extolled Storch as a spiritually gifted layman (Rupp 1969:259), but also hailed the status of all laymen on a par with that of prelates and ministers (Seidemann 1842:110 quoted by Hoyer 1988:85-98). This indicates that he, more than any other Reformers, not only promoted lay preaching, but also publicly proclaimed it as an alternative to the work of ordained priests (Hoyer 1988:90). In light of this, some scholars (Wappler and Gritsch in particular) see a rapid and total capitulation of Müntzer to Storch's extreme spiritual mysticism during the Zwickau period (Wappler 1966:30, Gritsch 1967:36). By contrast, Gordon Rupp insists that Müntzer led, rather than was led by, the Zwickau prophets (Rupp 1969:167). Max Steinmetz attributes the Storchian influence on Müntzer to Melanchthon's pejorative creation (1963:160 quoted by Hoyer 1988).

[7]Scholars suggest that the direction of this travel was no accident because (1) Luther's support of John Hus at the Leipzig Disputation made Müntzer become more sympathetic with the Hussite tradition, and (2) the proximity of Zwickau to Bohemia had brought him into contract with the Hussites (Hillerbrand 1967:6, Klaassen 1992:36).

Prague Manifesto,⁸ which shows his theological outlines as a combination of anti-clerical sallies and mystical soteriology (Gritsch 1967:56). In one sense, it is the gateway which runs through the present and future of Müntzer's theology. Everything that he did and wrote later is basically present here, only needing to be worked out, deepened, and sharpened by concrete situations (Goertz 1982:33). In the *Menifesto*, he rejected the legitimation of the priests of the official church, instead elevated lay people who had been seized by the Spirit (Klaassen 1992:36). Also, he presented himself as the prophet of the apostolic church and thus as the tool of God in the imminent judgment of the world in which the elect would be separated from the godless (Goertz 1982:34-5). This certainly was the significant shift in emphasis from his previous Lutheran position (Hillerbrand 1967:7).

Müntzer was unable to remain long in Prague, however. After several failed attempts to locate himself in the Saxon Thuringian area, he finally obtained a pastorate in the town of Allstedt on Easter 1523. Here he married a former nun (Steinmetz 1956:59 quoted by Hillerbrand 1967:8). With his translation into German of the liturgical offices, psalms, and hymns, people from surrounding territories began crowding to the Allstedt services. Soon his sermons and liturgies became an event (Goertz 1982:35).⁹ In this reform of worship, he pursued the goal of educating the common people, trying not only to lead them to the experience of faith, but also to make them the bearers of the new order. This enabled him to establish a "covenant,"¹⁰ a secret military organization for the defense of the new gospel (Goertz 2007:23).

Müntzer also attacked infant baptism by challenging the 'scribes' to cite a single scripture passage that a child was baptized by Christ or his disciples (Baylor 1993:25-6). To him, only adults were accepted (Oyer

---

⁸Three versions of the Manifesto are present (in German, in Latin, and in Czech). The two vernacular versions, especially, contain emphatic attacks upon the learned and educated (Hillerbrand 1967:168, note 11).

⁹This suggests that Müntzer's reforming activities were more people-oriented than Luther's. Notably, he antedated Luther's liturgical efforts and was even superior to Luther's in terms of his translation from Latin into German. Luther, instead, saw nothing wrong in principle with the continued use of Latin (Hillerbrand 1967:9).

¹⁰Robert Friedmann saw that, from onwards, this "covenant" has been called everything from a conspiratorial secret society in a negative way to the prototype of the Anabaptist concept of church in a positive way (Friedmann 1957:75).

1964:108).[11] This meant that baptism was not a sacrament but only a symbol (Hillerbrand 1967:10). That stance quickly stimulated the enmity of the Catholic rulers and officials in the neighbourhood and even enraged Luther in his growing distrust of Müntzer (Baylor 1993:25).

As the disorder around Allstedt increased, particularly after Müntzer's supporters destroyed the chapel at Mallerbach, the court at Weimar found itself obliged to investigate the situation (Hillerbrand 1967:12). Yet it was Müntzer who took the initiative to turn the tables. Now he would have to present a trial sermon at the castle in the presence of Duke John and his son John Frederick, both of whom stood under the influence of the Wittenbergers (Klaassen 1992:37). Filled with confidence, he interpreted the dream of Nebuchadnezzar about the collapse of the world empires in Daniel 2, his intention being to win the princes for his "invincible" future Reformation (Matheson 1988:244). The princes must help it to victory against the resistance of the godless; otherwise (he threatened) God would take the government from them and give it to the common people (Baylor 1993:30-32).[12] This was the forthright and bold sermon to be known as "The Sermon Before the Princes." However, the Saxon court refused the prophetic offer of this "new Daniel" (Williams 1957:64-5).[13] Making the political situation in Allstedt too volatile, he was forced to leave in August 1524 (Gritsch 2006:75).

---

[11]Muntzer, however, did not push it through to inaugurate believer's baptism for his emphasis was not on the outward ceremony but on the inner baptism of the Spirit (Oyer 1964:107-8, Friedmann 1957:80).

[12]Here the contemporary scholarship is willing to agree that, as explicitly expressed in his later letter, Müntzer's sermon to the princes was not revolutionary; instead, it asserted the necessity of a new *Bund* (covenant) among the truly elect. Müntzer seemed to have no intention of being against the secular rulers but rather offered an olive branch to them by saying that "a proper covenant must be established so that the common men and the pious ruler unite for the sake of the Gospel." At point here was not that the people would rise against the godless rulers, but that the pious people and rulers should unite for the "sake of the Gospel." In short, Müntzer's *Bund* was to unite the rulers and the common people against all the godless, and the godless against the people. This implies that his *Bund*, by nature, stood closer to revolution "from above" than to revolution "from below" (Hillerbrand 1967:15, 20).

[13]At this juncture, Luther intervened. In his *Letter to the Saxon Princes about the Rebellious Spirit*, he had aggressively warned against Müntzer, though he conspicuously avoided mentioning Müntzer by name. Luther's treatise constituted ample proof that Müntzer's activities at Allstedt were widely viewed with concern and associated with civil insurrection. All this made Müntzer's attempt less convincing and less successful (Hillerbrand 1967:14-5).

Again his life on the run, Müntzer nevertheless was now more politically active than ever. He cooperated with Heinrich Pfeiffer, a runaway lay-preacher, in trying to initiate a radical Reformation in the Thuringian imperial city of Mülhausen (Josipovic and McNiel 1996:444). In an effort to give his goal organizational support, he founded the "Eternal Covenant of God," an even more radical form of the previous covenant in Allstedt, which had taken on a military character (Goertz 2007:23, Bainton 1982:12). After some turbulent episodes, both he and Pfeiffer were soon forced to leave the city.

This time, Müntzer journeyed to Nuremberg where he met Hans Hut who had secured the publication of his "Exposé of False Faith" (Hillerbrand 1967:18, Matheson 1988:327). Then near the end of 1524, he went to the territory of the peasant uprising in the Upper Rhine region where he also met with Johannes Oecolampadius in Basel and possibly with Balthasar Hubmaier in Waldshut (Staehelin 1927:389 quoted by Hillerbrand 1967:21).

Taking advantage of the disorder in the north, Müntzer re-admitted himself to Mülhausen in February 1525 (Josipovic and McNiel 1996:444). Meanwhile, the mood in that city had changed in his favour. The old council had been replaced with an elected "Eternal Council," and this gave him a chance to take over the pastorate at St. Mary's (Hillerbrand 1967:22). However, although that new council hesitated to follow his apocalyptic plans for conquest, it did give him a free hand to participate in the organization of peasant marches through Thuringia and the Eichsfeld (Hillerbrand 1967:22). He now committed himself totally to the uprising and spurred it on. Furthermore, his apocalyptic perspective interpreted the imminent confrontation with worldly might as the Last Judgment (Matheson 2012:105).

On May 1525, Müntzer joined the Frankenhausen crowd, which was the sole remaining and armed peasant group of any significance and, not surprisingly, immediately became their leader (Scott 1979:719, Blickle 1998:108). At the same time, an army led by Catholic and Protestant princes was approaching toward the town. While increasing pressure on the peasants, this joint army promised them a general amnesty on the condition that they would hand over Müntzer to the authorities (Blickle 1998:108). Against it, this charismatic leader consolidated his position, pledging for the peasant's victory in the upcoming battle (Rothbard

1990:146). He encouraged his followers promising that he would himself "catch all the bullets of the enemy in the sleeve of his coat" (Friesen 1990:261). However, it did not take long for the peasants to realize "the expected 'divine intervention' failed to materialize"—in a hail of artillery fire, the peasants soon fell into a panic and dispersed in all directions (Blickle 1998:108, Williams 1962:165). The battle was short-lived and its result catastrophic. As many as 5,000 out of 6,000 rebels lay dead and 600 were taken prisoner, whereas the whole princely army suffered only six fatalities (Rothbard 1990:146, Blickle 1998:108).

Müntzer was able to escape the field of battle but was soon discovered in an attic in the town (Williams 1962:165). In a subsequent interrogation under torture to force him to recant all his misdeeds, he admitted being in the wrong and wrote a farewell letter to his followers in Mühlhausem—a complete turnabout from his former position (Friedmann 1957:79).[14] On May 27, 1525, he was executed, so ending the life of Thomas Müntzer (Williams 1962:165), his body, plus that of Pfeiffer, being put on public display as a warning against further rebelliousness (Scott 1989, Goertz 1993).

Luther's call for stern punishment of the peasants was then justified. The Wittenberg Reformers also joined hands against Müntzer's tragic fate. They propagated it as God's victory over the assaults of the Antichrist and suppressed any scruples about the bloody massacres of the fleeing peasantry at Frankenhausen (Gritsch 2006:120). Nobody could afford to show mercy to the Antichrist and the devil, and Luther and his followers were unable to see it otherwise. To them, Müntzer's shameful end was the refutation of a theology that had falsely claimed the support of the Holy Spirit (Loewen 2015:6970). So, Luther came forth to defend his position: "I killed Müntzer; his death is on my shoulder. But I did it because he wanted to kill my Christ" (Brecht 1990:184-85). Succinctly, the battle was won for Luther, the moderate Reformation was beginning, while Müntzer lost the battle and was forgotten with his

---

[14]In retrospect, Müntzer was persuaded that the peasants had deceived him, since they had been more concerned about material gain than the gospel (Hillerbrand 1967:23). Contrary to his expectation of the peasants, "They sought only their own interests and the divine truth was defeated as a result" (Matheson 1988:160). But the reliability of this letter has been challenged by many scholars (Williams 1962:165).

revolution of the common men. Now we are ready to turn our attention to his theological perspective.

Theological Perspective

Anti-clerical Medieval Mysticism

In one sense, Thomas Müntzer's theology can be seen as a creative fusion of anti-clericalism and medieval spiritual mysticism (Goertz 1967:25-8). Both elements were closely intertwined and ultimately evolved into a theology of revolution (Gritsch 1986:59). Müntzer saw anti-clericalism not as a populistic, demagogic campaign of the early Reformation designed to attract support from the common people. Rather, he regarded it as the material that oriented his action on behalf of the revolution of the common men (Goertz 2007:25). This means his anti-clerical view served as his "theological point of origin" (Goertz 2007:24). Nowhere did he do more to sharpen his anti-clerical critique than in the *Prague Manifesto* of 1521, his first complete theological treatise, which was not published (Goertz 2007:24, Matheson 1988:357).

In his anti-clerical milieu, Müntzer made a sharp contrast between the damned priest and the elect layman (Goertz 2007:26). Emphasizing the experience of God or being taught by God, he elevated the lay person as the elect friends of God who were taught directly by the mouth of God (Baylor 1993:61, Goertz 2007:26-7), whereas the priests in their blind trust of the Word forgot the Spirit and thus relativized the experience of the Holy Spirit (Ojakangas 2013:75). Therefore, in Müntzer's eye, the clergy had failed to lead anyone in the right way to the "true exercise of the faith" (Matheson 1988:357). Instead, they were a "plague on the poor folk," "lords who only gobble and guzzle," "usurious, interest-extorting testicled doctors," and thus, all "devil's priests" who were damned (Matheson 1988:364-70).

Lamenting this situation, he had signed the *Manifesto*, "Thomas Müntzer, who wants to worship not a dumb, but a speaking God" (Matheson 1988:371). In it, he had rejected the legitimacy of the priests of the official church who could not hear the voice of God (Goertz 2007:25). Their claim that God long ago stopped the outpouring of his Spirit sparked his anger, thundering that "Whoever robs God of his speech becomes speechless himself; whoever shuts God's mouth . . . is responsible for *people's* spiritual degeneration" (Goertz 2007:25, *emphasis is mine*).

As his theology was being developed, Müntzer saw this lack of the Spirit in Luther's *sola scriptura,* even if he "swallowed a hundred thousand of the Bible" (Baylor 1993:105). For him, the problem was that Luther fell into the fallacy of "bibliolatry" (i.e., the worship of external letters) by putting the Bible in the highest court of appeal in spiritual matters (Loewen 2015:61). Instead, he insisted, true faith is always experienced even without the Bible (Lindberg 1983:81); "If one had throughout his entire life neither heard nor seen the Bible, he could still have a sincere Christian faith through the true teaching of the Spirit, as all those have who, without any books, have written the Holy Scripture" (Ozment 1973:88).

Müntzer's anti-clericalism eventually led to his open espousal of *solo spiritu* over *sola scriptura* in the direction of spiritual mysticism (Gritsch 2006:45). In fact, his appropriation of the mystical tradition was an essential component of an individual's path to salvation and inextricably linked to the pneumatological arguments of the Bible (Goertz 2007:26). In his thinking, one can gain access to God not through the Holy Scripture but through the Holy Spirit, because Scripture gives testimony but not faith, which is only given by the Spirit (Franz 1968:276 quoted by Lindberg 1983:82, Goertz 2007:26). To him, "faith was the result of the direct transmission of divine truth by the Holy Spirit" (Gritsch 1989:38-9).

In this way, Müntzer made clear that faith is founded not on the dead letter but on a living experience (Drummond 1979:65). By placing himself in the "poor in spirit," who rely on not themselves but God's Spirit (Scott 1989:102), he rejected the 'invented/contrived faith'—a faith that is only accepted outwardly, so that neither does it fundamentally change believers nor does it lead to their moral improvement (Lindberg 1983:83-4). To his dismay, the official priests claimed to be Christians but denied it by their lives. This was none other than a cheap grace—a grace entirely without cost (i.e., suffering and fear of God) and which leaves everything else as before, because it does not change anyone's life (Lindberg 1983:84, Rupp 1969:255). Rather, he developed the concept of 'experienced/authentic faith'—a faith that emphasizes emotional inner spiritual genuineness as well as the purity and practical application of the Word of God through suffering and tribulation (Baylor 1993:16-8).

Here once again, Müntzer deemed the Christian laymen true believers who had an experienced faith, namely faith in the Spirit through suffering and tribulation. For they recognized that, without the living Spirit, the Word of God had no significance (Baylor 1993:56, 62). He condemned the priests as the 'Spiritless Soft-Living Flesh' "who subvert the living Word by the appeal to Scripture" in their lack of 'experienced faith' (Lindberg 1983:82). "So the authority of the priests is shattered by the experienced authority of the speaking God" which is open to the laymen (Goertz 2007:25).

On the other hand, the conceptual arsenal of Müntzer's medieval mysticism was already manifested in the *Prague Manifesto*. It is quite evident for him that faith can be experienced only through the living voice of God in the depth of the soul without external means, including the letter of Scripture, the sacraments, the institutional church, or the ecclesiastical hierarchy (Goertz 1976:120). Thus, he argued that if the priests remained silent on the voice of the divine Spirit, it proved their office was invalid and irrelevant (Goertz 2007:25-6); "For anyone who does not feel the spirit of the Christ within him, or is not quite sure of having it, is not a member of Christ, but of the devil" (Matheson 1998:358). He saw all three externals—speechless, spiritless, and godless—in the same package (Goertz 2007:25-6).

This helped Müntzer build his idea of resignation in redemption—a mystical connection between suffering/pain of the soul and receiving of the Spirit of God (Oyer 1964:107). Using the colourful language of German mysticism, he had advocated the observance of several stages before God's invitation took place in individual believers.

> First, man has to get rid of all coarseness and sin (*Entgrobung*); second, he has to meditate and think on the new life in Christ and eternity (*Studierung*); third, he has to contemplate the sinfulness of sin and God's grace to man; fourth, he has to feel sorrow and repent genuinely of his former sinful life (*Langeweile*); last, he must attain to a state of perfect resignation before God (*tiefe Gelassengeit*) (Loewen 2015:61-2)

To him, this process begins anew again and again. The Spirit of the fear of God demands the self-mortification of man and in the "night, when wretchedness is at its highest, then Christ, the true Son of God, descends" into the depth of the soul (Goertz 1976:110-120).

Müntzer elaborates this process as if he draws a diagram thusly: (1) "The Spirit's visitation to person from within → (2) The Spirit's encounter with the believer through suffering → (3) The arrival of faith → (4) The birth of the Spirit-filled new men" (Goertz 2007:27-8). Then, he adds flowcharts to track each process cautiously; the Spirit permeates people from within; that the Spirit encounters believers in their innermost hearts to which no mere man or merely human word could reach; that this encounter produces a painful struggle to overcome the old man, but it leads believers into the "arrival of faith" (Baylor 1993:18, Goertz 2007:27); and that such faith creates new Spirit-filled persons who will obey only God; and these 'new persons' through suffering submission to God's work allow themselves to be purified of creaturely attachments (Goertz 2007:27).

Such an idea of salvation around the suffering and tribulation, then, became the trademark of Müntzer's theology which led him to preach not a "sweet Christ" but a "bitter" Christ (Matheson 1988:200, Scott 1989:35).[15] Here, once again, he accused the priests of making the way to salvation too easy, so that the common people sought to avoid all sufferings (Loewen 2015:61). The priests taught that Christ had suffered for them and that his suffering was sufficient. Thus he argued that such teaching may have been more inviting but was invented and fictitious because it deprived Christ of his relevance for life and turned him into a "cute and fantastic idol"—a honey-sweet Christ (Nipperdey 1963:14581 quoted by Lindberg 1983:84).

Müntzer rather held that the true gospel required suffering (Baylor 1993:81). "As Christ was crucified, so believers enter into Christ through suffering" (Holder 2009:124). For him, suffering is a prelude to the Spirit's visitation for all his glory (Rupp 1969:188, Lindberg 1983:84). Thus, the preaching of a 'sweet Christ' represents a turning away from the gospel (Baylor 1993:71, Holder 2009:124). Instead, he believed that it

---

[15] Yet this preaching of the "sweet" and "bitter" Christ was not Müntzer's original invention. Such a theme was, in fact, popular in the late medieval German mysticism (Hoffman 1980:82, 84).

is the 'bitter Christ' who must be grasped by believers. But this 'bitter Christ' comes with a task, and believers must take up the task that Christ sets before them—namely, experience of the cross (Holder 2009:124).

This led him to look suspiciously at Luther's theology of justification (Lindberg 1983:85). Indeed, Luther's teaching on the 'theory' of imputation was foreign to Müntzer's view of justification (Lindberg 1977:35-50). Luther's 'justification' consisted of declaring the unjust justified based on the vicarious satisfaction wrought by Christ (Harnack 1903:208, Clark 2006:278). Müntzer saw this 'vicarious substitution of guilt' as merely an intellectual conception (Gritsch 1963:180).[16] His own stated view was that justification is not static and rigid but rather dynamic and holistic (Goertz 2007:27, 38). It involves more than a once-and-for-all divine declaration, rather it must embrace mortification, perdition, and dying and rising with Christ in correspondence with his life (Gritsch 1963:180, Lindberg 1983:83-4).

Müntzer even went so far as to argue that justification was part of the process of deification, for it leads believers to the *unio mystica*—namely, the uniting of man with God (Lindberg 1983:84, Goertz 2007:27): "Fleshly, earthly people should become gods through the incarnation of Christ, and thus with [Christ] be God's pupils, taught by him, deified by him, and indeed much more, completely transformed into him, so that earthly life changes into heavenly" (Matheson 1988:278, Mayer 1992:128-29). Thus, each person has to bear his own cross and must not (like Luther) assume that Christ suffered for him with no more human accountability (Baylor 1993:38, 213).

From his faith in the Spirit and his experience of the cross, Müntzer set forth his own synergistic position on justification (Baylor 1993:38); "suffering was the means of purification"; therefore, "the 'bitter Christ' has to be experienced first before the 'sweet Christ' will bring comfort" (Packull 1977:31, Nipperdey 1980:109). This drove him to accept justification as sanctification plus deification (Goertz 2007:27, Lindberg 1983:84), for in justification, man is renewed and totally transfigured into God through Christ (Nipperdey 1980:110).

---

[16]Many scholars, however, see Luther's justification not merely as a legal and forensic concept but as a dynamic and open one, including both as an event (justification) and process (sanctification). For more details, see Hillerbrand (2004:941-945).

Müntzer further tried to synchronize this inner spiritual sphere of persons with an external reality (Goertz 2007:28). That is, as one becomes transformed through suffering produced by the Spirit, so must the entire world be changed into a purified Christian World (Gritsch 1963:181). Thus, he no longer distinguished between the inner and outer word (Goertz 1967:133-49), for the inner transformation that he envisioned included a transformation of outer conditions; "it opened the gate of the 'kingdom of God'—a kingdom already established in the heart of human beings, which equipped the individual with new insight into the conditions of this world" (Goertz 2007:28, Nipperdey 1980:115). In his dialectic of inner and outer, renewal of the individual logically links to a renewal of the church, government, and society (Goertz 2007:27).

Here, the essentials of Müntzer's justification can be expressed in concepts of time; not an objective past or a completed, fossilized cross, but as a decisive, present process (Nipperdey 1980:110). As the Christ for believers becomes real only as Christ in them, his suffering for them becomes real only as Christ suffers in them (Baylor 1993:61). In this light, the believers become contemporaries of Christ. The eschatological promises of the coming of the Kingdom of God are not only for the future, but also are already present in believers (Nipperdey 1980:110, Goertz 2007:32). Thus, his justification becomes effective and vital. Fear of God is part of the process of salvation and election and an important step for believers that leads to the transformation of not only man but also the entire world (Drummond 1979:67).

At its very core, linked to his faith in the Spirit through suffering was his hope for the establishment of the Kingdom of God on earth. So, in Müntzer's theology, this mystical impulse, paired with his anti-clericalism, paved a way for the evolution of his theology of revolution (Goertz 2007:28-9, Packull 1977:31).

Theology of Revolution of the Common Men

Müntzer's idea of dialectic of inner and outer enabled him to become more than a mystical theologian; it erected him to be an "apocalyptic crusader" against the *Obrikeit*—the godless temporal rulers (Stayer 1972, Goertz 2007:29). Once he was certain that the (inner) movement of the Spirit in the individual corresponded with the (outer) movement of society, he began to extend his apocalyptic accent in his theology, proclaiming the end of the eschatological tension within the church (Gritsch 1963:181). With a conviction that now would be the time for inauguration of the new age, his struggle against the sacred realm (the clergy and priest) as hindering its advent was the logical corollary, leading to his advocacy of revolt over against the secular realm (the ruling authorities) in the alliance of the godless (Goertz 2007:28-9, 31).

Since he saw the elect as being God's servants in this undertaking, Müntzer called for "the Spirit-led cleansing of the godless not only from the [church], but also from the world" (Lindberg 1977:43). This perspective had decisive consequences in two ways. First, the human race was divided into two categories—the elect *(ausserwelten)* and the godless *(gotlosen)* (Bainton 1982:8), the elect being those who had 'experienced/authentic' faith and the godless being those who had only 'invented/contrived' faith or had stolen it out of the Holy Scripture. Second, this distinction stoked his emphasis on the separation of the wheat and the tares in preparation for the new age (Bailey 1983:35): "One must remove the enemies, for otherwise the church cannot return to her origin. One must tear out the weeds from the vineyard of God if the harvest is to come. Only then is the wheat able to grow" (Matheson 1988:371).

To this end, Müntzer founded "the covenant of the elect" *(Bund der Auserwählten)*, which would institute the age of the Spirit (Gritsch 1963:190). This was the logical conclusion, leading to his theology of revolution, a right of resistance against the godless *Obrikeit* (Goertz 2007:30). In the inner process, it cleansed the inner man and destroyed the power of sin—mortification and suffering with submission to the divine work (Lindberg 1983:83-4). In the outward process, it appeared in man's activity to resist oppression by the world; to transform, change, and even annihilate the existing worldly conditions (Goertz 1980:125). In it, both God and man would be active—God acting in, through, and with man (Goertz 1980:126). "It is through his presence in the elect… that God will purge society of the ungodly. God's mystical immanence thus became for Müntzer the foundation of political activism" (Myers 1992:162).

Thus, in its synergistic interaction, the elect no longer remained as mere passive, pessimistic instruments of God but rather as his ardent agents who were called to work with the Spirit to transform the world by smashing all earthy powers, especially the state-church system (Goertz 2007:28-29).[17] Then, sooner or later, the kingdom of this world would be given to the elect (Matheson 1988:371). Here we can detect the evolution of Müntzer's apocalyptic vision (Bailey 1983:34). The grounding was derived from the mystical process of salvation, but the consequence was to be a great confrontation between the godless and the elect, which would assume apocalyptic dimensions (Goertz 1982:34-5).

Furthermore, in Müntzer's thought, this apocalyptic transformation (or to be more specific, the Christianization of the world) could not be postponed to an indefinite world to come but must be realized here and now, *secula seculorum* (Franz 1968:505 quoted by Bailey 1983:35). "Where God is clearly speaking... of the transformation of the world. In the last days he will bring this about... and pour out his spirit over all flesh; and our sons and daughters will prophesy and have dreams and visions" (Matheson 1988:244). Indeed, the Kingdom of God did not take place aside from the world but rather in it (Nepperdey 1980:115); and like the Joachimist third age, it would be eternal (Hinrichs 1952:19-21 quoted by Bailey 1983:35). To him, the Armageddon-like sweep of the Peasants' War into Thuringia would be a sign that the end was drawing closer, and he was alerted to his role in the last days (Gritsch 1963:190, Stayer and Packull 1980:105, 116). Since the time had come to separate the godless from the elect and the Spirit to be given to the poor masses over the aristocracy, his theology resulted in demands for a revolutionary transformation of society as well as church (Drummond 1979:66).

Müntzer's experience at Zwickau provided a basis for his social program. He had seen how "poverty benumbed the spirit and impeded faith" (Bainton 1982:6), the townspeople suffering from unemployment and the development of nearby silver mines forcing most weavers into bankruptcy (Gritsch 1967:13). The enthusiastic response to his preaching in Zwickau and Allstedt, where the guildsmen and the poor

---

[17]This shows that Müntzer's reference to chosen ones (the elect) stood in stark contrast to the Reformation framework of predestinarianism. Müntzer's reference must be understood within the context, meaning self-selected instruments of God (Packull 1977:190).

rallied behind his reform, tended to confirm his own sense of mission and his status as a special prophet who would lead mankind to the revelation of God (Bailey 1983:38-9). This might have been one reason why he identified with the common people as the elect (Friesen 1990:131, Goertz 2007:32). "While the elect could not easily be spotted, he sought them primarily among the poor and oppressed, among artisans and peasants" (Blickle 1998:24).

Yet Müntzer's pendulum at the outset oscillated. His "Sermon Before the Princes" proved that he attempted to gain the support of those princes for his revolutionary program (Gritsch 1967:190, Goertz 2007:31). So when he faced the two princes—John of Mansfeld and Frederick the Wise—at the castle of Allstedt (July 13, 1524), he tried to convince them through his own allegorical interpretation of the Book of Daniel (Baylor 1993:30-32, Friesen 1986:156). By setting himself up as "the new Daniel," he appealed to the Saxon authorities of his qualification to distinguish false from true revelation and thus suggested that they give him a place of prominence, as Nebuchadnezzar did in making Daniel his advisor (Baylor 1993:32, Bailey 1983:39).

Müntzer's conclusion was that "The godless have no right to live except the elect grant it to them" (Matheson 1988:248), so "Let the princes do their duty" (Bainton 1982:11). In this way, he sought the revolution "from above" (Lindberg 1977:44), despite the fact that he saw the revolution of the peasants as being the end of the fifth period described in the Book of Daniel (Gritsch 1967:190). Yet it was Müntzer himself who had taken the initiative in this matter. In that same sermon, he threatened that power would be taken from the princes and given back to the common people (i.e., the elect), if the princes refused to protest against the godless (Matheson 1988:250):

> But our scholars come and—in their godless, fraudulent way—understand Daniel to say that the Antichrist should be destroyed without human hands when it really means that he is intimidated already, like the inhabitants of the Promised Land when the chosen people entered it. Yet as Joshua tells us, he did not spare them the sharp edge of the sword...they did not win the land by the sword, but by the power of God, but the sword was the means used, just as eating and drinking is a means for

us to stay alive. Hence, the sword, too, is necessary to eliminate the godless (Rom. 13). To ensure, however, that this now proceeds in a fair and orderly manner, our revered fathers, princes, who with us confess Christ, should carry it out. But if they do not carry it out the sword will be taken from them (Daniel 7), for then they would confess him in words but deny him in deeds (Titus 1) (Matheson 1988:249-50).

According to Müntzer, if a ruler gives cause for fear of the creature instead of making place for the fear of God, he has lost all claims to legitimate authority and will lose his power to the people (Matheson 1988:249-50). A government that resists the Word of God *ipso facto* legitimizes the resistance of the common men (Hinrichs 1952:8 quoted by Drummond 1979:66); "Everyone should properly receive according to his need. Any prince, count, or lord who refused to do this even when seriously warned should be hanged or have his head chopped off" (Blickle 1981:148).

When his appeal to the Saxon authorities failed, Müntzer changed his mind to replace Luther, who was in the favour of the princes, as Daniel replaced the unilluminated scribes (Cohn 1961:239). Rather, he decided to become the new Daniel for the common people. Then he began to extend his attack from the priests to worldly rulers (i.e., the princes), saying, "The lords do the same as the rest of the godless so that the poor man becomes their enemy. They do not want to do away with the cause of rebellion" (Franz 1968:326-27 quoted by Bailey 1983:42).

To this new Daniel, the increasing theological and political alliance proved that the princes were still too far from God and how easily theology could be abused as a prop for the existing order (Lindberg 1977:44). Such bolstered Müntzer's conviction that the Kingdom of God on earth could only be established by destruction of the godless by the elect, and that the common people were now the elect who would wield the sword for extermination of the ungodly (Matheson 1988:249-50, Goertz 2007:32). Thus he urged; "Christendom truly has no more time to lose. Beloved brethren ... multiply, it is time. Wait no longer, summer is at the door" (Friesen 1990:129).

Therefore, the peasants' rebellion was inevitable as a righteous uprising because the princes had failed to fulfill their God-given duty, and their right was now given to the congregation of the elect—i.e., the common men (Bailey 1983:42). Müntzer thundered that "The rising sought to level all Christendom and to kill all lords opposed to the gospel" (Franz 1968:548 quoted by Blickle 1998:24) and led him to the point of widening the category of those he called the godless. At first, these godless were only the clergy, who were obsessed by their false authority. But soon, also included were the major Reformers with Luther, who had claimed to have a monopoly over the interpretation of Holy Scripture, and ultimately all unrepentant political rulers (Scott 1989:87). This even highlighted his identification with the common men. He now became a revolutionary, being-in-the-common-men.

This was the critical moment when Müntzer's theology of suffering and the cross was transformed into a theology of revolution (Scott 1989). He wanted to transform the inner experience into an external social program, and the Peasants' War of 1525 served to consolidate his theology of revolution (Gritsch 1963:190). Taking a cue from Joachim of Fiore's Trinitarian interpretation of history, he identified the age of the Spirit with his own time (Gritsch 1963:188): "Indeed, Joachim himself stated that in the new era the individual would have immediate contact with God, that the written Word would become superfluous for the religion of the Spirit would reign supreme" (Friesen 1973:17).

Müntzer used the peasants' rebellion as motivation and rationale for a revolutionary transformation of society. His apocalyptic interpretation (based on third-age Joachimist tradition) gave the Peasants' War of 1525 a new character (Bailey 1983:43). No longer was it simply an armed resistance fired with indignation over the plight of the peasants (Bainton 1982:12); but now it was "the cataclysmic transformation of the world" from below, including "the necessity of rooting out evil within the secular and religious spheres" (Bailey 1983:43). The final battle had begun, so that he aroused the elect (the common men) to action with the following words:

> Dear Brothers: May the true fear of God be with you. How long will you sleep? Why don't you serve God's will? Do you think God has let you down? Oh! How often have I told you that God can reveal himself only to the wholly committed *(gelassen)*? Otherwise your excruciating heartache is worthless. You must

start all over again with suffering. I tell you, unless you are willing to suffer for God's sake, you will be the devil's martyrs. Pull yourselves together. Do not sag. Be not lazy. Pander no more to perverted knaves, the godless scoundrels. Pitch in. Fight the Lord's war. It is high time ... The bands are coming in from the French, German, and Italian lands. The peasants in the Schwartzland number now 3,000, and there will be more.

If you were utterly committed to God, you would not fear 100,000. So now, on! on! Run down the rascals like dogs. On, on, on. Have no mercy. Give no heed to the whining of the godless. Rally the peasants, the town folk, the miners especially, and other good chaps. We must sleep no longer. Join the dance. On! On! While the iron is hot. Let not your sword grow cold. Smite! *Pinke Panke!* God leads. On! On! God says, "Fear not." Recoil not before the great horde. It is not your war. It is God's. Play the man. The shield of the Lord is about you (Franz 1968:414-15 quoted by Bainton 1982:12-3).

Yet a rendezvous between Müntzer's apocalyptic campaign and the Peasants' War ended in a tragedy. Opposed to Müntzer and his *Bund* was a coalition of three of the princes —"Duke George of Albertine Saxony, a rabid Catholic; Philip of Hesse, a belligerent Protestant; and the Elector John of Ernestine Saxony, a moderate" (Bainton 1982:13). With the joint forces dominating the battle, Müntzer could not turn the tide all alone. He and his *Bund* fought and became the victims of a bloody massacre.

In the long run, although Müntzer's ambitious goal in the separation and destruction of the godless failed, his third-age apocalyptic revolutionary activity established important lines of continuity, including some Anabaptists and Münster Anabaptism (Bailey 1983:44). To be sure, in his dialectic of inner and outer, Müntzer was initially a mystic but later a revolutionary who integrated it into an apocalyptic vision, putting himself to the point of being-in-the-common-people as the new Daniel.

Theology Over and Against Luther

Although Thomas Müntzer and Martin Luther were two powerful voices of the time and had in common the fact that both started their theology from "a dialectic of the Word of God (Scripture) and the Spirit of God (Revelation)" (Blickle 1992:114), they unfolded their theologies quite differently. The contrasting theologies between the two became visible when Müntzer intensified a hermeneutic of Spirit, while Luther deepened a hermeneutic of Scripture (Lindberg 1977:38). The former "stressed the subjectivity of a faith experienced through the Spirit," whereas the latter "accentuated the objectivity of a faith transmitted through Scripture" (Blickle 1992:114).[18] Müntzer saw in Scripture an objective effect, for it attested to the faith of those who wrote it but it did not constitute revelation that could transform man (Blickle 1992:114, Gritsch 1989:38-9). To him, only when revelation becomes a subjective experience can one be transformed (Gritsch 1963:179).

Yet, to his disappointment, Luther's teachings put too much emphasis on man's passivity—incapacity to raise himself up, passive reception of grace, and suffering obedience (Steinmetz 1980:139, Vogel 1986:249). In prioritizing the Holy Scriptures as the only and complete divine revelation, Luther defined the Christian as a justified sinner *(simul justus et peccator)* by faith alone, waiting for the fullness of the kingdom of heaven in Christ's second coming (Vogel 1986:261). This ultimately

---

[18]In some sense, this made Luther and his colleagues judgmental about any attempt in relation to spiritual hermeneutics. They looked suspiciously at the uneasy connection between Bible reading and the heretical Spirit hermeneutic. In their eyes, with misuse and overuse by Müntzer and his followers, the healthy balance between the Word of God and the Spirit of God was in trouble. To them, more problematic was that, by declaring that every person cannot only read the word of God for herself/himself but be a judge of it, the radicals criticized Luther and the ruling authorities. This perhaps explains one reason why the sixteenth-century Lutherans later turned their emphasis from Scripture toward the catechism, where there was nothing to judge but only to memorize and repeat, for the traumatic experience of the 1520s had left behind the lesson that even trained minds had fatally misread the Bible and urged people to meet the Bible on their own terms (Strauss 1978:116-17).

enabled him to assert the doctrine of two kingdoms,[19] with Christians to serve God by obeying both secular and spiritual authority (Steinmetz 1995:112-25, Blickle 1979:239).

Against this, Müntzer developed a theology of the Spirit or of *"Anfechtung"* (tribulation) (Bornkamm 1926:44:6 quoted by Gritsch 1963:178). In his view, Luther's doctrines, especially that of justification by faith alone, was an invented doctrine, for "Christ had come to fulfill the law" (Lindberg 1977:43). Unlike Luther, he saw the Holy Spirit as a source of knowledge and principle of transformation being independent of the letter of Scriptures (Friesen 1990:126, 129). So, it must be the Spirit who converted the sinner into being God's instrument through the "justification by law" (Gritsch 1967:90).

Thus, "The justification of the sinner [was] not achieved solely through faith in what Christ did, *sola fide*, but through the voluntary acceptance of the punishment of the law, *sola lege*" (Gritsch 1963:180).[20] Since those who experienced the cross (*Anfechtung*) could cleanse themselves of the stain of original sin (Lohmann 1931:47 quoted by Friedmann 1957:83), they "became rather Christ-like, filled by the Holy Spirit and thus justified before God" (Myers 1992:128, Blickle 1992:114). Here, contrary to Luther's justification, Müntzer's emphasis was given to the fulfilment of the law as "a continual process of purification through suffering" (Lindberg 1983:84).

Furthermore, from his pneumatological perspective, Müntzer saw in Lutheran theology, especially that of the two kingdoms, an all-

---

[19]"God has ordained two governments; the spiritual, by which the Holy Spirit produces Christians and righteous people under Christ; and the temporal which restrains the un-Christian and wicked so that–no thanks to them–they are obliged to keep still and maintain an outward peace" (quoted by Wright 2010:135). The gist of this doctrine is that God ordained both the spiritual and temporal authorities, thus Christians should serve God by obeying both of them. This doctrine served to constitute Luther's own theological purposes. From it, he separated himself from the violent actions of the peasants, declaring them his enemy. In his two kingdoms theory there was no place for the peasants who were rebellious against the temporal authority, which is ordained by God.

[20]In this sense, Müntzer argued that "The target is missed by far if one preaches that faith makes us righteous and not works. It is a presumptuous teaching. Nature is not shown thereby how man must come to faith through God's work, which he must await above all else . . . For the more nature grasps after God, the more it is alienated from the working of the Holy Spirit. . . . Indeed if man understood the presumption of the nature light he would without doubt not seek help from stolen Scripture as the scholars do with one or two little passages (Isaiah 28, Jeremiah 8); instead he would soon feel the working of the divine word spring out of his heart (John 4) . . . Our scholars . . . confuse nature with grace without any distinction" (quoted by Irwin 1972:71).

consuming social passivity toward the reality of oppression and injustice (Lindberg 1977:44). In his view, Luther's theology gave less weight to the political and social conflicts than obedience to the will of God (Stayer and Packull 1980:116). Thus it created to some degree (albeit unwittingly) a license for the nobles to commit oppression and injustice, that was antithetical to the standards of Scripture (Seebass 1980:109).

Acknowledging Luther's flawed response to temporal injustice and oppression, Müntzer came to hold vastly different approaches to reform from that of Luther. Indeed, he was more concerned with bringing the transformation of both the sacred and secular realms (Franz 1968:505 quoted by Bailey 1983:35) and this transformation was by nature apocalyptic, which resulted in a plain separatism between the elect and the godless—between those who had experienced the cross and the Spirit and those who had not (Matheson 1988:244, Friesen 1990:112).

Then special attention was paid to the role of the elect, those who had endured the most severe *Anfechtung* (spiritual cleansing); they should work with the Spirit in order to ultimately usher in the Kingdom of God on earth (Matheson 1988:244). Further, Müntzer included in their role revolutionary activism (physical cleansing), having the elect purge the godless temporal power which failed to act justly (Janz 1999:167, Mayer 1992:200-1). Thus his call for urgent changes necessarily accepted bloodshed for social and economic justice (Whitford 2001:46-7). This is what released Müntzer to resist the godless and social injustice in his link between the mystical concept of *Anfechtung* and God's work in the outer order (Bailey 1983:40).

This contributed significantly to Müntzer's way of engaging with the world. Just as people became inwardly transformed through suffering and the cross, so those who experienced the Spirit (i.e., the elect) must change the entire world outwardly (Bailey 1983:40, Lindberg 1983:84), for they were called to work with God in order to make the godless aware of his law (Gritsch 1963:181). As such, this transformation included the possibility of violent revolution against the godless *Obrigkeit* (Janz 1999:167, Goertz 1993:21). The elect would go above and beyond temporal law when it hindered the work of the Holy Spirit (Gritsch 1967:8). Thus, he argued, it was their duty to fight against oppression and injustice perpetuated by the godless authority, and once again, this required an outward war that involved the physical destruction of powers of this world (Goertz 2007:27-8).

This is why Müntzer saw the peasants' rebellion as a sure sign that the power of the sword was given to the Spirit-filled common people (Friedmann 1957:79). So he approached this revolution of the common men in a more defensible way. Indeed, he did not struggle to justify the use of violence to execute God's law and fulfill his will (Janz 1999:167, Steinmetz 1980:139). For in his theology of *Anfechtung* (tribulation), without its concomitant revolutionary work in the outer order, neither man's salvation nor the advent of the Kingdom of God on earth could begin (Bailey 1983:40).

Yet Luther differed drastically from Müntzer. Although Luther's message and view had the revolutionary nature, especially in terms of the peasants' quest for political and economic rights (Hillerbrand 2007:143-44), he nonetheless opposed any efforts by those peasants to overturn the social order, but rather remained an ardent defender of the *Corpus Christianum* (Williams 1974:302-303, Janz 1999:171). Since he required support of the nobility to keep his Reformation, he did not lend his support to any Spirit-filled mob action such as Müntzer had instigated (Hillerbrand 1968:43-4, Seebass 1980:109). Instead, in his dualistic doctrine of two kingdoms, Luther divorced the spiritual realm from the secular, God from Caesar (Moltmann 1984:70), and even encouraged the authorities to quell the revolt of the common men, which resulted in thousands of them being killed (Janz 1999:177).

Müntzer, however, refused to separate the two realms and gave the commoners a rationale for divine justice grounded in Scripture (Blickle 1981:93, 188). Whereas he linked the process of reformation with the destiny of the common men and harnessed their revolutionary power in his intervention in the peasants' revolt (Drummond 1979:63, Blickle 1998:24), Luther trusted the Reformation to the protection of the secular authorities, who began to control the political and the ecclesiastical arenas (Gonzalez 1975:60-1).

Consequently, the two men's incompatibility led to an outcome that determined the weal and woe of ruler and subject (Balyor 1993:39). Blood flowed on both sides, but more on the common people's side than on the side of the princes and their servants (Ozment 1980:284, Lindberg 1996:165). Neither Luther nor Müntzer managed to stop it, despite both trying to convey a conciliatory Christian message of justice, peace, and salvation for both peasants and princes (Kolb 2009:142). Yet soon that message was divided into a gospel for rulers and a gospel for common people (Edwards 2003:198). The princes didn't want Müntzer to be a 'new Moses' in the peasants' revolt, and Luther worked hard to keep him invalid (Tappert 1967:170).

The conflict between Luther and Müntzer became critical enough for them to take every opportunity to attack each other. Ironically, Luther condemned Müntzer as a satanic prophet who created chaos in the *Corpus Christianum* (Bainton 1950:263), whereas Müntzer denounced Luther as the satanic defender of the *status quo* (Franz 1968:341 quoted by Drummond 1979:64). Luther even portrayed Müntzer as one of Satan's "fifth column" (Gritsch 1994:18-9). In his eyes, the principal issue in Müntzer's *Schwärmerei* (enthusiasm) was his confusion of God's judgment and his law with God's mercy and his gospel (Whitford 2011:76). Thanks to this confusion, Müntzer's *Schwärmer* (enthusiasts) had even justified their burning and destroying of the images and chapels under the pretext of restoring the Mosaic Law, which was already fulfilled in Christ (Gritsch 1963:181, Friesen 1990:189-98). Luther berated them to say that such a claim simply transformed Christ's gospel into a legalistic mandate that manifested nothing but the most visible work of Satan (Whitford 2011:76). Thus he condemned Müntzer as the ringleader of *Schwärmer* who failed to respect the temporal authority ordained by God (Dejonge 2017:191).

From Luther's two kingdoms theory, this kind of *Schwärmerei* had no place, for he saw "the identification of any political program . . . with the will of God is to subvert both politics and gospel" (Lindberg 1990:691). His own preoccupation with the work of the devil fed his impatience with Müntzer and his followers, which had been marked by subjectivist judgments and speculations (Headly 1963). In contrast, Müntzer hurled at Luther the term "malicious raven"—the first messenger from Noah's ark, who did not return with the message of peace—while at the same time portraying himself as the "dove" who properly continued the work and completed it (Gritsch 2006:88).

In the end, Müntzer became Luther's worst enemy, precisely because he began on the ground Luther won but was betrayed by him (Nipperdey 1980:106). An interesting circular antagonism erupted between them—"Doctor Liar" (Luther) rejecting the "Satan of Allstedt" (Müntzer) and *vice versa*. No doubt "Luther's time was Müntzer's time, the Last Days" (Brady 2009:200). However, Müntzer's theology released him to resist the injustices of the temporal authority, while Luther's theology led him to a doctrine of the two kingdoms, which resulted in a chilling indifference (even offense) toward resistance to the injustices of that authority (Steinmetz 1995:113-14). To be sure, for Müntzer, the key to reform was a call for "destruction of all secular lordship" and for Luther, the key was a call for "confirmation of princely authority" (Blickle 1998:24).

In summation, in the chaotic sixteenth-century Reformation context, Müntzer battled against Luther's teaching by setting up his own theology, which had these chief components: (1) the teaching of the Spirit as the constant divine revelation, (2) the teaching of the cross as a person's purification through suffering, and (3) the teaching on the sword, consisting of the right to resist the godless rulers (Steinmetz 1980:135). These components were outright contrary to Luther's theology, which included (1) the teaching of the Scripture as the sole and definitive source of revelation (*sola Scriptura*), (2) the teaching of justification without any human contribution (*sola fide et gratia*), and (3) the teaching of the "pathos of obedience," namely, suffering obedience since all governments were established by God (Steinmetz 1980:136). This eventually places Müntzer a radical theologian over and against Luther.

Summary: Müntzer—the Radical Reformer as Being-in-the-Retributive-Common-People

The terrible ordeal of the Peasants' War of 1525 left Müntzer a shameful legend. His name became a dirty byword for heretic and *Schwärmer* (Gritsch 1987:61). No doubt this dishonor had been hastily decided by his major opponents—the Wittenberg theologians: Luther, Melanchthon, and Bullinger who were hostile to Müntzer's commitment to the naked sword (Rupp 1969:247). So they disparaged his enthusiasm as being the devil's [21] and his death as God's judgment. [22] Yet this dominant defamatory portrait of Müntzer as a maverick revolutionary is not without controversy. Ironically, it is the widespread and one-sided criticism that calls for a more critical assessment of this sixteenth-century *Schwärmer*. This includes the necessity of positing the following three-part consideration of him from the perspective of the common people.

First, Müntzer was anti-clerical and mystical. In fact, no other reformers of the sixteenth-century came nearer to contact with the late medieval German mystics than he (Rupp 1969:247, Friesen 1988: 63, Gritsch 2006:17). Indeed, his anti-clerical and mystical conviction contributed to the idea of the separation between the damned priest and the elect layman on one hand and the dialectic between internal and external order on the other (Goertz 1982:29-44). For Müntzer, restoration of the inner order—i.e., the unity of God and the elect—was indispensable to the transformation of the outer order (Packull 1977:31-2). At the same time he saw the outer order as the sinful structure of the world that had been corrupted by the damned priest, which resulted in the separation of the elect and the godless, ultimately leading to an active apocalyptic transformation (Goertz 1990:30).

Here, Müntzer's apocalyptic vision balanced his anti-clericalism and mysticism (Stayer 1976:74). By integrating mystical-religious elements into an apocalyptic framework, he developed his social and political theology (Bailey 1983:43). Taking a cue from the Joachite interpretation of history, he was convinced that a new age was about to dawn (Friesen 1973:13-4, Stayer and Packull 1980:105, 116). Despite the world pointing forward to the coming conflict between the godless and the elect, the former had to be rooted out by the latter (Matheson 1990:87, Myers 1992:162). If the princes would not do it, then the common people must clash with the present ungodly politico-religious order so that the kingdom of this world would be given to God's elect for all time (Matheson 1988:244, 246).

In this sense, Müntzer's *Bund*—the covenant of the elect—was nothing other than an effective instrument to make his apocalyptic

---

[21]"... whoever has seen Müntzer may say that he has seen the devil himself in his greatest wrath. . . ." (quoted by Gritsch 1988:77).

[22]"... since Thomas has failed, it is quite clear that he used God's name but spoke and acted in the name of the devil. . . ." (quoted by Friesen 1988:59-80).

dream come true. Not only did he identify himself with the new Daniel (an apocalyptic figure), he also made plain to his followers that theirs was "a transcendent battle in the name of God, a holy war against the reprobate and obdurate" (Scott 1989:154). Despite the fact that his position changed or developed over time, Müntzer had finally equated the elect with "the common folk, the poor, and the materially oppressed" (Scott 1989:168). Thus, his call for rule by, of, and for the elect "tapped a ready vein of [the common people]" who had suffered a type of social *Anfechtung* (Scott 1983:213). Beating the drum for a better world, both Müntzer and the common people came to realize that this demand could be achieved only after a revolutionary overthrow of the existing socio-economic structure (Goertz 1993:161, 170).

Müntzer's *Bund* was good enough to be the spearhead of, but not strong enough to be a savior of, the whole peasant army, the result being its destruction by the advancing princely army at Frankenhausen in 1525 (Friesen 1990:261). He attributed this downfall to his misplaced faith in the peasants, who had not been properly prepared to act as God's agents (Bailey 1983:42-3). Yet his concept of the elect provided the whole dynamic of his leagues, his apocalyptic, and his participation in the peasants' struggle, and earned him the epithet 'mystic with a hammer' (Goertz 1976).

Second, Müntzer never ceased to be spiritual. The Spirit was of ultimate importance for him and was the motif for his theology (Lindberg 1977:44). He was convinced that it was the Spirit who would make true baptism, who would teach the elect faith with the fear of God, and who would begin the divine work at every stage in salvation (Rupp 1969:267-72). This resulted in his persistent concern for the timeless power of the Holy Spirit in, through, and for all Christians (Friesen 1973:9, Gritsch 1963:178-79).

Müntzer's spiritual mysticism served as a litmus test to separate the elect from the godless. True believers must always be overshadowed by the Spirit before they can become the League of the Elect *(Bund)* as the bearers of inner turmoil *(Anfechtung)* (Matheson 1988:290). This reflected his highly dynamic spirituality. To become the elect meant to become the agent of the Spirit, who began to undertake the transformation of the world into the Kingdom of God (Gritsch 1963:188). Therefore, it was this spirituality that led Müntzer, like Elijah, to the prophetic mission (Matheson 1988:250, 300) and eventually to the peasants' revolt under the banner of the sword of Gideon to herald the age of the Spirit (Matheson 1988:149).

Increasingly, spiritual hermeneutics ruled Müntzer's ideas and praxis. To him, the Spirit defined the Word, not *vice versa* (Snyder 1995:161). Hence, the Scripture without the Spirit was the dead word of God (Gritsch 1988:61). This advocacy of the Spirit over Scripture drove him to throw his gauntlet down to Luther. Undoubtedly his *solo spiritu* (by Spirit alone) went directly against Luther's *sola scriptura* (by Scripture alone) (Irwin 1972:71). He accused Luther and the Wittenberg theologians of separating Scripture from Spirit and thus neutralizing the power of the revelation, blaming them as false scribes who had "stolen the Scripture" (Matheson 1988:235-36, Packull 1977:29). It was clear to him that the Scripture testified the revelation—dreams and visions—of God's Spirit as the living Word, not the dead letter (Williams 1957:62). The Spirit speaks here and now, and Scripture becomes alive only in the Spirit (Matheson 1988:274). Here, his message was explicit. Since he had the Spirit and Luther did not, true believers must join him in battle on the Lord's side (Williams 1957:47).

Yet Müntzer's spirituality was not exclusive. Instead, it ran parallel with his being full of knowledge about the Scripture (Rowland 1988:97, Gritsch 1963:176). Despite his primacy of the Spirit over Scripture, he was well aware of the need of dynamic tension between the two (Rupp 1966:476). To this end, he adopted a new hermeneutic—an interpretation of the works of the Spirit as a verification level, appropriated only as long as those works did not contradict the Word of God (Goertz 1967:90-1, Nipperdey 1963:150 quoted by Lindberg 1976:366). Actually, such a balanced position made him fully spiritualist and fully biblicist (Bailey 1983:33).

Interestingly, this reunification of Spirit and Scripture played a major role in shaping his radical attitude towards both the major Reformers and the secular authorities (Kolb 1978:119-22). Deeply anchored by the Spirit-Scripture interplay, Müntzer rejected infant baptism as a groundless relapse of the 'old church' (without Scripture) (Stayer 1981:102), while espousing the Peasants' War of 1525 as groundbreaking progress to the advent of the 'new church' (with the Spirit), the "*Kairos*" (Lindberg 1976:369).

In this light, Müntzer came to identify the peasants' revolt with the physical embodiment of dialectic of the external Word and the internal Holy Spirit—namely, the dynamic interplay between Spirit and Scripture (Gritsch 1963:180). "Rulers usurped the place of God in their subjects' hearts; landlords exploited their peasants," so that the outer order had to be transformed by the common people "spiritually humbled and yet socially and politically aroused by oppression" (Goertz 1967:143-44 quoted by Stayer 1969:149). This led him to be 'the Spirit-filled revolutionary' in the common people, who "were usually quicker to respond to God's revelation" (Franz 1968:252 quoted by Bailey 1983:40). Bearing on his body the marks of the Spirit, he had marshaled the elect, (the common people) to usher in a new age where Spirit and Scripture would work together.

Third, Müntzer appeared as a 'staunch defender of the League of the Elect,' consisting of the common people (Friesen 1990:271). There was coherence about his belief in the elect. In principle, the elect were not a small band of chosen saints, but the whole community of Christ connected by suffering (Matheson 1988:260). Against the easy and sentimental promises of the major Reformers, his consistent stress was on the solidarity of the elect and their conformity to Christ in the fellowship of his suffering (Scott 1989:35). Indeed, he was not merely an armchair critic; "not reading and speculating, but living, dying and being damned" made him an angry young man who lent a sympathetic ear to the suffering of the mass (Rupp 1969:304).

His first-hand experience of the plight of the peasants under the feudal system widened his definition of the elect (Bainton 1982:12). From it, he began to extend his League of the Elect from the volunteers of Christ's suffering to the victims of the secular lords who lost their opportunity to conform to the suffering Lord (Lindberg 1976:370). This explained why his theology of suffering, of the Cross, and of the 'bitter Christ' paid homage to the common people as the elect. Since he began to identify the elect with the poor and downtrodden—the materially as well as spiritually poor, the victims of the powerful (Bailey 1983:42, Baylor 1989:51)—his defense of the common people soon was inseparable from his defense of the gospel as the divine law against the ungodly rulers (Goertz 1993:170).

Yet this did not drive him to be the sixteenth century Bolshevik. Instead, "Müntzer never spoke of force, nor did he call for a show of force, but only of counterforce" (Goertz 1976:106). His aggressive actions in the peasants' revolt were defensive in nature and "rhetorical and hyperbolic" in particular (Josipovic and McNiel 1996:446). He was not attributing the cause of the Peasants' War of 1525 either to his theology or to the demands of the suffering peasants (Goertz 1976:106). Rather, he saw it only in the "antisocial, exploitative behaviour of the ungodly rulers" (Goertz 1976:106). It was the temporal rulers who had abused God's command, and this kind of abuse caused the peasants to riot (Franz 1968:326-27 quoted by Bailey 1983:42). Such a notion enabled him to extend his violent aim only to the "ungodly rulers" responsible for his and his followers' suffering (Josipovic and McNiel 1996:446).

Thus, "Force that was employed in this situation . . . was counterforce and to Müntzer it seemed to be ethically required. He did not decide lightly to issue the call for counterforce. He tried to form an alliance with the princes who favoured the Gospel or who refused to persecute people for their faith, to keep the ungodly rulers in check and thereby to avoid a bloody insurrection, while there was still time," though "the transfer of rulership to the common people would eventually come to pass." (Goertz 1976:107).

This resisted a one-sided interpretation of his violent participation in the Peasants' War of 1525. There was an urgent need to get the common people to arise as an instrument of self-defense, no longer based on civil obligations and allegiance but on a new religious covenant with a suffering God (Scott 1989:49). This was the power of suffering against the suffering of the power; and he strove to harness the suffering peasants to the suffering elect as "a necessary, unavoidable counterforce," being aligned himself to the common men, God's elect people (Goertz 1976:108).

To summarize, Thomas Müntzer was the prototype and outstanding figure of the Radical Reformation, the responses to him oscillating between "fascination and repulsion" (Goertz 1993: xiii). His name, "to the little band of the poor and needy, . . has the sweet savor of life; while to those who pursue the pleasures of the flesh, it is a gruesome abomination presaging their speedy downfall" (Matheson 1988:68). This pendulum rejects any simple definition of Müntzer. Indeed, he was neither a Lutheran nor a Zwinglian nor an Anabaptist. His apocalyptic vision, infused with mystical-spiritual tenets drove him to expect the immediate coming of God's kingdom on earth, not in a passive way, but through the active revolutionary assistance of the suffering people as God's chosen elect. It grew clear that he was predestined to destroy and overcome the worldly order by following Christ in the cross and suffering by the repudiation of all worldly possessions and all human passions.

Müntzer's intentions were not merely aimed at any reform of existing conditions or the restoration of past conditions, but at complete revolution in order to bring about the immediate rule of God. This was the establishment of Christian freedom and equality on earth to be achieved, not within the framework of the old governmental and social order, but only through its revolutionary overthrow (Scott 1993:206). In his view, man could "become righteous" *(Gerechtmachung)* rather than merely be "accounted righteous" *(Rechtfertigung),* and so could the church and society (Gritsch 1963:180-81). The Peasants' War of 1525 acted as a catalyst for the formation and radical development of his theology for appealing to the rural peasants and urban burghers (i.e., the common people). Thus, he was able to urge them to take actions in righteous indignation as God's elect people.

All in all, a real portrayal of Müntzer appears at the intersection of various characteristics: anti-clerical/mystical, apocalyptic/spiritual, and common people-centred. As each single picture maximizes his distinct characters through an incongruous and seemingly self-contradictory element, ironically enough, these different features make his profile coherent in a collision with one another. When such plural characters intersect, they come together with power. A popularized and familiar image of Müntzer, then, transforms into a new oxymoron, one which embraces positive tensions between his polarity and coherence, between glory and suffering, and between success and failure, emphasizing retributive divine justice from below against the ungodly temporal rulers. Thus, Müntzer is born again who is the radical reformer as being-in-the-retributive-common-people.

Chapter 4

Profiles of the Radical Reformers

Hans Hut (1490-1527)

Biographical Sketch

Hans Hut, known as a founder of Anabaptism in south Germany, has remained a controversial figure (Stayer 1965:181). Despite there being no detailed picture of his life, he was a self-taught rather than a formally educated man (Stayer 1965:181).[1] He was more concerned with the Christian social order than the sinner's standing before God, which was raised theologically by the monks and professors at Wittenberg (Seebass 1982:54). From that background came his strong affinity with Thomas Müntzer, who was diametrically opposed to the theology of Luther and major Reformers (Klassen 1959:267-304).

As a book peddler, Hut supervised publication of Müntzer's major pamphlet, the *Manifest Exposé of False Faith*, in 1524 (Brandt 1933:243 quoted by Klassen 1959:280),[2] which implies that he may have met with Müntzer on various occasions and formed a special friendship with him (Seebass 1972:168 quoted by Packull 1975:58). Once Müntzer and Karlstadt stigmatized pedobaptism (infant baptism) as "a spineless

---

[1] There is a document, originally published by the City Council of Nuremburg, which described the portrait of Hut: "The highest and chief leader of the Anabaptists . . . a well-educated, clever fellow, rather tall, a peasant with light brown cropped hair and a blonde moustache. He is dressed in a grey, sometimes black, riding coat, a broad grey hat, and grey pants" (Schornbaum 1934:19 quoted by Klaassen 211).

[2] In late September 1524, Müntzer stopped in Bibra and spent a night and a day in Hut's house and likely delivered his publication. Hut later recounted that visit during his interrogation in Augsburg, but insisted to the judges that he had no specific business with Müntzer during that visit (Ozment 1973:98).

character of Christianity," he, refusing to have his three children baptized, risked going into exile from his native village, Bibra (Klassen 1959:280). This was enough to prove that Hut was in league with Müntzer. From then on, he was blacklisted and he became a planetary vagabond, wandering from Wittenberg to Erfurt to Nuremberg (Rupp 1969:333).

In the spring of 1525, Hut found himself in the town of Frankenhausen, where a peasant revolt was taking shape under Müntzer's leadership (Klassen 1959:178-79). There he was taken captive, possibly because of the books that he had brought into Luther's city (Klassen 1959:268). But he was released at the command of his old friend, Müntzer (Packull 1975:59). The fact that his name appeared on the list of Müntzer's *Bund* indicates that he likely witnessed the beginnings of the peasant uprising in Thuringia (Williams 1962:78-9, Seebass 1972:168 quoted by Packull 1975:58).

He was a "sympathetic spectator" of Müntzer's fiery sermon on the eve of the great battle with the princes' forces (Franz 1963:523 quoted by Friesen 1974:178) and he did participate in the Frankenhausen debacle, which Müntzer identified with the last great conflict between the godly and ungodly before the return of Christ (Matheson 1988:148-49). Although Hut managed to escape from that fiasco (Klassen 1959:179), it seems evident that Müntzer's person and his message nevertheless remained decisive for him (Klassen 1959:179, Packull 1975:59).

At the end of May 1525, Hut re-appeared in his home town of Bibra and, at the request of Jorg Haug of Juchsen (a pastor elected by the peasants), delivered a sermon on May 30 (Seebass 1972:105-11 quoted by Packull 1975:59). That sermon was not only religious in nature but also political (Klassen 1959:179). As a kindred spirit with Müntzer, in it he succeeded in inciting the defeated peasants to rise again against the rulers and kill them while the sword was still in their hand (Loserth 1893:130-31 quoted by Stayer 1965:182). Echoing Müntzer's lament, he argued persuasively that God had destroyed the peasants because they had not been pure but had sought their own in place of God's honour (Meyer 1874:241-42 quoted by Klaassen 1981:273, Packull 1986:53).[3]

---

[3]Similarly Müntzer had even scolded the common people, criticizing their selfish ambitions and, in so doing, reminded them of the deeper roots of his "righteous uprising"

Although the peasants' revolt failed, Hut appeared undeterred and applied the event to his own sense of new mission. With the bodies of Müntzer and Pfeiffer not yet buried but rather put on spikes, he began to identify them with the two witnesses of Revelation 11:3-9, whose bodies were to lie unburied for 3½ days (Seebass 1972:180-81, 190 quoted by Packull 1975:60). Thus, instead of disregarding the revolt as a failure, he redefined this great tragedy as both a sign of another 3½ years of tribulation and a sign of testing for the faithful before the Second Coming (Meyer 1874:239 quoted by Stayer 1972:153). This gave the Peasants' War of 1525 a new momentum—it being not the end but the beginning of the apocalyptic tribulation of 3½ years (Stayer 1972:153). In Hut's new schema, the end was then newly expected for Pentecost 1528 (Deppermann 1987:175-76), which would begin again the judgment on the ungodly and the realization of the Kingdom of God on earth (Williams 1962:163).

But who would assume the role of the godly? Hut found the answer in the Anabaptist group that he joined through Hans Denck (Waite 1990:24). He had met Denck (1495-1527), another of Müntzer's covenanters, in Augsburg on the Day of Pentecost 1526, and there Denck baptized him (Meyer 1874:223, 245 quoted by Klassen 1957:180). From his baptism emerged a distinctive picture of Hut, who formed the dynamic link between the revolutionary Müntzer and the reactionary Denck (Packull 1973:327-38, Klassen 1959:171-205).

However, this does not mean that he immediately converted from the social revolutionary peasant (Saul) to the religious, peaceful Anabaptist (Paul) (Seebass 1974:161 quoted by Packull 1977)[4]—"He was baptized but not converted, so to speak" (Friesen 1984:155). Rather, while remaining a faithful disciple of Müntzer, he found in the Anabaptists the separatist elect who would vindicate the defeat of the peasants, seeking to inspire hope through an apocalyptic end-time forecast (Stayer 2007:85). So adult (believer's) baptism became totally

---

(Matheson 1988:160, 341).
    [4]In fact, many Anabaptist scholars, who have little sympathy for Müntzer, have interpreted Hut's baptism by Denck as a regenerative experience. According to them, from that point on, Hut's inheritance from Müntzer had transmitted to the Swiss Brethren, and thereby his teachings were the noblest and most conciliatory (Bender 1953:16). But this view has gained little support due to its exclusive focus on his political ethic. For the critical view on this interpretation, see especially Packull (1977:63-4).

integrated into his apocalyptical speculations as a sign of the seal between God and man (Seebass 1974:158 quoted by Packull 1977).

At any rate, this gave Hut's mission a vibrant impulse. While it did not permit him to remain for long in any one place, he became the major south German Anabaptist missionary (Kiwiet 1957:227-59). For the next year and a half, he was constantly on the move from his home territory in Franconia through Austria to as far away as Moravia (Klassen 1959:179-80).[5] Everywhere he went, he dispensed adult (believer's) baptism to seal the faithful remnant—namely, the apocalyptic assembling of the elect (Seebass 1974:158 quoted by Packull 1977).

From then forward, Hut saw himself as the man of Daniel 12:6 and Ezekiel 9:2-5 (Meyer 1874:21 quoted by Packull 1975:61), whose duty it was to mark the sign of the cross on the foreheads of as many as possible of the 144,000 elect in the approaching judgment, as the opposite of the sign of the beast on the foreheads of unbelievers (Packull 1975:61): "He took two fingers, dipped them in water, and made the sign of the cross on his forehead. Whoever does not have this cross will find God sending his angel who will strike him dead. And all who are unbaptized will be slain by the angel" (Armour 1966:87).

Restless and secretive activities then ensued. In Franconia, Hut had particularly appealed to fugitive veterans of the peasant rebellion who longed for the day of vengeance (Seebass 1974:140-56 quoted by Stayer 1978:62). But he told them to put their swords in their sheaths until the final tribulations began—"A Christian may certainly have a sword, but he must keep it sheathed until God tells him to draw it" (Meyer 1874:242 quoted by Klassen 1959:204). According to him, before the Day of the Lord, Turks would invade the land to annihilate the ungodly (Meyer 1874:367 quoted by Packull 1975:60) and the remnant of the ungodly—i.e., the princes and priests—would be destroyed by the little band of Anabaptists, the special Christian elect (Wappler 1913:231 quoted by Stayer 1965:185).

Echoing Müntzer's most bloodthirsty rhetoric (Packull 1977:35-117), Hut provided the veterans of the peasants' uprising a rationale for

---

[5]During this period, an apocalyptic expectation had remained a live option for those who continued to hope for the reform of society, despite the fact that it had increasingly been abandoned by the majority of Hut's followers in Austria and Moravia (Snyder 1995:201).

their distress and suffering (Seebass 1982:57), saying that suffering had to be endured awaiting the vengeance of the godly upon the ungodly. Once again, this demonstrated himself to be an erstwhile disciple of Müntzer rather than an Anabaptist (Friesen 1984:155). In this sense, his identity stood closer to patient revolution, which is Müntzerism, than to peaceful Anabaptism (Ozment 1973:101). To put it another way, his brand of Anabaptism signified him nothing less than a patient revolutionary as "Müntzer's *Erbe* (legacy)" (Packull 1976:64).

This explains why, in the eyes of important Anabaptist leadership, Hut remained an intruder, despite his conversion into Anabaptism under Denck (Kiwiet 1958:25). One example should suffice for this. The theologically trained Balthasar Hubmaier wanted no part of Hut's end-time fantasies (Stayer 1965:189). The result was a sharp confrontation between the two, culminating in the so-called Nikolsburg Debate of May, 1527 (Seebass 1972:279 quoted by Packull 1975:59).[6] Hubmaier attempted to create a magisterial Anabaptism from above (Zieglschmid 1943:50 quoted by Rothkegel 2007:170), which secured places for the learned and the powerful, while Hut was too convinced of his idea of communitarianism so far as to encourage commoners to sell temporal goods in view of Christ's return (Balint 2014:140-41).[7] This resulted in both sides constantly failing to narrow differences.

---

[6]Gottfried Seebass considers this event as "the first head-on collision between a spiritualistic, apocalyptic Anabaptism dependent on Müntzer and a humanistic, Biblicist Swiss Anabaptism, even though the latter was represented in the form developed by Hubmaier. The subject of the debate was not political ethic but Hut's eschatology" (Seebass 1972:279, 257-59 quoted by Packull 1975:59). Hubmaier feared that Hut's apocalyptic expectations would offend the magistracy so as to lead to the demise of his successful establishment of Anabaptist reformation in Nikolsburg. Indeed, Hut's message of apocalyptic violence and community of goods had created discord within the Anabaptist community in Moravia, which had been built by Balthasar Hubmaier, who led the rebellion of Waldshut against the Habsburg during the Peasants' War. Hubmaier was concerned that his new religious establishment in Nikolsburg, Moravia, was threatened by large numbers of property-less Anabaptist refugees from all parts of south Germany and Switzerland. They rallied around the travelling missionary Hans Hut, who visited Nikolsburg as the staunch advocate of the chiliastic ideas and the community of goods. Under these present circumstances, Hubmaier retorted that his baptism was the very opposite of Hut's. Furthermore, he complained that the two were as different "as heaven and hell, Orient and Occident, Christ and Belial" (Packull 1977:99-106). Nevertheless, Hut's kind of Anabaptism prevailed there (Stayer 1995:261).

[7]According to the testimony of one of Hut's followers, it was believed that Nikolsburg was to be one of the cities where the elect were to gather for the unfolding of the eschatological events (Schornbaum 1934:212 quoted by Rothkegel 2007:179).

Leonard of Liechtenstein, the local prince, called for an open disputation between the two which, when it occurred, focused primarily on Hut's apocalyptic interpretation of Scripture (Rupp 1969:333, Seebass 1972:257-59 quoted by Packull 1975:59). In the long run, the conflict ended with Hut's temporary imprisonment by the prince's noble patron, who supported Hubmaier's position (Williams 1962:225-26).[8] Only by flight was Hut able to escape a threatened deportation (Klassen 1964:52). This charge, however, continued to plague him as a "scarlet letter."

In the summer of 1527, major meetings of Anabaptist leaders of various backgrounds were held in Augsburg (Klassen 1959:184). Later referred to as the "martyrs' synod" (because many of those present shortly thereafter fell to the sword of executioners) it eventually singled out Hut as an outsider of mainline Anabaptism (Williams 1962:177-78, Stayer 1965:187). This forced him to restrain his apocalyptic predictions as a sort of esoteric teaching only to be shared with selected followers in private (Muller 1938:12, quoted by Clasen 1972:163).

At these meetings, Hut seemed to break with other Anabaptist leadership to stand on his own (Klassen 1959:283). He rejected both the "Sermon on the Mount Ethic" (Seebass 1972:512-25 quoted by Packull 1975:62) and the "Schleitheim Articles" as the outright manifestos of the Swiss Brethren (Yoder 1972:35-47 quoted by Stayer 1996:113).[9] Since from the beginning Hut had treated the end-time expectation as secret doctrines reserved only for an initiated few, he could not set aside the secretiveness for those who eagerly wished to hear it (Seebass 1982:59,

---

[8]Court records dated November 4, 1527 reported Hut recalling the following theses in which Hubmaier had composed for the debate of Hut's no-fewer-than 52 heretical teachings—(1) that Christ was not God's son; (2) that Christ was merely a prophet; (3) that Mary had more sons after Christ; (4) that the angels should have become man with Christ; (5) that when a man is possessed by a good angel he can do only good, and when possessed by a bad angel only evil; (6) that Hut and his followers put stock in vision and dreams; (7) that they forecasted a specific time for the last day; (8) that with Scripture one receives lies as well as the truth; (9) that Christians wish to rule the world; (10) that no prince or power in this world has accepted or recognized the truth; and (11) that power should be taken from the government and given to Christians (Meyer 1874:232 quoted by Friedmann 1967:393). Hut countered that only two of these propositions—numbers 6 and 8—accurately represented his teachings. He twice maintained that Hubmaier acted "from anger and envy" (Williams 1962:284-85).

[9]Through his contact with Jacob Grofi (an Anabaptist from Waldshut), Hut had become acquainted with Schleitheim's separatist ordinance concerning oaths and had rejected it. He had argued that "this [i.e., oaths] was not contrary to God, nor was it forbidden" (Meyer 1874: 229, 231 quoted by Snyder 1984:97).

Stayer 1972:157). In fact, his eschatology was by nature a secret teaching not revealed to everyone (Meyer 1874:239 quoted by Stayer 1965:187).

A few weeks later, Hut was arrested in Augsburg (Klassen 1959:185) and his trial, with tortures, lasted several months. For the Augsburg authority, his connection to Müntzer and the peasants, as well as his expectation of judgment upon the present order *(Obrigkeit)*, were enough to call for his execution and the burning of his body (Stayer 1965:187), which actually occurred in September 1527 despite an attempt to escape by premature death (Klassen 1959:175).

As to the actual cause of Hut's death, the reports conflicted. One such report was that, having a premonition of a miserable death, he attempted to make an escape by setting fire to the straw in his cell, which resulted in death by asphyxiation (Meyer 1874:253 quoted by Klassen 1959:185). However, according to his son, Hut was in a comatose condition when released from the torture room, which prevented him escaping a fire accidently set by a candle left by the guard in his cell (Wolkan 1923:47 quoted by Klassen 1959:185).

Whatever the true story, Hut perished without honour (Williams 1962:179). The trial had created a deep abhorrence of his eschaton; and the court pronounced sentence on his corpse, which was to be burned at the stake the following day (Loserth and Friedmann 1956:849 quoted by Estep 1975).

Theological Perspective

Gospel of All Creatures

Hut's theology was shared across boundaries between Müntzer and Anabaptism. From one aspect, like Müntzer, he was more likely to understand Scripture through the lens of mysticism (Goertz 2008:588-96), which put strong emphasis on the *unio mystica*—namely, mystical reunion between God and man as its theological axiom (Klaassen 1981:89-90). So, he valorized the mystic ideas, such as 'God's grace through an abyss of the soul,' 'the necessity of suffering,' and 'the reception of a living Spirit in all believers' (Seebass 1972:512-15 quoted by Packull 1975:62). This intimacy and intensity of mysticism—"less emphasis on sin and greater emphasis on becoming like Christ through suffering"—made his theology "a cruder version of Müntzer's basic assumptions" (Buschart 2006:63, Seebass 1982:57). Indeed, the influence of Müntzer on Hut can easily be traced (Klaassen 1962:19, Liechty 1994:63). Especially, Müntzer's mystical approach to suffering with the concept of "yieldedness" (*Gelassenheit*)[10] contributed significantly to Hut's theology of the 'gospel of all creatures' (Packull 1975:62).

Hut's 'gospel of all creatures' characterized the relation of creature to humanity and humanity to God (Finger 2004:263), "which instructed agriculturalists and craftsmen that, just as they use plants and animals to fulfill the will of man, so God uses human beings to fulfill his divine purpose" (Stayer 2007:86, Liechty 1994:63). In order to extend this exposition, he introduced the medieval concept of *Ordnung Gottes* (the Order of God)—that being, "as man rules over the creatures, so God reigns over man" (Seebass 1972:435 quoted by Packull 1975:63). Further, he developed it with his mystical idea of the necessity of suffering as a prerequisite for redemption (Packull 1986:54).

According to Hut, God revealed in all creation the fundamental 'gospel' that lower orders of creation must suffer the will of the higher orders (Packull 1986:54). Just as animals must suffer at the hands of human beings, so also human beings must be subject to, and suffer at the hands of God (Klaassen 1981:49, Liechty 1994:70). He called this chain of being 'dying and rising with Christ,' and even identified it with the suffering of Christ (Muller 1938:17 quoted by Klaassen 1962:217, Baylor 1991:158).

Here, once again Hut echoed Müntzer (Packull 1977:68). By insisting that suffering itself was "the medium and the justice" through which justification was obtained (Packull 1977:75)[11] and by insisting that

---

[10]To a large degree, Hut's teaching of "yieldedness," seemed to extend Müntzer's criticism of the current social and economic order. In his major writing, "On the Mystery of Baptism," Hut attacked the mainstream Reformers' conservative affirmation of temporal wealth and status with a rhetorical question: "Everybody says each of us should stay in his vocation. If this is so, why didn't Peter remain a fisherman, Matthew a tax collector—and why did Christ tell the rich young man to sell what he had and give to the poor? . . . Oh, Zacheus, why did you give up your property so frivolously; according to our preachers, you could have kept it and still been a good Christian!" (Stayer 1991:115, Rupp 1969:392).

[11]"Suffering is the medium on account of which the Lord justifies His own. This happens through penitence and bitterness . . . Therefore I say . . . there is no other way, we must step into the footpath of Christ" (quoted by Packull 1977:75).

the suffering of Christ was the prototype of human suffering (Seebass 1972:516 quoted by Packull 1975:62), he had a theological expansion for true righteousness as something attainable only in the experience of the 'bitter Christ,'[12] only those who had experienced the suffering Son becoming partakers of the Spirit (Packull 1977:68).

From this vantage point, Hut could call the believer's suffering as Christ's suffering and Christ's merit as the believer's merit: "Everything that such persons suffer is all called Christ's suffering and not ours, because we are in Christ one body in many members, united and allied in the bond of love. Wherefore . . . Christ accepts such persons as His own body because Christ's suffering must be fulfilled in every member. . . . For just as Christ, the lamb, has been slain from the beginning of the world, so also is He still crucified until the end of the world, that the body of Christ be perfected according to the length, width, depth and height in the lover of Christ" (Packull 1977:75).

This led him to regard Christ's suffering not as vicarious but as the example of faith (Seebass 1972:516 quoted by Packull 1975:62). "No one can come to blessedness other than through the suffering and grief which God works in him, just as all of Scripture, and every creature also, show nothing but the suffering Christ in all his members" (Muller 1938:3:17 quoted by Gregory 2007:472). It was his belief, then, that Christ's conception, birth, passion, and resurrection were to be repeated in every true follower of Jesus (Packull 1977:68). Thus he argued that "By yielding themselves fully to God, suffering Christians 'complete the suffering of Christ' and fulfil his redemptive mission" (Stayer 2007:86).

Hut's emphasis on the mystical experience of the cross and suffering did not even harmonize with Luther's teachings on justification (Seebass 1972:465-66 quoted by Packull 1975:62), but rather he saw suffering as the process of justification (Packull 1986:54, Klaassen 1962:222-25).[13] Therefore, the overall framework of his theology did not permit predestinarianism, which was a logical prerequisite for Luther's *iustitia*

---

[12]"Whoever does not want to follow these footsteps and this way, and has not carried the cross of Christ, or does not want to carry it, he does not have or recognize the Son, and whoever has not the Son, he does not have or recognize the Father, and can also not be illuminated through the goodness of the Holy Spirit" (quoted by Packull 1977:68).

[13]Furthermore, by permitting dreams and visions as a mode of special revelation, Hut began to set himself apart from the major Reformers (Seebass 1972:430-31 quoted by Packull 1975:64).

passiva (the passive righteousness) and *sola gratia* (by grace alone) (Seebass 1972:499-50 quoted by Packull 1975:62). Like Müntzer, he minimized the effect of original sin (Packull 1975:64) and continued with the principle of *cooperation*—namely, the dynamic interplay between divine grace and human will as regarding salvation (Packull 1976:76).

On the other hand, Hut's teaching of the 'gospel of all creatures,' especially his call to accept suffering as a precondition for redemption, sounded very much like the Swiss Brethren, whose emphasis was on their discipleship, each individual having to take up the suffering cross in conformity with Christ (Bender 1944:415). The acceptance of his followers into the non-resistant Anabaptist leadership—such as Jakob Hutter and Pilgram Marpeck—also seems to support this assumption and place him in the circle of peaceful Anabaptism (Stayer 1965:181). Yet it was unable to circumvent Hut's dependence on Müntzer totally (Rupp 1960-61). To be sure, Hut under Anabaptism was an insignificant figure versus Hut under Müntzer (Stayer 1965:185). Thus, the suffering theme in his 'gospel of all creatures' proved that he was a student of Müntzer, the revolutionary rather than that of the Swiss Brethren who rejected violence (Seebass 1972:512-15 quoted by Packull 1975:62).

This explains why Hut's 'gospel of all creatures,' his "signature notion of Anabaptism," even served as a powerful tool for the common people (Ozment 1973:106). For, from their daily activities, the common people—peasants, artisans, goldsmiths, weavers and farmers—were more readily taught in the creatures than the Scriptures, his message, mostly described by creatures and parables, more easily and immediately appealed to them than that of the scholars in Wittenberg, whose teaching was false and had the wrong order (Muller 1938:13-4, 16-7 quoted by Klaassen 1962:217, Packull 1986:54-5). So, the common people must turn to the common people, for "from the creatures they learned that they must renounce the world and depend on God" (Klaassen 1962:220).

Thus Hut argued that the world, created in the 'gospel of all creatures,' was "not purely spiritual, [but] political or economic" (Bechtel 2002:10). This drove him to encourage the common people to participate in the expected punishment of "the money preachers" and "hypocritical scribes" (Packull 1986:54-5); ". . . If God has use of us or will have benefit of us, we must first be justified and made pure by Him, both inwardly and outwardly; inwardly from greed and lust, outwardly from injustice in our way of living and our mission of the creatures" (Liechty 1994:70). Here his 'gospel of all creatures' became part of the common people's movement which contained the egalitarianism and anti-clericalism (Packull 1986:55, 66, Bechtel 2002:8);

All in all, to Hut, the entire Bible declared nothing but the 'gospel of all creatures,' first by the law and ceremonies through Moses in the Old Testament and then by suffering and the cross in the New Testament (Seebass 1972:47 quoted by Packull 1975:63) (Muller 1938:95 quoted by Finger 2004:263),[14] and it could be clearer to the illiterate peasants (common people) than to the scholars (Liechty 1994:67-72). In this light, his teaching of the 'gospel of all creatures' became a gospel for the common people, who were "transformed and transforming new beings in the world" through suffering and the cross (Boyd 1992:152).

Doctrine of the Sword

While the 'gospel of all creatures' included Hut's focus on encouraging the common people—especially the fugitive veterans of the revolt in 1525—to strike back "against the unjust system and to stone the clergy" (Packull 1986:54), this idea was further elaborated in his apocalyptically inclined messages and finally incorporated into his violent doctrine of the sword. His position was all about "Yes" to the use of force and therefore the connection was very close between Hut and Müntzer in this regard (Stayer 1965:184, Klaassen 1962, Seebass 1972).

Hut's teachings on the sword cannot be fully understood without considering his early association with Müntzer, he actually being Müntzer's comrade-in-arms (Loserth 1893:130-31 quoted by Stayer 1965:182). From Müntzer's exile from Mulhausen in 1524 to his last battle at Frankenhausen in 1525, he had been in Müntzer's *Bund*, the League of the Elect (Packull 1975:59). This implies that he must have been deeply affected by Müntzer's apocalyptic crusade during the latter's zenith (Bailey 1983:44). Hut's admiration for his master remained active even after the crushing defeat at Frankenhausen (Seebass 1972:322, 564 quoted by Packull 1975:60). While venerating the memory of Müntzer,

---

[14]This view distinguished him from the Swiss Brethren, who maintained the difference between Old and New Testaments (Seebass 1972:453 quoted by Packull 1975:63).

he continued to give some sense of hope to the remnant peasants in order to reshape the role of the common people for the future kingdom (Deppermann 1987:201, 219, Packull 1986:53).

In the wake of the absence of Müntzer, his lord, Hut acted as Joshua in the post-Moses period. Shortly after the debacle of the revolt of 1525, from an open pulpit on May 31, 1525, he did not hesitate to advocate use of the naked sword for apocalyptic vengeance, which was no other than an extended version of Müntzer's revolutionary activism (Stayer 1972:151). "The subject should kill all rulers, because the right time has come now that they have the sword in hand" (Meyer 1874:241, 251 quoted by Stayer 1972:151). This utterance was strong enough to hail him as Müntzer *redivivus*, 'the destroyer of the godless,' who continued to encourage his followers to drink from Müntzer's revolutionary wells and thus reshape their roles in God's apocalyptic program (Stayer 1972:150-51, 2007:85).

Indeed, from the beginning, Hut appeared as a man of the sword and the edge of his sword was not blunted, even after converting to Anabaptism (Vedder 1905:157-70, Stayer 1965:184-88, 1972:156). Both external and internal records prove that his teaching consistently advocated the violent sword of vengeance, despite that it was to remain in the sheath until the right time (Stayer 1965:185). As to the external, Sebastian Franck, the sixteenth-century German chronicler, was one of the first outsiders to mention him as the Anabaptist leader with the violent sword in a somewhat negative way (Klassen1959:176), writing in 1531,

> ... [Hut] thought from reading of Moses and the Prophets that they, as the children of God, must, like Israel, root out the ungodly—but not before God would summon and prepare them for this task. Many of the Anabaptists spoke and wrote against him [Hut], and this opinion [of Hut] is held none of them any longer (or only by very few whom I cannot find out about). For they absolutely disapprove of this opinion, condemn it in Hut and speak of it as a lapse and an error (quoted by Stayer 1972:156-57).

Similarly the Hutterites's Great Chronicle draws a violent portrait of him;

> all assembled at Nikolasburg in the castle to hold a disputation about whether the sword should be used and carried or not. Also about whether taxes should be paid for war.... They were not able to come to an understanding, however, and parted from one another in disagreement. Hans Hut, however, who did not choose to agree with Lord Leonhard von Lichtenstein to maintain the sword, was detained in the Nikolsburg castle....
> (quoted by Stayer 1972:162-63)

These two sources depicted him as a man of violence and explained why Hut was an unwelcome guest in the peaceful Anabaptist camp (Stayer 1965:182). Indeed, he appeared to be neither the warlike *Schwertler* (sword bearer), nor the peaceful *Stäbler* (staff bearer) (Stayer 1991:114, Klassen 1959:177-78). Thus many Anabaptists condemned him as a *Schwertler* in *Stäbler*'s clothing, who "[stirred] up conspiracy and rebellion under the appearance of the baptism and communion of Christ, as if it were necessary to assault with the Sword and the like" (quoted by Stayer 1972:156).

The internal evidence sheds more light on Hut's violent doctrine of the sword. There are a good number of his Anabaptist converts who firmly testified of his violent teachings on the sword from within (Stayer 1965:184). For example, George Nespitzer and Marx Maier (significant Anabaptist disciples of Hut) clearly echoed their master's hardline manifesto on the sword, which was now given to them (Klassen 1959:182). Nespitzer confessed that "Christ will give the Sword and revenge to them, the Anabaptists, to punish all sins, stamp out all governments, make all property common and slay those who do not permit themselves to be rebaptized" (Schornbaum 1934:188 quoted by Stayer 1965:184). Maier also reported the Anabaptist leaders of Augsburg who believed that "The government does not treat the poor people properly and burdens them too heavily. When God gives them revenge they want to punish and wipe out the wicked" (Schornbaum 1934:198 quoted by Stayer 1965:184).

Furthermore, Thomas Spiegel, one of Hut's converts at Konigsberg in Franconia, was witness to Hut prophesying an imminent invasion by the Turks and a special mission, given to his followers (Stayer 1965:184). Anabaptists were expected to wait "until the Turk invades. Whom the Turks allows to survive—princes, monks, priests, or noblemen—shall be killed by the little band [the Anabaptists]. . . ." (Wappler 1913:231 quoted by Stayer 1965:184-85). All such 'disciples' suggested, then, that Hut's teaching never played down the use of the sword but rather it "exhaled revolutionary fire" of his followers to anticipate the righteous upheaval against the ungodly, like hawks, not doves (Wappler 1913:242-44 quoted by Stayer 1965:184, 1972:155).

However, Hut was not merely a copycat of Müntzer as to the sword. Instead he did reshape it in a more creative and critical manner. On the one hand, like Müntzer, he separated the elect (Anabaptist) from the godless (the *Obrigkeit*), declaring that the power of the sword was given to them—"Yes" to the use of force (Stayer 1972:75-6). On the other hand, unlike Müntzer, he elaborated a so-called "interim ethic," which allowed for the temporary rule of Christian magistracy before the Second Coming— "Wait" to the use of force (Stayer 1972:158, 1965:185).[15] This interim ethic required a significant caveat that "Until Christ came Christians could fight and rule within the compass of the legitimate magistracy," allowing its waver on the vengeance of the elect upon the godless—namely, the doctrine of the 'sheathed sword' (Stayer 1965:185, 1972:158).

Nonetheless this does not cast a shadow over Hut's violent position on the sword. For here his real motive was not sheathing but unsheathing the sword, not just waiting for but actively participating in divine judgment (Stayer 1965:185). The ultimate aim behind his interim ethic was the holy war accompanying the punishment of the ungodly—for one day "[the saints] will slay a thousand, two will slay ten thousands [of ungodly]" (Stayer 1965:185).

> "A Christian can indeed have a sword, as long as he allows it to remain in the sheath until the Lord tells him to draw it. [That

---

[15]In this sense, Hut insisted that he "neither said nor heard that magistrates were not Christian" (Meyer 1874:229, 243 quoted by Stayer 1965:183).

time would come] after they had been dispersed and tested. Finally, the Lord would reassemble them and come to them with his *parousia*. At that time the saints would punish the others, the sinners who had not repented. Then the priests who had preached falsely would have to give an account of their teaching and the powerful of their government" (Meyer 1874:242 quoted by Stayer 1972:154)

Therefore, what Hut really expected was the speedy advent of the Day of Judgment when God, in close collaboration with the saints (the Anabaptists), would punish the evil authorities and all sinners (Meyer 1874:231, 239 quoted by Stayer 1972:156). Put differently, Hut heated his sword up with Müntzer's furnace and cooled it down with Anabaptism; he used the same sword that Müntzer used but kept it in the scabbard for the last chance. This meant, as to the doctrine of the sword, he was an Anabaptist of a different kind, being far more subversive and vibrant in his defense of the "sheathed sword" with the emphasis on the Last Judgment (Stayer 1965:189). All this proved that he was a man of the sword who, from first to last, never dropped it from his hand (Stayer 1965:184).

Violent Eschatology

Hut's teachings on the sword placed him as a critical and creative imitator of Müntzer, who reshaped his teacher's naked sword into his own sheathed sword (Stayer 1972:167, Loewen 2015:114). Once again, the genuine intention behind this teaching was not the declaration of non-violence, but rather its temporal suspension until the Second Coming (Stayer 1995:258). This served as both a stigma and a stimulus for the development of his violent vengeful eschatology (Stayer 1972:153).

Many of his early followers were "little Müntzers," elevating him as a great protégé of Müntzer who was able to revive his apocalyptic vision (Stayer 1972:152). Their unswerving loyalty to him remained alive even after his conversion to Anabaptism in 1526, because his proclamation still echoed the Müntzerite revolutionary crusade—"What captivated and inspired these men in Hut's proclamation was certainly not an

Anabaptism living in imitation of Christ and denial of violence—it was the threatening judgment of the godless . . . in which they wanted to participate" (Seebass 1972:202 quoted by Packull 1975:59-60).

Yet since the collapse of Müntzer's League of the Elect at Frankenhausen in 1525 posed a conundrum for Hut and his apocalyptic zealots, its rehabilitation was not an option but must be done. This drove him to seriously pursue a sort of tailor-made approach to the abortive revolution of 1525 as well as those compromised by it (Packull 1975:59). Thus, he began to "readjust his general apocalyptic expectation to the changed circumstances" (Packull 1975:59) and in this vein, his chiliasm, violent and vibrant eschatology, served as an apologia for the disaster of the revolt in 1525 (Stayer 1972:153, Packull 1975:66).

The traditional figure of 3½ years revisited Hut's new interpretation (Williams 1962:163). By identifying Müntzer and Pfeiffer with the two prophets of Revelation 11:3-10, he renewed his schema (Packull 1975:60). Taking a cue from the fact that both of them lasted 3½ years in ministry and their bodies lay in the street without being buried (Seebass 1972:180-81, 190 quoted by Packull 1975:60), he justified predicting the millennium for 3½ years after the Peasants' War of 1525 (Meyer 1874:239 quoted by Stayer 1965:186). Therefore, the end of the world would come in the summer (Pentecost) of 1528 from the outbreak of the revolt of 1525 (Packull 1975:60, Williams 1962:163).

From it, the peasants defeated at Frankenhausen gained new momentum. It was not the end but the new beginning "allotted for repentance before the end of the world" (Meyer 1874:239 quoted by Stayer 1965:186). Thus it turned his Anabaptism into "an urgent, hurried and apocalyptic mode" (Snyder 2010:73). Under the prediction of the imminent end of the world, he and his followers felt a sense of urgency to baptize adults so as to mark them as members of the 144,000 elect of the last days (Snyder 2010:73).[16] In his apocalyptic-chiliastic vision, the Peasants' War of 1525 became an end-time event and the Anabaptists

---

[16] The passage in Ezekiel 9 provided a main supporting text for the apocalyptic mode of baptism practiced by Hut and his followers (Packull 1986:59). However, such references to the sign on the foreheads of believers seemed to have confused some of his followers. Evidently, Hut and his disciples had not baptized them but had given them the sign (Mecenseffy 1964:18-21), even though they had used the words, "I baptize you," when they did so (Schornbaum 1934:79, 80, 87) (both quoted by Clasen 1972:101).

the special end-time Christian elect (Hillerbrand 2007:117).

This overriding zeal made Hut a chiliastic prophet (Stayer 1965:184, 1972:153). While recognized by his followers as Jeremiah-*redivivus* ("a prophet sent of God") to the nations (Williams 1962:164), he considered himself the end-time Elijah for the faithful remnants (Seebass 1972:398-99 quoted by Packull 1975:61). Encouraged by that commission from on high,[17] he even signed one of his letters, "Hans Hut from the den of Elijah," reflecting on the prophet's miraculous nourishment during the 3½ years of drought (Seebass 1972:21, 398-99 quoted by Packull 1975:61). The testimonies of his important followers also supported his strong chiliasm (Stayer 1965:186).

Two of his ardent disciples—Marx Maier and George Nespitzer—portrayed Hut as a chiliastic prophet who proclaimed the 3½-year millennium after the Peasants' War of 1525 (Schornbaum 1934:188, 198 quoted by Stayer 1965:186, Packull 1975:60, Williams 1962:163). Leonhard Schiemer, his Anabaptist convert and subsequent follower, spoke of the same mid-1528 millennium under Hut's influence (Stayer 1975:154). Fully absorbing his master's thought patterns, Schiemer even considered the suffering persecution of Anabaptists in Switzerland at Solothurn as a sign of the imminent end of the world (Muller 1938:54-6 quoted by Stayer 1965:186).

At any rate, Hut stood out with his vibrant chiliasm, which was attractive to the majority of his contemporaries, especially the broken common people after the Peasants' War of 1525 (Deppermann 1987:201). His violent eschatological impulse was strong enough to re-awaken their lost hope, stirring up nostalgia for the apocalyptic dreams of Thomas Müntzer (Klassen 1959:177). This explains why "remarkably many" of his followers were veterans of the revolt of 1525 (Seebass 1972:186 quoted by Packull 1975:60). By identifying the magistrates and the upper class with the ungodly and by promising the vengeance upon the ungodly with the imminent *parousia*, his vengeful eschatology provided them with reason and justice for both the past and future events (Packull 1975:60, Stayer 1965:188).

Thus, like his doctrine of the sword, his chiliasm was essentially

---

[17]In fact, Hut told Urbanus Rhegius (1489-1541), the chief Lutheran pastor at Augsburg, about his commission at night (Seebass 1972:396 quoted by Packull 1975:61).

revolutionary (Packull 1977, Stayer 1965:185). Hut never denied that he defended "violent eschatology" (Deppermann 1987:202). To him, if the *parousia* meant the Day of Judgment, it was by its very nature vibrant and violent (Stayer 1965:186). So, his violent eschatology justified the use of force.

But the true significance was the sequence and direction between the two; the former (violent eschatology) always precedes the latter (the sword), not *vice versa*. In other words, the role of the saints (the Anabaptists) would be determined by the rule of God (Stayer 1972:154). Despite having the sword in their hands, they must wait until God finally confirmed its execution. Here, his code of conduct was clear and irreversible—"A Christian can indeed have a sword, as long as he allows it to remain in the sheath until the Lord tells him to draw it" (Meyer 1874:242 quoted by Stayer 1972:154). Even during persecution, the sword was to remain silent. Only after the Second Coming would the sword be held for apocalyptic vengeance upon the ungodly (Stayer 1972:154-55).

Put differently, although Hut promised God's imminent inauguration accompanying the destruction of the godless (Deppermann 1987:202), this demanded being in the proper order—first the Lord's return, then wielding the sword by the saints, and lastly the end of this world (Klassen 1959:180). In this sense, his violent eschatology embraced the *already*-but-*not-yet* tension. The Anabaptists *already* had the sword in their hands to actively take part in that, but they should *not yet* draw it from its sheath of their own will.

This led to Hut's idea of double-vengeance on the ungodly—action by God and action by man (Stayer 1972:156, Packull 1975:60). Here, he emphasized the role of the saints being in parallel with that of God (Goertz 1996:17). Figuratively speaking, his chiliastic rhapsody had two main characters—God and the saints (Anabaptists)—and reached its climax in their mutual punitive sanction upon the ungodly (Seebas 1972:219 quoted by Packull 1975:61). To Hut, despite eschatological vengeance belonging to God, it was also assigned to the saints as a special joint mission (Stayer 1972:156).

So instead of removing the sword, his eschatology sharpened its blade for the final judgment in which God would work in close collaboration with his elect in punishing the wicked (Stayer 1965:191,

Seebas 1972:402 quoted by Packull 1975:61). Indeed, he believed that on one hand, the Kingdom would come, not be advanced, and Christians must receive the Kingdom, but in the other, he and his followers would play an active role on the Day of Judgment for they were called to punish the ungodly as the special Christian elect (Packull 1975:61). This made his eschatology violent and vibrant enough (Scribner 1994:753).

In short, while Hut had struggled with the abortive revolution of 1525, his chiliasm, violent eschatology, shed new light on this tragic event, not as a tombstone but as a birthplace of new prophecy; hence it became a decisive point in history (a *kairos*) which would inaugurate the *parousia*—the Second Coming. It was, then, characterized by his open espousal of the vengeance upon the ungodly in close collaboration between God and the saints (namely, the Anabaptists). Evidently he never left the Last Judgment in the hand of God alone, rather encouraged his followers to draw their sword and become the joint force for the sake of the Kingdom. In a word, Hut was a chiliastic prophet who held eschatological revenge both patiently and passionately.

Theology of Baptism: Baptism in Blood

Another explicit theme of Hut's teaching was baptism. Encouraged by an eager expectation of the return of Christ, he developed a concept of "eschatological baptism" (Spinks 2006:86, Clasen 1972:100). Over his lifetime, he had bred a sort of love-hate relationship with baptism. From about 1521 onward, like the other radicals, he was an opponent of infant baptism to the extent of refusing to have himself and his children baptized (Rupp 1969:333, Klassen 1959:280).

Much of Hut's attacks on infant baptism followed in the footsteps of his master, Thomas Müntzer—i.e., faith preceded baptism and was made real in suffering (Klassen 1965:178, Packull 1975:64). The true significance of this view was his allegiance to adult or believer's baptism (Snyder 2010:73). It was the Anabaptist leader Hans Denck (1495-1527) who introduced him to the practice of adult baptism and made him an apostle of Anabaptism in South and Central Germany (Williams 1962:162). On Pentecost 1526, Denck baptized Hut (Williams 1962:80, Meyer 1874:223, 245 quoted by Klassen 1957:180), and this experience was decisive to the extent of distinguishing him from his previous life and activity under Müntzer (Klassen 1965:177-78).

However, that did not mean Hut's baptism led him to be a man in different kind—from being a disciple of apocalyptic Müntzer to being an apostle of peaceful Anabaptism (Stayer 1965:181-91). While his theological and eschatological framework was already complete before his baptism and showed a strong indebtedness to Müntzer (Seebass 1972:198 quoted by Packull 1975:59), his baptism experience served not as a separation and a relegation, but as an extension and even an elevation of Müntzer's influence on him (Packull 1975:66).

Of course, a dynamic link between Hut under Müntzer and Hut under Denck mediated from his baptism (Packull 1975:66); but his "theology of baptism" was essentially more compatible with Hut the apocalyptic revolutionary than Hut the non-violent Anabaptist (Stayer 1965:185). Just as his eschatology eventually served to sharpen (not sheath) his sword, so his baptism urged him to espouse (not eschew) Müntzer's revolutionary ideas at its core (Seebass 1972:402 quoted by Packull 1975:59).

At any rate, after his own baptism, Hut was carried along by eschatological baptism mediated by both Müntzer and Denck (Armour 1966:76, Packull 1973:333-35). On one hand, he developed his baptismal theology from Müntzer's "confirmationist" point of view (Seebass 1972:481 quoted by Packull 1975:61).[18] Taking a cue from Müntzer's stress on Christian confirmation through the impartation of the Spirit (Rupp 1969:270), he began to apply it to baptism (Seebass 1972:478-79 quoted by Packull 1975:61). For example, not only was Hut himself baptized at Pentecost, he also baptized his followers using the TAU as a sign of the cross upon the forehead in seeking to recruit the 144,000 saints (Schornbaum 1934:90-93 quoted by Packull 1973:332, Klaassen 1981:320-21, Clasen 1972:101). From this vantage point, some of his followers argued that they had only received a sign on the forehead with the traditional rite of confirmation, not of baptism (Packull 1973:332-33). In overtones reminiscent of Müntzer, he set a peculiar mode of baptism—namely, eschatological baptism sealed with and by the Spirit as a rite of confirmation (Rupp 1969:272, Seebass 1972:478-79 quoted by

---

[18]In this light, G. Rupp has proposed the necessity of considering Müntzer as a confirmationist rather than an Anabaptist (Rupp 1969:271-72).

Packull 1975:61).

On the other hand, Hut was also greatly indebted to Hans Denck regarding baptism (Kiwiet 1958:21).[19] Like Denck, he found the basic premise of his baptism in the Great Commission of Matthew 28 and Mark 16:15:

> The word which stands in Mark 16:15 had moved him [Hut] to preach, namely, that preaching was first, afterwards faith, and thirdly baptism. And man must let the word of the Lord stand. [He is] not to do anything apart from it, [and] also shall depart neither to the right nor the left, according to the last of Matthew [Ch. 28:19-20], that one shall first teach and afterwards baptize (Williams 1962:162-63).

As for him, the Scripture gave no example of infant baptism (Meyer 1874:223 quoted by Klassen 1959:192-93, 295) but rather the clear order in the preaching-faith-baptism sequence (Packull 1975:64, Klaassen 1981:170, Armour 1966:77, 92-3). Encouraged by it, he developed a three-fold baptism—that of the Spirit, that of water, and that of blood—based on 1 John 5:6-8 with the emphasis on the concept of covenant (Seebas 1972:468-69 quoted by Packull 1975:61, Williams 1962:163, Klassen 1959:271). Here, baptism as the covenant was singled out as one of the most important points of his theology (Klassen 1959:193, 271-72).[20]

The first type of baptism (of the Spirit) was the inward covenant, a sealed contract between the believer and God through the action of the Holy Spirit (Williams 1962:163, Klassen 1959:194). In this baptism, the Spirit "washed, purified, and justified men from their lusts, sins, and evil deeds" through the process of the so-called "water of all affliction" (*Wasser aller Trubsal*), which served as the means by which "man sinks into the death of Christ" (Schornbaum 1934:21 quoted by Klassen 1959:194). Hut emphasized the anteriority of this baptism; it did not begin with Christ but rather with all the elect friends of God from Adam

---

[19] Denck saw "the prerequisite for a genuine baptism" as "the oral confession of faith" (Kiwiet 1958:21).

[20] Denck defined baptism as "covenant of a good conscience with God" (Kolde 1887:408 quoted by Kiwiet 1958:21).

onward (Schornbaum 1934:21 quoted by Klassen 1959:194).

The second baptism (of water) served as the external covenant, considering a commitment of obedience to God and to fellow Christians (Williams 1962:163, Klassen 1959:193-94). It "manifested itself in godly love to brothers and sisters with body, life, property, and honor, regardless of the criticism of the world" (Schornbaum 1934:20 quoted by Klassen 1959:272). The sign of baptism was given and offered by the Christian community so that whoever would desire to be a disciple of Christ must be baptized before a Christian congregation, the Body of Christ (Klassen 1965:193-94).

However, he considered both Spirit and water baptism not as separate but as integrated—the outward baptism of water was the inward struggle of Spirit baptism and vice versa (Finger 2004:27). This led him to see baptism as 'a dual covenant'—"between the believer and God and between the believer and the *Gemeinde* (community)" (Packull 1975:61).

The third baptism (of blood) is what made Hut's baptism unique, being the culmination of his baptism that true Christians should experience (Klassen 1959:192, Rupp 1969:395). This baptism in blood was related to suffering and persecution; it was the baptism with which Christ was baptized, but his saints still shed their blood in this world (Williams 1962:163, Klassen 1959:291). In his end-time schema, this baptism in blood was even tied to the suffering of the elect who would experience the last three and a half year tribulation as the apocalyptic sign of covenant (Seebass 1972:138-64 quoted by Kim 2013:133, Packull 1975:61, Snyder 2010:73). Indeed, he was convinced that Spirit and water baptism enabled believers to accept baptism in blood, "consisting of daily mortification and perhaps literal martyrdom" (Finger 2004:27). Thus, his three-fold baptism served as a coherent whole that culminated in the final point—baptism in blood.

> Baptism consists of three things, Spirit, water and blood. In essence, they are one and give testimony on earth. The Spirit refers to trust in the Word of God and commitment to live according to it. The Word calls this the covenant of God that he makes by his Spirit in the hearts of men. Beyond this, God gave water as a sign or covenant that a man might reveal himself openly and testify of his desire to lead an irreproachable life in

true obedience to God and to all Christians. Whoever transgresses and sins against God and his brother should be disciplined orally by the others. This is the ban that God refers to as the witness before the Church. Blood is the baptism that Christ mentioned to his disciples when he asked, 'Do you desire to receive the baptism with which I have been baptized?' This is the baptism that gives testimony throughout the world when the blood of one who has received it is spilled (Meyer 1874:227 quoted by Klassen 1959:195).

To summarize, Hut's teaching on baptism shows the dynamic interconnection between Hut under Müntzer and Hut under Denck (Kim 2013:132-23). At the first stage, his baptism grew under Müntzer's inner baptism of the Spirit through suffering; then it was linked with Denck's baptism as the external covenant in his three-fold formula; and lastly, it was integrated into eschatological baptism—namely baptism in blood—as the apocalyptic sign of the elect on the Last Day. To be sure, both Müntzer and Denck's baptism contributed to his baptism in blood as the culmination of baptism in Spirit and covenant.

Summary: Hut the Radical Reformer as Being-in-the-Restorative-Common-People

As a "zealous unschooled missionary," Hans Hut left an indelible impact on the early South German Anabaptism (Stayer 1965:181). His career as a book binder and a book salesman made him close to "peasants and proletarian townsmen"—the common people (Stayer 1965:181, Klassen 1959:179). From the personal involvement in the revolt of 1525, he became acquainted with Thomas Müntzer and after the debacle at Frankenhausen, began to share the shattering experience of this abortive revolution in 1525 (Klassen 1959:179, Packull 1986:53). His radical teachings and actions, focusing on encouraging the untrained mass in general and the fugitive veterans of the revolt of 1525 in particular, served to give impetus to the post-revolutionary reality, providing striking parallels to Müntzer's revolutionary activity (Klaassen 1962:220, Packull 1975:59).

His baptism by Hans Denck served as a turning point in his life and ministry but it did not lessen but rather strengthen his connection with Müntzer. Indeed, "On all essentials Hut remained a faithful disciple of his master" (Seebas 1972:564, 322 quoted by Packull 1975:60). This was made clear by his radical teachings such as 'gospel of all creatures,' 'doctrine of the sword,' 'violent and vibrant eschatology' and 'baptism in blood.'

First, as to the 'gospel of all creatures,' Hut put an emphasis on the concept of the 'Order of God': the creatures witness to God (Seebass 1972:435 quoted by Packull 1975:63). In this principle of hierarchical chain of being, God was the centre and the creatures fulfilled His purpose by their submission to the order above them (Packull 1986:54). This included the necessity of suffering, which ultimately pointed to the crucified Son of God (Klaassen 1962:217). Thus suffering served as a prelude to God's redemptive work (Seebass 1972:435, 447-48 quoted by Packull 1975:63).

The true significance of this teaching was easily accessible to everyone except for scholars, priests and princes; all illustrations and parables were tailor-made especially for the common people and thus "opened to [them] the possibility of hearing the gospel directly" (Packull 1986:54, Liechty 1994:67-72). In this way, his 'gospel of all creatures,' infused by Müntzer's egalitarian and anti-clerical thought, became a gospel for the common people and served as a great arsenal for his influence on the common people's movement in general and Anabaptism in South Germany in particular (Packull 1986:54, 66).

Second, Hut's doctrine of the sword served as a creative extension of Müntzer's violent revolution. From the beginning, his position on the sword was radical enough to put his name on the list of Müntzer's League of Elect (Seebass 1972:168 quoted by Packull 1975:58); he would not rule out the use of force if necessary. As he unfurled the banner of the 'gospel of all creatures' for the common people, his teaching on the sword became more and more hostile against the magistrates so far as to identify them with the godless (Packull 1986:54).

His stress on the violent sword was especially well received by veterans of the revolt of 1525, who still wished to join those revolutions again, expecting the punishment of the godless *Obrigkeit* (Seebass 1972:202 quoted by Packull 1975:60). Yet in his teaching, he made clear that the attitude to the use of force and the way to use of the force was especially different. While justifying the use of force, he encouraged his followers to put time limits on it.

This resulted in his advocacy of an interim ethic—a temporal rule of Christian magistracy before the Second Coming—which turned Müntzer's naked sword for now into his sheathed sword for tomorrow (Stayer 1972:158, 1965:185). It meant not giving up the sword but *reculer pour mieux sauter*—delaying the inevitable; the sword should remain sheathed until the Lord would come again. In essence, he never changed his belief in justification by the sword; while patiently waiting for the Last Day, he had passionately inspired his followers to take up arms against the ungodly.

Third, Hut's violent eschatology was singled out as the verification of his violent sword. Borrowing much of his specific end-time program from Müntzer's chiliasm (Seebass 1972:341-44 quoted by Petersen 1993:84), he gave the abortive revolution of 1525 apocalyptic significance not as the failure but as the fulfillment of prophecy for a future kingdom (Seebass 1972:180-81 quoted by Packull 1975:60). This drove him to move his thought further toward the revolutionary goal, emphasizing eschatological vengeance upon the ungodly.

This was created by him as the end-time Elijah and his followers as God's special elect both of whom would play an active role in punishing the wicked (Seebass 1972:402 quoted by Packull 1975:61). What was striking was that his eschatological vengeance was two-fold; both God and the saints (Anabaptists) were responsible for annihilating the ungodly (Stayer 1972:156, Packull 1975:60). This also showed the systematic evolution of his thought regarding the use of force. His idea of mutual sanction upon the ungodly was justified by the doctrine of the violent sword, backed by an interim ethic. All this made him an end-time chiliastic prophet who proclaimed the threatening judgment upon the wicked.

Fourth, Hut's allegiance to eschatological vengeance led him to espouse eschatological baptism—namely, baptism in blood as the apocalyptic sign of the elect. Like other Anabaptists, especially Hans Denck, he saw baptism as a covenant sign that incorporated believers into the fellowship of the Church, emphasizing a three-fold baptism of

Spirit, water and blood (Schornbaum 1951:43 quoted by Klaassen 1981:169, Friedmann 1959:36).

Yet his willingness to resort to suffering, drawn from Müntzer's mystical idea, was more responsible for moving him toward vibrant baptism in blood than non-violent Anabaptist teachings. In his belief, baptism was more than a covenantal sign of the elect, which sought out persecution and martyrdom from worldly Christians. Instead, it was the sign of the self-conscious willingness to suffer according to God's will as part of the 'gospel of all creatures' (Gregory 2007:472). Thus it came to be included within the pattern of violent eschatology which brought about the eventual compensation (or vindication) against the worldly power (Williams 1962:226).

By linking his baptism to an eschatological symbol to seal the 144,000 elect of the Last Days, Hut gave his followers a conviction that they had received the gifts of the Spirit so as to actively participate in the violent eschatological event as the special Christian elect (Packull 1975:61, 1976:80).

In short, since Hut wished to rekindle the dying embers of Müntzer's enthusiasm through Anabaptism, his concern was focused on not an either-or but a both-and distinction. This was created by his intriguing synthesis of Müntzer's active revolution and Anabaptism's passive non-violence. He was convinced that the followers of Müntzer were to be more rationalized, while the adherents of Anabaptism were to be more radicalized. This resulted in his advocacy of an interim ethic—the doctrine of the sheathed sword—as a sign of the 'patient' revolution for the former (the followers of Müntzer), though he continued to resort to the use of force.

On the other hand, his open espousal of baptism in blood—the apocalyptic sign of the elect—encouraged the 'passionate' reaction for the latter (the followers of Anabaptism), leading to the eventual vindication of the suffering saints (Anabaptists) on the Last Days. All this depicted Hut the radical reformer as being-in-the-restorative-common-people, who tried to embrace both Müntzer's revolution and Anabaptism's non-violence both patiently and passionately.

Chapter 5
Profiles of the Radical Reformers

Melchior Hoffman (1495-1543)

Biographical Sketch

When it comes to radical religious leaders in the sixteenth century context, many of them were renegade Catholic priests (like Luther), but there were also a remarkable number of others, having no formal religious training before embarking on their 'new faith' (Stayer 1965:181, MacKay 2007:12). One such man was Melchior Hoffman (1495-1543), a godfather of Anabaptism in northern Germany and the Netherlands. "As an artisan and lay preacher, he naturally denigrated the higher education which his more learned opponents had openly turned against him" (Waite 1988:297-98). "Born in 1495 in Schwabisch Hall in southwestern Germany, he was a furrier by trade," a vocation in which he took great pride throughout his life (Neff 1956:778-85, MacKay 2007:12). Indeed, he saw himself as following in the footsteps of the apostle Paul (Deppermann 1987:35).[1]

In 1526, Hoffman burst onto the historical stage as one of the Lutheran lay missionaries of Livonia (Krahn 1968:82).[2] This marked the start of his wandering life for the next ten years as 'the prophet against the learned' (Deppermann 1987, Waite 1990:90). From that point and

---

[1] Hoffman asserted his right to preach without official training or knowledge of Latin based on the fact that many types of builders helped to erect Christ's temple (Pater 1984:209).

[2] At that time, Hoffman was granted the required certification to preach. Luther had generously published Hoffman's letter, along with his own and that of Bugenhagen, Luther's own father confessor, to the Livonians (Bailey 1990:175-90).

onward, he got himself into trouble in assorted German towns along the eastern Baltic, where his preaching resulted in an iconoclastic riot (Noll 1973:48-9, MacKay 2007:12-3). It was both his lower social status and his popularity among the common people that often prevented his arrest as a result of the trouble he stirred up (Greschat 2004:119).

In the small Teutonic city of Wolmar, although proclaiming Luther's gospel of 'righteousness by faith alone' (Noll 1973:48), Hoffman was distinguishing himself from the Wittenberg Reformers by combining his messages with threats of imminent judgment on the monks, knights, and prelates (Lindberg 1983:89). This inevitably resulted in him being expelled from the city (Deppermann 1987:36, Pater 1984:310-66).[3] However, he soon relocated in Dorpat, where the magistrates supported the evangelical movement (Packull 1990:146). It was here that he found himself surrounded by the most violent iconoclastic outbursts (Deppermann 1987:36).[4]

Regardless of his level of involvement, the situation proved that Hoffman was again in trouble (Pater 1984:190). The city councilors and the official Lutheran preachers called for tough measures against the religious radicalism and hammered those who had kindled it (Bailey 1990:177). The differences in background, training, and personality had created a gap between this lay preacher and the learned Lutheran pastors

---

[3]Hoffman's earliest activities were summarized by Karlstadt thusly—"The furrier spent some time in Livonia. He was visited by God with grace, and his eyes were opened unto him with the recognition of the Word of divine truth and of Christ. Thus he began to preach the Word of God in a town called Wolmar under the jurisdiction as they call it of the master of the Teutonic Order. There he suffered much persecution until, at last, he was expelled at the lord master's command for the sake of truth" (Pater 1984:173).

[4]At that time, the whole city revolted because, in the futile attempt by the provost of the bishop to arrest Hoffman, mercenaries killed four of his followers and wounded 20 others. In revenge, armed masses stormed every church in the city on January 10, 1525, demolishing images and altars (Pater 1984:190). Yet no blood was shed in the course of the iconoclastic outburst itself, and no evidence was found that Hoffman had called for the destruction of churches or expulsion of the canons before his attempted arrest (Deppermann 1987:87).

(Krahn 1968:82, Pater 1984:174).⁵ Fearing that the simmering social revolution might spread to the peasants, the landed aristocrats withdrew their support of Hoffman (Pater 1984:173) and forced him to leave the area (Deppermann 1987:87-8).

By 1526, Hoffman held a new position as a preacher in Stockholm (Sweden), where he found an audience among the wealthy German merchants, who were interested in his radicalism to protest the king's "half-hearted" religious reforms (Deppermann 1987:93-4). With the help of these merchants (Deppermann 1987:91), he published his first major work—a charge against the Livonians (Pater 1984:203). Since his preaching had caused rioting, the king saw him as a threat to public order so expelled him from the city in 1527 (Pater 1984:174).⁶ Taking refuge in the Baltic port city of Lübeck (Germany), he again found himself in the midst of violent followers (Deppermann 1987:84, Pater 1984:218). Taking note of the radical nature of his preaching, the municipal authorities prompted him to leave (Bailey 1990:177).

Hoffman (with his wife and child) sought to establish himself in Schleswig-Holstein, at that time a part of Denmark (MacKay 2007:13). Surprisingly, he received a letter of safe conduct from the king of

---

⁵With regard to the differences, the controversy was brought into the open. The learned scholars laughed at Hoffman because he was an artisan. They thought it impossible for "a layman or a furrier to be able to expound God's word as truly as their own scribblings, because they have been taught Scripture since childhood. A furrier should have spent the same amount of time in study as a Cathedral priest or monk if he is to preach" (quoted by Deppermann 1987:64). This disagreement did not die down even after Hoffman went to Wittenberg (June 1525) to testify before Luther and Bugenhagen as to his orthodoxy. There was indeed no reason that the mainline Reformers could have refused to testify to Hoffman's theological orthodoxy, for his eschatological speculations were, to a large extent, an expression of the views of the Wittenberg Reformers, and his works clearly stressed all of Luther's most important ideas, such as justification by faith alone, faith as a gift of divine grace, need for Christian to renounce use of force and any vengeful desires, etc. (Deppermann 1987:61-62).

⁶On January 13, 1527, the king forbade Hoffman from continuing to preach publicly, issuing the following decree: "It appears from the experience of those who have heard his preaching that Hoffman has been very fanatical and that his words have been indiscreet. Thus he is ordered to stop his public preaching before the general populace" (Deppermann 1987:92).

Denmark, Frederick I (Pater 1984:174, Bailey 1990:177).[7] Thanks to this recommendation, he was appointed deacon at the church of Nikolai in Kiel and received permission to preach in the area (Krahn 1968:83). As the king intended for this untiring itinerant preacher to undermine the Catholic Church in the territory, he attained riches and honour—temporarily (Deppermann 1987:96).

Under this favourable circumstance, Hoffman became the proprietor of the first printing press in Kiel and utilized it to defend himself against the attacks of his opponents (Bailey 1990:176, Fudge 2007:246-47). Yet his involvement in doctrinal disputes with the Lutheran preachers forced him to travel to Wittenberg in 1527, expecting Luther's endorsement of his orthodoxy (Pater 1984:174-75). This time Luther repudiated him and no longer sanctioned his ministry[8] by warning that his iconoclasm and allegorical interpretation of Eucharist were not orthodox (Deppermann 1987:67, Lindberg 1983:90, Pater 1984:174-75).[9] To Luther, Hoffman sounded like a 'little Müntzer' in his apocalyptic visionary expressions (Klaassen 1986:15).

In 1529, a meeting in the duchy of Schleswig-Holstein (Flensburg) was set up to seemingly test Hoffman's views (Bailey 1990:179); but it was actually intended to provide an authoritative venue in which to reject him (Pater 1984:175, MacKay 2007:13). So to prepare himself, Hoffman requested help from Andreas Bodenstein von Karlstadt, who accepted an invitation to defend his views but then received no permission to be present (Bailey 1990:183-84, Krahn 1968:84). Thus his condemnation was predestined (Deppermann 1987:127).

---

[7]"The same furrier arrived in the country of Holstein with his wife and child. There he was summoned to King Frederick of Denmark, who wanted to hear his sermons. As he rightly preached the Word of God, the King appointed him as his servant, giving him a letter and seal that permitted him to preach God's Word in the whole land of Holstein. The King loved him and established him as a preacher in Kiel and granted protection to all his possessions. He protected his wife, child and all he owned in a just and Christian way" (quoted by Deppermann 1987:96).

[8]Hoffman's account in Wittenberg shows that he felt insulted after a sharp exchange over his exegesis. "When I revealed such an explanation to my teachers in Wittenberg and clearly wanted to follow Scripture, I—poor worm—was considered a great sinner and a dreamer, and thus I was terribly mistreated, maligned, and despised" (quoted by Pater 1984:174).

[9]Krahn in particular saw what brought Hoffman into disfavour and led to his final break with Lutheran pastors, primarily that being his anti-Lutheran position regarding the Lord's Supper—spiritualization of the meaning of the Eucharist (Krahn 1968:84).

In April, this radical lay preacher was forced to either recant or leave (Lindberg 1983:90). Being duly banished, he was expelled from the city, leaving behind all his belongings, including his printing press (Deppermann 1987:136, Bailey 1990:184).[10] This, of course, gave him a bad image of Lutheranism as a whole, which he now considered as the new "papacy," no less tyrannical and blasphemous than the old church (Deppermann 1987:136-37).

Hoffman's next stop was the city of Emden in East Frisia, where he found Karlstadt, who also had been expelled from the city of Kiel and collaborated with him under the protection of Ulrich von Dornum, the influential counselor (Lindberg 1996:135, Krahn 1968:85-6).[11] His success in Emden was immediate, to the extent that he re-baptized about 300 persons, which understandably caught the attention of the city's clergy (Snyder 1996:249), while a growing tension brought him into temporary alliance with Karlstadt (Krahn 1968:85-6).[12] In June 1529, once again running into trouble with the Lutherans, he fled to the city of Strasbourg, one of the great centres of Reformation thought (Williams and Mergal 1957:209-10).

Here, Hoffman found himself in relatively favourable conditions, because the local leaders appreciated the limit of their authority unless major social unrest occurred (Lienhard 1977:204-5). This city's policy remained appealing to many religious dissenters (including the Anabaptists) and thereby made it easy for him to find attachment and followings (Deppermann 1987:218).

At the beginning, this lay preacher was welcomed by Martin Bucer, leader of Strasbourg's reforming clergy; he introduced Hoffman to his co-workers, including Caspar Schwenckfeld, who at the time was a house

---

[10] Nonetheless, Hoffman still clung to the delusion that he had simply been the victim of the new Lutheran orthodoxy, not of the new princely church government. He continued to trust Frederick I, so after his banishment he dedicated the commentary on Revelation to the king. In it, he presented Frederick as one of the two Christian kings who would protect the suffering church from annihilation at the hands of the beast (the emperor) in the course of the apocalyptic disturbances (Deppermann 1987:137).

[11] Karlstadt and Hoffman had joined the Court of Emden. There they had written a book about the Flensburg disputation. (Deppermann 1987:159).

[12] Even if both agreed on the issue of the Eucharist and thus opposed to Lutheranism, their collaboration was only temporary due to some differences, such as the hermeneutical weight on Revelation. Most of all, Karlstadt was not comfortable with Hoffman's apocalyptic ideas (Deppermann 1987:159).

guest of Wolfgang Capito (Krahn 1968:88). But soon his radicalism earned him the enmity of the local Zwinglian religious leaders (Haude 200:92, MacKay 2007:13). Their advice to him was to stop preaching and return to his profession as a furrier! (Deppermann 1987:160). Greatly disappointed, he charged that the Strasbourg Zwinglians and the Wittenberg Lutherans were all cut from the same cloth—namely, 'Scripture wizards' (*Schriftgelehrte*) who knew the Scriptures but lacked the Holy Spirit (Greyerz 2008:164).

The rejection from the religious authorities drove Hoffman to consort with the Strasbourg radicals, a group of lower-class individuals who were open to the Spirit (Brady 2009:204, MacKay 2007:14). These "poor in spirit lying in the dust" (Friesen 1984:158) were the so-called 'Strasbourg Prophets,' led by Lienhard and Ursula Jost, who claimed to receive direct visions from God (Deppermann 1987:178-80, Waite 2013:496). The 'Strasbourg Prophets' began to convince him that the last days were drawing closer, which had the effect of heightening his apocalyptic excitement (Deppermann 1987:218-19), while at the same time, the 'Strasbourg Prophets' deemed Hoffman as the prophetic Elijah-figure for whom they had been waiting. Thus, he soon held the most esteemed position in the apocalyptic strand of Strasbourg Anabaptists (Deppermann 1987:218).

What really made Hoffman become an Anabaptist?[13] Primarily it was because of their view pertaining to the covenant or the fellowship of believers as well as their dedicated Christian life and witness (Krahn 1968:90). Therefore, in April 1530, he identified himself with them and then "rashly petitioned the Strasbourg city council to grant the Anabaptists a church" for public worship (MacKay 2007:14, Krahn 1968:90), a petition which the magistrates flatly refused (Pater 1984:176).

By the next month, when Hoffman was back in East Frisia, he became further radicalized in spreading the doctrine of Anabaptism, including the practice of believer's baptism (Deppermann 1987:218). He acquired several hundred followers in this area, including John

---

[13]In this regard, Pater has suggested that Karlstadt may have had renewed impact on Hoffman when they met in East Frisia. For after that encounter, Hoffman revised his view of baptism, repudiated predestination, and began to teach the typically Karlstadtian combination of a universal offer of salvation by God (Pater 1984:175-76). But this question still remains open.

Matthjisson, a baker from Haarlem, and David Joris, a glass-painter from Delft (Snyder 1995:212). He then was shocked when he received news that ten of his followers were beheaded in The Hague in December 1531 due to the practice of re-baptism (MacKay 2007:15). As a result, he reportedly ordered a halt to adult baptism until the end of 1533, when the world was to end anyway (Deppermann 1987:226-31, Snyder 1995:212).[14]

In March 1533, Hoffman returned to Strasbourg full of expectations. By officially declaring Strasbourg as the 'New Jerusalem,' he brought a whole new dimension into the city, emphasizing its significant role as "the center of resistance against the godless in the impending cataclysm" (Klaassen 1992:86, MacKay 2007:14).[15] The city council had recently opted for Lutheranism and was not at all pleased with this restless prophet's declaration, so ordered his arrest (Packull 1983:98, MacKay 2007:15). In May, he was accused of plotting rebellion (Snyder 1995:213), an accusation that he welcomed, since it was part of the apocalyptic last days, and he believed his stay in prison would be brief (Pater 1984:176). Encouraged by the prophecy of an old man, he "went willingly, cheerfully, and well-comforted to prison" (Deppermann 1987:293).[16]

However, Hoffman had to spend a much longer jail term than he expected (Deppermann 1987:380). This radical preacher was on the city authorities' blacklist. Even if there was no proof of any plot to rebel, he had large numbers of ardent followers who honoured him as the second Elijah, one of the two witnesses in the last days (Barrett 1992:278-79, MacKay 2007:15).

Hoffman's apocalyptic faith in the world's demise was not only

---

[14]Thus is followed by the critical question as to whether or not Hoffman had really regarded re-baptism as the central point of his teaching. This goes further to whether or not he did give his followers the suspension order. Here, some scholars argued that he never ordered a suspension of baptism but suggested it and thus there might never have been an actual suspension of the administering of baptism (Krahn 1968:134).

[15]Before Hoffman proclaimed it, there were already prophecies that identified Strasbourg as the place where the last great end-time battle would be fought (Peuckert 1976:159, 161 quoted by Klaassen 1992:86).

[16]Obbe Philips (1500-1568), one of Hoffman's followers, wrote later on; "He [Hoffman] beat his hat from his head, threw his shoes away, raised his fingers to heaven, and swore by the living God that he would not enjoy any other food or drink but water and bread until his stretched arm would point to the one who had sent him; this is the way in which he entered the prison, prepared, joyous and comforted" (quoted by Jelsma 1998:52-3).

theologically flawed, but also dangerous to the city's welfare (Packull 1983:98). So the authorities eventually declared a shocking ruling—a life sentence (Packull 1983:95, Deppermann 1987:380), which gave him a chance "neither to leave nor to become an outright martyr" (Krahn 1968:117). The only way out for this great lay preacher was to die a natural death. As a result, he remained incarcerated in a closed and isolated prison cell until he died in 1543 (Deppermann 1978:165-66 quoted by Packull 1983:94, MacKay 2007:15). His name and passion then had passed into oblivion.

Theological Perspective

Prophet against the Learned

Without formal theological training, Hoffman had drunk from his own spiritual wells (Deppermann 1987:69). He especially drew theological water from apocalyptic texts[17] like Daniel, the fourth book of Ezra, and Revelation, which were obscure to the official Reformers but fascinating to the common people (Packull 1986:32). The Book of Revelation held a special place in his theology, serving as a keyhole through which to see the rest of Scripture (Packull 1986:32). He believed that the written word concealed the mystery of God's revelation (Waite 1988:302). So concentration on spiritual discernment was to be his distinguishing mark as 'the prophet against the learned' (Deppermann 1987, Waite 1988:297). Against more learned opponents, he asserted that "God's wisdom is not perceived with fleshly eyes, but only with spiritual eyes, which do not look upon the person, nor upon the position of rank" (Deppermann 1987:58).

Thus Hoffman's spiritual hermeneutics were created on the premise of a sharp distinction between letter and spirit (Waite 1988:298, Klaassen 1986:22). In this Spirit-oriented hermeneutics, he boldly affirmed that

---

[17]Here, the attention should be given to the different use of the concepts of eschatology, apocalyptic, and millennialism. Eschatology is that part of Christian doctrine that deals with the last things inclusively. Apocalyptic denotes the understanding that the great cosmic struggle between good and evil is about to be concluded in cataclysm and includes a precise identification of times and time periods as well as of actors in the drama. Millenarianism is the expectation of a reign of peace, plenty, and justice on earth before or after the Second Advent of Christ (Klaassen 1986:18).

the Church needed people of the Spirit (not the letter) who were called by God rather than by a human agency (Pater 1984:209). On the strength of the popular anti-clerical sentiment of the time, this prophetic lay preacher found ready supporters among the lower classes (Waite 1988:298). To them, his different type of Bible reading and interpretation was marked by a voice from the wilderness against the pope, the emperor, and the university theologians (Bailey 1990:189-90).

In contrast to learned opinion, Hoffman played up "the spiritual sense which lay concealed under the letter" (Waite 1988:298). By giving more weight to a hidden meaning behind the Scripture, which disclosed itself only to those who were led by the Spirit (Goertz 2008:593), he insisted that a true meaning must be a "comprehension of the spiritual [hermeneutics] as a whole" (Waite 1998:298). In his thinking, the spiritual meaning could offer a new angle of approach to a literal meaning, which had become encased in a conceptual system of this or that tenet (Waite 1988:298). Thus for him, the axiom was that one should open, allege, argue, enforce, and apply the biblical message from the mind of the Spirit—for "without the Holy Spirit, every figure was nothing but empty letter" (Goertz 2008:593-94).

Zeal for this spiritual exegesis became a trigger for Hoffman's Christocentric hermeneutics (Waite 1988:298). He saw the hermeneutical key in the "mystery of Christ's work in history, which is revealed in Scripture, particularly its prophetic passages predicting the course of events, past, present, and future" (Waite 1988:298). Here, the Old and New Testaments had one grand meaning and conveyed one leading message that was full of allegory, symbols, and images (Deppermann 1987:216). In his view, this culminated in the return of Christ and coming of the Kingdom as an apocalyptic promise (Packull 1986:32-61). Thus, the deepest ontological basis of his Christocentric hermeneutics included the idea of apocalyptic calamity—namely, the coming judgment on the evils in the church and Christendom (Deppermann 1987:212-13, Packull 1986:32).

Via this "spirit-under-the-letter motif," Hoffman's famous use of the 'cloven hoof' was born (Waite 1988:298). This 'cloven hoof' method resulted from his observation that "All God's words are doubled or twofold, the one against the other" (Goertz 2008:594). Thus, he saw the Old and New Testaments as two inseparable parts; two parts are equal but different, analogous to the two parts of the hoof of a clean animal (Williams 1962:830-31). By applying this method to his hermeneutical metaphor, he sought to resolve outward contradictions in Scripture (Goertz 2008:594). This led to his conclusion that "All events in the Old Testament are images to which some happenings in the New Testament, or yet to take place, correspond" (Williams 1962:831).

This was the reason why, despite the fact the 'cloven hoof' analogy did not fully fit into his typological/allegorical exegesis (Deppermann 1987:214), Hoffman remained obstinate in interpreting the rest of Scripture through this distinctive method (Waite 1988:298). By believing that this 'cloven hoof' was a key to maintain the essential unity of the Word of God, he attempted to "find the middle" between the two opposing statements—two parts of the hoof—in Scripture (Waite 1988:298, Goertz 2008:594, Deppermann 1987:214).

In addition, the concept of the apocalyptic 'key of David'[18] played an important role in this purpose (Waite 1988:298). While defining it as the revelatory tool for spiritual illumination, "which was given to all those who lived in the pure fear of God," Hoffman combined this 'key of David' into his 'cloven hoof' method for unlocking the secrets of Scripture, especially its apocalyptic passages (Packull 1987:363-74, Waite 1988:298).

> History, thought Hoffman, is determined by God and furthermore, a description of the future course of history has been hidden in prophetic Scripture. Since this was so, a "figurative" interpretation of all of Scripture—Old Testament as well as New—was possible for those who, through the Spirit, possessed the crucial interpretive "key of David." Those who held the interpretive key would be able to apply the principle of the "cloven hoof," which harmonized apparent Scriptural contradictions (Snyder 1995:167)

In short, from the beginning, Hoffman set himself up as 'the prophet against the learned,' emphasizing spiritual discernment as distinct from

---

[18]The "key of David" had been granted to the church of Philadelphia, the sixth church of the Book of Revelation (Rev. 3:7).

the learned interpretations. This drove him to elevate spiritual hermeneutics as a key to open the true meaning of Scripture, based on a sharp contrast between Spirit and letter (Deppermann 1987, Visser 2006:100). Both the 'cloven hoof' and the 'key of David' were his special tools, which enabled him not only to "explain the apparent contradictions between the Old and New Testaments," but also to "discover the fulfillment of scriptural images in the present age" (Deppermann 1987:216, Waite 1988:298). This "spirit-under-the-letter" conviction led him to take a step further toward 'the prophet of the last days.'

Prophet of the Last Days

The Restitution

Hoffman's nickname, 'the prophet against the learned,' had a twofold implication; one was his close affinity with the lower classes and the other was his prophetic role as a layman, including the end-times prophecies (Kuhles 1969:377-90 quoted by Packull 1985:134). In fact, "Hoffman saw, in the poor, God's instrument for historical change," and his primary support also came from them (Packull 1985:134).[19] That role was virtually bolstered when he encountered the 'Strasbourg Prophets,' who held a strong apocalyptic bent (Stayer 1971:268). From then onward, he stood as 'the prophet of the last days' and it gave him overlapping roles (Waite 2013:485-506). Since, like many Radical Reformers of his time, he believed he was living in the last days, the theme of restitution—i.e., the restoration of all things—became the central leitmotif of his theology (Waite 1990:94).

This was epitomized by Hoffman's idea of the apocalyptic conception of history (Deppermann 1987:60). Following Joachim of Fiore and radical Franciscans, he used as his basic schema a Trinitarian division of history (Deppermann 1987:217)—namely, the Old Testament

---

[19]This does not mean that Hoffman was a "class-conscious revolutionary," as Kuhles had argued (1969:377-90). Rather, in his reformation, he had consistently sought to promote the revolution *from above;* he attempted to work though the authorities. "Nevertheless, voluntarily or involuntarily, [Hoffman] found himself on the side of the common person" (Packull 1985:135).

age of the Law (Father), the New Testament age beginning with Christ (Son), and the present age of empowerment by the Holy Spirit (Reeves 1969:491-92). In his thinking, "The second and the third ages were even subdivided into seven periods corresponding to the visions of sevens in the Apocalypse" (Packull 1986:29).

This made Hoffman's expectations of reform of church and society far more visible. At its core, he anticipated "the church of his own day to be restored to its New Testament condition" in all aspects (Packull 1986:31); this was nothing but the end-time church "to be completed with the sixth seal in his own day" (Packull 1986:53). Furthermore, he was convinced that the age of the Spirit was beginning with him (Klaassen 1986:21) and that he was co-opted as the promised prophet who possessed the spirit of Elijah for its sake (Deppermann 1987:218). The culmination came to his bold prediction that the world would end in 1533 after the cataclysmic war between the chosen of God and the ungodly (Klaassen 1986:17, MacKay 2007:14).

Hoffman's conviction as to the outpouring of the Holy Spirit in three stages appeared to enhance this end-time belief all the more (Packull 1986:16). He saw that the first outpouring of the Spirit lasted only 100 years, the second took place at the time of John Hus, and the third and final began in 1526, when he wrote his commentary on Daniel (Packull 1986:40). Thus the preaching of the two witnesses (Enoch as Hoffman and Elijah as Polderman, his follower) and with them the great persecution of believers could be expected in the next few years (Barrett 1996:278-79, Snyder and Hecht 1996:274). The bottom line was that the final judgment upon the ungodly would occur in 1533 and Strasbourg would play a significant role as the New Jerusalem (Deppermann 1987:67). This singled him out as the end-time prophet, whose role was harnessed and internalized by both the radical 'Strasbourg Prophets' (led by Lienhart Jost, his wife Ursula, and Barbara Rebstock) and the non-violent Strasbourg Anabaptists.

First, with regard to the radical 'Strasbourg Prophets,' they served to legitimize Hoffman's prophetic role, affirming him as Elijah and accepting him as their leader (Barrett 1996:278-79). Also, he granted that their visions and pneumatology were authentic and published the visions of both Josts,[20] despite the fact that there were some bizarre and ecstatic forms of prophecies (Goertz 2008:28). He nevertheless equated their prophecies with those of Isaiah and Jeremiah (Klaassen 1986:23).[21]

In one sense, their visions highlighted Hoffman's role as 'the prophet against the learned.' From the beginning, he was proud of his laity as the distinguishing mark of God's special revelation (Waite 1990:90, Goertz 2008:593). For him, God loved to reveal his secret to the lowly and despised (Klaassen 1986:21, Bailey 1990:180-81). His belief in 'God's preferential option for the poor' was enhanced and even radicalized by the 'Strasbourg Prophets' who were mostly found in lower-class circles (Mackay 2007:14).[22] For in their vision, God as imbuing the poor with dignity and meeting their needs did not simply ensure the poor a heavenly reward, but promised to judge their wealthy oppressors (Nafziger-Leis 1996:258-72, Snyder and Hecht 1996:273-87, Deppermann 1987:210). Thus, the 'Strasbourg Prophets' promoted his apocalyptic prediction in an even more radical way (Clasen 1972:130), eventually identifying the city as the New Jerusalem in which king and prophet reign in harmony (Deppermann 1987:211, Klaassen 1986:24).

Here, Hoffman's role as the prophetic layman took on a wholly different character. In his thinking, the council of Strasbourg was chosen for this global theocracy that would accompany the cataclysmic struggles (Deppermann 1987:388-89). This meant these godly magistrates were responsible for mobilizing the war against the hellish trinity—namely, the pope, the emperor and the false teachers—while the Anabaptists (the elect) were not to soil their hands with blood (Stayer, Packull and Deppermann 1975:118), but to support this military struggle through

---

[20]The fact that Hoffman had published and promoted accounts for the two Jost prophets—in 1530 for Ursula Jost and in October 1532 for Lienhart Jost—suggested that they were in close relationship (Clasen 1972:130).

[21]It is to be remembered that, while Hoffman granted Ursula had the gift of vision, he did not find her capable of interpreting those revelations. According to him, this was the only distinction of the prophetess, saying, "So then it is apparent that this lover of God [Ursula]...has a high gift of godly Spirit; visions of divine revelation, but not an understanding of their interpretations, other than what the Spirit reveals to her and teaches. And this will be offered farther to another" (Barrett 1992:65-66). Presumably, it seems evident that Hoffman saw himself as the chosen exegete of such divine visions as the end-time prophet (Haude 2007:436).

[22]Notably, the Strasbourg Prophets belonged to the lower class. For example, the prophetic couple, Lienhard and Ursula Jost, was engaged in the butchery work (Mackay 2007:14).

their prayers (Deppermann 1977:217).[23] Thus, ironically enough, what this 'prophet against the learned' really expected was a revolution 'from above' in which a military breakthrough would occur with the help of the ruling authorities (Deppermann 1977:218).

However, his passionate offer fell on deaf ears. While the council accused him of inciting rebellion and ordered his incarceration in a Strasbourg prison (Snyder 1995:213), Hoffman was willing to contrive his own imprisonment in 1533 as a necessary step to usher in the end-time divine program (Klaassen 1986:24).

Second, with regard to the non-violent Strasbourg Anabaptists, Hoffman's role as the end-time prophet gained further momentum through his acquaintance with them and especially Hans Denck, who had been influenced by Thomas Müntzer (Deppermann 1987:181-84, Snyder 1995:126-27).[24] Denck advocated the mystical theology of synergism, stressing the cooperation of man's will with God's inner Word (Packull 1977:191-99). When he accepted Denck's ideas, it enabled him to be distinguished not only from the major Reformers, but also from the Swiss Brethren (Stayer, Packull and Deppermann 1975:85).[25]

Once Hoffman began to replace Luther's doctrine of predestination with Denck's universal grace and human free will (Packull 1982:185), the lines between justification and sanctification became blurred (Deppermann 1977:217). Instead, he saw both of them as a single process that could "be accomplished through cooperation between the divine illumination and the striving of the human will" (Deppermann 1977:217). He then followed Denck a further step to say that God not only desired all men to be saved, but also enabled them to do salvific good works (Deppermann 1987:190).

This drove him to maintain the doctrine of the divinized man purified by suffering (Deppermann 1987:83-4). By identifying the goal of the process of salvation with a deification of man (Deppermann

---

[23]From this came Hoffman's ambiguous view on political ethics, which had affected his followers (namely, the Melchiorites) in serious ways. It will be discussed later with more details centering on the event of the Anabaptist Kingdom of Műnster.

[24]This has triggered the scholarly concern that there might be the strongest link between Hoffman and Hut, who was baptized by Hans Denck (Packull 1973:322, Stayer 1986:143-59, and Isaak 1986:66-82).

[25]His followers in Strasbourg even appeared to have been distinguished from other Anabaptist groups (Stayer 1971:267).

1977:217, Stayer, Packull and Depperman 1975:121), he argued that man could become divinized in this life when taught directly by God (Deppermann 1977:217). In this manner, the Swabian furrier posed a threat to the Reformation's discovery of justification by faith alone, *sola fide* (Goertz 1996:41-43, Packull 1977:35-61).

Echoing the Strasbourg Anabaptists, Hoffman expressed his position on baptism and Lord's Supper clearly (Williams and Mergal 1957:193). Since he saw baptism as a sign of betrothal between God and man (Williams 1962:447), the only baptism worthy of a mature free human being was that based on the confession of faith—namely, believers' baptism (Stayer 1995:267). Thus, he rejected infant baptism and was himself re-baptized (Deppermann 1987:259-63, Friesen 1984:158). Taking a cue from this covenantal relationship, he interpreted the Lord's Supper as the marriage of the believer to Christ, and bread and wine as the wedding ring, representing this mutual binding based on faith (Williams 1957:193-95, Krahn 1968:99).

All proved then that Hoffman's sojourn in the city of Strasbourg made a great contribution to his role as 'the prophet of the last days' (Goertz 2008:28). It was here that his apocalyptic end-time prophecies were confirmed and consolidated by both the non-violent Strasbourg Anabaptists and the radical 'Strasbourg Prophets' (Deppermann 1987:218-19). From the former, he accepted the idea of baptism upon one's confession of faith as the inner purification (discipleship/spiritual cleansing), while at the same time, from the latter, he developed outwardly the militant-activist apocalypticism (revolution/physical cleansing) (Goertz 2008:28).[26]

However, these two groups were seemingly on the opposite side of the apocalyptic end-time view and thus were difficult to reconcile; the non-violent Strasbourg Anabaptists were inclined to wait peacefully for God to bring about his justice, whereas the radical 'Strasbourg Prophets' insisted that the "world had to prepare itself for the return of Christ through an act of great cleansing" (Friesen 1984:158). Here, his role as

---

[26] Among them, Lienhard Jost (husband of Ursula) announced that "from this city the 144,000 elect would go forth into the whole world as apostolic emissaries. After a futile attempt of the emperor to besiege Strasbourg, the emissaries will rule the godless with an iron rod. The blood of the martyrs will be avenged and the new covenant will be established by baptism upon confession of faith" (Deppermann 1987:193).

'the prophet of the last days' came in handy. By redefining the pacifist idea of the Strasbourg Anabaptists and the violent apocalyptic vision of the 'Strasbourg Prophets' within his prophetic and lay-mystic context, he successfully constituted a new form of his theological leitmotif—a two-stage restitution (Packull 1985:146, Waite 1990:96). In other words, his purification in an Anabaptist way was recreated to complement his apocalyptic vision in the 'Strasbourg Prophets' for the final restitution of church and society (Packull 1986:31, Waite 1990:96).[27]

From it, the message of Hoffman took a new form. In his end-time scenario, the theme of restitution became manifest in his idea of the extermination of the godless before the final judgment plus his prediction of the earthly reign of saints until the return of Christ (Deppermann 1987:390, Packull 1985:146). In the first stage, the entire host of false teachers, including the "bloodsucking anti-Christian Lutheran and Zwinglian preachers," would perish by the sword of pious magistrates. In the second stage, the 'invulnerable' and 'invincible' 144,000 apostolic messengers (Anabaptists)—spearheaded by the two end-time witnesses (Hoffman and Polderman)—would go on a mission to the whole world, dispensing the (re)baptism of faith rather than shedding blood (Deppermann 1977:217, 1987:193, 211). Then they would come to the New Jerusalem, which would be ruled by the pious king and the Spirit-filled prophet in harmony as once in the old Israel under Solomon (Isaak 1986:79, Deppermann 1987:390).

This was an entirely new concept of the final stage of history. The previous notion of establishing the reign of God non-violently through suffering was muted by his cosmic transformation accompanying the volatile military defense of the New Jerusalem (Strasbourg) against the powers of darkness (Deppermann 1977:217, Klaassen 1981:326-28, Barrett 1996:15).

In conclusion, as 'the prophet of the last days,' Hoffman's end-time message of restitution of church and society had sparked lost hope in the poor and the oppressed, heavily disappointed by the unjust religious and secular authorities (Packull 1985:146, Deppermann 1987:390). Encouraged

---

[27]Although Hoffman did not directly use the term "restitution" in the works consulted, it seems evident that he took the theme of restitution as his central theological motive by arguing that the church of his own day was in a great need of returning to the New Testament condition (Packull 1986:31).

by both the radical 'Strasbourg Prophets' and the non-violent Strasbourg Anabaptists, he developed a two-stage apocalyptic end-time program, which held both revolutionary and reactionary tenets in it. A number of common people were enthusiastic about his idea of destruction of the godless before the last judgment and welcomed his apocalyptic programme of restitution (Pater 1984:173-253). But that was certainly not the view which some milder and less extreme characters had of him. Thus, his theme of two-stage restitution left open the possibility of the use of violence among them.

Political Ethics: Doctrine of the Sword

What Hoffman appeared to have done in Strasbourg was to integrate two different elements into one (like a cloven hoof method), combining both the peaceful (McLaughlin 1985: 265-78, Stayer 1971:268, Clasen 1972) and the radical (Boyd 1989:58-76, Stayer 1991) Anabaptist tenets into his concept of restitution (Goertz 1996:105). Yet in this dialectics of non-violence and revolution, his political ethics gave his followers an ambivalent message: "Should we wield the sword or not?" (Packull 1985:130-46, Stayer 1971:266, Deppermann 1987:22). For it was more compatible with a *both/and* category than an *either/or* (Isaak 1986:77).

In one sense, Hoffman's political ethics stressed pacifism, for he never approved of the use of aggressive violence (Isaak 1986:79)—"The sword existed to punish evil, [but] it had no authority over the church, which followed Jesus' suffering way" (Finger 2004:297). This led to his consistently peaceful teachings of "enduring all suffering for Christ until his expected second coming" (Krahn 1968:118). Here we find the pacifist Hoffman who taught his Anabaptist followers not to participate in the "slaughter of the prophets of Baal;" not even during the holy war were they to bear arms (Klaassen 1981:329, Deppermann 1977:218).

But in another sense, his apocalyptic conviction created a mess on his pacifism (Stayer 1971:268). In his thinking, since a ruler can be a Christian, use of force and Christianity were not mutually exclusive (Deppermann 1987:10, Stayer 1971:271). Although he was against the militarization of believers for the sake of transforming the world into the Kingdom of God, his political ethics left room for the worldly sword being used by pious magistrates (Stayer 1971:271). Here we find the revolutionary Hoffman who took the lead.

To Hoffman, God gave the sword to rulers to punish evil (Isaak 1986:79), which is why he provoked the Strasbourg magistrates to take up arms in expectation of a New Jerusalem. Just as the godly authorities were given the right to carry out the sword in order to secure the military victory of the Heavenly Jerusalem (Strasbourg) against the Hellish Trinity (Stayer, Packull, and Deppermann 1975:118), so too was the Strasbourg council; God chose it in his divine plan to fulfill his apocalyptic mission (Deppermann 1977:217). In his eschatological drama, once the pious magistrates defeated the "bloodthirsty hordes of Zwinglians and Lutherans," the (re) baptized apostolic messengers from Strasbourg would spread the knowledge of Christ and of believers' baptism throughout the whole earth (Deppermann 1987:211.

Thus, Hoffman's political ethics found more solace in revolution than non-violence. Encouraged by his apocalyptic conviction, he began to resort to an "eschatological revolution from above" (Goertz 1996:105), a revolution "conducted by a pious king, instructed by a prophet" (Stayer 1991:124). While disapproving of the violent uprisings by his followers, he anticipated the imminent military breakthrough with the help of the legitimate political authority *(Obrigkeit)* (Goertz 1982:187, Deppermann 1977:218)—i.e., "By order of the perfect, who do not defile themselves with blood, the faithful (the pious magistrates of the free imperial cities) must seize the sword of vengeance and exterminate the godless" (Goertz 1996:105).

In fact, Hoffman's desire for a revolution from above was not new: from his early days as a follower of Luther to his last days in prison, he had longed for recognition by the authorities (Krahn 1968:116).[28] This lingering desire for a pious *Obrigkeit* served as both an anchor and a trap for his political ethics (Deppermann 1977:219). It was complementary to his role as 'the prophet of the last days' but was contradictory to his role as 'the prophet against the learned.'

---

[28]For example, Hoffman asserted that the Lord had chosen Frederick of Denmark to be one of the two kings mentioned in Revelation, chapter 12, who would protect the spiritual Jerusalem. He belonged to the faithful servant of the Lord who helps the pious and is willing to do everything to the glory of God (Krahn 1968:89).

On the one hand, his role as 'the prophet against the learned,' which often led to iconoclastic riots by the common people, hardly recommended him to the magistrates of Dorpat, Stockholm, Kiel, and Strasbourg (Deppermann 1987:42-49). Instead, his consecutive imprisonments in and exclusions from these cities proved he lacked approval of the magistrates (Packull 1985:136). To their eyes, "[Hoffman] was perceived as a madman, fanatic or dangerous revolutionary" (Negru 2016:188). Thus, there was little chance of such for this uneducated lay preacher whose messages were defiant and subversive against bishop and magistrates (Packull 1985:139). "Only religiously chaotic and socially agitated situations" received him in piecemeal fashion.

Yet in their power struggle (the powers of the new faith), the "ruling princes, urban magistrates, nobles, Protestant clergy" had given tacit approval for Hoffman's message (Deppermann 1977:218). Thus, Lutherans used him as their theological arsenal to attack the old church or Zwinglians against Lutherans. But once they had squeezed the orange from him, they abandoned him quickly (Deppermann 1977:218-19). Nonetheless, the transitory support from the authorities—especially from the Livonian magistracy, the king of Denmark, and the East Frisian chancellor Ulrich von Dornum—constantly gave him an expectation of a pious *Obrigkeit* and thus he waited for a revolution from above, though his primary support came from the lower classes (Packull 1985:135, Deppermann 1977:219).

On the other hand, his role as 'the prophet of the last days' elevated a revolution from above as a central theme of his political ethics (Deppermann 1987:211). The necessity of "the military campaign against the godless" to usher in the Heavenly Jerusalem gave added urgency to his theocratic theme—namely, the establishment of an interim kingdom on earth, which holds the tension of the two kingdoms, the present-and-future, or already-not-yet, before Christ's *parousia* (Goertz 1996:105, Deppermann 1977:217, 1987:390).

In one sense, Hoffman believed the End was *already* here and he was living in the dying hours of the kingdom of the world and the age of antichrist, while assuming that the word of the Spirit was destroying that kingdom before his eyes (Kyle 1998:59, Deppermann 1987:76-8). This meant he had received the Spirit of the end-time, so that he was now living in the new age of the Spirit (Williams 1962:260, Klaassen 1986:25).

In another sense, he was certain that the End had *yet* to be consummated and thus was awaiting a definite sign from the Lord—that being "the collapse of the forces of Hell and the establishment of the New Jerusalem" (Goertz 1982:186-87). Believing that he was living in the overlap of the two kingdoms (i.e., the kingdom now and the kingdom not yet), he urged establishment of an earthly interim kingdom, prepared by both prophet and king and preceding the *parousia* (Stayer 1991:124, Krahn 1968:115-16, Deppermann 1977:217). To this end, the pious rulers, instructed by him, had earned the right to judge the godless and take their vengeance upon them (Deppermann 1977:217).

This was his manner of maintaining a theocratic theme as a sort of tacit manual (Finger 2004:532). By insisting on the extermination of the godless before the final judgment plus the reign of a theocratic intermediate kingdom on earth until the return of Christ (Deppermann 1982:187), he revealed the revolutionary character of his political ethics, which ultimately resulted in his desire for a revolution from above (Deppermann 1987:390, Boyd 1989:58-76, Goertz 1996:105).

Yet of greater concern to Hoffman was not *who* and *when*, but *how*—"How could this interim kingdom be built?" He saw the main thrust of this interregnum as a revolutionary one, which meant destruction of the godless (Snyder 1995:204-5). But his lesser interest as to *who* would be responsible for the purging and *when* the purging was to begin left his followers an ambivalent legacy (Packull 1985:146).

This ambiguous heritage culminated in Münster Anabaptism in 1534-35, which is to be discussed in depth in the latter part of the book. Suffice to say for now the radical Anabaptists who flocked to Münster wanted to expedite the *parousia* by establishing a global theocracy—a New Jerusalem (Pleysier 2014:59). For they believed that, if the pious authority hesitated to play its apocalyptic role, it was their (the radical Anabaptists') duty as the apostolic messengers to take the sword to usher in the Kingdom of God, which was drawn heavily from Hoffman's theocratic idea (Snyder 1995:219). Thus, his fame created the "intellectual progenitor of the kingdom of Münster," who provided its important ideological presuppositions (Deppermann 1982:187).

In summation, Hoffman's political ethics were not monotonous (Goertz 1996:105). Instead it crossed the boundaries of pacifism and radical violence (Packull 1985:146). In one sense, he held a strong commitment to non-violence, which was demonstrated by his disapproval of the elect (the Anabaptists) to take up the sword (Waite 1988:312). Even in his advocacy of revolution from above, none of the violence was to occur by their hands (Stayer, Packull and Deppermann 1975:118). In his thinking, the final vengeance would not be undertaken by the believers but by the pious rulers who tolerated the Anabaptists (Stayer 1976: xxvii, Waite 1988:312). So his political ethics "implied peace, not revolution, for his true believers" (Stayer 1972:211-26).

But in another sense, his position on the sword was not passive, but active and even went so far as to defend the violent revolution (Boyd 1989:58-76). In his apocalyptic end-time scenario, the physical destruction of the godless was certain, although the elect themselves were not to commit violence directly. Under the banner of militant apocalypticism, the godless were subject to the violent punishment—total annihilation, and he offered no explicit condemnation of violence that served this end (Stayer 1972:220). Most of all, it was Hoffman himself who encouraged the pious magistrates to fully participate in the violent military defense that would usher in the Heavenly Jerusalem (Stayer 1991:124). This would provide an ideological backdrop for establishment of Münster Anabaptism, the militant Anabaptist takeover in 1534-35 (Goertz 1996:105, Deppermann 1982:187).

In essence, by taking a mediatory position between the non-violence of the Strasbourg Anabaptists and the radical violence of the 'Strasbourg Prophets,' Hoffman's political ethics remained ambivalent even to the point of leaving a peaceful as well as volatile revolutionary legacy to his followers. This distinguished him from the Wittenberg theologians, especially from Martin Luther (Packull 1985:146, Deppermann 1987:22).

Prophet against Luther

Before Hoffman appeared as the 'prophet against the learned,' he was known as a Lutheran. In fact, there once was a time when he was under Lutheran influence, considering Luther his teacher and had embarked on his ministry as a Lutheran missionary (Packull 1990:146).

Luther's personal sanction of his ministry at Kiel proved how great his loyalty to Luther was (Tinsley 2001:98, 101). In principle, he shared Luther's view "on justification by faith, predestination and even obedience to unjust government" (Packull 1990:147). By using Luther's doctrine of the two kingdoms, he "permitted Christians to accept official positions in order to maintain general order" (Deppermann 1987:20). Indeed, he had once fallen within the purview of Lutheran loyalty to government (Deppermann 1982:178-90).

However, his strong apocalyptic tendency, which was latent from the beginning, plus his later conversion to Anabaptism had gradually pulled him away from the Lutheran reformers (Snyder and Hecht 1996:247) and led to frequent polemical disputes with them. Thus, he no longer fit Luther's reform movement and actually opposed Lutheran doctrines (Bailey 1990:57).

Hoffman's open break with Lutheran reformers centered primarily on the issues of baptism and the Eucharist (Lindberg 1983:94-5). He believed baptism was an internal rebirth accompanying purification through the blood of Christ (Deppermann 1987:341, Pater 1977:184, 186). To strengthen his position, he described baptism in covenantal terms, it being a sign of the betrothal of the believer to the heavenly bridegroom—namely, believer's (adult's) baptism (Williams and Mergal 1957:188-89). Pedobaptism (infant baptism), its religious counterpart which was taken for granted by the Lutheran reformers, he rejected outright due to its lack of biblical evidence:

> Pedobaptism is absolutely not from God but rather is practiced, out of willfulness by anti-Christians and the satanic crowd, in opposition to God and all his commandment, will, and desire. Verily, it is an eternal abomination to him. Woe, woe to all such blind leaders who willfully publish lies for the truth and ascribe to God that which he has not commanded and will never in eternity command. How serious a thing it is to fall into the hands of God and willfully to mock and desecrate the Prize of God the Highest? Yea, all who do this will be stricken with heavy, great, and eternal blindness, and they will inherit the eternal wrath of God. For God is the enemy of all liars, and none of these inherits or has a part in his Kingdom. Their inheritance

and portion is rather eternal damnation (Williams and Mergal 1957:193).

As with baptism, Hoffman gave the Lord's Supper a covenantal understanding and denied the doctrine of the real presence of Christ (Bailey 1990:183). To him, the Lord's Supper was the marriage feast in which bread and wine symbolized the ring (Williams 1957:193-95, Krahn 1968:99). But Christ cannot be contained in the bread or the wine. Rather, these earthly elements are only signs for the spiritual food which acted as a remembrance (Snyder 1995:211). Thus he affirmed that Christ

> . . . takes bread (just as a bridegroom takes a ring or a piece of gold) and gives himself to his bride with the bread (just as the bridegroom gives himself to his bride with the ring)... so that just as the bride eats a physical bread in her mouth and drinks the wine, so also through belief in the Lord Jesus Christ she has physically received and eaten the noble Bridegroom with his blood in such a way that the Bridegroom and the outpouring of his blood is [one] with hers. She [is] in him and, again, he is in her, and they together are thus one body, one flesh, one spirit, and one passion (Williams and Mergal 1957:193-94).

From this viewpoint, Hoffman developed his doctrine of the heavenly flesh of Christ (Lindberg 1983:95). He held that, in the incarnation, Christ had indeed become flesh but that this had a heavenly origin, since all human flesh had been corrupted because of the fall (Pleysier 2014:33). He reasoned that Jesus received his physical substance directly from heaven (not from Mary) so that "There existed only one nature, and a heavenly flesh" (Backus 2003:191):

> Jesus Christ is alone the Word of God, who himself became flesh through his divine power, and received nothing from the Virgin Mary; else she would not have remained a virgin. He is along [from] the seed of the Spirit. Even as the water in the jars at the wedding of Cana became wine through divine power, and took into itself no wine from the jars nor from any other wine. As the bread from heaven, he [Christ] fell from heaven and

became himself a seed [corn], but received nothing from the earth (Beachy 1977:80).

This doctrine grew out of his belief that "Only heavenly flesh was sufficiently strong enough to overcome the powers of evil" (Klaassen 1991:27-8, Williams 1962:330). However, the consequence of his doctrine of Christ's heavenly flesh was the return to monophysite Christology as opposed to Chalcedonian Christology, which had affirmed both Christ's deity and humanity (Deppermann 1987:201). In his Christology, Jesus was more divine than human being (Tinsley 2001:106). This departed from the orthodox Christology, thus he moved further away from Luther (Pleysier 2014:33).

Hoffman's such radical thoughts were well received (even advocated) by the radical Anabaptists in Strasbourg (Snyder and Hecht 1996:273-87). Influenced by Anabaptist Hans Denck—especially by his doctrine of the freedom of the will, he rejected the Lutheran doctrines of predestination and justification (Lindberg 1983:92, Packull 1982:185). Instead he held a synergistic view on salvation; God's saving grace was a gift, its acceptance being up to human beings (Finger 2004:126, Deppermann 1987:223-24). Thus, in his emphasis on man's part in the relationship with God, human was elevated into a place in the acquisition of salvation (Rainbow 1990:53). By stressing human cooperation with divine grace in the process of salvation, he turned Luther's *sola gratia* on its head (Lindberg 1983:92).

To sustain the link between divine grace and human free will, Hoffman turned to the notion of deification—man becomes a divinized man, leading to the *unio mystica* (Stayer, Packull and Depperman 1975:121). He believed that "divinization came through participation in Jesus' flesh" (Finger 2004:35)—i.e., with God becoming human, humanity could become divine and experience a form of divinization, which "had implication for believers and their transformed status" (Koop 2004:100, 2016:255). Thus he argued, salvation was divinization or, more specifically, becoming a perfected and spiritual man who had free will (Deppermann 1977:217, 1987:240).

It is true that Hoffman's doctrine of divinization became more radical as a result of his contacts in Strasbourg, especially with the so-called 'Strasbourg Prophets,' who had strong apocalyptic overtones

(Deppermann 1987:218-19). Harnessed by their militant-activist ideas, he expected his divinized converts to be nearly "invulnerable" and "invincible" as the "apostolic messengers" described in the Book of Revelation (Deppermann 1987:211). Thus was created by him a two-stage apocalyptic scenario.

The first stage was full of great cosmic struggles between the godly and the ungodly (Goertz 1996:105). Yet in it, the strategic role—use of the sword—was to be played by the pious authorities, not by the elect (Petersen 1993:92). The appointment of Strasbourg as a spiritual Jerusalem or earthly theocracy was the climax of a military campaign before the *parousia* (Krahn 1968:115-16). The second stage was characterized throughout by grace, victory, and hope (Rublack 2017:112). Only when the triumph of the godly—i.e., the baptized 144,000 apostolic messengers (divinized converts)—was complete would they go on a mission both "invulnerable" and "invincible" to fill the world with the light of the true Gospel (Deppermann 1977:217).

Here, it should be noted that Hoffman prevented the divinized converts (the Anabaptists) from taking up arms themselves at the first stage and it suggested Luther's two kingdoms theory was behind his two-stage apocalyptic scenario (Deppermann 1987:10, 20). Luther distinguished differences between the two as being the "worldly regiment as the left hand of the kingdom and the spiritual regiment of God's right hand" (Sanders 1964:29), but he purposed to show not two different kingdoms but the "organic unity of both realms"—i.e., of gospel and of law (Bauman 1964:49).

This meant in Luther's two kingdoms theory, "all *Obrigkeit* is *of* God and therefore *under* God" (Horsch 1951:38), so that Christians should offer obedience to the civil community and its officials (Barth 1960:159). Like Luther, Hoffman saw a closer relation between the two kingdoms and a more positive role for the secular *Obrigkeit* (Deppermann 1987:10). Thus, his acceptance of Luther's doctrine of obedience to secular authority made his apocalyptic program less lurid and thereby his role of resisting the ungodly *Obrigkeit* more vague and passive (Deppermann 1977:216, Goertz 2004:81).

Thus Hoffman's revolution from above was a winning alternative to the dialectic of his peaceful and radical strand (Deppermann 1987:57-75). By limiting use of force to pious secular rulers, his followers kept themselves from joining the military campaign (Goertz 2008:28). In this way, his end-time program could meet the needs of both the believers' non-violence and the false teachers' punishment—Luther's incompatible and Hoffman's compatible views on Christianity and the sword (Stayer, Packull and Deppermann 1975:117-18, Packull 1985:146).

At any rate, with the 'Strasbourg Prophets' embracing his apocalyptic vision and the common people enhancing his popularity (Packull 1985:136), Hoffman's radical stance greatly distressed Luther, especially owing to its lingering legacy of Müntzer and the Peasants' War of 1525 (Bailey 1990:180). When Luther came to consider Hoffman a dangerous *Schwärmer* who hindered his reforming movements (Williams 1962:388), their break was complete. Hoffman now became an independent sect leader whose apocalyptic enthusiasm anticipated the necessity of a final Elijah mission by force and thus was the opposite of Luther's (Petersen 1993:94).

To summarize, despite Hoffman beginning his career as a Lutheran and an active participant in Luther's movement of reform, he did not simply remain as a 'little Luther.' In fact, he pursued and retained his theological moves separate from Luther early on (Bailey 1990:175-90). His favourite identification as 'the prophet against the learned' hinted that he did not fit the "Lutheranizing trend" (Bailey 1990:179). Since he was influencing common opinion against Luther, he was considered a hindrance to Luther's reform and, thereby, was rejected by the one on whom he had set his hopes (Snyder and Hecht 1996:247).

Hoffman's radical thoughts, his challenge against the doctrine of Christ's real presence in the Eucharist, his adaptation of a monophysite Christology (namely, a heavenly flesh of Christ), his supremacy of believer's baptism over infant baptism, and his idea of man's divinization by suffering comprised a significant theological front against Lutheran reformers (Tinsley 2001:98-122). Thus, all served to highlight Hoffman 'the prophet against Luther,' although Luther's two kingdoms still remained in him as a deterrent against his militant apocalyptic ideas.

Summary: Hoffman the Radical Reformer as Being-in-the-Revelatory-Common-People

One can hardly deny Hoffman's pivotal role in the history of Anabaptism. Although he was a furrier, having no formal education, he carried the movement from Strasbourg through the Rhineland to Münster, Hesse, Frisia, the Netherlands and even to England (Packull 1990:146, Stayer 1971:265). Even if his career began as a Lutheran missionary, he was outside the tent. His anti-clericalism based on God's preferential option for the poor and the oppressed, his end-time prophecies of the imminent end of the world and the advent of the *parousia* began to distinguish him from the Wittenberg Theologians. It was his 'different' teachings which put the crowd into a wave of enthusiasm and gave him a three-fold prophetic role—namely, 'the prophet against the learned,' 'the prophet of the last days' and 'the prophet against Luther.'

First, from his affinity to and privilege for the poor and the illiterate, 'the prophet against the learned' was Hoffman's favourite. His primacy of Spirit over Scripture, paired with his anti-clericalism, drove him to sharply contrast between the learned and the unlearned; the former he disparaged as the people of the letter, representing the upper classes, including the clerics and the University theologians, while the latter he deemed as the people of the Spirit, representing the lower classes, including the poor and the common people (Pater 1984:209).

Thus, he had fiercely attacked the monopoly of the learned clergy in expounding Scripture and it was harnessed theologically by his 'cloven hoof' and the 'key of David' motifs, his special tools for spiritual hermeneutics. The benefit of such tools was two-fold; they would serve to bring about both the right understanding of the Bible (right hermeneutics) and its right application to the present situation (right practice), especially regarding the apocalyptic passages.

Second, in addition to the first, Hoffman's role as 'the prophet of the last days' became visible. Encouraged by support of the lower classes, he began to channel his expectations of reform of church and society in an apocalyptic direction. A group of radical Anabaptists in Strasbourg (mostly 'the Strasbourg Prophets') became his strongest supporters for solidifying his end-time program under the theme of restitution

(Balserack 2014:36). Thus, their militant-activist ideas inspired violent actions in him (Deppermann 1987:218-19). Linking his apocalyptic calculations on two 3½-year periods to the last judgment in 1533 (Deppermann 1987:67), he declared the Anabaptists as being 'apostolic messengers' (or divinized converts) and the city of Strasbourg as the spiritual New Jerusalem (Isaak 1986:79).

Yet mixed with Denck's peaceful Anabaptism, his violent theme of restitution became specialized in an idea of interim kingdom on earth both as present-and-future, or already-not-yet, and as a result, his theocratic theme evolved into a two-stage program like a cloven hoof analogy; the first half accepted the cataclysmic struggle between the godly and the ungodly, but its military breakthrough was assigned to the pious rulers only, while the second half celebrated the victory and the re-baptized 'apostolic messengers' prevailed, spreading the true gospel around the whole world without soiling their hands with blood (Stayer, Packull and Deppermann 1975:118). Consequently, although his political ethics were inclined to a revolution from above, it remained ambivalent, holding both peaceful and violent dimension.

Third, Hoffman 'the prophet against the learned' and 'the prophet of the last days' couldn't go together with Luther. His early dependence on Luther paled into insignificance when especially his apocalyptic excess became manifest through the radical 'Strasbourg Prophets.' His merciless verbal attack on the existing church as the 'whore of Babylon' plus his belief in the necessity of enacting vengeance on religious and secular tyrants (Goertz 1996:105) marked him as Luther's diametrical opposite.

Nonetheless Luther's two kingdoms theory was still behind Hoffman and served as a sort of regulator for his militant apcalypticism, reminding him of obedience to the pious *Obrigkeit* (Packull 1990:147). This was because he elaborated a two-stage end-time scenario in which violent and peaceful potentials coexisted under the auspices of the legal authorities—a revolution from above. This eventually oscillated his position between the two spectrums—peaceful and revolutionary and thus two divergent followers. Here, the progression from Hoffman to Münster Anabaptism became apparent as his radical followers led the political takeover of the city of Münster in 1534-35 (Depperman 1982:187).

All in all, as the sixteenth-century prophetic layman, Hoffman's messages attracted a large number of the common people in North Germany and the Netherlands and gained a strong following among them. His three-fold prophetic role—'the prophet against the learned,' 'prophet of the last days' and 'the prophet against Luther'—hailed him the second Elijah, while only a few political powers temporarily interpreted his radical thoughts for their own advantage and quickly withdrew their support if necessary. This established him firmly as the radical reformer as being-in-the-revelatory-common-people.

John Bockelson (1509-1536)

Biographical Sketch

John Bockelson, also known as John of Leiden, was born in 1509 as the illegitimate child of the burghermaster of a village near Leiden (Holland) and a bondwoman from Westphalia (Bax 1903:114). His educational opportunities being limited, young Bockelson learned the tailor's trade and travelled to various provinces of the Netherlands as well as to England (Bax 1903:115). In Leiden, he married the widow of a boatman and opened a tavern (Baring-Gould 1891:254, Arthur 1999:70). He also engaged in mercantile enterprises but was unsuccessful (Krahn 1968:134). In literary societies, called the 'Chambers of Rhetoric' at Leiden,[29] he became a prominent figure and was popular as an actor and a poet (Verduin 1960:196, Horsch 1935:135).

In consequence of his failure in business, Bockelson secretly left his family in the summer of 1533 and went to the city of Münster for several weeks (Arthur 1999:70). While there, he focused his efforts on theology, specifically studying the writings of Thomas Müntzer and the 'prophet' John Matthjisson (Bax 1903:115). Returning to Leiden, he made common cause with Matthjisson, who baptized him (Bax 1903:115).

---

[29]Bockelson was known as an active rhetorician in his early years. Based on the fact that several groups of Radical Reformers used the 'Chambers of Rhetoric' to perform some forms of Dutch popular drama, some scholars have suggested that the Chambers had played a role in the rise of Anabaptism, especially of Dutch Anabaptism (Verduin 1960:192-96, Waite 1991:227-55).

Following his baptism, Mathjisson sent Bockelson back to Münster as an 'apostle' (Krahn 1968:134). During his stay, he made significant contacts with prominent figures, including the famous Lutheran pastor and theologian Bernhard Rothmann and the wealthy merchant Bernhard Knipperdolling, whose daughter he later married (Arthur 1999:70-1). Bockelson was in Münster over those crucial days of change in its religious, social, and political life, which enabled him to provide Matthjisson an eyewitness account of what was taking place (Krahn 1968:134-35).

Returning to Münster on January 13, 1534 (along with Matthjisson), they found it already taken over by Anabaptist fervor (Cohn 1961). Under the initiative of Matthjisson's emissaries Bartholomeus Boekbinder and Willem de Kuitper, mass conversions and re-baptisms swept the city of Münster; in its wake, Rothmann (with the help of other prominent figures) became a re-baptizer (Krahn 1968:135). Matthjisson's arrival in early February 1534 was the climax of the Anabaptist campaign, giving the city "a fierce militancy" (Cohn 1961:260). By drawing an enormous amount of charismatic enthusiasm (Krahn 1968:138), this immigrant 'prophet' had a grip on the city and enforced many of his policies with divine authority (Krahn 1968:138). For instance, all property was held in common, the Catholic and Lutheran population was expelled, and any who remained were forced to be re-baptized (Klotzer 2007:234). Then he identified Münster as the New Jerusalem (Bax 1903:143).

However, Matthjisson died suddenly just a few months later, and the power of gravity fell to his next in command, John Bockelson, (Goertz 1996:30-1). Next to his predecessor, Bockelson's credentials were not very impressive (Rammstedt 1966:75 quoted by Eichler 1981:47); he had been of secondary rank compared with other prophets; and his career up to age 25 had been as a tailor, a salesman, and an amateur actor (Klaassen 1992:82). Nevertheless, young Bockelson boldly claimed that God had told him in a dream he was to be Matthjisson's successor (Horsch 193

5:135).[30] Thus by invoking God, he stressed the divine nature of his ordination (Arthur 1999:69-72). This convinced the Münsterites who came under attack from the prince-bishop, Franz von Waldeck, and thereby prepared them for resistance under a new leadership (Dawson 2010:113-132).

Following a vision, Bockelson proclaimed himself king of Münster as the New Jerusalem (Vidmar 2005:204), and immediate actions were essential to solidify his authority. The main such action was the city council dissolution and replacement by 'the twelve elders of Münster' (most of whom were his friends) in order to rule the New Jerusalem (Horsch 1935:136, Baaker 1986:114). He also began instituting other changes in the city's organization, primarily along Old Testament lines, Münster thus becoming transformed into a theocracy, but also the practice of polygamy (Stayer 1972:255-74). Regarding this issue Bockelson faced a backlash from within (Williams 1962:372), but his leadership became even stronger once opposition had died down by force (Williamson 2000:29).[31] He himself eventually took sixteen concubines, among whom was a daughter of Knipperdolling as well as his leading wife Divara, Matthjisson's widow (Horsch 1935:138).

Thanks to his consistent military successes against the prince-bishop's mercenary army, Bockelson began to establish his authority all the more (Klaassen 1992:83). In September 1534, following another victory against the army of siege, he attempted to use the triumph as a chance to make his position even more secure (Rothbard 1990:151-52). This manifested in his deification, identifying himself as the Messiah (Rammstedt 1966:79 quoted by Eichler 1981:51). Dusentschur, a self-

---

[30]This implies that Bockelson's act, consciously or unconsciously, served as both a religious and a political maneuver. The following illustrates how his religious behaviour affected and appealed to the people in Münster politically. Early in May, 1534, in a frenzy, Bockelson ran naked through the city then fell into a silent ecstasy for three days. When speech returned to him, he announced before the population God's revelation to him—namely, the replacing of the city's old constitution by a new one under his leadership (Cohn 1961:291-92).

[31]Not only did Rothmann and other preachers resist Bockelson on this point, but also many common Münsterites complained publicly against this proposed offensive practice. Among them, a group of citizens led by Henry Mollenhecke had even imprisoned Bockelson on July 29 in an effort to force him to abandon polygamy. However, he was freed again with the aid of his followings, and Mollenhecke and 48 others were cruelly put to death. So polygamy was practiced without any further hindrances (Williams 1962:372).

proclaimed prophet in the city, anointed Bockelson as son of David who was to rule over the whole world (Snyder 1995:149). Now, he had become both Messiah and king (Rothbard 1990:152).

However, with the siege of Münster by the prince-bishop intensifying, this tailor-king realized that, despite its successful defenses, the city could be saved only by outsider assistance (Mackay 2016:4). So he sent twenty-seven apostles (mostly prominent ministers) to new Anabaptist sympathizers in other towns to help defend Münster (Cohn 1961:276). The result was that most of them who responded fell into the hands of the authorities and were executed (Williams 1962:374-75). In addition to failure of the promised deliverance from outside, famine ravaged the besieged Münsterites by the end of that winter (Rothbard 1990:154). This two-pronged situation worked against this new tailor king, generating widespread discontent which mitigated his earlier success (Mackay 2016:4).

Despite this terrible situation, 'King Bockelson' made an effort to amuse his subjects by throwing feasts in the market place, followed by dancing in which he himself took part till late night (Rothbard 1990:154), and also putting on theatrical plays. But all failed to satisfy the starving people of the city as "the famine increased from day to day" (Horsch 1935:142). Regardless of his last ditch attempt to maintain control and loyalty, thousands of Münsterites were driven by "starvation and terror" to escape the city (Arthur 1999:208). At last, Münster's formidable city wall was breached not by outside forces but by inside treason, revealing weaknesses in the city's defense to the prince-bishop's army (Mackay 2016:4-5). Thus, the New Jerusalem finally came to a bloody end on June 25, 1535 (Rothbard 1990:154).

Many of the inhabitants were promptly and ruthlessly slaughtered (Cohn 1961:279-80, Kirchhoff 1962:77-170 quoted by Driedger 2016:17).[32] Among the Anabaptist leaders taken were Bockelson and his close collaborators, Bernhard Knipperdolling and Bernhard Krechting (Williams 1962:574). After a period of questioning and imprisonment, they were tortured to death with red-hot tongs in February 1536 (Horsch

---

[32]It is assumed that some 3,500 to 4,000 women and an unknown number of children survived the conquest of the city. But a year later, only 216 women and 19 men in the city had renounced their vices and were found to be innocent (Kerssenbroch 2007:700, 736, 833-56, Krahn 1968:159-60).

1935:143). Eyewitnesses to this bloody scene were the prince-bishop, Franz von Waldeck, sitting in a special armchair, as well as a large crowd (Hsia 1988:51-70). Bockelson's, Knipperdolling's and Krechting's remains were placed in iron cages and hung from the tower of St. Lambert's Church as a warning against heresy and rebellion (Mackay 2016:5, Snyder 1995:150). The name Bockelson, legendary tailor-king, became a byword of scorn and opprobrium.

Theological Perspective

Bockelson was not a professional theologian. Although he was once enthusiastic about Thomas Müntzer's writings (Bax 1903:115), he did not relate to the persistent interest in theology; indeed, he provided no clear-cut picture about his theological positions. Yet parts of his theological perspective can be seen in his eclectic role between the two power groups in Münster Anabaptism. During his reign in Münster Kingdom, he constantly faced power struggles both from within and from without and it appeared to give a glimpse of his theological stance through his response to, defense of and compromise with the given situation. Thus, Matthjisson's death was the very moment when Bockelson's theological traits were revealed.

The sudden death of Matthjisson provided Bockelson with both an opportunity and a challenge. He moved to fill the leadership vacuum but realized his lack of charismatic authority.[33] In this regard, he was nowhere close to his predecessor, whose acts were "sanctioned by his pneuma" (Rammstedt 1966:75 quoted by Eichler 1981:47). To solve the problems of succession, Bockelson did so via a process of bureaucratization and "routinization of charisma" (Weber 1978:249). Under him, "prophecy [was] completely in the service of institution" (Eichler 1981:49). Thus, he attempted to work through the Münster citizens, especially Bernhard Rothmann, who had never received much attention under Matthjisson (Eichler 1981:47).

---

[33]Since O. Rammstedt had posed this question based on Max Weber's theory of the routinization of charisma (1966), that line of interpretation was seconded by K. H. Kirchhoff (1973), J. M. Stayer (1986) and R. Klotzer (2007), whereas other scholars tended to consider Bockelson as a charismatic leader. Magrit Eichler (1981) in particular had emphasized his prophetic leadership by revising the aspect of Weber's theory.

Matthjisson's simple division of people as the godly and the ungodly was no longer beneficial for legitimating Bockelson's position (Eichler 1981:47). Instead, he decided to reconfirm the earlier categorizations of 'immigrants' and 'natives' (Rammstedt 1966:75 quoted by Eichler 1981:49). This meant his legitimacy would involve considerable give-and-take between the immigrant radicals and the native reformers (Klotzer 2007:244). Indeed, he recognized that he was caught in the middle between the power of Matthjisson as the representative of the immigrant prophetic group and Rothmann as the representative of the native civic elites (Klotzer 2007:234).

Bockelson's theological perspective found its rightful place in a mediatory role between the immigrant radical prophets and the native reactionary reformers in the city of Münster. Thus, the conjuring of his extraordinary powerful leadership does not make for sound interpretation. In fact, much closer to his real figure was his parasitic relationship with the dual power structure—namely, the immigrant radicals and the native reactionaries (Klotzer 2007:234). Since he suffered from a lack of authority, he depended on his eclectic leadership, with his political, socio-economic, and religious tactics designed to appease the concerns of both the radical prophets of Matthjisson's group and the reactionary reformers of Rothmann's group (Kirchhoff 1973).

The question then arises as to whether Bockelson was really a genuine charismatic leader or just an ordinary successor whose legitimation derived from the preceding leader's charisma. If he was an eclectic leader, how did he maintain that balance between the two different power groups? And how was that important for his 'deification,' which culminated in the recognition of him as the Messiah, as it related to the people's recourse to the Münster Kingdom? These are questions to address significantly, so much so that it will be dealt with separately in Chapter 11. By looking anew at Bockelson's relationship with Matthjisson and Rothmann on one hand and with the common people in Münster on the other, it will help us to arrive at a clearer understanding of his role as the Radical Reformer—i.e., as being-in-the-rhetorical-common-people.

Summary: The 16th Century Radical Reformers as Being-in-the Dialectic-of-*Guru-Avatar*

It becomes evident that the four Radical Reformers—Thomas Müntzer, Hans Hut, Melchior Hoffman, and John Bockelson—had inexorably set themselves up in a certain way of being-in-the-common-people. To be sure, this so-called bastard line *(sic)* of radicals was willing to share their lot with the commoners via different emphases. This was created by the distinctive characteristics of each, namely, (1) Thomas Müntzer as being-in-the-retributive-common-people, (2) Hans Hut as being-in-the-restorative-common-people, (3) Melchior Hoffman as being-in-the-revelatory-common-people, and (4) John Bockelson as being-in-the-rhetorical-common-people (this will be dealt with in depth later).

There are close ties between these four and the common people, the former being conceived of only in their close relationship with the latter and *vice versa*. This mutual and dynamic correlation proves that both are no longer bound to the dualistic principle of *either/or* but are in *both/and* categorization. With this understanding, the sixteenth-century Radical Reformers and the common people are neither two nor one but are more than one and even more than two.

Furthermore, such mutual interdependence between the two attends to a new connecting thread—the dialectical unification of *guru-avatar*. In one sense, what is unique about the sixteenth-century Radical Reformers is to be seen not in their *guru*-ship but in their *avatar*-hood (i.e., the incarnation of themselves into the common people). As eyewitnesses to the oppressive conditions of the simple folk, these four radicals could not neatly separate the religious reform from the secular one (Matheson 2007:4). Instead, they found the need for the reformation in the reality of the suffering common people by becoming the *avatar* themselves. In another sense, the common people were changed in a significant and innovative way, "becoming visible" or "wising up" through this close encounter with the radicals (Matheson 2007:260).

In this way, the common people came to the forefront in the Reformation as well as the sixteenth-century Radical Reformers. They critically and creatively began to accommodate their own self to the Reformation as the *guru* of the sixteenth-century Radical Reformers.

This eventually led to the dynamic interconnection between the two agents as a coherent whole—the sixteenth-century Radical Reformers as the *avatars* of the common people and the common people as the *guru* of the sixteenth-century Radical Reformers.

Like the Mobius strip, both *guru* and *avatar* are not juxtaposed nor is the one absorbed by the other, but rather they remain in a reciprocal and dynamic correlation. Therefore, depicting the sixteenth-century Radical Reformers as the *avatars* of the common people does not diminish their theological *guru*-ship; nor does characterizing the common people as the *guru* of the sixteenth-century Radical Reformers dispense with their potential *avatar*-hood. Here, the principle of *guru-avatar* underlines the mutual interpenetration and interdependence of the two agents, who must paradoxically be regarded together as the co-agent of the sixteenth-century Radical Reformation.

From this vantage point, Thomas Müntzer, Hans Hut, Melchior Hoffman, and John Bockelson (John of Leiden) were a whole that consisted of both a *guru*-ship and an *avatar*-hood element. Therefore, this bastard line *(sic)* of sixteenth-century Radical Reformers stood as *guru* of the common people and at the same time *avatar* of the common people. Significantly enough, since each of the sixteenth-century Radical Reformers in their chain of connection left a (in)direct impact on the rise of Münster Anabaptism, this dialectic of *guru-avatar* is singled out as a significant aspect to give the Münster Kingdom a new and dynamic portrait.

Part 3

RE-READING KOREAN MINJUNG THEOLOGY AS BEING-IN-THE-KOREAN-MINJUNG

Chapter 6

Korean Minjung Theology as the Keyhole to the Radical Reformation

Taking a cue from the dynamic interplay between the sixteenth-century Radical Reformers and the common people, this chapter revisits the twentieth-century theological movement in Korea—namely, Korean Minjung Theology, a fully contextualized form of theology that has taken seriously a combination of Jesus and *minjung* (common people) in favour of Christian political and social responsibility. More specifically, it is a critical and creative attempt to look anew at the sixteenth-century Radical Reformation and especially Münster Anabaptism through Korean Minjung Theology, emphasizing the non-dual relationship of Jesus and *minjung* on one hand and the radicals and the common people on the other.

This dynamic synthesis presupposes a so-called 'double-mirror reading',[1] a reading from the *avatar-hood* of the sixteenth-century Radical Reformers (the first mirror reading) to that of the twentieth-century Korean *minjung* theologians (the second mirror reading). Just as the first mirror is supposed to project an image of the sixteenth-century

---

[1] The term 'mirror-reading', as its letter indicates, refers to looking at an 'image' (part of a conversation) and trying to discern the original 'object' (original discussion or context) (Gupta 2012:362). Mirror-reading the New Testament is well recognized as necessary since John Barclay made a key contribution to the practice of interpreting Paul's letters (Galatians) (1987:73-93). Here the researcher adopts this approach to rediscover the nature and role of the common people (*minjung*) behind the four sixteenth-century radical Reformers and further extends it to the relation of the twentieth-century Korean *minjung* and *minjung* theologians. Especially, this double-mirror reading serves to constitute the dynamic correlation between the radicals and the common people in Münster Anabaptism.

Radical Reformers, being-in-the-common-people, so the second mirror reveals the non-dual relationship of twentieth-century Korean *minjung* theologians and Korean *minjung*.

Deserving of special note here is the role of the common people, or *minjung*, being reflected in these two mirrors. For these dynamic relationships help the *minjung* stand out not as mere recipients (*avatars*) but as active participants (*gurus*) of these two movements—the sixteenth-century Radical Reformation and the twentieth-century Korean Minjung Theology. Thus, Korean Minjung Theology serves as the keyhole to the sixteenth-century Radical Reformation—especially Münster Anabaptism, being in the creative tension between the Radical Reformers and the common people, the *minjung* and the Messiah. Let's turn our attention to Korean Minjung Theology.

Rise of Korean Minjung Theology

Korean Minjung Theology[2] was "a contextual theology of the suffering people in Korea" (Moltmann 2000:252). It is one that includes the suffering *minjung* (民衆)[3] as its central subject. It was born out of an experience of faith amid Korea's pressing socio-political problems in the 1970s (Daniel Park 1985, Lee 1993:63). The portrait of the 1970s in Korea was two-fold (Kim 1995:3). It was a time when the Korean economy developed very quickly by the government, but also a time when the Korean people (*minjung*) engaged in socio-political struggles against General Park Chung-Hee's military dictatorship (Kim 1998:53). Their struggle slowly but surely laid bare the truth of the brutal reality of a

---

[2]The peculiarities of Korean Minjung Theology can be characterized primarily as the discovery of the *minjung* (民衆, the mass or the common people) and their *han* (恨, unresolved inner wounds or bitterness). Its description can be epitomized by these five categories—methodology/hermeneutics (*minjung* as the hermeneutical key), exegesis (*minjung* as the biblical reference), Christology (*minjung* as the messiah), ecclesiology *(Missio Dei*/Minjung church), and political theology (*minjung* as the subject of history).

[3]The term *minjung (*民衆) carries a constellation of meanings, and its definition is still a debating point even among Minjung theologians. Hence they maintain that "Minjung cannot be defined by objective and socioeconomic conditions . . . thus, Minjung is, first of all, a political concept, which should be differentiated from the proletariat defined by socioeconomic conditions...Minjung, whoever they become, are the people who are placed on the side of the oppressed under the powers that be" (Kim 1982:372).

development dictatorship. Indeed, there were inwardly malicious sacrifices of the lower strata of society behind the outwardly miraculous economic growth under Park's regime (Na 1988:139).

The famous miracle on the Han River (*han* 漢, large)[4] river was but another name for the misery of *han* (恨; unresolved bitterness), which deprived the welfare of both urban workers and rural peasants (Chang 2007:208). Propagating a bogus justification, the military government continued to impose a fiercely exploitive pattern of economic development (Sin and Kim 2003:127-8), which only aggravated the social conditions in Korea (Hwang 2013:105), whereby the rich-poor disparity increased and the pain of dehumanization upon the *minjung* became more intensified (Kim 1995:3). Consequently, Korean society plunged into a serious pitfall—the further experience of economic booming and the further impoverished life of the labourer (Chang 2007:29-30). Being stuck in the middle, the *minjung* were forced to become scapegoats (Kim 1995:39-60).

An event involving a young labourer, Chun, Tae-Il (全泰壹), proved to be a catalyst for the *minjung* movement in Korea (Kim 1995:3). On November 13, 1970, Chun set himself on fire to protest the dehumanizing working conditions, and his death became a symbol of resistance all over the country (Chai 2003:540). In its wake, many workers and students staged protests against political oppression and economic deprivation (Sebastian Kim 2007:46). However, Korea's Christian leadership responded differently. A majority of churches denounced interference with politics as not conforming to the Gospel, while only a minority of progressive Christians felt the need to take it as the voice of Christ for their time (Ryu 1976:171, Hwang 2013:108-9). The latter began to interpret the meaning of Christian faith from the *Sitz-im-Leben* of the suffering *minjung* and stood for (and with) the poor, oppressed, and despised (Yoo 1984:258-59, Eckert 1990:365).

This spurred Christian participation in activities for human rights and liberation (Lee 1988:7). Especially the "1973 Theological Declaration of Korean Christians" became the basis for Christian involvement in

---

[4]"South Korea was unrivalled, even by Japan, in the speed with which it went from having almost no industrial technology to taking its place among the world's industrialized nations" (Vogel 1991:59).

society (Kim 1995:7, Lee 1996:69). While acknowledging the current situations of oppression and injustice, it clearly declared that "In the salvation of human beings, individual or spiritual salvation is not to be separated from social and collective salvation, and it does not have any priority" (Kim 1995:7-8). This declaration served as the starting point of Minjung Theology, affirming the Church's involvement in politics "as a matter of faith in action" (Lee 1996:69, Clark 1995:89) and the Church's mission as following the footsteps of Jesus Christ—i.e., "living among our oppressed and poor people, standing against political oppression, and participating in the transformation of history, for this is the only way to the Messianic Kingdom" (Billings 1983:79, 81).

This created such a great momentum that Christians began to use the term *minjung* (Grayson 2006:21, Yoo 1997:43). As progressive theologians started to use the term as the master symbol in construction of their version of liberation theology (Chang 2007:197). The populace's identification with *minjung* or "minjung imagery" became the rhetoric of Christian protest (Abelmann 1996). This heralded the birth of Korean Minjung Theology. A group of theologians had embroiled themselves in a fight for human rights and social justice, emphasizing "*minjung* as their concern and the theme of a new theology" (Kim 1996:168). Thus, Minjung Theology, in its emphasis on solidarity with the suffering *minjung*, emerged as a rhetorical weapon of Christian dissenters in the discursive struggles against socio-political oppression and injustice (Chang 2007:197).

A watershed moment for Korean Minjung Theology came with a conference in 1979 (Oct. 22-29), cosponsored by the Christian Conference of Asia and the National Council of Churches of Korea (Niles 1981:6, Küster 2010:25). The papers presented at that conference were published in English and German, and this served as a momentum to make Korean Minjung Theology internationally known (Kim 1996:168). Indeed, "The 1979 conference volume had become something like the manifesto of the movement" (Küster 2010:26). The centerpieces for the publications included these forerunners of Korean Minjung Theology: Ahn, Byung-Mu (1922-1996), Suh, Nam-Dong (1918-1984), Hyun, Young-Hak (1921-2004) and Kim, Yong-Bock (1938-). "All they wanted was to function as mediators, by learning from the *minjung* themselves. Their theology was simply supposed to give the *minjung* a voice" (Küster 2010:25). Here "Minjung Theology set up the decisive frame of reference for doing theology" as a critical reflection on Korea's socio-political problems (Kim 1995:9, Park 2003:197).

Focusing on the perspectives of the Bible and church history for the poor and oppressed, Korean Minjung Theology had further come to grips with the people's predicament in its theological frame (Suh 1981:171). In that frame, there is the link between suffering Jesus and the suffering *minjung*, the Jesus event and the *minjung* event (Ahn 182:177). As Jesus is present in the suffering of the *minjung*, the Jesus event continues in the life of the *minjung* today (Ahn 1990:256). Thus, in Korean Minjung Theology, the suffering *minjung* and their struggle for liberation is redefined as "the setting of the revelation event" (Chai 2003:540) and in this way, the *minjung* become the Messiah who save themselves in the *minjung* event (Ahn 1982:103, Suh 1983:116).

Korean Minjung Theology also speaks of "the convergence of two stories"—the encounter between the *minjung* tradition in Korean history and in the Bible (Suh 1983:66). By believing that God's salvific actions are not limited to the Bible, it highlights the synchronic nature of the *minjung* tradition and the biblical tradition of liberation (Suh 1981:171). God who took side with the biblical *minjung* stands with today's *minjung* for their liberation and invites them to participate in this liberation movement (Lee 1998:19, Suh 1983:116), "The *minjung* have risen up to be subjects of their own destiny, refusing to be condemned to being objects of manipulation and suppression" (Moon 1985:72).

It gives the *minjung* new dignity—i.e., the *minjung* as subjects of history, having their own power and authority not only in making and sustaining their destiny, but also in opening up a new history (Suh 1983:34, Kim 1990:157-78, Moon 1985:72). Thus the subject-hood of *minjung* becomes "a key theme of Minjung Theology" as "a theology by the people, for the people, and of the people" (Kwon 1990:23, Lossky 2002).

Development of Korean Minjung Theology

No doubt, Korean Minjung Theology as a Protestant affair found its strongest support in the Presbyterian Church in the Republic of Korea (PROK; *Kichang* in Korean) (Küster 2010:131). Development of the unique identity of Minjung Theology can be largely divided into three periods—the 1960s through the 1970s, the 1980s, and the 1990s (Suh 2000:143, Chang 2002:125). However, this distinction of generations fluctuates due to a "more thematic than biological" categorization (Küster 2010:131), for each generation of *minjung* theologians has done theology through the reading of the contemporary conditions with critical and distinctive foci (Kim and Lee 2002:158). This resulted in different interpretations of *minjung* in each generation (Kim 1993:21-47).

The first generation of *minjung* theologians regarded minjung as a living essence and refused to make a definition of it in the western sense (Choi 2008:213); they generally interpreted *minjung* as the "deprived people" (Kim and Lee 2002:158). The second generation of *minjung* theologians tried to define it with a new knowledge of Marxist social method (Choi 1992:78-99); in this sense, their understanding of *minjung* tended towards "class solidarity" (Kim and Lee 2002:158, Cho 1996:4, 11-14), which created a new synthesis of *minjung* as being both Christian and Marxist (Kim and Lee 2002:164).

The third generation of *minjung* theologians, unlike the first two, gives much attention to a subjective existence (normalistic being) of *minjung* (Choi 2008:214). By stressing the importance of diversity and changeability in *minjung's* new post-modern reality, this third generation has wrestled with a new task—that being, how *minjung* can claim their subjectivity under this drastically changed reality (Kang 2000). From it, the main question has changed from "Who are the *minjung*?" to "How are the *minjung* as a historical subject being made up?" (Kim and Lee 2002:158). Thus, the task of the third generation is to search for a new Christian identity in a now-changed situation; in this light, a new Korean Minjung Theology is in the making.

Background of Korean Minjung Theology

Historical Background

From the rediscovery of *minjung* as the subject of history, Korean Minjung Theology provides a new perspective for understanding a *minjung* historiography (Kim 1995:9, Suh 1983:155-82). To the minjung theologians, the subject-hood of *minjung* cannot be fully understood apart from Korea's people and history, because it was a reflection on the *minjung* movements in Korea (Lee 1988:4). To give the word *minjung* a new meaning, these theologians tried to find the *minjung* movements in Korean history as a basis for their theology. In Korean Minjung Theology, three major events are regarded as historical antecedents for the minjung movements—the *Donghak* Peasant Revolution (東學農民革命) of 1894-95, the March 1st Independence Movement (三一獨立運動) of 1919, and the April 19th Student Revolution (四一九學生革命) of 1960 (Suh 1983:233-34).

Donghak Peasant Revolution (東學農民革命) of 1894-1895

Donghak (東學, Eastern Learning) was a typical religion of the oppressed Korean people of low estate during the late nineteenth-century (Ryu 1967:62-3, Shin and Lee 2008). The late period of the *Yi* (李朝) or *Choseon* (朝鮮) dynasty (1392-1910) was characterized by social turmoil, resulting from the class struggle between the privileged (*yangban* [兩班]) and the underprivileged (*cheonmin* [賤民]) (Kim 2007:1020, Nahm 1988:100-101). In the Confucian-structured society that emphasized the hereditary nature of social status, all ruling powers and privileges became centralized in the hands of a few elite groups—namely, the *yangban* classes or the gentry (Cho 2010:55, Adams 1985:193). Thus, the poor masses were exploited and constantly threatened for the sake of the noble bloods (Moon 1998:25).

The corrupt government officials had imposed heavy taxes on the peasants,[5] which exacerbated the lives of the lower class (Lee 1996:53, Noh 1987:49). Thus, the social and economic oppressions became more the norm among the poor (Moon 1988:151). This fomented a revolutionary backlash against the autocratic and hierarchical society

---

[5]There was an oppressive and absurd tax system at that time. "Even dead people and small babies were expected to pay taxes. People were responsible for paying taxes of their relatives and their neighbours who did not, or could not pay. According to one report, a village of less than 100 households was forced to pay 108,900 sok of grain (about 450,000 bushels) for governmental loans, plus the interest which had accumulated over several years. It would take the villagers about 20 years to produce the grain. Tax exploitation on the various levels was too heavy for people to survive and many peasants died of hunger every year" (Noh 1987:49).

(Kim 2002:279-97). As a corollary, the unfair economic extraction had mitigated escalation of class tension and turned into more of a class struggle (Kim 1981:78-152).

Yet the causes of confrontation between the *yangban* (elite groups) and the *cheonmin* (grassroots) were much more complex and dynamic than to simply ascribe it to the theory of class struggle, for it explained only part of the whole (Kim 2007:1021). Larger social and economic changes also played important roles in making the popular rebellions in *Choseon* Korea (Pak 2005:18, Kim 2007:1020-21).

Toward the end of the nineteenth-century, Korea was no longer safe from the expansion of western imperialism (Bretzke 1991:114). Competition between the foreign superpowers (particularly Japan and western colonial-oriented countries) had turned the Korean Peninsula into an arena of proxy war for their own benefits (Moon 1998:25). The primary prey of such hostile changes was none other than the ordinary, rank-and-file members of society—namely, the Korean *minjung* (Paik 1998:32). From this inherent and long-festering oppression, a number of *minjung* found themselves in *de facto* slavery (Ahn 1997:69-71). This sense of blockage urged them to lean toward violent struggle (Kim 2007:1019); for when the oppressed decided to take the matter into their own hands, an open resistance/rebellion seemed the only remedy against the current malicious conditions (Kim 1981:116).

The *Donghak* Peasant Revolution arose out of these circumstances. With the *Yi* dynasty already on the verge of disintegration (Ahn 1997:71), a series of peasant rebellions (*Hong, Kyung-Rae's* rebellion in 1812, the *Chinju* uprisings in 1862, and the *Donghak* Peasant Revolution in 1894) was a counter-proof of the *Yi* regime's inability to rule well (Moon 1998:24).[6] In addition, western colonial expansion further fueled the already deteriorated situation. Now the peasants and others were in desperate need of new teaching that could channel their grievances into radical action (Ahn 1997:71).

It was at that very moment *Donghak* came into being as a new way to resist the cynicism of power (Ahn 1997:73-5). By challenging the injustice caused by both the internal aristocracy and external

---

[6]The peasant uprisings became the hallmark of the 19th century in Korean history, which is often called "the age of rebellions." Even the late 19th century saw revolts on average of about 20 each year, but most of them were not successful (Kim 2007:1020).

imperialism (Hong 1968:45), *Donghak* could justify or legitimize the rebellion from below against the abuse of power by twin empires (Hong 1968:47). Thus *Donghak* as the initial cause against oppression of the helpless was soon converted to *Donghak* as the final cause for liberation of the hopeless (Ahn 2001:66-7). This explains why, from the beginning, it evolved around a form of political protest and populist nationalism, even if it was actually initiated as a new religious movement (Bell 2008:85).

Donghak was founded in 1860 when a man named Choi, Jae-Woo (崔濟愚, 1824-1864) experienced a divine revelation that compelled him to form a new religion (Choi 1997:106).[7] Choi formulated his own version of religious salvation through a critical synthesis of different elements (Chung 1969:118-32, Kang 1968:39). He took ethical aspects from Confucianism, pure-mind from Buddhism, incantation and ecstasy from Shamanism, and monotheism from Catholicism (Ryu 1967:76, Kim 1977:114-15, Noh 1992:218-19), the sum of which would serve as the conceptual basis of *Donghak*, that basis being, all humans bear God (侍天主, *Si-Cheonju*) (Ahn 1997:82). This theme later became the epitome of *Donghak*'s teaching—namely, *In-Nae-Cheon* (人乃天, humans and heaven are one) (Ahn 2001:62-7, Ryu 1965:117) and gradually evolved into the doctrine of egalitarianism (Ryu 1967:77)—the doctrine that all humans (gentry, peasants, slaves) are the same in their essential nature thus have a right to freedom and equality (Ahn 2001:66-7).

Criticizing inequality and corruption that prevailed in the current autocratic and hierarchical structure, Choi sought a new order wherein all could enjoy equality and prosperity (Moon 1998:28). Thus, the teaching of *Donghak* stood in stark contrast to that of Confucianism, which justified the class system as a state ideology (Han 1970:356-57). In the highly status-oriented society of the late *Yi* dynasty, one's social and economic station was determined by one's social status (Choe 1974:611-

---

[7] Choi, Jae-Woo was born to a disgraced noble family as an illegitimate child and thus occupied a lower position in the social hierarchy (Ahn and Park 1980:283). From this background, he rejected both Confucianism and Buddhism as means to the improvement of the lot of the masses and sought a way of salvation from the woes of the personal life. A crisis of Choi's personal affairs coincided with the reception of his spiritual revelation. It is said that in the fourth moon of 1860, he received the revelation of the doctrine, which was most unexpected to him (Clark 1932:265).

31).[8] This meant the lower class, who were arbitrarily distinguished by their birth, had almost no hope of social advancement (Kim 2007:994). Not surprisingly, *Donghak's* doctrine of *In-Na-Chun*—'Human is Heaven/God'—had great appeal to the disaffected masses *(cheonmin* class) as a hope for a new world order based on human equality (Lee 1996:118), whereas from the ruling class' perspective *(yangban* class), the *Donghak* followers were now political rebels bent on sending clear messages of violent uprising (Bretzke 1991:118).

Choi's call for change to the contemporary social conditions became more acute with the influx of western imperial influence (Ahn 1997:75). He soon realized that the common people had been doubly oppressed by the elites of their own Confucian regime and by the western colonial powers (Bell 2008:85-6). For him, individual equality was inseparable from nationalistic equality (Moon 1998:28-9); thus, peasant liberation should be seen as coinciding with national liberation (Kim 1963:232-33).

This was why Choi strongly rejected the West's encroachment into Korea, denouncing it as the intrusion of foreign economic exploitation and ideological domination on Korean society (Bell 2008:85-6). This led to the naming of his new religion, *Donghak (東學)*, meaning, "Eastern Learning" (Clark 1932:262). The name was intentionally chosen to be the explicit opposite of *Seohak (西學)*, "Western Learning," which threatened to supplant earlier Korean religious traditions (Bell 2008:86, Ahn 1997:75). Further, he ascribed the power of the West to the Christian belief (Roman Catholicism) as the 'Heavenly Way' and believed there would be another heavenly way for the East, revealed especially in Korea. "I was born in the East and received the teachings of the East. The *do* (道, "Way") is *chondo* (天道, "the Heavenly Way"), but the *hak* ("學", "Learning") is *Donghak* ("東學", "Eastern Learning")" (Paek 1956:13).

---

[8]Even in comparison with China, Korea's stratification system was far more rigid. In it, there was almost no social mobility. For example, regarding the examination system that led directly to office holding, eligibility for examinations was not open to the *cheonmin* class—i.e., slaves, entertainers, outcast groups, shamans, and illegitimate sons of *yangban* (the gentry). In practice, eligibility appeared to have been confined almost exclusively to those of inherited *yangban* status (Choe 1974:611-31). Furthermore, even if members of the *yangban* failed examination, they still belonged in the *yangban* class (Hong 1968:45).

Both Choi and his new teaching were a pain in the neck for the ruling class. The aristocrats saw his egalitarian ('Human is Heaven/God') ethic as a treasonable plot in disguise and that he deluded the poor peasants by this false doctrine to take action against the *yangban* elite group (Flaherty 2004:30). This resulted in Choi's immediate arrest and execution at Taegu on March 10, 1864 on a charge of "agitating the public with impure thought" (Ahn 1997:101, Bell 2008:86). A cruel irony was that Choi was beheaded as a Catholic though he had strongly criticized Catholicism as being a propagandist of western imperial power (Weems 1964:7-12).[9] Against all expectations of the elite group, his death became a catalyst for the political change sought by the *Donghak* movement.[10]

After Choi, Jae-Woo's death, his nephew Choi, Si-Hyung (崔時亨, 1827-1898) succeeded him as leader, whose efforts succeeded in making *Donghak* live on as an underground movement (Ahn 1997:105). However, it was Chun, Bong-Joon (全琫準, 1854-1895),[11] a member of *Donghak* in Kobu (古阜), who actually led the radical uprising, known as the *Donghak* Peasant Revolution of 1894 (Kim 2007:1020).[12] Thus, in 1892 a generation after its founding, the followers of *Donghak* had united in protest against the government, demanding official vindication of Choi, Jae-Woo (Yi 1960:345, Clark 1932:149). Over against ongoing

---

[9]It is partly because, in its initial state, *Donghak* was suspected of being another form of western learning (Roman Catholicism) due to the use of the same name of the deity—namely, *chun-ju* (天主, the Heavenly Lord) (Bucknell and Bierne 2001:204).

[10]Yet this campaign seemed a sort of petition movement in which the *Donghak* leaders beseeched the government for religious tolerance (Palais 1979:103). In fact, Choi, Jae-Woo did not suggest any specific program for revolutionary action. Although his new teaching appealed greatly to the downtrodden masses under severe conditions, salvation was rather promised in the form of a mystical millennial renewal, rather than a direct revolution against the oppressive government. Before his execution, Choi even said that *Donghak* was not essentially different from the Confucian idea of love (Kim 1977:60).

[11]Chun, Bong-Joon was known as the son of a local *yangban* who had been beaten to death by an official (Lew 1990:14980).

[12]There was a split within the *Donghak* leadership between the northern and southern parishes. The southern parish, located in *Chulla* province (全羅道), under the leadership of Chun, Bong-Joon, had been more active and involved in peasant politics than the northern parish in *Chungchong* province (忠清道), led by Choi, Si-Hyung. The northern parish was more committed to religious than political objectives, which made them less active to join in the fighting (Lew 1990, 101).

government persecutions, this drive took a more political direction under the leadership of Chun, Bong-Joon (Lee 1993:79, Lee 1996:122).

In the wake of an unequal treaty with Japan in 1876,[13] the *yangban* class intensified their unjust and violent oppression against the poor peasants, with Kobu, the most fertile land for rice production, being a key object of exploitation (Kim 2008:39). An arbitrary and sudden tax increase became widespread, and people paid taxes even without knowing why they had to do so (Bell 2004:127). When their plea that these heavy and illegal taxes be lifted was rejected, the peasants' accumulated anger finally exploded, propelling a protest into a full-scale uprising (Ahn 1997:106). Some 600,000 peasants gathered around Chun, Bong-Joon and he led them to victory (Park 2004:643-47, Kang 1968:41). This tax-riot became the spark that set off subsequent waves of popular revolt on the Korean Peninsula in the late nineteenth-century (Weems 1964:37-41).

The *Donghak* peasant army conquered most of the cities in the south and marched on the capital city, Seoul (Kang 1997:33, Bell 2004:127). The panic-stricken government officials, being unable to cope with such fearless peasants,[14] called upon China for aid in suppressing the rebellion (Ahn 1997:107). Japan, fearing a Chinese monopoly in Korea, also sent in troops without being asked (Ahn and Park 1980:317, Kim 2008:39-40). The battle near Kongju (公州) in December 1894 was a fatal blow to Chun and his *Donghak* peasant army and they were never able to recover the initiative (Young 2016:102, Lee 1984:281-90).[15] Further, the SOS-call for foreign powers would soon prove suicidal for the government ruling party as well as the *Donghak* peasant army. By providing an excuse for those powers to conduct a brutal crackdown, both experienced humiliating defeat (Ahn 2001:67-9, Kang 1968:38-42).

---

[13]By signing this unequal treaty, Korea was forced to sell rice at a cheap price to Japan, who was also forced to buy the goods from the western nations (Ahn 1997:106).

[14]For the *Donghak* believers, Choi's sign and formula, namely *jumun* (呪文)—a 21-syllable incantation— and *yeonbu* (運附)—a magical talisman—were supposed to protect them against bullets of the enemy (Bucknell and Beirne 2001:201 -22).

[15]Government and Japanese troops defeated the *Donghak* peasant army near the city of Kobu in Chulla province. In March 1895, the revolution's leader Chun, Bong-Joon, was executed in Seoul. In the *Donghak* rebellion, which lasted about a year, an estimated 300,000 to 400,000 had been slain (Yi 1960:345).

After the violent suppression of the *Donghak* peasant army and Chun, its leader, via foreign forces (Lee 1996:120-27), "Korea soon found itself caught between two Asian superpowers"—Japan and China (Bretzke 1991:118), the Sino-Japanese War in 1894-95 being the result of the confrontation between the two (Ahn 1997:107). An exclusive grip on the entire Korean peninsula was guaranteed when the victory was given to Japanese imperialism (Bell 2008:86). Korea was further subjugated as a Japanese protectorate in 1905, which effectively terminated its political sovereignty (Bell 2004:127). An inevitable corollary was Japan's annexation of Korea in 1910, which formally marked her end as an independent country (Park 1989:55-7, Son 2000:22-6).

The way to assess the *Donghak* movement is divided. On the one hand, the *Donghak* peasant uprising was unsuccessful as an abortive rebellion (Ahn 1997:107-9). It failed to bring forth a new way, new world, and new humanism in which all could live as equals in dignity and prosperity (Kang 1997:33, Chongsan 2012:3). Instead, in its aftermath, the economic disaster, religious persecution, and official exploitation became even more intense (Lee 1963:33), leaving the poor and the lowly completely destitute (Bell 2008:86). Further, its goal to change the contemporary social status quo ended in failure, its ideas of egalitarianism and social justice going underground (Kang 1968:3842). As a result, the *Donghak* Peasant Revolution made Korea too vulnerable to aggressors like Japan (Cumings 1997:115-20).

Yet, on the other hand, the movement was successful (Lee 2007:56) in the sense that the *Donghak* belief as to equality, freedom, and justice not only awakened, but also instilled a sense of calling to transform a corrupt society with regard to the oppressed (Ryu 1965:103). In fact, the recognition of each and every human being as a bearer of the divine (*In-Nae-Cheon*) had revolutionary potential (Ryu 1965:103). It became the spearhead of the *minjung* revolution against a double predicament—internally the corrupted Confucian regime and externally the covetous western imperial power (Kang 1997:34). Therefore, the *Donghak* Peasant Revolution was a clear manifestation of self-consciousness of the suffering *minjung*, whose aim focused primarily on their liberation from all men-inflicted sufferings (Lee 1984:287-88).

Furthermore, the idea of *In-Nae-Cheon*, in its advocacy of an integration of heaven (universe) and human beings, was the attainment of the new messianic kingdom of heaven on earth (Han 1970:356-57). It had boldly proclaimed that humanity (especially the powerless and the marginalized) was its own saviour, that would bring holistic salvation— namely, a religio-socio-political (national) salvation (Ahn 1997:103). This marked the *Donghak* movement as an unending outcry in the suffering history of Korea (Joe 2000:96).

The legacy of this *minjung* revolution, despite its fearful losses, was bequeathed to the next generations awaiting new opportunity and new leadership that could rekindle other grassroots movements, such as the *minjung* democratization and human rights ones of the 1970s (Choo 1981:6977). Thus, *minjung* theologians regarded the *Donghak* revolution as the first indigenous *minjung* movement in Korea, which had an important implication for their theology (Kim 1981:188-89, Suh 1981:170-71).

March 1st Independence Movement (三一獨立運動) of 1919

The changed situation had changed the *telos* of the *Donghak* movement. In the wake of Korea's annexation to Japan in 1910, the adherents of *Donghak* were motivated to take anti-Japanese action over anti-government resistance (Palais 1979:105). Also at that time, *Donghak*'s leadership passed to its third revered founder, Sohn, Byeong-Hui (孫秉熙, 1861-1922) (Bell 2008:86). Since Sohn inherited mental leadership from the moderate Choi, Si-Hyung rather than from the revolutionary Chun, Bong-Joon (Hong 1968:49), his concern was more committed to religious reforms than to political activities (Bell 2008:88). In 1905 Sohn renamed *Donghak* (東學; "Eastern Learning") to *Chondogyo* (天道教; "Religion of the Heavenly Way") (Oh 1959:135-36) and took the title *taidoju*, "Ruler or Head of the Faith" (Beaver 1962:118). Priority was then given to religious revival of the *Donghak,* following the standardization of both its theory and its practice (Bell 2008:88, Oh 1959:135-36, Ko 2007:33-49).

It was from this background that *Donghak*'s political and revolutionary components against the existing government paled into relative insignificance (Flaherty 2011:335). Rather, under Japanese rule, activities were more and more oriented toward nationalism (Kang

1968:41). This explains why Sohn, despite his emphasis on religious activities versus political action, became the first signer of the "1919 Declaration of Independence" (Flaherty 2011:333). As a religious leader, he inserted himself into the political struggle for national independence (Chung 2007:58-9). Here, *Donghak* (*Chondogyo*) once again was to play a crucial role in inaugurating a mass demonstration against Japanese rule in Korea[16]—namely, the March 1st Independence Movement of 1919 (Young 2002:65, Kang 1968:41).

The movement actually began with a group of Korean students who were studying in Japan (Baldwin 1969:389). On February 8, 1919, they assembled at the Tokyo YMCA demanding the independence of Korea (Lee 2010:37-8). This student demonstration was a prelude to the mass participation on the Korean Peninsula (Lee 1993:79). Emboldened by it (and also encouraged by U.S. President Woodrow Wilson's theory of self-determination), leaders within the homeland organized a nationwide independence movement, with thirty-three top leaders of Protestantism, *Chondogyo (Donghak),* and Buddhism sharing in the effort (Baldwin 1969:45-6, Chung 2009:160, Kim 1989:17-24).[17]

This triumvirate of the religious leadership, all being representatives of the people, inscribed their names on a "Declaration of Independence" (Lee 2010:38). Then, on March 1, the movement finally broke out. Shortly after the Declaration was read at the Pagoda Park in Seoul, thousands of Koreans (men, women, young, old) became a great wave of protest for liberation and independence (Lee 2009:84). Every participant without exception was in a happy delirium, shouting, *"Taehan Tongnip Manse!"* (Long live Korean independence!) (Lee 2010:38).

Within days, the movement spread like a wildfire to every corner of the country, with over two million participating in this people-oriented

---

[16]An official Japanese source proved the significant role of *Donghak* (*Chondogyo*) in the 1919 Independence Movement. According to this report, "The independence disturbances principally owed their origin to the theory of self-determination as enunciated by President Wilson of the United States of America. This theory strongly appealed to the imagination of *Sohn Byeong-Hui* [sic] . . . and other leaders of the sect, who were discontented with the annexation of Korea by Japan and hope for opportunity to recover the independence of their country" (Nakarai 1921:8-10 quoted by Kang 1968:41, *italics are mine*).

[17]Among them, 16 were Protestants, 15 were Chondogyoists, and two were Buddhists (Lee 2009:83).

uprising (Lee 1984:344). Indeed, the March 1st *(Samil)*[18] Independence Movement was a pan-Korean phenomenon in which all segments of the society were involved (Robinson 2007:48, Baldwin 1969:231).

Sadly, it did not take long for the joyful shouting to turn into tragic crying. Taken by surprise, the Japanese authorities commenced to commit bloody atrocities against the non-violent demonstrators in an attempt to suppress all hope for national liberation and independence (Lee 2009:84).[19] The Japanese blind crackdown on protestors continued for the rest of the year with tragic results (Lee 2000:137).[20] According to a report by the Japanese authorities, 19,525 demonstrators were arrested,[21] 7,645 killed, and 15,961 wounded (Lee 1984:344, Baldwin 1969:232-35).

Because of their deep involvement, both *Chondogyo (Donghak)* and Protestantism became prime targets for Japanese persecution (Kim 1989:17-24, Yi 2000:335-55). For instance, of those arrested during the demonstrations, 14.9% were Chondogyoists, 14.8% Presbyterians, 3.4% Methodists, 0.35% Roman Catholics, and 5.74% other religions (Osgood 1951:292, Palmer 1986:66). Interestingly, the charges brought by the Japanese authorities against the Protestant and *Chondogyo* created among the people a sense of public credibility and support for both religions (Min 1999:119). People looked them as "comrades in spirit,"

---

[18]*Samil* is simply Korean-Chinese for 3-1, which is how dates are rendered. Thus, the 3rd month, 1st day is March 1st.

[19]The March 1st Independence Movement was meant to be nonviolent. It started that way but failed to remain so in the end. When the Japanese authorities had indiscriminately beaten and shot at the demonstrators, the peaceful demonstrations soon turned into violent uprisings (Timothy Lee 2000:134).

[20]A pamphlet under the title, *The Korean Situation: Authentic Accounts of Recent Events by Eye Witnesses,* published by the Federal Council of the Churches of Christ of America (FCCCA) in July 1919, proved how the Japanese government used brutal tactics against the demonstrators (Lee 2000:137).

[21]Against it, Korean nationalists claimed about 45,000 arrested (Rees 1988:66-7, Cumings 1997:154).

even though they sometimes took a nonpartisan stance (Kim 1985:24-40).²²

What is crucial is that the March 1st Independence Movement of 1919 was a people's movement for freedom and human rights (Choi 2015:55). Of those involved in it, 59% were common people, especially the poor and the lowly class (Kang 1995:33). Certain religious affiliations paled into insignificance compared to public ecumenical participation in the movement (Choi 2015:55). It was evident, then, that the leading people were neither Protestants nor Chondogyoists but rather the nameless commoners who had suffered from social distress and political oppression (Ahn 2013:92). Given this condition, both *Chondogyo* and Christianity were positioning themselves as the religion of the oppressed people (Lee 2009:67), which meant both were seen as the agents of hope to the hopeless (Koschorke, Ludwig and Delgado 2007:131). Against

---

²²The scholarly consensus is that the 'March 1st Movement' was the culmination of the political awakening of Korean Christians, despite the fact that foreign missionaries had been taking a politically neutral stance (Baldwin 1973:197). It is a historical irony that, although there had been strong religious intentions of Christian mission, many people in Korea, from the first, responded to the Christian message as embodying a social and political hope for liberation from Japanese rule (Choo 1981:69-70, Park 2003:5). In this sense, the 'March 1st Movement' was an unintended gift of missionary teaching (Lee 2003:153-57). This nationwide uprising at first had alarmed the missionaries and made them apolitical (Ryu 2003:174-203). They had attempted to depoliticize the Christian message and activities with a pessimistic view of any political action undertaken by Christians (Min 1974, Park 2004:252). It was at this vantage point, most Protestant missionaries to Korea had espoused a policy of political neutrality and thus became pro-Japanese (Hutchison 1974:110-31). "We (missionaries) felt that the Korean church needed not only to repent of hating the Japanese, but a clear vision of all sin against God, that many had come into the church sincerely believing in Jesus as their Saviour and anxious to do God's will... We felt... that embittered souls needed to have their thoughts taken away from the national situation to their own personal relation with the Master" (Paik 1970:369). Such a non-political stance was made in subsequent revival movements, emphasizing personal and spiritual relation with God as purely religious experiences (Kim 2002:242-67, Moon 1985:16). But it is quite doubtful if this policy was really politically neutral. Though espousing political neutrality, the missionaries actually did more than disallow political activities within the Church (Lee 2009:82). They discouraged their flocks from harbouring nationalistic sentiments, thus eventually welcoming the status quo—namely, Japanese rule over the Korean people. As a result, many Koreans conceived the Church as being politically institutionalized and thus led their exodus from it (Min 1983:111). In its irony, the missionaries' efforts to depoliticize the church had succeeded in galvanizing many Korean Christians into political action (Lee 2009:83). However, there were some exceptions among the missionaries. A few of them had supported the Koreans in their struggle for independence (Moffet 1962:200-201). One in particular was Homer B. Hulbert, a Methodist missionary, who would serve as a royal emissary to Washington in 1905-1906 and to The Hague Peace Conference in 1906-1907 for the sake of Korea's independence (Han 1970:450-51, Yun 1997:219-20).

Japan's harsh rule, the March 1st Movement was the desperate effort of Korea's common folks to gain self-identity as an independent nation and people (Lee 1984:342-43). Indeed, the movement was the culmination of "the common people nationalism," the voices and outcries for liberation from below (Suh 1981:172).

Although the March 1st Movement failed in its immediate intent to secure Korea's independence, it did expose the subject-hood of common people in her history (Ahn 2013:92). This mass uprising, like the *Donghak* revolution, would result from people's self-awakening, self-consciousness, and self-determination (Robinson 2007:47). They became more aware of their plight in society and banded together to fight for liberation and independence from the Japanese colonial power (Kim 1981:191). It was nothing but the suffering Korean people who consciously determined to be involved in a life-or-death struggle to disarm the principalities and powers (Lee 1988:70-75). Thus, the March 1st Movement is marked as a genuine people's movement from below in which the numberless and nameless grassroots had played decisive roles as subjects, not objects, of their own history (Yun, Sin and Ahn 1977, Ahn 1971:2-3).

Further, this particular people's movement reshaped the awareness of Christianity (and *Chondogyo*) into a "politically oriented faith and a religion of hope and power for the oppressed and suffering people" (Moon 1985:13, 17). From that vantage point, the *minjung* theologians began to see the March 1st Movement as a landmark event, which paved the way for recovery of "People-o-logy" in Korean history (Lee 2009:83), while at the same time rediscovering the suffering Korean *minjung* who "transformed Christianity into its own grassroots color and created a Koreanized Christianity" (Kim 1981:194, Choi 2008:209).

April 19th Student Revolution (四一九學生革命) of 1960

While Japanese colonial power was weakened in the wake of the Korean people's consistent independence movement, Korea was finally set free from the 36-year yoke of Japanese rule when the emperor of Japan signed an unconditional surrender to the Allied Forces in August 1945 (Lee 2009:86, Wainstock 1999:3). But the euphoria of its independence did not last long, for she was soon again plunged into crisis

(Millett 2004:21). When the Cold War ensued, the Korean Peninsula became the battlefield for a proxy war between the Soviet Union and the United States (Bretzke 1991:114). This new confrontation, known as the Korean War (1950-1953),[23] resulted in the country being divided into North (a communist state) and South (a U.S. ally)—a condition that exists to the present day (Kim 2008:88, Cyhn 2002: 78-79).

The war helped Rhee, Syng-Man (李承晚), relying on the U.S. aid, to seize the power in 1948 and become president of the Republic of Korea (i.e., South Korea)—a reign that would last twelve years (Millett 2004:44, 51). As a descendent of the *Yi* dynasty royal family and a Presbyterian minister (Kleiner 2001:107), Rhee was too reactionary to deal with a Korean bourgeois class that had prospered by collaborating with the Japanese colonial power (Eckert 1996). Thus, most such collaborators went unpunished because the newly elected president needed their help both in safeguarding his position and in setting up a pro-U.S. regime (Cumings 1990:208-18).

However, Rhee's strong desire for power caused him to make some false steps (Chang 2015:50, Kleiner 2001:111-12). Not only did he decree a National Security Law on Dec. 24, 1958, aimed at eliminating any political rivals, he also led crooked elections through ballot rigging to prolong his stay in power (Kim 2000:30, Han 1975:92-4). This act enraged the people, resulting in mass demonstrations (Kang 1984:182). Soon, strong protests were occurring all over the country against the electoral corruption of the Rhee regime (Kern 2009:307).

On April 11, 1960, the discovery in Masan Bay of the body of a student, Kim, Chu-Yol (金朱烈), allegedly killed by police during a demonstration, added fuel to the public protests (Kleiner 2001:126).[24] Eight days later (April 19), thousands of students marched from Korea University to the Blue House (the presidential mansion), demanding Rhee's resignation (Oh 1961:62, Han 1980:143-61). His response was to

---

[23]It is estimated that during the Korean War (1950-53), nearly one million South Korean civilians and 320,000 South Korean soldiers were killed; about 25% of the people became refugees; and five millions were forced to live on relief (Rees 1988:441, Cole and Lyman 1971:22). Also, much of South Korea's infrastructure and productive capacity were almost in ruins (MacDonald 1986:258).

[24]Kim, one of the missing protesters, was found with a tear gas cartridge embedded in his right eye, which instigated the populace of Masan to protest against the government (Oh 1968:61).

declare martial law in order to suppress this and future demonstrations (Kern 2009:307). In Seoul alone, about 180 people died and at least 1,000 were wounded when the police opened fire on the unarmed student protestors (Kang 1984:182-84, Cumings 1997:344). However, the government's violent response backfired on Rhee's regime (Stone 1974:136). Far from quenching protest, the blood of the students sparked a chain reaction that led to a large-scale people's movement (Park 2008:65).

Volcanoes of wrath and anger against the unjust, undemocratic authorities beat within the hearts of most all Korean people (Woo 2011:66). Protests mushroomed and continued in every city, despite the Rhee government's crackdown (Kim 2000:36). The student demonstrations escalated into mass rallies for freedom and democracy, and even led to U.S. withdrawal of support for the regime (Kluver 2014:220). Rhee waved the white flag when some 250 university professors joined the students in preparing for another mass protest (Kim 2000:36, Kim 1964:83-92) and the martial-law commanders refused to intervene in the demonstrations (Cole and Lyman 1971:20, Stone 1974:137). Rhee stepped down from power on April 26 and fled to Hawaii, where he spent his last days in exile (Lee 2009:128-29, Oh 1968:63-5).[25]

Here again, the common people emerged as a leading force in the formation of anti-regime groups demanding urgent actions (Choi 1993:33). This April uprising was considered by the *minjung* theologians as yet another touchstone of a people's movement (Choo 1981:76). To them, the April 19th Student Revolution of 1960 was an heir to the spirit of the March 1st Independence Movement of 1919, "inspired by the ideals of equality, justice, liberty, and democracy that were taught by Korean Christians" (Suh 1981, 29).

To sum up, the *minjung* theologians have considered and accepted the events that unfolded in 1894-95, 1919, and 1960 as the paradigmatic people-oriented movements in Korean history (Lee 1993:65, Kim 1981:187, Suh 1983:63). First, these theologians take account of the *Donghak* Peasant Revolution in 1894 as their touchstone in bringing

---

[25]After resigning, Rhee never returned to Korea. He died of stroke in Hawaii on July 19, 1965 (Kleiner 2001:128).

about transformation of the Korean history (Kwon 2008:62). Here the oppressed *minjung* defined themselves as the subject of their own history who could not only deconstruct the unjust reality, but also reconstruct the new future with revolutionary zeal (Suh 1981:171). Second, they insist that the *minjung*-based movement in 1894-95 reappeared in the March 1st Independence Movement of 1919. In their eyes, that March 1st event was nothing less than the heir of the *Donghak* Revolution, which heard the outcry and protest of the *minjung*, who rose up in solidarity with them to decry Japanese colonialism (Kim 1981:189). Third, the theologians have also seen the resurgence of the March 1st Movement in the April 19th Student Revolution of 1960 as being another eruption of the *minjung's* outrage against the corrupt and unjust ruling government (Suh 1981:29). To them, it was the *minjung* who were the motivating force of the movement (Kim 1981:189)

In essence, the *minjung* theologians begin to rediscover *minjung*-oriented movements in the Korean history and see the Church's mission as being the church for and of the *minjung* (Choo 1981:76). They have found the historical root in the *Donghak* Revolution, the March 1st Independence Movement, and the April 19th Student Revolution as prime examples of the *minjung's* struggle for self-liberation (Ahn 1984:223). At its core, these events exhibit the framework of historical subject-hood of the *minjung*—"[*Minjung*] may be conquered, trampled upon, enslaved, but cannot be perished; [they], like the sun that dies every morning, will rise again from the dead" (Costa 2002).

Socio-Economic-Political Background

As noted above, the victory of the April 19th Student Revolution of 1960, which toppled the corrupt and incompetent Rhee regime, was short-lived (Minns 2001:180). Rhee's abdication was followed by a brief period of transition to democracy but not to the direct installation of that democracy (Chang 2007:199). In these confusing times, the blossoming of political liberalization abruptly ended when former Japanese imperial officer General Park, Chung-Hee (朴正熙) took power via military coup on May 16, 1961 (Küster 1994:109-110, Kern 2009:294). Park began a discursive campaign to justify his political takeover (Kim 1987:251).

First, he emphasized the necessity of a strong authoritative government for the sake of national security because of a threatened invasion by North Korea (Chang and Kim 2007:332). Second, he continued to advocate political dictatorship as a means of achieving economic growth (Oh 1999:52).

The result was open espousal of collectivist nationalism, which buttressed both political authoritarian rule and state-led economic development (Glassman, Park, and Choi 2008:351). Based on these logics, the Park regime tactically combined national security with economic growth to justify its illegitimate seizure of power (Vogel 1991:51, Chai 2003:540). Sensing that the result of economic growth would affect the existence of his political fortunes, (Jang 2004:140), Park established a government-led developmental-ism to facilitate the intensive mobilization of capital and labour (Chang 2007:195-96). Favouring economic growth at all cost, this authoritarian leader aggressively deployed an outward-looking strategy (Chang 2007:195), which manifested itself in export-oriented industrialization by granting favours to Korean big businesses—namely, the "*chaebols*" (Minns 2001:180, Caiden and Jung 1981:303-4).[26]

This concentration of economic gigantism worked for a while. Under the Park regime, the pace of industrialization in South Korea was rapid and its economic growth rate extraordinary to the extent it was called "the miracle on the Han River" (Lee 1992:36-45).[27] Park's uneasy alliance of state and *chaebol* led South Korea away from an agrarian society to one of the leading capitalist nations in East Asia (Shin 1998:1309-51). However, this 'miracle' did not come about cheaply (Lie 1998:285-300). Park's propagation of a growth-first model had provided bogus justification for its continued promotion of a strategy of unequal distribution (Minns 2001:181). In fact, South Korea's rapid economic

---

[26]The term *chaebol*, which is equivalent to the Japanese *zaibatsu*, literally means 'financial clique' (Minns 2001:193). It generally represents a large, private business conglomerate but also has negative connotations in relation to greed and corruption. Hyundai, Samsung, and LG are typical examples of it in Korea (Hwang 2003:364).

[27]Upon seizing power, General Park established the so-called "Five-Year Economic Development Plan." Under this government-led program, South Korea's economy had continued to grow. The first-five-year plan (1962-1966) resulted in its GNP increasing at 7.8%, and the second-five-year plan (1967-1971) resulted in a 10.5% rise (Chang and Kim 2007:332). But this was achieved mostly at the expense of the numerous Korean *minjung*.

growth resulted mainly from an abundant supply of cheap, disciplined rural migrant labourers, who had flocked to the urban centres (Jang 2004:140, Leggett 1997:64-76).[28]

This government policy, which favoured the urban sector at the expense of the rural, was inevitably accompanied by many social problems, including unemployment, crime, and the urban poor (Light and Bonacich 1988:111-2). In particular, large groups of urban labourers (especially women factory workers) found themselves working under brutal conditions, which made them into another "urban underclass" (Chang and Kim 2007:337). Destruction of their dignity as human beings was ignored and their individual values, needs, and interests appropriately sacrificed for the sake of state-*chaebol's* profits (Choi 1989:127-28). Indeed, in just a short time, such rapid industrial change began to give priority to material goods over human value (Lee 1996:17).

In its wake, the Korean society became vulnerable to a wide disparity between employers and employees, haves and have-nots, powerful and powerless (Cho 1984:13). Driven to get more profit, human rights and justice for the Korean people had been subordinated to economic growth (Bello and Rosenfeld 1990:24). Increasingly, economic development itself became less concerned with people as people (Choi 1989:127-28). As the military dictatorship-*chaebol* power elites (obsessed with expansion and development of the capitalist system) continued to create and implant the image of mammon in the public sphere, it was natural that the social disparities, growth of poverty, and inequality became pressing issues in Korean society (Kim 1987:251, Lee 1996:17).

Soon, the powers and principalities of capitalism's "invisible hand" even crouched at Korean churches' doors. It was much to do with the rapid industrialization and urbanization under Park's dictatorship that inevitably alienated the poor and underprivileged people from society under the principles of "Social Darwinism" (Chang 2007:208, Robinson 1988:28-37).[29] Out of this desperation, the people (especially labourers)

---

[28]Indeed, there was a rapid decrease in rural population in a relatively short period. It had made up 58.3% of the population of Korea in 1960 but only 28.9% by 1979 (Cho 1984:13).

[29]Here, 'Social Darwinism' means the social version of Darwin's evolutionary theory—i.e., evolutionary selection of the fittest. As a stepchild of the spirit of capitalism, it regards inequality in social classes as natural differences among people and thus reinforces people to worship profit (Sumner 1883:167-68).

began looking to the Church for some form of relief (Suh 1984:246). In one sense, this explained why the explosive growth of Korean churches coincided with the rapid expansion of national economy in the 1970s (Jang 2004:140, 143). When the fate of alienation was fostered by materialism, the mass of grassroots people, as the primary victims of this economic development, turned to the Church as an alternative community to relieve their sense of insecurity and fear (Buswell and Lee 2006: 195, Kim 1985:71).

However, these urban fringes soon discovered that often the Church was no longer a refuge; for with its rapid growth, it already shared "a rigid dichotomous belief system and a conqueror's attitude" that prevented it from standing with the least of the people (Jang 2004:141). A bigger-is-better mentality had penetrated deep into many Korean churches, their interest now the pursuit of power and money (Kang 1983:385-6, Lee, Lee and Park 2012:7). In a more simplistic way, as rapid-but-uneven modernization had forcefully planted extreme materialism into every inch of Korean society, churches likewise had become contaminated with its sweet poison—greed and self-centeredness (Jang 2004:143, Han 1999:71). By moving hand-in-hand with the "religio-economic entrepreneurship,"[30] Korean Protestant churches at that time became used to serving two masters—God and mammon (Han, Han, and Kim 2009:334).

To be sure, a single-minded devotion to mammon became ingrained in many churches (Kim 1985:62) and as a result, "the church was not a refuge from materialism, but rather another institutional embodiment of it" (Han 1997:60). In other words, the rapid industrialization drive under a military dictatorship had aggravated not only the social orders in Korean society, but also the social responsibility of the churches, asserting the separation of church and politics (Han, Han, and Kim 2009:336, 353).

Thus, the Korean churches in the times of modernization tended to be strangers to the poor and indifferent to political, social, and economic oppressions, with not many volunteering to be involved (Jang 2004:142). As such, it was an unfortunate aspect of the "bigness syndrome" of the

---

[30]This term was first used by Dearman (1982:175) in her study of the Korean church in the United States.

Church that blindfolded itself to the suffering people (Kim 1985:71-2, Buswell and Lee 2006: 195). By joining the powers and principalities of the times to beat the drum for "a healthier and richer life" (Cho 2014:315), the Korean Church turned itself from being the place of defense of the little ones to being the place of offense against them (Pak 1983:19-21, Hong 1986:11).

However, there were some critical and progressive Christians who resisted falling into this web of compromise (Park 2003:188-99). They rather held the legitimacy of resentment and grievance of the suffering people on the underside of Korea's 'economic miracles'. Taking side with the marginalized, these theologians (allied with activists) became embroiled in protests to defend human rights and social justice, emphasizing the Church's socio-political responsibility (Kim 2003:75, Clark 1995:96-7). This drove them to give more weight to the social and political dimensions of sin, than its individualistic and personal ones (Ryu 2000:309-10, Ucko 2002:76), which soon turned into the focal point of Minjung Theology (Park 2003:197).

Philosophical Background

Hegel and Feuerbach

Korean *minjung* theologians, who became very active regarding political freedom and labour conditions, owed their modern concept of God to German philosophers Georg Hegel (1770-1831) and Ludwig Feuerbach (1804-1872) (Lee 1993:84). Hegel's concept was, in turn, deeply impacted by Spinoza's pantheism—that God is in the world and the world is in God (Spinoza 1957:167). From this vantage point, Hegel emphasized the historicity of God, who externalized himself to the world throughout history. For him, God is the living God, always active in history (Hegel 1900). Thus, it came as no surprise that he saw in history the foundation of theology (Kung 1978) and "a pantheistic historical God" leading the world to himself (Kim 1987:3), though he tended to give much of the spotlight to ideas (Pippin 1989:16).

Yet this triggered a negative backlash from a group of young Hegelians (Wartofsky 1977:175). Feuerbach (1804-1872) especially challenged Hegel's idealism, resulting in his reduction of man's essence to self-consciousness (Wartofsky 1977:216-17). Instead, he sought increasingly to develop an anthropological, rather than a theological, essence of religion (Feuerbach 1957:75). For him, theology is anthropology because man (not God) is the essence of religion, which is Christianity (Feuerbach 1980:19), and because man (not God) created God in his own image (Kung 1978:200). Thus it was Feuerbach's central claim that "Man was already in God, was already God himself, before God became man" (Feuerbach 1957:50).

Against the Hegelian concept of a historical God, Feuerbach had insisted on an "anthropological atheism" (Kim 1987:250-95), which interpreted God as an imaginary projection of man. What is significant is that both Hegel's and Feuerbach's concepts of God influenced *minjung* theologians to understand the doctrine of synergism—i.e., a partnership of man with God in salvation—that emphasized both God's active involvement in Korea's history and Korean *minjung's* struggles for self-liberation from the structural violence (Kim 2009:21).

Marxism

Feuerbach had inspired deeply another young Hegelian, Karl Marx (1818-1883). In fact, Feuerbach's critique of Hegel's absolute idealism set the agenda for Marx's future path (Marx 1978:145). At first, he presented himself as a pupil of Feuerbach, who had restored materialism to its rightful place; but he soon turned away from his master, who still remained in the traditional idealist fetters (Marx and Engels 1975:652-54). For Marx, matter is primary and the material world is the only reality (Chaurasia 2001:523). He extended this materialism to the contemporary society and applied it critically to the practical activities of the proletariat or working class (Granter 2014:536).

The poverty and misery of the working class, particularly in the present phase of capitalism, motivated Marx to sharpen the concept of materialism.[31] Indeed, he was a living witness to the social and economic

---

[31] Engels, Marx's lifelong friend, witnessed the misery of the working class in Manchester, UK, as follows; "He [Engels] saw the working people living like rats in the wretched little dens of their dwellings, sometimes even without beds to sleep on when all the furniture had been sold for firewood, sometimes living in the same room with the pigs; spending their lives, without a sewage system, among the piles of their excrement and garbage; spreading epidemics of typhus and cholera" (Wilson 1972:160).

realities of his day and it had transformed him from being a proponent of Feuerbach's anthropological atheism to being a progenitor of his own socio-political atheism (Lee 1993:86). He became convinced that human beings as the creators of society and history could transform the world by changing the circumstances in which they lived (Patterson 2009:39-57, Fromm 1961:26).

This conviction for human beings' subjectivity in history and society became the foundation for Marx's historical materialism (Tabak 2012:25-50). He understood society to be the outgrowth of collective economic activities (Patterson 2009:103). That being the case, each economic system (i.e., mode of production) in human history contained within it a contradiction that would eventually lead to its demise to be replaced by another, more advanced stage of economic and social life (Tabak 2012:50-52). Thus, an epoch of new social change only begins in the womb of the old society itself (Patterson 2009:57).[32]

Marx did not see change proceeding smoothly, without conflict or upheaval. Rather, he saw it taking place by means of the revolutionary overthrow of old relations of production and the establishment of new ones. In other words, history could only progress by eliminating the "bad side" (Callinicos 1983:85). In his view, this meant the current capitalist system was pregnant with revolution (Marx and Engels 1975:174). For capitalism's main feature was the acute class struggle between the exploiters (those who own the means of production) and the exploited (those who do not) (Callinicos 1983:106). Here, the working class stood out as a new political power that could abolish the existing relations of production and their upholders (Callinicos 1983:183, Marx and Engels 1975:183, 187).

Marx's historical materialism turned capitalist fetishism on its head. While redefining human history as being the result of class struggle by its relationship to the means of production (Marx and Engels 1975:9), he predicted the economic breakdown of capitalism, characterized by exploitation of the bourgeoisie (the owning class) and alienation of the

---

[32]To Marx, "Force is the midwife of every old society pregnant with a new one" (Marx and Engels 1975:603).

proletariat (the working class).[33] His final goal was, then, creation of a new man in a classless society through revolution and it was epitomized by communism, a system whereby the means of production would be owned by all (Berghoef 1984).

Marx's critical insight into the reality of class struggle was brought back into the spotlight by the liberation theology of Latin America (Miranda 1974: xv). Under a context of continuing economic exploitation, Latin American theologians concluded that poverty was an "institutionalized violence" and "social sin," and they called for liberation from repressive economic and political structure (Ellacuria and Sobrino 1994). This drove them to accept Marxist social and political theory as an indispensable tool in transforming their society (Gutierrez 1973:273-74, Brown 1978:64-7). Although these theologians attempted to put theological flesh on the Marxist bones (Nunez, Emilio and William 1989:252-58), their theology and praxis were also nourished by the Second Vatican Council (1962-1965), which openly opted for the poor (Verkuyl 1978:289).

This radical reassessment of theology had influenced Korean *minjung* theologians both theologically and practically (Lee 1988:47). Taking their cue from Latin American liberation hermeneutics, especially from Paulo Freire's "Pedagogy of the Oppressed" (1968), Korean *minjung* theologians began to acknowledge that a political reading of the Bible was not only legitimate, but also highly desirable in the Korean context (Kim 1990:150-51). Doing theology based on a socio-economic analysis of Christian truth resonated powerfully with them because they lived in a similar socio-political troublesome situation (Kim 1992:28-9).

Nevertheless, Korean *minjung* theologians were careful not to be thought of as 'Marxist-lite' by the *minjung* who suffered from the Marxist 'temptations' during the Korean War (Lee 1993:87). This not only kept *minjung* theologians distant from the Marxist ideological language, which tended to interpret the Bible in the category of class or class

---

[33] For Marx, 'alienation' meant human beings do not experience themselves as the acting agent in their grasp of the world, but that the world remains alien to them. Alienation is essentially experiencing the world and oneself passively and receptively as the subject separated from the object (Fromm 1961:44).

struggle (Son 2000:36-7). [34] It also differentiated Korean Minjung Theology itself from Latin American liberation theology, which pronounced an essential identity between Marxism and Christianity (Bonino 1988:157-68, Chae 1994:72).

This is why, in Korean Minjung Theology, the Marxist tools of social and political analysis failed to legitimize it as theology proper; it would remain un-Korean and ineffective, despite there having been a certain degree of mutual interaction and impact (Pieris 1988:80). By recognizing the fact that the problem of and oppression from the unjust society and structure prevailed even before the introduction of capitalism into Korea (Park 1984:9), Korean Minjung Theology has stood out as a distinctively Korean style of 'doing theology', which was deeply rooted in the pathos of the Korean *minjung* or their "social biography" (Park 1984:9-10, Kim 1984:66-78).

Theological Background

Despite Korean Minjung Theology being contextual to the core, it is also influenced deeply by various modern theological thoughts and perspectives. Indeed, like a jigsaw puzzle, Korean Minjung Theology has taken its form with a set of interlocking and mosaiced theological pieces,

---

[34]However, this stance was not in dispute among *minjung* theologians. In fact, it was challenged by the so-called second-generation *minjung* theologians, who had called for a critical dialogue between Minjung Theology and Marxism. These younger theologians had maintained the need of the ideological stance (or materialistic paradigm) of Minjung Theology in a scientific way (Kim 2009:21, Choi 2008:214). Some elaborations on this matter will be discussed later.

such as the secular theology,[35] the theology of hope,[36] process theology,[37] the theology of history, [38] liberation theology, [39] political theology, [40]

---

[35]'Secular theology', which sounds somewhat oxymoronic, has its root in Dietrich Bonhoeffer, Paul Tillich, and Neo-Orthodoxy. In the wake of the 1960s "Death of God theology" and Robinson's theory of "Honest to God," secular theology argues that theology must address the immanency, secularity, or shared world of human experience over transcendence (Crockett 2001:1-2). In this sense, secular theology rejects the idea of "God up there," but recognizes the idea of God to be "the ground of our being" (Robinson 2013:1-40). In it, God's continuing revelation to humanity goes beyond the confines of religion or church. Thus it even maintains that "in a pluralistic world it is not religion [humanity] has in common. What [humanity] has in common is the secular." In essence, secular people rather require a secular theology (Vahanian 2005:21).

[36]'Theology of hope' is one of the modern theological perspectives that takes faith in God and expectation of the future seriously. Its main task is to rediscover the "logos of hope" inherent in Christian eschatology (Moltmann 1967:28). In this perspective, Christian hope itself is born from contradiction, from the contradiction of the resurrection to the cross (Moltmann 1967:14). This idea has been developed by both Pannenberg (1928-2014) and Moltmann (1926-), who see the future as a divine mode in the light of the eschatological message and history of Jesus (Braaten 1967:224). Here, the 'theology of hope' is both a theology of the resurrection and a theology of universal history (Braaten 1967:218). It therefore urges the Church to take its "practical eschatology or eschatological praxis" as mission in world history, but that transcends this world (Braaten 1967:226).

[37]'Process theology' is a theological movement influenced by the "process philosophy" of Alfred North Whitehead (1861-1947), Charles Hartshorne (1897-2000), and later John B. Cobb (1925-). As its term "process" indicates, this theological movement rejects static actuality and affirms that all actuality is process. In that light, 'process theology' denies at least five kinds of the common connotations of God's existence—(1) God as Cosmic Moralist; (2) God as the Unchanging and Passionless Absolute; (3) God as Controlling Power; (4) God as Sanctioner of the Status Quo; and (5) God as Male (Cobb and Griffin 1976:7-11).

[38]"Historical theology is the branch of theological inquiry which aims to explore the historical development of Christian doctrines, and identify the factors which were influential in their formulation and adoption. Historical theology therefore has direct and close link with the disciplines of church history and systematic theology" (McGrath 2013:8). It is generally agreed that the origins of 'historical theology' lies in the 16th century in the wake of an intense debate over Christian authenticity between the Protestant and Catholic reformations (McGrath 2013:9).

[39]'Liberation theology' appeared as a response to suffering. This theological perspective, therefore, holds the affirmation of the significance of experience and social location in one's theological formulation and identifies theology with liberating praxis for the poor and oppressed. In a variety of forms, Latin American Christians demand this liberating praxis on the history of colonialization, feminist Christians on the male dominance of ecclesiastical structure and theological system, black Christians on the white picture of Jesus and the segregation of Christian fellowship, and German political theologians the bourgeois gospel of apathy and consumerism (Chopp 1986:2-3).

ecumenical theology,[41] and practical theology[42]—in both critical and creative ways (Kim 1980:19, Na 1988:139).

For example, from Karl Rahner (1904-1984) and Dietrich Bonhoeffer (1906-1945), Korean *minjung* theologians have learned a new perspective on both Christ presenting in "anonymous Christians" (Suh 1976:78, Rahner 1983:288-95) and history incarnating in the reality of the suffering people (Bonhoeffer 1971:17). German Reformed theologian Jürgen Moltmann has also left an indelible imprint upon development of Korean Minjung Theology (Kim 1998:55). He helped *minjung* theologians take issue with the "history of God" in Trinitarian formulae (Moltmann 1992) and "the crucified God,"[43] or "the pain of

---

[40]'Political theology' is the analysis and criticism of political arrangement, which is related to politics, society, and economics (Scott and Cavanaugh 2004:1). As an academic discipline, it began during the latter part of the 20th century, partially as a response to the work of both Carl Schmitt (1888-1985), German jurist and political theorist, and the Frankfurt School (Schmitt 1922:64-66). The theme of revolution, liberation, and *minjung* can belong to this category.

[41]'Ecumenism' is the quest for unity among Christians now divided by denominations; and in this sense, it is to be distinguished from religious pluralism, even if it is sometimes called a "wider ecumenism." As ecumenism "is not the effort to find some generic essence of religion that might minimize conflicts between the religions," it is far from a "relativistic pan-religious pluralism," but is to be understood as the quest for specifically Christian unity (Harmon 2010:3).

[42]'Practical theology' can be defined as "empirically descriptive and critically constructive theory of religious practice." It was once considered only as the application of the so-called foundational theological disciplines, such as exegetical, historical, and systematic theology; but now it presents itself at the academic level as a separate branch of theology. The term 'practical theology' serves as a "theological theory of action" (Heitink 1999: xv-xviii). Don S. Browning (1934-2010) succinctly defines a fundamental practical theology "as critical reflection on the church's dialogue with Christian sources and other communities of experience and interpretation with the aim of guiding its action toward social and individual transformation" (Browning 1991:36). In its wake, the main focus of practical theology has been broadened to include the common good, on a personal as well as structural-societal level (Osmer & Schweitzer 2003:216).

[43]The idea of the passibility of God has been condemned as heresy (patripassianism, or Sabellianism) in the orthodox tradition of church. However, many theologians have held the idea of God's pain and suffering, despite their denial of patripassianism (i.e., the belief that, since Father had become incarnate in Christ, he had suffered). Among them are Saint Anselm *(divine wound)*, Martin Luther *(theologia crucis)*, Kazoh Kitamori *(the pain of God)*, and Jürgen Moltmann *(the Crucified God)* (Park 1993:111-27).

God," [44] in light of the hope of a future—namely, an eschatological resurrection (Moltmann 1970:8, 23).

In addition, Alfred North Whitehead's (1861-1947) thesis that "God creates the World, as the World creates God" (Whitehead 1978:343) also proved helpful to these theologians by contributing to the advent of holistic humanism—namely, the elevation of humanity as the centre of the evolutionary process of development (Lischer 1979:2-3, 9). From Wolfhart Pannenberg (1928-2014), they learned not only how to interpret God's revelation in human history, but also how to negate the effects of transcendentalism (Pannenberg 1970:15, 19, 98). Also it was Latin American liberation theology that urged them to apply socio-economic hermeneutics to the contemporary situation, opting for the Korean suffering *minjung* (Gutierrez 1973:2607).

Further, Paul Loffler (1931-2010), a German political theologian, motivated these progressive theologians to interpret the cross of Christ and Kingdom of God not in substitutionary but in political terms (Loffler 1979:10914, Kim 1990:125-29). And Kenzo Tagawa (1935-), a Japanese theologian, introduced them to the political concept of *minjung*, which became a keyhole to the socio-political conflict between the rulers and the ruled (Tagawa 1983:13-4, 272-74). Even ecumenical theology resonated with Korean Minjung Theology when the World Council of Churches (WCC) began marshaling its interest to the social issues of human rights and political injustice (Lee 1993:93). The *Missio-Dei* theology of the Bangkok Conference held under the theme "Salvation Today" (1972-1973) was also crucial to *minjung* theologians for redefining the Church's mission as "the catalyst of God's saving work in the world . . . not merely the refuge of the saved" (Moltmann 2007:173).

All this proved that Korean Minjung Theology has been influenced heavily by various modern theological perspectives and thoughts (Kim 1998:61-2). However, this does not mean that it was formed as a mosaic product of theologies through a process of blind synthesis. Rather, Korean Minjung Theology came about as being independent of other

---

[44]Like Moltmann, but prior to him, Kazoh Kitamori (1916-1998), a Japanese Protestant theologian, saw the very essence of the gospel in the idea of the pain of God. Thus, Kitamori's book "The Theology of the Pain of God," published in 1946 (one year after the Japanese surrender to the Allies in the World War II) was used by Moltmann, but not vice versa.

theologies not only by constituting significantly a critical challenge to the modern theological stream (Chung 2010:156-57), but also by seeking authentically Korean expressions of Christian faith (Choi 2008:213). In short, Korean Minjung Theology has emerged not as a spin-off from western versions of modern theologies, but as a spearhead of the Korean version of contextual theology.

Chapter 7
Contextualization of Korean Minjung Theology

Korean *minjung* theologians have learned—and accepted—various modern views, not to be imitators but rather initiators of their own theology, and they have continued their search for a theological identity with its own unique background. This has amounted to a project for a 'contextual' theology deeply anchored in the concrete reality of Korean *minjung*. That 'contextual' theology would be one that lives in solidarity with the suffering *minjung* and speaks out against oppression and injustice (Chung 2007:1). In this pursuit of a Korean version of 'contextual' theology, Minjung Theology develops its distinctive characteristics—namely, theology of *minjung* (民衆; common people), of *han* (恨; unresolved bitterness), and of *Hyun-Jang* (現場; life-field/*Sitz-im-Leben* of the *minjung*) (Park 1985).

Theology of *Minjung* (民衆; Common People)

The term *minjung*'[1] is a "dangerous" word (Suh 1981:15). As it has its own connotation and history that is peculiar to the Korean context, no single equivalent in any other language renders all the shades of this unique Korean word (Lee 1988:3). Thus, a more useful way is to prune out any pseudo terms that cause confusion. For instance, "Paik-sung"

---

[1] As already mentioned in the previous chapter, *minjung* is a Korean word composed of two Chinese characters, "min" (民) and "jung" (衆);" the former means "people" and the latter means "the mass." Thus, combining these two words can be translated into English as "the mass of people" or simply "the people" (Moon 1985:1). But the true significance of this term can be found in its untranslatability due to its thick and dynamic meanings.

(百姓; subjects in monarchy) and "Dae-jung" (大衆; mass) are not equivalent to *minjung* because of their impersonal and non-political nature (Suh 1983:225); "In-min" (人民; people, used primarily in the Democratic People's Republic of Korea) does not fit because of its ideologically and politically biased nuances (Hyun 1985:4); and "proletariat" is not acceptable either because of its ideological and economic slant (Suh 1983:183, Son 2000:37). Rather, *minjung* demands more personal, dynamic, and contextual interpretations in Korean vernacular usage (Kim 1984:66-78).

Despite its untranslatability, a general consensus among *minjung* theologians is that *minjung* can be defined as "the common people" literally and "the underdogs" figuratively (Na 1988:138). However, its contextual meaning prefers to denote it as "the lower echelon of the Korean society" that has long been marginalized unjustly (Kim 1981:80). Yet the most popular definition of *minjung* refers to the people who are "politically oppressed, economically exploited, socially marginalized, and culturally alienated" (Lee 1988:4). But even this definition is not sufficient to render its full essence. The fact that many efforts have been made to define *minjung* proves that none of them truly captures its crux in a satisfactory manner (Kim 1996:168). Indeed, unlike 'black theology', 'feminist theology', 'Dalit theology', etc., trying to identify *minjung* theologically with a concrete, tangible group has been difficult, to say the least (Kim 2011:121).

In fact, the term *minjung* has a much broader and deeper meaning, for it must be experienced in order to be understood (Park 2008:138).[2] Conversely this means the term is pretty indefinable (Ahn 1987:27).[3] In other words, the ambiguities and inconsistencies of any of the above definitions do not coincide with a definite categorization and

---

[2]Moon, Dong-Hwan (1921-), an OT scholar and a leading *minjung* theologian, once said that "The term [*minjung*] came to be used first during the *Yi* Dynasty (1392-1910) when the common people were oppressed by the *yangban* (the gentry) class, the ruling class . . . at that time anyone who was excluded from the *yangban* class was a *minjung*. During the Japanese occupation (1910-1945), most Koreans were reduced to *minjung* status except for a small group who collaborated with the Japanese imperialists. Today the term *minjung* may be used for all those who are excluded from the elite who enjoy prestigious positions in the present dictatorial system" (quoted by Lee 1988:4).

[3]Ahn, Byung-Mu, even says that he does not explain who the *minjung* are because once it has its conceptual definition, it is separated from the *minjung*'s reality (Ahn 1987:284).

conceptualization. Hence it leads to the indefinable definition of *minjung*—namely, the idea of self-emptying of *minjung* as a holistic, dynamic, and changing reality that transcends any fixed formula (Kim 1996:168-69, Suh 1983:42, Kim 1981:183, Bonino 1988:159).

In Korean Minjung Theology, the idea of self-emptying of *minjung* has to do with that of self-identifying of *minjung* in a paradoxical way (Oh 2015:1105), which implies that "Minjung cannot be defined by others but can be defined only by themselves" (Park 2008:123). In this light, the name of *minjung* has been a symbol of both oppression and liberation (Kim 2011:217-32). It refers to, in one sense, the victims who are oppressed and exploited yet, in another sense, the victors who are called not only to survive in the midst of misery, but also to fight for their own liberation with revolutionary zeal (Kim 1981:184). Here, the idea of self-identifying of *minjung* is incorporated into that of self-liberating of *minjung* (Kim 2009:77), which represents itself as the subject or prime mover of historical development, not merely as a byproduct of socio-economic classification (Lee 1994:140-41, Kim 1983:184-85). For *minjung* could include but should transcend the proletariat, the Marxist idea of the working class (Kim 1996:168).

Again, this recalls the indefinable, dynamic nature of *minjung*, encompassing "women who are dominated by men, or an ethnic group ruled by another group, or a race when it is ruled by another powerful race" (Kwok 1995:15, Kim 1981:136). In other words, *minjung* appear as various groups of self-emptying, self-identifying, and self-liberating people, such as students, intellectuals, workers, peasants, church activists, writers, and other democratic forces, rather than strictly taking up a specific social class, especially the proletariat (Koo 1987:103, 112, Kim 1981:185).

As such, the 'Three-Self' formula—self-emptying, self-identifying, and self-liberating—proves that it's not the proletariat but the *minjung* who have a transcendent power to tell their own story (Kim 1984:66-78). That story is often expressed in religious hope and aspirations as well as in historical and socio-economic struggles and suffering (Kim 1981:184-85). What is crucial is that this 'Three-Self' constitutes another self-image—namely, its self-transcending nature. In this light, *minjung* can refer to not only the oppressed Korean people, but all the people in the world who suffer from inequalities and injustices, regardless of religion or nationality (Wielenga 1999:48). In short, 'Three-Self enables *minjung* to transcend themselves (self-transcending) in a dynamic and coherent way (Ahn 1987:116).

On the other hand, the indefinable character of *minjung* leads to a dynamic and rightful juxtaposition of the biblical and the Korean *minjung* (Ahn 1983:138-51). It is part of a hermeneutical awakening from *minjung* theologians in their search for biblical equivalents to the concept of *minjung* as God's people (Park 1984:10). In the Old and New Testaments, they are pointed to as the *am ha'arets* (the people of the land), the *ochlos* (the outcast), the *habiru* (the Hebrew), the "my people" of Micah, and *anawim (ptōchoi,* Greek for "the poor") (Na 1988:142). In these biblical references, *minjung* theologians have first found in the *am ha'arets* and the *ochlos* the sociological meaning, referring to the poor and powerless class as victims of the society of that time,[4] which is reminiscent of the contemporary Korean *minjung* (Ahn 1983:150).

Minjung theologians then have developed the concept of *minjung* theologically by identifying the *habiru (*the Hebrew)[5] in Egypt with the oppressed *minjung* (Moon 1985:4). Here, the *habiru* has a twofold meaning; the objects of Pharaoh's oppression and the objects of God's liberation as his specific elect (Park 1982:133-39). Furthermore, regarding the Exodus event, a greater concern to these theologians is the Hebrew outcry to Yahweh (Kim 1988:231-32). What is crucial for them is that this outcry of the oppressed *habiru* (the *minjung* of that time)

---

[4]Some western scholars have also held a similar line of argument. For example, Joachim Jeremias (1971:108-113) sees the *am ha'arets* and the *ochlos* (the outcast) as being the same. He even posits that Jesus' opponents could call his followers (under the heading 'the poor') either sinners or *am ha'arets* (the *ochlos)* without distinction. Yet others, such as S. Westerholm (1978), E.P. Sanders (1983:32-3, 1985:189), and James D.G. Dunn (1988), have argued that identification of the *am ha'arets* (the *ochlos)* and sinners *(hamartoloi)* is incorrect. Rather, the sinners should be identified with the wicked *(resha'im),* with tax collectors, and with others who had renounced the covenant. Here, Jesus offended the people, especially Pharisees *(haberim),* and was killed, not because of his association with the *am ha'arets* (the *ochlos),* but because he included the sinners in the Kingdom without requiring repentance as traditionally understood (Sanders 1985). However, this claim that Jesus scandalized his fellow Jews due to such inclusion without repentance is also a subject of scholarly debate (Allison 1987:57-78).

[5]Originally, the term *habiru* was often considered as mercenary soldiers, people under treaty, and prisoners of war in one sense (Astour 1976:382-85), and as outlaws, outcasts, and those who stood outside the dominant social system in another sense. At any rate, the term suggests antagonistic characteristics against the prevailing social or power structure (Chaney 1983:39-90).

preceded God's divine action (Croatto 1981:18). This means their painful outcry served as prerequisite to bringing God's redemptive work (Kim 1988:233). For the outcry of the oppressed *habiru* itself motivates Yahweh to take action against the oppressors—"Whenever Israel cried in distress, God gave relief" (Batten 1972:369). It is the great eureka moment that enables these theologians to look anew at God's salvific act in the light of the *minjung's* struggle against the present situation (Park 1985:14245). In their eyes, it's the suffering *minjung's* outcry that actually embarks on *Heilsgeschichte* (salvation history) (Kim 1988:232, 236).

This emboldened *minjung* theologians to re-interpret the calling for "my people" in Micah as the calling for *minjung* in the Korean society and it turned the course of their theology (Moon 1985:45, Na 1988:142). By seeing "my people" as the victims of social injustice, these theologians began to recognize that a conflict between "my people" (the oppressed) and "this people" (the oppressors) is still in progress here and now (Moon 1985:35). This creates a double-identification, one being "my people" as *minjung* and the other being Micah as the theologians who speak as *minjung* and live among them (Moon 1981:127, 1985:49). Like Micah, these theologians have sought to find "my people"—i.e., today's suffering *minjung*—then have tried to share in their suffering (Moon 1982:104-32, 1985:47-9).

Furthermore, these theologians see 'the poor' *(anawim* in Hebrew, *ptōchoi,* in Greek) as another scriptural equivalent of Korean *minjung* (Suh 1983:109, 356-57). In their thinking, 'the poor' in the Bible included the captives, slaves, widows, orphans, prostitutes, sick, and demon-possessed (Ahn 1990:120) and they were nothing but the sociologically exploited and oppressed powerless *minjung* (Kim 1995:10, Suh 1983:109).

The theologians, then, give 'the poor' a dual-character: they are not only the oppressed under antagonistic social structures, but also the privileged of the Good News (Kim 1986:280-85, Suh 1983:53-55). To them, it is the sociologically 'poor' who have learned from their powerlessness and thus place their whole trust in God (Suh 1983:398-99). Thus, the sociologically poor are the spiritually poor—namely, 'the poor in spirit' of Matthew's beatitudes (Matt.5:3) (Suh 1983:399). They hunger for bread but also for salvation as the original recipients of the Kingdom of God (Kim 1995:10). Although not invited at first, they eventually become the guests of God's grand banquet (Lk. 14:21-23) (Suh 1981:155-82).

This enables *minjung* theologians to look anew at the *minjung* as the materially and spiritually poor who are not the passive victims of history, but rather the active participants in the Covenant Code (Suh 1981:160, Kang 1990:91-4)—"the Code of Protection for the weak" or "the Code of Social Justice" (Suh 1983:264-66). What's important here is their new dignity as the poor of God who could bring their sufferings and struggles into salvation (Sugirtharajah 1993:172-174).

From this affinity between the biblical and Korean *minjung* as God's people, these theologians take a further step by seeing in the suffering *minjung* a messianic role (Suh 1983:51, 53, 107-8)—that is, the *minjung's* own power not only to liberate themselves from the suffering reality, but also to become the subject of their own history (Kim 1984:517-35). In this way, Korean Minjung Theology finds the Gospel in the *minjung* and the *minjung* in the Gospel. Thus, the story of Jesus in the Gospels "is not a personal biography of an individual but a 'social biography'" (Ahn 1982:177). Such belief in the *minjung's* transforming power culminates in the idea of their self-salvation—namely, a doctrine of the *minjung*-Messiah (Suh 1983:54, 191, Moon 1998:29).

By emphasizing what the *minjung* are "saved for" rather than what they are "saved from" (Wilson 2002:186), *minjung* theologians begin to rediscover both centripetal and centrifugal forces found in the suffering *minjung* (Suh 1981:179). Thus, they argue that Jesus not only meets the *minjung* through suffering as centripetal force, but also sets them free from suffering as centrifugal force (Ahn 1987:32-3). In this dynamic connection, Jesus is found in *minjung* and *minjung* is found in Jesus (Suh 1983:54, 191); they become the saviour and deliverer for their own liberation, just as Jesus does (Ahn 1975:17, 50, Yim 2002:99-101).

Yet the idea of *minjung*-Messiah raises the ontological question in the relationship between the two (Son 1998:87-98). Here, differentiation of 'identification' and 'identity' serves as a useful tool (Suh 2010: xiv). Even if *minjung* theologians identify minjung with Jesus and Jesus in the Bible as *minjung*, this does not necessarily mean that he and the *minjung* are the same 'identity' (Suh 2010: xiv). Rather this means *minjung* have to be understood as an experiential entity 'identified' with the Jesus event—i.e., his crucifixion and resurrection (Kim 2011:121-22).

No doubt "There is unambiguous distinction between *minjung*, who is functionally messianic and Jesus as the Messiah" (Kim 2009:52). But by participating in Jesus' life and death, *minjung* become part of the Jesus event and, in that sense, they are Jesus (Ahn 1987:19, 96, Choi 1998:345-69). Thus, these theologians insist that the idea of "Jesus as *minjung* and the Jesus event as the *minjung* event" is valid and effective (Suh 2010: xiv). This sheds further light on their argument that the Jesus-event is not the only messianic event in history (not the once-and-for-all salvific event) but that it happens here and now as the *minjung* event where the *minjung* would play a decisive role as the subjects of their own salvation (Ahn 1990:104, 284, Kim 1993:21, Suh 1981:169).

All in all, Korean *minjung* theologians have rediscovered the relationship of Jesus as *minjung* and *minjung* as Jesus in the Bible and in Korean history (Ahn 1982:177). Elucidating that relationship, these theologians attempt to amplify the *minjung's* messianic character in the Jesus event (the *minjung* event) (Suh 1983:187-89, Yim 2002:99-101). Rather than engaging in theologizing for theologizing's sake, they have begun listening and sharing the stories of the suffering *minjung* by putting themselves on the side of the *minjung* (Suh 1993:189). Here, they are not merely story-tellers for the *minjung*, but are story-makers of the *minjung* who would retell stories against the oppressive and exploitative power elite (Kim 1993:21).

In so doing, *minjung* theologians have become the *minjung* themselves (Suh 1995:144-45), for they see *minjung* as the "alternative consciousness"[6] of Korean society, history, and theology, which died on the Cross with Jesus 2,000 years ago, but is dying and rising everyday again in the present for their own salvation (Ahn 1990:104, 284). It is this essential continuity between Jesus and *minjung* that enables them to proclaim a new resurrection of Jesus in the suffering Korean *minjung* as a recurrence of the Jesus event (the *minjung* event) (Kim 2009:61). This affirms *minjung* as the key for theological reflection and Korean Minjung Theology as a theology of *minjung*.

---

[6]Walter Brueggemann (1933-) coined this term as a "movement of protest which is situated among the disinherited and which articulates its theological vision in terms of a God who decisively intrudes, even against seemingly impenetrable institutions and orderings" (1979:162).

Theology of *Han* (恨: Unresolved Bitterness)

Another distinctive characteristic of Korean Minjung Theology has to do with a particular form of suffering known as *han* (恨) (Lee 1988:8, Shu 1981:55-69). As with the term *minjung*, this word is essentially untranslatable (Kim 2008:81), its meaning hard to grasp as a whole.[7] Although derived from Korean shamanism (Hyun 1985:445-56), *han* is popular in other Asian countries where dominance-subordination has persisted for centuries (Song 1986:70-71). This explains why the term is often described as the depth of human suffering (Park 1993:15).

But in the Korean context, more than suffering itself, *han* is the deep-seated lamentation of the Korean *minjung*, inherited and transmitted to each generation and thereby has become a DNA in their blood (Suh 1983:64).[8] Whereas *han* in China *(hen)* and Japan *(kon)* is similar to "grudge," "resentment," or "waging a counter-attack" (Kim 1999:126), *han* in Korea is a feeling of defeat, of nothingness, of having no specific target of anger. Thus, it is typically resolved by releasing or healing rather than by taking revenge (Kim 1999:126-7, Hyun 1985:445-56). Thus, for Korean people, *han* is much closer to "frustrated hope," "collapsed feeling of pain," "resentful bitterness," "letting go," and "wounded heart" (Park 1993:20), like the "blues" in the U.S. black experience (Cone 1981: xi).

This feeling of inward frustration is attributed mainly to the Korean *minjung's* painful and resentful experiences (Suh 1983:25). Figuratively speaking, the distinctive feature of *han* is born in the womb of the Korea's suffering history (Suh 1981:58). Behind *han* is a long history of oppression, poverty, and dehumanization inflicted on the *minjung* by foreign invasions and internal exploitations (Hatada 1969:142, Ham 1983:71-2). This double oppression by powerful foreigners and by ruling

---

[7]Often rendered as bitter grief or feeling of sorrows, *han* carries with it thick connotations. Indeed, *han* possesses a constellation of meanings, which is never innocent (Joh 2006:25-7). It is "a pent-up force looking for a place to vent," based in aggression, resignation, and nihilism (Padgett 2010:41). Despite its "thick descriptions," *han* is akin to an anthropology that refers to a "wounded heart" or "black hole" in the soul as the residue of violence unleashed upon the innocent (Park 1993:15-20).

[8]Kim, Chi-Ha (金芝河, 1941-), the ex-*minjung* poet, once defined "*han* as a people-eating monster" (quoted by Suh 1981:64).

elites of their own society turns *minjung's han* inward, hardening and sticking to their heart as a deep wound (Moon 1985:1-2, Park 1993:15). Just as Korea's history is nothing but one of suffering, so the *minjung* is nothing but the suffering people captured by the *han*-ridden society (Hyun 1985:7).

It's not too much to say that "[The Korean minjung] were born from the womb of the *han* and brought up in the womb of the *han*" (Yoo 1988:222); therefore, *han* became part of the blood and breath of minjung throughout history (Kim 1999:125, Lee 2004:158-68). Since "*Han* is a hallmark of the Korean *minjung*" (Moon 1985:1-2) and "The inner reality of *minjung* is *han*" (Lee 1994:136), knowing the Korean *minjung* is inseparable from knowing its *han* (Son 2000:33). This points to a close connection of *han* to the *minjung* experiences.

Taking *minjung's han* as the keyhole, Korean *minjung* theologians attempt to turn the anthropology of *han* into a theological rhetoric of the *minjung* (Suh 1983:105, Ahn 1984:141-42). To put it differently, these theologians begin to transform the sighs of the *han* into "the voice of Christ knocking on [*minjung's*] doors" (Suh 1981:68). What is crucial here is not only how *han* affects the *minjung* but how it is affected by the *minjung* (Lee 1994:141-42). Recognizing the positive potential of *han*, the theologians pay close attention to the power of resurrection—namely, a "tenacity of will for life" (Suh 1983:58) and it changes *han* from a feeling of defeat and nothingness to righteous indignation against abusive and unjust violence (Suh 1983:54, 59). Here, *han* is sublimated into the dynamic energy for revolution, which would provide the *minjung* hope in situations of no hope (Suh 1981:27, Song 1986:71).

Linking the power of *han* to that of revolution, *minjung* theologians, then, have devoted themselves to making a *minjung*-centered historical view—namely, the re-reading of Korea's *han*-ridden (suffering) history from the perspective of the *han*-ridden (suffering) *minjung* (Park 1993:77-81). This quickly resonated with the idea of *Ci-al*[9] (씨알, taken from the Korean word for "seed"), which sees the *minjung* as a collection

---

[9]This idea of *Ci-al* was coined by Ham, Suk-Hon (1901-1989), a well-known people's leader in Korea during the Park dictatorial regime. His understanding of Korean history as a history of suffering *Ci-al* (*minjung*) had made a great contribution to the development of Minjung Theology.

of individual *Ci-al* and Korean history as the collective experience of the suffering *Ci-al* (Ahn 1982:21, Kim 1985:125-81, Park 1989:50).[10]

It helps broaden their horizons even to the point of looking at Korean society as a breeding ground for the *minjung*'s *han* that makes visible its social dimension (Moon 1998:61-2, Suh 1981:55-69). Alongside Latin American liberation theology, these theologians view the structural (systematic) evil as the root cause that reinforces oppression and alienation of the *minjung* (Suh 1981:55-69). To them, *han* comes from the evil social structure and it perpetuates a vicious circle of making Korean *minjung* a *han*-ridden people and Korean society a *han*-ridden society (Suh 1981:15-37). Thus, they propose an analysis of *minjung's han* not as a natural phenomenon or inevitable outcome of one's *karma*, but rather as the systematic consequences of social injustice and exploitation (Lee 1988:8, Phan 2000:47). Therefore, when one speaks of *han*, the stress should fall on the systemic aspect that lies beyond the individual, for it subordinates, through coercion of the system, to increase social injustice and functions as a structure of control and domination in which the few oppress the many (Suh 1983:25).

This has enabled *minjung* theologians to distinguish *han* from sin (Suh 1983:106). In other words, they have realized that *minjung's* victimization, which the rulers labeled as sin, is in fact the reality of *minjung's han* (Park 1993:69). They then stress the uniqueness of *han* not as sin itself but as the result of the sins of an unjust society that entangles and oppresses the lives of the *minjung* (Suh 1988:6). "When the oppressors commit sin, the oppressed are harmed by the sin of the oppressor and come to have and deepen their *han*" (Hwang 2013:220). Thus, it makes no sense to talk about sin from the experience of *minjung's han*. For sin is the volitional act of sinners, whereas *han* is the pain of the sinned-against who are the victims, not the perpetrators, of sin (Park 1993:12). These theologians then alert themselves to the polarization of two realities—sin labeled by the rulers belongs to the oppressors, and *han* expressed by the *minjung* belongs to the oppressed (Hwang 2013:220).

---

[10] *Minjung* theologians have further elaborated it to the point of distinguishing *minjung* (a socio-political term) as the subject of history from *Ci-al* (a cosmo-ontological term) as the subject of cosmos (Suh 1981:63, 182).

This leads to a two-fold task of Minjung Theology—resolution of the *minjung's han* in one sense and resistance against structural sins in another sense (Suh 1981:68, Kim 1981:15). Yet they should not be separated, even as they are distinct. As *han* exposes the *minjung's* pain and suffering, Minjung Theology needs to be a '*han*-solving' theology (Kim 1970:90, Suh 1981:55-69). Also, as *minjung's han* results primarily from the sins of the oppressive social and economic structure, Minjung Theology needs to be a 'sin-solving' theology (Moon 1998:84). Thus, '*han*-solving' is inseparable from 'sin-solving' (Suh 1981:27-8). As Minjung Theology sees that sin produces *han* and is construed as an obstacle in the way of salvation, personal salvation or personal '*han*-solving' is closely interconnected with social liberation or social 'sin-solving' (Lee 1996:53, Paik 1998:32, Suh 1983:25).

Taking into consideration such a two-fold task, *minjung* theologians argue that justice needs to be stressed for there could be neither '*han*-solved' *minjung* nor '*han*-less' society without justice being done (Suh 1983:58, Lee 1993:101). This is why they prefer to be more cautious about the love-without-justice approach, while quickly finding themselves embroiled in producing justice prior to forgiveness and love, even if it may at times provoke revolution (Lee 1984:10, Lee 1994:5). For them, reflection from the experience and vantage point of power of *han* demands that justice alone can release *minjung's han* and thus restore the *minjung* to the rightful place (Lee 2010:206, 224). This encourages them to insist on a necessary and radical change in the social order rather than an easy and partial solution, which may alleviate oppression but not lead to liberation (Kim 1989:1005-16).

The method of resolving *han* is evolved into a more elaborate form, known as *dan* (斷) (Kim 2008:96).[11] *Dan* means 'cutting off'—cutting off

---

[11] It should be noted that Minjung theologians borrow from Kim, Chi-Ha (1941-), a well-known dissident poet, not only the concept of *han* but that of *dan*. His story of Chang Il-Dam vividly shows the idea of *dan*. According to the story, when Chang Il-Dam, the preacher of liberation and of *han*, is betrayed, arrested and eventually executed by the ruling group, his head is chopped off; but strangely enough, it appears on the betrayer's body while the betrayer's head appears on Chang's body. In this way, Chang's *han* is resolved through *dan* (quoted by Suh 1981:67). This is how Kim lifts up a "violence of love" associated with a socio-political practice of *dan*. Reflecting upon Thomas Aquinas' argument that people have the right to overthrow a tyrant, he continues, "I reject dehumanizing violence and accept the violence that restores human dignity. It could justly be called a violence of love…I welcome the violence of love, yet I am also an ally of true nonviolence. The revolution I would support would be a synthesis

the chain of *han* (Suh 1983:65). More specifically, it is an "attempt to destroy the greed which is at the center of the oppressor-oppressed cycle" (Moon 1985:55). To the oppressor, *dan* means the negation of being greedy and oppressive; while to the oppressed, it means the negation of being vengeful and violent (Moon 1985:10). Via the concept of *dan*, *minjung* theologians intend to create the dialectical unification of *han* and *dan*; the more *han* is accumulated, the more necessary *dan* is. Thus they argue that "on the other hand, there is the fearful *han* which can kill, cause revenge, destroy and hate endlessly, and on the other, there is the repetition of *dan* to suppress the explosion which can break out of the vicious circle, so that *han* can be sublimated as higher spiritual power" (Suh 1981:61). In short, *dan* allows the *han*-ridden *minjung* to experience justice, healing, and peace, leading to a *han*-less society (Suh 1981:61, Lee 1994:154).

This explains why *minjung* theologians take a keen interest in *han-pu-ri* (한풀이; releasing from *han*),[12] practiced by shamans (Kim 1999:127, Hyun 1985:445-56). But its catharsis and ritual oriented tendency have left them critical of its validity to seek for a radical change of the reality in which *han* has been generated (Ryu 1978:345-46). In their eye, by overlooking the evil of structure, it simply attempts to patch up peace and reconciliation among people in conflicts (Ryu 1965:30). For they are more concerned with the total transformation of the oppressed society and culture than the one-sided psychological and emotional release of the individual (Suh 1981:28).

Thus, *minjung* theologians have put their special emphasis on the collective dimension of *dan* that does not remain as self-denial, but curtails the vicious circle of revenge in society (Suh 1981:64-5). This leads

---

of true nonviolence and an agonized violence of love" (Kim 1977:8-15). Kim continued, "It is an expression of Chang's conflicting thought that this is revenge but at the same time also the salvation of vicious men" (ibid, 67). This is a reflection of his belief that God and revolution are intertwined (Lee 1988:9-11)—the salvation from *han* is being embraced by the *minjung* through a personal and political practice of *dan.* To some degree, this understanding corresponds to what John de Gruchy, the internationally esteemed political theologian of South Africa, tried to show in his book, "Reconciliation: Restoring Justice" (2002).

[12]The term *han-pu-ri* comes from Korean shamanism. This is a ritual means through which *han* is resolved. In Korea, this is also called *kut*. It is known that there are three general movements throughout the duration and various steps of a *kut*—"speaking and hearing," "naming," and "changing" (Chung 1988:27-36).

theologically to the bold link of *dan* to the death of Jesus, which has deconstructed the evil structures that reinforce injustice and oppression, thus cutting off the vicious chain of *han* (Son 2000:59).[13] Here, the Cross is redefined as "God's ultimate negation of *han*"[14] and Jesus' crucifixion as "the very *dan* of God for the *minjung*" (Son 2000:59). So, "*dan* is eventually to overcome *han*" (Suh 1983:65) for the Jesus event (i.e., his crucifixion and resurrection) would transform *han* into *dan* which has its focus in reconciliation and healing of both personal and social *han* (Son 2000:59).[15]

All this motivates *minjung* theologians to be both "the priest of *han*" and "the prophet of *dan*" (Kim 1977:65, Suh 1981:55-69) who are called to bring healing for the *minjung's han*, eventually leading to a *han*-less society—namely, a free, just, and non-exploitative *han*-free (or *han-pu-ri*) society (Suh 1986:602, Park 1985:4). Thus, the theology of *han* (*dan*) becomes one of Minjung Theology's most famous landmarks.

Theology of *Hyun-Jang* (現場; Life-Field/Sitz-im-Leben of the *Minjung*)

As the priest of *han*, *minjung* theologians do not bring a ready-made theology to impose on the situation, but struggle to bring *dan* that illuminates the situation. This is why "Minjung Theology prefers praxis

---

[13] Here, *minjung* theologians owe their approach to *Chondogyo* (Heavenly Way) or *Donghak* (Kim 2008:98). Under the banner of *In-Nae-Cheon* (人乃天; humanity is heaven) and *Hu-Cheon Gae-Byeok* (後天開闢; the great opening of the latter heaven), *Chondogyo* taught the four stages of personal and social *dan*—namely, "worshiping the divine embodiment" *(Shin-chonju)*, "nurturing the divine embodiment" *(Yang-chonju)*, "practicing the divine embodiment" *(Haeng-chonju)*, and "transcending the divine embodiment" *(Sang-chonju)* (Kim 1982:24). All would then be incarnated in Minjung Theology as a new type of *dan*, that being the process of salvation of *minjung* both personally and socially. Then the *minjung* is "to realize God in [their] hearts," "to allow the divine consciousness to grow in [them]," "to participate what [they] believe in God," and "to overcome injustice through transforming the world" (Lee 1988:11, Suh 1981:66-7).

[14] In this connection, Rauschenbusch's insight is noteworthy. He observes that Jesus was crucified not just by individuals but by "constitutional forces in the Kingdom of Evil," such as "religious bigotry, the combination of graft and political power, the corruption of justice, the mob spirit, militarism, and class contempt" (1961:257).

[15] In this sense, Karl Barth's understanding of salvation resembles the perspective of *han* and *dan* in terms of his idea of healing the broken relationship between God and man and between man and man (1969:4:2:314).

to theory" (Kim 1995:10). It understands itself not as "Theo-LOGOS" or "Theo-LOGY" but as Theo-PRAXIS" (Suh 1986:602). In it, rediscovery of the *minjung* as the hermeneutical key becomes formative for doing theology (Kim 1995:10). For as it begins to see society and history from the perspective of the socially and economically marginalized, the socio-political role of the Church and Christians emerges as an indispensable part to authentic Christian theology (Ahn 1982:25, Kim 2008:100, Moon 1998:104, Kim 1995:10).

Emboldened by this *minjung*-centred perspective, these theologians stress liberating praxis as a "mutually critical correlation"[16]—namely, a critical link between the social and political experience of oppression and liberation, and the Christian witness (Suh 1981:166). Thus, unlike the academic type of traditional theology, which is divorced from action, Minjung Theology claims Christian praxis toward justice and liberation, standing at the side of the *minjung* (Kim 1995:8, Kim 2008:100-101, Park 1995:196). Thus, it turns on its head the Augustinian and Lutheran legacies of "two kingdoms," which teaches Christians to neglect social and political renewal (Segundo 1976).[17]

Being seen as the task of church liberating praxis from the current de-humanistic structure of de-humanized society, Minjung Theology rather insists on the need for a "prophetic church" that listens to and speaks for the suffering *minjung* (Ahn 1984:186-208, Kim 1995:8). This is embodied in the so-called '*minjung* church movement', initiated by pastors "who committed themselves to witness to the liberating gospel as seen from the *minjung* perspective" (Park 2003:198). Focusing on the *minjung* and their vital context as the "epistemological foundation" for doing theology (Kim 1995:13, Suh 1981:229), this '*minjung* church movement' has evolved to become a church of *Hyun-Jang* (現場)[18]— namely, the *Sitz-im-Leben* of the *minjung*.

By articulating the image of *Hyun-Jang* as the very place where Jesus

---

[16]David Tracy (1984:167-80) originally coined this term.

[17]According to Luther, God has established two kingdoms, one ruled by the law and the other by the Gospel. This theory has contributed largely to the dualistic idea of western theology by separating the realm of religious life from secular life (Chung 2008:117-18).

[18]The first syllable *Hyun* means "present," the second *Jang* means "location" (Suh 1981:57).

is incarnated, Minjung Theology further elaborates it as the very place the Korean *minjung* have confronted in their everyday lives and thereby where the *minjung* movements have actually been revealed (Suh 1981:57).[19] Thus, *"Hyun-Jang* [becomes] a precondition of doing theology" which aims at making the Church practically relevant and theologically contextualized (Enns 2013:159, Park 2003:198). By placing the Church at the centre of *Hyun-Jang,* the concrete life place of the *minjung,* Minjung Theology is to bridge the gap between theology and the life of *minjung* (Suh 2010: xiii, Kim 2008:286). Here, the Church must do violence to itself by having the *minjung* as its audience and by achieving the fusion of horizons between theology and praxis, which is not to be alienated from the life-situation of the *minjung* and not to be confined to the academic guild (Kim 1995:11, Moon 1998:105, Kim 2008:286).

In its emphasis on the fusion of theology and praxis, the *Sitz-im-Leben* of Jesus is cast in a new light—Jesus present with the poor and the suffering *minjung* of his time (Suh 1982:237-76). Not only did he, as one of the suffering *minjung* (Ahn 1987:288), carry out his public ministry in Galilee, the first-century Palestine *Hyun-Jang* (Suh 1981:142, Ahn 1990:18-31).[20] He also, as the suffering Messiah, died on the Cross for the sake of the *minjung's* liberation (Suh 1981:161, 214). In this light, Jesus did achieve the fusion of theology and praxis by incarnating himself into *Hyun-Jang,* the *Sitz-im-Leben* of the *minjung* (Ahn 1990:138, Suh 1983:297).

This sheds further light on Jesus' Cross event, not as a once-and-for-all (*ephapax*) but as a continuing and recurring event embodied in the suffering reality of the *minjung,* which is *Hyun-Jang* (Ahn 1987:104, 284, Suh 1991:243-45). As one of the *minjung,* Jesus can be found not only in Galilee (the first-century *Hyun-Jang*), but also in the Korean society (the contemporary *Hyun-Jang*), where the scandal of the Cross is erected everyday (Lee 1988:11, Ahn 1987:104, 284). This means *Hyun-Jang* becomes a living witness; for wherever the *minjung* suffer, there is the

---

[19] This church of *Hyun-Jang* can also be translated as "field church," or "church on the spot" (Suh 1981:68). By presenting a *minjung*-oriented characteristic, Suh, Nam-Dong, a leading *minjung* theologian, has even argued that this *Hyun-Jang* church is a third form of the Church, besides the Catholic and the Protestant (Suh 1981:57).

[20] As such, about 70% of the inhabitants of Galilee were peasants at that time (Saldarini 1988:200-209).

agony of God on the Cross, not as a "symbol of escape" but a symbol of "ultimate vindication" (Roberts 1988:104-5). This is a radical rethink of the trans-phenomenon of Jesus event into *Hyun-Jang*—i.e., Jesus' crucifixion happens again and again in the contemporary *Hyun-Jang* as the collective death of the suffering *minjung* (Suh 1976:67, Song 1988:81).

Such a notion that the Cross event is still alive today even leads to the radical concept of the unity of God (spiritual renewal) and revolution (structural renewal) (Suh 1981:179, 1991:239). By being fused with the idea of *Hyun-Jang* as the vital context of the *minjung*, the Cross is to be seen as the *Hyun-Jang* of the Jesus event which exposes God's protest against the dominant and unjust structures (Park 2001:52, 2009:81). So, whenever the *minjung* suffer from the contemporary *Hyun-Jang*, it has to be proven in action. As for Jesus, the resurrection signifies that there is more to the life of Jesus than the Cross (Sobrino 1993:254-71). Similarly, for the *minjung*, the resurrection signifies that there is more to their hope and liberation than their oppressive experience (Ahn 1987:98-9, 118).

Thus *Hyun-Jang* comes to the *minjung* as an eschatological reality to encounter and realize God as the liberator in the present suffering context, which involves the ongoing creation of justice (Yewangoe 1987:293). From this vantage point, *Hyun-Jang* is sublimated into a crossroad where the crucified Jesus (suffering) and the risen Jesus (liberated) are meeting together (Suh 1983:180-81), and where the suffering *minjung* and the liberated *minjung* are living together (Moon 1998:71, Ahn 1987:104, 284).

In short, in Minjung Theology, *Hyun-Jang* is nothing less than the vital context for both Jesus and the *minjung*. It's the place where Jesus experiences the *minjung's* suffering (the human *han*) and the *minjung* understands Jesus' suffering (the divine *han*). It's also the place where Jesus and the *minjung* transform the suffering *Hyun-Jang* into the eschatological place where the *minjung* is making promise of the future here and now (*dan*). Here we clearly note one significant theological characteristic of Minjung Theology which attempts to achieve the fusion of theology and *Hyun-Jang* (praxis), the *Sitz im Leben* of the *minjung*.

New Understandings of Korean Minjung Theology

The contextualization of Minjung Theology can be epitomized by the theologies of minjung (民衆; common people), of *han* (恨; unresolved bitterness), and of *Hyun-Jang* (現場; life-field, *Sitz-im-Leben* of the *minjung*). This three features are complementary to one another and thus help Minjung Theology establish its characteristics of (1) *minjung* as the hermeneutical key for the Bible and history; (2) the church as the priest of *han* and *dan* (3) the fusion of theology and *Hyun-Jang*, the place of *minjung*. Against the inherited ways of seeing, thinking, and theologizing, Minjung Theology has uniquely developed its ways of doing theology, that being the so-called Korean version of biblical, historical, and spiritual understanding of Christian theology. In other words, this Korean contextual theology provides evocative and challenging perspectives of the Bible, church history, and the Holy Spirit in presenting its own appreciation of Christian theology from inside the Korean reality.

New Understanding of the Bible

Having analyzed critically the socio-economic situation of the scriptural context, *minjung* theologians try to read the Bible from the *minjung* perspective (Park 1995:196, Lee 1993:110). Through this socio-economic interpretation of the Bible, they discover the biblical *minjung*, which is the suffering people of Israel (Kim 1995:13, Suh 1991:243-45). Thus, to them, the liberating act of God for the suffering people of Israel is the Bible's main theme (Ahn 1987:78). Yet they also find it is the outcry of the suffering *minjung* that results in God's salvific action (Kim 1988:229-39). Here, biblical history bears witness to God's participation in the *Sitz-im-Leben* of the suffering *minjung* and, on the flip side, to the story of the *minjung's* self-liberation (Suh 1981:179, 1983:11, 21, 168).

Understood in this way, the outcry of the *minjung* is no longer regarded as one of despair but rather one of hope in the liberating God, who hears and protects those suffering unjustly (Kasper 1976:118, Kim 1988:229-39). Taking into consideration the dynamic interconnection between God and *minjung* in the Bible, these theologians focus on the Exodus event in the Old Testament and Jesus' crucifixion in the New Testament as the liberating event's core (Ahn 1987:79, Suh 1991:243-45). In their thinking, both are inexorably bound together as pivotal events for the sake of the biblical *minjung's* salvation (Suh 1981:159-59).

Thus, *minjung* theologians argue that in Exodus the stress should fall on the suffering Hebrews *(habiru)* (the politically, economically, and socio-culturally downtrodden *minjung*), who were being forced to serve as slaves under an oppressive Egyptian system (Moon 1981:125, 1985:3-4). On the other hand, Yahweh also needs to be stressed because he heard the Hebrews' groaning and came down to rescue them from the power of Egypt, the harbinger of the vicious circle of the Hebrew's *han* (Exod. 3:7-8) (Moon 1987:182-83, 1981:124). No doubt, the Exodus narrative is showing Yahweh as being on the side of the oppressed, the *han*-ridden *minjung* (Moon 1981:124-25).

Yet there is the suffering *minjung* as well as Yahweh behind the event of the Exodus (Moon 1985:5). Indeed, the *minjung's* outcry provoked Yahweh to rise up against the oppressive Pharaoh and this really attracts *minjung* theologians' attention (Kim 1988:236). Thus, the Exodus event comes to them as a theology of *Heilsgeschichte*—i.e., the Old Testament Yahweh is the God of the *minjung* and the *minjung* are the people of God who play an active role for their own liberation (Croatto 1981:18, Moon 1981:124-25).

The story of the Cross and the resurrection of Jesus is another archetype example of *minjung* liberation (Suh 1981:161, Ahn 1983:99). In one sense, the liberal idea of the so-called "historical Jesus movement" [21] contributed to development of the idea of *minjung* Christology, or *minjung*-Messiah (*minjung's* ability to save themselves) by making Christ radically historical (Son 2008:52). While minjung theologians, like the circle of Jesus movement, put more emphasis on the

---

[21] Here "the historical Jesus" refers to the discrete historical work of such men as H. S. Reimarus (1694-1768) and D. F. Strauss (1808-1874), whose focus was on Jesus' rational, humanistic impulse over against the excesses of supernaturalism (Reimarus 1962, Strauss 1972). They are credited by some (especially Albert Schweitzer) with initiating historians' investigation of the historical Jesus. From then onward, the history of historical Jesus studies has generally been divided into recognizable periods—the Old Quest, from 1778 to 1906; an interim period or "No Quest," from 1906 to 1953; and the New Quest, from 1953 to the present (Ladd 1993).

life of historical Jesus than on theological dogma (Ahn 1999:48-56), their persistent interest in *minjung* began to distinguish them from the latter (Ahn 1981:85, 1993:166) even to the point of criticizing it for overlooking the people around Jesus—i.e., the suffering *minjung* (Moon 1998:69-70, Ahn 1987:228-53). For it is far more relevant to them to ask the question "Who is Jesus Christ for the *minjung* today?" than "Who is the historical Jesus Christ?" (Moon 1985:48-50).

Such a focus on Jesus-with-the people or Jesus-with-the-Galilean-*minjung* opened a new hermeneutical grid in interpreting those around him and resulted in the discovery of *ochlos-minjung* in the Gospel of Mark (Ahn 1981:141, 151). In it, Jesus' messages were targeted particular at the social outcasts, which is *ochlos*—i.e., a crowd, the ignorant multitude, the populace, the common people, those oppressed by the ruling powers (Ahn 1981: 149-50, 1982:90, Suh 1981:142). Therefore, it becomes evident that the word *ochlos* is a sociological term that Mark used intentionally to indicate victims of the society of that time (Ahn 1983:139-41). In fact, the *ochlos* were the followers of Jesus as the *minjung* of his time, differentiated from not only the ruling class, but also the disciples (Ahn 1982: 90).

What is crucial for *minjung* theologians is the dynamic relationship between Jesus and *ochlos*. Jesus identified himself with the *ochlos-minjung*, had compassion for them, and sided with them (Ahn 1981:96, Suh 1983:12), while promising them the coming of the Kingdom of God, a message of hope, without imposing any conditions (Ahn 1990:122-25). Further, because Jesus, with the *ochlos-minjung* appeared as a counter community, contrasting to the political power groups (Ahn 1982:91), he was crucified as being the political Messiah of the *ochlos-minjung* by the Roman officials and Jewish leaders who feared the 'Jesus-movement' (Ahn 1981:149-50, 1990:18-31). It serves to make explicit Jesus' special affinity for the *ochlos-minjung*; he is the one who not only was with them but was one of them (Ahn 1985:183, Suh 1983:129).

To these theologians, Jesus without the *ochlos-minjung* is abstract and unreal, for his life and passion are part of the social biography of the *ochlos-minjung*, rather than that of an individual (Suh 1981:211, Ahn 1982:177). In keeping with this indivisible intertwining between the two, they even regard Jesus as "the personification and symbol of the [*ochlos-minjung*]" and his crucifixion and resurrection as the *ochlos-minjung*'s struggle for their own liberation (Suh 1983:54, 191, 1991:245). Thus, it is not the individual Jesus but rather the collective *ochlos-minjung* who were crucified on the Cross (Ahn 1982:183, 1987:99) and in that sense, Jesus being raised means the *ochlos-minjung* of Galilee were raised (Ahn 1982:184, 1987:99). This leads to a radical turn of *minjung* Christology from "the Saviour-saved schema" to "the Jesus-*minjung* schema" (Ahn 1990:259-60, Moltmann 2000:256).[22]

Yet this does not mean that *minjung* Christology comes to terms with low Christology.[23] Instead, it constructs a radical new Christology that even deifies the *minjung* (Chang 2007:206).[24] So its focus lies primarily not on the "personal saviour" motif but on the "Jesus-event" as the *ochlos-minjung* event (Chang 2007:206). By seeing Jesus' ministry in the Gospels as the first *minjung* movement, these theologians emphasize the Jesus event in the Gospels not as a time-bound unique story but rather

---

[22]This idea essentially concurs with the work of M. M. Thomas, a renowned Indian Christian theologian. He regards "the struggle for Human Dignity as a preparation for the gospel," saying, "If theology is christologically oriented, it needs not be opposed to anthropology" (Thomas 1971:14).

[23]Christology in systematic theology has to do with beliefs about Jesus Christ. Broadly speaking, notions of Christ are categorized as either "high Christology" or "low Christology." While high Christology focuses on Jesus as the divine Son of God and equal to God, low Christology highlights his humanness and life on earth (Chang 2007:206).

[24]Here comes the problem of deification of the *minjung*. The concept of *theosis* or divinization is one of the important themes of the Eastern Church. Theologians like Iranaeus, Clement of Alexandria, and Origen worked with concepts related to *theosis*. These concepts often dealt with the notion of the divine image in humanity and how human beings become children ('adopted sons' as Scripture says) of God. For example, Irenaeus wrote about "the Word of God, our Lord Jesus Christ, who did, through his transcendent love, become what we are, that He might bring us to be even what He is Himself" (Iranaeus *Adversus Haereses* 3, 19:1 quoted by Bingaman 2014:67). Also, Athanasius said that "the Word (Logos) was made man that we might be made God" (Athanasius *On the Incarnation* 107, quoted by Bingaman 2014:67). As biblical support for this statement, reference is made to 2 Peter 1:4, which states, "so that through them you may participate in the divine nature" (see also Eph 3:19, John 1:14, 16, 17:22-23, 2 Cor 3:17-18, Gal 4:19, 1 John 3:2). In the modern era, it is noteworthy to remember Karl Barth's argument that, in Jesus, the "Lord as Servant" is an indication of the way in which the divine wants to live among us, and the "Servant as Lord" is an indication of how humans can be related to the divine. In Jesus God is not separated from humans and humans are not separated from God (Barth 1969). In a similar vein, D. Bonhoeffer says that "Man becomes man because God became man" (1971:84). In Minjung Theology, the *minjung*-Jesus represents his identification with the *minjung* in suffering. In this way, he becomes one with the *minjung*, and they become one with him (Ahn 1987:31, Moltmann 2000:256). This *minjung*-messianism will also be dealt separately in later parts of the book.

as a common story enacted through the lives of all suffering *minjung* (Ahn 1990:259-60, Chang 2007:213).

As a result, in *minjung* Christology, just as Jesus is inseparable from the *ochlos*-minjung, so the Jesus event is inseparable from the *minjung* event. In this way, Jesus and the *ochlos-minjung* are one and the Jesus event and the *minjung* event are the same historical event, taking place here and now (Ahn 1975:183, Yim 2006:136). With the idea of *minjung* -Messiah, the salvation of God and liberation of the *ochlos-minjung* go hand in hand (Suh 1983:11, 21).

To summarize, through their socio-political interpretation, *minjung* theologians find the suffering minjung in the Bible to be the protagonists of their own history and destiny (Lee 1993:110, Suh 1981:5569). To them, the Exodus event in the Old Testament and the crucifixion-resurrection event in the New Testament are the two poles of the *Heilsgeschichte* running through the whole story of the Bible (Suh 1983:164). Thus, what both events reveal is the true meaning of the Gospel as the dynamic interaction between the biography of the suffering *minjung* and God enacted in the biography of Jesus (Song 1988:122).

Here, it is the *ochlos-minjung* who have galvanized Yahweh to rise up against the oppressors through their outcry (Kim 1988:231-32); who have broken the vicious circle of violence through their crucifixion and resurrection with Jesus (Suh 1981:159); and who have ultimately redeemed themselves from their own suffering through the *minjung-*Messiah interplay (Ahn 1977:717-57, Kim 1987:254).

New Understanding of Church and Korean History

Taking a cue from the new understanding of the Bible, *minjung* theologians have developed their own outlook on church history (Kim 1987:253-57), which manifests in two different ways. One is an explosive critique of the transcendental view of the Church. The other is a creative confluence of church history and Korean history (Suh 1982:237-76).

On one hand, it is from their observation that the deformation of the Church started with the adoption of a Hellenistic worldview—i.e., the rise of a Greek cosmological and metaphysical view, taking precedence over a Hebraic historical and eschatological one (Suh 1983:299, Ahn 1985:154). Such Hellenistic predominance in the church proved to be problematic as it began to confine the Jesus event to purely a spiritualized concept, apart from political features (Suh 1982:248). This resulted in the de-politicization of the Jesus movement—i.e., the historical Jesus of Nazareth (the Son of Man), a political messiah, was superseded by the supra-historical divine Jesus Christ (the Son of God), a religious one (Ahn 1982:161, Considine 2015:120). Thus, the political implication of the Cross degenerated almost into a religious symbol under the cloak of the doctrine of reconciliation (Suh 1982:248).

To continue this critical assessment, these theologians point out that the notion of the days of Constantine as a period of the Church's triumph does not clearly convey the truth (Suh 1982:248-49). They rather insist that from that point on, Christianity served as the ideology of the ruler (Kim 1987:256). This means the Church lent its justification to the existing order at the expense of its original apocalyptic and revolutionary character (Suh 1983:301-304). Thus, the emphasis fell on the theology of domination *(Herrschende Theologie)* (Suh 1983:258), leading to the Church's systematic elimination of the subversive memory and praxis of Jesus on the Cross (Suh 1982:249). The corollary was that for Christian churches of the post-Constantinian era adaptation and submission to the existing order was a necessity (Suh 1982:248-49).

This tragedy was constitutive for the Church as such: not only was Constantinianism the "bad beginning" that spoiled Christianity as a religion of rulers (Ahn 1990:115), but it was a "hard habit to break" that pushed Christians toward metaphysics, being separated from the particular and concrete human history (Hauerwas 1991:18-9, Suh 1982:249). Although it started with the mutual connection between the Church and imperial policies, as the ideology of the empire was imposed on the Church's theology, the radical pronouncements of Christian believers were muzzled and held in check (Suh 1981:162-63, Na 1988:138, Kim 1987:256).

Through the above-mentioned forced silence and compromise of the Church, another distortion became interwoven to the point of misrepresenting the original concept of the Kingdom of God (Suh 1982:249-50). To their dismay, these theologians found out that the original apocalyptic expectation, including the radical and total renewal of society through revolution, degenerated into an idea of a temporal kingdom that was apart from human history (Moon 1998:100). It is here that the Church under the Constantinian framework entered into the realm of the Kingdom of God and was deprived of its power to transform history (Ahn 1990:115). Thus, its essence as the historical establishment of God's justice on earth was replaced by the symbol of utopia ("no place"), which would only be possible beyond this world (Suh 1983:131).

On the other hand, from that vantage point, *minjung* theologians have sharpened their argument, ultimately leading to a creative confluence of church and Korean history. To them, the post-Constantinian position of the Church that limited the Kingdom of God to the realm of an other-worldly or next-worldly dimension calls for a kind of responsibility that evokes its historical and sociopolitical significance (Suh 1981:162-63, Kim 1987:256). What must happen is the return to the Kingdom of God that Jesus taught. The coming of the Kingdom of God was at the heart of Jesus's teaching and his ministry was essentially the Kingdom of God movement which was closely linked with the poor and oppressed—namely, the Galilean *minjung* (Ahn 1987:238). In fact, his original intention for the Kingdom had to do with liberation of the *minjung* from suffering reality (Kim 1992:243-44, Suh 1983:356). Thus, they argue that there is no liberation that does not involve justice and social transformation, so that the Kingdom of God Jesus taught should not be the symbol of utopia or an idealized place, but a concrete historical reality where the suffering people are to be liberated (Song 1988:81).

From this understanding, *minjung* theologians propose that being saved does not mean merely going to heaven (Ahn 1990:146), rather it means to be delivered now from the forces of alienation that have enslaved the *minjung* unjustly (Song 1988:81). Here, the deeply ingrained soteriological kingdom motif has given way to a more integral understanding of salvation as fullness of life (Lee 1996:147). It turns salvation of souls as a post-mortem affair into a call to share the divine life—the grace, mercy, love, blessings—with others here in this life (Park 1990:527)—namely, salvation *hic et nunc* (here and now) (Suh 1982:250-51, Kim 2007:74-5).

This enables them to identify the Kingdom of God with the messianic society, where the power of the powerless is found and restored (Suh 1983:133, Ahn 1990:104-5). Under the utopian shell of other-worldliness, it would be a mirage, having no connection with anything that happens on earth and no effect on the day-to-day struggles of the suffering *minjung* (Lee 1996:147-48). Thus, these theologians insist on the realization of the Kingdom of God in this world, which aims at transforming the oppressive social system or political power in the present (Ahn 1990:232)—i.e., the Kingdom's re-incarnation into the concrete life situations of the suffering *minjung* (Park 1990:527, Suh 1983:131).

More in line with this articulation is the idea of the Millennium. By refusing Constantinian Christianity as the *minjung*-less and history-less dystopia, these theologians pay special attention to the concept of the Millennium (Rev. 20:1-7)—namely, establishment of the messianic kingdom on earth (Suh 1982:249-50). It is from this shift of emphasis that the biblical metaphor of the Millennium, which guarantees salvation of the poor, marginalized, and oppressed, turns into the reality of historical achievement (Song 1988:15961, Considine 2015:120). This drives them to contrast the differences between the Kingdom of God and the Messianic Kingdom (i.e., Millennium) (Suh 1983:249). In their thinking, whereas the Kingdom of God is prone to the other world after death by securing salvation of the individual under the ideology of the rulers, the Millennium is rooted in this world by seeking out social justice and transformation through the *minjung's* own struggles (Kim 1987:256, Park 1985:45- 50).[25]

The *minjung* theologians have further elaborated on the following five major differences between the concept of the Kingdom of God and that of the Millennium.

- The Kingdom is a heavenly or ultimate symbol beyond human reach; the Millennium is a historical and semi-ultimate symbol within human reach.

---

[25]This is reminiscent of Jan Amos Komensky's millenarianism or chiliasm. As a pioneer of the Czech Reformation, Komensky (1592-1670) took a vigorous view in defending the theological and practical grounds for the chiliastic hope. While distancing himself from fanatical versions of faith in the millennial kingdom, he was openly advocating "true Chiliasm" as integral to Christianity, which sustained Christians already within earthly history and set it in motion in the direction of the Kingdom of God. He thus understood that reformation of the Church, culture, and society was developed in a down-to-earth way in the chiliastic, eschatological prospective of the coming and already beginning sovereignty of Jesus Christ (Lochman 1980:83).

- The Kingdom appears as the symbol of a resting place where people enter after death; the Millennium is a new living society that people construct together.
- The Kingdom guarantees the individual's salvation; the Millennium offers collective, social salvation.
- The Kingdom presupposes salvation through Jesus' vicarious work; the Millennium presumes salvation by the *minjung* themselves.
- The Kingdom has been used as the ideology of the rulers; the Millennium stands for the hope of the *minjung* (Suh 1981:162-63, Oh 2005:55-6).

Despite their preference for the latter to the former, the emphasis of these theologians is not on the polarity between the Kingdom and the Millennium (Suh 1983:193). Rather, they argue, the stress should fall on its complementary, not contradictory, relation between the two (Lee 1988:14-5, Koyama 1988:145-46). For the latter does not neutralize but rather materializes the former by focusing on the reality of God's salvation in the present (Suh 1976:102, Ahn 1975:108). In other words, the Millennium is to include and encourage, not to exclude and discourage, the Kingdom in the messianic-transformative role (Suh 1983:177). Thus, though with different emphasis, the two concepts need to go together in order to understand better the character of the messianic kingdom on earth that Jesus taught.

The theologians further argue that the idea of the Millennium as the messianic kingdom on earth is congruent with the liberating praxis of *dan*—i.e., the realization of *han*-solved *minjung* and *han*-less society here and now. There is no other way of achieving *han*-less society (i.e., Millennium) that bypasses the *han*-ridden *minjung* but always in and through them. To push further, the *han*-ridden *minjung* is not simply part of the Millennium but the Millennium has become the *han*-ridden *minjung*; it is achieved in and through them (Suh 1981:163). Thus, the Millennium constitutes the "aspiration of the suffering *minjung*" (Kim 2007:74) and envisions a *han*-less society as the realized eschatology by transforming individual and spiritual salvation into historical and political liberation for the *han*-ridden *minjung* (Song 1988:159-61, Considine 2015:120, Ahn 1979:108).

It is from this perspective that the *han*-ridden *minjung* are not considered simply the object of the Kingdom, but rather they are the power to achieve their historical call (Kim 1982:371). With no Millennium apart from the *han*-ridden minjung, they are destined to be the protagonists of their own history in exercising their messianic role to advance the Millennium on earth (Suh 1982:250-51). Thus, the Millennium is the kingdom of '*han*-solved' *minjung* —namely, the '*han*-less' society where freedom, justice, and equality prevail (Kim 2007:74, Park 1990:527, 530).

The notion of the Millennium as the creation of a '*han*-less' society culminates in the idea of the confluence (conjunction) of the biblical tradition and the Korean *minjung* tradition (Suh 1983:66-8, Yi 1996:143-44)—i.e., a critical and creative fusion of biblical stories to Korean history or, re-reading of biblical stories within the framework of Korean history (Suh 1983 237-76). Conversely, it is a radical attempt to incorporate Korean history into Christianity as part of the *minjung* movement (Suh 1983:17-86). To strengthen their critical view, the theologians contend that Jesus' ministry is to be justified as "the liberation of humanity" (Suh 1983:13) and Jesus is to be understood as the model for the revolutionaries in Korea—i.e., as one who is always with the Korean people "as a symbol, or paradigm of *minjung* deliverance," though anonymously so (Yi 1996:143, Lee 2010:146).

Thus, these theologians have boldly argued that there had been the presence of God within Korean history even before Christianity was introduced to Korea (Hyun 1981:54, Camp 2000:167). This means God's redemptive acts are not limited to the Bible but can and must be found in the history of Korean *minjung* (Suh 1983:299). In this light, God's ongoing activities are intertwined with the various *minjung* movements in Korea's history to the point where two currents of tradition are confluent to one, the Millennium or *han*-less society [26] —for the '*han*-ridden'

---

[26] The confluence of these two traditions makes the message of the Gospel more relevant to the Korean context because "the stories of the *minjung* reveal not only their rendering of reality of who they are and what the world is. They also tell about their struggles for peace, justice and integrity as God's people in Korean history. The Bible includes the same kind of stories of God's people, be it Hebrews and Gentiles; how they have tried to understand themselves, the world, and God's acts in their specific historical context" (Park 2008:133).

minjung by the '*han*-ridden' *minjung* (Suh 1982:271, 1983:256, Yi 1996:143-44).

The true significance of the parallels between the *minjung* movement in the Bible and the current Korean *minjung's* context is the liberation tradition that unites the two as a coherent whole, much like two rivers flowing into each other to form one river (Park 2008:209, Moon 1998:115). In fact, liberation events like the Exodus and the Jesus event (his crucifixion and resurrection) prove that there is no gap between the two traditions, but rather they cast "the significance of theological interpretation of liberation for the oppressed, the poor, or the dominated" (Lee 2005).

As such, Korean history, like church history, has embodied the liberation movement of the suffering *minjung* from its inception (Lee 1976:34, Ham 1983:71-2). Just as the Christian *minjung* tradition is deposited in the events of Exodus and Jesus' crucifixion, so is the Korean *minjung* tradition deposited in Korea's history, in how they have struggled for their own liberation (Kim 1981:187, Suh 1981:167). The theologians then describe the *minjung* movement in Korea's history— from the period of the Three Kingdoms (300 CE) up to the recent human rights movement—as evidence of the *minjung's* struggles for historical subjectivity (Suh 1981:169-71).

The key to these movements is the *minjung's* messianic praxis for their own liberation (Suh 1986:158). Here, the *minjung* subjectivity stands out as the authentic communication medium of God's redemptive acts (Suh 1983:177). This means the social reality of suffering *minjung* serves as precondition for God's salvation history or Jesus events (Lee 2005). As the Exodus narrative indicates, before God appears as liberator, the *minjung* have to confront the pharaohs of the world, who had infringed upon their rights and freedom (Moon 1985:6-7, 1987:181-82). That confrontation with oppressors conscientizes them about their suffering reality so that they realize their responsibility to resist and fight back (Moon 1987:185).[27]

---

[27] Yet these theologians are, at the same time, aware of *minjung's* sinfulness (Park 1992:180-202). For example, in the Exodus narrative, the motif of the Hebrew *minjung's* complaining in the wilderness demonstrates that not only Pharaoh but they themselves can be stumbling blocks to their own liberation (Lee 2005).

Alongside the *minjung* subjectivity, God is considered as "an immanent force" who "lives along with *minjung*, is immanent within *minjung*, and is equal to *minjung*" (Suh 1983:79). This creates the idea of God as a "co-suffer of the *minjung*" who considers suffering in human history through injustice and violence as his own (Kim 1982:15, Moon 1987:183). One important aspect here is that God acts justly for the *minjung* liberation by intervening in history (Moon 1987:183), but is not the sole actor; the *minjung* are also offered opportunity to participate in this liberation movement in the context of the Covenant Code between the two (Kim 1986:281, Lee 2005).

This sheds further light on the *minjung* subjectivity that sees the *minjung* not only as the first bearers and transmitters of the liberation tradition, but also as partners with God who continue to form the Jesus event in the Covenant Code (Moon 1987:185, Sye 2001:60-117). In the dialectic between *minjung's* accountability and God's sovereignty, the theologians begin to integrate 'the confluence of two traditions' into the doctrine of synergism—a partnership of *minjung* with God in salvation (Suh 1982:250-51, 1983:78).

In the biblical stories, God sides with the oppressed and fights for them (Moon 1987:183), while in Korean history, the *minjung* are involved in the fight for their liberation, in striving for salvation here and now (Ahn 1982:177-84, Suh 1981:171). Therefore, a confluence of two traditions represents the mission of God—or more specifically, "pro-*minjung* mission in Korea" that takes place in the present historical context (Suh 1983:19, Jung 2012:124). It is from this outlook that the Church's history and the Korean *minjung's* history are not separated (Suh 1982:237-76), but converged in the concept of *Missio Dei*—namely, God's on-going struggle for establishment of his justice and freedom on earth through the *minjung's* active participation as reflecting the doctrine of synergism (Suh 1982:250-51, Küster 2010:1).

To sum up, what Korean *minjung* theologians strive to do is to link the liberation traditions of the *minjung* in the Bible to the Korean *minjung* movement (Lee 2014:60). In this dynamic confluence, the story of biblical *minjung* is no longer the story of the past to Korean *minjung*, who are now suffering here and now (Suh 1982:237-76), but rather is integrated and fused into their own story (Suh 2007:64). Here, the suffering *minjung* in Bible times revisit the suffering *minjung* in the present and it even re-invites the God of the *minjung* who sides with them to the present historical context (Suh 1982:244, Kim 2009:137). Thus, discovery of the biblical *minjung* coincides with discovery of *minjung* today for they are not dead but living; they still speak to, for, and with the Korean *minjung* (Ahn 1987:249).

In this light, the biblical *minjung* story is a long preface to the Korean *minjung's* stories in its liberation tradition (Park 2008:21). The story they are experiencing now is a continuation of the biblical story, which makes it part of their story, leading to the confluence of God and *minjung* in *Missio Dei* (Lee 1988:20-1, Ahn 1999:248). Certain here is that God, who has stood on the side of the biblical *minjung*, still stands on the side of the today's *minjung* (Lee 1998:19, Cone 1975) and as covenant partners of God, the Korean *minjung* are invited to play a messianic role for their own liberation (Suh 1983:116-19, Ahn 1987:25-6). Thus, in Minjung Theology, the doctrine of synergism serves as a critical paradigm for dynamic interplay between God and *minjung* in salvation (Suh 1982:250-51).

New Understanding of the Holy Spirit

It is apparent from the *minjung* theologians' view that the emphasis on *Missio Dei* ("mission of God") is the emphasis on the Holy Spirit (Lee 1988:13). Indeed, there is a connection between the notion of *Missio Dei* and the liberating works of the Holy Spirit. In the dialectic of biblical and Korean *minjung* traditions, their view of God's on-going intrusion into Korea's history requires both socio-historical and pneumatological-synchronic interpretations (Suh 1982:78-9, Kim 1994:134). The former needs to be stressed because it underscores their socio-political responsibility (Kim 2003:75). Here the Jesus event is understood as a historical one in which God's action takes places on behalf of the suffering *minjung*. On the other hand, the latter is necessary to become embroiled in "the Holy Spirit's transforming power and movement for the creation of a new society" (Suh 1983:20-1).

As to the latter, the Holy Spirit is the driving force in actualizing the two *minjung* traditions here and now (Chung 2008:189, Park 2008:21). It is the Spirit who transforms the Jesus event into the *minjung* event as the ultimate liberating phenomenon (Chung 2008:189-90). At this point, the Jesus event is not a once-and-for-all but a recurring historical event, inspired and empowered by the Holy Spirit (Lee 1988:11, 15, Kwon 2010:155-56).

For these theologians who prefer a pneumatological-synchronic interpretation rather than a classical Christological-diachronic one (Suh 1981:163, Chung 2008:190), God's revelation in Jesus Christ is exemplary, while "the Holy Spirit is ascribed the role of the one in whom the *minjung* is imitating Jesus Christ" as a reenactment of the Jesus event (Küster 2010:118). Thus, the *minjung* event in Korea, like that of *Chun, Tae-Il (全泰壹, 1948-1970)*,[28] becomes transparent for the Jesus event where the *minjung* would play the role of Jesus with the Spirit (Kwon 2011:57).

This constitutes the *minjung* pneumatology—namely, a dynamic fusion of the Spirit and the *minjung*. The former is working today in the lives of *minjung* and empowering them to transform the oppression of the present situation (Suh 1983:79, Bretzke 1997:329-30), while the latter participates in the Jesus event for their liberation with the Holy Spirit who inspires them "to become real subjects of their own history" (Suh 1982:79, Kang 1990:84-107). In this dynamic interconnection, the liberating movements of the Korean suffering minjung continue to reemerge with the Spirit here and now (Bretzke 1997:325).

The pneumatological-synchronic perspective also serves to legitimate minjung ecclesiology—namely, "the Church of the Holy Spirit," or "the Church of Minjung" (Park 2008:210). In keeping with Joachim's three successive historical periods, *minjung* theologians hold that just as this age is neither of the Father nor of the Son but of the Holy Spirit, so is the church; it is neither Catholic nor Protestant but the third Church of the Spirit (Suh 1976:124, Lee 2009:79). What is crucial as this third age of the Spirit is to go far beyond the institutionalized church and written scripture (Suh 1981:166-67). It is to emerge as a mysterious and democratic community that is totally liberated from fear, class,

---

[28]Chun, Tae-Il, a sewing machine operator and textile worker, was sympathetic towards the young, assisting his fellow workers in small factories who were paid little and became diseased from extended work hours and their workplaces' dust-filled and polluted environment. He organized fellow workers and finally immolated himself in protest against the structures that created such miserable situations. As he set fire to himself on November 13, 1970, he cried out, "We are not machines!" His suicide became a touchstone for the Korean *minjung* (labour) movement (Kwon 2011:57).

monopolizing of wealth, and domination by the unjust ruler (Suh 1983:58). By identifying the *minjung* with the spiritual men of the third age, they argue that today is the age of *minjung* (Suh 1976:132, 1982:253, Moltmann 1981:205). "The third age of [Spirit] is therefore of, by, and for the *minjung*" (Lee 1990:363, Suh 1976:58-9).

Understood this way, the stress falls on the liberating works of the Holy Spirit rather than old dogmas that focus only on the Father and the Son (Kim 2009:33). This is why the minjung church is called a third model "beyond the Catholic sacramental and the Protestant proclamation models of church" (Min 1996:30, Suh 1981:167). To these theologians, the Church is not to be "an institution, a fixed form, a building;" rather it is to be "an event, the event of the encounter between the Spirit and the minjung" (Min 1996:30). At this point, they are convinced that the minjung church is the most appropriate to the third age of the Spirit in which the minjung redeem themselves with the Spirit's outpouring (Lee 1988:13, Park 2008:211).

Not surprising then is the fact that *minjung* theologians give more credence to pneumatology than to Christology (Suh 1983:161-64). To them, as the Bible reveals it's the Holy Spirit who empowers the Christian Church (the Pentecost) (Ahn 1987:220-21) and now is the time of the Spirit who is shown to be Christ's successor (Suh 1981:164), God as the Spirit is thus more relevant than God as the Son (Lee 1988:13).

However, this Spirit-centred ecclesiology is interrupted when the West's orthodox theology posits an undue emphasis on Christology (Suh 1983:163). In their thinking, the most fundamental error of this classical Christology is its justification of dualism—i.e., giving priority to the transcendent, sacred, and divine over the immanent, secular, and human (Ahn 1984:148-49). Despite the fact that both church and secular history are the warp-and-woof of history, in traditional Christology, God's salvation history is limited merely to church history (Suh 1983:131-32, Lee 1990:187-88). As a result, God's saving realm is confined to the Church, excluding and relegating world history (Suh 1983:58).

To *minjung* theologians, what makes it even worse is that in this dualistic understanding, God as the Spirit loses its significance (Koo 2007:177), there being no room for the Spirit as freedom who keeps on engaging in human history (Suh 1983:61-2). Instead, a lopsided other-worldliness and individualistic pietism occupy a central place in order to suit its dogmatic claims and prejudices (Park 1985:56). In this light, the this-worldly God as the Spirit is eventually superseded by the other-worldly God as the Son (Suh 1983:162).

For this reason, these theologians emphasize the necessity of restoring pneumatology which makes Christianity truly universal and inclusive (Lee 1988:13). By refusing God's salvific activity to be reducible simply to the mission of the institutionalized church (Song 1984:493), they hold that it must embrace the world and society as the sphere of the Holy Spirit's work (Suh 1983:58). For the movement of the Spirit is itself ecumenical (Kim 2016:132-38) to the point of embracing both Christianity and the secular world (Moltmann 1992, Moon 1998:113).[29]

Thus, every event in the secular world turns into "the language of God" (Suh 1983:51), and any act that implies liberation of the powerless has a new meaning in Korean Minjung Theology (Bretzke 1997:329-30). It is from this perspective that these theologians' emphasis on all events of liberation as a point of reference to God's mission acquires legitimacy (Suh 1983:58). Their pneumatological-synchronic perspective tells that the Holy Spirit transcends both sacred and secular histories. Yet, on the other hand, it is the Holy Spirit who creates these histories by carrying out the works of justice and liberation (Suh 2007:61, Kim 2008:179). To put it differently, there is anteriority of the Spirit to both histories, but the pneumatological-synchronic perspective points to the power of the Spirit which submits two histories to the liberating concept of *Mission Dei*:

> Prior to the human and ecclesial mission in the world, God has already been engaged in God's own mission of liberating the oppressed with a preferential love . . . This liberating *Missio Dei* undercuts all the traditional dualism including that of church and society to the extent that God's mission is not the monopoly of the Christian churches. In this regard, [it] highlights the role of the Holy Spirit as the universal, eschatological, and liberating presence of God beyond the borders of Christian history. The Spirit is at work wherever and whenever selfishness is

---

[29] Ahn, Byung-Mu once said that there is no border between Christians and non-Christians when both suffer. He even further insisted that Jesus could not be a Messiah for the whole world if he was crucified only for Christians (Balasundaram 1995:61).

transcended and the existing order is eschatologically renewed (Min 1996:28-9).

To summarize, emboldened by the Spirit's liberating and ecumenical power, *minjung* theologians venture to claim that, in God's salvation-history, there is the dynamic unification of God as the Spirit and *minjung* as the Spirit-filled Christians (Suh 1976:129-30). To them, the Spirit enables the oppressed *minjung* to fight for their own liberation against unjust reality. In that light, "God as *das ganz Andere* (the Wholly Other)"[30] in the third person pales into insignificance against "God-as-for-us," who directly speaks and acts in the first person for and with the suffering *minjung*. The *minjung* theologians have integrated such a notion of God as freedom and liberation into the praxis of *minjung*, resulting in the Koreanized *minjung* pneumatology—namely, a dynamic unity between the Spirit and the *minjung*.

In pneumatological-synchronic perspective, these theologians have attempted to wed together the ecumenical movement of the Spirit with the struggle for *minjung's* liberation in the Korean context. This is fully articulated in the idea of the liberating *Missio Dei*, which unites church and secular histories as the *minjung* movement in the Spirit. The Jesus event is the culmination of this liberating *Missio Dei* as the point of reference for both the Church and secular movements.

Thus, they argue that the liberating presence of the Holy Spirit makes the Jesus event not as a unique revelatory event but as a reiterating event throughout history (Ahn 1990:104, Kim 2009:34). Here, "Jesus continues to suffer, die and rise again in his people. The Holy Spirit has been poured out upon all creation even before the arrival of Christian missionary" (Min 1996:29). Indeed, they find the liberating Spirit, who drives ecumenism, where two histories come together as tributaries and form a river (Kim 2007:8). In short, these theologians find the Spirit already there with the *minjung*: in the beginning was the Spirit and the Spirit was with the *minjung* and the *minjung* was the Spirit.

---

[30]This term was first coined by Rudolf Otto then developed by the well-known contemporary Catholic theologian Walter Kasper in his understanding of the doctrine of revelation (Kasper 2008:164 quoted by Huhtanen 2016:66).

Distinctive Characteristics of Korean Minjung Theology

Minjung theologians have contextualized their theological concerns into the Korean context from a *minjung* -centred perspective. In this way, Korean Minjung Theology is part of doing theology, its fundamental concern being for liberation of the suffering *minjung*. This manifests in three distinctive characteristics—a theology of *minjung* (民衆; common people), a theology of *han* (恨; unresolved bitterness), and a theology of *Hyun-Jang* (現場; *Sitz-im-Leben* of the *minjung*).

All three contribute to a new understanding of Minjung Theology—namely, that of the Bible, of church and Korean history, and of the Holy Spirit. In brief, the theology of *minjung* has found the *minjung* as the hermeneutical key to understanding the Bible and history; the theology of *han* has emphasized the *han*-ridden *minjung* as the subject of church and Korean history through the praxis of *dan*; and the theology of *Hyun-Jang* (as the meeting place of Jesus and *minjung*) has redeemed the role of the Holy Spirit who not only initiates but reiterates the *minjung* event in history. However, there are three other distinctive characteristics of Minjung Theology that merit special attention—*minjung*-Christology, *minjung* -soteriology, and *minjung*-biblical hermeneutics.

Minjung-Christology

minjung -Christology constructs a radical new Christology—namely, *minjung*-Messianism, which emphasizes the messianic character of *minjung* (Suh 1983:51, 53, Ahn 1987:32-3). By recognizing sin as political and economic inconsistencies, *minjung* theologians regard the plural mass of the *minjung* (not Jesus individually) as "the lamb of God" who carries the sin of the world (John 1:29) (Ahn 1987:19, 96, 105). Here, like Jesus, the *minjung* play a messianic role to take away the sin of the world, which is suffering (Ahn 1975:17, 50). "They are hungry because of others; they are thirsty instead of others, [but] they save the world from its own suffering" (Choi 2008:207).

This radical outlook leads these theologians to claim "the subversive interpretation of the Good Samaritan story" (Luke 10:25-37) (Choi

2008:207). *Minjung*-Christology answers differently the question, "Who is the Saviour in this story?" (Hwang 2013:215). Unlike the traditional western interpretation, which says it's the Good Samaritan, *minjung* theologians say the messianic role goes to the robbed man (Suh 1983:180). In their thinking, it is this wounded one who takes the initiative through his suffering. In other words, the *han* of the person who was attacked and beaten by the robbers encourages the Samaritan to act in love (Choi 2008:207). It's the cry of his suffering that touched the Samaritan's heart to respond (Ahn 1987:117-18). Thus, they continue, it's none other than the calling of Jesus to participate in God's messianic mission (Lee 1996:234). In this way, the robbed man's burden, pain, and suffering coincide with "the meaning of Jesus' suffering, cross, and death" (Choi 2008:207). It is from this notion that they create the distinctive concept of *minjung* -Christology—that is, the one who plays the role of the Saviour is but "the person is who attacked by the robbers" (Suh 1983:107).

Korean poet Kim, Chi-Ha's play, "The Golden-Crowned Jesus," is another example that crystallizes this *minjung*-Messianism. In the play, Jesus is imprisoned in a concrete statue inside the church, and he asks a beggar to set him free and to remove the golden crown from his head. The dialogue carried out is as follows:

> *Beggar*: What can be done to free you, Jesus? Make you live again so that you can come to us?
> *Jesus*: My power is not enough. People like you must help to liberate me. Those you seek only the comforts, wealth, honour, and power of this world, who wish entry to the kingdom of heaven for themselves only and ignore the poor and less fortunate, cannot give me life again . . . Only those, though very poor and suffering like yourself. . ., can give me life again.
> *Beggar*: Jesus, as you can see, I am helpless. I cannot even take care of myself. Howe (sic) can I help you?
> *Jesus*: It is for that exact reason that you can help me. You are the only one who can do it. It is your wisdom, your generous spirit, and, even more, your courageous resistance against injustice that makes all this possible. Come closer, come closer and liberate now my body as you freed my lips. Remove this

prison of cement... The crown of gold is merely the insignia of those ignorant and corrupt people who value only displays of external pomp and showy decoration (Kim 1978:24).

Here, when "seen from the angle of the forsaken, naked, and castigated *minjung*," Jesus is no longer Christ of the Church with his golden crown (Chung 2009:190-91). Rather, the crown is a symbol of God forsaken, thus the outcry for salvation (Moltmann 1973:126-53): "Take it please! For too long a time have I been imprisoned in this cement. Eventually, you have come and made me open my mouth. You have saved me" (Ahn 1995:163-64). At its core, the suffering *minjung* become the liberators who hear Jesus' crying for salvation and free him from the burden of the crown that was imposed on him by the privileged and powerful (Orevillo-Montenegro 2006:37).

To summarize, *minjung*-Christology is not concerned about reproducing a classical Christology in an individualistic-forensic sense, but rather about actualizing and deepening Jesus in solidarity with the *minjung* through suffering and struggle (Chung 2008:265). In this understanding the suffering *minjung* are the Messiah who could liberate themselves (Choi 2008:207). Yet in a Christology of a *minjung*-Jesus, he is not replaced by the *minjung*; rather it emphasizes both Jesus' presence among the suffering people and *minjung's* liberating act with Jesus (Chung 2008:266). Thus, an authentically *minjung* -Christology recapitulates the dialectic of *minjung* -Messiah—" *minjung* cannot exist without God, and God cannot exist without *minjung*" (Choi 2008:207).

Minjung-Soteriology

Minjung-Soteriology is inextricably linked with *minjung*-Christology. Indeed, the liberating character of *minjung*-Messianism points to salvation of the suffering *minjung* (Suh 1981:166)[31]—or more specifically, the connection of *minjung*-Messianism and *minjung*-

---

[31]It is noteworthy to say that here the term "salvation" is in line with the definition suggested by Belgian Roman Catholic theologian Edward Schillebeeckx (1914-2009), who proposes moments of fragmentary salvation that are God's incomplete but realized works of healing, liberating, forgiving, and reconciling in this world that will not come to fulfillment until the eschaton (Schillebeeckx 1981:646-842).

soteriology has resonance in the dialectic of *han* and *dan* (Kim 1989:1007, 1014). In this dynamic correlation, *minjung* is justified as the Messiah who could bring their own salvation by resolving their *han* through *dan* (Ahn 1987:98-9, Suh 1983:309-10). As the praxis of *dan* involves both personal and social dimensions (Park 1987:121), the concept of *minjung* -soteriology must deal with both personal salvation and social transformation as a meaningful and coherent whole (Suh 1983:81). The central question about *minjung*-soteriology is then two-fold—"What is the concept of sin and salvation at the personal level?" and "What is the relationship between salvation and social justice at the social level?"

The idea of "the conscious absence of sin" as a distinctive characteristic is essential to understanding the salvation theme in Minjung Theology (Chang 2007:206). For salvation, of greater concern to *minjung* theologians is *han* rather than sin—"One must be saved not from personal sin, but from the collective *han* stemming from social injustice" (Chang 2007:206). Criticizing the prevalent Protestant emphasis on sin, they contend that sin is the language of the oppressor, while *han* is the language of the oppressed (Hwang 2013:220); that is, the former commits sin while the latter suffers from the sin committed (Park 1993:69). Although both are related to each other, the subject of sin and *han* are separated (Hwang 2013:220). In light of this distinction, "Sin is of the sinners and *han* is of the sinned-against" (Park 2004:115); hence, salvation is for the sinner and healing or liberation for the sinned-against (Park 2008:141).

This distinction is very crucial in understanding these theologians' view of salvation. To them, the problem of sin is not sin itself but the social conditions that cause one to sin (Suh 1983:243-34). And the condition of the *minjung* as the sinned-against has to do with certain forms of oppression as social sin which produces the *minjung's* collective *han* (Oh 2005:55). In short, social sin is the great perpetrator of the *minjung's han*. Based on this construal, they give the idea of *dan* a soteriological meaning (Kim 1981:24). Since the Korean *minjung* are in dire need of releasing their collective *han*, which is caused by both personal and social sins, the praxis of *dan* appears as the Church's mission for the salvation of the *minjung* and their liberation from every oppressive system (Suh 1983:101, Park 2008:141).

In *minjung*-soteriology, the praxis of *dan*, therefore, suggests that action for justice and social transformation are at the heart of salvation (Kim 1989:1005-1016). From this understanding, the traditional, exclusively soul-saving approach to soteriology is no longer attractive (Küster 2010:223, Bacote 2002:99). Rather these theologians see salvation as both an individual-spiritual and a concrete social-structural process. Thus, "Any personal salvation is but a [key] constituent element in social salvation" (Kang 1980:214)

The notion of salvation as both personal and social transformation affirms that *dan* ultimately liberates *han*, thus liberating the *minjung* (the people of *han*) from their *han*-ridden society (Suh 1983:166, Lee 1994:154). This means, through this dual process, the *minjung* can cut off the cycle of oppression and restore justice and freedom (Kim 1982:384). Thus, *minjung* theologians continue to insist that salvation for the *minjung* can only be achieved through their struggle for justice (*dan*) against the power of injustice *(han)* (Chang 2007:212-13, Park 1987:121). It leaves open the possibility of establishment of a *han*-less society as the historical realization of the Kingdom of God (Moon 1985:173-74).

To sum up, in *minjung*-soteriology, salvation for the *minjung* is closely linked with personal and social transformation (Ahn 1982:177-84). It reiterates the idea of the dialectic of *han* and *dan* because *dan* is a practice to overcome both personal and collective *han* of the *minjung*, stemming from injustice and oppression of the structure (Suh 1982:274). Indeed, "Through *dan*, the *minjung* can invade *han*" (Hwang 203:130) and thus transform their *han*-ridden society into a *han*-less society (Lee 1994:154, Oh 2005:57). What *dan* ultimately pursues is the historical realization of a *han*-less society—a new social reality based on justice and freedom—as the foundation of the Kingdom of God (Lee 2008:241, Moon 1985:173-74)

Minjung-Biblical Hermeneutics

Minjung Theology is proposing a new paradigm of biblical interpretation—the so-called *minjung*-biblical hermeneutics (Knitter 1995:80). By emphasizing the epistemological privilege of the *minjung* in its hermeneutics (Park 1995:196), this methodology approaches the Bible from the *minjung's* perspective (Ahn 1983). Due to its primary concern for the sociological context or *Sitz-im-Leben* of the scriptural text, it is often called a "sociological biblical interpretation" (Kim 1995:12). This *minjung*-centred outlook has a two-fold aspect: it enables *minjung* theologians not only to read the Bible sociologically, but also interpret Korean traditions of *minjung* theologically (Suh 1983:49-55, Na 1988:141). It is apparent from their interpretation that the core of the Bible is the "liberating movement"—namely, the history of the liberation of the suffering *minjung* (Ahn 1990:78). In this sense, *minjung*-biblical hermeneutics serves as the connecting thread that unites the Bible's social-political dimensions and the Korean *minjung's* contemporary historical situation (Suh 1983:57-8, Lee 1993:106).

These theologians call their special attention to the Exodus and Jesus' crucifixion event as a testimonies of liberation (Suh 1983:164, Lee 2005:69). To them, the Exodus event represents the history of the Hebrews' liberation from economic exploitation and political oppression (Kim 1982:29-57, Gottwald 1980:223). It was the oppression and injustice of the Egyptians that galvanized them to take action to escape (under Moses' leadership) Egypt's cruel and merciless bondage (Suh 1983:158). Here, Exodus is read as "a political revolution which took place in a socioeconomic context" (Moon 1995:240, Kim 2008:123). Thus, they conclude that the salvation of Israel from Egypt was a political (not a spiritual) liberation primarily rooted in history and politics (Suh 1983:235, Ahn 1990:78).

In the same way, they interpret Jesus' crucifixion as a political execution committed by political injustice (Suh 1983:317-18). He was crucified by the ruling class because of his political resistance for the human rights of the *minjung* of his time (Suh 1983:54, 191). This means for them, the crucifixion was a political event for the liberation of the *minjung* (Suh 1981:161). It is from this view that these theologians have further elaborated the event of the Cross into the event of *minjung* today (Ahn 1987:26). In their thinking, since Jesus is a personification or symbol of the *minjung* (Suh 1983:54), his death and resurrection coincide with the death and resurrection of the *minjung* (Ahn 1990:99) –i.e., Jesus' death and resurrection are not those of an individual but of collective *minjung*, taking place here and now (Ahn 1975:16-7, 1987:25-6, 1990:99).

In short, it is apparent from *minjung*-biblical hermeneutics that "theological interpretation ought to start from the social context of the *minjung* and a commitment to their liberation" (Suh 1995:12, Suh 1981:157-58). Shifting their hermeneutical eye to the context of *minjung*, these theologians reinterpret the biblical events—from Exodus to the Cross event—not as a unique once-and-for-all event but as "a repetitive suffering and liberating event of *minjung* throughout history" (Ahn 1990:104, 284, Kim 2008:125, Suh 1981:158).

Chapter Summary:
Korean Minjung Theology as a New Radical Reformation in the Making

Korean Minjung Theology was formulated in the 1970s as a protest against both conservative evangelical theologies and the unjust structural system in Korea (Kim 2007:48). To continue its critical view, Minjung Theology began to look anew at the suffering reality of the Korean *minjung*—"the locked-out, the exploited, the downtrodden, and the have-nots" (Louie 2005:383)—from which it derives its essence. "[Minjung] Theology is of practical use only in the measure in which it is practiced by the [*minjung* themselves]; otherwise it remains a merely intellectual activity indulged in by comfortable academics" (Kalilombe 2006:443).

Historically, development of Minjung Theology can be seen in three phases and foci. The first generation in the 1970s paid more attention to "the *minjung* in theological and biblical terms" (Lee 2015:159); they considered their task as witnessing the *minjung* based on their experience and thus a theology of witness (Choi 2008:213, Kim 1993:22). The second generation in the 1980s envisioned *minjung* as both a religious and a socio-political concept, trying to theorize the social movement of Christianity from a Marxist position (Kim 2009:21); this enabled them to advocate "the theology of transformation/revolution" (Kim and Lee 2002:165). The third generation in the 1990s and forward took as its mission to integrate the national horizon of Minjung Theology into the whole global horizon (Choi 2008:205). Acknowledging the phenomenon of globalization, this younger generation has proposed non-dialectical, non-dualistic, and relational methods and approaches as the central theological topics (Lee 2015:159-60).

Methodologically, Minjung Theology is "inductive and not deductive, descriptive and not normative, storytelling and not system building, biographical and not theological construction, and it is open to dialogue and not closed and final as in dogma and fundamentalism." This results in "not a theology of the Word, but a theology about the world and for the world. It is to change the world, and not to explain the world" (Suh 2010 xiv). Furthermore, by choosing the biblical *minjung* as the text and the Korean minjung movement as the context, it attempts to remake "a truly contextual and indigenous Korean theology" (Son 2000:50). It is from this radical approach that Minjung Theology has a two-fold emphasis—to be faithful to the contemporary social and political realities on one hand and to the Christian faith as attested in the Bible on the other (Suh 2010: xiv).

Theologically, the discovery of *minjung* in both biblical and Korean *minjung* traditions opens a new perspective for Minjung Theology. In the dialectic of *han* and *dan,* the *minjung* of Minjung Theology appear as the people of *han*, victimized by economic exploitation and political oppression throughout Korea's history (Suh 1983:64). This leads to the task of Minjung Theology as the ministry of *dan—i.e.,* the release of the *minjung's han* (Suh 1981 64-5, Moon 1998:85). In so doing, it is to articulate the subject-hood of *minjung* in both history and theology, epitomized by the concept of *minjung* Christology and *minjung* soteriology (Kwon 2011:67).

All this proves that Minjung Theology is to be understood not as *the* Korean theology but as *a* Korean theology in the making (Park 1984:1), holding a tension between the old and new frame of reference (Chung 2007:1). This means Minjung Theology of the 1970s and 1980s needs to revisit the new situation and the new *minjung*, which is the post-colonial *minjung* who are certainly politically oppressed, economically exploited, and culturally alienated by the impact of the global and post-modern situation (Kim and Lee 2002:175). Here, a Korean Minjung Theology is being constructive as part of a new Radical Reformation which aims at reinventing and transforming itself into the *minjung's* new reality here and now (Küster 2010:148-49).

Chapter 8
Profiles of Four Key Korean Minjung Theologians

Korean Minjung Theology, as a doing theology, aims at self-reinventing and self-transforming; that is, it contains its challenge from within as it approaches and struggles with a new situation. This results in a paradigm shift—from the political and populist *minjung* frame of reference in the 1970s and 1980s towards a "spiritual and multi-religious *minjung*" frame of reference in the 1990s and onwards (Chung 2007:1). Further, such shift of reference contains the socio-political reality of *minjung* under economic globalization. In this sense, the Minjung Theology of the past is a gateway to that of the future; and studying that previous generation leads to identifying the differences and tensions between *minjung* and theology, between *minjung* and minjung theologians; and between the past and present generations.

Thus, is the rationale for taking a close look at the four prominent forerunners of Minjung Theology who initiated it using their own distinctive methodologies. These four devoted themselves to bringing about *dan* in the *han* of the *minjung* both critically and creatively and, in so doing, attempted to present Minjung Theology more as public theology[1] than as church theology (Kwon 2004:56). In this light, they could stand as the "Radical Reformers" who had dreamed of a new Reformation in Korea for, by, and of the *minjung*. The four include: Suh, Nam-Dong (1918-1984); Ahn, Byung-Mu (1922-1996); Kim, Yong-Bock

---

[1]Public theology here refers to a "theological articulation of the rationale for giving voice to marginalized groups and promoting socio-political change" (Kim 2008:10). For more details on this matter, see Bacote (2005:11), Stackhouse (1997:165-179), and Thiemann (1991).

(1938-); and Hyun, Young-Hak (1921-2004), whose lives and theology merit serious attention.[2]

Suh, Nam-Dong (徐南同; 1918-1984)

Biographical Sketch

Suh, Nam-Dong was born into a well-to-do family in Jaun-do (慈恩島), a small island about 40 kilometers northwest of Mokpo (木浦) in the province South *Chulla* (Küster 2010:79). When a fifth-grader, he moved to *Mokpo*, where he first encountered Christianity. After finishing middle and high school in *Chun-Ju* (全州), the provincial capital of North *Chulla*, he went to Doshisha University in Kyoto, Japan, in 1936 to study theology. Earning his BA degree in theology, he returned to Korea in 1941 (Küster 2010:79), taught one year at the *Pyongyang Johan Theological Seminary*, and then pastored three different congregations (Küster 2010:79). Thanks to his undiminished enthusiasm for learning, Suh was extremely well-read in the theological books (both domestic and international). In 1952, became a professor at Hanguk Theological Seminary, which had staked out a progressive position (Küster 2010:79).

In 1951, Hanguk allowed Suh to go to Canada to further his studies at Toronto University's Victoria Seminary (Lee 1990:179, Küster 2010:79). This experience fueled his theology afresh as well as earned him a Th.M degree. Returning to Korea in 1961, he joined the faculty of Theology of Yonsei University, where he began introducing western theology's general trends into Korea's theological society, earning him the nickname, "the antenna of the Korean theological circle" (Chung 2007:7, Küster 2010:79). Although Suh's passion and expectations about theological study were on another level, he had shown no noticeable interest in socio-political issues until the Chun, Tae-Il event in 1970 (Kim 1992:164). This turned his relatively lukewarm response on its head and galvanized him to carefully but actively participate in anti-

---

[2]These four minjung theologians' biographical sketches and theological perspectives are owed primarily to Küster's summary of them (2010:59-102).

government protest (Chang 2015:105). Then in 1973, together with a group of Christian dissidents, he played a leading role in developing "The 1973 Theological Declaration of Korean Christians," the first public statement that defined theologically Christian protest as a Christian duty (Chang 2015:105), which reads, in part,

> The present dictatorship in Korea is destroying rule by Law and persuasion. . . . Our position is that no one is above the law except God. . . . If anyone poses himself above the law and betrays the divine mandate for justice, he is in rebellion against God. The present regime is destroying freedom of religion... (UCLA Archival Collection on Democracy and Unification in Korea, Box 08-01, folder 1973).

This declaration served as a prelude to Minjung Theology, with Suh spearheading its position that would uphold democracy and human rights. While his 1975 article titled, "Jesus, Church History and Korean Church," marked the beginning of his minjung theology (Suh 1983:29), it was his participation in the World Council of Churches (WCC) at Nairobi that same year which would escalate Minjung Theology into full-blown development (Chae 1994:40). At this ecumenical meeting, he was introduced to Europe's political theology, to South America's liberation theology, and to the USA's Black theology. These 'introductions' triggered him to rethink and reapply *minjung* poet Kim, Ji-Ha's idea of *han* and *dan* to Minjung Theology (Küster 2010:81). Such explains Suh's theological affinity with Kim's, which he well described in his dictum on the "unity of God and revolution" (Küster 2010:82). Indeed, by incorporating ecumenical discussions into the specific Korean situation, he established his own theological foundations based on the *minjung's* struggles and hopes (Küster 2010:82).

All this influenced Suh to become an acting intellectual. Time and again, he played a leading role in waging Christian protests for democracy and human rights—to the extent that he was discharged from his academic position under both the National Security Law and the Anti-Communist Law (Chang 2007:220). Repeated imprisonments and releases making it impossible to return to the university, Suh took the job of director of the Mission Education Centre (Küster 2010:79). Ironically, this 'underground period' helped crystallize his minjung theology—not only the key concept of his theology (i.e., "confluence of two stories" and "the priest of *han*"), but also more specified theological methodologies. In this way, he continued to characterize uniquely his minjung theology, emphasizing "the participation of the *minjung* in God's works of salvation" (Küster 2010:85), as epitomized by his *minjung* messianism, which defined the *minjung* as the subject of history appointed by God (Jung 2018:108).

Due to the chronic after-effects of torture and imprisonments Suh was subjected to a markedly shortened life. He died on July 19, 1984 (Küster 2010:85). Although it had only been for nine years that he had 'take off his coat' to Minjung Theology, nevertheless over that brief time, he left an indelible imprint on the next generation of minjung theologians. The immediate task was to do theology in the current Korean context—to discern what God was doing in and through the *minjung* and anticipating the liberating *Missio Dei* in Korean history for the sake of the suffering *minjung* (Suh 1982:239).

Theological Perspective

From Western to Anti-Western Theology

Suh, as one of the two pillars of Minjung Theology along with Ahn, Byung-Mu (安炳茂),[3] had developed his distinctive theology in a progressive and synchronic way—from inside the Church to outside the Church (Moon 1998:44). Following his theological training in Japan under the strong domination of liberalism (Suh 1976:7, Chae 1994:30-1), he broadened his spectrum, which would be characterized by these four periods on his theological journey—(1) existential theology in the 1950s, (2) secular theology in the 1960s, (3) scientific theology between the late 1960s and early 1970s, and (4) Minjung Theology as political theology after the early 1970s (Park 1991:182).

<u>First period.</u> Regarding existential theology, Suh took seriously the theme of personal subjectivism (along with the idea of the here and now)

---

[3]In this regard, Suh is often considered "the systematic alter ego of the exegetically oriented Ahn" (Küster 2010:79).

as being the proper way to understand the concrete life situations of the people. Thus, he had no hesitation confessing his theological heritage coming from Paul Tillich and Rudolph Bultmann (Suh 1976:181-87, Moon 1998:47-9). Yet those Westernized scales already began to fall from his eyes when influenced (from the 1940s) by Ham, Suk-Hon (1901-1989), the "Korean Gandhi" (Chae 1994:31-2). Especially, Ham's interpretation of Korea's history as one of the suffering "Ci-al" (an independent *minjung*; literally means "the seed"), had widened his concerns ranging from existential individualism to the social condition of human living, particularly embodied in the Korea suffering *minjung* (Suh 1983:49).

Second period. Secular theology encouraged Suh to develop the idea of the so-called Jesus who came to us as an "incarnated-suffering neighbor" (Suh 1976:65-77, 1984:552). Taking Bonhoeffer's question "Who is Jesus for us today?" as the meaningful text,[4] he was committed to exploring the significance of the Korean context, which could encounter the suffering Christ who worked among the poor and oppressed *minjung* in their real-life situations (Suh 1983:8). For him, the present Christ within the life of *minjung* and his self-identification with the suffering *minjung* were not different. This attempt culminated in his interpretation of the parable of the Good Samaritan (Lk. 10:29-37).

Here, Suh reshuffled the traditional interpretation by identifying Jesus Christ with "the wounded person on the road," not with the Good Samaritan (Suh 1983:107). To him, Jesus is to be understood as the crying victim among, yet beyond, a helping hand for the suffering *minjung*. In other words, the present Jesus is no other than the suffering neighbours who are beaten and stripped by the unjust attackers today.

> The moaning (Han) of the person, who was attacked, deprived of his money, beaten by the robbers and almost dead, is the calling of Christ to passers-by. One's attitude to the moaning person is exactly his or her attitude to Christ. On the response and action to the moaning, a latent humanity within a human

---

[4]Pointing out the historical responsibility of Christians for Auschwitz, Metz, in his essay, writes a quotation by Soren Kierkegaard: "In order to experience and understand what it means to be a Christian, it is always necessary to recognize a definitive historical situation" (Metz 1984:26).

being either awakens or disappears. Therefore, on this moaning, the crossroads between Salvation and Damnation exists (Suh 1983:107).

On the other hand, this is a re-contextualization of Bonhoeffer's intriguing question from the perspective of the suffering *minjung*—namely, "What does Jesus mean for the poor and oppressed Korean *minjung* today?" (Moon 1985:48-50) In this sense, the core of Suh's secular theology relies on the "re-mythologization" of "the holy one in the secular one" (Ro 2000:50) –namely, the "incarnated suffering" Jesus in the earthly neighbours who need help (Kim 1984:490-91).

This served Suh as a stepping stone to a more distinctively Korean way of theologizing on the socio-political orientation. For his secular theology had its root in the teaching of *Donghak* ("東學", "Eastern Learning"), the religion of the Korean *minjung* (Moon 1998:51). In fact, his understanding of Jesus as a suffering neighbor was consonant with *Donghak*'s doctrine of *In-Nae-Cheon* (人乃天, humanity is Heaven)— i.e., the belief that humanity is the bearer of the divine and thus that human beings are God in disguise.[5] This identification of Jesus and *minjung* came to Suh not only with a faith principle, but also with a political and ideological statement (Suh 1976:227, 1983:168), emphasizing an ethos of equality between human beings and human beings, and between human beings and the divine (Suh 1983:166).

Third period. Scientific theology fascinated Suh between 1969 and 1974. Especially, the idea of the "Omega Point Theory" of Teilhard de

---

[5]In this sense, it is reminiscent of the Apostle Paul's claim, "Christ in me" (Gal. 2:20, Phil. 1:21). Paul seemed to be aware that all his life activities were the works of Christ, who was once revealed "in me" and now "lives in me," in order that human life is at the same time divine. This constituted the unity of the human and the divine. From that vantage point, it can be further said that, when Jesus was incarnate divine-human and called himself the son of man, he was aware of himself as a divine being (Yagi 1987:127).

Chardin (1881-1955)[6] caught his attention (Suh 1983:49). During this period, he attempted to build a new synthesis of religion and science—i.e., of biblical truth and scientific methodology (Moon 1998:51), which led to a significant turn in his theological perspective—from the Church to nature (Moon 1998:44). Emboldened by this scientific/religious concept, he tried to expand his theological emphasis into the field of cosmology (Chae 1994:32-4).

This fueled Suh's strong criticism of Westernized Christianity, which reduced God's revelation to historical events only, and thus failed to recognize Christ in the realm of cosmos (Suh 1972:95-6). To be sure, his new fusion of science and religion had a two-fold aspect. First, it challenged the traditional idea of placing revelation in God's sole property; and second, it propounded the methodology of natural theology as a new pathway of human consciousness toward spirit, culture, and history (Kim 1984:147-151). Thus, knowledge of God does not need to begin only in God's historical revelation in Jesus Christ. It was from this understanding that Suh made preparation to expand his theological perspective into the history of the whole world, having no separate boundary between Church and society—i.e., between sacred and secular (Suh 1976:492). In his thinking, God is not an object of religion but really the Lord of the world.

<u>Fourth period.</u> After the early 1970s, the theology of contextualization became Suh's theological motto under the banner of Minjung Theology (Suh 1976:9). The advent of liberation theology of Latin America and Black theology of North America spurred this shift (Moon 1998:64). By showing sympathy with a theology of social change, he participated in the conference of the World Council of Churches (WCC) at Nairobi in 1975, which was his Road to Damascus (Kim

---

[6]Even if the "Omega Point Theory" is a physical one derived from scientific materialism rather than revelation, it becomes "a model for an omnipresent, omniscient, omnipotent, evolving personal God who is both transcendent to space time and immanent in it" (Tipler 1989:217-53). The term was popularized by the French Jesuit priest Pierre Teilhard de Chardin (1881-1955) (Castillo 2012:393-5). In his book, "Activation of Energy," he articulated that the "Omega point" is "the centre, at once one and complex, in which, bound together by the person of Christ, may be seen enclosed one within the other (one might say) three progressively deeper centres: on the outside, the immanent ('natural') apex of the humano-cosmic cone; further in, at the middle, the immanent ('supernatural') apex of the 'ecclesial' or Christic cone; and finally, at the innermost heart, the transcendent, triune, and divine centre: The complete Pleroma coming together under the mediating action of Christ-Omega" (Chardin 1978:9).

1984:523). From then on, Suh's theology focused on the present predicament of the suffering people in Korea under the dictatorship of President Park, a Korean pharaoh. This "theological conversion" enabled him to become actively involved in the socio-political struggles of the suffering Korean *minjung* (Suh 1983:81, Kim 1984:488-90). To him, theology should be one of urging the Church and every Christian to wield the sword of truth and justice directly at the various cycles of violence and injustice where exploitation and oppression are prevalent (Kim 1984:490).

More specifically, it must bring forth true *metanoia* not only as a cognitive change, but also as a socio-economic and political turning to God's justice (Park 1993:90). In this sense, Suh saw Minjung Theology as "the most suitable one in the Korean context and for Korea's churches" (Suh 1976:9). By taking the *han*-ridden society as the point of departure for his theological reflection, he emphasized liberation of the oppressed *minjung* as the essence of divine work. This also led him to develop a deeper understanding of the role of the Church in relation to the concept of *Missio Dei*—i.e., God's missionary activity on earth.

Such a realization made him unable to remain neutral to what was happening around the *minjung*. Instead, it was from this *minjung*-ness that he would be involved with and committed to the suffering reality of the *minjung*. This in return helped him establish the "Church of Galilee" as the beginning of the Minjung Church (1975) (Chae 1994:42). Put succinctly, Suh found a Christian hope in the Church's incarnation into the place of *minjung*—namely, *Hyun-Jang (*現場; *Sitz-im-Leben* of the *minjung*) as the agent of the coming of the Kingdom of God.

Not surprisingly, Suh's theology and action greatly irritated the military government of that time. Thus, he was forced to leave his teaching position at the university and later imprisoned for his severe criticism of Park's dictatorship (Moon 1998:45).[7] However, all these challenging situations seemed to have the effect of encouraging him to

---

[7]With him were a number of other minjung theologians who had been dismissed from their university teaching posts. In 1975 alone some 13 professors (all were members of the Korean Christian Faculty Fellowship) were fired by the government (Suh 1995:159-60). In addition, hundreds of students and labour union workers were either under arrest or imprisoned for alleged violations of the so-called "Emergency Decree No. 9," which could punish any act criticizing the Park's regime.

actualize and radicalize Minjung Theology *hic et nunc* (here and now) (Suh 1983:353).

In short, Suh transformed all other stereotypes, the occidental theological ideas (e.g., existential, secular, and scientific theology) into Korean Minjung Theology as a critical response to the concrete life situations of the *minjung*, his snappy slogan being, "The only way out was in." By shifting his focus from western to anti-western theology, or by releasing Christianity from western theological captivity, Suh had begun doing theology from below and soon become involved in the Korean *minjung's* struggles for humanity, justice and life.

From Christology to Pneumatology

Suh's involvement in the World Council of Churches opened his eyes to the relationship of Church and world both theologically and pragmatically (Hyun 1984:523). Alongside the WCC's concern for human rights in general, he in particular began to uphold the Church's responsibility for the Korean *minjung*, "those who suffered outside the wall of the Christian church" (Chae 1994:36-7). He saw the inhumane social phenomenon in Korean society as the byproduct of structural sin. The poverty, hunger, and misery of the *minjung* were common causes in their unrighteous political and economic relations under Park's military dictatorship (Suh 1983:174). Thus, it became clear that participation in the struggle for the *minjung's* justice and freedom was to be the Korean Church's central task (Suh 1983:132). As a result, he actualized and radicalized his theology to the point of being the political praxis against injustice and violence, which aimed at transforming all social relations (Suh 1983:55-69).

To Suh, doing or restoring justice was a dimension of God's mission, and thus the Church's participation in the struggle for justice meant its participation in God's mission—"To know God is to enter into a covenant justice-oriented relationship" (Abraham 1996:35). Thus, Christian involvement in changing and renewing the dominant social structure that had produced a vicious cycle of structural injustice coincided with God's mission (Suh 1983:167). Suh linked it to the concept of salvation, he even argued that as sin was neither committed in the abstract, nor remained in the individual level, so salvation must be concrete and corporate expression in relation to the humanization of collective existence (Thomas 1971:1-19).

It was from this notion that Suh identified the mission of God with the mission of social justice for liberation of the suffering *minjung* (Moon 1998:93). Since salvation must include liberation from the structures of sin—i.e., oppression, injustice, depravity, and death, God's mission was primarily political, which demanded action. This led him to accept radical action for liberation from oppression and transformation of society as an indispensable and integral part of salvation.[8]

From this arose Suh's distinctive concept of *Missio Dei* in the Spirit, leading to a messianic community of Christ's reign on earth with his people—namely, the suffering Korean *minjung* (Moon 1998:93). He continued to say that the Kingdom of God is to be found and fulfilled "here and now" (Suh 1983:133), the very place where justice is broken and dead, so that "the blood of the [*minjung*] is crying aloud to heaven." Thus, his understanding of *Missio Dei* in the Spirit was the contextualization of Trinitarian mission.[9] In one sense, his view found resonance in a traditional Trinitarian mission, which was epitomized by God's act of sending the Son and the Spirit for the world. It echoed the orthodox idea of God's mission as Trinitarian activity (Newbigin 1995:29).

Yet in another sense, Suh's concept of *Missio Dei* in the Spirit had a distinctive character of its own. Here, a form of pneumatological-synchronic interpretation came into light (Kim 1992:243). What was crucial here was the shift of emphasis from a Christological-diachronic to a pneumatological-synchronic interpretation (Suh 1991:272). While

---

[8]Here Suh's idea of salvation stands closer to what liberation theologians in Latin America have maintained (Gutierrez 1973, Ellacuria and Sorbrino 1995:251-89).

[9]"The Trinitarian concept of *Missio Dei* was introduced in discussions at the world missionary conference in Willingen, Germany in 1952. It was an attempt to overcome the crisis of the western missionary project by giving it a new theological foundation in God's acting in history. Before, during, and after the Willingen conference, there were always two competing interpretations. One that perpetuated the old salvation history model in disguise (i.e., the church understood as the agent of God's mission); the other one influenced by the American social gospel and Barthian theology that focused on God's promise to be with the creation. In the prolongation of the latter the *relecture* of the *Missio Dei* concept in liberation theologies took place" (Küster 2010:1). A good summary of its development can be found in the work of David Bosch, best known for his book, *Transforming Mission: Paradigm Shifts in Theology of Mission* (1991:389-93).

the former focused on Christ's atoning work as a once-for-all event "for the sake of my sin," the latter construed the Jesus event as a permanent reality that can be revived here and now in the work of the Holy Spirit, emphasizing that "I replay Jesus" (Kim 1992:243). By giving priority to the Spirit in God's mission, Suh attempted to connect the Spirit's work to social movements as well as to spiritual revival. In so doing, he brought the Holy Spirit into God's salvific drama as the concrete face (Suh 1983:162-67).

Not surprisingly, Suh's attempt at re-reading *Missio Dei* in the Spirit resulted in his contextualizing the Korean society, where the Spirit is working here and now, with, and for, the suffering *minjung* (Suh 1976:132). He saw the current precarious situation of society not as the absence, but rather the presence of God in the liberating *Missio Dei*, which had a missional direction for liberating the oppressed, exploited, and suffering people from socio-political injustice (Suh 1983:57). Indeed, his conviction regarding liberation of the Korean minjung was inspired primarily by his conviction of the liberation motif of *Missio Dei* in the Spirit (Kim 1976:41). For him, God's on-going mission cannot be fully understood apart from the Spirit's liberating activity for the world (Moon 1998:93).

It is in this light that the Exodus motif (both Old and New Testament alike) had become central to Suh's understanding of the concept of *Missio Dei*.[10] In resonance with a notion that the biblical Exodus event did not exhaust God's liberating mission in salvation history, he

---

[10]One of the critics of this perspective can be found in the so-called historical peace churches, their claim focused on the fact that the apocalyptic and the whole of NT literature belongs not to the "Exodus-paradigm" but to the "Exile-paradigm." The epistemological privilege in reading the biblical apocalyptic and NT texts is, according to this interpretation, on the side of Exile-communities (Yoder 1972).

attempted to plant this Exodus theme into the Korean context.[11] With this idea, his central argument took on the dimension of liberation. In other words, he unfurled the banner of *Missio Dei* in the Spirit as a major breakthrough in the concrete reality of socio-political injustice of his time, and thus tried to bring about the Good News in the lives of the suffering *minjung* and the society in Korea (Suh 1983:58). Here his concept of *Missio Dei* in the Spirit was sublimated into liberation and justice for the suffering Korean *minjung*, which responded with Christian hope for a different world and a different order of society (Suh 1991:243-45).

This even led Suh to claim that the Holy Spirit would play a more proactive role in mission than Jesus. To him, the illustration that best conveyed this idea was the Spirit's present work, embodied in the struggles of the oppressed Korean *minjung* here and now. Yet such an affirmation was introduced not as a contradiction, but as a complement to the Christ-centred interpretation (Suh 1983:162-67). While not negating that there was continuity between the Father's mission, Jesus' mission, and the ongoing mission of the Spirit (Newbigin 1995:29), he disagreed with the doctrine of absolute grace through Jesus only that accompanied ignorance and indifference to the believer's responsibility toward the society (Moon 1998re:137).

---

[11] Joining the historian Lee, Ki-Baek, Suh presents the history of Korea as a process characterized by "a progressive expansion of the social base of the ruling power" that culminates in the subject-hood of the *minjung* and in the democratization of Korean society (Suh 1983:167-69). Lee has proposed 16 eras and their corresponding social systems, which have been widely discussed in Korea. According to him, periodization of Korean history can be divided into: "(1) Neolithic period: since ca. 4000 BC—Communal clan-centred society, (2) Bronze age: since ca. 800 BC—Walled town states and confederated kingdoms, (3) Three kingdoms: since ca. 50 BC—Aristocratic societies under monarchical rule, (4) Since ca. 650—Fashioning of an authoritarian monarchy, (5) Since ca. 750—Age of powerful gentry families, (6) Since ca. 950—Hereditary aristocratic order, (7) Since ca. 1200—Rule by the military, (8) Since ca. 1300—Emergence of the literati, (9) Since ca. 1400—Creation of a *yangban* society, (10) Since ca. 1450—Rise of the neo-Confucian literati, (11) Since ca. 1650—Emergence of landed farmers and wholesale merchants, (12) Ca. 1800-1850—Instability of the *yangban* status system and outbreak of popular uprisings, (13) Ca. 1850-1900—Growth of the forces of enlightenment, (14) Ca. 1900—National stirrings and imperialist aggression, (15) Since 1919—Development of the nationalist movement, (16) Since 1945—Beginnings of democracy" (quoted by Suh 1983:167-69).

What Suh criticized most was orthodoxy's emphasis on the so-called "Jesusology,"[12] which seldom, if ever, told about the Spirit's degeneration into an egoistic and heteronomous spirit (Moon 1998:136-37). It had centred so much on metaphysical 'answers' propositionally given by traditional theology and doctrines that the connection between the Word of God and every-day realities became secondary, in fact almost irrelevant (Song 1990:13-4). This meant the ready-made Jesusology dictated by academic theology needed its critical conversion to the *minjung's* life-field *(Sitz-im-Leben)* where material deprivation, violations of human rights, and sheer exploitation were the most pressing concerns (Suh 1983:57). Thus, the suffering *minjung's* life-field, according to Suh, should be the mission-field of the liberating God (Suh 1983:57, Chae 1994:170).

In summation, it was not a Christological-diachronic but a pneumatological-synchronic interpretation that opened Suh's eyes to the Spirit's working in and through the suffering *minjung* here and now (Moon 1998:104-105). In his thinking, the concept of *Missio Dei* in the Spirit pointed to the Spirit's liberating activity in solidarity with the suffering *minjung* in Korean history—namely, God's on-going intervention into the history of the suffering Korean *minjung* through the work of the Holy Spirit (Kim 1991:29-57, Moon 1983:123-37). In short, the traditional Christological horizon was stretched by his pneumatological horizon based on the liberating *Missio Dei* movement in the Spirit.

From Saviour (Jesus) to Saved (Minjung)

Suh's idea of *Missio Dei* in the Spirit that widened his narrow vision of Christ pointed out that knowledge of the Spirit must precede knowledge of Jesus (Suh 1983:163-64). Now he went even further to contend that knowledge of the *minjung* must antecede knowledge of the Spirit (Moon 1998:134). From it, the liberating *Missio Dei* movement in the Spirit was closely related to his concept of *minjung*-Christology (Moon 1998:76-7). According to him, both were in fact two sides of the

---

[12]T. E. Fretheim, a professor of Old Testament in Lutheran Seminary (1984:3), originally coined this term.

same coin; one cannot know Jesus without knowing the *minjung* at the same time: one cannot talk about Jesus if one does not talk about the *minjung* simultaneously (Suh 1983:157, 165-66, Song 1996:216). Here, his interest in Jesus was not the triumphant hero "who had overcome the whole world" but a human son who identified himself with the suffering people who strove for freedom and justice with the Spirit (Suh 1983:142, 211, Song 1996:147).

Suh was convinced that reinterpretation of Jesus in the light of the *minjung* was indispensable and it was from this radical identification with them, the outcry of Jesus on the Cross became the *cantus firmus* ("the leading voice") to which all voices of the suffering *minjung* were joined (Suh 1976:76, 1983:177, 243-45). By understanding the Cross event of Jesus not as the vicarious suffering, but as the example of the direct link between Jesus and *minjung* in body and in spirit, he insisted that Jesus was "the crucified *minjung*" and vice-versa (Song 1996:210, 216). In other words, it was by this involvement in the suffering of *minjung* that Jesus became the Messiah and, in this sense, the suffering *minjung* also became the Messiah (Suh 1983:188-89).

This enabled him to see possibilities for realization of the Cross event of Jesus in the present *minjung* event that was at work through the messianic role of the *minjung*—namely, their self-salvation through the work of the Holy Spirit (Moon 1998:83-4). It was apparent from the fact that Jesus suffered and died for the suffering people in his time that they were none other than the 'secular Christ', the source of salvation (Suh 1991:243-45, Kim 1992:239).[13] This means Jesus' Cross event served as a prelude to the *minjung's* self-salvation in solidarity with all victims of evil—i.e., those who were relegated to the underside of history (Lee 1988:11).

In a simplistic way, Jesus on the Cross paid the price for the *minjung's* salvation of today, where the outcry of Jesus and the outcry of countless *minjung* were "both annulling and preserving, of both passing-

---

[13] Following this, Suh even argued that Jesus was no longer to be identified with the Good Samaritan, but rather with a victim who had been assaulted by thieves and left by the side of the road half-dead. To him, this man of sorrow was Jesus himself who lived here and now not only *as* but also *with* the suffering *minjung* (Suh 1976:65-84). Thus, it was evident to Suh that the stripped, robbed, and half-dead victim could complete the salvation of the *minjung* themselves (Suh 1976:67).

over and taking-up" (Sobrino 1978:231, Hodgson 1987:224). Suh saw it as affirmation that the suffering Jesus was present with the suffering *minjung* in the power of the Spirit. Therefore, he continued to argue that Jesus' crucifixion must be present in the *minjung's* day-to-day struggles that led to their freedom and victory (Song 1980:158-75). The suffering *minjung*, then, no longer remain silent as the object; rather they would speak out their hope as the subject of their salvation (Suh 1991:245). To Suh, this was the way by which the Spirit empowered the suffering *minjung* to play a messianic role in society and history (Suh 1990:133).

In this sense, Suh did not hesitate to consider the event of Chun, Tae-Il,[14] as a resurgence of Jesus' Cross event in Korea (Moon 1998:87). To him, Chun's suicide at the Peace Market in Seoul was nothing but Jesus' Cross event to save the *minjung* from the existing unjust structure of the Korean society (Suh 1983:353). With a powerful *déjà vu* of Jesus' crucifixion from Chun's self-immolation for others, Suh intended to highlight the universality of the Cross event that continued to happen today with the suffering *minjung* (Suh 1983:223, 353, Ahn 1990:133).

Understood in this way, Suh boldly insisted that the *minjung's* self-salvation even embraced Jesus' salvation (Moon 1998:90). If the crucified *minjung* gained salvation in solidarity with Jesus as the crucified *minjung*, it must be the crucified *minjung* who could liberate Jesus as the crucified *minjung* who suffered from the oppressive status quo here and now (Suh 1976:76, Lee 1988:11). His radical understanding coincided with the image of Jesus with the 'golden crown' who was freed by the

---

[14]Here it deserves extra attention to the story of Chun, Tae-Il (全泰壹, 1948-1970). Chun was a worker in a garment factory in the Tongdaemun-ku (東大門) district in Seoul. He became involved in labour organizing and formally petitioned the government: "We understand well the working procedures which are specified in the Labour Standard Law. However, we cannot receive the least benefit of the Labour Standard Law and what is more 90% of the 20,000 employees are on average 16-year-old girls. Even without the Labour Standard Law, as human beings how can you force girls to work 15 hours a day?" Chun's appeal continued, describing non-existent health facilities, wages that forced workers to fast through lunch, crowded conditions, and lack of days off. The dual imperatives, clearly of ideological rather than practical necessity, of a vicious internal anti-communism and export-led economic development worked against any compromise with regard to unionization or even the enforcement of labour laws already on the books. Deeply disturbed by working conditions and the lack of any positive remedial action, official or otherwise, on November 13, 1970, Chun entered the Peace Market and, shouting "Comply with the Labour Standard Law! We are not machines! Do not enslave the workers!" committed self-immolation in a desperate display of protest" (Yi 1993:454).

poor beggar on the street—i.e., the Korean poet, Kim Ji-Ha's famous play. Here the subject of salvation was completely changed, "from the golden-crowned Jesus to the homeless beggar Jesus"—namely, the crucified *minjung* (Küster 2018:19, Moon 1998:90): "People like you [*beggar*] must help to liberate me [*Jesus*]. . . . Only those, though very poor and suffering like yourself . . . , can give me life again" (Kim 1978:24, *italic is mine*). It was from this view that the golden-crown Jesus cannot save himself apart from the salvation of the *minjung* Jesus. Thus, salvation must be the salvation of the crucified *minjung* as well as the crucified Jesus (Pang 2008:170).

Yet Suh refused to see the salvation of the *minjung* Jesus as a sort of surrogate for Jesus' atonement (Kim 1992:238), there being an intrinsic correlation between the two: the former are the partners of the covenant with the latter, so that both are to be understood as complementary rather than contradictory, as synchronic rather than diachronic (Kim 1976:41). Thus, it has been pointed out that Suh's radical Christology affirmed the balance between Jesus and *minjung*—or Jesus-messianism and *minjung*-messianism (Kim 1983:187).

To sum up, Suh had strived not only to incorporate the suffering Jesus into the present socio-political context of the Korean *minjung*, but also to impart Jesus' messianic role into the suffering *minjung*, to the extent that Jesus meant the crucified *minjung* and vice versa, and thus, salvation came from the *minjung* Jesus not from the golden-crown Jesus (Suh 1983:78, Küster 2018:19). This signified a critical Christological conversion from the Saviour to the saved; from Messiah to *minjung*. In this sense, "[*Minjung*] are the ones [*minjung*] have been waiting for"[15] as the subject of history and salvation. Here the concept of *Missio Dei* in the Spirit came to him as the prophetic witness that Jesus' Cross event would continue to happen today with the *minjung* in the dynamic tension between *minjung*-ness of the Spirit and the Spirit-ness of *minjung*.

---

[15]This phrase originally came from the poem of June M. Jordan (1936-2002), the Caribbean-American bisexual poet and activist who used the term "*minjung*" instead of "we" (Jordan 1980:42-3).

From Other-Worldly Kingdom of God to This-Worldly Messianic Millennium

Linked with the idea of universality of Jesus' Cross event, Suh saw the coming of the Kingdom of God as the hallmark of Jesus' own preaching and ministry (Suh 1983:261).[16] Further, his notion of *Missio Dei* in the Spirit as God's liberating activity to the world motivated him to look anew at Jesus' message of the Kingdom, not as an abstract and theoretical concept, but as a concrete, organized historical reality here and now (Suh 1983:131). While describing the *minjung* as being the permanent reality of the historical Jesus—namely, the object of the *han*-ridden society, he at the same time prescribed them as the champions of the Kingdom of God—namely, the subject of the *han*-free society on earth (Suh 1983:131). Here he spoke of a two-fold characteristic of the Kingdom of God as denouncing and announcing. The Kingdom was to take the process of denouncing the *minjung's* suffering as injustice on one sense and of announcing its total transformation on the other (Suh 1983:177).

Here, Suh pointed out that the genuine litmus test of the Kingdom was whether the *minjung* were liberated from their suffering reality, which is *Hyun-Jang* (Sitz-im-Lenben) (Suh 1983:57). To him, Jesus' Kingdom message was present in the day-to-day struggle of the people of Galilee (the 1st-century suffering *minjung*) and became Good News to them with a new vision of social order where the *minjung* were to be the centre—"Blessed are the *minjung*; they shall inherit the kingdom of God!" (Kasper 1976:72) This meant that, from its inception, the Kingdom was closely related to liberation of the poor and oppressed—namely, the suffering *minjung* (Kim 1992:243-44). As long as they suffered in dehumanized conditions, there was Good News to be proclaimed beyond time and space.

Suh took God's predilection for the *minjung* as the critical gospel paradigm for his time, that being, "God of the oppressed": he loves the poor, marginalized and disadvantaged (Suh 1983:142). Thus, he argued that the concrete life-situation of the suffering *minjung* joined at a divine

---

[16] G. R Beasley Murray also claims that the Kingdom of God was the very centre of Jesus' own message (1986:5).

place where God's liberating activity for his people was taking place (Suh 1976:80). In this light, the *minjung*'s *Sitz-im-Leben* (life-setting) could serve as a prism through which the Kingdom of God can shine. It represents in microcosm where heaven and earth would meet, where Jesus is present, and where the Kingdom is realized as a complete reversal of the status quo (Kim 1992:234).

Consequently, Suh's appraisal of the *minjung*'s life-field as the incarnation of the Kingdom of God found expression in the Messianic Millennial Kingdom as the realization of the new heaven and new earth in the present (Suh 1976:102). This presupposed his negation of the spiritualization of God's Kingdom, apart from the liberating *Missio Dei* movement in the Spirit—i.e., God's transforming act in this world (Suh 1983:58).

To clarify his position, Suh began re-reading church history and pointing out that Christianity was changed and debased by the Constantinian compromise, the compromise with the worldly power (Moon 1998:99-100). To him, Constantine's elevation of Christianity to being the official religion (AD 313) proved to be disastrous, which made it a lackey to the Empire (Suh 1983:258). Because, from that point on, it became a better advocate for the oppressive Roman rulers than for the oppressed, as part of a scheme to build and maintain the Holy Roman Empire (Suh 1983:258). In short, Constantine's Christianity degenerated into being a tool in the hands of the privileged to safeguard their interest under the banner of a *henotikon* (act of union), a formula for Christian unity.[17]

In its wake, according to Suh, a tendency toward centralization of power and systematic suppression of freedom came into the Church, to the point of abandoning Jesus' revolutionary ethic of justice and peace

---

[17]The *Henotickon* was an imperial edict issued by Emperor Zeno in 482 to reconcile the differences between Chalcedonian supporters and their opponents, which were the Monophysites. Yet its promulgation actually satisfied no one, instead resulting in the so-called Acacian schism between Rome and the East, which lasted until 518, due in part to its mollification of the moderate Monophysites.

(Suh 1983:258). Soon the "political economy" of truth[18]—"a form of critical reflection on governmental practice" which gradually changed the way people think and act—became its norm (Foucault 1979:819). Thus, within the circles of the powerful, it reduced Christians to silence about their responsibility regarding socio-political issues, the Church no longer opposing oppression, instead becoming the ultraconservative prop of the existing power structure (Moon 1998:129-30).

It was apparent from this observation that the Church's close relationship with the power from above had justified its willful ignorance to the outcries from below (Suh 1983:301-304). Thus, Suh argued that "Doing nothing is in fact doing something."[19] What was worse was that such a shift of church that benefited the powerful but victimized the powerless, camouflaged itself by absorbing into an individual and spiritual category under the pretext of the Church's sake. As a result, it changed the Church from a movement of the people-centred to the institutional structure and shifted its focus from God's reign in this world to getting people into heaven in the next. To be sure, it reduced the 'this-worldly' Church to resort to the 'other-worldly' Kingdom of God as a place of pilgrimage which fostered an a-historical and a-social retreat to heaven (Suh 1976:129-30).

This galvanized Suh to distinguish the term "Millennium" from the Kingdom of God, ascribing it rather to *minjung*-messianic aspirations, which would embrace both spiritual salvation and historical-political liberation as a whole (Suh 1976:102, 1983:162-63, Ahn 1979:108). In a word, he made a distinction between the *minjung*-oriented this-worldly emphasis on the Millennium and the power elite-oriented other-worldly emphasis on the Kingdom of God (Suh 1983:193).

Drawing the analogy of a messianic feast open to all, Suh proposed an analysis of the apex of the Millennium that did not trample the poor and oppressed, but vindicated them, taking seriously the advent of the

---

[18]Michel Foucault (1926-1984), a French philosopher (1980:131), originally coined the term and defined it as such: "Political economy is . . . a type of knowledge . . . which those who govern must take into account. But economic science cannot be the science of government and economics cannot be the internal principle, law, rule of conduct, or rationality of government. Economics is a science lateral to the art of governing. One must govern with economics, one must govern alongside economists, one must govern by listening to the economists, but economics must not be and there is no question that it can be the governmental rationality itself." (Foucault 2008, 286).

[19]This came from Joseph Hough Jr (1993:65).

messianic Kingdom on earth (Suh 1983:131, 193). To him, it became evident that the implication of this parable was the necessity of the praxis of the powerless in this world, which should be distinguished from that of the powerful toward other-worldly discourse (Moon 1998:97). Whereas the latter was the praxis of conspiracy from above, promoting alienation, oppression, and domination over the powerless, the former was the praxis of liberation from below, encouraging the powerless to stand up, protest, and struggle for their rights, for participation, and for justice (Moon 1998:100).

Suh believed it to be a liberating praxis that had to do with the power of the powerless (the *minjung*) inherited from Jesus' own struggle against the established powers and authorities of his time (Moon 1998:101, 156). In Suh's thinking, there is no doubt that Jesus, as the suffering Messiah, suffered and died for bringing the power of the keys back from the privileged to the underprivileged, from the oppressor to the oppressed, from the powerful to the powerless (Moon 1998:101). Thus, it was Suh's conviction that the other-worldly Kingdom of God must be replaced by the this-worldly Messianic Millennial Kingdom (Suh 1983:162-63, 1991:243-45).

This notion of the Millennium as the messianic Kingdom on earth found expression in the liberating *Missio Dei* movement in the Spirit. Just as God's liberative and transformative mission to the world is interconnected both cosmically and eschatologically, the Messianic Millennial Kingdom is inclusive of both spiritual-vertical and social-horizontal dimensions (Suh 1983:133, Kim 1992:24344). To Suh, *shalom* before God here on earth must come together with the everlasting *shalom* before God in the hereafter. In this connection, he insisted that realization of life in all its fullness (including the spiritual and material bases) is an indispensable part of the Messianic Kingdom of God in the eschatological reversal, which is imminent. In short, Suh was convinced that the Millennial Kingdom would be a physical manifestation of God's salvific action in the Spirit for the liberation of the *minjung* here and now (Suh 1983:131).

To summarize, in Suh's outlook, God's Kingdom is never abstract but is open to the concrete life situations of the minjung. It cannot be understood conceptually in some a-temporal fashion but must be reckoned with in any effort to bring it into the minjung's day-to-day struggling. Therefore, to him, the matter is not *when* the Kingdom comes, but *how* it can come. By reinterpreting the suffering *minjung* as both guests and hosts of the messianic banquet, Suh gives the powerless *minjung* a new impetus as the subject of salvation, being exercised a liberating praxis, and thus, creating a brave new world here on earth— namely, the Messianic Millennial Kingdom as the historical-eschatological realization of the liberating *Missio Dei* movement in the Spirit.

Summary: Suh, the Radical Reformer as Being-in-the-*Minjung* in the Liberating *Missio Dei* of the Spirit

Suh found in the liberating *Missio Dei* of the Spirit the apex of *dan*. Taking seriously the reality of the suffering *minjung* in Korean society (especially in the 1970s), he began reinterpreting it from a perspective of God's liberating action in the works of the Spirit. To him, God as the Spirit always opted for the victim's cry for justice. Explicit is that the Spirit is the Good News of God, who brings down from their thrones the mighty and exalts the lowly (1 Cor. 1:26-29). This motivated Suh to link the Exodus motif with Korean society, seeing God's on-going mission in human history, including the Church's history. In this sense, the Exodus event in the Old Testament was a close nexus not only of Jesus' Cross event in the New Testament, but also of the *minjung* event in Korea's history as a presage and presentiment of a new Exodus.

Suh's emphasis here was two-fold. In one sense, he emphasized the continuity of the Father-Son-Spirit's mission in the history of the Korean *minjung*; while in another sense, he represented the close affinity between the *minjung's* suffering and God's suffering on the Cross. From this perspective, the liberating *Missio Dei* movement in the Spirit served as a signature of the relationship between idea and action, church and world, spirit and body, knowledge of God and practice of liberation, and Messiah as *minjung* and *minjung* as Messiah.

This led to Suh's complete change: (1) from western to anti-western theology, (2) from Christology to Pneumatology, (3) from the Saviour (Jesus) to the saved (*minjung*), and (4) from the other-worldly Kingdom of God to the this-worldly Messianic Millennial Kingdom. To be more specific, linking critically the idea of *Missio Dei* in the Spirit to the reality of social injustice in the Korean context, he first endeavored to break the shell of western models of theology that were not suitable to that context. Next, he tried to reshape a Korean version of contextual theology based on the *minjung's* perspective. This resulted in his emphasis of pneumatology over Christology, a pneumatological-synchronic interpretation over a Christological-diachronic one, which reappraised the Holy Spirit for liberation of the *minjung* not only from the socio-economic oppression, but also from the spiritual cul-de-sac where "Jesusology" disguised itself as Christology.

Suh's Spirit-centred outlook forged a new connection between Jesus and suffering *minjung* in the liberating *Missio Dei* movement in the Spirit, that being Jesus-messianism and *minjung*-messianism as a Spirit-Christology. In it, there was a holistic view of *minjung* (the saved) and Messiah (the Saviour) in the Spirit—i.e., *minjung*-ness of the Spirit and the Spirit-ness of *minjung* that did resist injustice and oppression. Further, it drove him to distinguish the Messianic Millennial Kingdom from the Kingdom of God when the latter appeared as the other-worldly utopianism, apart from the *minjung's Sitz-im-Leben*—namely, *Hyun-Jang*. Here, his conspicuous concern was to turn the Kingdom of God into the Messianic Millennial Kingdom as realization of the liberating *Missio Dei* movement in the Spirit—i.e., "God's saving *coup d'etat*" (Barth 1969:620) for a wholesome, liberative, and *han*-less society in the here and now by the power of the powerless *minjung* in the Spirit.

In short, Suh had radicalized the theology of *Missio Dei* by accepting worldly occurrences as divine intervention or the work of the Spirit. Beyond Christological teaching of justification in an individualistic and forensic sense, he tried to actualize the Jesus event *hic et nunc* (here and now) in an on-going pneumatological-synchronic manner. This, in turn, characterized him the Radical Reformer as being-in-the-*minjung* in the liberating *Missio Dei* of the Spirit.

Ahn, Byung-Mu (安炳茂, 1922-1996)

Biographical Sketch

Born in Shinanju (新安州), which currently belongs to North Korea, Ahn, Byung-Mu's life had been precarious from the outset. Soon after his first birthday, his family fled to Manchuria because of Japan's colonial threat (Küster 2010:59).[20] Due in part to his father's dissipation and in part to personal curiosity, Ahn, despite a Confucius background, converted to Christianity in childhood (Küster 2010:59-60). However, the price of his involvement with Christianity was high. His father disowned both him and his mother, which resulted in him (as the first son) having to be the family's breadwinner (Küster 2010:60).

Despite the difficulties, Ahn was able to enter the Canadian Presbyterian Mission's secondary school in Youngjung (Longjing; 龍井), where he formed close relationships with his future comrades-in-arms as there are several names given, including Ham, Sok-Hon (咸錫憲, 1901-1989), the 'Gandhi of Korean'; Kim, Chai-Joon (金在俊, 1901-1987), co-founder of Hanguk Theological Seminary[21] of the Presbyterian Church, Republic of Korea (PROK, in Korean: *kichang)*; and Moon, Dong-Hwan (文東煥, 1921-), a pioneer of the pro-democracy movement in Korea (Küster 2010:60).

After graduating from the mission school in 1940, like many of his fellows, Ahn studied in Japan; but unlike them, he did not major in theology. Instead, not wanting to be a pastor, he focused on literature, especially the writings of Kierkegaard (Küster 2010:60). However, in the midst of his studies he fled to Manchuria in order to avoid Japan's forced military service (Küster 2010:60). It was not until Korea's liberation from Japanese colonial rule in 1945 that Ahn was able to return home. From then on, his public life centred round Seoul, the nation's capital. He then took on the formidable task of supporting his family during the day and resuming his studies at Seoul National University at night, finally earning

---

[20]Ahn later compared this situation to that of Galilee in Jesus' time (Küster 2010:59).

[21]This seminary was the predecessor of Hanshin University in 1980.

a degree in sociology in 1950, "choosing religious studies as a minor" (Küster 2010:60).

The Korean War (1950-53) left an indelible imprint on Ahn both negatively and positively. On the one hand, he despaired of the war's chaotic aftermath, ceaseless ideological confrontations between left and right; and endless desperation and frustration of the common people. On the other hand, hoping against hope, he focused on how to awaken the nation's spirit not only to break the impasse, but also to transform society. Wanting to encourage people, he developed a concept of lay mission and introduced the *Hyang-rin* (香隣; good neighbour) church as an alternative to the current crisis (Küster 2010:61). Concurrently, he served as senior lecturer at Chungang Seminary.

During this time, Ahn continually pursued the question of the historical Jesus, which motivated him to go to Germany for further study. He did so in 1956 at Heidelberg University under Gunther Bornkamm, one of Rudolf Bultmann's top pupils (Küster 2010:61). His main focus was not on the Christ confessed in kerygma but rather the Jesus of history. Receiving his doctorate in 1965, his thesis, "Kung-Tse and Jesus about Love," pried into the distinction between the historical Jesus and the kerygmatic Christ and proved his theological focus laid deeply in a specific and practical love, not in an abstract and conceptual ideology (Küster 2010:61).

In 1966 Ahn returned to Korea and accelerated his role as a thinker-in-action. He not only resumed teaching at Chungang Seminary, but also served as a professor at Hanguk Theological Seminary. In 1973, he also founded the Korea Theological Study Institute, which opened a new chapter in the theological forum for both lay people and theologians (Küster 2010:62).

But 1970 marked a turning point in Ahn's theological thinking as a result of the young labourer Chun, Tae-Il's self-immolation for the sake of human rights (Ahn 1990:257). From then on, he began to see theology through the *minjung's* eye and no longer separated it from human rights issues (Küster 2010:62). To him, theology was not simply a methodology but rather a resistance movement against the military dictatorship. As a result, governmental monitoring and repression was meted out against him, including his dismissal from the college in 1975 (Küster 2010:63).

This created in Ahn a momentum that would embody his theology into *minjung's* life-situations. Teaming up with other dissidents, such as Suh, Nam-Dong (徐南同, 1918-1984), the brothers Moon, Ik-Hwan (文益煥, 1918-1994)[22] and Moon, Dong-Hwan (文東煥, 1921-2019), and Lee, Oo-Jung (李愚貞, 1923-), Ahn established the "Galilee congregation" for those who were politically persecuted (Küster 2010:63). This stimulated him to more fully personify Jesus and the suffering *minjung* in their mutual correlation and to see Galilee as *Hyun-Jang*, the very place where Jesus and the *minjung* were to meet together (Suh 1981:57).

In 1976, Ahn took charge of the Mission Education Centre, which served as an outpost for urban and rural mission (UIM/URM) (Küster 2010:63). On March 1, he became involved in the "Declaration of Democracy and National Salvation," resulting in his 1½-year incarceration (Küster 2010:64). It is interesting to note that, in his experience of prison, he began to realize what Jesus, a friend of sinners, meant to him and penned the following:

> This was the turning point for me, I started to look at the world with different eyes. I asked myself what the church and Christianity would look like from their perspective. Intellectual speculation, philosophy and theology did not make any sense to these people. Their language emerged from the center of their own lives. I really lived in an entirely different world and I thought through what *minjung* means. Of course, we had already started with the Galilee congregation. But then it was mostly the parents of (sic) family of those in prison. Our standards had to change. So, I read the Bible anew—after some time I had received a Bible—and I read it from the beginning, without any commentary. My view had changed dramatically. What seemed senseless to me before now appeared full of sense to me and vice versa. . . . It was like I was born again. I will never forget that experience (Küster 2010:65).

---

[22]Moon, Ik-Hwan was a South Korean pastor, theologian, poet, and activist engaged in various social movements. Earning his master's degree from Princeton University in the U.S., he returned to South Korea and began to lecture in the Old Testament at Yonsei University and Hansin University.

In 1979, the 'Seoul Spring', which took place after the assassination of President Park, allowed for Ahn's release and return to the seminary. However, shortly after, Chun, Doo-Whan and his military faction seized power, and Ahn was again dismissed from his position. At this juncture, he established the sisterhood, *Diakonia*, which focused primarily on a congregation of women sharing Jesus' love with the suffering *minjung* (Küster 2010:66). This created momentum that characterized his theology of *Kong* (公 , public) as an alternative to that of materialism/capitalism.

In July 1984, Ahn was again reinstated and served as dean of Hanshin University's Graduate School until his retirement in 1987 (Küster 2010:66-6). Thanks to his great affection for the next generation, he nurtured many students and leaders. He also published more than 20 books and periodicals during his lifetime.[23] On October 19, 1996, Ahn passed away, leaving a lasting legacy of Minjung Theology.

Theological Perspective

Encountering Western Theology

In general, Ahn's theology can be divided into two periods: before Minjung Theology and after Minjung Theology (Kim 2013:32). While well-organized, this distinction can simply be a tool of obfuscation without referring to Bultmann,[24] whom he ardently admired (especially in its early stage). Thus, to say that "before Minjung Theology, Ahn was an existentialist" is not an exaggeration (Küster 2010:66). Indeed, despite his interest in Bultmann's analysis of synoptic tradition, what really attracted Ahn was Bultmann's existential approach which helped him recognize text and context as an inseparable part of reality (Küster 2010:66). Yet he was not a blind imitator of Bultmann; he was more concerned with a collective and socio-political dimension than his

---

[23] Among them are *A Voice from the Wilderness*, *Presence*, *Theological Thoughts*, *Sallim* and so on.

[24] In an interview, Ahn once said that "Bultmann has been the only teacher with a large influence on me, as a theologian and a New Testament scholar at the same time . . . If I had not encountered Bultmann, I would never have started doing theology. He showed me how to do theology" (Küster 2010:66).

'master'. While giving blanket consent to Bultmann's sociological reading of the Bible, his existential orientation pushed him forward to the *Sitz im Leben* of Korean society after the civil war in his theologizing (Küster 2010:66).

Ahn's struggle for human rights and democratization (triggered by Chun, Tae-Il's death in 1970) took solace in Dietrich Bonhoeffer's theology (1906-1945). In particular, revealing to him was Bonhoeffer's protest against German Christians and the Nazi regime through the confessing church, which showed the parallels in the current Korean context, especially groaning under the conservative church and Park's military dictatorship (Küster 2010:67). Like Bonhoeffer, Ahn was looking at the significant role of suffering from the *minjung's* reality:

> The Bible directs humanity to God's powerlessness and suffering: only a suffering God can help . . . Christ helps us, not by virtue of his omnipotence, but by virtue of his weakness and suffering . . . To be a Christian . . . is to be a human—not a type of human, but the human that Christ creates in us. It is not the religious act that makes the Christian but participation in the suffering of God in the secular life (Bonhoeffer 1966:188, 190)

Furthermore, Bonhoeffer's statement—"Before God and with God we live without God"—gave him a new dignity, defining the suffering *minjung* as the ones who "stand before God but live without God" (Ahn 1987:56). This led to his new *minjung* Christology in which he found Jesus in the suffering of the *minjung* and even identified Jesus with them. To him, Jesus suffered with the *minjung*, who were present not only inside but also outside the Church (Küster 2010:67).

To sum up, Ahn's theology was, to a large extent, drawn from the western well (Küster 2010:67-8),[25] but that water never satisfied him, which is why he critically reinterpreted it in the Korean context (Küster 2010:68). It was apparent from this perspective that his western theology had served as a stepping stone to his own unique style of theology, not as contradictory but as complimentary (Küster 2010:68). This enabled him

---

[25]"I was educated by Western theology. I cannot divert from it. It is within me; it is part of me. My thoughts, my language, also logics plays a role . . . I admit it, whether I like it or not, consciously or unconsciously, I cannot reject it" (Küster 2010:68).

to continue to develop the independent Korean theology—namely, Korean Minjung Theology. Thus, he argued that the locus created a certain perspective, and it was the locus of theology that determined its content (Segundo 1976:8). To him, the locus was the *Sitz im Leben* (i.e., the life-situation of the suffering *minjung*) and its content is Korean Minjung Theology (Ahn 1987:12-16). In short, Ahn was a dwarf standing on a giant's (western theology's) shoulder, which allowed him to see the farther of the two.

Discovering the Ochlos-*Minjung* in the Gospel of Mark

Ahn's uniquely Minjung Theology was introduced in his article, "Nation, Minjung, and the Church," published in *Christian Thoughts*, April 1975 (Ahn 1990:25). Although being the first article which interpreted *minjung* as *ochlos*, it was his later one titled "Jesus and Ochlos" that developed the quintessence of his theory of *minjung* and *ochlos* in a full measure (Kim 2013:39). From then on, the term *ochlos* was the trademark of his own way of discovering *minjung*.

Ahn defined the term *ochlos* in the Gospel of Mark as excluded people (the crowd) "deprived of the place to which they belong" (Kim 2013:40). Here, *ochlos* rendered those who existed but were regarded as nonexistent (Kim 2011:43). This definition went beyond that of Genzo Tagawa, who first categorized the word *ochlos* as a group of low-class people that included the sick, the tax-collectors, the prostitutes, and the demon-possessed (Kim 1983). While Tagawa reduced *ochlos* to the place of 'audience' in the Gospel of Mark, Ahn identified them with the masses around the historical Jesus, "who come together wherever Jesus appears during his public life" (Küster 2010:68). In fact, Ahn's theory of the Gospel of Mark identified *ochlos* as God's people who were poor, marginalized, and despised—namely, the suffering *minjung* of Galilee.

This led to Ahn's radical interpretation of a reciprocal relation between Jesus and the *ochlos-minjung*. By paying special attention to Jesus' preferential option for them, he even boldly represented Jesus as the *ochlos-minjung*. As evidence, not only did Jesus spend most of his time with them, he also proclaimed the Kingdom of God as their future (Moltmann 2000:255, Küster 2010:70). In short, Jesus was willing to identify himself with the *ochlos-minjung* as being one of them. Thus, Ahn argued that the core of Jesus' messianic mission was not only to be with them, but also to suffer with them even unto death on the Cross (Lee 2005:524). Here, Jesus and *ochlos* are inseparable—"[T]here is no Jesus without the *ochlos-minjung*, as conversely there is no *ochlos-minjung* without Jesus" (Chung 2009: 190-91). By seeing Jesus "from the angle of the forsaken, naked, and castigated *minjung*" (Chung 2009:190-91), he came to conclude that "Jesus becomes the Messiah not because he is in fact God, but because he is a fellow *ochlos* (*minjung*)" (Chang 2006:207).

Encouraged by that, Ahn began to develop his radical reinterpretation of Christology which proposed its immediate application to Korea's contemporary context (Chung 2009:189-90). Alongside the theme of Kim, Chi Ha's play, "The Golden-Crowned Jesus," he urged the Korean church to cut itself off from the classical Christology formulated by western traditions and thus to become "the liberators of the colonial Christologies" (Orevillo-Montenegro 2006:37, Lee 2005:524). It was his conviction that Jesus was imprisoned by Christian dogma and only "the poor, the miserable, and the persecuted"—namely, the *minjung*—could set Jesus free and remove the golden crown from his head (Chung 2009:190).

In conclusion, Ahn no longer portrayed Jesus as Christ of the Church with the golden crown, but rather as the liberated one by and with the *ochlos-minjung*. Therefore, it was not Jesus but the *ochlos-minjung* who could save themselves from despairing and giving up.

Theology of Event: Jesus Event as Minjung Event

From his radical Christology, Ahn's distinction between the Jesus event and kerygma became visible. He argued that the Christ of the kerygma and the historical Jesus were two different concepts. While the kerygma "was primarily concerned with the meaning" as the dogmatic formulation, the historical Jesus focused on "the description of the Jesus event" (Ahn 1984:30). Thus, the former was transmitted primarily by the institutionalized church, whereas the latter by the *ochlos-minjung* (Ahn 1984 28):

To Ahn, the kerygma paradigm not only de-historicized the Jesus-event, but it also propped up the authority of the church. He criticized the paradigm because, in his view the Christology in this Kerygma has greatly served as an ideology to preserve the Church, but at the cost of silencing [historical] Jesus (Orevillo-Montenegro 2006:38).

This explains why Ahn was not satisfied with Bultmann's theology, which ignored the question of the historical Jesus (Küster 2010:70). Against Bultmann's kerygmatic theology, he thereby proposed the so-called "theology of event,"[26] by arguing that "[I]n the beginning there was the event, not the kerygma" (Ahn 1984:27).

Ahn's theology of event was theorized by his focus on the Gospel of Mark. Here he provided this remarkable insight—that there was oral transmission by *ochlos* between Jesus and the Gospel of Mark (Ahn 1982) and that such transmission was in the form of narrative, especially rumors (Ahn 1984:37, Küster 2010:71). The conclusion he reached through this approach was that the subversive and dangerous memory of Jesus was spread via rumors by the *ochlos-minjung* of Galilee (Küster 2010:72). In this sense, they were not only the audience of the Gospel of

---

[26] Ahn stated about the event, "Western theology asks only who Jesus is, about his *persona*. Its answer is that his person is this or that. Western theologians find comfort in such answers. But I do not think that is right. My response is Jesus is an event! And God is also an event! I came to realize it. Regarding Jesus as a person is wrong! This enlightenment has become a turning point in my theological journey. Event, not a Person! The person of Jesus two thousand years ago in Galilee, Palestine has no significant meaning for me. Event is more significant. This enlightenment came to me late in my life. Jesus was an event! This awareness made me turn from study on historical Jesus to Minjung Theology. In the past my study on historical Jesus focused on the person of Jesus. However, a new insight into Jesus opens up a new road that leads anew to my search for historical Jesus. I would like to see Jesus as the event of *minjung*, a collective event. The event of Jesus was not a complete, once and for all event two thousand years ago. It happens again and again not only in the church, but in history. This awareness lets my theology of the event easily pass over to Minjung Theology. . . . I liken the event of *minjung* to the magma of volcano (molten rock below ground) by analogy. An amount of magma erupts at a certain time in history. In Jesus time, a large volcano erupted and overflowed magma, which is the event of Jesus. Other eruptions have taken place at different historical moments. The events of *minjung* that are taking place today are not disparate and separate ones, but are connected to the event of Jesus two thousand years ago. Jesus appears to us through the events of *minjung*! It is nonsense to quest for the Jesus of two thousand years ago, or to quest for the Christ in doctrine. Important is where Christ of today –in my word, today's event of Jesus –appears" (Ahn 1987:25-6, 35).

Mark, but also the transmitters of the rumors, including the suffering of Jesus on the Cross and his resurrection—namely, the Jesus event (Kim 2013:45). Thus, Ahn's theory of rumor through the Gospel of Mark was a Copernican revolution in historical Jesus studies (Kim 2013:42).

Ahn's creative understanding of the *ochlos-minjung* as transmitters of the Jesus event was a prelude to his next theological subject—the *ochlos-minjung* as the subject of the Jesus event. Here, his radical interpretation of the Gospel of Mark once again played an important role. To him, Mark's Gospel included "the salvific story of the Jesus event" whose main performers and transmitters were the *ochlos-minjung* of the time (Kim 2013:45). What was decisive here was that they did not remain the object, but were actively involved in the Jesus event as the subject (Kim 2013:45). "Through interpreting Christ's suffering on the cross as sharing their lot, the [*ochlos*]-*minjung* who are alienated in their suffering can and should re/construct their identity and become the subject of history" (Küster 2010:75).

However, Ahn's discovery of the *ochlos-minjung* as the subject of the Jesus event would not diminish or disqualify the role of Jesus as Messiah; rather it served as an occasion to overcome the subject-object dichotomy through event (Kim 2013:45). Jesus had brought about the event together with the *ochlos-minjung*; while at the same time, the *ochlos-minjung* brought about the Jesus event together with Jesus (Kim 2013:45). Just as Jesus was the *ochlos-minjung*, so, the Jesus event was the *ochlos-minjung* event as the event of salvation (Kim 2013:46).

Ahn now went one step further. By postulating an analogy between the Markan *ochlos* and the Korean *minjung*, he began to synchronize the Jesus event with the present *minjung* event in Korea (Küster 2010:74), the decisive proof being the Chun, Tae-Il event in 1970. However, despite he read the event of Chun as an epiphany of the Jesus-*minjung* event in Korea (Kim 2013:46), that did not mean a direct and ontological identification of Jesus with Chun, Tae-Il, but rather "a realization of the genealogical continuity between the Jesus-event and the Chun, Tae-Il event in Korea" (Kim 2013:46).

In summation, with insight from theology of event, Ahn found the answer to the question that had long troubled him—"Who is Jesus for us today?" By considering a *corporate theologia crucis*, or Jesus' social biography with the *ochlos-minjung* as the hermeneutical key to the event of salvation of the *ochlos-minjung* (Küster 2010:75, Chung 2009:189-90), Ahn came out to see and witness the Jesus event where the *ochlos-minjung* have struggled for justice and life, realizing Jesus as an event and the Jesus event as the *ochlos-minjung* event, recurring in Korea here and now.

Summary: Ahn, the Radical Reformer as Being-in-the-*Minjung* in the Jesus Event

Ahn's theology began with his rediscovery of the suffering *minjung*, which came not from seminary or church but out of *Hyun-Jang*, the *Sizt-im-Leben* of the *minjung*. Refusing to do theology sitting on a couch, he was willing to anticipate the place of *Hyun-Jang* where he could encounter the suffering Christ in the suffering *minjung*. This affirmed his theology as being deeply rooted in the suffering *minjung* to whom Jesus did show his unconditional love and support, making it possible for him to reinterpret the Bible from below, apart from the western point of view. This led to his idea of the *ochlos-minjung*, a most critical and creative theory on Minjung Theology.

In his quest for the historical Jesus, Ahn drew a sharp distinction between the Christ of kerygma and the historical Jesus. While rightly paying attention to a deficit of the former, he focused on the latter, who related to the *ochlos-minjung*. This was culminated in his radical notion of Jesus as the *ochlos-minjung*. In identifying with them, "Jesus was not suffering *for* but *with* the [*ochlos*]-*minjung*" (Küster 2010:116). This sociological interpretation of *ochlos* in the Gospel of Mark brought progression in Ahn's *ochlos-minjung* theology. By defining Markan *ochlos* as a social group (i.e., "the masses deprived of the place to which they belong"), Ahn constituted his unique theory of the *ochlos-minjung* as transmitters of the Jesus event primarily by means of rumor.

Furthermore, Ahn began to contextualize his theology of the *ochlos-minjung* in Korean society. By re-reading the Chun, Tae-Il event as a reappearance of the Jesus-*minjung* event, he represented the *ochlos-minjung* as not only the audience, but also the transmitter and the subject of the Jesus event. Thus, it was apparent from this perspective that the quintessence of Ahn's theology was brought forward—that being, Jesus as the *ochlos-minjung* and the Jesus-event as the *ochlos-minjung* event. In this light, Ahn can rightfully be identified as the Radical Reformer as being-in-the-*ochlos-minjung* in the Jesus event today.

Chapter 9
Profiles of Four Key Korean Minjung Theologians

Kim, Yong-Bock (金容福, 1938-)

Biographical Sketch

Although Kim, Yong-Bock was by far the youngest among the first generation minjung theologians, it has never been an issue that he holds a key position in the spirit of Minjung Theology (Küster 2010:95). Born in 1938 in Gimje (金堤) of *Chulla* province, Kim's childhood was not a happy one. He lost his father at an early age and lived at an uncle's with his mother and sisters (Küster 2010:95). Since his aunt was a Christian, he went to church for the first time with his cousin. His life pressed by household chores in the uncle's house, the church served as a haven for him (Küster 2010:96) and would eventually affect his future plans.

In the midst of desperate conditions, Kim became convinced that getting involved in 'spiritual work' would make his life more worthwhile; so, he decided to study to become a pastor (Küster 2010:96). However, harsh reality would push him to a crossroad regarding what to pursue as a field of study—theology at the Presbyterian Theological Seminary or philosophy at Yonsei University. He decided on the latter, rationalizing that doing philosophy was a prerequisite for doing theology (Küster 2010:96).

So, in 1957, Kim entered Yonsei University and almost immediately began distinguishing himself academically, even to the extent of earning a scholarship (Küster 2010:96). However, in 1960, Korea's April 19th

Student Revolution shook his university life; and he played a leading role in this movement for democracy and was arrested with other strike organizers (Küster 2010:97). After 40 days in jail, he returned to his studies, eventually graduating in 1961. Difficulties, especially financial, only hardened his desire to study abroad—this time, theology (Küster 2010:97). That desire was realized when he was accepted (with a full scholarship) by Princeton University (Küster 2010:97), which he entered in 1963 after being discharged from Korea's military air force.

At Princeton, Kim pursued and retained his distinctive theological methodology, which was markedly different from that of most other students (Küster 2010:97-8). Wanting to preserve himself as an Asian Christian, he requested and was granted an interdisciplinary study of theology and East Asian history, which included Japanese and Chinese rather than German and French as the language requirement (Küster 2010:97).

Kim's dissertation, "Historical Transformation, People's Movement and Messianic Koinonia," in 1976 was a healthy combination between his bold, creative methodology and Princeton's open and inclusive policy (Küster 2010:98). This "historical-theological sketch" enabled him to see the Bible and Korean history from the *minjung's* eyes. "[T]he language of the Bible was directly applied to the history of the Korean people. It was becoming a historical language and not just a 'church' language" (Kim 1981:108). Based on this, he developed a new theological methodology, that being the "social biography" of the *minjung*. The red thread of this concept was rediscovery of the *minjung* as the subject of history (Kim 1981:187).

From then on, Kim's main concern was subject-hood of the *minjung*, or the concept of *minjung* messianism. Yet he refused to allow that concept to be identified with deification of the *minjung* (Küster 2010:101). His focus was not on ability of the *minjung* to redeem themselves but on "their corporate subjectivity in participating in the Messianic Kingdom" (Kim 1981:187). This resulted in his clear distinction between "messianic politics" and "political messianism" (Küster 2010:101). Calling these two types of messianism "Jesus messianism" and "power messianism," respectively (Kim 1981:189), he advocated choosing the former not the latter, for all powers must be judged under the rule of Jesus (Yewangoe 1987:134). His focus on *minjung* messianism has evolved a step further by not confining it to just Korean *minjung* but to all Asian's struggle for liberation within the framework of the wider ecumenical movement (Kim 1987:628-30).

Kim's active involvements after his studies at Princeton were in line with this way of expansion. Between 1974 and 1977, he served as a senior adviser to both the Christian Conference of Asia in Japan and to the World Council of Churches; he also helped in establishing the Documentation for Action Groups in Asia program in Tokyo (Küster 2010:95). His aim in so doing was to strengthen the *koinonia* of Asian churches and Christian communities as an extended version of Jesus/*minjung* messianism (Kim 1981:189).

As can be seen from his emphasis on *koinonia*, Kim began paying attention to the issue of economic justice in Asia. His adoption of Calvinist covenant theology in the 1980s, therefore, could be understood as a continuing effort to overcome the negative aspects of globalization, which had systematically fostered economic injustice and ecological destruction in Asia (Küster 2010:101). Kim's response to such perversion of neoliberal capitalism was to call for a state of *status confessionis*.[1] Because it would not only drive people against life but cause them to live in despair, the Church must stand up for "the integrity of the Gospel" to bring a halt to such injustice (Küster 2010:101). In his view, economic justice was closely related to the people's struggle for social rights and life at all levels and in all places (Kim 1986:280-85).

In the 1990s, Kim continued to lead an active life as head of Hanil Theological Seminary (1992-1999), the Korea Association of Christian Studies (1994-1995), the South East Asia Graduate School of Theology, and the Korea Association of Minjung Theology (1999-2000). Based on these experiences, he then decided to start his own school that would focus on the study of life (*salim*), a decision that eventually bore fruit in 2010 with establishment of the Asia Pacific Graduate School for the Integral Study of Life (Küster 2010:102). This vision to expand the

---

[1]This term literally means a state of confessing, but also renders the technical sense of an individual or the Church's doctrinal stance/protest on socio-political questions, based on the integrity of the gospel. "For Protestantism, a *status confessionis* is by definition a moment of truth, "a moment in which a Christian community are of the opinion that a situation has developed, a moment of truth has dawned, in which nothing less than the gospel itself, is at stake, so that they feel compelled to witness and act over against this threat'" (Smit 1984:21-46)

concept of *salim* in the Asian context echoed in a group of progressive minjung theologians who considered it a new theological impetus to spur a "passionate theology of life" (Küster 2010:148). Such portrays Kim as a living legacy who is still prolific, productive, and making many significant contributions to Minjung Theology as "the last of the core group of first generation minjung theologians," together with David Suh (1931-) (Küster 2010:101).

Theological Perspective

History as the Social Biography of the *Minjung*

In general, Kim's theological motive coincides with the goal of Minjung Theology, which is resolution of the *minjung's han*. However, he distinguishes himself by adopting and developing his own theological methodology, using the Korean *minjung's* "social biography" as his theological frame of reference (Kim 1984:66-78):

> The identity and reality of the *minjung* is known not by a philosophical or scientific definition of their essence or nature, but rather through their own stories—their social biographies which the *minjung* themselves create and therefore can tell best. This story of the *minjung* as their social biography is told vis-à-vis the power structure that rules the people; and therefore, power is the antagonist in the story, while the people are the subjects. The *minjung* themselves are the protagonists. Thus, the story of the *minjung* entails story and destiny (Kim 1981:184).

Looking anew at *han* as "a collective feeling in the collective social biography of the oppressed *minjung*," Kim stresses the immediate need of re-reading Korea's history from below—i.e., from the *minjung's* point of view (Kim 1981:188, Suh 1981:24). Seen from the social biography of the *minjung*, that history sheds a different light on his perspective:

> The social biography is not merely social or cultural history; it is political in the sense that it is comprehensively related to the

reality of power and the 'polis,' namely, the community. . . . Social biography functions to integrate and to interrelate the dimensions and components of the people's social and cultural experiences, especially in terms of the dramatic scenario of the people as the historical protagonists (Kim 1982:369-89).

This provides Kim a key to reinterpreting Korean history as a dynamic conflict between "the *minjung* as protagonists and those in power as antagonists" (Kim 1981:184, Küster 2010:100). Rather than having history always happening to them, the *minjung* can make history happen. In this light, he continues, they can become the subject of rather than just the object of history (Kim 1981:184-85).

It is apparent from this perspective that *minjung* movements in history not only mirror subject-hood of the *minjung*, but also produce its legitimacy (Kim 1981:187); it serves as a testimony that they have their own power and authority in making and sustaining history (Kim 1981:188). Recognizing the concern that the *minjung's* subject-hood can be dismissed into Marxist ideology, Kim points up the distinction between the *minjung* and the Marxist proletariat (Kim 1981:184). To him, unlike the latter, *minjung* have not a static but rather a dynamic nature that encompasses socio-economic-political as well as religious-cultural biography, which ultimately points to their subjectivity. "The proletariat is defined socio-economically, while the *Minjung* is known politically . . . the *Minjung* as historical subject transcends the socio-economic determination of history—a 'beyond' history which is often expressed in religious form" (Kim 1981:184).[2]

While Kim defines the *minjung* in a political concept determined mainly by their relation to the political power (Kim 1981:184), he also identifies them with the poor in the Covenant Code as a spiritual reference (Kim 1986:281). However, most interesting is his claim of a link between the subject-hood of the *minjung* and the messianic movement in Korean history (Kim 1981:185-86). In his view, many

---

[2]In the same vein, Suh made a distinction between the two. "While the proletariat of Marx's theory is rigidly defined in socio-economic terms in all political circumstances, the notion of *Minjung* provides a framework of theology which takes into consideration the socio-economic, cultural, messianic praxis and political history of Korea and the socio-political biography of the Christian koinonia in Korea" (Suh 1981:19).

Korean traditions and movements are messianic. "History is the process in which the *minjung* realize their own destiny to be the free subjects of history and to participate in the Messianic Kingdom" (Kim 1981:186, 1982:371). And since the *minjung* "realize their corporate subjectivity in participating in the Messianic Kingdom," their subject-hood is an eschatological one (Kim 1981:187). It is 'already' but 'not yet' given to them (Kim 1982:371, Küster 2010:100-101):

> In the historical reality the *minjung* do not become the subject of history but are defined by the ruling system. Thus, the *minjung* find themselves situated to be ruled by the ruling class, and consequently the historical experience of the *minjung* is characterized as suffering. Seen from the eschatological perspective of history, the *minjung*, though suffering at present, are in the process of becoming the subjects of history depending on the hope and promise that they will become the subjects of history. Thus, the *minjung* struggle to become the subjects of history (Kim 1982:372).

Within this framework of ideas, Kim has further developed the dynamic relationship of the Messianic Kingdom and *minjung* history, observing that the Messianic Kingdom is realized by the struggle of the *minjung* in history (Kim 1981:187). In this sense, he lists a number of messianic movements in Korean history as evidence—e.g., Maitreya Buddhism;[3] the tale of *Hong, Kil-Dong* (a Korean version of Robin Hood, who collected a gang to rescue the poor and attack the rich); the *Donghak* religious movement; and the March 1st Independence Movement (Kim 1981:187-89). The red thread that runs through all of these is the suffering *minjung*; for it triggers Messianism, which is "the collective

---

[3] In early Korean history, the Buddha Maitreya is considered as a liberating figure and triggers the *minjung* to participate in many revolutionary movements (Suh 1981:175-76). Besides, the name "Maitreya" (taken from "the Sanskrit word *maitri*, meaning "kindness," "love," "benevolence," "friendship," "friendliness" or "goodwill") indicates a coming Buddha or a future Buddha. Thus "Maitreya" has been referred to as "Loving One" or "Friendly One," "embodiment of all-encompassing love" (Prophet 2006:32). Since he is considered by his disciples to be a messiah who would rescue the world, even today "many Buddhists await Maitreya's coming in much the same way that Christians await Jesus' second coming" (Prophet 2006:4).

longing for an ideal leader to institute the Messianic Kingdom of justice, *koinonia* (fellowship), and *shalom* (peace)" (Lee 1996:42, Kim 1981:187).

The Christian movement in Korea in this light receives a new perspective. Kim reads the central biblical stories, such as the Exodus and the Jesus event (i.e., his life, death, and resurrection) as the stories of the *minjung* in their struggle for liberation and justice that reconstruct the identification of Messiah with them (Kim 1981:189). "Thus, the language of Jesus' Cross was the language of the suffering of the Korean people" (Kim 1981:117) who "recognize their own suffering in the suffering of the Cross" (Küster 2010:99).

Here, the two stories became transparent and ultimately dovetail into the messianic *minjung* movement (Kim 1981:109). This leads Kim to conclude that "the biblical logic of suffering led from the suffering messiah to the coming of the messianic kingdom; thereby encouraging Christians to believe that they suffered on behalf of the whole Korean people, and so Christianity developed the characteristics of a messianic movement" (Kim 1981:183-93 quoted by Kim 2010:224). Thus, these messianic movements are the core of history for which the suffering people, the poor, and the oppressed continue to struggle.

Yet Kim also makes clear that subject-hood of the *minjung* is closely related to the divine intervention of Messianic Kingdom into history, which renders him quite sensitive to any possibility of achieving their subject-hood through revolts. He rejects the notion of revolt as a way to realize subject-hood (Kim 1982:372). For he is convinced that it is realized only when the eschatological Messianic Kingdom intervenes into history, which leads to his critical separation of the messianic politics of Jesus from the political messianism that deserves our close attention (Kim 1981:187).

The Messianic Politics of Jesus against Political Messianism

Linking the Messianic Kingdom to *minjung* history, Kim develops his own *minjung*-messianism based on the *minjung's* subject-hood in history. Against rampant speculation that his *minjung*-messianism is deifying *minjung*, he makes clear that the ultimate Messiah is Jesus, the Suffering Servant (Lee 1996:42), then uses the subject-hood of the *minjung* as a boundary marker between *minjung*-messianism (the messianic politics of Jesus) and power (political) messianism (Kim 1981:191).[4] Here, "The messianic politics of Jesus is a radical challenge to all forms of political, royal, and power messianism" (Kim 1981:187).

Pointing to Japanese colonialism, North Korea communism, and modern technocracy as examples of power (political) messianism in Korea, Kim recounts their antagonism against the *minjung* as his focal point. In claiming absolute power, he argues, it makes the subject-hood of the *minjung* a historical nothing so as to reduce them as merely an object of its messianic claim (Kim 1981:190-91). He then compares that to the messianic politics of Jesus which helps the *minjung* realize their historical subject-hood and thereby makes them the masters of their own destiny (Kim 1981:191). This means, by placing all powers under Jesus' messianic politics, the *minjung* recapture their own identity as the subject of history. In short, the messianic politics of Jesus takes precedence over political messianism as true messianism, which epitomizes the subject-hood of the *minjung* (Kim 1981:191).

This sheds further light on the relationship between the Messiah and the *minjung*. In this dynamic, Kim interprets "the *minjung* as subject and the Messiah as their function" (Kim 1981:191)—that is, through messianic politics, Jesus the Messiah performs his messianic role, while at the same time the *minjung* realize their historical subjectivity in joining with the Messiah (Kim 1981:191):

> [The messianic politics of Jesus] is concerned with saving and transforming the *minjung* so that its subjecthood may be realized. Hence, all powers must be under the rule of Jesus the Messiah, who came to be the Servant of the *minjung*, who died for them, and who rose from the dead so that the *minjung* may rise from the power of death historically and not just at the end of time (Kim 1981:187).

Kim precludes any possibility of performing the messianic politics of Jesus by and with a ruler or an elite; for the Suffering Servant is to

---

[4]Kim also calls it, respectively, "power messianism" vs. "Jesus messianism"; "ruler messianism" vs. "*minjung* messianism"; and "political messianism" vs. "messianic servanthood" (Kim 1981:187).

identify himself with the suffering *minjung* (Kim 1981:191). The implication here is two-fold—one being his identification with the suffering *minjung*, the other his function as servant to the *minjungs'* aspiration for liberation (Kim 1981:191). From it, Kim proposes that the critical task of the Christian community is to serve not only as agent for the suffering *minjung* but as center stage of their messianic struggle (Kim 1981:192). Thus, he calls for a complete purge of political messianism from the Church (Kim 1981:192). Since the Messiah "emerges from the suffering [*minjung*] and identifies with the suffering [*minjung*]," the Church's task is to be carried out not in the power messianism, but in the servant messianism, following the footsteps of Jesus, the Suffering Servant (Kim 1981:191):

> To be sure, there are many images or models in the Bible which will help to illuminate this notion of messianic politics. For instances, there is the model of King David; there is the figure of the Son of Man in apocalyptic literature; and other kingly (the anointed) images of the Messiah. However, these have a corrupting influence, for we see the Messiah as a power personality (political messianism) who embodies self-righteousness and triumphalism. However, the most appropriate and convincing of all messianic images is that of Jesus as Suffering Servant, in the light of which we must examine and reshape other images like that of David, Son of Man, etc. (Kim 1981:191).

This enables Kim to further elaborate on the nature of the subject-hood of the *minjung*. Although recognizing its eschatological aspect, he regards their subject-hood as essentially a historical-eschatological reality. To him, the idea of "the sudden intervention of messianic politics" (i.e., the Messianic Kingdom) of Jesus crystallizes this paradox between the historical 'already' and the eschatological 'not-yet' (Kim 1982:371). On one hand, since the *minjung* become the subject of history through their participation not only in history but in the Messianic Kingdom, their subject-hood is by nature eschatological (Kim 1981:186-87). But on the other hand, by this messianic politics of Jesus, the Messianic Kingdom is realized into history and the *minjung* are transformed into the subject of history (Kim 1984:67, 1982:371-72).

Also, by this sudden intervention of the Messianic Kingdom into history, a new history emerges—one in which suffering is transformed into hope (Kim 1982:372). To Kim, this represents the triumph of Jesus' messianism over power (political) messianism; and thus, the inauguration of realized eschatology (historical-eschatological reality) accompanying the messianic rule of justice, *koinonia* (participation), and *shalom*" here and now (Kim 1981:193).

What is crucial here is Kim's emphasis on the historical sovereignty of God. To him, it is God, not the *minjung* themselves, who makes their subject-hood a historical-eschatological reality (Kim 1982:371); it is God, not the *minjung* themselves, who stands as the Lord of history (Kim 1984:73). This once again saves his *minjung*-messianism from a danger of deifying the *minjung* by saying that "The *minjung* realize their corporate subjectivity in participating in the Messianic Kingdom" (Kim 1981:187). Thus, his *minjung*-messianism finds expression in a dynamic interplay between the Messiah and the *minjung* in history:

> This God of history is not a God of transcendence, Who does not like dirty [sic] His hands by touching the problems within history. He is not a God Who overlooks the historical problems. He is not a God Who takes part in history only in principle, but not in actuality. Rather because God is the God of history, Who is not alienated from history, He prevents the evil of suffering from becoming a permanent reality in history and thereby the Minjung will not lose their bases as a historical entity (Kim 1984:73 quoted by Yewangoe 1987:136).

To sum up, Kim's social biography of the *minjung* provides a new impetus to reinterpret Korean history in the messianic movement that defines *minjung* as the subject of history through suffering and struggle. Yet his emphasis on the subject-hood of *minjung* does not eschew, but espouses Jesus as the Messiah, who not only emerges from, but also identifies with the *minjung*. Thus, the subject-hood of *minjung* can only be realized not by political (power) messianism but by Jesus messianism that all powers are subjected to the rule of Jesus.

Here, his stress falls on a dynamic interplay between the Messiah and the *minjung* in history. In his view, the notion of *minjung* as the subject of history is congruent with that of God as the Lord of history (i.e., the One who is still active in history and is sovereign over history). For the former anticipates the latter to gain their subjectivity in history, while the latter gives the former a special power to fight the existing evil forces in history (Kim 1981:191, 1984:73). This dynamic interplay between the two culminates in his idea of the sudden intervention of messianic politics into Korea's history.

Summary:
Kim, the Radical Reformer as Being-in-the-*Minjung* in the Messianic Politics of Jesus

Kim, Yong-Bock's contributions to Minjung Theology can be found primarily in regard to Korea's historical domain—the re-reading of its history from below (Kim 1982:370). Especially, he has emphasized "the need to understand the collective spirit—the consciousness and the aspirations of the *minjung*, through social biography" (Kwok 1995:15). For the *minjung*, reality is known only through its biography, its story, its hope, and its suffering (Kim 1982:372). Unfurling the social biography of *minjung* as his theological banner, Kim has tried to understand Korea's history as a messianic movement and thereby to redeem Korean *minjung* as historical protagonists. In short, Korean *minjung* are the subject of history and their social biography is the predicate.

However, Kim also finds in the subject-hood of the *minjung* in history an eschatological and transcending dimension, "a beyond history, towards the Messianic Kingdom" (Kim 1981:184, 187). This leads him to preclude any possibility of achieving their subject-hood through revolts, but rather to claim a dynamic link by arguing that the subject-hood of the *minjung* is ensured only as long as they participate in the Messianic Kingdom (Kim 1982:371).

To continue this articulation, Kim then provides a conceptual distinction between the messianic politics of Jesus and political (power) messianism (Kim 1981:191). In his view, Jesus' messianic politics is critical of the political (power) messianism, which has been to force the *minjung* into servitude, and thus, to negate their historical subjectivity that eventually renders them a historical nothing (Kim 1981:191).

Instead, by challenging "all forms of political, royal, and power messianisms," the messianic politics of Jesus helps *minjung* realize their historical subject-hood under the rule of Jesus (Kim 1981:187). In Messiah's identification with the powerless, Kim urged, the *minjung* become the subject. This leads to the dynamic solidarity of the Messiah and the *minjung*—that being "a relation between the *minjung* as the subject and the Messiah as their function" (Kim 1981:191).

This line of understanding also opens the way for Kim's idea of "the sudden intervention of the Messianic Kingdom into history" (Kim 1982:371). To him, the dynamic interplay between the Messiah and the *minjung* ushers in a new order that serves to bring the Messianic Kingdom into history, and thus, transforms the history of suffering into one of hope (Kim 1982:372). Indeed, it makes the subject-hood of the *minjung* a historical-eschatological reality—namely, a critical tension of the historical 'already' and the eschatological 'not-yet' (Kim 1984:67, 1982:371-72). However, Kim never loses his emphasis on God's sovereignty over the *minjung's* subject-hood as its verification level (Kim 1984:73).

Not surprisingly, when "the sudden intervention of the Messianic Kingdom" has fallen into Korea's history, Kim has not hesitated to choose the power of the powerless (namely, the *minjung*) by becoming himself the Radical Reformer as being-in-the-*minjung* in the messianic politics of Jesus, who "emerges from the suffering *minjung* and identifies with the suffering *minjung*."

Hyun, Young-Hak (玄永學, 1921-2004)

Biographical Sketch

Hyun, Young-Hak, a theologian of *han* (恨, bitterness) and *heoung* (興, fun), was born in 1921 in *Hamheung* (咸興), the capital of South Hamgyong province, the first child of his father, a pastor and mother, a Christian 'modern-woman' who conformed to Western education but confronted with Japan as a colonial power. (Küster 2010:87). He was sickly from birth but regained his health thanks to his mother's dedicated care. Upon his father's untimely death, he would be raised (very strictly and correctly) by his now-widowed mother. Hyun's original career plan—to be a doctor to support his family—had to be withdrawn in order to follow his father's wish that "one of his sons would follow in his footsteps" (Küster 2010:87). Thus, after graduating from high school in 1938, with the help of a missionary friend, he entered Kwansei Gakuin University (関西學院大學) in Japan to study theology (Küster 2010:87).

At that time, Kwansei Gakuin University was under the influence of liberal theology; ideas of Albreht Ritschl (1822-1889) and Friedrich Schleiermacher (1768-1834) forming the mainstream of theological discussion (Hyun 1985:29). At first, Hyun had come to terms with this theological atmosphere and even enjoyed it. Yet soon he himself began posing some thorny questions, such as, "What has Schleiermacher to do with Moses who liberated his people from Egypt?" and "What is the use of studying liberal theology for my people who currently suffer from Japanese colonial power?" These questions, which stemmed from his recognition of the contradictions of the times, took on fresh meaning when he visited some Korean churches in Japan, which were located in the slums of *burakumin* (部落民; ぶらくみん)[5] (Küster 2010:87). Here, he witnessed and experienced a great gap between the seminary teaching and reality (Hyun 1985:30) and came to realize that a theology removed from reality could be hopeless and helpless (Küster 2010:87).

Upon completing his studies in 1943, Hyun (still treasuring what he saw and experienced) began his pastoral ministry at the Korean church in *Kobe* (Küster 2010:88). However, faced with the Japanese army's forced conscription, he scrapped his ministry in Japan and returned to Korea in 1944 (Küster 2010:88) and worked for a metal company in *Na-*

---

[5]The *burakumin* (literally it means village people, from the words *buraku* (部落), meaning hamlet or small village, and *min* (民), meaning people like 'min'-jung) has been pejoratively applied to descendants of outcast communities from the feudal era society. The history of anti-*buraku* attitudes is long and deep-rooted. From the Tokugawa period (1600-1868), the leather and butchery workers were considered polluted and thus they were excluded and disadvantaged by other Japanese who did not want to be in contact with or 'polluted' by them. This discrimination had permanently and irretrievably infected not only those who carried out such tasks, but also their descendants and associates in all future generations (McLaughlan 2006:1). In this sense, the *burakumin* are social outcasts rather than an ethnic or racial group. The marginalization and prejudice are real and ongoing. Although "ethnically speaking purely Japanese," they are still victimized by the increase of derogatory and formal discrimination against them in contemporary Japan (Küster 2001:163-77).

Heung (羅興). When Korea was liberated from Japan's colonial rule in August 1945 (Küster 2010:88), he worked there for one more year, after which time he was invited to become an assistant professor at Ehwa Women's University on account of his studies in Japan (Küster 2010:88). Yet, feeling the need for further study in theology, he declined the offer, and instead, enrolled at the Biblical Seminary of New York via a scholarship. Acquiring his bachelor's degree in 1949, he moved on to Union Theological Seminary (also in New York), where he was exposed to the theology of Reinhold Niebuhr (Küster 2010:88).

At that time, Hyun developed a special interest for Niebuhr's idea of Christian Social Ethics, which, coupled with his personal experience of the *burakumin* in Japan, reminded him of that burning question: "What has the biblical message to do with current reality?" The more he attended Niebuhr's lectures and read his books, the more he aligned himself to Niebuhr's idea (Küster 2010:88).

When Hyun returned to Korea in 1955 with a Th.M degree, he had already become a 'little Niebuhr' who actively spread his theological bent to the students at Ehwa Women's University, where he resumed his teaching career (Küster 2010:88). However, being a faculty member, he soon found himself unable to concentrate on academic work, but rather was bogged down with many administrative duties, which prevented him from committing to further studies. This motivated his decision to re-enroll at Union Theological Seminary in 1964 at age 43 (Küster 2010:88).

Waiting to greet Hyun there was the Secular Theology of Harvey Cox (1929-). At first, he was shocked at Cox's advocacy of the secular fashion of God, which sounded very un-Christian to him (Küster 2010:88). But, the more he thought about Cox's argument, the more sympathetic he became to this radical idea (Küster 2010:88). What attracted him most was that Secular Theology called for theology from below, which was exactly opposite of theology from above. In his eye, as "theological thinking has to start with the reality we live in," secularization itself is none other than biblical faith (Küster 2010:88-89).

This resulted in Hyun's complete break with Niebuhr and development of his own theological methodology with Cox's Secular Theology as the important nexus that could turn the "secular city" into a place where the sacred was present. Based on this, he attempted to re-contextualize Cox's secular city onto Korean soil by arguing that "The reality I had to start from is not the American secular city, but the secular world of Korea or better: the non-Christian world of Korea" (Küster 2010:89).

From then on, Hyun began paying more attention to the reality of Korean society, which marked another turning point in his theological journey. Yet, it was not until after his involvement in the urban and industrial mission (UIM) in the 1970s[6] that he entered the road to Minjung Theology in earnest (Küster 2010:89). Even though completely shocked when he witnessed the reality of the poor in the slums, there he found "the sacred in the secular city," the incarnated Jesus in the underdog—namely, the suffering *minjung* (Hyun 1985:29-31). This ultimately enabled him to be a theologian who chose to side with the *minjung*, thus making his theology a Minjung Theology.

Beyond abstract and conceptual theory, Hyun's theology began to take on a new form—a theology of body, or a theology of "Oh-Jang-Yuk-Bu" (五臟六腑, the whole internal organ) that embodied the struggles and hope of the *minjung* as the basic principle of theology (Hyun 1985:354-59). His next step was to focus on Korea's folk cultures, especially the Korean mask dance, which he saw as a prime example of theology of body language of the *minjung* who in this way broke their *han* and thus experienced the "critical transcendence" over their suffering situation (Hyun 1981:47-54). This culminated in his "Christology of Fools," which led the *minjung* to the presence of God in the midst of suffering (Hyun 1981:47-54).

As an ardent proponent of this kind of theology of body, Hyun joined forces with other *minjung* theologians for the democracy and human rights of Korea's *minjung*. This stance resulted in Chun, Doo-Hwan's new military group discharging him from the university in 1980 (Küster 2010:92). Although reinstated in 1984, two years later, he had to leave again due to having reached mandatory retirement age. After

---

[6]President Park's government-led economic development left an increasing number of the city poor and the industrial workers in Korea's society, while widening further the incoming gulf in a rich-get-richer, poor-get-poorer society. At this juncture, some progressive Christians came to feel a sense of duty to protect the urgent human needs of workers, and this led to the creation of urban and industrial missions (UIM). It was their conviction that to continue this industrial evangelism, they had to experience directly the reality of workers, and thus, many of them actually became laborers for six months to a year (Suh 1981:38-41). Hyun felt an acute need to join this action-oriented organizational movement and became involved in it.

retiring, he continued as emeritus professor of Ehwa Women's University and visiting professor of Kwansei Gakuin University. In 1997, even though struggling with illness, Hyun wrote his significant article, "Mask Dance of Jesus," in 1997. On January 4, 2004, this outstanding *minjung* theologian died at his home at age 84.

Theological Perspective

Once a Neibuhrian ethicist and a follower of Cox's secular theology, Hyun has now become a strong advocate of a theology of body, or of the whole internal organ that bore the marks of people in agony (Hyun 1985:28-40). In resonance with C. S. Song's argument that theology must "body forth" from the people (Song 1982:165-66), Hyun has strived to reveal the sweat, tears, and laughter of the *minjung* in his studies of Korean *minjung* cultures (Hyun 1997:71). In his observation, through their paintings, songs, stories, *pansori* (one-man opera), and mask dances, the *minjung* are both lamenting their miserable lot and expressing their hopes and wishes. By singing, narrating, and dancing the incongruities of reality, they not only can create distance from their own situation but can transcend their *han* (Hyun 1985:35, Park 1988:124).

Here, Hyun focuses particularly on the critical transcendence experience as 'communicated' via mask dance; for it serves as a theology of body language not only to disclose their hidden *han*, but also to transcend it with tears and laughter. From it comes his distinctive understanding of the *minjung* as the clown (comic hero) and a Christology of Fools (Hyun 1985:13-4).

Minjung as the Clown (Comic Hero)

The mask dance in Korea (탈춤, *talchum*), the origin of which can be traced back to shamanistic village rituals, is a popular form (Lee 2007:194) consisting "not only of dance, but also of rhythmic instrumental music, songs and dialogue between the performers and the musicians, and between the performers and the audience" (Hyun 1981:47-48). It is usually performed outdoors with no particular type of stage; and the players act on the basis of a clumsy plot line or synopsis of each scene—thus, spontaneity and improvisation play a decisive role (Cho 1982:43).

In his studies, Hyun looks specifically at the satirical nature in the mask dance, which culminates in the high degree of comic sense and critical spirit (Hyun 1981:47-54, Yewangoe 1987:121). It includes a great deal of humor, satire, and bawdy language (Hyun 1981:48) that are mostly used to ridicule and criticize the oppressors of ordinary people (the *minjung*) (Hyun 1981:50). Thus, he points out that the mask dance serves as a vent for the *han* of the oppressed (Park 2011:17) in which they can address their grievances (*han*) against the upper class through the vehicles of satire, laughter, and debauchery (Küster 2010:90).

Hyun highlights vividly the nature of the Korean mask dance by focusing on the "Bongsan Mask Dance," one of the best known styles today. Among its seven acts, he speaks of three key episodes with the main characters being the *Nojang* (an old Buddhist monk), three *Yangban* (aristocrats/noblemen), *Miyal-Halmi* (an old woman); and *Maltugi* (servant of the *Yangban*) (Hyun 1981:43-49). Here, each character represents an entire class rather than an individual—i.e., the former two (*Nojang and Yangban*) portraying the upper class and the latter two (*Miyal-Halmi and Maltugi*) portraying the commoners (Kim 1985:51). With the story's main aim being to reveal the hypocrisy and misbehavior of the monk and the noblemen, they are comically caricatured and occasionally mimicked by their servant *Maltugi*, which evokes laughter from the audience which is comprised of common people (Kim 1985:8).

Hyun finds in such laughter a laughter of the *minjung*. They ridicule the *Nojang* (the old monk), who is being saturated with metaphysical abstraction, and thus, provides no concrete answer for their real lives. They also play jokes on the three *Yangban* (aristocrats/noblemen) by mocking them as the blind literati of the blind. The ordinary people, on the contrary, identify themselves with *Miyal-Halmi* (the old lady), who first is separated from her husband for a long time when he goes off to war, but then is beaten to death when he returns with his new concubine (Hyun 1985:13).

From all this, Hyun draws his theological implication of a "critical transcendence" (Hyun 1981:51). His insight is that, through the experience of the mask dance, the *minjung* begin to look at their life-situation afresh. By satirizing and laughing at the aristocrats, they "can become their own 'over against'" (Küster 2010:90), a satire or metaphor of the upper class that encourages them to transcend the status quo in their laughter (Hyun 1981:50-3). This experience of critical transcendence pales the absurdities of society into insignificance. In it, the tensions of *han* can be released and even sublimated into humor, satire, and laughter, which helps the *minjung* in transcending their own precarious conditions (Hyun 1985:354-59).

That explains how the *minjung* can shed tears and burst into laughter at the same time (Hyun 1985:13), or how they can laugh in tragedy which transforms a tragedy into a comedy, the suffering *han* into the liberating *dan*. Here, such so-called "tragic laughter"[7] serves as a vehicle for the *minjung's* self-emancipation—namely, "Their *han* breaks free in liberating [tragic] laughter" as a form of resistance against traumatic reality (Küster 2010:90, Ostrower 2015:184 quoted by Claassens 2015:671). What is crucial is that this resistance is not destructive but constructive, not malefic but therapeutic, not tragic but comic (Amaladoss 1997:5). For "where there is humour (laughter), there is hope and *vice-versa*" (Eckardt 1992:411 quoted by Claassens 2015:670).

At this point, characteristics of critical transcendence (or "tragic laughter") in the mask dance is self-defensive. By laughing, not only at oppressors but also at themselves, the *minjung* are defending themselves against the danger of self-righteousness (Hyun 1985:13), and thus, distinguishing themselves from the oppressive ruling powers who seek revenge (Amaladoss 1997:5). This even opens up the possibility of reconciliation. By forgiving their worst enemies, "the *minjung* are already enjoying the experience of the eschatological reality, the Kingdom of God" (Hyun 1985:13). Here, Hyun's interpretation of the mask dance has reached its apex; a dynamic interplay of resistance and reconciliation. It encourages the *minjung* to resist the oppressors, while

---

[7]The term "tragic laughter" is originally from Jacqueline Bussie, who defines it as laughter that emerges in a context of trauma, which "interrupts the system and state of oppression, and creatively attests to hope, resistance, and protest in the face of the shattering of language and traditional frameworks of thought and belief" (2007:4). However, greater insight on it came from an article, "Rethinking Humour in the Book of Jonah: Tragic Laughter as Resistance in the Context of Trauma" (2015:655-73), written by J. Claassens, the Old Testament professor of Stellenbosch University.

at the same time drawing them into reconciliation through their tears and laughter (Hyun 1985:13).[8]

In conclusion, it is in the notion of tragic laughter of the *minjung* that Hyun's emphasis on the critical transcendence in the mask dance acquires intelligibility (Hyun 1985:13). In one sense, it serves as a vent for the explosion of their *han* in the collective resistance against their enemies. In another sense, it brings resolution of *han* (*dan*), reconciling them through their tears and laughter. This enables him to depict a new identity of the *minjung* as "the clownish comic figure" that transcends "the tragic hero of revolution" (Hyun 1985:14). In short, Hyun describes the *minjung* in the mask dance as the clown (or comic hero) who transcends their suffering with both tears and laughter ("tragic laughter") and thus transforms tragedy (*han*) into comedy (*dan*), the victim into the victor.

Christology of Fools

Viewing the Korean mask dance as an interplay of *minjung's han* and *dan* (i.e., of their resistance and reconciliation), Hyun develops his own Christological interpretation, the so-called "Christology of Fools." Like other *minjung* theologians, he focuses on the significance of *han* for his Christology and distinguishes three faces of *han*—the priestly, the prophetic, and the Servant-King's (Hyun 1985:354-59). Whereas the priestly face of *han* (*jung-han*; 情恨) is more passive and patient in the painful situation, the prophetic face (*won-han*; 怨恨) is seeking justice actively through anger, revenge, and revolution (Hyun 1985:359). However, it is the Servant-King's face of *han* that crystallizes his uniquely Christological interpretation into Minjung Christology; this 'face', marked by humor, satire, and laughter is the "Christology of Fools" which culminates in the critical transcendence (or "tragic laughter") in the mask dance (Hyun 1985:359).

---

[8]Hyun delineates it in this fashion: "The *minjung* are revolutionaries, but no simple revolutionaries. If they are, after repeatedly getting beaten up, imprisoned, and killed, they would soon fall into despair and give up. Yet, they do not give up. In the process of repeated beating, the *minjung* rather have developed wisdom to survive in the most adverse conditions with human dignity. They have developed a capacity to laugh and to play clown, a way for the victim to become the victor" (Hyun 1985:12-3).

In his Christology, Hyun pays special attention to the figure of *Maltugi*, a servant-slave of the *Yangban* (aristocrat/nobleman). In the mask dance, the *Yangban* is originally depicted as the master of *Maltugi*. However, when they appear together, everything is upside-down (Yewangoe 1987:122), with *Maltugi*'s sense of humor and biting satire turning the *Yangban* into a laughing stock for all to see and jeer at (Hyun 1981:47-54). In so doing, *Maltugi* becomes known by the spectators as the protagonist, while the *Yangban* is seen as the idiot. This shows the power of paradox—servants beginning to take the place of their masters and making fun of them with audacious and abusive language (Kim 1985:40-64), as this dialogue demonstrates:

> *Maltugi*: (Suddenly jumps up and goes over to the ARISTOCRATS and hits their faces with his whip). You damn pigs... (Mimes driving pigs). Soo-ee, nose...
> *Second Aristocrat*: You wretch, Maltugi, how dare you think of us as pigs? [...]
> *Maltugi*: Damn you aristocrats, stray dogs, stop barking (After improvised abusive language, he calls the ELDER ARISTOCRAT again). Hey, Master, in order to find you, I went to your home. Your mistress greeted me and brought me a drink from the wall cabinet. I drank the rice wine, realized the mistress' intentions, and rode her belly. (In a chanting tone) Oh-oh-oh, ah-ah-ah... (All dance for a while to the music) (Lee 1985:153).

Here, *Maltugi* vents his bottled-up *han* upon his foolish master in the way, not of tragedy and seriousness but of humor and satire (Chae 1982:204). Thus, laughter and humor are the idioms of protest against the unjust situation.[9] More specifically, *Maltugi*'s actions serve as a

---

[9]In this regard, David Suh, Kwang-Sun, another famous *minjung* theologian, claims that "If revolution is humourless, and the *minjung* laugh at revolutionary seriousness, the revolutionaries would be the ones who might at the end take away laughter and humour from *minjung* for whom the revolutionaries claim to work. The humourless Zealots departed from Jesus. And the humourless Romans took Jesus' humour by giving him the royal robes and by forcing down the thorny crown on his head, even to the point of putting up the inscription on the cross: 'King of the Jews'. Jesus was, indeed, a big joke. But it was a joke of critical transcendence, a serious joke and a dangerous one, dangerous

channel to connect him to the audience in a "strangely warmed" manner. In this way, the *minjung* begin to perceive the world through the humor and laughter of *Maltugi* and "to takes his side to laugh at the false dignity of their ruling masters" (Hyun 1981:46, Massey 2011:17). In keeping with this indivisible intertwining of the two, *Maltugi* becomes a symbol of the *minjung*, who begin to realize their potential as protagonists of their own life through this mean but smart, powerless but powerful servant (Suh 1981:75).

This affinity between *Maltugi* and *minjung* is epitomized by a common dance in the final scene. This is a 'feast of fools' where the audience joins the performers. Here, shedding blood together on a cross is immediately followed by smiling and laughing together in the dance; *Maltugi* and the *minjung* are united and begin singing, dancing, and shouting together (Hyun 1981:45). Thus, Hyun argues that:

> They become one in expressing their deep-seated *han*, their unresolved angry feeling of injustice and the hunger stored deep in their hearts and stomachs. In this moment they become critical of the existing order and social system. As they shout with *Maltugi* in the mask dance, letting out their *han*, their frustration, their desire for resistance, *han* as the deep feeling turned inside is coming out in the open. The *minjung* and audience join with *Maltugi* in shouting for a fight against injustice and oppression. In the mask dance play, *Maltugi* is no longer a subservient slave boy but an independent fighter, ready to resist and cut off the vicious circle of oppression. In the laughter and shouts of the *minjung* audience, we hear their cry for liberation—and sense the storm coming (Suh 1991:171-72).

Inspired by this 'feast of fools', Hyun even elevates *Maltugi* as a Christ-like figure, a liberator who brings *dan*—namely, the resolution of *minjung's han* (Küster 2010:90). By anticipating the mask dance, the *minjung* find in *Maltugi* the Christ, who is singing, dancing, and shouting together with them. In this light, Hyun's Christology has parallels to that of C. S. Song, a renowned Taiwanese theologian. Song

---

enough to be killed on the cross" (Suh 1983:69).

not only defines Jesus as the mask of God, the God of the poor, the lost, the outcast, which is the suffering *minjung*, he also claims a close link between the mask dance of God and mask dance of people (Song 1986:221-23). To him, a 'feast of fools' becomes a place of realized eschatology where the *minjung* grasp Jesus who is wearing a *Maltugi* mask and Jesus, the mask dance of God, grasps the *minjung* at the same time:

> He [Jesus] stages the mask dance of God so that they [*minjung*] can hear, see, and touch God. And as Jesus goes on dancing the mask dance of God, he creates a community of hope—a community with a capacity for suffering as well as for rejoicing, a capacity for pain as well as for comfort, a capacity for tears as well as for laughter, a capacity for desire as well as for hope a capacity for dying as well as for living (Song 1986:223).

The uniqueness of Hyun's Christology reaches its climax in his portrayal of Jesus as the *Dokaebi* (도깨비),[10] a Korean goblin (Hyun 1985:9). Looking beyond Jesus as the *han*-ridden "ghost"[11] with the suffering *minjung*, he seeks to find a new aspect of Jesus as the *Dokaebi* who chuckles and laughs at the precarious reality of the people (Hyun 1985:2-14). "In the place of the ghost of Jesus on the cross dripping with blood, [Hyun] begins to see Jesus the *Dokaebi* or rather hear the sound of the *Dokaebi*'s hearty laugh" (Hyun 1985:9).

This notion of Jesus as the *Dokaebi* helps advance Hyun's Christology aptly; his Christology begins with him finding Jesus as *Maltugi* (i.e., a representative of the *minjung* in the mask dance), who ridicules the absurdities of the existing social order; then he develops the idea of Jesus as the mask dance of God, who is laughing and shouting

---

[10] "Dokaebi'(도깨비) is another supernatural being like the ghost. But unlike the ghost who resembles real people, 'Dokaebi' has his own features. He is tall, has horns on top of his head, and the whole body is painted red. Usually he plays havoc on people, mostly jokes, in the dark of night. By the time you discover that you have been cheated and misled during the confusion of the night, the 'Dokaebi' is already gone, but you can hear his chuckles and laughter" (Hyun 1985:9).

[11] Hyun has intentionally used the term "ghost," for "Spirit" is too abstract and metaphysical, while "image" too aesthetic and dispassionate. To Hyun, "ghost" is more material and concrete in expressing *han* (Hyun 1985:7).

together with the *minjung*; and lastly, he puts Jesus as the *Dokaebi* in the *minjung* at its centre. In essence, Hyun's Christology ends in a big joke that embraces "the ghost with tears and the *Dokaebi* with laughter of Jesus and his God in the Minjung of Korea" (Hyun 1985:14).

Summary: Hyun, the Radical Reformer as Being-in-the-*Minjung* in the Mask Dance

In his focus on a theology of body language, Hyun has sought to establish possibility of theological epistemology in the Korean *minjung* culture. His major contribution is especially attributed to his theological look at the Korean mask dance as a process for the resolution of *minjung's han* (Hyun 1981:51). By interpreting the mask dance as a collective experience of critical transcendence, he found in it the liberating dimension that gives *minjung* the wisdom and energy to overcome unjust reality with humour and laughter, the courage to fight for change and freedom, and an act of self-defense against self-righteousness—all without seeking for revenge (Kang 2018:17).

To Hyun, this is the moment when the *minjung* are conscientized and transformed from "the tragic hero of revolution to the comic hero of reconciliation" (Hyun 1985:14). Here, he gives them a new dignity as the clown who transcends their suffering with "tragic laughter" and thus cuts off the vicious cycle of bloody revenge based on self-righteousness. In his thinking, through the experience of critical transcendence, the *minjung* not only can transform their reality from tragedy (*han*) to comedy (*dan*), but also can transform themselves from victim to victor.

It is from this concept of critical transcendence that Hyun proposes his unique Christology—namely, "Christology of Fools," a radical reinterpretation of a 'feast of fools' in a common dance occurring at the end of the mask dance. He regards it as the dance's climax in which the performers and audience join together, and thus, *Maltugi* and *minjung* become one as they sing, dance, and shout. Here, he draws parallels between *Maltugi* and Jesus who can bring both liberation and reconciliation to the *minjung*. Hyun's view of *Maltugi* as a Christ-like figure who plays a messianic role in resolving and healing the *minjung's han* finds expression in the Servant-King's face with humour, satire, and laughter (Hyun 1985:359), leading to another parallel between the mask dance of God and the mask dance of people. By joyfully laughing and dancing together, this 'feast of fools' turns into a place of realized eschatology where Jesus with the mask of *Maltugi* grasps the *minjung* and the *minjung* grasp Jesus as the mask dance of God at the same time.

The culmination of Hyun's Christology comes with his claim of Jesus as the *Dokaebi*, the Korean goblin. Indeed, Christology of Jesus as the *Dokaebi* stems from his parallel of Jesus with *Maltugi* (a mean but smart servant), which demonstrates the power of paradox. While *Maltugi* is dangerous due to his biting satire and sheer criticism against the status quo, he is nonetheless regarded as a comic figure who is powerless and even foolish. Similarly, his notion of Jesus as the *Dokaebi* reveals that his salvific work on the Cross is comic as well as tragic, joyful as well as tearful, playful as well as dreadful. For in his crucifixion, the *minjung* can see his tears and blood but at the same time they can hear his chuckles and laughter. Thus, his Christology of Jesus as the *Dokaebi* provides the *minjung* with hope against hope that's based on the "tragic laughter" of the Servant-King's face, "so that [they] could really laugh heartily, enjoying and celebrating the resurrection of Jesus the Christ as well as his crucifixion" (Hyun 1985:24).

All in all, encouraged by his "Christology of Fools," Hyun is willing to act like a fool and even to enjoy the status of being a fool who has sought to humanize the revolution with "tragic laughter." This enables him to further devote himself to be the Radical Reformer as being-in-the-*minjung* in the mask dance.

Chapter Summary (8 and 9)

Korean Minjung Theology as Being-in-the Dialectic of Messianic and Prophetic Practice

Korean Minjung Theology defines its main task to bring *dan* into the *minjung's han*. This goal has been dealt with creatively by four outstanding *minjung* theologians who used different methodologies—Suh, Nam-Dong via the liberating *Missio Dei* of the Spirit; Ahn, Byung-Mu via socio-biblical analysis of the *ochlos* (the outcast) in the Jesus event; Kim, Yong-Bok via Messianic Politics; and Hyun, Young-Hak via the Korean mask dance.

First, Suh, Nam-Dong (1918-1984) has argued that it is to be a people's theology not only to solve *han* of the *minjung*, but also to transform it for constructing God's Kingdom on earth. Thus, the mission of Minjung Theology is two-fold—one being to be the priest of *han* and the other being to be the prophet of *dan* (Suh 1982, Moon 1998:85). With his pneumatological-synchronic interpretation, Suh gives the practice of *dan* a new impetus as the apex of the liberating *Missio Dei* movement in the Spirit with the *minjung* (Suh 1983:355). Soon it serves as his theological frame of reference that emphasizes the role of church to cut the vicious chain of violence and oppression (*han*) and thus to bring a liberative and *han*-free society here and now (*dan*) (Suh 1983:58).

Second, Ahn, Byung-Mu (1922-1996) has interpreted the Bible from a socio-economic perspective as part of efforts to resolve the *minjung's han*. In the Gospel of Mark, he has found the Greek term *ochlos*—the crowd gathered around Jesus, mostly the poor, the oppressed, the sick, and those who were opposed to the ruling classes. For Ahn, Mark's intentional distinction of *ochlos* from *laos* (people) has significant theological implications; they were followers of Jesus as the socially oppressed *minjung* of the Galilee with whom Jesus identified himself. It is from this identification of Jesus and the *ochlos-minjung* that Ahn defines them not only as the transmitter but also as the subject of the Jesus event that continues to take place with the present *ochlos-minjung* event in Korea as the liberating praxis of *dan* against *han*.

Third, Kim, Yong-Bok (1938-) has sought to unpack the *minjung's han* by reinterpreting Korean history as the messianic movements that emphasizes the subject-hood of *minjung* (Kim 1981:77-118). Despite their historical reality as being the powerless, Korea's *minjung* had played a messianic role to liberate themselves from the presently gloomy structure of oppressive power. To him, the social biography of *minjung* is a keyhole through which to identify the *minjung* with Messiah. Kim thus reads the story of Jesus in the story of "messianic politics," which stirs the hopes and imagination for liberation of the *minjung* (Kim 1984:193). In this dialectic of "the *minjung* as the subject and the Messiah as their function," *minjung* become the people of the Messianic Kingdom which transforms the history of suffering (*han*) into one of hope (*dan*).

Fourth, Hyun, Young-Hak (1921-2004) has explored the traditional Korean mask dance in relation to *han* of the *minjung*. In the dance, the *minjung* express their *han* behind masks by lampooning the unjust rulers (Hyun 1982:351), in this way recognizing the absurdity of their present situation and experiencing the "critical transcendence" of the injustice (*dan*) (Park 1985:6). For Hyun, therefore, the goal of the mask dance is to give the *minjung* wisdom and power, not only to survive, but also to create new hope for change and freedom (Hyun 1982:52). In this process of social catharsis ('feast of fools'), they transform themselves from "the tragic hero of revolution to the comic hero of reconciliation," and thus, transform their suffering reality from tragedy (*han*) to comedy (*dan*).

Although these four *minjung* theologians have used different methodologies, they are mutually united in presenting *minjung* as real and historical subjects who can and should play the "messianic practice" for their own salvation. This "messianic practice" provokes the theologians to carry out the task of their *avatar*-hood that involves doing the "prophetic praxis" designed to confront, reform, and transform the current injustice in Korea.[12] In other words, the "messianic practice" of *minjung* galvanizes the theologians into their "prophetic practice." More figuratively, when they heard a call to "take the crucified people down from the cross" (Sobrino 1993:48), these theologians are caught up in their *avatar*-hood—i.e., the transformative participation in the *minjung's* messianic practice. This constitutes unique characteristics of Korean Minjung Theology as being-in-the-dialectic of (*minjung's*) messianic and (*minjung* theologians') prophetic practice.

Korean Minjung Theology as Being-in-the-Double-Mirror Reading

The dialectic of messianic-prophetic practice in Korean Minjung Theology opens a new path for a creative synthesis between the 16th century Radical Reformers and the 20th century Korean *minjung*

---

[12]The terms "messianic practice" and "prophetic practice" and their correlation are hinted at from the works of Jon Sobrino (1938-), a Jesuit Catholic priest and theologian. In an effort to build a Latin American "saving history" Christology starting with the historical reality of Jesus, Sobrino, a native of Spain, introduces Jesus' "messianic practice" and "prophetic practice" as a unified whole, which alters the historical reality of 1st-century Israel (1993).

theologians. It draws a so-called double-mirror-reading—namely, a synchronic reading of the 16th century Radical Reformers from the *minjung's* perspective. It begins with the *avatar*-hood of the 16th century four Radical Reformers (Thomas Müntzer, Hans Hut, Melchior Hoffman, and John Bockelson), who had been caught up in the common people's messianic practice. This is what the first mirror-reading reflects. Then it moves to the second mirror-reading that reflects the Korean minjung's messianic practice through the *avatar*-hood of the 20th century Korean *minjung* theologians, who have carried out their prophetic practice to "take the crucified [*minjung*] down from the cross."

To be more specific, by fusing the methodologies of the 20th century Korean minjung theologians (Suh, Nam-Dong via the liberating *Missio Dei* of the Spirit; Ahn, Byung-Mu via socio-biblical analysis of the *ochlos* [the outcast] in the Jesus event; Kim, Yong-Bok via Messianic Politics; and Hyun, Young-Hak via the Korean mask dance) with those of the 16th century Radical Reformers, it attempts to construct a radical new interpretation of history from below—i.e., re-reading the 16th century Radical Reformation, especially Münster Anabaptism from the 20th century Korean Minjung Theology as one way of being in the *avatar*-hood for the common people (the *minjung*). In this way, the double-mirror-reading approach (or reading from a diachronic-synchronic way) can serve as the point of departure to reshape a new portrait of the 16th century Radical Reformers, not only being refined and elaborated by the Korean minjung theologians, but also being renewed and transformed by the *avatar*-hood of the common people (or the crucified *minjung*).

Ultimately, this way of re-reading history from below leads to a new picture of Münster Anabaptism as the place of hybridity which holds potential for both the *avatar*-hood of the 16th century Radical Reformers and the *guru*-ship of the common people, or of the prophetic practice of the 16th century Radical Reformers and the messianic practice of the common people, which will be dealt with further in the next chapter.

Part 4

RE-READING MÜNSTER ANABAPTISM FROM KOREAN MINJUNG THEOLOGY

Chapter 10

Another Look at the Anabaptist Kingdom of Münster

One of the most enigmatic events of the 16th-century Reformation was the Anabaptist rule in the city of Münster in 1534-35,[1] which was epitomized with "a variety of Anabaptists who proceeded to institute polygamy and a form of collective ownership of property and to elect a Dutch tailor as their king" (Mackay 2007:1). Not surprisingly, most scholarly accounts of Münster Anabaptism shared a hostile attitude toward such "freaks of fanaticism" as exemplified by the following:

> The whole crisis is often constructed as an extreme outworking of some latent tendencies within Reformation thought. Luther's widespread influence had greatly diminished the role of the priest as a mediator between the layman and God, thereby increasing the importance of the Bible and personal conscience in directing the layman's spiritual journey. The outcome of this change was that many laymen gave birth to radical interpretations of scripture—interpretations which often carried dangerous social and political implications. The prophetic claims of the two principal prophets at Münster,

---

[1] Admittedly, there are two major contemporary sources on Münster Anabaptism—one is a personal account written by the shoemaker Heinrich Gresbeck, who betrayed the city to the besieging troops, and the other is the historical work of the Münster schoolmaster Herman von Kerssenbroch. While the former's depiction of events was written nearly 40 years after the occurrence, the latter recorded his observation a decade after the Anabaptist kingdom's fall. Both primary sources have been translated into English under the titles *False Prophets and Preachers: Henry Gresbeck's Account of the Anabaptist Kingdom of Münster* (2016) and *Narrative of the Anabaptist Madness: The Overthrow of Münster, the Famous Metropolis of Westphalia* (2007), respectively.

[John Matthjisson and John Bockelson], support this view. Both men drew an enormous amount of prophetic authority from Scripture (sic) and wielded it with disastrous social and political consequences (Howard 1993:48).

While this unfriendly memory of the Anabaptist takeover has long been an attractive subject for many scholars and historians, "odious opprobrium" against Anabaptist rule in Münster is almost monolithic among them (Bender 1944:8). Indeed, the enduring dark image of Münster Anabaptism has been retained and repeated until it has hardened into fixed anti-Anabaptist histories of the contemporary scholarship (Driedger 2016:3), even though it results from "their narrow starting points or misjudgments of the sources" (Reventlow 2010:176). In her studies, Sigrun Haude (1959-), a prominent female scholar of Anabaptist Münster and the German Reformation, especially points out that, under the reproduction of polemical frameworks, the tragic Münster episode has become the paramount example of historical chains of riots and heresies (Haude 2000:1). She further says:

> Anabaptists, together with the Turks, were the great enemies of the sixteenth-century Holy Roman Empire, and "Münster" displayed the worst example of this heretical movement yet. As representations of them in the daily press and in learned writings reveal, the Anabaptists conjured up images of the criminal and the vagabond, the foreigner and the rebel, the devil's handmaiden and the blasphemer, the insurrectionist and the barbarian. A polyphony of fears, some more powerful than others, converged in the Anabaptist (Haude 2000:20).

Yet there are a few challengers to this predominant view. Since the pioneering work of C. A. Cornelius (1819-1903), there has been some scholars who began to put forth their critical views about the deeply contested Anabaptist reign of Münster, while reconstructing a more sympathetic view of the Münster's Anabaptists accused of heresy and rebellion (Driedger 2016:15, Kautsky 1897:249, Kirchhoff 1962:77-170, Stupperich 1958:12). In this light, the co-existence of the radical and the peaceful Anabaptists in Münster has emerged as a new controversial subject (Kirchhoff 1970:357-70). However, this is not technically new. In response to the opponents of Anabaptists who have tended to lump them all as fanatical and revolutionary, the Mennonite writers have constantly strived to differentiate between the revolutionary enthusiasts and more peaceful, biblical Anabaptists (Klotzer 2007:217-56).

For example, the Anabaptist scholarship, especially spearheaded by the Marxist historians, such as Karl Kautsky (1854-1938), had insisted that Münster Anabaptism was a revolutionary movement, not a religious reformation (Kautsky 1897). In keeping with Kautsky, Karel Vos (1874-1926), an outstanding Dutch Mennonite historian, identified the Anabaptist movement in Münster as a revolutionary one, despite the fact that the Münster debacle created momentum that turned it into a peaceful movement (Vos 1920:311-90). Similarly, E. B. Bax (1854-1926), a British socialist and historian, contended that Münsterites were "the forerunners of Modern Socialism" (Bax 1903) and a kind of "medieval communism" (Bender 1957:36).

W. J. Kühler (1932-), the Dutch Mennonite historian, also agreed the Münsterite development as a deviation from the Anabaptist biblical line while disagreeing its absolute revolutionary violence by arguing that "the peaceable . . . exist before Münster, during Münster and after Münster" (Kühler 1932 quoted by Brock 1972:89). Even in the eyes of the Reformed historian Henry E. Dosker (1855-1926), the Anabaptists of Westphalia were the 16th-century bolshevists (Dosker, 1921:65). Following Vos, Dutch historian A. F. Mellink (1915-1987) aligned himself with the Kautsky-Marxian line by saying that the Dutch Anabaptists were not pacifists but revolutionaries. In his view, the whole problem was attributed to an economic struggle of the desperate masses, with the immigrant radical Anabaptists using religious vocabulary to express their needs (Mellink 1953 quoted by McLaughlin 2008:105).

Some even exceed these revolutionary interpretations by claiming that all Anabaptists were the "left wing of the Reformation" (Bainton 1941:124-34, Armitage 1887:399); and furthermore, historian Andrew Miller (1810-1883) added claim by defining them as the "scandalous fanatics" (Miller 1994:189-190). Alongside this line of interpretation, a remarkable course of Anabaptism in the Westphalian metropole has been variously interpreted as follows: a "revolution of the common man" (Brendler 1966), an "anticipated urban insurrection" (Schilling

1975:193-238), a "sectarian revolution" (Rammstedt 1966), a "reign of terror" (Wolgast 1976:179-201), a "millenarian psychodrama" (Herwig 1979:173-84), an "episode in collective religious fanaticism" (Stupperich 1965), and the "final aftershock of the 'Early Bourgeois Revolution'" (Laube 1974:345-52) and so on.

However, recent research has begun to take on a different aspect. Karl-Heinz Kirchhoff (1925-2014), the expert of Münster historiography, especially offered a pungent critique against such approaches to Münster Anabaptism as politically revolutionary violence. His re-examination of the social structure of the Münsterite Anabaptists, plus their access to power, has brought an entirely new dimension to the interpretation of Münster Anabaptism. Here, its dominant view as the "Protestantism of the poor" alone pales into insignificance (Kirchhoff 1970:357-70). Instead, his interpretation based on quantitative studies has shown that Anabaptism in the Low Countries had no single class, rather, it was a broad movement of all classes and estates (including the upper hand). Thus, the Münsterites were a complex group that included the well-to-do as well as the poor (Kirchhoff 1973:87, Stayer 1986:288).[2]

Implicit in Kirchhoff's studies was that the Anabaptists and their takeover of Münster cannot simply be seen as a proletarian revolution which stereotyped Münster's Anabaptists as just the lower echelon of society (Kirchhoff 1970:357-70). For him, social revolutionary motives were something, but not everything. Thus, to argue that Münster Anabaptism possessed a unilateral revolutionary character appeared to Kirchhoff "a sign of ignorance or dishonesty"; it rather demonstrated that the Anabaptists in Münster had relatively enjoyed prosperity in collaboration with the traditional elite group (Kirchhoff 1970:357-70). It is from this interpretation that Anabaptism in Münster was seen by Kirchhoff as a necessary move for the sake of two groups (Bakker 1986:105): it, though, came from without (primarily run by Matthjisson and Bockelson, the Dutch immigrants),[3] found a ready hearing among

---

[2] Yet some have criticized Kirchhoff's interpretations, questioning that his studies rest primarily on slim documentary basis covering only 5% of the populace, thus do not represent the general public in Münster (Oltmer and Schindling 1990:481).

[3] In his studies, Kirchhoff suggests that in Münster roughly 800 of the 1,600 adult males and 1,600 of the 4,800 adult females were immigrant Melchiorites (Kirchhoff 1973:24 quoted by Bakker 1986:111).

the Reformers within (primarily led by Rothmann and Knipperdolling, the native notables).

From it, the two new main characters of Münster Anabaptism come into being—i.e., the immigrant Melchiorites (the radicals) and the native civic reformers (the reactionaries), and it even leads to a new portrait of the Anabaptist Kingdom of Münster as the critical and creative tension between the two—i.e., between the native noble elites and the immigrant religious dissenters (Hsia 1988:55). This leaves open the possibility for the co-existence of radical and peaceful Anabaptists in Münster where both parties were intertwined, not as contradictory but as complementary (Waite 1992:459).

Kirchhoff's study also challenges that Anabaptist violence at Münster is to be understood in the context of events in and around the city. To be sure, the rising influence of Anabaptism there alarmed Franz von Waldeck, the Catholic bishop of Münster (ruled 1532-1553) and gave him, as territorial ruler, reason to increase pressure on the city (Reventlow 2010:179). As von Waldeck's mandate and the military siege began in earnest, Münster's defense grew stronger: all of the city's inhabitants united themselves against their common enemy (Reventlow 2010:179), with war between Münster Anabaptists and the prince-bishop being an inevitable corollary (Driedger 2013:4). To Kirchhoff, therefore, the violence of Münster was a sort of defensive activity against the threat of the aggressive siege army (Kirchhoff 1962:77-170, 1970:360, Kautsky 1897:249). Thus, it's reasonable to assume that "Anabaptist rule in Münster was the rule in the emergency conditions of a defensive war" (Driedger 2013:4).[4]

However, what Kirchhoff's interpretation was lacking is his silence to the common people in Münster. In one sense, his new trend of interpretations (Kirchhoff's) helps explain that Münster Anabaptism was carried out by a critical and creative tension between the two parties—the immigrant Radicals and the native Reformers. But in another sense, it fails to 'discover' the common people in Münster, who played a decisive role not only in sustaining the Radicals-Reformers in tension, but also in creating a new check-and-balance between the two.

---

[4]For this line of interpretation, see also Kirchhoff (1989:277-422 quoted by Klotzer 2007:219).

Conversely, this demands that particular attention be given to the representatives of both parties—namely, John Matthjisson (the radical) and Bernhard Rothmann (the reactionary). But it also includes the necessity of expanding its criticism with a particular focus on the lack of perspective from the common people in Münster.

Anabaptist Kingdom of Münster as a Place of Hybridity

While Münster Anabaptism is notorious for its strange and violent characteristics, few know that the cities served as a catalyst in developing and spreading the Protestant Reformation, especially a Lutheran-oriented reformation and Münster, the North Rhine-Westphalian city in western Germany, was not an exception. In its structure, the Evangelical movement in the city followed that in many other German cities (Moeller 1982),[5] which generally consisted of these steps:

> A popular preacher echoed Luther's message and called for reform, attacking monasticism and clerical abuses; citizens rallied to his cause, adding their resentment of the church's economic competition to the call for moral regeneration; spontaneous sacramental and liturgical innovations were tolerated by the magistrates, who disagreed regarding their response; the reform movement became part of the struggle between burghers and magistrates, which often took the form of opposition between the guilds and the city council, and a final, usually bloodless constitutional reform incorporated many of the demands of the Evangelicals, while averting a social

---

[5]Bernd Moeller (1931-), a German church historian, in his pioneering work, showed the important point of departure for the Reformation in cities. According to his studies, the cities had acted as harbingers of the Reformation, and the Reformation was therefore undertaken by the city council (1972:39-115). From it came the notion that there was neither an evangelical movement outside of, or opposed to, the council. He added that there would have been no chance of success for an evangelical popular movement in the face of a hostile council. As a result, slow and gradual reform outperformed fast and radical reform in the cities and all fanatic stirrings or attempts to draw socio-revolutionary consequences from the Gospel were firmly rejected by the council with the support of the city preachers (Seebass 1972:24-30). Yet, it should be noted that there was in the city an alternative group inclined to resistance, that is, the lower level of the population were invoking Christian freedom, and thus, a Radical Reformation as a new spearhead. The city of Münster was not an exception in this regard.

revolution; cloisters were closed, clerics took civic oaths, ecclesiastical properties were secularized, and reforms institutionalized in a new Evangelical church ordinance; and finally the magistrates came out with more authority, a few ruling families lost power but the social order was preserved and protected (Hsia 1988:53).

Before turning to Anabaptism, the chain of events in Münster from 1531 to the spring of 1533 was common in nature with this model of urban reformation (Moeller 1972:39-115). As such, Bernhard Rothmann (1495-1535), Münster's leading Protestant preacher, began appealing to the city council "to take up the cause of religious reform", while at the same time criticizing clerical abuses of the prince-bishop (Hsia 1988:53). As the struggles between Catholics and Protestants and between the prince-bishop and city council escalated, "the Evangelical movement turned into a popular political movement" (Hsia 1988:53).

The close affinity between Rothmann and the guilds of Münster pressured the city council not only to protect him against the Catholic prince-bishop, but also to declare Münster an evangelical city (Bakker 1986:106-8). Backed by the guilds and Rothmann's Reformation party, the civic election in February 1533 "returned a solidly Evangelical city council, with the guild elite replacing the Catholic patriciate, who had evacuated the city; and an Evangelical ordinance was promulgated in April to consolidate the gains of the Reformation" (Hsia 1988:53). This resulted in establishment of the Protestant reform in Münster, carried out via cooperation between the city council (magistrates) and Rothmann and his followers in the guilds (Bakker 1986:106-7).

Because Rothmann's reforming activity smacked of Zwinglianism, which placed the real religious authority not in magisterial monopoly, but in congregational autonomy (Hsia 1988:54), it soon caused concern to the Lutheran magistrates, who were inclined towards the oligarchies away from the 'Swiss way' (Hillerbrand 1969:39-46). Rothmann's radical sacramental position, having its root in the Wassenbergers who tended toward Zwinglian reform, added further fuel to their concern (Bakker 1986:109), as a result damaging this reformers-magistrates alliance (Bakker 1986:106-7). The split became public in the summer of 1533 when Rothmann and his followers aligned themselves with the teachings (i.e., baptism and Lord's Supper) of radical preachers (Anabaptists) from the Netherlands and confronted Lutheran ministers (Hsia 1988:54).

With the city council now in a dispute, the common people (represented by the guilds) once again pledged support for Rothmann and opposed the magistrates who were attempting to exile him (Hsia 1988:54). Such context of "intra-evangelical party struggle" forced Rothmann to choose; eventually his allegiance to the guilds moved him closer to the common people than to the council (Bakker 1986:109). In the long run, this led Rothmann's camp to regain control of the city.

Encouraged by Rothmann's actions, two Dutch prophets—John Matthjisson and John Bockelson—sent two apostles to Münster to proclaim believer's baptism and Melchiorite teachings. In January 1534, Rothmann and his followers had themselves baptized and soon 1,400 people were baptized (Bakker 1986:109). On February, when Matthjisson arrived at Münster, Catholics and Lutherans fled, and the civic election affirmed that the city of Münster had finally become Anabaptist (Hsia 1988:54). Thus, Matthisson boldly declared that the end of the world was at hand and that all Christian believers should seek refuge in Münster as the New Jerusalem (Stayer 1995:268-69). This resulted in thousands of future Dutch Anabaptists flocking to Münster, the holy city, despite massive executions being carried out there by the magistrates (Jensma 1979 quoted by Stayer 1995:269).

Rothmann saw such developments as part of the larger picture of religion and politics in Münster's reformation (Bakker 1986:109-10). However, conversely, this Anabaptist turn in Münster made the city vulnerable. Since the Imperial law had defined Anabaptism as a capital crime, this provided prince-bishop Franz von Waldeck legal authority to retaliate against Anabaptist Münster via a military campaign (Driedger 2016:3-4). So, he immediately placed the city under siege and threats of the army, which consisted of both Catholics and Protestants (Hsia 1988:54). Under these circumstances, Münster needed to protect itself, and it became inevitable that the new leadership had to take more extreme measures, such as "the enforcement of re-baptism on all inhabitants and the exile of dissidents," "war communism" and "polygamy" as a way to defend the city from the mounting pressure from without (Hsia 1988:54).

This sheds new light on the violence, or terror of Münster Anabaptism: it "was not an expression of the group's very nature. Instead, violence, or terror was a reaction to worsening conflicts" (Driedger 2016:17). To be sure, the new Anabaptist leadership evoked tension between the immigrant Dutch Prophets and the native Reformers (Hsia 1988:54). It was an unstable but creative mixture of Prophets-Reformers; despite the fact that the former resorted to "their personal charismatic and extra-institutional power" (Hsia 1988:55), while the latter were neither prophet-hireling nor inspired by the prophets' courage when they responded to this challenging situation. The Prophets-Reformers alliance also provided a good counterbalance where both could render the other neutral. Here, "the remaking of Münster into the New Jerusalem depended on the critical tension between the old civic elite and the new religious leadership"—i.e., between the reactionary Münsterites and the radical Melchiorites (Hsia 1988:55).

From this vantage point, three phases of the Melchior-Münsterite movement came into being, each having its own main characteristic. "The first phase extended from the summer of 1533, when Rothmann adopted the radical sacramental position of the Wassenbergers, until February 1534. During this period, the Melchiorite movement was powerful, but it still lacked official sanction and still responded to its opponents with peaceful avoidance. The second phase was from February 1534, with its "political miracles," to Easter of that year, with Anabaptist Münster at the focal point of an apocalyptic crisis which legitimized the prophetic authority of the immigrant John Matthjisson of Haarlem. Militancy and radial community of goods corresponded to this crisis. The third phase ran from April 1534 to the demise of the Anabaptist regime in June 1535. Although Münster's apocalyptic enthusiasm was in decline, desperate efforts were nonetheless made to preserve the energies and idealism of the earlier periods under the inventive, institution-building leadership of John Bockelson of Leiden as the eclectic mix of the radical Prophets and the reactionary Reformers (Stayer 1991:131).

However, all of this must be seen in the dynamic interplay of the common people of Münster who had existed before, during, and after the Anabaptist takeover of Münster. Both as the point of contact and the point of action, they had tried to take the matter into their own hands, not only by radicalizing the Reformation but also rationalizing it in the dialectic of the Prophets-Reformers interplay (or the dialectic of the *guru-avatar* interplay).

From it emerges a new portrait of the Radical Reformers—namely, (1) John Matthjisson as being-in-the-immigrant-Melchiorite-prophets, the radicals; (2) Bernhard Rothmann as being-in-the-native-civic-reformers, the reactionary; (3) John Bockelson as being-in-the-eclectic between the two power structures—and the common people (the *minjung*) in Münster, whose role was even beyond the radical, the reactionary, and the eclectic. This dynamic interconnection turns Münster Anabaptism into the place of hybridity, wherein the *avatar*-hood of the Radical Reformers and the *guru*-ship of the common people are closely intertwined for the realization of a new type of Communal Reformation.

Chapter 11
Profiles of the Münster Reformers

John Matthjisson as Being-in-the-Immigrant-Melchiorite-Prophets, the Radical

It is undisputed that Melchior Hoffman, the furrier-turned-Anabaptist preacher, "brought Anabaptism from Southwestern Germany to the Netherlands, where it won mass support such as it never again attained elsewhere in Europe" (Stayer, Packull and Deppermann 1975:111). Despite spending only a brief time preaching at Emden in East Frisia (spring 1529 to summer 1530), Hoffman stamped his own personality, theology, and apocalyptic mood upon the Dutch Anabaptist movement to the point that its adherents were called Melchiorites or Hoffmanites (Stayer 1972:205, Jones 1909:398).

His message appealed mostly to the common people, who had been deprived of the material and cultural goods enjoyed by others and who longed for a more meaningful religious experience (Krahn 1968:124). Just as the peasants in the South were inspired by Thomas Müntzer to appeal to divine law, so the laymen in the North were inspired by Hoffman (Waite 1989:175). And being an artisan, his preaching was greeted warmly by that same social stratum (Waite 1990:29). Given that the Melchiorites were overwhelmingly from the artisanal stratum (Waite 1986:250), only a few of their leaders had any kind of religious training (Krahn 1968:213). Therefore, it would be natural for them to look for leadership from within their own ranks. That's the reason many of the movement's famous leaders, such as John Matthjisson (baker), John Bockelson (rhetorician and merchant), and David Joris (glass-painter), fit this description (Waite 1986:252-53).

Coupled with Hoffman's imprisonment in March 1533 in Strasbourg, the prohibition against believer's baptism created ferment among the Melchiorites of the Low Countries (Mackay 2007:16-7). Believer's baptism was paramount to them, many identifying it as "the seal that distinguished the pious from the godless in Apocalypse" (Mackay 2007:17). This was heightened by a climate where the dreaded events in the Apocalypse could occur in their lifetime, leading them to align with the early Christians—"The stronger the persecution and suffering of the faithful, the greater was the hope and expectancy" (Krahn 1968:130).

Despite their higher apocalyptic enthusiasm, the Melchiorites had no clear conception of the Second Coming, engendering such questions as, "Would the Kingdom of God be ushered in by Him with or without the help of His saints?" (Krahn 1968:130). In this context, radical elements started to exploit the situation, and John Matthjisson (a baker from Haarlem) became the initiator of a new trend by taking advantage of their disappointment in the delay of the Apocalypse, which Hoffman, their spiritual father, had set (Jelsma 1998:53).

Soon after Hoffman was imprisoned, Matthjisson, whom he had baptized, began his prophetic activity in Amsterdam (Pleysier 2014:60). The city became his headquarters from which he sent emissaries to the various Melchiorite communities in the Low Countries (Mackay 2016:12). This enhanced his leadership to the point where even some of Hoffman's earlier adherents were subdued (Mackay 2016:12), one of whom was John Bockelson of Leiden, who would eventually succeed Matthjisson (Krahn 1968:134).

Led by dreams and visions, Matthjisson proclaimed himself the Enoch of the Last Days[1] and reinstated believers' baptism, which had been suspended by Hoffman (Stayer 1976:227-28). Echoing Hans Hut's "eschatological baptism" (Spinks 2006:86), Matthjisson connected it to the mark of the 144,000 elect who would oppose the Antichrist in the Apocalypse (Deppermann 1987:289). At a certain point, this included the distinctly millenarian and militant view that "crystallized into an urge

---

[1] It was said that Matthjisson's wife had likely rejected his claims to be a prophet called by God. Meanwhile, he had met the brewer's daughter who knew the Gospel well. They then came to an agreement that she would be his wife and they would leave secretly to get away from her parents to begin their mission in Amsterdam (Klaassen 1992:46).

to take up arms and fight" (Cohn 1961:21). He believed that the world was sunk in corruption and had to be cleansed before Christ's return and that the people to carry out that task were the baptized ones, the Anabaptists (Klaassen 1992:46).

Münster was one of the few cities most receptive to Matthjisson's radical messages. His two emissaries (Bartholomaus Boekebinder and Willem de Kuiper), who arrived on January 5, 1534, quickly obtained influence among the radical city preachers (including Bernard Rothmann) and baptized them (Bakker 1986:109). Within a week, some 1,400 citizens (about a fourth of the population) plus previously arrived immigrants from Holland were also baptized (Dulmen 1977:289 quoted by Klaassen 1992:47). John Bockelson, being encouraged by this mood, appeared in Münster with others of Matthjisson's emissaries another week later (Kirchhoff 1970:362).[2]

These favourable conditions also inspired Matthjisson himself to come to Münster in early February (Worth 2005:115). Yet, his stormy entrance into the city threw the radical group there into confusion. Hoffman, their spiritual father, had suspended baptism, and they had received no other instructions; now along came a new leader claiming that he was called to reinstate believers' baptism to prepare for Christ's return (Pleysier 2014:61-2). It was prophet against prophet, inspiration against inspiration (Klaassen 1992:46)—so who was right?

However, Matthjisson's prophetic authority and power (the rising prophet) seemed to far surpass Hoffman's (the fading prophet).[3] He extended the time of grace from Christmas 1533 (the time Hoffman had expected the end of the world) to Easter, April 5, 1534 (Kirchhoff 1985:24 quoted by Stayer 1986:275). Furthermore, he even attempted to speed up the coming of the Lord by calling on the saints to help with establishment of the New Jerusalem as opposed to waiting for God or the 'pious

---

[2] When Bockelson arrived at Münster on January 13, he had already found the Anabaptist influence in the city. About one fourth of the adults were baptized, and of these, the majority was probably women (Kirchhoff 1970:362).

[3] Why was Matthjisson taken so much more seriously than his predecessor or successors? One possible answer is that all of his deeds were sanctioned by the Spirit, thus they were beyond examination and criticism. The only applicable comparison is the actions of the prophets in the Bible. Even the maddest commands of Matthjisson received meaning through appeal to God. His decisions, therefore, were not tied to established ordinances or traditions but rather were dependent only on spontaneous revelations and, accordingly, were irrational (Rammstedt 1966:62-3 quoted by Stayer 1986:275).

magistrates' to act (Bax 1903:112). Finally, he relocated the setting for the New Jerusalem from Strasbourg to Münster (McDaniel 2007:66, Klaassen 1981:329).

Exercising his personal charismatic power, Matthjisson quickly assumed the real leadership of the city (Eichler 1981:46), despite its formal authority structure (i.e., the city council and elected mayors) continuing to exist (Hsia 1988:55). Even the external and internal situations benefited Matthjisson and his radical followers. First, the political decentralization of the Holy Roman Empire, invariably ruled by a Habsburg, allowed for Melchiorite unrest in the Low Country in general and their takeover of Münster in particular (Vogler 1988:110-15).[4] From that weakening of imperial control, Münster simmered with tension between civic independence and episcopal rule, which provided an excuse for the immigrant Melchiorites to take control of the city (Driedger 2016:4). Second, the local authorities' religious and political inability would also offer grounds for Matthjisson's attempt to take power without strong opposition (Williamson 2000:27).

In fact, by failing to immobilize the radicals' activities, the local authorities rendered themselves somewhat obsolete (Krahn 1968:135-61) and thereby gave ammunition to the radicals (McLellan 2012:25). Indeed, before Matthjisson and Bockelson came to the city, Bernhard Rothmann had persistently refuted the authorities, despite them having ample opportunity to regulate him (Stayer 1972:227-80). But their repeated inaction allowed him to continue to influence the city (Jelsma 1998:54) and eventually made the whole community vulnerable to the outside influence—namely, the immigrant Dutch Prophets (McLellan 2012:25). It was through both these external and internal conditions that Münster bowed to pressure and underwent a radical Anabaptist turn.

The Anabaptist takeover in February 1534 elevated Matthjisson's status even to the rank of *Enoch-redivivus* (Williamson 2000:29). To the Melchiorites, they were now firmly in control of the city and it was a miracle akin to the Red Sea crossing for the Israelites (Kuratsuka

---

[4]In the early sixteenth century, the various territories in the Low Countries were simply another part of the Empire in which German dialects were commonly spoken; and this similarity of language would contribute to the ease with which the Melchiorite movement of the Low Countries was so readily received in neighbouring Münster. The events of Münster played themselves out against this situation (Vogler 1988:110-15).

1985:261 quoted by Stayer 1999:268)—and behind it all was Matthjisson. Moreover, "The content of the miracle was the deliverance of the peaceful Münster Anabaptist congregation from the overwhelming numerical superiority of their enemies" (Stayer 1986:276). Here, his apocalyptic militancy gained momentum, the end was indeed at hand, and God had given the sword to the elect (the Anabaptists) to keep the hope for imminent salvation alive among themselves (Kirchhoff 1970:357-70).[5] In short, since God's hand was so visible now, Matthjisson's violent apocalypticism had engaged and captured the minds of Münsterites.[6]

On the other hand, this political miracle sanctioned Matthjisson's charismatic dictatorship, as he now claimed all authority in Münster (Williamson 2000:29). Those who would not listen to the "prophet John" were to be expelled (Snyder 1995:148). In addition, an anti-intellectual tendency prevailed in the city, declaring that it was the unlearned who had been chosen by God to redeem the world. This established a monopoly as to interpretation of the Bible and resulted in destroying all books except the Bible (Dulmen 1974:90-1 quoted by Klaassen 1992:48). Under Matthjisson's absolute power and the top-down system, "All other works had to be brought to the cathedral square and thrown upon a great bonfire. This act symbolized a complete break with the past, a total rejection of the intellectual legacy of earlier generations" (Cohn 1961:290). His unchecked power went a step further in constituting a

---

[5]From this came the hypothesis that apocalyptic militancy in Münster was a product of Matthjisson. "It is basically correct to describe the whole period from the summer of 1533 to late February 1534 as a peaceful Melchiorite phase of the Münster Reformation" (Stayer 1986:276-77). Yet this interpretation seems to pale under the new perspective which sees the Münster event as the critical and creative tension between two groups—namely, the immigrant radical Melchiorites and the native civic notables.

[6]One of the visible signs on which that conviction among the Münster Anabaptists rested was the fact that they had a city. There was much more to this reality than the simple physical control of the episcopal city, which had come into their hands quite legitimately. For Münster was not only a physical fact, but also the product of the imagination, nurtured primarily by the image of Jerusalem, the city of God (Klaassen 1992:84).

form of forcible communalism[7] in the city, substantiated by the book of Acts (Williamson 2000:29). "It was by no means required, but all who refused became prospects for expulsion" (McLellan 2012:26).

Yet Matthjisson's power abruptly ended. As a result of his prophecy that the Second Coming would take place at least by Easter 1534, citizens lined the city walls in expectation of viewing the spectacle of God destroying the heathen (Dulmen 1974:16 quoted by Klaassen 1992:50). But since that 'salvation' would not come until Easter made it too tantalizing for Matthjisson to stand still. So, being convinced by his own self-prophecy, he decided to desperately sally forth with a few companions,[8] the result being that he was quickly slaughtered by the prince-bishop's besieging soldiers.[9] This turned out to be a foolish rush and shocked the entire citizenry who witnessed it.

To sum up, it is evident that Matthjisson was a special charismatic figure, hailed by the radical Melchiorites in the Low Countries, whose views were different and distinctive from the native Münsterites. Exercising charismatic authority, he quickly emerged as the new prophet and played a decisive role in turning the city into radical Anabaptism. His connecting believers' baptism to millennial eschatology allowed his followers not only to embrace apocalyptic militancy as the prelude to the Second Coming, but also to relocate Münster as the New Jerusalem, the place of salvation for God's people. This characterized Matthjisson's role as a charismatic leader of the immigrant radicals who strove for accelerating the Second Coming with the help of revolutionary saints—

---

[7]Some have argued that the communism in Anabaptist Münster should be distinguished from the mainstream of Anabaptism. They maintain that the vast majority of Anabaptists supported voluntary giving but definitely not compulsory communism. For the Anabaptists in general, the concept of property as a God-given trust was inseparably united with a belief in mutual aid. Thus, to them, "all things in common" meant they did not permit another to be in want—"Their communism was a communism of need." It is therefore to be noted that Anabaptist communism was to be regarded as an expression of the love-ethic for a spiritually united group and was never intended for society as a whole, although there was, of course, a noted exception to this—namely, the Hutterites (Klassen 1964:28-49, Krahn 777-82).

[8]"Matthjisson may have sought death in order to fulfill the prophecy in Revelation 11 that Christ would return after the death of his two witnesses: one was Hoffman, still in prison in Strasbourg, and the other was himself, the second witness, who had now fulfilled his commission on Easter 1534" (Laubach 1993:187 quoted by Klotzer 2007:237).

[9]Even so, some in the city believed that Matthjisson would arise and visibly ascend into heaven, according to Revelation 11:12 (Fast 1962:336 quoted by Klaassen 1992:50).

i.e., the Anabaptists in Münster. In short, Matthjisson emerged as being-in-the-immigrant-Melchior-Prophets, the radical.

Bernhard Rothmann as Being-in-the-Native Civic Reformers, the Reactionary

Before the radical Melchiorite Anabaptists had immigrated into Münster, there were in the city a group of native notables, the civic intellectuals (reformers). They sometimes confronted but also cooperated with these radical immigrants in order "to safeguard their power and to prevent the disintegration of the congregation" (Rammstedt 1966:70 quoted by Eichler 1981:51). Prior to the Anabaptist takeover, such 'insiders' had led the evangelical movements, and after the takeover, they still remained a significant force to counterbalance the radical Melchiorites. These native reformers, on the one hand, had used the immigrants' prophetic authority for their religious and political stability and yet at the same time, checked and controlled the immigrants' level of radical activities.

One of the examples was Bernhard Knipperdolling's objection to Matthjisson, who was now sole leader of Anabaptist Münster (Loffler 1923:64-66 quoted by Eichler 1981:50). Against Matthjisson's radical plan to put to death the 'godless' (i.e., all adult citizens who refused to be baptized) remaining in the city, Knipperdolling (1495-1536), both as the mayor and as an Anabaptist, made a counter-proposal to drive them out of the city and his demand was accepted (Kerssenbrock 1899-1900:517, Baring-Gould 1891:273).

Yet most of all among the native reactionary groups, it was Bernhard Rothmann (1495-1535) who played the leading role in the Münster Reformation (Hsia 1988:52-3). As a historical figure, he is totally bound up with its Reformation. Apart from his activities between 1529 and 1535, almost nothing about him was clearly grasped. His career fell into two distinctive phases—the first being as a civic reformer in his own right, and the second being an ideologue and propagandist for the radical Melchiorites who eventually replaced him (Bakker 1982:191).

Born about 1495 in Stadtlohn, a town in the north-west of North Rhine-Westphalia, as the son of a blacksmith, Rothmann had been raised in poverty, stirred the social conscience by the Peasants' War of 1525, and began to challenge the Church for its failure to support the peasantry (Arthur 1999:14-5). He received his education at the Cathedral School in Münster and with the Brethren of the Common Life in Deventer (Krahn 1968:123). In 1529, he resurfaced as an assistant at St. Mauritz, a church just outside Münster, and began to preach the Gospel as an admirer of Luther (Bakker 1982:191). In 1531, this young Protestant preacher visited the so-called Reformation centres, such as Marburg, Wittenberg, and Strasbourg, and in 1532 he led the introduction of a Reformation in Münster (Krahn 1968:123).

The situation in Münster when Rothmann arrived was complicated. To be more specific, the institutional structure of the city was broadly determined by three mutually antagonistic forces—the regent class, who controlled the city council; the popularly based guilds, who wielded increasing power; and the clergy, which was headed by the Catholic bishop (Bakker 1986:106-7). Behind a facade of Polybian constitutional harmony in which the bishop reigned, the council ruled, and the guilds acted as tribunes of the people, this three-cornered power struggle dominated political developments in Münster (Bakker 1982:192).

Such struggles for power in government did work to the advantage of Rothmann and his reforming activities. The first effects of the Münster Reformation were anti-clericalism and iconoclasm (Bakker 1982:191-93). Attempts to silence Rothmann did not work, primarily because of the city council's tacit consent to keep in check the privileges of the Catholic clergy (Bax 1903:126). In this light, the actual tactic of reform was simple—(1) Rothmann would preach against the Catholic clergy and thus stir up popular enthusiasm for the Reformation; (2) the bishop's threatening response would antagonize the population; and (3) the council would use the civic and religious outrage as an excuse for tolerating Rothmann's biting sermons against the clergy (Bakker 1982:193-94). After a few cycles in this process of escalation, the council, pressed by the guilds, announced that only Rothmann's Gospel preaching would be tolerated in the city's churches (July 1532), and the bishop was forced to acknowledge the Münster Reformation, which was ratified by the Treaty of Dülmen on February 1533 (Bakker 1982:194, Hsia 1988:53).

The victory of the Münster Reformation shifted the locus of religious authority from clergy to laity, making the aristocrat's position obsolete (Bax 1903:133). However, it was not yet clear which party of the laity was to gain control. The regents, as the dominant group of council, assumed the authority would be theirs, while the guilds, from the standpoint of their communal ideology, assumed it would reside in the community. The issue of religious authority, therefore, turned into another political power struggle, which gave Rothmann the leverage to legitimize the position of either the council or the guilds (Bakker 1982:194). As expected, he leaned more in the direction of the guilds (Bakker 1986:109).

At this juncture, in September 1532, Heinrich Roll (-1534), an ex-Carmelite but now a Sacramentarian, came to the city from Wassenberg to make Münster an 'evangelical city' (McLellan 2012:24). His sacramental theology, with its stress on a new people of Israel, found a ready audience. By this time, Rothmann was already at odds with Lutheran theologians (Hsia 1988:53). For instance, he no longer saw the Lord's Supper like they did as a means of the divine grace, but rather interpreted it as a confession of discipleship (Klotzer 2007:227).[10] Encouraged by that, Roll and his associates ("Wassenbergers") extended their covenantal implications of sacramental theology to baptism,[11] arguing that infants should not be baptized (Bakker 1982:197). At first, Rothmann resisted them, but after further discussions, he had also received a Zwinglian conception the sacrament; he rejected of infant baptism and supported adult baptism (Stupperich 1970:229-30 quoted by Stayer 1986:271, Bax 1903:135-36).

---

[10]It is now generally recognized that, despite his Lutheran position, Rothmann's doctrine, both in theology and in political ethic, was closer to Zwingli than to Luther (Bakker 1982:194-95). Current scholarship has found that Rothmann's view on justification as well as sacraments possessed more deep resonance with a Reformed covenantal sign than a Lutheran promise of grace (Ozment 1975:153). But a far more decisive factor was Rothmann's interest in a Christian *Obrigkeit* as important for Christians to be involved. All this implied that the substance of his theology was primarily Reformed. The nuts and bolts of that theology were thus found in its compatibility with a people-of-God conception, resulting in a natural alliance with the guilds in the civic power struggle (Bakker 1982:196).

[11]From here, some (Brecht and Klotzer) argued that Anabaptist ideas were introduced into Münster first by the evangelical preachers Rothmann, Roll, and other Wassenbergers rather than by John Matthjisson's disciples (Breach 1985:66 quoted by Snyder 1995:156, note 32). Furthermore, since Melchiorite apocalyptic teachings were not present in Münster before 1534 and Hoffman had suspended adult baptism during that period, it seems not possible to identify Melchiorite influence on the issue of baptism in Münster (Klotzer 2007:251).

In August 1533, the council called Rothmann to account for his opposition to infant baptism, and this disputation ended in a victory for him (Kuratsuka 1985:248 quoted by Stayer 1986:273). In addition, Lutheranism in Münster was waning, and an attempt to import an effective Lutheran reformer for the city turned out to have come too late (Stayer 1986:273).

Rothmann's leaning to the 'Swiss way' earned the Lutheran theologians' suspicion and thereby brought into Münster a new intra-Protestant controversy over the baptism issue. This rekindled religious strife that once again divided the population into three antagonistic groups (Williamson 2000:28)—the remaining Catholics; the Lutherans, who were backed by the council (magistrates); and the Reformed Rothmannists, who were supported primarily by the guilds (burghers) (Bakker 1982:198).

Because anti-pedobaptism (anti-infant baptism) was against imperial law, the council sought to remove Rothmann (Stayer 1986:285). However, since any struggle between the two evangelical parties increased the risk of a Catholic restoration, the guilds persuaded the council to settle for a compromise (Bakker 1982:198)—that being, expelling Roll and his associates and allowing Rothmann but forbidding him to preach (Klotzer 2007:229). As it turned out, this solved nothing, for the religious agitation continued and a new uneasy stalemate prevailed. Soon, popular support for Rothmann increased and he regained control of all which even sparked the return of the banished Roll and the "Wassenbergers" (Klotzer 2007:229-30).

On January 5, 1534, with a couple representatives of John Matthjisson present in Münster, Rothmann, Roll, and other leading figures accepted re-baptism and baptized their congregations (Krahn 1968:124). Such was the situation John Bockelson encountered when he arrived in January (Bakker 1982:198). The city's sentiment had shifted in favour of the Anabaptist faction (Cornelius 1965:370 quoted by Stayer 1986:273), and some 1,400 adults already had accepted re-baptism (Snyder 1995:147, Klotzer 2007:230). Shortly thereafter, those so baptized faced mortal danger, for the prince-bishop was demanding arrest of the persons responsible for initiating this new baptism. In addition, a rumor spread that the prince-bishop was on his way to

Münster with a troop of mercenaries to recapture the city (Stayer 1986:287).

In its wake, for those within the city, support for the Anabaptist party seemed to be the best option for its independence, given the exigent circumstances. With many political opponents (both Catholics and moderate reformers) having already left the city, the February 23 election for city councilors fell to the Anabaptists (Stayer 1986:281), among whom Bernhard Knipperdolling was elected.[12] Against it, the prince-bishop had already set up military headquarters in the nearby town of Telgte in preparation for a siege (Stayer 1986:281). The next day, at Knipperdolling's invitation, John Matthjisson entered Münster claiming prophetic authority, the result being all non-baptized inhabitants of Münster were forced either to leave or to accept re-baptism (Snyder 1995:147).

In the long run, the arrival of 'Prophet John' in February 1534 would permanently sweep Rothmann from centre stage. Having lost his ability to directly influence developments, he was gradually reduced to articulating and propagandizing the religious ideology of the besieged community under the leadership of Matthjisson then of Bockelson (Bakker 1982:199). Indeed, Rothmann's internal role was that of stabilizer, whereas his external role was that of propagandist for the Melchiorite leadership (Klotzer 2007:251). In this light, the final fall of Münster would mark the final fall of Rothmann. After June 25, 1535 when the city was taken by the prince-bishop, he never again appeared in the historical records (Kerssenbrock 1899-1900:842 quoted by Krahn 1968:160).

Although Rothmann's authority in Münster had ebbed and flowed under Matthjisson and Bockelson, his most important published tracts dated from the period between October 1534 and January 1535 (Wray 1962:229-38). Three of them especially—"Restitution," (1534), "On Vengeance," (1534), and "The Hiddenness of the Word of God" (1535)— helped shape both the ideological development of Münster Anabaptism and the theological foundation of the New Jerusalem (Waite 1990:89, Reventlow 2000:180). Here, "The general impression he aimed to give

---

[12]On that day, six council members were re-elected, while 18 others were chosen to this office for the first time. It is notable that about half of them belonged to the higher socio-economic stratum (Kirchhoff 1973: 68 quoted by Klotzer 2007:233).

was that the Münster Anabaptists were about to play a crucial role in a comprehensible, historically delineated drama of salvation" (Stayer 1967:181).

This gives a glimpse into Rothmann's advocacy of synergism. That is "Not only did God himself choose different means from age to age in realizing human salvation, his eternal end: human beings, too, were required to change the ethical means by which they cooperated in that salvation. At one period God required of his people patient suffering, at another he summoned them to glorious revenge. To know how to serve God, one must be able to locate himself in the temporal unfolding of Providence" (Stayer 1967:181). On the basis of this notion Rothmann could argue that "vengeance belonged not to Christ, but to the saints" (Stayer 1972:249), that the enemies of Christ must be subdued by God "with and in his saints" ("The Hiddenness" 77 quoted by Stayer 1967:190).

Emboldened by it, Rothman developed a theory of Christian revolution. He interpreted history as a succession of apostasy and restitution (Klaassen 1981:330-33, Reventlow 2010:181) and here restitution meant reparation of apostasy—i.e., the time of re-establishing all those things God has ever mentioned through his prophets (Stupperich 1970:215 quoted by Reventlow 2010:181). In another connection, Rothmann elaborated his concept of the three ages—the first having disappeared through the Flood; the second being the present one which will perish by fire and be purified by it; and the third to be the New Heaven and New Earth in which the people would live in justice ("The Hiddenness" 65 quoted by Vogler 1988:106).

Undoubtedly, Rothmann paid special attention to the end of the second age (i.e., his own time) (Stayer 1967:182). While considering the present day as the final apostasy (Reventlow 2010:181), he understood the Reformation as "the major sign of the end of that age" which was pregnant with "the nearness of the Second Coming"—namely, the final and eternal 'Restitution' (Stayer 1967:186, Stupperich 1970:219 quoted by Reventlow 2010:181). He likewise held that, although 'Restitution' began with the Reformation when God awakened Luther, it had not yet been concluded (Klaassen 1992:77). Since the "learned" magisterial Reformers like Erasmus, Luther, and Zwingli had abandoned the cause, its right was now given to Melchior Hoffman, John Matthjisson, and

John Bockelson, "who were regarded as completely without worldly learning" ("Restitution" 16-7 quoted by Klaassen 1981:333, Stayer 1967:186).[13]

Such emphasis on the 'Restitution' here and now by the unlearned prophets placed Münster at the centre of cosmic crisis and John Bockelson and his followers God's saints who would take vengeance on the godless ("Restitution" 104-105 quoted by Stayer 1967:190, Reventlow 2010:183): "The glory of all the Saints is to wreak vengeance.... Revenge without mercy must be taken of all who are not marked with the sign [of the Anabaptists]" ("Vengeance" 69 quoted by Cohn 1961:274).

To Rothmann, in this time of 'Restitution', God would rally his people in order to put an end to the king of the whole world (Pleysier 2014:67-8). The wrong order would be eliminated, even though government authority was a God-ordained order. "This order has long been wrong because the authorities not only forgot their duties and took unfair advantages but also turned against God himself and his world" (Stupperich 1970:219 quoted by Vogler 1988:107). Thus Rothmann argued that "Now, dear brother, the time of vengeance has come to us. God has awakened beloved David; arm for vengeance and punishment on Babylon and its people" (Stupperich 1970:297 quoted by Reventlow 2010:184).

By conceiving the 'Restitution' in Münster as a prelude to "the great eschatological climax", Rothmann justified Münster's role as "the embryonic Kingdom of Christ"—namely, the in-breaking of the Kingdom of God which included the restoration of the fallen throne of David (Stayer 1967:183, 192, Reventlow 2010:183). Yet interestingly enough, he identified Solomon, not David, with Christ: "We well know that up to now, and perhaps still, David is understood as Christ. But this does not make sense at all and is completely wrong, for not David but Solomon is symbolic of Christ" ("Vengeance" 77 quoted by Stayer

---

[13]This is reminiscent of Hoffman's teaching that, whereas Christ revealed himself and his will to the poor and simple, Antichrist revealed himself to the leaders and scholars in the Church (Klaassen 1986:20).

1967:191).¹⁴ In his schema, it was in Münster that God has established the throne of David "in the image prepared by battles and punishments a peaceful kingdom for Solomon . . . then the peaceful Solomon is come, ruled in peace and high-priestly glory the whole of Israel and built in marvelous wisdom God's temple" (Stupperich 1970:295 quoted by Reventlow 2010:184).).

Rothmann here looked back on the basic miracle of the deliverance of the Anabaptists on February 9-11 as the seal of God's apocalyptic blessing on Münster (Stupperich 1970:280-81 quoted by Stayer 1986:277). Thus it was no accident but rather fulfillment of prophecy that 'Restitution' in Münster would come in the form of self-defense against the prince-bishop (Stayer 1967:189). For it was the Lord who would lead the Münster Anabaptists to wield the sword through "spiritual revelation" ("Restitution" 110 quoted by Stayer 1967:190). It was from this understanding that Rothmann assumed Bockelson would take "the stool of David in order to hand it over in a short time to Christ, the peaceful king of Solomon" (Kirchhoff 1989:400, Laubach 1993:198-200 quoted by Klotzer:2007:243). "Thus, most of the mayhem associated with the Day of the Lord became the business of the 'king of Münster', and [John Bockelson] was assigned the status of a sort of mystical father of Christ" (Stayer 1967:191).

In summation, Rothmann's theological journey represented his self-perception of before-and-after the Anabaptist turn in Münster's Reformation. In the pre-Anabaptist stage, he led that Reformation, the success of which he owed heavily to his close affinity with the guilds (Hillerbrand 2007:120). He was unwilling to have the council dictate to him the nature and extent of the Reformation. The council, in return, was equally unwilling to have his religious innovations jeopardize the community's security (Bakker 1986:107-8). That conflict led him to claim that the council's authority in matters of religion was legitimate only to the extent that it corroborated and reinforced his authority as the community's prophet (Bakker 1986:109). This claim found ready

---

¹⁴"Rothmann's identification of Christ with Solomon rather than David was made to justify the glorious vengeance of the saints as a prelude to the Second Coming of Jesus" (Stayer 1967:191). Yet this is also related to John Bockelson's desperate attempt to maintain his position through the praxis of institutionalization of leadership as the eclectic leader between the two power structures. Details on this matter will be discussed in the later part of the next section.

support among the guild membership, for it was the exact analogue of their long-standing claim that the council's authority was legitimate only so far as it was corroborated by them as the people's tribunes (Bakker 1982:201-202).

The character of Rothmann's theology remained intact despite the advent of the radical Melchiorites (Bakker 1986:113). Their influx into Münster from the Netherlands certainly influenced both the course and tone of development of the city's Reformation (Kirchhoff 1973:24 quoted by Bakker 1986:111). Although this admixture of Dutch prophets had introduced the major distinctives of Melchiorite doctrines, such as monophysite Christology, they "merely extended some elements in Rothmann's previous theology; they did not in any fundamental way change it" (Bakker 1986:111). Yet as threats of the siege intensified, Rothmann's apocalyptic expectancy was transformed "from the restrained warning to the crusading spirit" (Bakker 1986:112). At that time, he used his pamphlets as blatant Anabaptist propaganda and to gain support from the apocalyptic followers of John Matthjisson, regarding them as only "genuine, unconstrained statements of Münsterite self-understanding" (Bakker 1986:113).

However, Rothmann's high apocalyptic tone was once again replaced by a "note of resignation" when defeat was staring Münster in the face (Bakker 1986:112). His last pamphlet, written just before the fall of the city on June 25, 1535, proved that he had returned to his original eschatology—i.e., patient suffering as a prelude to the final triumph (Bakker 1986:112). Here, his political legitimacy had become "radically a-political *faute de mieux* (because there is nothing better available)" (Bakker 1986:112-13, *parenthesis is mine*).

To be sure, as a representative of the native notables, Rothmann remained engaged in Anabaptist Münster by history and by choice, shaping the balance of power that favoured rationalization of radical reform. Under his leadership, this body of civic-minded notables reluctantly sided with the radical Prophets, who were riding on the massive Anabaptist immigration from the Netherlands, as the only means to preserve the city's endangered religious and political freedom (Kirchhoff 1963:7-21 quoted by Bender 1970:357-70). The precarious besieging situation required their temporal tolerance, with external threats preventing them from engaging the open power struggle with the immigrant prophets (Bakker 1986:114). "Hence they could attenuate, but not openly oppose the more spectacular measures of the Dutch prophets" (Bakker 1986:114).

This resulted in a strategic partnership—that being, the radical Melchiorites (Prophets) could only make headway with a measure of the native Münster notables (Reformers), which meant that self-help effects in Münster went both ways to rescue itself and survive the danger and pressures of the siege. What was distinctively Anabaptist Münster, therefore, was the co-existence of twin powers that kept each other in check. Thus, a crucial part of Münster Anabaptism is found in the creative and dynamic tension between the Prophet-Reformer interplay. In this way, the distinctive portrait of Rothmann was singled out as being-in-the-native-civic-Reformers (the reactionary) to counterbalance the immigrant Prophets (the radicals).

John Bockelson as the Eclectic between the Two Power Structures

Such the Prophet-Reformer interplay in Münster sheds new light on the portrait of 'King John' Bockelson. From the outset, the Anabaptist takeover of Münster on Easter 1534 was a collaboration between the immigrant Prophet and the native Reformer. Yet 'Prophet John' Matthjisson's death that day (in effect, a suicide) caused a serious imbalance in this twin-power structure. Most of all, it came as a shock to the Münsterites, trapped within the city walls, thinking that the prophetic authority—one pillar of the new Kingdom—could collapse (Kirchhoff 1970:39 quoted by Stayer 1986:279). Under this situation, young John Bockelson as second-in-command was given a huge challenge in restoring the damaged authority of the Prophets. Thus, his most immediate task was to ride out the current leadership crisis, caused by the disgraceful death of his predecessor. This was the reason why Bockelson was considered by the panic-stricken Münsterites the best figure who could fill the prophetic vacuum, despite his lack of charismatic and spiritual authority, compared to his predecessor (Rammstedt 1966:68-86 quoted by Stayer 1986:275).

In this sense, the famous portrayal of John Bockelson as "King of the World" was part of a defamation campaign by the prince-bishop, who needed further help for the battle against Münster (Kirchhoff 1989:400, Laubach 1993:198-200 quoted by Klotzer 2007:243). Instead, from the beginning, Bockelson had claimed for himself the role of mediator between the council and the people, between the immigrant Prophets and the native Reformers[15] (Klotzer 2007:234).

Thus, much closer to his real figure was an eclectic leader who stood between the immigrant Melchiorites and the native Münsterites, between Matthjisson (the radical Prophet) and Rothmann (the reactionary Reformer): like chameleons, he used to change his approach based on what the circumstances required. Bockelson must have been aware that he never regained Matthjisson's prophetic legitimacy and authority as well as Rothmann's theological insights and knowledge. Instead, the only possible option this less charismatic tailor-king chose was to create a 'halo effect' by associating himself with such two key figures, who continued to be held in high esteem by the public, with a hope that it would give people more reason to respect him than they had reason to doubt (Stayer 1991:131). In this sense, the true portrait of 'King John' is to be found in his process of negotiation between the two powers rather than his bizarre performances and megalomaniac leadership (Kirchhoff 1973).

From this standpoint, king Bockelson's various attempts at constructing an extreme form of "Anabaptist reform" in Münster could rather be seen as reflecting his lack of personal charisma that failed to take control of the entire power (Rammstedt 1966:68-86 quoted by Stayer 1986:275). Contrary to his notorious nickname ('King John') as being a charismatic leader, this new king was actually losing his ground due to his lack of prophetic authority that had already been proven through "the pathetic failures of his attempts to raise uprisings at Oldeklooster in Frisia and in Amsterdam in the spring of 1535" (Stayer 1995:270).

His prophetic ineptness continued in the period of his reign in Münster as a king. For instance, when Münster's status as the New Jerusalem was disputed after the death of Matthjisson, Bockelson had toyed with an idea (unthinkable in Matthjisson's reign) to abandon the

---

[15]In this light, it is noteworthy that Bockelson titled himself "King in the new Temple" (Klotzer 2007:244).

city for an armed invasion of the Netherlands (Jansma 1979:41-55, Stayer 1991:129). Since then, doubt was cast upon the legitimacy of Bockelson even to the point that some hardline Dutch Melchiorites attempted to replace him by John Batenburg, a hawkish Anabaptist leader, by using the failure of Bockelson's prediction that Münster would be delivered before Easter 1535 as an excuse to oppose him (Stayer 1986:277, 1991:129).

With public doubt and distrust against Bockelson rising, the resident notables strongly advised him to withdraw from the earlier institutions imposed by Matthjisson and Rothmann, adding a request that would include reshuffling of the community of goods and redistribution of houses and landed property (Stayer 1991:270). Implicit in it was how regularly and cautiously his authority was being checked by the resident notables and other leading figures behind the Anabaptist 'King of Münster' (Stayer 1991:270). Since these elites remained powerful, Bockelson's government institutions (e.g., the Twelve Elders and Davidic Kingship) would play a secondary position, a subservient position to the dual power structure, i.e., the "careful power-sharing" between the resident civic notables (the reactionaries) and the immigrant newcomers (the radicals) (Stayer 1991:270).

In this connection, Bockelson's extreme and even gruesome behaviours and politics can be read differently. Even the instituting of polygamy in summer 1534, which was known as his original creation to satisfy his personal lust, was actually a sort of tacit, implicit agreement between a less charismatic king and a more powerful elite group. Indeed, the latter had joined hands with him to impose the practice of polygamy "as an attempt to officer the numerous women by dividing them into patriarchal households" (Stayer 1991:270).[16] After all, if this collective noble leadership behind King John had not accepted it, the idea of polygamy could never have commenced in Münster. Furthermore, toward the final days of siege, turning the community of goods into little more than "wartime rationing" was another outcome decided by this "careful power-sharing arrangement" (Stayer 1991:123-38).

All this implies that the bright pageantry of Bockelson's rule had

---

[16]This could be confirmed by the fact that these polygamous relationships included women beyond childbearing years (Grieser 1995:32).

nothing to with his real personal power (Kirchhoff 1973, Rammstedt 1966 quoted by Stayer 1999:270). Instead, more plausible is his eclectic leadership as a mediator between the native notables and the immigrant newcomers (i.e., the civic Reformers and the radical Prophets). Thus, the essence of his leadership in political, socio-economic, and religious dimensions is much closer to the careful and eclectic compromise between the radical Prophets (from Matthjisson's group) and the reactionary Reformers (from Rothmann's group) rather than to the exercise of unchecked powerful and prophetic authority.

Political Eclectic

Despite his lack of prophetic authority, Bockelson, who recognized Matthjisson's sudden death, started organizing the situation well even to the point of bringing political and religious stability back to Münster. At first glance, it seemed to be quite successful so that a new biblical order appeared to have come with the reign of King John in Münster, the New Jerusalem:

> ... [T]he preacher baptized [the people] with three handfuls of water from a pail in the name of the Father, Son, and the Holy Spirit and gave them a copper token with the inscription "DWWF"[17] to wear around their necks.... The token served for admission into the gates. The quote from the Gospel of John meant that God's word had begun to take on reality. With the introduction of baptism as the new basic order, the old structures of estates and social status were abolished. Under the reign of King John, now there were only Christian brothers and sisters—no clergy or burgers, no nobles or serfs (Klotzer 2007:234-35).

But more accurately, just like a duck, remaining calm on the surface but paddling like crazy underneath, there were constant veiled power games among the ruling groups, all of which were built up to create

---

[17]"DWWF" (Das Wort wird Fleisch) meaning, "the Word becomes flesh" (Cornelius 1965:27-8, Lippe and Reck-Malleczewen 2008:18).

tensions (Stayer 1991:129). Notable was that the guilds had surprisingly grown fast and become a pillar of the power structure in the city. In recognition of their collaboration in reconstructing the Anabaptist community in Münster, the native Münsterites took on many of the new positions of power, which was a sort of political compensation. For the guilds—the representative of native Münsterites—had played a pivotal role in bringing about Anabaptist rule in Münster, it gave them legitimacy to demand their power sharing with the city council (Hsia 1988:67). And since they were primarily the guildsmen, it was Rothmann (the native Reformer), not Bockelson (the immigrant Prophet), who was solidly behind them.

The catch here is that these newly elected ones were those "who had at most held minor civic offices before, and none had served on the city council before 1533" under the Evangelical council (Hsia 1988:67). Also, as they were "more committed [to] radical religious ideas and to more thorough transformation of society," they were more receptive to the Anabaptist vision that "informed the egalitarian ethos of the guilds" (Hsia 1988:67-8). Sympathizing with Rothmann's ideas, they supported the Anabaptist movement, thinking it would bring them corporatist communal politics, which defended the equality of the community as a whole (Hsia 1988:68). Here again it was Rothmann, not Bockelson, who encouraged them in their struggle "to restore corporatist politics in Münster against the elitist domination of the self-styled *Obrigkeit* (political authority)" (Hsia 1988:69).

Thus it became evident that there was twin political leadership in Münster, apart from 'King' Bockelson—namely, the Prophets and the Reformers (the immigrant Melchiorites and the native notables) (Kirchhoff 1973:68-77 quoted by Stayer 1991:129). Both accepted Anabaptism as a new governing ideology (religious belief), but their points of emphasis were quite different. The native Reformers regarded adult (believer's) baptism as a useful tool to integrate citizens and non-citizens as well as men and women, while the immigrant Prophets saw it as a kind of apocalyptic sign for the *parousia* (Klotzer 2007:235). This was the reality behind the appearance of absolute power vested in tailor 'King John'. Although Bockelson was 'officially' a king of Münster, the major political decisions were 'practically' controlled and constrained by power-sharing arrangements.

After Easter 1534, under permission of the civic notables, King Bockelson dissolved the elected council and replaced it with the so-called "Twelve Elders", a divinely sanctioned administration, modeled after the institutions of the ancient Israelites (Klotzer 2007:238). As such, the council of "Twelve Elders" assumed an excessive concentration of power "as identical with the divine will, as superior to all law" (Baring-Gould 1891:290). However, in reality, this council was just a part of a power-sharing maneuver between the elite notables (Reformers) and Bockelson (Prophets) to make their position secure by getting rid of those previously elected officials who were devoted to Matthjisson (McLellan 2012:26-7).

Membership in the "Twelve Elders" showed how carefully composed it was for the sake of the twin political leadership. Along with selection of men from various origins (including Münster, Westphalians, Netherlands and so on), this council had reshuffled its organization into two: "half were residents, half new arrivals" as part of efforts to cement the current leadership in power (Klotzer 2007:238). Furthermore, given the city's exposure to war, a special task was given to these twelve 'god-fearing men'. Officially, "the chief task of the Elders was jurisprudence based on the divine law derived from Scripture" (Klotzer 2007:238); however, much of their efforts went into establishing a strict system of vigilance against potential attacks by the prince-bishop's forces (Baring-Gould 1891:290-91).

This kept the twin political leadership in power and allowed the bureaucratic organization to grow. Under the carefully planned power-sharing arrangements, a 'divinely sanctioned administration' had eventually become institutionalized, the "Twelve Elders" being completely in the service of the institution (Eichler 1981:45-61). A case in point was when, in a public ceremony, 'King John' gave "to the first [Elder] a naked sword and ordered him to fight according to God's command, then he gave the sword in the same way to the second, to the third, and so on until the last", which were little more than a formality for 'King' Bockelson, who walked a tightrope between the immigrant Prophets and the native Reformers (Geisberg 1856:248 quoted by Klotzer 2007:238).

Bockeslon had tried to maintain this political eclecticism by giving each Elder a new position in the 'royal household' (Bax 1903:199). On the surface, by virtually dissolving the board of town elders and confiscating the sword of justice, he seemed to have bolstered his sole headship. Indeed, the authority of the city council was effectively bypassed when Bockeslon appointed Knipperdolling (his right-hand man) as official sword-bearer with the power over life and death (Lippe and Reck-Malleczewen 2008:47-8). However, behind the scene, there were the careful power-sharing arrangements. More precisely, from the very beginning, the institution of the 'royal household' was being carefully regulated not by Bockelson, but by the twin leadership: its inner-circle comprised of nine persons, including Bockelson, four outsiders, and four Münster residents (Klotzer 2007:243-44).[18]

Furthermore, among the 148 official members of King John's court, half came from Münster and 25 were former office-holders. Despite not being the majority, these former office-holders nevertheless had a more prominent position in the court, meaning that the creation of the royal court served the interest of a privileged minority, untouchable even by Bockelson himself (Kerssenbrock 1899/1900:68-77). In one of the "Twelve Elders" early decrees, King John gave explicit recognition to a right of inheritance, which had never been interrupted in Anabaptist Münster, the administrator of inheritances being none other than Knipperdolling, burgher-master (Kerssenbrock 1899/1900:586).

All this implies that Bockelson was being kept in check by the twin political leadership: not only were the elite notables reluctant to align themselves with him, but even Knipperdolling, his close aide, once attempted to set up his own spiritual kingship against him (Baring-Gould 1891:314-17). Yet Knipperdolling's immediate restoration to office after this aborted plot once again demonstrated how Bockelson's political leadership was inept and incompetent (Cornelius 1965:149-50, Williams 1962:374).

In short, under the careful power-sharing arrangements between the immigrant Prophets and the native Reformers, King Bockelson's leadership was constantly checked—and sometimes seriously challenged. Although this tailor King tried to let some of the tension go

---

[18]Those are Bockelson, Knipperdolling, Bernd Krechtinck, Gerrit Boekbinder (former priests), Heinrich Redecker (city council member), Gert Reininck (brother of Bernd Krechtinck), Heinrich Krechtinck (an alderman), Hermann Tilbeck (a court master), and Bernhard Rothmann (as royal spokesman) (Klotzer 2007:243).

out of the situation, he seemed to always end up entangled in his own net because of his lack of charismatic authority and political power.

Socio-Economic Eclectic

On the other hand, King Bockelson's lack of prophetic authority was both the cause and result of the power-sharing arrangements between the immigrant Prophets and the native Reformers in Anabaptist Münster. Indeed, he was losing his ground as a king due to the continued tension between the two power groups as well as his prophetic ineptness. In a sense, his eclectic position provided an outlet for the Münster twin leadership to effectively release their cacophony of conflicts and disputes. This explained the reluctance of Münster's native Reformer leadership to align itself with the immigrant Prophets, as the latter began to stall and limit the former's previous legacies (McLellan 2012:26).

It especially appeared to have an "erosion of the strict community of goods instituted by John Matthjisson", a leading figure of the Prophets (Stayer 1991:129). At the outset, this belief in communal property was legitimized through Biblicism, particularly as substantiated in Acts 4 (McLellan 2012:18). Therefore, the institutionalizing of this practice was seen as the realization of the "New Jerusalem" into Münster (Reventlow 2010:179). Also, it was accepted as a necessary response to the city's emergency to counter against an external threat by the prince-bishop.

In February-March 1534, a significant exchange of population took place in besieged Münster—about 2,000 non-Anabaptists being expelled and about 2,500 Anabaptists immigrated in (Stayer 1991:128). This changed situation urged Matthjisson to take immediate action; and as part of it, he enforced the practice of community of goods to maximize efficiency and accomplishment but to minimize possible confusion and disorder (Kirchhoff 1973:24 quoted by Stayer 1991:128):

> The possessions of deserters and those expelled, as well as the property of the church and the monasteries, became public property which was managed in accordance with the newly developed laws and regulations. Many refugees from the surrounding places as well as the Netherlands arrived in Münster. These people had left all their possessions behind.

They found shelter in the various monasteries and were cared for out of public funds. Community living was a natural development (Krahn 1968:142).

As such, Matthjisson's community of goods was closely connected to a "refugee problem" (Stayer 1991:128). His leadership was tested by crisis and thus he had to prove his problem-solving ability. However, regardless of his original intention, Anabaptist propaganda for communism had attracted many immigrants from neighbouring towns, especially women and the poor (Stayer 1991:129).[19] Encouraged by it, Matthjisson began to legitimize the reordering-of-property arrangements by preaching that "the possessions of the emigres should belong in common to those who remained" (Kerssenbrock 1899/1900:556-58, Stayer 1991:129). Rothmann stood firmly together with him about this issue, preaching that "All things are common to every Christian" (Stayer 1991:129). Thus, a series of regulations were imposed to ensure the practice of the community of goods, including "outlawing the use of money inside Münster; confiscating ecclesiastical properties and the possessions of burghers who had fled the city; and appointing twelve elders who were to supervise the stockpiling of surplus food, clothing and wealth in communal stores and to oversee their distribution to the needy" (Hsia 1988:55).

The main executors of the community of goods in Münster were the deacons who moved according to their leader Matthjisson's command in an orderly but swift manner.[20] They did preserve and distribute the goods of emigres chiefly to assist immigrants but in principle to aid all needy members of the community. In fact, during summer 1534, "Ten to twelve hundred oxen were consumed, together with a quantity of other meat, butter and cheese, besides codfish and herring" (Bax 1903:186). This indicates that application of communal property had a double

---

[19]One example of it was a letter from a woman from Münster requesting that her sister send her daughter to join her in Münster. "I'm not concerned whether she has clothes or not. Send her to me; she'll have enough here . . . and the poorest have become as rich through God's grace as the burgher-masters or magistrates of the city" (Rammstedt 1966:90, quoted by Stayer 1991:129).

[20]In this regard, the various sources conflict. Kerssenbrock referred to seven deacons, while Gresbeck wrote of three deacons from each parish or 18 altogether (Kerssenbrock 1899/1900:69, Cornelius 1965:34).

purpose—"one was ideological and the other practical. The first was rooted in Christian Anabaptist tradition and the second in the unique situation in which the besieged Anabaptists found themselves" (Krahn 1968:141). Not only "acting according to the historical example of the earliest Christian communities recorded in the Acts of the Apostles," but also "responding to the real need to house, clothe, and feed the many immigrants," the radical Anabaptists in Münster played a leading role in abolishing private property in the city (Hsia 1988:55).

However, upon King Bockelson's reign, the community of goods took on a new meaning and began to deviate from its original purpose. Behind it all was the native elite group who pulled the strings to keep their vested interests. That's mainly why—despite establishment of the community of goods—the social structure of Anabaptism property-holders native to Münster remained intact (Kirchhoff 1973:35-44 quoted by Stayer 1991:125) and "Persons who had been rich property-owners in the old order were represented in disproportionate numbers among the political leaders of the new regime" (Stayer 1991:125).

Discounting the principle of community of goods—"all things in common", distribution of wealth among the Münsterites was even deteriorating. While all who were in high standing still enjoyed their privileges, a majority of the poor and of women were forced to share the burden (Kirchhoff 1973:87). The practice of community then became the shadow of communism, being "nothing like the egalitarian transformation of patterns of life and work" achieved by the early Christians (Plumper 1972:186 quoted by Stayer 1991:124). Further, as the siege of the prince-bishop intensified, its alteration grew worse (Krahn 1968:143). Not only was community of goods reshaped into a kind of war-rationing, but also women, children, and old men who could not fight were forced to leave the city (Kerssenbrock 1899/1900:172-73). All this was done under the native elites' initiative; King Bockelson just agreed with the need for affirming military defense and appeasing their demands (Stayer 1991:126-27).

Under Matthjisson's charismatic leadership, community of goods corresponded to the apocalyptic crisis as a form of social control (Stayer 1991:131). But when this enthusiasm declined as a result of Matthjisson's death, it gave rise to confusion and division within the city. Since a consensus was developing that a certain action should be taken, the city leadership inevitably had to make a strategic choice to preserve the energies of 'the good old days.' To put it more simply, Bockelson was selected by the ruling elites as the next best option, so that his leadership had inherently its limitation over the native notables in power. Indeed, "Bockelson's authority was personal and indirect, so the actual promulgation of community of goods came from a consensus of the prophets, preachers and Council" (Stayer 1991:134). The upshot of all this was that the status as the egalitarian community in Münster, based on equal distribution of communal goods, was reduced only to a new aristocracy where "the hegemony of the ruling elites over common men continued" (Stayer 1991:130).

In line with that, in July 1534, King Bockelson had also instituted one of his most controversial innovations—the practice of polygamy—which was actually made out of a need to align himself with prominent native notables in a way to secure his position (Smithson 1935:106-7, Hsia 1988:55-6). Having abruptly assumed the throne–half by his will and half by others'—after Matthjisson's death, this immigrant tailor king found himself in a vulnerable situation; he was lacking in everything—experience, personal charisma, solid political support base and age. Thus such disadvantages galvanized him to marry Divara van Haarlem (Matthjisson's young widow), whom her followers esteemed as a prophetess, for gaining more stable and public support (Williamson 2000:31). Since he was already married to the daughter of Bernhard Knipperdolling—the first Anabaptist mayor of Münster, the only way that allowed him to marry Divara would be a divinely sanctioned system of polygamy. This served him in two ways—elevating his status as a prophet through the union with Divara and maintaining his close ties with the native Münster notables (Kobelt-Groch 1996:302).

Later on, there arose a more practical and urgent reason for instituting polygamy. With pressure of the prince-bishop's heightening, polygamy was necessary if Bockelson was going to maintain control of Münster's remnants (Williamson 2000:29). Since the city's population now consisted of about three times the number of women than men,[21] and since adultery and fornication were both capital crimes, polygamy

---

[21] While the estimates varied, clear was the significantly higher number of women than men, one estimate being 2,000 men, 8,000-9,000 women, and 1,000-1,200 children (Cornelius 1965:107 quoted by Jelsma 1998:68).

was the only way to address the women's sexual needs on one hand (Bakker 1986:115). Also, Bockelson and the ruling elites were concerned as to whether that vast number of women were allegiant to his leadership (Williamson 2000:32). Thus, legitimizing polygamy through Biblicism (especially the Old Testament patriarchs) was seen as a way to effectively control and check the women on the other (Roper 1991:405-8).[22]

Furthermore, as defense of the city was more successful than anticipated, the Anabaptist leadership in Münster began to take into account the possibility of their prolonged rule. They realized that the city had to remain inhabitable but that the average age should not rise too much. They also realized the importance of increasing the number of births but that every woman who remained barren represented 'a lost opportunity' (Jelsma 1998:68-9). So it seemed plausible to encourage individual men to impregnate multiple women (Arthur 1999:93).[23]

However, unlike the community of goods, which no one could speak against, the matter of polygamy brought internal tensions from the outset (Hsia 1988:55). After several days of intense discussions with the city's preachers, King Bockelson on July 23 had officially proclaimed the instituting of polygamy (McLellan 2012:27). But the disgruntled voices could not be silenced, partly because of his lack of authority, but mostly because of its destructive impact on family structure (Snyder 1995:282). Therefore, in an attempt to overcome the resistance (including Rothmann's), intense pressure was applied to convince the local preachers that it was God's will for all to marry and procreate (Williamson 2000:29). Nonetheless, the issue even sparked a violent revolt by the native Münsterites who had severely denounced it and even Bockelson was arrested and imprisoned by these raging citizens (Pearse 1998:89, Cohn 1961:269). They vowed to continue their protest to call for the withdrawal of polygamy. The severity of the resistance was seen in these all-encompassing demands—rescinding of polygamy 'mandate'; returning to each person his property; reinstating the burgher-master,

---

[22] Examples of polygamy in the Old Testament refer to Exodus 21:10; 2 Samuel 5:13; 1 Chronicles 3:1-9, 14:3; 1 Kings 11:3; 2 Chronicles 11:21; and Deuteronomy 21:15 (McLellan 2012:18).

[23] Bockelson set a personal example in the matter of multiple marriages. In the fall, he had four wives; in the winter, six; and by the following spring, sixteen. Yet it seemed not that he was driven by the sensual passions, considering that none of his wives became pregnant by him (Klotzer 2007:244).

council, and all other usual practices; and even surrendering the city to the prince-bishop unless King Bockelson would accept their demands (Horsch 1935:138).

However, Bockelson was bailed out of his dilemma (at least temporarily) with the help of the ruling elites who feared that such rebellious party might have delivered the city over to the prince-bishop (Horsch 1935:138, Pearse 1998:89). Thus this failed revolt, in which many women took an active part, ended all possibility of further challenge to 'King John' and the power elites behind him (Pearse 1998:89). There followed a propaganda campaign by the ruling clique that was reminiscent of Rothmann's rationalization for polygamy and for the Davidic Kingship, both of which served to justify of Bockelson's political rehabilitation with the connivance of ruling notables (Bakker 1986:114-5).[24] This once again left King Bockelson awkwardly cast as 'piggy-in-the-middle'.

To sum up, the practice of communism and polygamy in Münster was introduced as part of the chief responses to the threats of the prince-bishop's siege from without and the connected refugee problem from within. It reached a high point under Matthjisson's reign with an iron fist. Afterwards, it showed its crude reality as a war on communism, modified and made more unappealing by Bockelson's responsiveness to the power elites' needs, who played 'piggy in the middle' role (Stayer 1986:134). In a nutshell, in his Machiavellian diplomacy, community of goods and polygamy addressed concerns of King Bockelson who remained an eclectic between the two ruling powers—namely, the native Münster notables and the immigrant Melchiorite radicals.

Religious Eclectic

When he assumed Matthjisson's position, King Bockelson found himself in an unenviable double job—to keep apocalyptic enthusiasm

---

[24]However, some have tried to see the role of polygamy in Anabaptist Münster not only as social and political, but also as a religious and spiritual complex by emphasizing both Bockelson's prophetic status and Rothmann's religious motivations. For more details in this regard, see Williamson (2000:27-38), Bakker (1986:105-16), and Hillerbrand (1988:507-11).

among the rank-and-file of the besieged city and to also maintain a balance between the two political powers (i.e., the immigrant radicals and the native notables). Although less of a charismatic leader than his predecessor, Bockelson was more of a politician (McLellan 2012:26). Utilizing his background as a player and poet, this tailor king distinguished himself with his oratory ability and succeeded in convincing his communicants to accept him as their new leader (Bax 1903:198, Cohn 1961:268).

Nonetheless, Bockelson was an unfortunate competitor under the shadow of the charismatic Matthjisson. Indeed, as a self-appointed prophet, Matthjisson had possessed "a personal magnetism that enabled him to claim, with some show of plausibility, a special role in bringing history to its appointed consummation" (Cohn 1961:285). Thus, "His acts were sanctioned by his pneuma," and nobody could speak against him (Eichler 1981:47). Coupled with chiliastic expectations, his prophetic leadership appealed to his followers to assume his "messianic roles to shape and change the political and social institutions" of Münster (Lerner 1983:6).

Bockelson's situation, however, was almost opposite that of Matthjisson, for he suffered from a lack of authority, principally due to his questionable prophetic gifting and accompanying lack of personal charisma (Rammstedt 1966:75 quoted by Eichler 1981:47). "His prophecies were highly rational and consequently were not satisfying to the congregation," which was accustomed to Matthjisson's charismatic and powerful authority (Rammstedt 1966:76 quoted by Eichler 1981:47). Thus, Matthjisson's death cast Bockelson both as an anchor and a trap. Even though he had quickly risen through the ranks of the stunned community to become its new leader, that didn't allay the congregation's doubts regarding his spiritual authority. In fact, it continued to render him as a comparison to his charismatic predecessor and heightened their concern as to his leadership ability (Rammstedt 1966:76 quoted by Eichler 1981:47).

This motivated Bockelson to devise ways of legitimizing his position. At first, he began pledging to seek support from the native notables, especially Rothmann and Knipperdolling, while at the same time planning and organizing spontaneous mass assemblages (made up largely of those who questioned his leadership) to be a threat (Eichler

1981:48). From it arose a new tactic—the institutionalizing of prophecy (Weber 1978:249, Eichler 1981:49). To compensate for his own lack of prophetic leadership, he began to exercise a variety of theatrical and bizarre performances, which often manifested the cruelty and terror of his religious cult (Rammstedt 1966:79 quoted by Eichler 1981:48). Thus, prophecy and punishment worked together to elevate his status which ultimately led to the form of "institutionalization of leadership" or "routinization of charisma" (Eichler 1981:57).

The purpose of his exercising of the routinization of charisma was clear. It led to the exoneration of his unrealistic prophecies and failed promises. For example, when the besieged congregation expected relief from the Netherlands, Bockelson declared as prophecy its fulfillment by Easter (Koltzer 2007:248). But when no salvation had come, he promptly switched his vision that the promise of deliverance meant "in an inward, spiritual sense, not as an external reality" (Koltzer 2007:248). "For all events supernatural forces were made responsible in order to feel one's dependence in one's behaviour on God, in order to live in a deterministic world" (Rammstedt 1966:79 quoted by Eichler 1981:48). Thus, the problem was given not to his prophecy but to the congregation who relied on outside help rather than on God.

Furthermore, in this process of the routinization of charisma, the fears and terrors of his religious cult were vindicated as new prophecy. By shifting responsibility onto the congregation's shoulders, Bockelson had suddenly reclaimed that Christian vengeance should be withdrawn (Cornelius 1965:130 quoted by Klotzer 2007:248). The city responded instantly to this new vision. Soon, military exercises in the cathedral square turned into a sort of sporting event (Klotzer 2007:248), and while anticipating the upcoming battle, he continued to encourage the contingents, who were celebrating communion, by riding from communion service to communion service (Klotzer 2007:239).

As part of such efforts, King Bockelson even began to ensure his court with a high level of sophistication (Cornelius 1965:85-6 quoted by Klotzer 2007:244). "Whenever in public, he would appear accompanied by members of the court, splendidly dressed in the finest robes, and adorned with one of his two gold crowns" (McLellan 2012:28). This was not an expression of vanity and exhibitionism but a desperate effort to make up for his shortfalls: he was choosing to replace his prophetic ineptness with various theatrical performances and religious ceremonies (Bax 1903:220). Indeed, he was resorting to every stratagem to retrieve his lack of charisma to the bitter end. Even during the final stage of the siege, Bockelson did not shrink from the institutionalization of leadership even to the extent of organizing a 'mocking mass' against Catholic practice (Jelsma 1998:68). Begun as a religious activity, it mocked the prince-bishop by sacrificing rats' heads, bats, and bones and its theme revolved around the victory of good over evil (Cornelius 1965:150 quoted by Jelsma 1998:68). In this carnival-like ridicule, the dearth of his charisma was compensated for by the congregation, which began to align itself with the institutionalization of leadership:

> The more hopeless the situation of the besieged became and the more incredible their faith in the *parousia* appeared, so much the more heightened grew their desire for miracles. Despite the complete institutionalization of community life, no conflict between institution and prophecy arose, since the latter also became institutionalized. Prophecy was completely in the service of the institution (Rammstedt 1966:80 quoted by Eichler 1981:49).

All this brings King John Bockelson's surreal, bizarre performances to a whole new dimension. The cruelty and terror of his regime, while often cloaked in religious expressions, were primarily a means of compensating for his lack of prophetic leadership. By turning-prophecy-into-institution, he expected a two-fold vindication—recognition of his good leadership by the ruling elites and compensation for lack of his personal charisma by the congregation.

Thus, Bockelson's cultic activities, which became a religiously justified ideology, are not to be read as pride of his dignity and power, but as a sort of desperate outcry and 'tragic laughter' resulting from his lack of charismatic authority. This further indicates that there must be much negotiation and compromise behind his religiously bizarre and theatrical performances. Indeed, he tried to set about dissolving the existing tensions and doubts through more-or-less cathartic religious activities as a means of appeasing both the ruling elites and the congregation.

To summarize, a careful reading of Münster Anabaptism reveals that John Bockelson's leadership was more than the vanity and lust of a former tailor and innkeeper. Merely characterizing him as a cunning demagogue is not convincing nor are his theatrical performances to be simply linked to his prophetic authority—or lack thereof. For he was not a charismatic Prophet or a learned Reformer. Rather, he found himself caught between the immigrant radical Melchiorites and the native reactionary notables throughout his reign. Thus his distinctive characteristics can be found not in cruelty and terror but in conspiracy and compromise. It is more plausible then that a true portrait of King Bockelson is seen in his eclectic role between the radical Prophets of Matthjisson's group and the reactionary Reformers of Rothmann's group. In short, he was neither radical nor reactionary, but the eclectic as being-in-the-two-power-structures.

Chapter 12
Profiles of the Münster Minjung: Beyond the Radical, Reactionary, and Eclectic

Profiles of the sixteenth-century Radical Reformers are remarkable in that it alerts one, who used to read Münster Anabaptism in a mono-dimensional presentation of history, to distinctive and dynamic tension among various groups. Especially, this manifests in three leading figures—John Matthjisson as being-in-the-immigrant-Melchiorite-Prophets (the radical), Bernhard Rothmann as being-in-the-native-civic-Reformers (the reactionary), and John Bockelson as the eclectic between the two power structures, which enhances the need for a closer and more critical reading of Anabaptist Kingdom of Münster.

Finding the common people (the *minjung*) in Münster among the *dramatis personae* is one of the important contributions to this reading. It is because, by positing this long-excluded group as among the historical protagonists, a more comprehensive picture of Münster Anabaptism comes to the fore. More precisely, reinterpreting Münster Anabaptism through the common people (the *minjung*) in Münster opens the possibility of both a sympathetic and a critical reading.[1] It is open to a sympathetic reading in terms of witnessing to their *han* (sorrow, suffering, and sinned-against), but also to a critical reading in terms of participating in their *dan* (praxis of agonized violence of love). This shift-in-perspective sheds new light on the Münster simple folks, especially women, who played an even greater role in shaping and

---

[1] I owe this terminology and its extended meaning to Margaret Miles (2005: xiv).

reshaping Münster Anabaptism, going beyond the three main groups—namely, the radical, reactionary, and eclectic.

Women in Münster as Victims and Participants

The Überwasser Nuns

It is far from the truth that the Anabaptist movement in Münster was the product of a social revolution by the low strata of society. Rather from its inception, it was welcomed by all strata of the population (Rammstedt 1969:122 quoted by Jelsma 1998). More remarkable was the positive role of women at that time (who comprised an overwhelming portion of the city's population), who made Münster 'the Anabaptist event' (Jelsma 1998:70).

Perhaps the Anabaptist teaching that there was neither male nor female, neither slave nor free in Anabaptism, came to these women as fresh hope, a way of liberation (Jelsma 1998:69). And in fact, the reality of Anabaptism in Münster was that they did play a greater role than elsewhere (Jelsma 1998:70); despite their otherwise limited gender role, a goodly number of the Anabaptist women there were very active in prophesying and in missionary work (Haude 2007:426). Indeed, in Münster, ability to prophesy was generally recognized as being God's instrument, which resulted in female Anabaptists' advent to take the lead:

> During this first stage in Münster, women began to preach, for example, the daughter of tailor, Georg thom Berge, who addressed a huge crowd for two hours on 8 February. Another woman then walked through the town shouting, until her voice gave up. Then she tied a sheep's bell to her girdle in order to continue her alarming work. Gesturing she pointed to heaven from where the judgment would come. It was also a woman who already in this initial stage prophesied that the King of Zion would descend from heaven to renew Jerusalem. At that moment John Matthjisson had not even arrived in the city (Jelsma 1998:71).

Yet, not all citizens had empathy for these phenomena. Instead, external behaviours of some of these women were met with ridicule and contempt from many of the male leaders, who simply scorned them like lunatics—"They began to see apocalyptic visions on the street, and of such intensity that they would throw themselves on the ground, screaming, writhing and foaming at the mouth" (Cohn 1961:283). This also provided a stumbling block to a number of wealthy citizens who left the town, considering it to be a dangerous precursor to a rebellion against them (Loffler 1923:27 quoted by Jelsma 1998:71).

Such a negative view from outside was not new among the Anabaptist women (Haude 2007:429-31). Even within Anabaptism, male leadership, which viewed men as shepherds or patriarchs of their communities, had become more mainstream (William and Mergal 1967:207). In this environment, "Women remained entirely subordinate, both at home and in church" (Irwin 1979: xxi). They even were expected to call their husbands 'lord'—"All of women, both young and old, have to be ruled by the men" (Stupperich 1970:258 quoted by Jelsma 1998:71). In all the regulations, "Women were to their husbands as their husbands were to Christ; the salvific path for women was, therefore, a tortuous one through a double intermediacy of men and Christ"[2] (Stupperich 1970:269 quoted by Hsia 1988:59). Thus it came as no surprise that Anabaptist male leaders in Münster saw such religious ecstasy and prophecy by women in a negative light (Weber 1922:104).

Since women's active roles and practices were considered to be potential threats to the patriarchal order (Waite 2013:496), the male leadership was determined to come up with a counter-measure against it, among which were these—the messages of women visionaries were forcefully silenced and direct access to salvation and sanctification were

---

[2]Bernhard Rothmann even wrote that "Man must re-appropriate his dominion over woman with a manly attitude. Everywhere women have got the upper hand. They lead men just like a bear is led on a chain. As a result the whole world has been immersed in adultery, impurity and fornication. Almost everywhere the wife wears the breeches. But God places everyone in his order, the man under Christ, the woman under the man, and that in full submission. Women must be obedient in quietness" (Stupperich 1970:258 quoted by Jelsma 1998).

fully denied to women (Hsia 1988:59).³ Thus, in the early stage, some women spoke out and held the esteemed position, but now it ended up strengthening patriarchal structures and accelerating the emancipation of women all the more (Goertz 2004:76).

In its wake, the initial promise of Anabaptism now turned into the new ball-and-chain regarding the reality of Anabaptist women (Haude 2007:437). To be sure, within the shell of the movement's initial excitement and promise, the substance of Anabaptism in Münster was men's subjugation of women "by restricting their social and religious roles, by transforming them into obedient wives and daughters of a polygamous, patriarchal and sacred tribe" (Hsia 1988:60). This evidently defines Anabaptist women in Münster as victims! "[They were] victims of the husbands and male family members who left them in the city to tend family property, while the men themselves fled the Anabaptist takeover; victims of an Anabaptist leadership intent on instituting an even stronger patriarchy by introducing polygamy; victims of starvation, fighting, repression after the city's fall" (Grieser 1995:33).

On the other hand, however, many of these Anabaptist women were not merely the passive victims who remained silent (Shantz 2009:21-34). In the midst of Münster's deteriorating external conditions, disciplines and regulations had been strictly enforced to ensure the defense of the city. Thus, essential tasks were allotted to both men and women either as artisans or in the maintenance and repair of the fortifications (Baring-Gould 1891:293). While the guards on the walls were inspected by the Elders day and night, most of all, the women played a crucial role in practical senses (Baring-Gould 1891:290-91). On one hand, when the city was bombarded in an attack by the besieging army, they (both young and older) worked all night to repair the damaged walls (Baring-Gould 1891:293). On the other hand, when the prince-bishop's troops tried to take the city by storm, they were greeted not only with cannon-shots but also stones, boiling water, and flaming pitch from Anabaptist women who defended the city, which led to the display of many of the guns as a trophy of the victory (Baring-Gould 1891:311-12, 353).

---

³Anabaptist men, especially many husbands, who faced persecution and execution, left a considerable amount of spousal guidance, which was expressed as concern for one's wife's salvation. In this way, they tried "to exercise their control over their wives even after their death" (quoted by Haude 2007:454-55).

Although at first, the task was forced against their will, acknowledging the severity of the situation, many Anabaptist women were actively engaging themselves in strengthening the besieged city wall and fighting back against threats from the outside. Thus, it was these ordinary women who took an active role in securing and defending the city of Münster both desperately and voluntarily for their existence.[4] In other words, "Despite their generally inferior position, [Anabaptist] women were essential for the maintenance, growth, and survival of the [Münster Kingdom]" (Haude 2007:430-31).

All this indicates that Anabaptist women in Münster were voluntary actors "taking control of their lives" (Grieser 1995:33). It was these 'obedient' wives and daughters who played dominant roles in defending the 'New Jerusalem' through their strength, courage, steadfastness, boldness, and bravery. Indeed, "They prophesied, they agitated for reform, they resisted the leadership, and they fought alongside the men" as willing participants (Grieser 1995:33).

The record of the chronicle of Überwasser Convent had provided ample examples, demonstrating that it was collaboration between the Überwasser nuns and the laywomen which made for the reform in Münster Anabaptism (Grieser 1995:38). According to a historical report (Kerssenbrock), on January 4, 1534, protests against allowing Lutheran influence into the city were being waged by a group of women, who were seeking to get rid of Lutheran minister Fabricius, whose popularity was extremely low (Stupperich 1973:9-50 quoted by Grieser 1995:37). The next day, these nuns, who had aligned themselves with Rothmann, acted in concert with the local women and marched toward the city council chambers, calling for Fabricius's expulsion (Grieser 1995:37). Their complaint against this Hessian Lutheran was two-fold—his theology and his manner of speaking, especially his ignorance of the local dialect (Grieser 1995:37).

---

[4]There have been scholarly concerns regarding what motives might have incited many ordinary women to join the Anabaptist movement in general and Münster in particular. One possible motive was the religious aspect, especially the persuasiveness of Anabaptist teaching. Yet other motives like economic safety or familial inducement likely also played decisive roles. As to the former, see Irwin (1979:20-1), Wyntjes (1977:168); for the latter, see Clasen (1965:182), Haude (2007:449-49), and Hsia (1988:51-69).

When their demands were refused by the councilors, "The women ridiculed them, called them papists, and threatened their eternal punishment" (Kerssenbrock 1899-1900:6:467-68 quoted by Grieser 1995:37). In aligning with the protesting women, the Überwasser nuns were demonstrating their belief that "the Word of God be preached in language accessible to the [ordinary] people" (Grieser 1995:38). The crucial point here was that Münster women (both the nuns and the laywomen) placed themselves at the forefront of agitating for the radical reform (Grieser 1995:34).

Furthermore, judging from the fact that these nuns were the first 're-baptizers' by Rothmann (Grieser 1995:38), there must have been strong ties between them and the reform party in the city (Grieser 1995:39). This allowed them to be the 'reforming' nuns who risked their lives to reform and resist the city: "Their boldness in going before the city council, their willingness to preach on the street, and their efforts to convert their unwilling sisters, all suggest that these nuns were activists, taking control not only of their own religious lives, but seeking to shape the religious life of the whole city" (Grieser 1995:39). In short, by actively participating in the religious interest, the Überwasser nuns, together with laywomen, proved that they became the subject of their own reformation not as mere victims but as willing participants (Grieser 1995:38).

Hille Feicken: Judith of the Münster *Minjung*

Another example comes from Hille Feiken, a committed young Anabaptist woman. Although the sources are silent about much of her biography, it seems evident that Hille Feicken was a devout Anabaptist from Sneek in Friesland (Snyder and Hecht 1996:289-90). She came to Münster at the end of February or beginning of March 1534, "not for curiosity or material need, but for reasons of faith," having given away all her possessions (Snyder and Hecht 1996:289). According to her later confession, she was married to a man named Psalmus, who introduced her to the Anabaptist life and faith (Snyder and Hecht 1996:290). There has been much scholarly debate about the exact identity of her husband.[5] Some doubted that this man had ever existed because Hille Feiken simply invented her marriage to Psalmus. Others assumed that his identity could well have been Peter Simon, who was "by-no-means ordinary" (Lippe and Reck-Malleczewen 2008:64) and probably occupied a high rank in Münster as a member of the "Council of Twelve" (Snyder and Hecht 1996:290).

Though it was not clear if this young and committed Anabaptist woman was satisfied with a new life in Münster, the chosen city, her solidarity with the Anabaptist community produced a strong conviction that God had led her to this place (Snyder and Hecht 1996:292); and at some point, the increasing threats and dangers from the outside likely awakened her consciousness about the mission of God. While actively participating with other women in Münster's defense efforts (Snyder and Hecht 1996:292), this beautiful fifteen-year-old young woman began to see the prince-bishop as the great Holofernes (a notorious general of Nebuchadnezzar) and to see herself as the heroic biblical Judith who rescued her people from their deep distress[6] (Lippe and Reck-Malleczewen 2008:27-8).

Hille was so thoroughly convinced that she had received this commission from God that "Day and night God gave her no rest carrying about this mission" (Lippe and Reck-Malleczewen 2008:66). Thus, daring to risk the extraordinary, she would eventually decide to fulfill her commitment to save Münster from the episcopal siege (Haude 2000:14). Her goal was to re-enact Judith's siege of Bethulia to behead the Assyrian

---

[5]Scholars have tried to identify this prominent Frisian man as the one in the Anabaptist group who stormed the Oldeklooster (Old Cloister) near Bolsward in Friesland and was killed in the battle. Peter was also considered as the brother of Menno Simons, the pacifist leader who opposed John Bockelson vigorously (Snyder and Hecht 1996:290).

[6]"In the Old Testament tale of Judith and Holofernes from *The Book of Judith* (not included in the Hebrew or Protestant biblical canons), the beautiful Judith's home city of Bethulia was under siege by Holofernes, a general of Nebuchadnezzar. After becoming drunk at a banquet, Holofernes repairs to his tent with Judith, who kills him and brings his head back to Bethulia, which had thus been saved from conquest" (Lippe and Reck-Malleczewen 2008:36). From it came a plausible assumption that the Münsterites considered the Old Testament a higher priority than the New Testament, since Judith is an Apocryphal heroine of the Old Testament period. This might be one of the distinguishing marks of Münsterites from other Anabaptists whose priority was mostly on the New Testament (Prokhorov 2013:200). G. H. Williams has also assumed the prevalence of Old Testament sermons preached in Münster (Williams 1992:570).

commander Holofernes while he slept (Williams 1992:570). Believing that the Lord God would show her the way (Cornelius 1965:404 quoted by Klotzer 2007:240), on June 16, 1534 (just weeks after the prince-bishop's first attack against the Münster), Hille crossed the enemy line to carry out that God-given task (Snyder and Hecht 1996:288). To liberate the besieged city, her plot was to kill the prince-bishop "using, if necessary the same feminine wiles" (Lippe and Reck-Malleczewen 2008:64). Having "enhanced her already general attributes of beauty" with fine clothes and jewels (Arthur 1999:86), she brought with her a handsome "Nessus shirt"[7] that she had soaked in poison (Lippe and Reck-Malleczewen 2008:64).

Hille's mission to murder the prince-bishop made the consequent differences between her and biblical Judith less lurid. Unlike Judith, she was not a rich widow; unlike Judith, she did not enter the enemy's camp with a maid but alone and not at night but in broad daylight; and unlike Judith, she did not bring a sword, but a poisoned shirt as the 'murder weapon' (Lippe and Reck-Malleczewen 2008:64). Yet these differences did not affect her decision because of her deep trust that God (not she) wanted it that way (Snyder and Hecht 1996:292).

When she went to the camp, Hille expected to be let in, but instead this young Anabaptist woman was arrested (Williams 1992:570) and taken to the prince-bishop's high bailiff for interrogation (Baring-Gould 1891:295). Pretending that she wished to betray Münster (Williams 1992:570), this Anabaptist Judith told him that she and her husband were disillusioned with their preachers' teachings plus wanted safety for themselves (Baring-Gould 1891:296). In return for that safety, she would share with the prince-bishop what she had learned from her husband about the city's defenses so Franz von Waldeck (prince-bishop), could conquer it without a single casualty (Arthur 1999:87). Her story and offer must have been persuasive, for the bailiff decided to take her to the prince-bishop (Baring-Gould 1891:296).

---

[7]"The Shirt of Nessus comes from Greek mythology. Hercules requested that the centaur Nessus carry Hercules's wife Deianira across a river, during which Nessus molested her. Hercules then shot Nessus with a poisoned arrow, which prompted Nessus to give Deianira his tunic as a gift for Hercules, which would supposedly make him love only her. However, the shirt was poisoned and eventually led to Hercules's death" (Lippe and Reck-Malleczewen 2008:69).

As it turned out, however, she was no more successful than John Matthjisson had been some ten weeks earlier. For at this same time, another Münster resident, Herman Ramert, who was in truth seeking asylum (Lippe and Reck-Malleczewen 2008:64), offered a more timely 'gift' than Hille's fancy shirt—that gift being that her story was a lie (Baring-Gould 1891:296) and, in fact, she was on a mission to assassinate the prince-bishop (Lippe and Reck-Malleczewen 2008:64). This revelation was followed by an immediate interrogation under torture, resulting in her confession that "she had intended to become a second Judith to try to save her city from the prince-bishop" (Arthur 1999:87, Haude 2000:14). After further torture on the wheel, Hille faced execution with a smile and the conviction that "she would return safe and sound to [New] Zion" (Baring-Gould 1891:296).

Implicit in all this is that Hille's plot was not a secret in Münster (Lippe and Reck-Malleczewen 2008:64). In fact, it was an open secret among Münsterites that this devoted young woman had planned to kill Franz von Waldeck by means of a poisoned shirt. Not surprisingly, she had shared her plan with the city's leadership—namely, Bockelson, Knipperdolling, and Rothmann (Lippe and Reck-Malleczewen 2008:66). Although they considered it too prosaic to implement, recognizing that they had nothing to lose, Münster's top bosses allowed her to take the risk (Arthur 1999:86). For if successful, "the siege would surely collapse and their fame would be immeasurably enhanced. If she failed, little was lost save her life" (Arthur 1999:86).

However, their permission did not mean that Hille had aligned herself completely with Münster's male leadership. In fact, as her interrogations revealed, she was quite critical of them, "since she did not feel responsible for any earthly authority, but to God alone" (Snyder and Hecht 1996:291). In her eyes, God's chosen city was still far from experiencing gender equality, for its strongly patriarchal organization had endowed men with power and authority while stressing women's subordination and silence (Snyder and Hecht 1996:291). Her negative judgment of governmental authorities was engendered by the reality that all Anabaptist leadership in Münster only talked the language of 'brotherhood' (Haude 2007:428). Thus, this committed Anabaptist woman was doubtful and even dissatisfied with the manner of male leadership, particularly the way it treated the simple women in Münster.

It seemed to her that "God's word had been lost somewhere *en route*", as something she was compelled to do (Snyder and Hecht 1996:291-92).

Hille's emulation of the biblical heroine Judith nonetheless left important consequences. First, it shed a completely different light on the death of John Matthjisson by showing that she had inspired (not was inspired by) Matthjisson (Snyder and Hecht 1996:293). From the outset, her inspiration was recognized by this charismatic leader as a welcome guest (Snyder and Hecht 1996:293). For the retelling of the Judith story, who was led and protected by God, could be the perfect solution for the New Jerusalem, which was in deep trouble (Snyder and Hecht 1996:293). But the one problem was that the biblical hero happened to be a woman whose independent image was not favoured by Münster male leadership (Snyder and Hecht 1996:293).

This spawned an adaptation of the story which better fitted the male-dominated milieu (Snyder and Hecht 1996:293). In his discretion, Matthjisson utilized Hille's inspiration to dissolve the problem and continue to maintain the gender roles. "As a male, it was not possible for him to take the role of the biblical heroine himself, but it was possible that he appropriated her way of thinking, her spirit, and her success" (Snyder and Hecht 1996:293). This explained Matthjisson's somewhat enigmatic sortie that eventually led to his tragic demise. In the process of adaptation, Hille's inspiration was completely in the service of Matthjisson, and this consequently provoked him to embark on a new mission to save his people from the besieging army, despite its turning out to be a suicidal rush (Snyder and Hecht 1996:293).

In addition, Hille's action showed that she was a subjective yet active participant in her destiny. Indeed, she was willing to risk going into the enemy camp out of her own volition, no one having sent her (Lippe and Reck-Malleczewen 2008:64, Snyder and Hecht 1996:294). Thus, the death of Matthjisson would not catch up with her. Rather, she made it as an opportunity to "hold tenaciously to her intention and seek to realize her plan" as the Judith of Münster (Snyder and Hecht 1996:294).

Hille's strong commitment to her mission even made the consent of male leadership obsolete, because she refused to serve "as a tool for someone else" (Snyder and Hecht 1996:294). This conversely proves that there was considerable distrust and discontent of the male leaders about her plan. Before attempting to carry it out, she had to overcome barriers in the form of male leaders of Münster—first John Matthjisson and later John Bockelson (Snyder and Hecht 1996:294). Indeed, Hille's 'Judith plot' was not put into action under Matthjisson's rule. Although he as a charismatic leader gave credence to the plan, she could carry it out only after his death (Snyder and Hecht 1996:294).

The same was true for John Bockelson. Although he had little interest in Hille's plot, he gave much attention to the spotlight she received. Being reluctant to endorse her independent actions, it became part of the reasons for him to introduce polygamy (Haude 2000:14). Out of his lack of prophetic authority, he perhaps saw her as a threat to his rule, just as he saw her husband Psalmus as a threat to his leadership (Arthur 1999:89-90). Despite all of these hindrances and disturbances, this 15-year-old Anabaptist woman nonetheless remained steadfast to put into action her plan to bring a new hope and deliverance to the New Jerusalem.

In summary, Hille Feicken, who had lived in Münster only a few months (Snyder and Hecht 1996:294), found in Judith of the Old Testament a role model that motivated her to want to become the Judith of Münster who would bring a magnificent rescue with God's help. However, the real significance of all this was not her blind imitation of the biblical heroine in every detail, but rather a new recognition of her identity as a woman which enabled her to look anew at the actual conditions in which she found herself (Snyder and Hecht 1996:294). With such new vistas, her goal to liberate the besieged city gained momentum. In this light, the consequent deviations between Hille and the biblical Judith served not as a deterrent but rather a catalyst that encouraged her to carry out her 'calling' as the Judith of Münster on behalf of the people—especially women—in Münster.

Further, Hille's commission to liberate the besieged city from the enemy mirrored a consciousness of its people, who decided to take matters into their own hands. In other words, this produced a self-awakening, self-consciousness, and self-determination of Münster's common people (*minjung*). In one sense, this 'power of the powerless' affected Matthjisson to the extent of adapting it according to his own discretion. But in another sense, it was seen as a threat that challenged the existing male-oriented leadership, which provided an excuse for the practice of Anabaptist masculinity, such as the introduction of polygamy. In this light, Hille Feicken played an exceptionally important role among both the external (i.e., prince-bishop) and the internal (i.e., Anabaptist male leadership) threats.

In short, although Hille Feiken, from her role as the Judith of Münster, failed to deliver the city from the prince-bishop's hands, she was successful in liberating herself from a traditionally passive female role as an obedient and submissive woman and thereby present a new model of Anabaptist women as principal actors who were willing to stand up against those in power (both the external and the internal), tilted primarily to the male-oriented milieu.

The Münster Common People (*Minjung*) as the New Psalmists as Well as the Protagonists

Both individually and collectively, the common people (*minjung*) of Münster were in one sense painful mourners but in another sense passionate singers. Even their besieged conditions failed to keep them from identifying with the psalmists, who brought a new meaning of hope against hope (Lippe and Reck-Malleczewen 2008:87). The few surviving sources consistently record that the city's Anabaptist congregations had sung "German psalms" and "songs of praise" (Cornelius 1965 quoted by Brecht 1985:362). Thus, it became evident that the singing of psalms was their daily bread in both the pre- and the post-Anabaptist Kingdom periods (Kerssenbrock 1899/1900:403 quoted by Brecht 1985:363).

How could that be possible? It was probably due to the apocalyptic mood of the city in which fear and hope, decadence and expectation both mixed and coexisted at the same time. It seemed to be evident that the Münster Anabaptists believed their city to be the New Jerusalem (Dulmen 1974:81, 103 quoted by Klaassen 1992:86). Since the charismatic leader Matthjisson had ruled the city, "A whole town had become a church; in other words, the church had been absorbed into the new kingdom. The people knelt as easily in the streets as in the church. Sermons were preached in the church buildings but also in the squares of the town, and psalms were sung, wherever people congregated" (Stupperich 1970:256 quoted by Jelsma 1998:55).

Under 'King John' Bockelson, although such had become routinized and institutionalized, even this trend did not subside, and "Psalms of

Münster" continued not by compulsion but rather by assent of the people (Eichler 1981:49). The Münster congregations sang at the conclusion of the preaching service, at communal meals, at observances of the Holy Communion, at celebrations, and even at Bockelson's coronation (Brecht 1985:363). Of particular feature here was the antiphonal and responsorial method—i.e., a call-and-response style of singing—which functioned by King Bockelson being cantor (i.e., caller) and the people being the congregation (responders): "During a celebration in the courtyard of the Münster cathedral, an Old Testament reading given by the king was followed by a German psalm sung antiphonally by the clergy and schoolmasters, and the soprano voices of the 'little boys' and the gathered people. Thereupon, another reading by the king was followed by another antiphonal hymn" (Brecht 1985:363).

All of these performances then would contribute to establishing a common heritage, the so-called people's song. The purpose was to involve both cantor and people in the song together and thus develop it as a dynamic and reciprocal congregational activity. By doing so, responders (people) led, rather than being merely led by the caller (Bockelson), and thus "the real function of [King Bockelson] as cantor has become extinct, and the reference to the people's song is avoided, as the cantor is no longer considered a people's leader" (Gouel 1991:73-85).

Such a performance of people's song was shifting from an option to a necessity with the besieged Münsterites concluding that they could and should remain psalmists to get out of the great cataclysmic struggle brought about by the prince-bishop's attack. Significantly enough, to the Münster congregations, there was a reason for the singing of specific songs, which is now known to be the following four songs that responded to the following four instances.[8]

1. *War Gott nicht mit uns diese Zeit* ("If God Were Not Beside Us in This Hour"). When Münster congregations were undergoing a period of transitioning from the evangelical-reformed faith to Anabaptism, the Überwasser Church became a target of an iconoclastic attack (Lippe and Reck-Malleczewen 2008:19). On Palm Sunday, April 5, 1533, Bernhard Rothmann, a city reformer, was celebrating communion there amidst the

---

[8]Here, the author is primarily indebted to the concentrated study of Martin Brecht (1985:362-66). The following four songs of the Anabaptists in Münster are mostly subject to his findings and interpretations.

antiphonal singing of the psalms (Baring-Gould 1891:232). One report says that they "croaked nasally the 124th Psalm passage, 'The snare has been broken and we have escaped'" (Kerssenbrock 1899/1900:191 quoted by Brecht 1985:363). The psalm's third verse, which referred to release of the bird from the fowler's snare, offered a sense of comfort and hope to the distressed congregations that were facing the insecurity of the besieging condition (Brecht 1985:363).

Here, the fact that this hymn was attributed to Luther was insignificant. Rather, the Münster Anabaptists were encouraged to adopt and sing this antiphonal psalmody following the repulsed attack on August 31, 1534 (Brecht 1985:364). While the entire population of Münster was desperate to rebuild the weakest wall, the ladies were singing (Lippe and Reck-Malleczewen 2008:87), reminding them that the first verse best reflected their own experience of that day—"If God had not been on our side, we should have had to despair" (Cornelius 1965:81 quoted by Brecht 1985:364).

2. *Allein Gott in der Hoh sei Ehr* ("Glory Be to God Alone on High"). Apparently, this so-called German Gloria became the Münster Anabaptists' favourite song (Brecht 1985:364, Baring-Gould 1891:290). It was sung on many occasions, including at 'King John' Bockelson's coronation (Lippe and Reck-Malleczewen 2008:90) and at the conclusion of a celebration in the cathedral courtyard (Cornelius 1965:83, 134 quoted by Brecht 1985:364). Ironically, it was also sung at the June 11, 1535, execution of Queen Elizabeth Wantscherer, one of King John's sixteen wives, who had criticized and rebelled against Bockelson's authority (Lippe and Reck-Malleczewen 2008:149).

What is important about such singing is that it provides a glimpse into the mentality of the Münster congregations. Phrases such as "God is pleased with us" represented the Anabaptists' self-consciousness in identifying themselves as his elect people (Brecht 1985:364). Whereas the petition in this song's fourth verse for protection from the "forces of the devil" reflected recognition of the currently besieging situation, it resulted not from their revolutionary conquest but from the surprising attack by the prince-bishop, which urged them to act in self-defense (Kirchhoff 1962:77-170, Stupperich 1958:12). Out of this conviction, the Münsterite people could sing this song as an expression of their unyielding spirit against a deadly threat to themselves.

3. *Ein feste Burg ist unser Gott* ("A Mighty Fortress Is Our God"). Against the evermore rigorous siege, King Bockelson had reshuffled those women remaining in the city and divided them into "platoons" to aid in its defense (Brecht 1985:364). While marching to their stations, such makeshift women-platoons began to sing "a German song called 'A Mighty Fortress Is Our God'" (Brecht 1985:364). This scene contributed in conveying an intense and dramatic theme of the song. In its rendering of the theme of Psalm 46, this hymn "reinforced their determination to resist" (Brecht 1985:364). Again, Luther's authorship of this hymnody paled into insignificance (Brecht 1985:364). Being encouraged by successful defense of the city on August 31, 1534 (Baring-Gould 1891:312), King Bockelson as the cantor had praised the aid of their mighty God and had led a "war song" by quoting from the second verse—"With force of arms we nothing can"—to keep the women-platoon's morale up (Cornelius 1965:81, 128 quoted by Brecht 1985:364).

4. "God Will Reveal a New Thing in This New Year." Although the songs of the Münster Anabaptists were mostly attributed to the hymnody of the Reformed, this was an exception (Brecht 1985:365). According to the testimony of one resident who had fled the besieged city only to be taken captive by the prince-bishop's forces, "It was prophesied that in a millennium no such joyous New Year had been rung in as the one which was about to begin; therefore [the Münsterites] had composed a psalm to be sung at the royal table: 'God Will Reveal a New Thing in This New Year'" (Dulmen 1974:194 quoted by Brecht 1985:365).

Judging from Rothmann's "Report of the Vengeance to Come," this expected 'new thing' could be seen either as the dawn of a day of vengeance against the godless or as the inauguration of the millennium (Stupperich 1970:284-97 quoted by Brecht 1985:366). In this sense, the 'new year' may best be reckoned to begin immediately after Christmas 1534 when Münster was filled with an intensive sense of immanence (Baring-Gould 189:313-14). In particular, two things in Rothmann's writing corresponded to the appellation in Psalm 149 reported by a runaway Münsterite. One was that verse 1 and verses 6-9, which related to vengeance against the heathen, were intentionally selected by Rothmann (Brecht 1985:366). The other was his interesting variation of verse 1. The original reading—"Sing to the Lord a new song"—was substituted for another reading—"A new song to the King of Zion"

(Brecht 1985:366). With that change, the psalm was re-made as homage to the 'King' of Münsterite Zion—namely, John Bockelson.

Rothmann's next verses spoke of his joyous expectation of a great turning point in history which was to reign in Münster that December— "The shrine now is broken. All doubt is put away. May we see David's kingdom. Come on earth this day, for which we rejoice always. The godless foes are all undone! O joy of joys!" (Stupperich 1970:294 quoted by Brecht 1985:366). This song fragment thus referred to the central hope of the Anabaptists in Münster who had a sense of satisfaction that 'political messianism' would be fully punished for the injustice and evil they had experienced (Brecht 1985:366). Here, the Münster Anabaptists did not recite Luther's hymnody parrot-fashion but rather determined themselves to be the new composers who expressed their collective expectation and hope in the midst of suffering. Thus this Rothmann-revised psalm should continue to be sung even if an imminent breakthrough was not forthcoming.

All this indicates that the Münster congregations stood as the new psalmists. Having undergone a transformation from lamentation to praise, from suffering to glory, the common people (*minjung*) of Münster could become the singers of lament but at the same time the singers of joy. Indeed, suffering, seen as being glorified with Christ, encouraged them. As was the case with Christ, so too was it with those who followed him—He would reward the suffering by ruling with him. Their certainty was that those who now oppressed them would be expelled from the renewed world. Thus to the Münster Anabaptists, suffering was the path to glory (Rom. 8:17); they should remain as the psalmists who saw suffering not as the end but as the beginning of glory. This allowed them to be the 'self-psalmists' singing in the fight and believing that the path to glory would go by way of the Cross. This created the new image of the common people (*minjung*) of Münster both as the protagonists *(gurus)* who had anticipated their liberation by themselves and the psalmists *(avatars)* who had received their salvation from the promised Messiah whom they continued to praise and admire in the midst of suffering.

Summary: Münster Anabaptism as the Hybridity in the Common People (*Minjung*)-Reformers Interplay

The problem of the traditional view on the Anabaptist Kingdom of Münster is exacerbated when we consider that it is increasingly becoming a kaleidoscopic diversity of portraits, which over time was backed by different dramatis personae—i.e., the immigrant radical Prophets, the native reactionary Reformers, the eclectic between these two power structures, and finally the common people (*minjung*) of Münster. This means the epitome of Münster Anabaptism should be seen in the creative and critical tensions among these various 'actors'. In a figurative fashion, the 'Münster rhapsody' was played by a quartet consisting of the radicals, the reactionaries, the eclectic, and the common people (*minjung*) as the key players.

More precisely, Münster Anabaptism requires a synchronic as well as a diachronic reading that recognizes the complexity and the interrelationships of these various dramatis personae. First were the immigrant radical Melchiorites (Prophets) under the banner of chiliastic and revolutionary belief; they considered themselves as the 144,000 elect whose obligation was to set up the Kingdom of God and destroy the ungodly. Second were the native civic notables (Reformers), who not only created the preconditions for the Kingdom, but also preserved their influence once it was established; the Prophets' radical activities were counter-balanced by these reactionary Reformers. Third was the eclectic leader John Bockelson, the Münster King, who found himself in the Prophet-Reformer tension; his compromise leadership was accepted by both parties as a temporary solution, given the reality of the city's precarious situation.

Last but not least were the common people (*minjung*) of Münster, whose role even went beyond the radical, the reactionary, and the eclectic. They rejected becoming either lamentable victims or merciless revengers, choosing instead to be the singers of Jesus, the suffering Messiah, moving from lamentation to praise, from suffering to glory. In so doing, they could stand still as the passionate psalmists who belittled death and pain to the point of singing hymns of victory while being attacked and even killed.

To be sure, refusing to merely be *tableaux vivants* (living pictures), they led, rather than were led by, these three groups (the radical, the reactionary, and the eclectic) to the 'Anabaptist Kingdom of Münster event'. Thus, it was these 'little' people who played an important role in making and sustaining Münster Anabaptism as the place of hybridity where both the common people and Münster Reformers interacted with and contributed to each other, as epitomized by the following:

First, in Münster Anabaptism, one underlying phenomenon was the sweeping apocalyptic expectations, the realization of which coincided with the active behaviour of the common people who held Radical Reformers sympathies. Passing through Luther's and Zwingli's reformations and the Radical Reformers' repudiation of them, it became apparent in the notion that the Reformation began with Luther but needed to be completed. That completion would involve destroying the old order and thereby establishing an alternative order—namely, the Anabaptist Kingdom of Münster. It was none other than the immigrant radical Melchiorites (the Prophets) who spearheaded this radical movement in Münster by justifying the city's role as the embryonic messianic kingdom on earth for God's chosen saints—namely, the Anabaptists.

This wave of excitement attracted a large number of common people in the Low Countries, especially those who were on the bottom rung of the social ladder. Captivated by this sudden, unexpected breakthrough— i.e., the Anabaptist bloodless takeover of Münster—these low-country commoners saw this political miracle in Münster as a sign of the new reality—namely, a community of love where the rich could no longer eat and drink the sweat of the poor (Stupperich 1970:256 quoted by Jelsma 1998:55). Thus, the radical Dutch Prophets, who had championed the powerless, became articulators of the intense yearning of ordinary people for liberation from all the age-old oppressions of the powerful (Jelsma 1998:55-6).

Second, beneath the Anabaptist rule in Münster was an undercurrent of the Prophet-Reformer power-sharing arrangements in accordance with a check and balance mechanism. Indeed, the immigrant radical Melchiorties and the native civic notables were the duumvirate of the Anabaptist Kingdom of Münster. Such a dual leadership made strange bedfellows: despite their contrasting positions, both had reached a tacit agreement that one shall follow the other as leader to preserve the city's religious and political freedom from outside threats.

This strategic alliance of two power groups even led to the eclectic leadership in Münster. With the sudden death of John Matthjisson (the radical Prophet), the power of gravity fell to 25-year-old John Bockelson, whose credentials (namely, tailor, salesman, and amateur actor) were hardly impressive compared with his predecessor. Thus, what this less-than-charismatic 'King' had long been struggling for was to keep the balance between the two political powers as the eclectic. To this end, Bockelson, even if he was Matthjisson's second-in-command, relied heavily on Rothmann and Knipperdolling, two native Münster Reformers who had been of no particular importance under Matthjisson, though it ended in another power struggle between themselves that proved to be a serious blow to his political standing as 'King'. Pressured by the native notables, Bockelson used to take a back seat when there was a conflict of interest between the two.

Socio-economic and religious matters were no exception to his eclectic approach. When both the internal and external situations became desperate, Bockelson reshaped and promoted the practice of 'community of goods' into war-time rationing and instituted the practice of polygamy with the approval of the ruling clique. Here, his mission as the eclectic was to compromise, not fight, with the native civic Reformers. This compromise, though far from a fundamental solution, was a realistic option he could have made under the present political condition.

Although Bockelson was in a dilemma—if he was accustomed to walking on eggshells in the native Reformers, he would never stand on his own two feet but just play second fiddle to them—it paled into insignificance beside what he would remain in power. He wished to hold his kingship even though that kingship was not 'imperial' or 'almighty'. This political maneuvering climaxed in his process of routinization of charisma which was channeled into religiously extreme and theatrical performances to compensate for his lack of authority.

Third, there were the common people (*minjung*) of Münster whose significance and contribution went beyond the radical, the reactionary, and the eclectic, although they had been minimized or ignored for a long time. By and large, the common people of Münster remained within bounds, even when they tried to defend the city against the attacks of the prince-bishop. This came as a strong sense of *déjà vu*, reminding them of the earlier event they experienced when the city council declared Münster an evangelical city and the bishop had tried to intervene with violence. At that time, they closed the gates to him with the burghers standing guard and none of the princes accused them of revolutionary action but rather doing what was their right to do—i.e., a justified act of self-defense.

However, now that the city had become Anabaptist, the prince-bishop laid siege again. The Münsterites were at first surprised to find themselves suddenly at war (Cohn 1961:286) then became indignant when the surrounding princes supported the bishop (Jelsma 1998:58-9): this was an unfair double standard! Time and again they returned to the same theme. Even though there had not even been a declaration of war (Stayer 1972:235), they were being treated as rebels instead of free citizens who had the right to defend their city against attack (Stupperich 1970:207-8, quoted by Jelsma 1998:59).[9]

From it was derived a significant revision that the decision to employ the sword would be a gradual process in response to external conditions and internal power struggles. Initially, the Münster Anabaptists were ambivalent or undecided about using the sword, and only gradually did they come to espouse its employment (Kirchhoff 1970:357-70, Stayer 1972:228, 230-33, Brady, Oberman and Tracy

---

[9]It is true to say that, in many cases, it was the harsh rhetoric and violent response of authorities that played a crucial role in the escalation of conflict. Government reaction produced the results they were intended to combat—in this case, the intensification of Anabaptist opposition (Driedger 2007:519-20). Driedger explains the relations between Anabaptists and government by the concept of "deviance amplification" or the spiral of mutual rejection (Wallis 1977:205-11, 214-24). This, too, seems fit to the situation of the Anabaptist Kingdom of Münster. The distinctive is that the common people of Münster responded to this governmental tactic both critically and creatively, not only as protagonists but also as psalmists, as already discussed above.

1995:269).[10] This pales the view that Münster Anabaptism had devised revolutionary plans or plans of conquest from its inception. Rather, it was to be considered as the right to govern itself and to defend its freedom against the destructive threats of the prince-bishop.

In addition, the Münster event especially raised the aspirations as well as opportunities of women (*minjung* of the *minjung*) as reforming pioneers. For example, it was the Überwasser nuns who took an active and leading role in the transformation of the city. In fact, these sisters were the protagonists of the movement, being protesters against the Lutheran ministers, being preachers for the unwilling fellow sisters, and being proponents of the city reformers.

These so-called 'second-class' citizens were also spiritual activists appealing to the call of the Spirit. In this sense, they acted as angry prophets who were against the existing society and inspired violent actions on the part of other believers. They even prophesied the impending advent of New Jerusalem before Matthjisson's arrival in the city. It was also women in Münster (especially single working women, spinsters, widows, and young servant girls) who took the lead in opposing polygamy and other internal oppressions. And it was fifteen-year-old Hille Feiken who confronted the attack of the prince-bishop alone, driven by the commitment to save the city. All this suggested that the ordinary women in Münster were not merely victims but rather willing participants of their own destiny.

Furthermore, the Münster commoners were the new psalmists who sang a song of the vision of New Jerusalem against the hopeless situation. How was that possible? Because in their suffering and broken context, they found the Cross of Jesus, the Messiah who showed the pattern of suffering as the path to glory. As such, they were convinced that the new

---

[10]This evolution in thinking on the sword among the Münster Anabaptists is well reflected in the writing of Bernhard Rothmann, chief ideologue and propagandist for the Münster Kingdom (Dipple 1999:91-105). However, there was stark contrast between Rothmann and the common people of Münster. While for Rothmann rationalization for the righteous to take up arms was rooted in the idea of an apocalyptic crusade for restoration of the Davidic Kingdom of John, the Münsterite commoners found its root from their own suffering situation. Thus, Rothmann wished him and John to remain the people's *gurus,* while the simple folk in Münster wished them to become their *avatars* as well as their *gurus.* Both agreed that the age of suffering was giving way to the age of vengeance but failed to agree to share their role-play in, for, and with the common people in Münster.

'Polis of Shalom' (Anabaptist takeover in Münster) revealed that the destructive power of the prince-bishop was broken and thus they were freed. This eschatological belief made them remain as the palmists as well as the protagonists, who could overcome suffering with new songs.

Fourth, all this suggests that Münster Anabaptism is to be seen as the place of hybridity, which holds the dynamic interconnection between the *avatar*-hood (prophetic practice) of the Radical Reformers and the *guru*-ship (messianic practice) of the Münster common people (*minjung*). In other words, in its dynamic tensions—among John Matthjisson as being-in-the-immigrant-prophets (the radical), Bernhard Rothmann as being-in-the-native-civic-reformers (the reactionary), John Bockelson as being-in-the-eclectic between two power structures (the eclectic), and the Münster common people as being-beyond-the-other-three (*minjung*)—the Anabaptist Kingdom of Münster initiated a process in which all *dramatis personae* were dialectically driven to maintain themselves both as *gurus* and *avatars*, subjects and objects, great men and common men, victimizers and victims, sinners and sinned-against.

To put it differently, Münster Anabaptism included a certain kind of dynamic interplay between the Radical Reformers and the Münster common people (*minjung*) in the dialectical unification of *han* and *dan*. For this place of hybridity is asymmetrical, uncertain, and in flux, but it holds the possibility of the praxis of *dan*—constructively resolving *han*. In it, there is the *avatar*-hood of the Radical Reformers—namely, incarnation of themselves into the *han*-ridden reality of the Münster common people (*minjung*). Also, there is the *guru*-ship of the Münster common people—namely, deification of themselves into the Radical Reformers that leads to the transformation of *han* into *dan*.

This place of hybridity, therefore, shows how the Radical Reformers and the Münster common people (*minjung*) converge (as well as collide) together in order to foster healing, liberation, and salvation on both sides, epitomizing the Anabaptist Münster Kingdom both as the place of *han*—where the common people suffer, and the place of *dan*—where the suffering of the common people is resolved and transformed.

Part 5
CONCLUSION

Chapter 13

Re-Reading Münster Anabaptism as the Minjung-Messiah Interplay

Münster Common People (*Minjung*) as Being-in-the-Messiah

This book aims to look at the sixteenth-century Radical Reformation, and especially Münster Anabaptism (1534-35), from a perspective of people's (or grassroots) history of Christianity. In this sense, it is a critical re-reading of history 'from below'—one that pays greater attention to the voiceless, the ordinary faithful. With this approach, the book uses a historical and constructive theological approach as the template for generating a counter-history of Münster Anabaptism, by inviting Korean Minjung Theology as its conversation partner. The goal of this volume is therefore to construct a critical and creative conversation between the twentieth-century Korean Minjung Theology and the sixteenth-century Münster Anabaptism.

More precisely, the choice of adopting this methodology brings with it the re-reading of the Reformation from below—that is, to look at how the common people have reacted and contributed to the Reformation both positively and negatively. By challenging the traditionally dominant interpretations, which were focused primarily on the great deeds of great men, the book has engaged itself in emphasizing not the famous princes and theologians but rather the ordinary peasants and simple folks, who have been little considered so far, as another element in the dramatis personae.

Then this serves as conceptual glue which holds together the Radical Reformation, Anabaptism, and the German Peasants' War of 1525 as a people's Christianity—how Radicals (Anabaptists) in particular and the ordinary Christians in general had engaged such important historical events in faithful and yet creative ways as the ones who were not just an add-on but were actually in the prime position. The point to be emphasized is that such re-reading of history from below can orchestrate these three movements into a harmonious whole—that being, both the Radical Reformation and Anabaptism were deeply anchored in the social and religious experiences of the Peasants' War of 1525, which was a revolution of the common men.

Here Radicals (Anabaptists) and peasants had strikingly the common desire to create a society that would "hear the gospel and live according to it". By interpreting the gospel as justification for social changes, both began to rise against their religious and political 'lords' ultimately leading to the Peasant Reformation. This Peasant Reformation became the Peasants' War, justifying their resistance with the Christian virtue of freedom and egalitarianism that emerged from their radical interpretation of the gospel. More precisely, their radical gospel appeared to have political and economic implications as well as theological ones, according to what they called 'divine law', which challenged the conservative Magisterial Reformers and the unjust existing political order, to the point of taking up arms to defend the word of God.

Such tenets that separated them from the major Reformers, who addressed strictly religious matters only, are nearly identical to the so-called 'bastard line' (*sic*) of the Radical Reformers who made the radical leap from religious and theological to secular and political in the Anabaptist Kingdom of Münster. This indicates that the dominant historiographical view that interprets in the Anabaptist Kingdom of Münster as a monstrous aberration of the Reformation is due for reexamination. In reality, Münster Anabaptism is rooted in the positive form of the Communal Reformation in collaboration with the Radical Reformers and the common people that suggests a new way of perceiving the Radical Reformers as 'being-in-the-common-people'—namely, Thomas Müntzer as 'being-in-the-retributive-common-people', Hans Hut as 'being-in-the-restorative-common-people', Melchior Hoffman as 'being-in-the-revelatory-common-people', and John Bockelson as 'being-in-the-rhetorical-common-people'.

The re-reading of history from below even sheds new light on this intricate connection of the two 'actors' to be read as the *guru-avatar* interplay—i.e., the dynamic combination of the *avatar*-hood of the Radical Reformers (incarnation of themselves into the common people) and the *guru*-ship of the common people (deification of themselves into the Radical Reformers). Here, like a Möbius strip, both *guru* and *avatar* are not juxtaposed, nor is the one absorbed by the other, but rather the relationship remains a reciprocal and dynamic one. Both are to be distinctly qualified to lead Münster Anabaptism in the form of Radical Reformation as being-in-the-Communal-Reformation.

This book's adoption of Korean Minjung Theology as its dialogic partner is meant to signal a commitment to such a dynamic correlation between the Radical Reformers and the common people (*minjung*). It is also meant to serve as a case study for a double-mirror reading—namely, re-reading Münster Anabaptism through the lens of Korean Minjung Theology. Thus, starting a conversation with the Korean *minjung* suggests linking them with the Münster common people (*minjung*) not as the object but as the subject of history. Such dynamic equivalence between the two has a two-fold implication: connectedness and openness. On one hand, they are closely connected with each other, who suffer socially, politically, economically, culturally, and religiously. On the other hand, they are not a homogeneous but a mixed group that encompasses both the great men and the common men, the victimizers and victims, the sinners and the sinned-against.

The book then invites reviews of four Korean Minjung theologians —the Korean Radical Reformers—with their distinctive methodologies as epitomized by (1) Suh, Nam-Dong's Spirit of *Missio Dei*, (2) Ahn, Byung-Mu's socio-biblical analysis of the *ochlos* (outcast), (3) Kim, Yong-Bok's Messianic Politics of Jesus, and (4) Hyun, Young-Hak's Korean mask dance. The common denominator is that all these challenge theology to be attentive to the suffering (or *han*) of Korean *minjung* and thereby urge theologians to be the priests of *han* who can bring *dan*, that is, the resolution of *han*. This is manifest in the dialectical unification of *han* and *dan*—i.e., the dynamic combination of the messianic practice of *minjung* and the prophetic practice of Minjung theologians.

Further, the book urges embrace of a theology of solidarity in suffering between Jesus and *minjung*, which culminates in the Jesus event and its correlation with Münster Anabaptism. By depicting Jesus as a co-sufferer of the *minjung*, Korean Minjung Theology reads Jesus' crucifixion as a crucifixion of the *minjung* and his resurrection as a resurrection of the *minjung*. In this sense, any kind of liberating event for the suffering *minjung* is transformed into the Jesus event where Jesus and *minjung* are one in suffering and hope—hence the adoption of the idea of *minjung*-Jesus or *minjung*-messianism. The telling point here is not the direct and ontological identification but the functional equivalence between Jesus and *minjung*. By participating in the suffering, the *minjung* become part of the Jesus event and, in that sense, are Messiah.

On this basis, Münster Anabaptism is being constructive as part of the Jesus event, that is, the *minjung* event, where the Münster common people have played a messianic role: they are powerless but they are also powerful, their suffering becoming a channel of transformation for themselves. Thus, inviting Korean Minjung Theology as a conversation partner brings about a major paradigm shift for interpreting Münster Anabaptism as part of the Jesus event, disclosing the messianic practice of the Münster common people (*minjung*).

Korean Minjung Theology even helps Münster Anabaptism re-appropriate its characteristics not as monophonic but as polyphonic—even as cacophonic—in nature, consisting of:

- John Matthjisson as being-in-the-immigrant Melchiorite Prophets (the radical),
- Bernhard Rothmann as being-in-the-native civic Reformers (the reactionary),
- John Bockelson as being-in-the-eclectic between the two power structures (the eclectic),
- The Münster common people as being-beyond-the-other-three (*minjung*).

Seen in this way, Münster Anabaptism in Korean Minjung Theology is being constructed as a place of hybridity where the prophetic practice (*avatar*-hood) of the Radical Reformers and the messianic practice (*guru*-ship) of the Münster common people (*minjung*) are becoming one and thereby becoming a place of *dan* where the *han* of the *minjung* is being resolved and transformed into the Jesus event where both Jesus and *minjung* are becoming one. To be sure, rediscovery of the Münster common people (*minjung*) as protagonist in Münster Anabaptism means the rediscovery of *minjung*-Jesus as protagonist in the Jesus event.

To sum up, at the heart of Münster Anabaptism lies the *minjung*-Messiah interplay—i.e., Messiah's radical rendezvous with the *han*-ridden Münster common people (*minjung*) for bringing about *dan*. Both, Messiah and *minjung*, have shaped and reshaped Münster Anabaptism into part of the Jesus event and in this connection, the Jesus event is itself the Communal Reformation, which necessitates an ongoing re-formation of the *minjung*-Messiah interplay. Here, not only is a history of Münster Anabaptism being constructive (not as a once-and-for-all but as a continuing and recurring historical event) as a place of hybridity as being-in-the-Jesus-event, but also the Münster common people (*minjung*) are being constructive both as *avatar* and *guru* as being-in-the-Messiah. Thus, Münster Anabaptism in Korean Minjung Theology becomes both analepsis and prolepsis of the Jesus event, where *Minjung Reformator* forms *Christo Reformator* and *Christo Reformator* reforms *Minjung Reformator* as *Minjung-Messiah Transformator*.

Epilogue

This book is not a historical comparison between two movements—the sixteenth century Radical Reformation and the twentieth century theological movement in Korea. Rather, it is a historical and constructive theological attempt at "shifting the emphasis to the process rather than the product" (Wyman 2017:314). Inviting Korean Minjung Theology as a conversation partner, the book attempts to generate a counter-history of the tragic Münster Anabaptism—that being, a place of hybridity that embraces a plethora of voices of the great men and the common men, the victimizers and the victims, the sinners and the sinned-against, who are affected by and seek to affect the realization of the Jesus event, not as a complete story but as an open-ended conversation.

To preserve this dynamic of the common people (*minjung*) as being-in-the-Messiah will and must be a continuing source of the Reformation studies. For this will encourage Christians to re-read and re-write not a new history but a counter-history, one that is constructive. Its own reading of the Reformation, then, generates its own leading of the Reformation and it is through the eyes of the common people (*minjung*) that the Church and its theologies need to be reformed time and again. But, at the same time, this ought to be attentive to *Reformatio Dei*, which sees and hears the Messiah as the subject of the Reformation; it does not juxtapose uncritically the "history of the people" with a "history of theology" (Vosloo 2009:61). Thus, it should be remembered that the common people (*minjung*) can and must proceed along a path of *ecclesia semper reformanda* as 'being-in-the-Messiah'.

However, the scarlet letter of Münster Anabaptism dies hard. It is still generally considered as the black sheep of the Reformation whose tragic end is attributed to its own karma. Thus, the Kingdom of Münster has remained as the Kingdom of Monster, the sin city like Sodom and Gomorrah. At this juncture, a historical and constructive theological approach as seen from Korean Minjung Theology raises changing and revised questions such as these: "Would this dark and ugly face of Münster Anabaptism not prove the prevalence of *han* as the wounds of sin and the people of *han* as the victims of sin there?" And "Would it not make sense to see Münster Anabaptism as the place of hybridity, which not only offers the coexistence of the sin of the victimizers and the *han* of the victims, but also holds potential for healing, liberation, and salvation on both sides?" If the term Messiah cannot have any meaning without being related to the suffering people (*minjung*), the madness of the Münster Kingdom should not be left as its own shame either. Paradoxically, therefore, the terror of Münster Anabaptism can serve as a case study for creating a new possibility of reconciliation and restoration.

Seen this way, there is a lot of reconstruction but also a lot of space for deconstruction in the Münster tragedy. Thus, the question once again comes up regarding whether to see Münster Anabaptism as a unique phenomenon or as an on-going paradigm; as a tombstone (*han*) or as a birthplace (*dan*) for the common people's (*minjung's*) reformation, leading to the Jesus event. But its answer can no longer take conventional claims and interpretations for granted. Rather, a historical and constructive theological outlook suggests that the emphasis must be given to its dynamic tensions that allow an open-ended and imaginative reconstruction. Realizing this provides us with a choice as to whether we take risks, and get involved in a process of counter-history, or to limit the interpretative possibility in a safe-but-rigid shell of the past.

Bibliography

Abelmann, Nancy. "Minjung Theory and Practice." In *Cultural Nationalism in East Asia: Representation and Identity*, edited by Harumim Befu, 139-65. Berkeley: Institute of East Asian Studies, 1993.

———. *Echoes of the Past, Epics of Dissent: A South Korea Social Movement*. Berkeley: University of California Press, 1996.

Abraham, K. C. *Liberative Solidarity: Contemporary Perspectives on Mission*. India: Christava Sahitya Samithi, 1996.

Adams, Daniel J. "The Roots of Korean Theology." Taiwan Journal of Theology, no. 7 (1985): 187-207.

Ahn, Byung-Mu. *Liberator Jesus*. Seoul: Hyundae Sasangsa, 1975.

———. "The Image of Jesus in the Korean Church: Its Centennial." *Theological Thought*, no. 19 (1977): 717-57.

———. "Jesus and the Minjung in the Gospel of Mark." In *Minjung Theology: People as the Subjects of History*, 138-154. Singapore: Commission on Theological Concerns, 1981.

———. "Jesu-s and Ochlos." In *Minjung and Korean Theology*, edited by Committee of Theological Study KNCC, 86-103. Seoul: Korean Theological Study Institute, 1982.

———. "The Historical Subject in a Perspective of the Gospel of Mark." In *Minjung and Korean Thought*, edited by CTC-CCA, 177-84. Seoul: Korean Theological Study Institute, 1982.

———. *A Sociological Exegesis of the Bible*. Seoul: Korea Theological Study Institute, 1983.

———. "Jesus and the Minjung in the Gospel of Mark." In *Minjung Theology: People as the Subjects of History*, edited by Yong-Bock Kim, 138-51. Maryknoll, NY: Orbis Books, 1983.

———. *History and Interpretation*. Seoul: Korean Christian Publishing Company, 1984.

———. "Transmitters of the Jesus-Event." Paper presented at the Christian Conference of Asia Commission on Theological Concerns Bulletin, Hong Kong, 1984.

---. "The Korean Church's Understanding of Jesus: An Historical Review." *International Review of Mission* 74, no. 293 (1985): 81-92.

---. *A Story of Minjung Theology*. Seoul: Korea Theological Institute, 1987.

---. *Christ in the Minjung Event*. Seoul: Korea Theological Study Institute, 1990.

---. *Jesus of Galilee*. Seoul: Korea Theological Study Institute, 1990

---. "Korean Theology." In *Dictionary of Mission: Theology, History, Perspectives*, edited by Theo Sundermeier, Karl Muller, Steven B. Bevans, and Richard H. Bliese, 246-50. Eugene, OR: Wipf & Stock Publishers, 1999.

---. *Theology for Reformation of Christianity*. Seoul: Korean Institute Theological Study Institute,1999.

---. *Jesus of Galilee*. Hong Kong: Christian Conference of Asia and Dr. Ahn Byung-Mu Memorial Service Committee, 2004.

---. "Minjok, Minjung and Church." In *Reading Minjung Theology in the Twenty-First Century: Selected Writings by Ahn Byung-Mu and Modern Critical Responses*, edited by Young Suk and Kim Jin-Ho, 91-100. Eugene, OR: Wipf and Stock Publishers, 2013.

Ahn, Byung-Wook. "Spirit and Significance of Samil Revolution." *Korean Quarterly* 13, no. 1-2 (1971): 1-10.

---. *History of the National Movement in Modern Korea*. Seoul: Dolbaege, 1980.

Ahn, Byung-Wook and Park Chan-Seung. "Historical Characteristics of the Peasant War of 1894." *Korea Journal* 34, no. 4 (1994): 101-14.

Ahn, Sang-Jin. *The Religious Synthesis of Choe Je-U as a Nineteenth Century Theological Paradigm for Korean Minjung Theology*. Toronto: Emmanuel College, Toronto School of Theology, 1997.

---. *Continuity and Transformation: Religious Synthesis in East Asia*. New York: Peter Lang Publishing, 2001.

Allison, Dale C. Jr. "Jesus and the Covenant: A Response to E. P. Sanders." *Journal for the Study of the New Testament* no. 29 (1987): 57-78.

Amaladoss, Michael. Life in Freedom: Liberation Theology from Asia. Eugene, OR: Wipf and Stock Publishers, 1997

Aravamudan, Srinivas. *Guru English: South Asian Religion in a Cosmopolitan Language*. Princeton: Princeton University Press, 2006.

Armitage, Thomas. *A History of the Baptists: Traced by Their Vital Principles and Practices: From the Time of Our Lord and Saviour Jesus Christ to the Year 1886*. NY: Bryan, Taylor & Co., 1887.

Armour, Rollin S. *Anabaptist Baptism: A Representative Study*. Scottdale, Pa.: Herald Press, 1966.

Arthur, Anthony. *The Tailor King: The Rise and Fall of the Anabaptist Kingdom of Münster*. NY: Macmillan, 1999.

Astour, M. C. "Habiru, Hapiru." The Interpreter's Dictionary of the Bible, Supplementary Volume. Nashville: Abingdon Press (1976): 382-385.

Backus, Irena. *Historical Method and Confessional Identity in the Era of the Reformation (1378-1615)*. Leiden: Brill, 2003.

Bacote, Vincent. "What Is This Life For? Expanding Our View of Salvation." In *What Does It Mean to Be Saved? Broadening Evangelical Horizons of Salvation*, edited by John G. Stackhouse Jr., 95-114. Grand Rapids, MI: Baker, 2002.

_____. *The Spirit in Public Theology: Appropriating the Legacy of Abraham Kuyper*. Grand Rapids, MI: Baker Academic, 2005.

Bailey, Richard G. "The Sixteenth Century's Apocalyptic Heritage and Thomas Müntzer." *Mennonite Quarterly Review* 57, no. 1 (1983): 27-44.

_____. "Melchior Hoffman: Proto-Anabaptist and Printer in Kiel, 1527-1529." *Church History* 59, no. 2 (1990): 175-90.

Bainton, Roland H. "The Left Wing of the Reformation." *The Journal of Religion* 21, no. 2 (1941): 124-34.

_____. *Here I Stand: A Life of Martin Luther*. New York and Nashville: Abingdon and Cokesbury Press, 1950.

_____. *The Travail of Religious Liberty: Nine Biographical Studies*. Philadelphia: Westminster, 1951.

_____. The Reformation of the Sixteenth Century. London: Hodder and Stoughton, 1965.

_____. "Thomas Müntzer Revolutionary Firebrand of the Reformation." *The Sixteenth Century Journal* 13, no. 2 (1982): 3-15.

Bakker, W. J. de. "Bernhard Rothmann: The Dialectics of Radicalization in Münster." In *Profiles of Radical Reformers: Biographical Sketches from Thomas Müntzer to Paracelsus,* edited by H. J. Goertz, 167-78. Scottdale, PA: Herald, 1982.

_____. "Bernhard Rothman: Civic Reformer in Anabaptist Münster." In *Dutch Dissenters: A Critical Companion to Their History and Ideas,* edited by Irvin Buckwalter Horst, 105-16. Leiden: Brill, 1986.

Bakker, W. J. de, John, James M and Stayer, and Michael Dennis Driedger. Bernhard Rothmann and the Reformation in Münster, 1530-35. Kitchener, ON: Pandora Press, 2009.

Balasundaram, Franklyn Jayakumar. Contemporary Asian Christian Theology. ISPCK, 1995.

Baldwin, Frank. The March First Movement: Korean Challenge and Japanese Response. Columbia University, 1969.

_____. "Missionaries and the March First Movement: Can Moral Men Be Neutral?" In *Korea under Japanese Colonial Rule. Studies of the Policy and Techniques of Japanese Colonialism,* edited by Andrew Chanwoo Nahm, 193-219. Kalamazoo, MI: Centre for Korean Studies, 1973.

Barclay, John MG. "Mirror-Reading a Polemical Letter: Galatians as a Test Case." Journal for the Study of the New Testament no. 31 (1987): 73-93.

Baring-Gould, Sabine. Freaks of Fanaticism and Other Strange Events. London: Methuen & Co., 1891.

Barrett, Lois Y. "Wreath of Glory: Ursula's Prophetic Visions in the Context of Reformation and Revolt in Southwestern Germany, 1524-1530." Ph. D dissertation: The Union Institute, 1992.

_____. "Ursula Jost and Barbara Rebstock of Strasbourg." In *Profiles of Anabaptist Women: Sixteenth-Century Reforming Pioneers,* edited by C. Arnold Snyder and Linda A. Huebert Hecht, 273-87 Waterloo, ON: Wilfrid Laurier University Press, 1996.

Barth, Karl. "Christian Community and Civil Community." in *Community, State, and Church: Three Essays*. Garden City: Doubleday, 1960.

———. *Church Dogmatics*. Edited by Thomas Forsyth Torrance Geoffrey William Bromiley Vol. 4: A&C Black, 1969.

Batten, L. W. *A Critical and Exegetical Commentary on the Books of Ezra and Nehemiah*. Edinburgh: T&T Clark, 1972.

Bauer, Walter. *Orthodoxy and Heresy in Earliest Christianity*. Edited by Robert A Kraft, Krodel, Gerhard Philadelphia: Fortress Press Philadelphia, 1971.

Bauman, Clarence. "The Theology of 'the Two Kingdom': A Comparison of Luther and the Anabaptists." *MQR* 38, no. 1 (1964): 37-49.

Bax, E Belfort. *Rise and Fall of the Anabaptists*. Macmillan, 1903.

———. Peasants War in Germany, 1525-26. Augustus M. Kelley, 1968.

Baylor, Michael G. "Thomas Müntzer's 'Prague Manifesto'." *MQR* 63, no. 1 (1989): 30-57.

———. *The Radical Reformation*. Cambridge: Cambridge University Press, 1991.

———. *Revelation and Revolution: Basic Writings of Thomas Müntzer*. Lindon: Lehigh University Press, 1993.

Beachy, Alvin J. *The Concept of Grace in the Radical Reformation*. Nieuwkoop: De Graaf, 1977.

Beasley-Murray, G.R. *Jesus and the Kingdom of God*. Grand Rapids: Eerdmans, 1986.

Beaver, R. Pierce. "Chondogyo and Korea." *Journal of Bible and Religion* 30, no. 2 (1962): 115-22.

Bell, Kirsten. "Cheondogyo and the Donghak Revolution: The (Un) Making of a Religion." *Korea Journal* 44, no. 2 (2004): 123-48.

———. "Pilgrims and Progress: The Production of Religious Experience in a Korean Religion." *Nova Religion* 12, no. 1 (2008): 83-102.

Bender, Harold S. "The Anabaptist Vision." *Church History* 13, no. 1 (1944): 3-24.

———. *Conrad Grebel (C. 1498-1526): The Founder of the Swiss Brethren*. Goshen, Ind.: Mennonite Historical Society, 1950.

_____. "The Zwickau Prophets, Thomas Müntzer, and the Anabaptists." *MQR* 27, no. 1 (1953): 3-16.

_____. "The Historiography of the Anabaptists." *MQR* 31, no. 2 (1957): 88-104.

_____. *The Anabaptist and Religious Liberty in the Sixteenth Century*. Philadelphia: Fortress Press, 1970.

Bensing, Manfred. *Thomas Müntzer. Bildbiographie 4*. Leipzig: VEB Bibliographisches Institut, 1989.

Berghoef, G. *Liberation Theology: The Church's Future Shock*. Grand Rapids: Christian Library, 1984.

Berman, Harold J. *Law and Revolution: The Formation of the Western Legal Tradition*. Cambridge, Mass.: Harvard University Press, 1983.

Biale, David. *Gershom Scholem: Kabbalah and Counter-History*. Cambridge MA: Harvard University Press, 1982.

Billings, Peggy. *Fire Beneath the Frost: The Struggles of the Korean People and Church*. New York: Friendship Press, 1983.

Bingaman, Brock. *All Things New: The Trinitarian Nature of the Human Calling in Maximus the Confessor and Jürgen Moltmann*. Princeton Theological Monograph Series. Vol. 213. Eugene: Pickwick Publications, 2014.

Blickle, Peter. "Peasant Revolts in the German Empire in the Late Middle Ages." *Social History* 4, no. 2 (1979): 223-39.

_____. *The Revolution of 1525: The German Peasants War from a New Perspective*. Translated by H. C. Erik Midelfort and Thomas A. Brady Jr. Baltimore: Johns Hopkins University Press, 1981.

_____. *Communal Reformation: The Quest for Salvation in Sixteenth-Century Germany*. Translated by H. C. Erik Midelfort and Thomas A. Brady Jr. Atlantic Highlands, NJ: Humanities Press, 1992.

_____. *From the Communal Reformation to the Revolution of the Common Man*. Translated by Beat Kumin. Studies in Medieval and Reformation Thought. Vol. 65, Leiden: Brill, 1998.

_____. "Communal Reformation: Zwingli, Luther, and the South of the Holy Roman Empire." In *Christianity: Reformation and

Expansion 1500-1660, edited by R. Po-Chis Hsia, 75-89. Cambridge: Cambridge University Press, 2008.

Bohmer, Heinrich. *Thomas Müntzer Und Das Jungste Deutschland*. Gotha: Flamberg, 1927.

Bonhoeffer, Dietrich. *Ethics*. London: SCM Press, 1971.

———. *Letters and Papers from Prison*. New York: Macmillan, 1966, 1972.

Bonino, Jose Miguez. "A Latin American Looks at Minjung Theology." In *An Emerging Theology in World Perspective: Commentary on Korean Minjung Theology*, edited by J. Y. Lee, 157-68. Mystic: Twenty-Third Publications, 1988.

Bornkamm, Heinrich. "Mystik, Spiritualismus Und Die Anfange Des Pietismus Im Luthertum." in *Vorträge Der Theologischen Konferenz Zu Giessen* 44. de Gruyter, 1926.

Bosch, David J. *Transforming Mission: Paradigm Shifts in Theology of Mission*. The American Society of Missiology Series. Maryknoll, NY: Orbis Books, 1991.

Boyd, Stephen B. "Anabaptism and Social Radicalism in Strasbourg, 1528-1532: Pilgram Marpeck on Christian Social Responsibility." *MQR* 63, no. 1 (1989): 58-76.

Braaten, Carl E. "Toward a Theology of Hope." *Theology Today* 24, no. 2 (1967): 208-26.

Brady, Thomas A. *Ruling Class, Regime and Reformation at Strasbourg 1520-1555*. Vol. 22, Leiden: Brill, 1978.

———. *Turning Swiss: Cities and Empire, 1450-1550*. Cambridge: Cambridge University Press, 1985.

———. "In Search of the Godly City: The Domestication of Religion in the German Urban Reformation." In *The German People and the Reformation*, edited by R. Po-Chia Hsia, 141-31. Ithaca, NY: Cornell University Press, 1988.

———. "Emergence and Consolidation of Protestantism in the Holy Roman Empire to 1600." In *Christianity: Reform and Expansion 1500-1660*, edited by R. Po-Chia Hsia, 20-36. Cambridge University Press, 2008.

———. *German Histories in the Age of Reformations, 1400-1650*. Cambridge: Cambridge University Press, 2009.

Brandt, Otto. *Sein Leben Und Seine Schriften. Jena*. Edited by Thomas

Müntzer. Thuringia: Eugen Diederichs, 1933.
Brauer,Siegfried and Helmar Junghans, eds. *Der Theologe Thomas Müntzer Untersuchungen zu seiner Entwicklung und Lehre.* Gottingen: Vandenhoek & Ruprecht, 1989.
Brecht, Martin. "The Songs of the Anabaptists in Münster and Their Hymnbook." *MQR* 59, no. 4 (1985): 362-66.
_____. *Martin Luther: Shaping and Defining the Reformation 1521-1532.* Translated by James L. Schaaf. Minneapolis: Fortress, 1990.
Brendler, Gerhard. *Das Tauferreich Zu Münster, 1534-1535.* Leipziger bersetzung Und Abhandlungen Zum Mittelalter, Reihe B 3. Berlin: Wissenschaften, 1966.
Bretzke, James T. "Cracking the Code: Minjung Theology as an Expression of the Holy Spirit in Korea." *Pacifica* 10, no. 3 (1997): 319-30.
_____. "Minjung Theology and Inculturation in the Context of the History of Christianity in Korea." *East Asian Pastoral Review* 28 (1991): 108-30.
Brinkman, Martien E. *The Non-Western Jesus: Jesus as Bodhisattva, Avatara, Guru, Prophet, Ancestor, or Healer?* Translated by Henry and Luch Jansen. Oakville, Conn.: Equinox, 2007.
Broadhead, Philip. "Rural Revolt and Urban Betrayal in Reformation Switzerland: The Peasants of St Gallen and Zwinglian Zurich." In *Religion and Rural Revolt,* edited by Janos M. Bak and Gerhard Benecke, 161-72. Manchester University Press, 1984.
Brock, Peter. *Pacifism in Europe to 1914.* Princeton University Press, 1972.
Brown, Robert McAfee. *Theology in a New Key.* Philadelphia: The Westminster Press, 1978.
Browning, Don S. *A Fundamental Practical Theology: Descriptive and Strategic Proposals.* Minneapolis, MN: Fortress Press, 1991.
Brueggemann, Walter. "Trajectories in Old Testament Literature and the Sociology of Ancient Israel." *Journal of Biblical Literature* 98, no. 2 (1979): 161-85.
Bubenheimer, Ulrich. "Thomas Müntzer" In *Protestantische Profile: Lebensbilder Aus Funf Jahrhunderten,* edited by Klaus Scholder and Dieter Kleinmann, 33-46. Frankfurt: Athenaum, 1983.

_____. *Thomas Müntzer: Herkunft Und Bildung. Studies in Medieval and Reformation Thought.* Vol. 46, Leiden: Brill, 1989.
Bucknell, Roderick and Paul Beirne. "In Search of the Yeongbu: The Lost Talisman of Korea's Tonghak Religion." *Review of Korean Studies* 4, no. 2 (2001): 201-22.
Buschart, W. David. *Exploring Protestant Traditions: An Invitation to Theological Hospitality.* Madison, WI: InterVarsity Press, 2006.
Buswell, R. E. and Lee, T. S. Ed. *Christianity in Korea.* Honolulu: University of Chicago Press, 2006.
Buszello, Horst. *Der deutsche Bauernkrieg als Politische Bewegung, mit besonderer Berücksichtigung der anonymen Flugschrift an die Versammlung gemayner Pawerschafft. Studien Zur Europäaischen Geschichte.* Vol. 8, Berlin: Colloquium, 1969.
Caiden, Gerald and Jung, Yong-Duck. "The Political Economy of Korean Development under the Park Government." In *Modernization of Korea and the Impact of the West,* edited by Changsoo Lee, 285-310. Los Angeles: University of Southern California, 1981.
Cairns, Earle E. *Christianity through the Centuries: A History of the Christian Church.* Grand Rapids, MI: Zondervan, 1996.
Callinicos, Alex. *The Revolutionary Ideas of Karl Marx.* Chicago: Haymarket Books, 1983.
Cameron, Euan. *The European Reformation.* Oxford University Press, 1991.
Carroll, Noel. "Interpretation, History and Narrative." *Monist* 73, no. 2 (1990): 134-166.
Castillo, Mauricio. "The Omega Point and Beyond: The Singularity Event." *American Journal of Neuroradiology* 33, no. 3 (2012): 393-95.
Cavanaugh, Peter Scott and William T. Ed. *The Blackwell Companion to Political Theology.* Oxford: The Blackwell Publishing Ltd, 2004.
Chadwick, Owen. *The Reformation.* Middlesex: Penguin Books, 1964.
Chae, Hee-Dong. *Minjung, the Holy Spirit, Life: The Life and the Thought of Jook-Jae Suh Nam-Dong.* Seoul: Han-Deul Press, 1994.

Chae, Hee Wan. "Cultural Movement in 1970s: Centering on Folk Drama Movement." In *Culture and Politics*, edited by Yoo Jae Chun, 168-219. Seoul: Minjungsa, 1982.

Chai, Soo-Il. "Missio Dei - Its Development and Limitations in Korea." *International Review of Mission* 92, no. 367 (2003): 538-49.

Chaney, Marvin L. "Ancient Palestinian Peasant Movements and the Formation of Premonarchic Israel." In *Palestine in Transition: The Emergence of Ancient Israel*, edited by D. N. Freedman and D. F. Graf, 39-90. Sheffield: Almond Press, 1983.

Chang, Jong-Sik. *Minjung Theology: Postcolonial Critique*. University of Birmingham, 2002.

Chang, Paul Yunsik "Carrying the Torch in the Darkest Hour: The Socio-Political Origins of Minjung Protestant Movements." In *Christianity in Korea*, edited by Robert E. Buswell Jr. and Timothy S. Lee, 195-220. University of Hawaii Press, Honolulu, 2007.

———. *Protest Dialectics: State Repression and South Korea's Democracy Movement, 1970-1979*. Stanford, CA: Stanford University Press, 2015.

Chang, Paul Y. and Byung-Soo Kim. "Differential Impact of Repression on Social Movements: Christian Organizations and Liberation Theology in South Korea (1972-1979)." *Sociological Inquiry* 77, no. 3 (2007): 326-55.

Chardin, Pierre Teilhard de. *Activation of Energy*. Translated by Rene Hague. William Collins Sons & Co. Ltd., London, 1978.

Chaurasia, Radhey Shyam. *History of Western Political Thought*. Vol. 2, New Delhi: Atlantic Publishers and Distributors, 2001.

Cho, Chuong-Kwon. "Han and the Pentecostal Experience: A Study of the Growth of the Yoido Full Gospel Church in Korea." Ph.D dissertation: The University of Birmingham, 2010.

Cho, Hee-Yeon. "The Democratic Transition and the Change of Social Movements in South Korea." in *The Annual Meeting of the Association for Asian Studies* Honolulu, 1996.

Cho, Kyun-Hoon. "Another Christian Right? The Politicization of Korean Protestantism in Contemporary Global Society." *Social Compass* 61, no. 3 (2014): 310-27.

Cho, Yo-Han. *The Struggles of the Korean Christianity. Korean Society and Christianity.* Seoul: Soungjeon University Press, 1984.

Choe, Yong-Ho. "Commoners in Early Yi Dynasty Civil Examinations: An Aspect of Korean Social Structure, 1392-1600." *The Journal of Asian Studies* 33, no. 4 (1974): 611-31.

Choi, Chung-Moo. "Hegemony and Shamanism: The State, the Elite, and the Shamans in Contemporary Korea." in *Religion and Society in Contemporary Korea*, 19-48. Berkeley: University of California, 1997.

Choi, Hee-An. "Minjung Theology." In The Hope of Liberation in World Religions, edited by Miguel A. De La Torre, 199-215, 293-295. Waco, TX: Baylor University Press, 2008.

———. *A Postcolonial Self: Korean Immigrant Theology and Church.* New York: SUNY Press, 2015.

Choi, Hyung-Mook. *The Movement for Social Transformation and Christian Theology.* Seoul: Nathan, 1992.

———. "Some Issues of Minjung Theology in 1990's." *Sidae ywa Minjung Theology* (1998): 345-69.

Choi, Jang-Jip. *Labour and the Authoritarian State: Labour Unions in South Korean Manufacturing Industries, 1961-1980.* Seoul: Korea University Press, 1989.

———. "Political Cleavages in South Korea." In *State and Society in Contemporary Korea*, edited by Hagen Koo, 13-50. Ithaca: Cornell University Press, 1993.

Chongsan. *The Dharma Master Chongsan of Won Buddhism: Analects and Writings.* Translated by Bongkil Chung. New York: Sunny Press, 2012.

Choo, Chai-Yong. "A Brief Sketch of Korean Christian History from the Minjung Perspective." In *Minjung Theology: People as the Subjects of History*, edited by Yong-Bock Kim, 69-77. Singapore: The Christian Conference of Asia, 1981.

Chopp, Rebecca S. *The Praxis of Suffering: An Introduction of Liberation and Political Theologies* Eugene, OR: Wipf and Stock 1986.

Chopp, Rebecca S. and Mark Lewis Taylor. Ed. *Reconstructing Christian Theology* Minneapolis, MN: Fortress Press, 1994.

Chung, Chai-Sik. *Religion and Cultural Identity: The Case of "Eastern Learning."* Westdeutscher Verlag, 1969.
Chung, Erin Aeran. "The Politics of Contingent Citizenship." In *Diaspora without Homeland: Being Korean in Japan*, edited by Sonia Ryang and John Lie, 147-67. Berkeley: University of California Press, 2009.
Chung, Hyun-Kyung. ""Han-Pu-Ri": Doing Theology from Korean Women's Perspective." *The Ecumenical Review* 40, no. 1 (1988): 27-36.
Chung, Ki-Yul. *The Donghak Concept of God/Heaven: Religion and Social Transformation*. New York: Peter Lang, 2007.
Chung, Paul S. *Martin Luther and Buddhism: Aesthetics of Suffering.* 2nd ed. Cambridge: James Clarke & Co, 2008.
———. *Constructing Irregular Theology: Bamboo and Minjung in East Asian Perspective*. Vol. 1, Leiden: Brill, 2009.
———. *Public Theology in an Age of World Christianity: God's Mission as Word-Event*. New York: Palgrave MacMillan, 2010.
Chung, Paul S., Kim, Kyung-Jae and Veli-Matti Karkkainen. Ed. *Asian Contextual Theology for the Third Millennium: A Theology of Minjung in Fourth-Eye Formation*, Princeton Theological Monograph Series 70. Eugene, OR: Pickwick Publications, 2007.
Claassens, L Juliana M. "Rethinking Humour in the Book of Jonah: Tragic Laughter as Resistance in the Context of Trauma." *Old Testament Essays* 28, no. 3 (2015): 655-73.
Clark, Charles A. *Religions of Old Korea*. New York: Fleming H. Revell Co., 1932.
Clark, Donald N. "Growth and Limitations of Minjung Christianity in South Korea." In *South Korea's Minjung Movement: The Culture and Politics of Dissidence*, edited by Kenneth M. Wells, 87-103. Honolulu, HI: University of Hawaii Press, 1995.
Clasen, Claus-Peter. "Nuremberg in the History of Anabaptism." *MQR* 39, no. 1 (1965): 25-39.
———. *Anabaptism: A Social History, 1525-1618: Switzerland, Austria, Moravia, South and Central Germany*. Ithaca, N.Y.: Cornell University Press, 1972.

_____. "Anabaptist Sects in the Sixteenth Century: A Research Report." *MQR* 46, no. 3 (1972): 25679.

Cobb, John B. and David Ray Griffin. *Process Theology: An Introductory Exposition*. The Westminster Press, Louisville, 1976.

Coggins, James R. "Toward a Definition of Sixteenth-Century Anabaptism: Twentieth-Century Historiography of the Radical Reformation." *Journal of Mennonite Studies* 4, no. 4 (1986): 183-207.

Cohn, Henry J. "Anticlericalism in the German Peasants' War 1525." *Past & Present* 83, (1979): 3-31.

Cohn, Norman. *The Pursuit of the Millennium*. 2nd Ed. New York: Harper Torch Books, 1961.

Cole, David C. and Princeton Lyman. *Korean Development: The Interplay of Politics and Economics*. Cambridge: Harvard University Press, 1971.

Cone, James H. *God of the Oppressed*. New York: The Seabury Press, 1975.

_____. "Preface" in *Minjung Theology: People as the Subjects of History*, edited by Christian Conference of Asia Commission on Theological Concerns, ix-xix. Maryknoll, NY: Orbis Books, 1981.

Considine, Kevin P. "Kim Chi-Ha's Han Anthropology and Its Challenge to Catholic Thought." *Horizons* 41, no. 1 (2014): 49-73.

_____. *Salvation for the Sinned-Against: Han and Schillebeeckx in Intercultural Dialogue*. Eugene, OR: Pickwick Publications, 2015.

_____. "The Han of the Sinned-Against: A Global Sensus Fidei in the Pope Francis Era." *New Theology Review* 27 (2015): 38-46.

Cornelius, C. A., *Berichte der Augenzeugen über das Münsterische Wiedertäuferreich 1853*. Münster: Aschendorff, 1965.

_____. Ed. *Berichte Der Augenzeugen Uber Das Münsterische Wiedertauferreich 1853*. Münster: Aschendorff, 1965.

Coser, Lewis A. *The Functions of Social Conflict*. NY: Free Press, 1956.

Croatto, J. Severino. *Exodus: A Hermeneutics of Freedom*. New York: Orbis Books, 1981.

Crockett, Clayton. Ed. *Secular Theology: American Radical Theological Thought*. London: Routledge, 2001.
Cumings, Bruce. *The Origins of the Korean War: The Roaring of the Cataract*, 1947-1950. Princeton: Princeton University Press, 1990.
_____. *Korea's Place in the Sun - A Modern History*. New York: W. W. Norton & Company, 1997.
Cyhn, Jin W. *Technology Transfer and International Production: The Development of the Electronics Industry in Korea*. Northampton, MA: Edward Elgar, 2002.
Davis, Kenneth R. *Anabaptism and Asceticism: A Study in Intellectual Origins*. Scottdale, Pa: Herald Press, 1974.
Davis, Natalie Zemon. "Some Tasks and Themes in the Study of Popular Religion." In *The Pursuit of Holiness in Late Medieval and Renaissance Religion*, edited by Charles Trinkaus and Heiko A. Oberman, 307-36. Leiden: Brill, 1974.
Dawson, Lorne L. "Charismatic Leadership in Millennial Movements." In *Oxford Handbook of Millennialism*, edited by Catherine Wessinger, 113-32. New York: Oxford University Press, 2010.
Dearman, Marion. "Structure and Function of Religion in the Los Angeles Korean Community: Some Aspects." In *Koreans in Los Angeles: Prospects and Promises,* edited by Earl H. Phillips and Eun-Sik Yan Eui-Young Yu, 165-84. Los Angeles: Koryo Research Institute, 1982.
Dejonge, Michael P. *Bonhoeffer's Reception of Luther*. Oxford: Oxford University Press, 2017.
Deppermann, Klaus. "Melchior Hoffman and Strasbourg Anabaptism." In *The Origins and Characteristics of Anabaptism*, edited by Marc Leinhard, 216-19. The Hague: Martinus Nijhoff, 1977.
_____. "The Anabaptists and the State Churches." In *Religion and Society in Early Modern Europe 1500-1800,* edited by Kaspar von Greyerz, 95-106. London: George Allen & Unwin, 1984.
_____. *Melchior Hoffman: Social Unrest and Apocalyptic Visions in the Age of Reformation*. Translated by Malcolm Wren. Edinburgh: T&T Clark, 1987.
Dickens, Arthur Geoffrey. *The German Nation and Martin Luther*. 2nd ed. London: Hodder Arnold, 1976.

Dictionary of the Ecumenical Movement. 2nd ed. Geneva, Switzerland: WCC Publications, 2002.

Dipple, Geoffrey L. "Sebastian Franck and the Münster Anabaptist Kingdom." In *Radical Reformation Studies: Essays Presented to James M. Stayer*, edited by Werner O. Packull and Geoffrey L. Dipple, 91-105. Aldershot: Ashgate, 1999.

Dosker, Henry Elias. *The Dutch Anabaptists*. Boston: The Judson Press, 1921.

Driedger, Michael D. "Anabaptists and the Early Modern State: A Long-Term View." In *A Companion to Anabaptism and Spiritualism 1521-1700*, edited by John D. Roth and James M. Stayer, 507-44. Leiden: Brill, 2007.

_____. "Münster, Monster, Modernity: Tracing and Challenging the Meme of Anabaptist Madness." In *Mennonites and the Challenges of Modernity over Five Centuries: Contributors, Detractors and Adaptors*, edited by Mark Jantzen, Mary Sprunger, and John Thiesen, 27-49. North Newton: Bethel College Press, 2016.

Drummond, Andrew W. "Thomas Müntzer and the Fear of Man." *The Sixteenth Century Journal* 10, no. 2 (1979): 63-71.

Dunn, James D.G. Ed. "Romans 1-8, 9-16." in *World Biblical Commentary*. Dallas, TX: Word Book, 1988.

Durnbaugh, Donald F. "Characteristics of the Radical Reformation in Historical Perspective." *Communio Viatorum* 29, no. 3 (1986): 97-118.

Edwards, Mark U Jr. "Luther's Polemical Controversies." In *The Cambridge Companion to Martin Luther*, edited by Donald K. McKim, 192-206. Cambridge: Cambridge University Press, 2003.

Eichler, Margrit. "Charismatic Prophets and Charismatic Saviors." *MQR* 55, no. 1 (1981): 45-61.

Eisenstadt, Schmuel N. *Fundamentalism, Sectarianism, and Revolution: The Jacobin Dimension of Modernity*. Cambridge: Cambridge University Press, 1999.

Ellacuria, Ignacio. "The Crucified People." In *Mysterium Liberationis: Fundamental Concept of Liberation Theology*, edited by

Ignacio Ellacuria and Jon Sobrino, 580-604. Mayknoll, NY: Orbis Books, 1994.

———. "The Historicity of Christian Salvation." In *Mysterium Liberationis: Fundamental Concepts of Liberation Theology*, edited by Ignacio Ellacuria and Jon Sobrino, 251-89. Maryknoll, NY: Orbis Books, 1995.

Elliger, Walter. Thomas Müntzer: Leben Und Werk. Gottingen: Vandenhoek & Ruprecht, 1975.

Elton, G. R. Reformation Europe, 1517-1559. New York: Harper & Row, 1963.

Engels, Friedrich. *Germany: Revolution and Counter-Revolution*. Vol. 13: International publishers, 1920.

———. *The German Revolutions: The Peasant War in Germany, and Germany: Revolution and Counter-Revolution*. University of Chicago Press, 1967.

Engels, Friedrich, Karl Marx. *Selected Works*. Vol. 2, Moscow: Foreign Language Publishing House, 1975.

Enns, Fernando. "The Freedom to Just Peace." In *Reading Minjung Theology in the Twenty-First Century: Selected Writings by Ahn Byung-Mu and Modern Critical Responses*, edited by Kim, Yung-Suk and Kim, Jin-Ho, 148-63. Eugene, OR: Wipf and Stock Publishers, 2013.

Enns, Fernando and Jonathan Seiling. Ed. *Mennonites in Dialogue: Official Reports from International and National Ecumenical Encounters, 1975-2012*. Eugene, OR: Pickwick Publications, 2015.

Estep, William Roscoe. *The Anabaptist Story*. Grand Rapids: William B. Eerdmans Publishing Company, 1975.

Feuerbach, L. *The Essence of Christianity*. New York: Harper Torchbooks, 1957.

———. *Thoughts on Death and Immorality*. Berkeley: University of California Press, 1980.

Finger, *Thomas N. A Contemporary Anabaptist Theology: Biblical, Historical, Constructive*. Downers Grove, IL: InterVarsity Press, 2004.

Flaherty, Robert Pearson. "Jeungsando and the Great Opening of the Later Heaven: Millenarianism, Syncretism and the Religion of Gang Il-Sun." *Nova Religio* 7, no. 3 (2004): 26-44.

———. "Korean Millennial Movements." In *The Oxford Handbook of Millennialism*, edited by Catherine Wessinger, 326-47. Oxford: Oxford University Press, 2011.

Foucault, Michel. *Power/Knowledge: Selected Interviews and Other Writings, 1972-1977*. Pantheon, 1980.

Franz, Gunther. Ed. *Quellen Zur Geschichte Des Bauernkriegs*. Munich: R. Oldenbourg, 1963.

———. Ed. *Thomas Müntzer: Schriften Und Briefe*. Gutersloh: Gerd Mohn, 1968. Fretheim, Terence E. *The Suffering of God: An Old Testament Perspective*. Philadelphia: Fortress Press, 1984.

Frey, Herbert. "Religion as an Ideology of Domination." in *Religion and Rural Revolt*, edited by Janos M. Bak and Gerhard Benecke, 14-30. Mancehster: Manchester University Press, 1984.

Friedmann, Robert. "Anabaptism and Protestantism." *MQR* 24, no. 1 (1950): 12-24.

———. "Thomas Müntzer's Relation to Anabaptism." *MQR* 31, no. 4 (1957): 75-88.

———. "Leonhard Schiemer and Hans Schlaffer: Two Tyrolean Anabaptist Martyr-Apostles of 1528." *MQR* 33, no. 1 (1959): 31-41.

Friesen, Abraham. "Thomas Müntzer in Marxist Thought." *Church History: Studies in Christianity and Culture* 34, no. 3 (1965): 306-27.

———. "The Marxist Interpretation of Anabaptism." *Sixteenth Century Journal* (1970): 17-34.

———. "Thomas Müntzer and the Old Testament." *MQR* 47, no. 1 (1973): 5-19.

———. "Philipp Melanchthon (1497-1560), Wilhelm Zimmermann (1807-1878) and the Dilemma of Müntzer Historiography." *Church History* 43, no. 2 (1974): 164-82.

———. *Reformation and Utopia: The Marxist Interpretation of the Reformation and Its Antecedents*. Mainz: Wiesbaden, 1974.

———. "The Radical Reformation Revisited." *Journal of Mennonite Studies* 2 (1984): 124-76.

_____. "Thomas Müntzer and the Anabaptists." *Journal of Mennonite Studies* 4 (1986): 143-61.

_____. "Thomas Müntzer and Martin Luther." *Archiv für Reformationsgeschichte* 79 (1988): 59-80.

_____. *Thomas Müntzer, a Destroyer of the Godless: The Making of a Sixteenth-Century Religious Revolutionary*. Los Angeles: University of California Press 1990.

Fromm, E. *Marx's Concept of Man*. New York: Frederick Ungar Publishing Co., 1961.

Fudge, John D. *Commerce and Print in the Early Reformation*. Leiden: Brill, 2007.

Fung, Raymond. "Compassion for the Sinned-Against" *Theology Today* 37, no. 2 (1980): 162-69.

_____. "Human Sinned-Againstness" *International Review of Mission* 69, no. 275 (1980): 332-36.

Garret, James L. "The Nature of the Church According to the Radical Continental Reformation." *MQR* 32, no. 2 (1958): 111-27.

Gauchet, Marcel. *The Disenchantment of the World: A Political History of Religion*. Princeton: Princeton University Press, 1997.

Gelder, H. A. Enno van. *The Two Reformations in the 16th Century: A Study of the Religious Aspects and Consequences of Renaissance and Humanism*. The Hague 1961.

George, Timothy. "Early Anabaptist Spirituality in the Low Countries." *MQR* 62, no. 3 (1988): 257-75.

_____. *Theology of the Reformers*. Nashville: Broadman, 1988.

Gerdes, Hayo. *Luthers Streit Mit Den Schwarmern Um Das Rechte Verstandnis Des Gesetzes Mose*. Germany: Gottingen 1955.

Glassman, Jim, Park, Bae-Gyoon and Choi, Young-Jin. "Failed Internationalism and Social Movement Decline: The Cases of South Korea and Thailand." *Critical Asian Studies* 40, no. 3 (2008): 339-   72.

Goertz, Hans-Jürgen. *Innere Und äussere Ordnung in der Theologie Thomas Müntzers*. Leiden: E. J. Brill, 1967.

_____. "The Mystic with the Hammer: Thomas Müntzer's Theological Basis for Revolution." *MQR* 50, no. 2 (1976): 83-113.

_____. "History and Theology: A Major Problem of Anabaptist Research Today." *MQR* 53, no. 3 (1979): 177-88.

_____. "Thomas Müntzer: Revolutionary between the Middle Ages and Modernity." *MQR* 64, no. 1 (1990): 23-31.

_____. "What a Tangled and Tenuous Mess the Clergy Is!": Clerical Anticlericalism in the Reformation Period." in *Anticlericalism in Late Medieval and Early Modern Europe*, edited by Peter A. Dykema and Heiko A. Oberman, 499-520. Leiden: B.J. Brill, 1994.

_____. *The Anabaptists*. Translated by Trevor Johnson. New York: Routledge, 1996.

_____. *Radikalitat Und Dissent Im 16 Jahrhundert*. Berlin: Duncker & Humbolt, 2002.

_____. "Radical Religiosity in the German Reformation." In *A Companion to the Reformation World*, edited by Pochia Hsia, 70-85. Oxford: Blackwell, 2004.

_____. "Karlstadt, Müntzer and the Reformation of the Commoners, 1521-1525." in *A Companion to Anabaptism and Spiritualism, 1521-1700*, 1-44. Leiden: Brill, 2007.

_____. "Spiritual Interpretation among Radical Reformers." In *Hebrew Bible/Old Testament: The History of Its Interpretation: From the Renaissance to the Enlightenment*, edited by Magne Saebo and Menahem Haran Christianus Brekelmans, 576-601. Gottingen: Vandenhoeck & Ruprecht, 2008.

Goertz, Hans-Jürgen, and Jocelyn Jaquiery. *Thomas Müntzer: Apocalyptic, Mystic, and Revolutionary*. Edinburgh: T&T Clark, 1993.

Goertz, Hans-Jürgen and Klaassen, Walter. Ed. *Profiles of Radical Reformers: Biographical Sketches from Thomas Müntzer to Paracelsus*. Scottdale, Pa.: Herald Press, 1982.

Gonzalez, Justo L. *A History of Christian Thought*. Nashville, Tennessee: The Parthenon Press, 1975.

Gottwald, Norman K. *The Tribes of Yahweh: A Sociology of the Religion of Liberated Israel: 1250-1050 B.C.E*. New York: SCM Press, 1980.

Gouel, Joelle. "The Psalmist." in *Les Cahiers Liturgiques, an Introduction to Theopoetic (I)* (1991): 73-85.

Granter, Edward. "Critical Theory and Organization Studies." In *The Oxford Handbook of Sociology, Social Theory, and Organization Studies: Contemporary Currents.* edited by Paul Du Gay Paul Adler, Glenn Morgan and Mike Reed, 534-60. Oxford: Oxford University Press, 2014.

Gray, A. "The Klein Bottle and a Different Klein Bottle." in *Modern Differential Geometry of Curves and Surfaces with Mathematica*, 327-30. Boca Ration, FL: CRC Press, 1997.

Grayson, James Huntley. "A Quarter-Millennium of Christianity in Korea." In *Christianity in Korea*, edited by Robert E. Buswell Jr. and Timothy S. Lee, 7-25. Honolulu, HI: University of Hawaii Press, 2006.

Gregory, Brad S. "Anabaptist Martyrdom: Imperatives, Experience, and Memorization." In *A Companion to Anabaptism and Spiritualism, 1521-1700*, edited by John D. Roth and James M. Stayer, 467-506. Boston: Brill, 2007.

Gresbeck, Heinreich. *False Prophets and Preachers: Henry Gresbeck's Account of the Anabaptist Kingdom of Münster.* Edited by Christopher S. Mackay Kirksville, Missouri: Truman State University Press, 2016.

Greschat, Martin. Martin Bucher: *A Reformers and His Times.* Translated by Stephen E. Buckwalter. Louisville: Westminster John Knox Press, 2004.

Greyerz, Kaspar von. Religion and Culture in Early Modern Europe, 1500-1800. Translated by Thomas Dunlap. Oxford: Oxford University Press, 2008.

Grieser, Dale Jonathan. "A Tale of Two Convents: Nuns and Anabaptists in Münster, 1533-1535." *The Sixteenth Century Journal* 26, no. 1 (1995): 31-47.

Gritsch, Eric W. "Thomas Müntzer and the Origins of Protestant Spiritualism." *MQR* 37 (1963): 172-94.

———. *Reformer without a Church: The Life and Thought of Thomas Müntzer, 1488?-1525.* Fortress Press, 1967.

———. "Thomas Müntzer and Luther: A Tragedy of Errors." In *Radical Tendencies in the Reformation: Divergent Perspectives*, edited by Hans J. Hillerbrand, 55-84. Kirksville, MO: Sixteenth Century Journal, 1988.

_____. *Introduction to Lutheranism*. Minneapolis: Fortress Press, 1994.

_____. *Thomas Müntzer: A Tragedy of Errors*. Minneapolis, MN: Fortress Press, 2006.

Grosheide, Greta. *Bijdrage tot de Geschiedenis der Anabaptisten in Amsterdam*. Hilversum: J. Schipper, Jr, 1938.

Gruchy, John W. de. *Reconciliation: Restoring Justice*. Minneapolis: Fortress Press, 2002.

Gupta, Nijay K. "Mirror-Reading Moral Issues in Paul's Letters." *Journal for the Study of the New Testament* 34, no 34 (2012): 361-81.

Gutierrez, Gustavo. *A Theology of Liberation: History, Politics, and Salvation*: Maryknoll, NY: Orbis Books, 1973.

Haas, Martin. "Der Weg Der Taufer in Die Absonderung." In *Umstrittenes Taufertum, 1525-1975 : New Forschungen*, edited by Hans-Jürgen Goertz, 50-78. Gottingen: Vandenhoeck & Ruprecht, 1975.

Ham, Sok-Hon. *The History of Korea in the Perspective of Meaning*. Seoul: Han Gil Sa, 1983.

Han, Gil-Soo. "Rapid Industrialization, the Birth of Religio-Economic Entrepreneurship, and the Expansion of Christianity in Korea." *Global Economic Review* 24, no. 2 (1997): 51-74.

Han, Gil-Soo, Joy J. Han, and Andrew Eungi Kim. "'Serving Two Masters': Protestant Churches in Korea and Money." *International Journal for the Study of the Christian Church* 9, no. 4 (2009): 333-60.

Han, Ki-Shik. "Underlying Factors in Political Party Organization and Election." *In Korean Politics in Transition*, edited by Edward R. Wright and Cho Suk-Choon, 85-103. Washington: The University of Washington Press, 1975.

Han, Mi-Jun. *The Group Preparing the Future of the Korean Church. A Survey Report of Activities and Beliefs of Korean Protestant Church-Goers*. Seoul: Hanguk Gaeleop, 1999.

Han, Sung-Joo. "Student Activism: A Comparison between the 1960 Uprising and the 1971 Protest Movement." In *Political Participation in Korea: Democracy, Mobilization, and Stability*, edited by Chong Lim Kim, 143-64. Santa Barbara, CA, 1980.

Han, Woo-Keun. *The History of Korea*. Seoul: Elyoo, 1970.
Harder, Leland. *Sources of Swiss Anabaptism: The Grebel Letters and Related Documents*. Vol. 4: Herald Press, 1985.
Harmon, Steven R. *Ecumenism Means You, Too: Ordinary Christians and the Quest for Christian Unity*. Eugene, OR: Cascade Books, 2010.
Hatada, T. A. *History of Korea*. Santa Barbara, CA: ABC Clio Press, 1969.
Haude, Sigrun. "The Rule of Fears: The Impact of Anabaptist Terror, 1534-1535." Ph.D diss.: The University of Arizona, 1993.
_____. *In the Shadow of "Savage Wolves": Anabaptist Münster and the German Reformation During the 1530s*. Leiden: Brill, 2000.
_____. "Anabaptism." In *The Reformation World*, edited by Andrew Pettegree, 237-56. London: Routledge, 2000.
_____. "Gender Roles and Perspective among Anabaptist and Spiritual Groups." In *A Companion to Anabaptism and Spiritualism, 1521-1700*, edited by John D. Roth and James M. Stayer, 425-66. Leiden: Brill, 2007.
Hauerwas, Stanley. *After Christendom? How the Church Is to Behave If Freedom, Justice, and a Christian Nation Are Bad Ideas*. Nashville: Abingdon, 1991.
Hegel, F. G. *The Philosophy of History*. New York: Willey Book Company, 1900.
Heitink, Gerben. *Practical Theology: History, Theory, Action Domains: Manual for Practical Theology*. Grand Rapids: William B. Eerdmans Publishing Company 1999.
Hendrix, Scott. "Martin Luther, Reformer." in Christianity: Reform and Expansion 1500-1660, edited by R. Po-Chia Hsia, 3-19. Cambridge: Cambridge University Press, 2008.
Hillerbrand, Hans J. "Anabaptism and the Reformation: Another Look." *Church History* 29, no. 4 (1960): 404-23.
_____. "The Origin of Sixteenth-Century Anabaptism: Another Look." *Archiv für Reformationsgeschichte* 53, no. 1-2 (1962): 152-80.
_____. *A Fellowship of Discontent: The Stories of Five Dissenting Actors in the Great Drama of Church History*. New York: Harper & Row, 1967.

_____. *The Protestant Reformation*. New York, NY: Harper & Row Publishers, 1968.

_____. "Zwingli's Reformation Turning Point." *Bibliotheque d'Humanisme et Renaissance* 31 (1969): 39-46.

_____. "The Reformation and the German Peasants' War." In *The Social History of the Reformation*, edited by Lawrence P. Buck and Jonathan W. Zophy, 106-36. Columbus: Ohio State University Press, 1972.

_____. *Radical Tendencies in the Reformation: Divergent Perspectives. Sixteenth-Century Essay & Studies*. Vol. 9: Truman State University Press, 1986.

_____. "Was There a Reformation in the Sixteenth Century?" *Church History* 72, no. 03 (2003): 525-52.

_____. *The Division of Christendom: Christianity in the Sixteenth Century*. Louisville, KY:Westminster John Knox Press, 2007.

_____. *A New History of Christianity*. Nashville: Abingdon Press, 2012.

Hinrichs, Carl. *Luther und Müntzer: Ihre Auseinandersetzung über Obrigkeit und Widerstandsrecht. Arbeiten zur Kirchengeschichte*. Vol. 29, Berlin: W. de Gruyter, 1952.

Hoffman, Bengt Runo. Ed. *The Theologia Germanica of Martin Luther. Classics of Western Spirituality*. New York: Paulist Press, 1980.

Holborn, Hajo. *A History of Modern Germany: The Reformation*. Princeton: Princeton University Press, 1959.

Holder, R. Ward. Crisis and Renewal: The Era of the Reformations. Louisville, KY: Westminster John Knox Press, 2009.

Holl, Karl. *Gesammelte Aufsatze Zur Kirchengeschichte*. J.C.B. Mohr, 1923.

_____. "Luther Und Die Schwarmer." in *Gesammelte Aufsatze Zur Kirchengeschichte I: Luther*, 420-67. Tubingen: J.C.M. Mohr, 1932.

Hong, Pan-Sik. "Modern Korean Church Challenged." *Research Journal of Church Affairs 5: What are the Problems with Korean Churches Today?* (1986): 7-14.

Hong, Suhn-Kyoung. "Tonghak in the Context of Korean Modernization." *Review of Religious Research* 10, no. 1 (1968): 43-51.

Horsch, John. "The Rise and Fall of the Anabaptists of Münster." *MQR* 9, no. 2, no. 3 (1935): 92-103, 129-43.

_____. *The Principle of Nonresistance as Held by the Mennonite Church*. Scottsdale AZ: Mennonite Publishing, 1951.

Howard, Tal. "Charisma and History: The Case of Münster, Westphalia, 1534-1535." *Essays in History* 35 (1993): 48-64.

Hoyer, Siegfried. "Lay Preaching and Radicalism in the Early Reformation." In *Radical Tendencies in the Reformation: Divergent Perspectives*, edited by Hans J. Hillerbrand, 85-98. Kirksville, MO: Sixteenth Century Journal, 1988.

Hsia, R Po-Chia. *Society and Religion in Münster, 1535-1618*. Vol. 131: Yale University Press, 1984.

_____. "Münster and the Anabaptists." In *The German People and the German Reformation*, edited by Hsia Po-Chia. Ithaca, 51-69. NY: Cornell University Press, 1988.

_____. Ed. *The German People and the Reformation*. Ithaca, NY: Cornell University Press, 1988.

Hudson-Reed, S. "Sixteenth Century Dutch Anabaptism. A Critical Examination of Its Origins, Basic Principles and Formative Influence." Ph.D diss.: University of Natal, 1989.

Huhtanen, Tiina. *Event of the Radically New: Revelation in the Theology of Walter Kasper*. Helsinki: University of Helsinki, 2016.

Humes, Thomas A. Forsthoefel and Cynthia Ann. Ed. "Introduction: Making Waves." In *Gurus in America*, edited by Thomas A. Forsthoefel and Cynthia Ann Humes, 1-13. Albany: State University of New York Press, 2005.

Hwang, Hong-Eyoul. "Searching for a New Paradigm of Church and Mission in a Secularized and Post-Modern Context in Korea." *International Review of Mission* 92, no. 364 (2003): 84-97.

Hwang, Nam-Duk. "The God of All the Earth: Contextual Theology in a Globalizing World: The Example of Korea." Ph.D diss.: University of Exeter, 2013.

Hwang, Yong-Yeon. "The Person Attacked by the Robbers Is Christ." In *Reading Minjung Theology in the Twenty-First Century: Selected Writings by Ahn, Byung-Mu and Modern Critical Responses*, edited by Kim Yung-Suk and Kim Jin-Ho, 215-31. Eugene, OR: Pickwick Publication, 2013.

Hyun, Young-Hak. "A Theological Look at the Mask Dance in Korea." In *Minjung Theology: People as the Subjects of History,* edited by Commission on Theological Concerns of the Christian Conference of Asia, 47-54. Maryknoll, NY: Orbis Books, 1981.
———. "Incarnation into Minjung and Korean Theology." In *Minjung and Korean Theology,* edited by KNCC Committee of Theological Study, 15-18. Seoul: Korean Theological Study Institute, 1982.
———. "The Cripple's Dance and Minjung Theology." *Ching Feng* 28 (1985): 30-35.
———. "Minjung Theology and the Religion of Han." *East Asia Journal of Theology* 3, no. 2 (1985): 354-59.
———. "Theology with Sweat, Tears and Laughter." *Inter Religio,* no. 7 (1985): 28-40.
———. "Three Talks on Minjung Theology." *Inter Religio,* no. 7 (1985): 2-40.
Ikegame, Jacop Copeman and Aya. Ed. *The Guru in South Asia: New Interdisciplinary Perspectives.* New York, NY: Routledge, 2012.
Irwin, Joyce Louise. "The Theological and Social Dimensions of Thomas Müntzer's Liturgical Reform." Ph.D diss.: Yale University, 1972.
———. Ed. *Womanhood in Radical Protestantism, 1525-1675.* New York: Edwin Mellen Press, 1979.
Isaak, H. "The Struggle for an Evangelical Town." In *The Dutch Dissenters: A Critical Companion to Their History and Ideas,* edited by I. B. Horst, 66-84. Leiden: E.J. Brill, 1986.
Jang, Suk-Man. "Historical Currents and Characteristics of Korean Protestantism after Liberation." *Korea Journal* 44, no. 4 (2004): 133-56.
Jansma, Lammert G. "De Chiliastische Beweging Der Wederdopers (1530-1535)." *Doopsgezinde Bijdragen, NR* 5 (1979): 41-55.
Janz, Denis. Ed. *A Reformation Reader: Primary Texts with Introductions.* Minneapolis, MN: Fortress Press, 1999.
———. "Forward." In *Reformation Christianity,* edited by Peter Matheson, xiii-xvi. Minneapolis, MN: Fortress Press, 2007.

Jelsma, Auke. Ed. *Frontiers of the Reformation: Dissidence and Orthodoxy in Sixteenth-Century Europe* in St Andrews Studies in Reformation History. Aldershot, UK: Ashgate, 1998.

Jeremias, Joachim. *New Testament Theology*. New York: Scribner, 1971.

Joe, Wanne J. A. *Cultural History of Modem Korea: A History of Korean Civilization*. Edited by Choe Hongkyu A. Seoul: Hollym, 2000.

Joh, Wonhee Anne. *Heart of the Cross: A Postcolonial Christology*. Louisville, KY: Westminster John Knox Press, 2006.

Jones, Rufus M. *Studies in Mystic Religion*. London: MacMillan, 1909.

Jordan, June. "Poem for South African Women." in *Passion: New Poems 1977-1980*, 42. Boston: Beacon Press (1980).

Josipovic, Mario and William McNiel. "Thomas Müntzer as 'Disturber of the Godless': A Reassessment of His Revolutionary Nature." *MQR* 70, no. 4 (1996): 431-47.

Jung, Mu-Sung. "Toward a Theology of Pareo Dei: Exploring a Contextual Theology of Mission Dei for the Missiological Reconciliation of the Korean Protestant Church." Ph.D diss.: Asbury Theological Seminary, 2012.

Kalilombe, Patrick A. "A Malawian Example: The Bible and Non-Literate Communities." In *Voices from the Margin: Interpreting the Bible in the Third World*, edited by R. S. Sugirtharajah, 442-53. Maryknoll, NY: Orbis Books, 2006.

Kang, Man-Gil. *Modern History in Korea*. Seoul: Changjak kwua Beepyung Sa, 1984

_____. "Contemporary Nationalist Movements and the Minjung." In *South Korea's Minjung Movement: The Culture and Politics of Dissidence*, edited by Kenneth M. Wells, 31-38. Honolulu: University of Hawaii Press, 1995.

Kang, Won-Don. "Discovering the Reality of the Minjung and a Search for Our Own." In *The Development of Korean Minjung Theology in the 1980s*, edited by Korea Theological Study Institute, 256-98. Seoul: Korea Theological Study Institute, 1990.

Kang, Wi-Jo. "Belief and Political Behavior in Chondogyo." *Review of Religious Research* 10, no. 1 (1968): 38-43.

_____. "Indigenous Tradition of Korean Religions." *Theological*

Forum 14 (1980).
———. *Christ and Caesar in Modern Korea: A History of Christianity and Politics*. Albany: State University of New York, 1997.
Kasper, Walter. *Jesus the Christ*. London: Burns & Oates, 1976.
———. *Der Gott Jesu Christi*. Freiburg: Herder, 2008.
Kautsky, Karl. *Communism in Central Europe in the Time of the Reformation*. London: Fisher and Unwin, 1897.
Kitamori, Kazoh. *Theology of the Pain of God*. 5th rev. Tokyo: Shinkyo Shuppansha, 1958.
Kern, Thomas. "Cultural Performance and Political Regime Change." *Sociological Theory* 27, no. 3 (2009): 291-316.
Kerssenbroch, Hermann Von. *Anabaptistici Furoris Monasterium Incliatm Westphaliae Metropolim Evertentis Historica Narratio*. Edited by Heinrich Detmer. Münster: Theissing, 1899/1900.
———. *Narrative of the Anabaptist Madness: The Overthrow of Münster, the Famous Metropolis of Westphalia*. 2 Vols. Translated with Introduction by Christopher S. Mackay. Leiden: Brill, 2007.
Kim, Andrew Eun-Gi. "South Korea." In *Christianities in Asia*, edited by Peter C. Phan, 217-32. Hoboken, NJ: Wiley-Blackwell Publishing Ltd., 2011.
Kim, Byong-Suh. "The Explosive Growth of the Korean Church Today: A Sociological Analysis." *International Review of Mission* 64, no. 293 (1985): 61-74.
Kim, Chang-Kyu. *Balthasar Hubmaier's Doctrine of Salvation in Dynamic and Relational Perspective*. Eugene, OR: Pickwick Publications, 2013.
Kim, Chin-Bong. "Resistance Movements of Peasants." In *History of Korea*, edited by Kulsa Pyoncha Wiwonhoe, 78-152. Seoul: Kuksa Pyonchan Wiwonhoe, 1981.
Kim, Chun-Hyong. *A Study of Sajok in Tansong During the Late Choson Period*. Seoul: Asea Munhwasa, 2002.
Kim, Chi Ha. *The Cry of People and Other Poems*. Hayama, Japan: Kanagwa-Ken, 1970.
———. "Declaration of Conscience." *Bulletin of Concerned Asian Scholars* 9 (1977): 8-15.

_____. *The Gold Crowned Jesus and Other Writings*. Maryknoll, NY: Orbis Books, 1978.

_____. "The Dream of Revolutionary Religion." in *Living Theology in Asia*, edited by England Jong, 21-25. Maryknoll, NY: Orbis Books, 1982.

Kim, Chong-Ik Eugene and Kim, Ke-Soo. "The April 1960 Korean Student Movement." *Western Political Quarterly* 17 (1964): 83-92.

Kim, Chang-Nack. "Minjung Theology as a Narrative Theology." *Shinhak Sasang* (1989): 5-24.

_____. "The Significance of Minjung in Doing Theology." In *The Development of Korean Minjung Theology in the 1980s*, edited by The Korea Theological Study Institute, 108-31. Seoul: The Korea Theological Study Institute, 1990.

_____. "Justification by Faith-A Minjung Perspective." *Register* 85, no. 2 (1995): 14-23.

_____. "Korean Minjung Theology: An Overview." *Register* 85, no. 2 (1995): 1-13.

Kim, Dong-Soo. "The Healing of Han in Korean Pentecostalism." *Journal of Pentecostal Theology* 7, no. 15 (1999): 123-39.

Kim, Dong-Kun. "Korean Minjung Theology in History and Mission." *Studies in World Christianity* 2, no. 2 (1996): 167-82.

Kim, Dong-Kun. *The Significance of the Historical Jesus in Contemporary Christologies: European, Latin American and Asian*. New College: Edinburgh University, 1992.

Kim, Duk-Ki. "Understanding the Kingdom of God in the Tension between Aphoristic and Apocalyptic Motifs: Towards a Hermeneutic of Liberation for Minjung Theology." *CTC Bulletin* 23, no. 2 (2007): 73-93.

Kim, Eun-Soo. "Minjung Theology in Korea: A Critique from a Reformed Theological Perspective." *The Japan Christian Review* 64 (1998): 53-65.

Kim, Ee-Kon ""Outcry": Its Context in Biblical Theology." *Interpretation* 42, no. 3 (1988): 229-39.

Kim, Grace Ji-Sun. *Colonialism, Han, and the Transformative Spirit*. NY: Palgrave MacMillan, 2013.

Kim, Hi-Heon. *Minjung and Process: Minjung Theology in a Dialogue with Process Thought.* Bern, Switzerland: Peter Lang AG, 2009.

Kim, Hyung-A. "Minjung Socioeconomic Responses to State-Led Industrialization." In *South Korea's Minjung Movement: The Cultural and Politics of Dissidence,* edited by Kenneth M. Wells, 39-60. Honolulu, HI: University of Hawaii Press, 1995.

Kim, Heung-Su, and Kim Seung-Tae. *History of Korean Christianity after Liberation. Yearbook of Korean Religion.* Seoul: Korea Institute for Religion and Society, 1993.

Kim, Heup-Young. "Toward a Christotao." *Studies in Interreligious Dialogue* 10, no. 1 (2000): 5-29.

———. *Christ and the Tao.* Wipf &Stock Publishers, 2010.

Kim, Il-Mok. "A Critical Analysis of the Relationship between Salvation and Social Justice in the Minjung Theology." Ph.D diss.: Andrew University, 2008.

Kim, In-Su. *A History of the Korean Church.* Seoul: Jangno-shinhak-daehakgyo Chulpanbu, 2002.

Kim, Jae-Joon. "Three Generations of Pastor and Suh, Nam-Dong's Minjung Theology." in *The Complete Works of Kim Jae-Joon,* 167-68. Seoul: University of Hanshin Press, 1992.

Kim, Jin. "Shamanism and the Theology of Han." *Theological Thought* 67 (1989): 984-1019.

Kim, Ji-Chul. "A Critical Observation on Minjung Theology's Bible Reading." *Shinhak Sasang* 69 (1990).

Kim, Jin-Ho. "Minjung as the Subject of History: Reappraisal on 'Minjung' of Minjung Theology." *Theological Thought* 80, no. 1 (1993): 21-47.

———. "The Hermeneutics of Ahn Byung-Mu: Focusing on the Concepts of "Discovery of Internality" and "Otherness of Minjung." In *Reading Minjung Theology in the Twenty-First Century: Selected Writings by Ahn Byung-Mu and Modern Critical Responses,* edited by Kim Young-Suk and Kim Jin-Ho, 25-42. Eugene, OR: Wipf & Stock Publishers, 2013.

Kim, Jin-Ho and Lee, Sook-Jin. "A Retrospect and Prospect on Korean Modernity and Minjung Theology." *The Journal of Theologies and Cultures in Asia* (2002): 157-75.

Kim, Jung-Joon. "God's Suffering in Man's Struggle." in *Living Theology in Asia*, edited by John C. England, 15-21. London: SCM Press, 1981.

―――――. "The Old Testament Foundations of Minjung Theology." in *The Minjung and Korean Theology*, edited by KNCC Committee of Theological Study, 29-57. Seoul: Korea Theological Study Institute, 1982.

Kim, John T. *Protestant Church Growth in Korea*. Ontario: Essence Publishing, 1996.

Kim, Kirsteen. "The Holy Spirit in the World: A Global Conversation." *Anvil* 25, no. 3 (2008): 177-93.

―――――. "Christianity's Role in the Modernization and Revitalization of Korean Society in Twentieth-Century." *International Journal of Public Theology* 4 (2010): 212-236.

Kim, Kyoung-Jae. "Theological Problems of the Korean Church in Tradition." *Theological Thought* 28 (1980): 18-28.

―――――. "Theological Thought of Jook-Jae Suh Nam-Dong." *Theological Thought* 46, no. 3 (1984): 517-35.

―――――. *Christianity and the Encounter of Asian Religions: Method of Correlation, Fusion of Horizons, and Paradigm Shifts in the Korean Grafting Process*. Zoetermeer, Netherlands: Boekencentrum Publishing House, 1994.

Kim, Myoung-Hyouk. "The Concept of God in Minjung Theology and Its Socio-Economico-Historical Characteristics." In *Trend of the Modern Church*, edited by Myoung Hyouk Kim, 250-95. Seoul: Sungkwang Publishing Company, 1987.

Kim, Sang-Il. *Hanism as Korean Mind: An Interpretation of Han Philosophy*. Los Angeles: Eastern Academy of Human Sciences, 1984.

Kim, Se-Yoon. "Is "Minjung Theology" a Christian Theology?" *Calvin Theological Journal* 22, no. 2 (1987): 251-74.

Kim, Sebastian C. H. "The Problem of Poverty in Post-War Korean Christianity: Kibock Sinang or Minjung Theology?" *Transformation* 24 (2007): 43-50.

―――――. *Theology in the Public Sphere: Public Theology as a Catalyst for Open Debate*. London: SCM Press, 2011.

_____. "'Justice and Peace Will Kiss Each Other' (Psalm 85. 10b): Minjung Perspective on Peace-building." *Transformation* 32 (2015): 188-201.
Kim, Sun-Hyuk. *The Politics of Democratization in Korea: The Role of Civil Society*. Pittsburgh: University of Pittsburgh Press, 2000.
Kim, Sun-Joo. *Marginality and Subversion in Korea: The Hong Kyongnae Rebellion of 1812*. Seattle, WA: University of Washington Press, 2007.
_____. "Taxes, the Local Elite, and the Rural Populace in the Chinju Uprising of 1862." *The Journal of Asian Studies* 66, no. 4 (2007): 993-1027.
Kim, Sung-Tae. "Religionists' Participation in the March First Movement and the Role of Christianity." *Journal of the Institute of Korean Church History Studies* 25 (1989): 17-24.
Kim, Sang-Yil. "Hanism: Korean Concept of Ultimacy" *Ultimate Reality and Meaning Toronto* 9, no. 1 (1986): 17-36.
Kim, Tuk-Hwang. *The History of Korean Thought*. Seoul: Hanguk Sasang Yongusa, 1963.
Kim, Yong-Bock. "Historical Transformation, People's Movement, and Messianic Koinonia: A Study of the Relationship of Christian and Tonghak Religious Communities to the March First Independence Movement in Korea." Ph. D. diss.: Princeton Theological Seminary, 1976.
_____. "Theological Tasks of Korean Church in the 80's." *Theological Thought* 28 (1980).
_____. "Korean Christianity as a Messianic Movement of the People." *Minjung Theology* (1981): 80-119.
_____. "Messiah and Minjung: Discerning Messianic Politics over against Political Messianism." In *Minjung Theology: People as the Subjects of History*, edited by The Commission on Theological Concerns of the Christian Conference of Asia, 183-94. Maryknoll, NY: Orbis Books, 1981.
_____. "The Social Biography of Minjung and Theology." In *Minjung and Korean Theology*, edited by Committee of Theological Study of KNCC, 369-89. Seoul: Korea Theological Study Institute, 1982.

———. "Theology and Social Biography of the Minjung." *CTC Bulletin* 5, no. 3 (1984): 66-78.

———. "Minjung Economics: Covenant with the Poor." *The Ecumenical Review* 38, no. 3 (1986): 280-85.

———. "The Bible and the Sociobiography of Minjung." In *The Development of Korean Minjung Theology in the 1980s*, edited by Korea Theological Study Institute, 157-78. Seoul: Korea Theological Study Institute, 1990.

———. *Theology of Indigenization and Minjung Theology*. Seoul: Korean Christian Literature Society, 1992.

———. "Messianic Spirit in the Life of the Minjung and All Living Beings." In *The Life, Legacy and Theology of M. M. Thomas: 'Only Participants Earn the Right to Be Prophets'*, edited by George Zachariah Jesudas M. Athyal, and Monica Melanchthon, 132-38. London and New York: Routledge, 2016.

Kim, Young-Gwan. "Karl Barth's Reception in Korea: An Historical Overview." *Evangelical Review* of Theology 27, no. 1 (2003): 73-85.

Kin, Yong-Choon. *The Chondogyo Concept of Man: An Essence of Korean Thought*. Seoul: Pan Korea Book Corporation, 1977.

Kirchhoff, Karl-Heinz. "Die Belagerung Und Eroberung Münsters 1534/35." *Westfalische Zeitschrift* 112 (1962): 77-170.

———. "Die Taufer Im Münsterland: Verbreitung Und Verfolgung Des Taufertums Im Stift Münster, 1533-1550." *Westfalische Zeitschrift* 113 (1963): 1-109.

———. "Was There a Peaceful Anabaptist Congregation in Münster in 1534?" 44 (1970): 357-70.

———. *Die Taufer in Münster 1534/1535*. Münster: Aschendorfsche Verlagsbuchhandlung, 1973.

———. "Die Endzeiterwartung Der Taufergemeinde Zu Münster 1534/35." *Jahrbuch fur Westfalische Kirchengeschichte* 78 (1985): 19-42.

———. "Das Phanom des Tauferreiches zu Münster, 1534/35." In *Fortschritte der Forschung und Schussbilanz*, edited by Franz

Petri, Peter Scholler and Alfred Hartlieb von Walthor, 277-422. Der Raum Westfalen, Part 1. Münster: Aschendorff, 1989.

Kiwiet, Jan. "The Life of Hans Denck" *MQR* 31 (1957): 227-59.

⎯⎯⎯. "The Theology of Hans Denck" *MQR* 32 (1958): 3-27.

Klaassen, Walter. "Hans Hut and Thomas Müntzer." *Baptist Quarterly* 19, no. 5 (1962): 209-227.

⎯⎯⎯. *Anabaptism: Neither Catholic nor Protestant*. Canterbury: Conrad Press, 1981.

⎯⎯⎯. *Anabaptism in Outline: Selected Primary Sources*. Vol. 3: Scottdale, PA. Herald Press, 1981.

⎯⎯⎯. "Eschatological Themes in Early Dutch Anabaptism." In *The Dutch Dissenters: A Critical Companion to Their History and Ideas*, edited by Irvin Buckwalter Horst, 15-31. Leiden: E.J. Brill, 1986.

⎯⎯⎯. *Anabaptism Revisited: Essays on Anabaptist/Mennonite Studies in Honour of C. J. Dyck*. Scottdale, PA: Herald, 1992.

⎯⎯⎯. *Living at the End of the Ages: Apocalyptic Expectation in the Radical Reformation*. Lantham, MD: University Press of America, 1992.

Klassen, Herbert. "The Life and Teaching of Hans Hut." *MQR* 33, no. 3 (1959): 171-205.

Klassen, Peter James. *The Economics of Anabaptism: 1525-1560*. London, Mouton, 1964.

Kleiner, Juergen. *Korea: A Century of Change. Economic Ideas Leading to the 21st Century* Vol. 6. London: World Scientific, 2001.

Klotzer, Ralf. "The Melchiorites and Münster." In *A Companion to Anabaptism and Spiritualism, 1521-1700*, edited by John D. Roth and James M. Stayer, 217-576. Leiden and Boston: Brill, 2007.

Klueting, Harm. "Problems of the Term and Concept "Second Reformation": Memories of a 1980s Debate." In *Confessionalization in Europe, 1555-1700*, edited by Hans J. Hillerbrand and Anthony J. Papalas John M. Headley, 37-50. New York: Routledge, 2004.

Kluver, Alan R. "Student Movements in Confucian Societies: Remembrance and Remonstration in South Korea." In *Student*

Protest: The Sixties and After, edited by Gerard J. De Groot, 219-31. London: Routledge, 2014.

Knitter, Paul F. *One Earth, Many Religions*. Maryknoll, NY: Orbis Books, 1995.

Ko, Byoung-Chul. "The Religion of the Heavenly Way's Sunday Service in Korea: Its Meaning and Structure." *The Review of Korean Studies* 10, no. 1 (2007): 33-49.

Kobelt-Groch, Marion. "Divara of Haarlem." In *Profiles of Anabaptist Women: Sixteenth-Century Reforming Pioneers*, edited by C. Arnold Snyder and Linda A. Huebert Hecht, 298-304. Waterloo, ON: Wilfried Laurier University Press, 1996.

Kolb, Robert. "The Theologians and the Peasants." Archiv fur Reformationsgeschichte-Archive for Reformation History 69 (1978): 103-31.

———. "Luther on Peasants and Princes." Lutheran Quarterly Review 23 (2009): 125-46.

Kolde, Theodor Hermann Friedrich. "Zum Prozess des Johann Denck und der 'drei gottlosen Maler' von Nürnberg." Kirchengeschichtliche Studien Hermann Reuter zum 70 (1887): 228-50.

Koo, Dong-Yun. "Pneumatologicala Perspectives on World Religions: The Cosmic Spirit and Chi." in *Asian Contextual Theology for the Third Millennium: A Theology of Minjung in Fourth-Eye Formation*, edited by Kim Paul S. Chung, Kyung-Jae and Veli-Matti Kärkkäinen, 165-78. Eugene, OR: Pickwick Publications, 2007.

Koo, Hagen. "Women Factory Workers in Korea." In *Korean Women in Transition: At Home and Abroad*, edited by E. Y. Yu and E. H. Phillips, 103-113. Los Angeles: California State University, 1987.

Koop, Karl. Anabaptist-Mennonite Confessions of Faith: The Development of a Tradition. Kitchener, ON: Pandora Press, 2004.

Koschorke, Klaus, Frieder Ludwig and Mariano Delgado. Ed. A History of Christianity in Asia, Africa, and Latin America, 1450-1990: A Documentary Sourcebook. Grand Rapids: William B. Eerdmans Publishing Company, 2007.

Koyama, Kosuke. "Building the House by Righteousness: The Ecumenical Horizons of Minjung Theology." In *An Emerging Theology in World Perspective: Commentary on Korean Minjung Theology*, edited by and Jose Miguez Bonino Jung Young Lee, 137-152. Mystic, CT: Twenty-Third Publications, 1988.

Krahn, Cornelius. Menno Simons (1496-1561): Ein Beitrag zur Geschichte und Theologie Der Taufgesinnten. Karlsruhe, Baden-Wurttemberg: Heinrich Schneider, 1936.

―――. Dutch Anabaptism: Origin, Spread, Life and Thought, 1450-1600. The Hague: Martinus Nijhoff, 1968.

Kuhler, W. J. Geschiedenis Der Nederlandsche Doopsgezinden in De Zestiende Eeuw. Haarlem, 1932.

Kuhles, Joachim. "Zur Ideologischen Differenzierung Der Reformatorischen Bewegung Im Ostbaltikum." In *Weltwirkungen Der Reformation*, edited by Steinmetz and Brendler, 377-90. East Berlin, 1969.

Kumin, Beat A. Reformations Old and New: Essays on the Socio-Economic Impact of Religious Change, c. 1470-1630. Routledge, 1996.

Kung, Hans. Does God Exist? Garden City: Doubleday Company, 1978.

Kuratsuka, Taira. "Gesamtgilde und Taufer: Der Radikalisierungs-prozess in der Reformation Münsters: Von der Reformatorischen Bewegung zum Tauferreich 1533/1534." Archiv fur Reformations-geschichte 76 (1985).

Kurtz, Lester R. The Politics of Heresy: The Modernist Crisis in Roman Catholicism. Los Angelis, CA: University of California Press, 1986.

Küster, Volker. "Minjung Theology and Minjung Art." Mission Studies 11, no. 1 (1994): 108-39.

―――. A Protestant Theology of Passion: Korean Minjung Theology Revisited. Vol. 4: Brill, 2010.

Kwok, Pui-Lan. Discovering the Bible in the Non-Biblical World. Maryknoll, NY: Orbis Books, 1995.

Kwon, Jin-Kwan. "The Emergence of Minjung as the Subjects of History: A Christian Political Ethic in the Perspective of Minjung Theology." Ph.D diss.: Drew University, 1990.

———. "A Preliminary Sketch for a New Minjung Theology." Madang: Journal of Contextual Theology 1, no. 1 (2004): 49-68.

———. "Is the Minjung Theology Still Relevant?" Theological Forum 52 (2008): 59-77.

———. "Minjung (the Multitude) Historical Symbol of Jesus Christ." Asian Journal of Theology 24 (2010): 153-71.

———. "The Subjecthood of Minjung in History through Han, Dan, and Event." Madang: Journal of Contextual Theology 16 (2011): 55-68.

Kyle, Richard G. The Last Days Are Here Again: A History of the End Times. Ada: Baker Books, 1998.

Ladd, George Eldon. A Theology of the New Testament. Revised ed. Grand Rapids, MI: William B. Eerdmans Publishing Company, 1993.

Laubach, Ernst. "Reformation und Tauferherrschaft." In Geschichte der Stadt Münster, edited by Franz-Josef Jakobi, 28-31. Münster, 1993.

Laube, Adolf. "Radicalism as a Research Problem in the History of the Early Reformation." In Radical Tendancies in the Formation: Divergent Perspectives, edited by Hans J. Hillerbrand, 128-41. Kirksville, Mo.: Sixteenth Century Journal, 1988.

Lee, Archie C. C. "Cross-Textual Hermeneutics and Identity in Multi-Scriptural Asia." In Christian Theology in Asia, edited by Sebastian C. H. Kim, 179-204, Cambridge: Cambridge University Press, 2008.

Lee, Byung-Ohk. Listening to the Neighbour: From a Missional Perspective of the Other. Eugene, OR: Pickwick Publications, 2015.

Lee, Chong-Sik. The Politics of Korean Nationalism. Berkeley: University of California Press, 1963.

———. "Historical Setting." In South Korea: A Country Study, edited by Andrea Matles Savada and William Shaw, 1-66. Washington, DC: Federal Research Division Library of Congress, 1992.

Lee, Gi-Baik. A New History of Korea. Translated by Edward W. Wagner. Seoul: Ilchokak, 1984.

Lee, Hong-Jei. "The Comparative Study of the Christology in Latin American Liberation Theology and Korean Minjung Theology." Ph.D diss.: The University of Glasgow, 1990.
Lee, Hong-Jung. "I Am at the Mercy of the Rats: Christological Images in Korean Folklore." *Studies in the Intercultural History of Christianity* (2000): 41-54.
Lee, Hyun-Hoon, Lee, Min-Soo and Park, Dong-Hyun. "Growth Policy and Inequality in Developing Asia: Lesson from Korea." ERIA Discussion Paper Series (2012): 1-30.
Lee, Jae-Hoon. *The Exploration of the Inner Wounds-Han*. American Academy of Religion Series. Atlanta, Georgia: Scholars Press, 1994.
Lee, Jae Won. *Paul and Politics of Difference: A Contextual Study of the Jewish-Gentile Difference in Galatians and Romans*. Cambridge: James Clarke & Co, 2014.
Lee, Jung Young. *The Theology of Change: A Christian Concept of God in an Eastern Perspective*. Maryknoll, NY: Orbis books, 1979.
_____. "Minjung Theology: A Critical Introduction." In *An Emerging Theology in WorldPerspective: Commentary on Korean Minjung Theology*, edited by Jung Young Lee, 3-34. Mystics: Twenty-Third Publications, 1988.
_____. "The Perfect Realization of Change: Jesus Christ." In *Asian Faces of Jesus*, edited by R. S. Sugirtharajah, 62-74. London: SCM Press, 1993.
Lee, Moon-Jang. "The Historical Jesus and Mokmin Hermeneutics with Reference to the Description of Jesus in Minjung Theology in Korea." Ph.D diss.: The University of Edinburgh, 1996.
_____. "Asian Biblical Interpretation." In *Dictionary for Theological Interpretation of the Bible*, edited by Kevin J. Vanhoozer, 68-71. Grand Rapids, MI: Baker Academic, 2005.
Lee, Nam-Hee. *The Making of Minjung: Democracy and the Politics of Representation in South Korea*. Ithaca: Cornell University Press, 2007.
Lee, Sang-Bok. "A Comparative Study between Minjung Theology and Reformed Theology from a Missiological Perspective." Ph.D diss.: Reformed Theological Seminary, 1993.

Lee, Sang-Hyun. *Essays on Korean Heritage and Christianity.* Association of Korean Christian Scholars in North America, 1984.

Lee, Soon-Chul and Shin, Jin-Young. *A Short History of the Donghak Peasant Revolution.* Translated by Rohini Singh and Chongmin Lee. Seoul: Donghak Peasant Revolution Memorial Association, 2008.

Lee, Sang-Taek. *Religion and Social Formation in Korea: Minjung and Millenarianism.* New York: Mouton de Gruyter, 1996.

Lee, Timothy S. "Political Factor in the Rise of Protestantism in Korea: Protestantism and the 1919 March First Movement." *Church History* 69, no. 1 (2000): 116-42.

_____. "What Should Christians Do About a Shaman-Progenitor?: Evangelicals and Ethnic Nationalism in South Korea." *Church History* 78, no. 1 (2009): 66-98.

_____. *Born Again: Evangelicalism in Korea.* Honolulu: University of Hawaii Press, 2010.

Lee, Yeong-Mee "A Political Reception of the Bible: Korean Minjung Theological Interpretation of the Bible." *SBL Forum*, 2005. Online: http://sbl-site.org/Article.aspx?ArticleID=457/

Lee, Young-Ho. "The Socioeconomic Background and the Growth of the New Social Forces of the 1894 Peasant War." *Korea Journal* 34, no. 4 (1994): 90-100.

Lee, Young-Hoon. *The Holy Spirit Movement in Korea: Its Historical and Theological Development.* Oxford: Regnum Books International, 2009.

Lee, Yvonne Young-Ja. "A Theological Reflection on the Korean People's Han and Hanpuri." In *Living Stones in the Household of God: The Legacy and Future of Black Theology*, edited by Linda E. Thomas, 158-68. Minneapolis, MN: Fortress Press, 2004.

Leedy, Paul D. *Practical Research: Planning and Design.* 11th ed. Boston: Person Education Limited, 2015.

Leggett, Chris. "Korea's Divergent Industrial Relations." *New Zealand Journal of Industrial Relations* 22, no. 1 (1997): 64-76.

Lerner, Robert E. *The Powers of Prophecy: The Cedar of Lebanon Vision from the Mongol Onslaught to the Dawn of the Enlightenment.* Berkeley, CA: University of California Press, 1983.
Lew, Young-Ick. "The Conservative Character of the 1894 Tonghak Peasant Uprising: A Reappraisal with Emphasis on Chon Pong-Jun's Background and Motivation." *The Journal of Korean Studies* 7 (1990): 149-80.
Lie, John. *Han Unbound: The Political Economy of South Korea.* Stanford: Stanford University Press, 1998.
Liechty, Daniel. Ed. *Early Anabaptist Spirituality: Selected Writings.* New York: Paulist Press, 1994.
Lienhard, Marc. Ed. *The Origins and Characteristics of Anabaptism.* The Hague: Nijhoff, 1977.
Light, I. H., and E. Bonacich. *Immigrant Entrepreneurs: Koreans in Los Angeles, 1965-1982.* Berkeley: University of California Press, 1988.
Lindberg, Carter. "Theology and Politics: Luther the Radical and Müntzer the Reactionary." *Encounter* 37 (1976): 356-71.
_____. "Conflicting Models of Ministry: Luther, Karlstadt, and Müntzer." *Concordia Theological Quarterly* 41, no. 4 (1977): 35-50.
_____. *The Third Reformation?: Charismatic Movement and the Lutheran Tradition.* Macon, Georgia: Mercer University Press, 1983.
_____. "Luther's Critique of the Ecumenical Assumption That Doctrine Divides but Service Unites." *Journal of Ecumenical Studies* 27, no. 4 (1990): 679-96.
_____. "Müntzeriana" *Lutheran Quarterly Review* 4 (1990): 195-214.
_____. *The European Reformations.* 2nd ed. Oxford: Blackwell, 1996.
_____. "Eschatology and Fanaticism in the Reformation Era: Luther and the Anabaptists." *Concordia Theological Quarterly* 64, no. 4 (2000): 259-78.
Lischer, R. *Marx and Theilhard.* NY, Maryknoll: Orbis Books, 1979.
Littell, Franklin H. "Spiritualizers, Anabaptists, and the Church." *MQR* 29 (1955): 34-43.
_____. *The Anabaptist View of the Church: A Study in the Origins of Sectarian Protestantism.* Boston: Starr King Press, 1958.

Lochman, Jan. Milic. *Reconciliation and Liberation: Challenging a One-Dimensional View of Salvation.* Translated by David Lewis. Philadelphia: Fortress Press, 1980.

Loewen, Harry. *Luther and the Radicals: Another Look at Some Aspects of the Struggle between Luther and the Radical Reformers.* Waterloo, Ontario: Wilfrid Laurier University Press, 1974.

———. "Luther and Müntzer: Unity of Opposites." In *Unity in Diversity*, edited by Nicolas A. Nyiri and Rod Preece, 159-80. Waterloo, Ontario: Wilfrid Laurier University Press, 1977.

———. *Ink against the Devil: Luther and His Opponents.* Waterloo, Ontario: Wilfrid Laurier University Press, 2015.

Lohmann, Annemarie. *Zur Geistigen Entwicklung Thomas Müntzers.* Leipzig, 1931.

Lohse, Bernhard. "Luther Und Müntzer," in *Luther*. Zeitschrift Der Luther-Gesellschaft, 12-32. Gottingen, 1974.

Lortz, Joseph. *The Reformation in Germany.* Translated by Ronald Walls. New York: Herder and Herder, 1968.

Loserth, Johann. Doctor Balthasar Hubmaier und die Anfänge der Wiedertaufe in Mahren Brunn, 1893.

Loserth, Johann and Robert Friedmann. "Hans Hut," in *Mennonite Encyclopedia* (1956): 846-50.

Louie, Miriam Ching Yoon. "Minjung Feminism: Korean Women's Movement for Gender and Class Liberation." In *Cultural Studies: From Theory to Action*, edited by B. G. Smith, 382-96. Oxford: Blackwell Publishing, 2005.

Loffler, Paul. "The Reign of God Has Come in the Suffering Christ: An Exploration of the Power of the Powerless." *International Review of Mission* 68 (1979): 109-14.

Luther, Martin. *Luther's Work, Vol. 43.* Edited by Jaroslav Jan Pelikan, Hilton C. Oswald and Helmut T. Lehmann. Philadelphia: Fortress Press, 1959.

MacCulluch, Diarmaid. *Reformation: Europe's House Divided 1490-1700.* London: Penguin Books, 2003.

MacDonald, C. A. *Korea: The War Before Vietnam.* London: Macmillan, 1986.

MacGregor, Kirk R. *A Central European Synthesis of Radical and*

Magisterial Reform: The Sacramental Theology of Balthasar Hubmaier. Lanham: University Press of America, 2006.

Mackay, Christopher S. "General Introduction," in *Narrative of the Anabaptist Madness: The Overthrow of Münster, the Famous Metropolis of Westphalia*, 1-64. Leiden: Brill, 2007.

_____. "Introduction," in *False Prophets and Preachers: Henry Gresbeck's Account of the Anabaptist Kingdom of Münster*, 1-48: Kirksville, Missouri: Truman State University Press, 2016.

Marx, Karl. "Theses on Feuerbach." In *The Marx-Engels Reader*, edited by Robert C. Tucker, 143-45. New York: W. W. Norton & Company, 1978.

Marx, Karl and Friedrich Engels. *Collected Works. Vol. 4*, London: Lawrence & Wishart, 1975.

Massey, James. "A Theology of Justice, Peace and Life: From the Perspective of Dalit and Minjung." *Madang* 16 (2011): 11-34.

Matheson, Peter. *The Collected Works of Thomas Müntzer*. Edinburgh, Scotland: T & T Clark, 1988.

_____. "The Hammer, the Sickle and the Rainbow: Sixteenth-Century Radicalism and Its Interpreters." *Theology* 93, no. 751 (1990): 20-6.

_____. "Thomas Müntzer's Marginal Comments on Tertullian." *Journal of Theological Studies* 41 (1990): 76-90.

_____. *A People's History of Christianity*. Reformation Christianity. Vol. 5, Minneapolis: Fortress Press, 2007.

_____. "Review Essay: Recent German Research on Thomas Müntzer." *MQR* 86 (2012): 97-109.

McDaniel, Charles A. "Violent Yearnings for the Kingdom of God: Münster's Militant Anabaptism." in *Belief and Bloodshed: Religion and Violence across Time and Tradition*, edited by Jr. James K. Wellman. Lanham, 63-79. Maryland: Rowman & Littlefield Publishers, 2007.

McGrath, Alister E. *The Intellectual Origins of the European Reformation*. Oxford: Blackwell Published Ltd., 1987.

_____. *Historical Theology: An Introduction to the History of Christian Thought*. 2nd edition. John Wiley & Sons, Ltd., 2013.

McLaughlin, R. Emmet. "Schwenckfeld and the Strasbourg Radicals."

MQR 59 (1985): 265-78.

———. "Radicals." In *Reformation and Early Modern Europe: A Guide to Research*, edited by David M. Whitford, 80-120. Kirksville, Missouri: Truman State University Press, 2008.

McLellan, Jaime Lenninger. "Theology of Revolution: Messianic Traditions and the Revolutions They Inspired." MA diss.: The University of Kansas, 2012.

Mecenseffy, Grete. Ed. "Osterreich, I. Teil." *Quellen zur Geschichte der Taufer 11*. Quellen und Forschungen zur Reformationsgeschichte 31. Gutersloh: Gerd Mohn, 1964.

Mellink, A. F. *De Wederdopers in De Noordelijke Nederlanden, 1531-1544*. Groningen: Wolters, 1953.

Metz, Johann-Baptist. "Facing the Jews-Christian Theology after Auschwitz." *Concilium* 175 (1984): 26-33.

———. "The Dangerous Memory of the Freedom of Jesus Christ: The Presence of the Church in Society." In *Love's Strategy: The Political Theology of Johann Baptist Metz*, edited by John K. Downey, 92-101. Harrisburg, PA: Trinity Press International, 1999.

Meusel, Alfred. *Thomas Müntzer Und Seine Zeit*. Berlin: Aufbau-Verlag, 1952.

Meyer, Christian. "Zur Geschichte der Wiedertaufer in Oberschwaben," *Zeitschrift des historischen Vereins für Schwaben und Neuberg* 1 (1874):227–228

Miles, Margaret. *The Word Made Flesh: A History of Christian Thought*. Oxford: Blackwell, 2005.

Miller, Andrew. *Church History*, 2 vols. Germany: GBV, 1994.

Millett, Allan R. "The Korean People: Missing in Action in the Misunderstood War, 1945-1954." in *Korean War in World History*, edited by William Stueck, 13-60. The University Press of Kentucky, 2004.

Min, Anselm Kyong-Suk. "Asian Theologians." In *A New Handbook of Christian Theologians*, edited by Donald W. Musser, 22-48. Nashville: Abingdon Press, 1996.

Min, Kyung-Bae. *History of the Formation of the Korean National Church*. Seoul: Yonsei University Press, 1974.

_____. *Korean History and Christianity*. Seoul: Daehankido-kyochulpansa, 1983.

_____. *Korean Christianity*. Seoul: Sejong-dae-wang-gi-nyeom-sa-eoup-hoe, 1999.

Minns, John. "The Labor Movement in South Korea." *Labor History 81* (2001): 175-95.

Miranda, Jose P. *Marx and the Bible: A Critique of the Philosophy of Oppression*. Translated by John Eagleson. Maryknoll: Orbis Books, 1974.

Mjaaland, Marius Timmann. *The Hidden God: Luther, Philosophy, and Political Theology*. Bloomington, IN: Indiana University Press, 2016.

Moeller, Bernd. *Imperial Cities and the Reformation: Three Essays*. Durham: Labyrinth Press 1972.

Mollat, Michel. *The Poor in the Middle Ages: An Essay in Social History*. Translated by Arthur Goldhammer. New Haven: Yale University Press, 1986.

Molnar, Amedeo. Die Waldenser. Geschichte und Europäisches Ausmass einer Ketzerbewegung. Gottingen, 1980.

Moltmann, Jürgen. *Theology of Hope: On the Ground and the Implications of a Christian Eschatology* New York: Harper and Row, 1967.

_____. *The Future of Hope*. New York: Herder and Herder Press, 1970.

_____. *The Crucified God: The Cross of Christ at the Foundation and Criticism of Christian Today*. London: SCM Press, 1974.

_____. *The Trinity and the Kingdom of God*. London: SCM, 1981.

_____. *On Human Dignity: Political Theology and Ethics*. Translated by M. Douglas Meeks. Philadelphia, PA: Fortress Press, 1984.

_____. *History and the Triune God: Contribution to Trinitarian Theology*. New York: Crossroad, 1992.

_____. *The Spirit of Life: A Universal Affirmation*. London: SCM Press, 1992.

_____. *Experiences in Theology: Ways and Forms of Christian Theology*. Translated by Margaret Kohl. Minneapolis: Fortress, 2000.

_____. *A Broad Place: An Autobiography*. Translated by Margaret

Kohl. London: SCM Press, 2007.
Moon, Cyris Hee-Suk. "An Old Testament Understanding of Minjung." In *Minjung Theology: People as the Subjects of History*, edited by The Commission on Theological Concerns of the Christian Conference of Asia, 119-35. Maryknoll, NY: Orbis Books, 1981.

———. "My People from the Perspective of Micah." In *Minjung and Korean Theology*, edited by Committee of the Theological Study, 104-32. Seoul: Korea Theological Study Institute, 1982.

———. *A Korean Minjung Theology: An Old Testament Perspective*. Maryknoll, NY: Orbis Books and Plough Publications, 1985.

———. "Culture in the Bible and the Culture of the Minjung." *The Ecumenical Review 39*, no. 2 (1987): 180-86.

Moon, Suk-Ho. "Ethics and Christology: A Critical Study of Korean Minjung Theology with Special Reference to Nam-Dong Suh" Ph.D. diss.: University of Stellenbosch, 1998.

Moon, Soon-Tae. "What Is Han?" In *The Stories of Han*, edited by Suh Kwang-Sun, 135-97. Seoul: Boree, 1988.

Moor, Tine De. "The Silent Revolution: A New Perspective on the Emergence of Commons, Guilds, and Other Forms of Corporate Collective Action in Western Europe." *International Review of Social History 53* (2008): 179-212.

Muller, Lydia. *Glaubenszeugnisse Oberdeutscher Taufgesinnter I*. Gutersloh: C. Bertelsmann, 1938.

Mullett, Michael A. *Radical Religious Movements in Early Modern Europe*. Allen & Unwin, 1980.

Myers, Glenn Earl "Thomas Müntzer's Neoplatonic Worldview: The Impact of Rhenish Mysticism Upon His Evangelical Theology, Charismatic Experience, and Revolutionary Activity." Ph.D. diss.: Boston University, 1992.

Na, Yong-Wha. "A Theological Assessment of Korean Minjung Theology." *Concordia Journal 14*, no. 2 (1988): 138-49.

Nafziger-Leis, Cheryl. "Margarethe Pruss of Strasbourg." In *Profiles of Anabaptist Women, Sixteenth-Century Reforming Pioneers*, edited by C. Arnold Snyder and Linda A. Huebert Hecht, 258-72. Waterloo, Ont.: Wilfrid Laurier University Press, 1996.

Nahm, Andrew. *Korea: Tradition & Transformation: A History of the*

Korean People. Seoul: Hollym International Corporation, 1988.
Neff, Christian. "Hofmann, Melchior." In *The Mennonite Encyclopedia II*, edited by Harold S. Bender and Henry C. Smith, 778-85. Scottsdale, Penna.: Herald Press, 1956.
Negru, Catalin. *History of the Apocalypse*. Raleigh, NC: Reason and Religion, 2016.
Niles, D. Preman. "Introduction." In *Minjung Theology: People as the Subjects of History,* edited by the Commission on Theological Concern of the Christian Conference of Asia, 1-11. Singapore: Christian Council of Asia, 1981.
Nipperdey, Thomas. "Theologie und Revolution bei Thomas Müntzer." *Archiv fur Reformationsgeschichte Archive for Reformation History 54* (1963): 145-81.
──────. "Theology and Revolution in Thomas Müntzer." In *The Anabaptists and Thomas Müntzer*, edited by J. M. Stayer and W. O. Packull, 105-17. Dubuque: Kendall, 1980.
Noh, Hong-Sun. *Religion and Just Revolution: Third World Perspective*. Seoul: Voice Publishing House, 1987.
Noh, Jong-Sun. "Donghak and Liberation." *Ching Feng 35* no. 3-4 (1992): 213-37
Noll, Mark A. "Luther Defends Melchior Hofmann." *The Sixteenth Century Journal 4*, no. 2 (1973): 47-60.
Nunez, Emilio A and William T. *Crisis in Latin America*. Chicago: Moody Press, 1989.
Oberman, Heiko A. "The Gospel of Social Unrest: 450 Years after the So-Called "German Peasants' War" of 1525." *Harvard Theological Review 69* (1976): 103-29.
──────. "The Gospel of Social Unrest." In *The German Peasant War of 1525: New Viewpoints*, edited by Bob Scribner and Gerhard Benecke, 39-51. London: Allen & Unwin, 1979.
──────. *Die Reformation: Von Wittenberg nach Genf.* Gottingen, 1986.
──────. *Luther: Man between God and the Devil*. Translated by Eileen Walliser-Schwarzbart. New Haven: Yale University Press, 1989.
Oh, Chae-Suk. *Biographies of Thirty-Three Representatives of the Korean People*. Seoul: Dongban Munhwasa, 1959.

Oh, John Kie-Chiang. *Korea: Democracy on Trial*. Cornell University Press, 1968.

―――――. *Korean Politics: The Quest for Democratization and Economic Development*. Ithaca, NY: Cornell University Press, 1999.

Oh, Jung Sun. *A Korean Theology of Human Nature: With Special Attention to the Works of Robert Cummings Neville and Tu Wei-Ming*. New York: University Press of America, 2005.

Oh, Wha-Chul. "Transforming Han: A Correlational Method for Psychology and Religion." *Journal of Religion and Health* 54 (2015): 1099-1109.

Ojakangas, Mika. *Voice of Conscience: A Political Genealogy of Western Ethical Experience*. London: Bloomsbury, 2013.

Oltmer, Jochen and Anton Schindlung. "Der Soziale Charakter Des Tauferreichs Zu Münster 1534-35. Anmerkungen Zur Forschingslage." *Historisches Jahrbuch 110* (1990): 476-91.

Orevillo-Montenegro, Muriel. *The Jesus from Asian Women*. Maryknoll, NY: Orbis Books, 2006.

Osgood, Cornelius. *The Koreans and Their Culture*. New York: The Roland Press Company, 1951.

Osmer, R & Schweitzer F. *Religious Education between Modernization and Globalization: New Perspectives on the United States and Germany*. Grand Rapid: William B. Eerdmans Publishing Company, 2003.

Oyer, John S. "The Writings of Luther against the Anabaptists." *MQR* 27, no. 2 (1953): 100-110.

―――――. "Anabaptism in Central Germany I: The Rise and Spread of the Movement." *MQR* 34 (1960): 219-48.

―――――. *Lutheran Reformers against Anabaptists; Luther, Melanchthon and Menius and the Anabaptists of Central Germany*. The Hague: Martinus Nijhoff, 1964.

Ozment, Steven. E. *Mysticism and Dissent: Religious Ideology and Social Protest in the Sixteenth Century*. Yale University Press, 1973.

―――――. *The Age of Reform 1250-1550: An Intellectual and Religious History of Late Medieval and Reformation Europe*. London: Yale University Press, 1980.

―――――. *The Reformation in the Cities: The Appeal of Protestantism to*

Sixteenth-Century Germany and Switzerland. New Haven: Yale University Press, 1980.

Packull, Werner O. "Denck's Alleged Baptism by Hubmaier: Its Significance for the Origin of South German-Austrian Anabaptism." *MQR* 47, no. 4 (1973): 327-38.

_____. "Gottfried Seebass on Hans Hut." *MQR* 49 (1975): 57-67.

_____. *Mysticism and the Early South German-Austrian Anabaptist Movement 1525-1531*. Scottdale, PA.: Herald Press, 1977.

_____. "A Response to History and Theology: A Major Problem of Anabaptist Research Today." *MQR* 3 (1979): 208-11.

_____. "'A Hutterite Book of Medieval Origin' Revisited: An Examination of the Hutterite Commentaries on the Book of Revelation and Their Anabaptist Origin." *MQR* 56 (1982): 83-111.

_____. "Melchior Hoffman -a Recanted Anabaptist in Schwabisch Hall?" *MQR* 57, no. 2 (1983): 83-111.

_____. "Melchior Hoffman's Experience in the Livonian Reformation: The Dynamics of Sect Formation." *MQR* 59, no. 2 (1985): 130-46.

_____. "A Reinterpretation of Melchior Hoffman's Exposition against the Background of Spiritualist Franciscan Eschatology with Special Reference to Peter John Olivi." In *The Dutch Dissenters: A Critical Companion to Their History and Ideas*, edited by Irvin Buckwalter Hosrst, 32-65. Leiden: E.J. Brill, 1986.

_____. "In Search of the 'Common Man' in Early German Anabaptist Ideology." *The Sixteenth Century Journal* (1986): 51-67.

_____. "The Sign of Thau: The Changing Conception of the Seal of God's Elect in Early Anabaptist Thought." *MQR* 61, no. 4 (1987): 363-74.

_____. "Melchior Hoffman's First Two Letters." *MQR* 64 (1990): 146-59.

Padgett, Keith Wagner. "Sufferation, Han, and the Blues: Collective Oppression in Artistic and Theological Expression." MA diss.: The Graduate School of the Ohio State University, 2010.

Paek, Se-Myong. *Donghak Thought and Chondogyo*. Seoul: Donghaksa,

1956.

Paik, Jong-Koe. *Constructing Christian Faith in Korea: The Earliest Protestant Mission and Ch'oe Pyon-Hon*. Zoetermeer: Uitgeverij Boekencentrum, 1998.

Paik, L. George. *The History of Protestant Missions in Korea (1832-1910)*. Seoul: Yonsei University Press, 1970.

Pak, A-Ron. "Church Growth Theology, What Is Wrong with It?" *Theological Guidance 199*, no. 9 (1983): 7-40.

Pak, Ung-Kyu. *Millennialism in the Korean Protestant Church*. New York: Peter Lang, 2005.

Palais, James B. "Political Participation in Traditional Korea, 1876-1910." *The Journal of Korean Studies 1* (1979): 73-121.

Palmer, Spencer J. *Korea and Christianity: The Problem of Identification with Tradition*. Seoul: Royal Asiatic Society, 1986.

Panikkar, Raimundo. *The Trinity and the Religious Experience of Man: Icon-Person-Mystery*. Maryknoll, NY: Orbis Books, 1973.

Pannenberg, W. *Basic Questions in Theology, Vol. 1*, Philadelphia: Fortress, 1970.

Park, Andrew Sung. "Minjung Theology: A Korean Contextual Theology." *Indian Journal of Theology 33*, no. 4 (1984): 1-11.

———. "A Theology of the Lament Psalms (I)." *The Theological Thought 48* (1985): 128-47.

———. "Minjung and Pungryu Theologies in Contemporary Korea: A Critical and Comparative Examination." Ph. D. diss.: Graduate Theological Union at Berkely, 1985.

———. "Minjung and Process Hermeneutics." *Process Studies 17*, no. 2 (1987): 118-26.

———. "Theology of Han (the Abyss of Pain)." *Quarterly Review 9*, no. 1 (1989): 48-62.

———. *The Wounded Heart of God: The Asian Concept of Han and the Christian Doctrine of Sin*. Nashville: Abingdon Press, 1993.

———. "The Bible and Han." In *Other Side of Sin: The Woundedness from the Perspective of the*

Sinned-Against, edited by Andrew Sung Park and Susan L. Nelson, 45-60. New York: State University of New York Press, 2001.

———. "Sin." In *Handbook of U.S. Theologies of Liberation*, edited by Miguel A. De La Torre, 110-16. St. Louis: Chalice Press, 2004.

———. "A Life Story Intertwined with Theology." In *Shaping a Global Theological Mind*, edited by Darren C. Marks, 205-13. Burlington, VT: Ashgate, 2008.

Park, Chung-Shin. *Protestantism and Politics in Korea*. Seattle: University of Washington Press, 2003.

Park, Daniel Kwang-Sun. "An Evangelical Evaluation of Munjung Theology in Korea." Th. M. thesis: Fuller Theological Seminary, 1985.

Park, Do-Woong. "Toward an Asian Ecclesiology Based on the Asian Liberation Theology and Minjung Theology." Ph.D. diss.: Drew University, 2008.

Park, Jae-Soon. "Jesus' Table Community Movement and Church." In *Development of Minjung Theology in the 1980s*, edited by Weolyo Sinhak Seodang, 87-120, Seoul: Korea Theological Study Institute, 1992.

———. "Critical Reflection on Christology and the Doctrine of Sin." In *Minjung Theology in Transition*, edited by The Editorial Committee of the Memorial Dissertation for Jukjae Rev. Suh, Nam-Dong, 180-202. Seoul: Korea Theological Study Institute, 1992.

———. *Minjung Theology for the Open Society*. Seoul: Hanul, 1995.

Park, Joon-Suh "God in the Old Testament: God of the Hebrews." In *Minjung and Korean Theology*, edited by KNCC Committee of Theological Study, 133-50. Seoul: Korea Theological Study Institute, 1982.

Park, Mi. *Democracy and Social Change: A History of South Korean Student Movements, 1980-2000*. Oxford: Peter Lang, 2008.

Park, Sang-Yil. *Korean Preaching, Han and Narrative*. New York: Peter Lang, 2008.

Park, Yong-Kyu. *History of the Korean Church 1784-1910*. Seoul: Saengmyeongui Malsseumsa, 2004.

Pater, Calvin. "Melchior Hoffman's Explication of the Songs (!) of Songs." *Archive fur Reformationsgeschichte 68* (1977): 173-91.
Pater, Calvin Augustine. *Karlstadt as the Father of the Baptist Movements: The Emergence of Lay Protestantism.* Toronto: University of Toronto Press, 1984.
Patterson, Thomas C. *Karl Marx, Anthropologist.* Oxford: Berg, 2009.
Payton, James R. *Getting the Reformation Wrong: Correcting Some Misunderstandings.* Downers Grove, IL: IVP Academic, 2010.
Peachey, Paul. "The Radical Reformation, Political Pluralism, and the Corpus Christianum." In *The Origins and Characteristics of Anabaptism,* edited by Marc Lienhard, 10-26. The Hague: Martinus Nijhoff, 1977.
Pearse, Meic. *The Great Restoration: The Religious Radicals of the 16th and 17th Centuries.* Carlisle: Paternoster Press, 1998.
Petersen, Rodney L. *Preaching in the Last Days: The Theme of "Two Witnesses" in the Sixteenth and Seventeenth Centuries.* Oxford: Oxford University Press, 1993.
Phan, Peter C. "Method in Liberation Theologies." *Theological Studies 61,* no. 1 (2000): 40-63.
———. "Whose Experiences? Whose Interpretations? Contribution of Asian Theologies to Theological Epistemology." *Irish Theological Quarterly 71* (2006): 5-28.
Pieris, Aloysius. *Asian Theology of Liberation.* Maryknoll, NY: Orbirs Books, 1988.
Pippin, Robert B. *Hegel's Idealism: The Satisfactions of Self-Consciousness.* Cambridge: Cambridge University Press, 1989.
Pleysier, Albert. *Henry VIII and the Anabaptists.* Lanham, Maryland: University Press of America, 2014.
Preus, James Samuel. *Carlstadt's Ordinaciones and Luther's Liberty: A Study of the Wittenberg Movement, 1521-22.* Cambridge: Harvard University Press, 1974.
Prokhorov, Constantine. "The Münster Tragedy." *Evangelical Journal of Theology 7,* no. 2 (2013): 193-207.
Prophet, Elizabeth Clare. *Maitreya on Initiation: The Coming Buddha Who has Come.* Gardiner, MT: Summit University Press, 2006.
Rahner, Karl. "On the Importance of the Non-Christian Religions for

Salvation." *Theological Investigations* 18 (1983): 288-95.
Rainbow, Jonathan H. *The Will of God and the Cross: An Historical and Theological Study of John Calvin's Doctrine of Limited Redemption.* Eugene, OR: Pickwick Publications, 1990.
Rammstedt, Otthein. *Sekte Und Soziale Bewegung: Soziologische Analyse der Täufer in Münster.* Cologne and Opladen: Westdeutscher, 1966.
Rauschenbusch, Walter. *A Theology for the Social Gospel.* New York: Abingdon Press, 1961.
Rees, David. *Short History of Modern Korea.* Ellan Vannin: Ham Publishing Co., 1988.
Reeves, Marjorie. *The Influence of Prophecy in the Later Middle Ages: A Study in Joachimism.* Oxford: Oxford University Press, 1969.
Reinhard, Wolfgang. *Probleme deutscher Geschichte 1495-1806/Reichsreform Und Reformation 1495-1555.* Stuttgart: Klett-Cotta, 2001.
Reventlow, Henning Graf. *History of Biblical Interpretation, Vol 3: Renaissance, Reformation, Humanism.* Atlanta: Society of Biblical Literature, 2010.
Ricca, Paolo. "The Reformation and Protestantism: An Inventory of the Issue." In *Martin Luther: A Christian between Reformers and Modernity (1517-2017),* edited by Alberto Melloni, 23-42. Berlin: De Gruyter, 2017.
Ritschl, Albrecht. *Geschichte Des Pietismus.* Bonn: Adolph Marcus, 1880.
Roberts, J. Deotis. "Black Theology and Minjung Theology: Exploring Common Themes." In *An Emerging Theology in World Perspective Commentary on Korean Minjung Theology,* edited by Jung Young Lee, 99-105. Mystics, CT: Twenty-Third, 1988.
Robinson, John A. *Honest to God.* London: SCM Press, 2013.
Robinson, Michael E. *Cultural Nationalism in Colonial Korea, 1920-1925.* Seattle: University of Washington Press, 1988.
———. *Korea's Twentieth-Century Odyssey: A Short History.* Honolulu: University of Hawaii Press, 2007.
Roper, Lyndal. "Sexual Utopianism in the German Reformation." *Journal of Ecclesiastical History* 42 (1991): 394-418.

Rosenfeld, Walden Bello and Stephanie. *Dragons in Distress: Asia's Miracle Economies in Crisis.* San Francisco: A Food First Book, 1990.

Rothbard, Murray N. "Karl Marx: Communist as Religious Eschatologist." In *The Review of Austrian Economics,* edited by Murray N. Rothbard, 123-79. Norwell, MA: Kluwer Academic Publishers, 1990.

Rothkegel, Martin. "Anabaptism in Moravia and Silesia." In *A Companion to Anabaptism and Spiritualism 1521-1700,* edited by John Roth and James M. Stayer, 163-210. Leiden: Brill, 2007.

Rothkrug, Lionel. "Icon and Ideology in Religion and Rebellion 1300-1600: *Bauernfreiheit and Religion Royale.*" In *Religion and Rural Revolt,* edited by Janos M. Bak and Gerhard Benecke, 31-61. Manchester University Press, 1984.

Rowland, Christopher. *Radical Christianity: A Reading of Recovery.* Cambridge: Polity Press, 1988.

———. "Apocalypse and Violence: The Evidence from the Reception History of the Book of Revelation." In *Apocalypse and Violence,* edited by Abbas Amanat and John J. Collins, 1-18. New Haven: Yale Center for International and Area Studies, 2004.

Rublack, Ulinka. *Reformation Europe: New Approaches to European History.* Cambridge: Cambridge University Press, 2017.

Ruether, Rosemary. "The Free Church Movement in Contemporary Catholicism." In *New Theology,* edited by Martin E. Marty and Dean G. Peerman, 271-72. New York: Macmillan, 1969.

Rupp, E. Gordon. *Luther Today.* Decorah, Iowa: Luther College Press, 1957.

———. *Patterns of Reformation.* London: Epworth, 1969.

———. *Thomas Müntzer: Prophet of Radical Christianity.* Manchester: The John Rylands Library, 1966.

Ruth, John L. *Conrad Grebel, Son of Zurich.* Scottdale, PA: Herald Press, 1975.

Ryu, Dong-Shik. *Korean Religion and Christianity.* Seoul: The Christian Literature Society of Korea, 1965.

———. "Rough Road to Theological Maturity." In *Asian Voices in Christian Theology*, edited by Gerald H. Anderson, 161-77. Maryknoll, NY: Orbis Books, 1976.

———. *The History and Structure of Korean Shamanism*. Seoul: Yonsei University Press, 1978.

———. *The Mineral Vein of Korean Theology*. Seoul: Jun Mang Sa, 2000.

Ryu, Dae-Young. "Treaties, Extraterritorial Rights, and American Protestant Missions in Late Joseon Korea." *Korea Journal 43*, no. 1 (2003): 174-203.

Saldarini, Anthony J. *Pharisees, Scribes and Sadducees in Palestinian Society: A Sociological Approach*. Wilmington, DE: Glazier, 1988.

Sanders, E. P. *Jesus and Judaism*. Augsburg Fortress, 1985.

Sanders, T.G. *Protestant Concepts of Church and State*. New York, 1964.

Schillebeeckx, Edward. *Christ: The Experience of Jesus as Lord*. New York: Crossroad, 1981.

Schilling, Heinz. "Aufstandsbewegung in der Stadtburgerlichen Gesellschaft des Alten Reiches. Die Vorgeschichte des Münsteraner Tauferreiches. 1525-1534." In *Der Deutsche Baurnkrieg, 1524- 26*, edited by Hans-Ulrich Wehler, 193-238. Gottingen: Vandenhoek & Ruprecht, 1975.

———. "Confessional Europe." In *Handbook of European History, 1400-1600*, edited by Jr. Thomas A. Brady, Heiko A. Oberman, and James D. Tracy, 641-75. Leiden: Brill, 1992.

Schmidt, Heinrich Richard. Reichsstadte, Reich und Reformation. Korporative Reichspolitik 1521-1529/30. Veröffentlichungen des Instituts für Europäische Geschichte Mainz. Vol. 122, Stuttgart: Franz Steiner, 1986.

Schmitt, Carl. *Political Theology: Four Chapters on the Concept of Sovereignty*. Chicago: University of Chicago Press, 1922.

Schornbaum, Karl. Ed. *Quellen zur Geschichte der Wiedertaufer*. Leipzig: M. Heinsius Nachf, 1934.

Schwarz, Reinhard. *Die Apokalyptische Theologie Thomas Müntzers und der Taboriten*. Tubingen: J. C. B. Mohr, 1977.

Scott, Tom. "The Peasants' War: A Historiographical Review: Part 1." *The Historical Journal 22*, no. 3 (1979): 693-720.

_____. "The Peasants' War: A Historiographical Review: Part 2." *The Historical Journal* 22, no. 4 (1979): 953-74.

_____. "The 'Volksreformation' of Thomas Müntzer in Allstedt and Muhlhausen." *Journal of Ecclesiastical History* 34 (1983): 194-213.

_____. *Freiburg and the Breisgau: Town-Country Relations in the Age of Reformation and Peasants' War*. Oxford: Clarendon, 1986.

_____. *Thomas Müntzer: Theology and Revolution in the German Reformation*. London: MacMillan, 1989.

Scott, Tom and Bob Scribner. *The German Peasants' War: A History in Documents*. Atlantic Highlands, N.J.: Humanities, 1991.

Scribner, Bob. "Practical Utopias: Pre-Modern Communism and the Reformation." *Comparative Studies in Society and History* 36, no. 4 (1994): 743-74.

Scribner, Bob and Gerhard Benecke. *The German Peasant War of 1525: New Viewpoints*. London: Allen & Unwin, 1979.

Scribner, Robert W. "Communalism: Universal Category or Ideological Construct?" *The Historical Journal* 37 (1994): 199-207.

_____. *For the Sake of Simple Folk: Popular Propaganda for the German Reformation*. Clarendon Press, 1994.

Seebass, Gottfried. "Müntzers Erbe, Werk, Leben Und Theologie Des Hans Hut." Ph. D. diss.: Heidelberg University, 1972.

_____. "Bauernkrieg und Taufertum in Franken." *Zeitschrift für Kirchengeschichte* 85 (1974): 140-56.

_____. "Peasants' War and Anabaptism in Franconia." In *The Anabaptist and Thomas Müntzer*, edited by Werner O. Packull and James M. Stayer, 154-63. Dubuque, Iowa: Hunt Publishing Company, 1980.

_____. "The Gospel and the Social Order: Luther's Understanding of the Gospel According to His Writings on the Peasants." *Lutheran Theological Journal* 14, no. 3 (1980): 105-13.

_____. "Hans Hut: The Suffering Avenger." In *Profiles of Radical Reformers: Biographical Sketches from Thomas Müntzer to Paracelsus*, edited by Hans-Jürgen Goertz, 54-61. Scottdale, PA: Herald, 1982.

Segundo, Juan Luis. *The Liberation of Theology*. Maryknoll, NY: Orbis

Books, 1976.
Shantz, Douglas H. "Anabaptist Women as Martyrs, Models of Courage, and Tools of the Devil." *Canadian Society of Church History* (2009): 21-34.
Shin, Gi-Wook. "Agrarian Conflict and the Origins of Korean Capitalism." *American Journal of Sociology 103*, no. 5 (1998): 1309-51.
Shorter, Aylward. *Toward a Theology of Inculturation*. Maryknoll: Orbis Books, 1988.
Sin, Gyu-Su and Kim, Woo-Suk. *The Newly Written Modern History of Korea*. Iksan, Korea: Wonkang University Press, 2003.
Smirin, Moises M. *Die Volksreformation des Thomas Müntzer und der Große Bauernkrieg*. 2nd ed. Berlin: Dietz, 1952.
Smithson, Robert Jamieson. *The Anabaptists: Their Contribution to Our Protestant Heritage*. London: James Clarke & Co., 1935.
Snyder, C. Arnold. *The Life and Thought of Michael Sattler*. Scottdale, PA: Herald Press, 1984.
_____. "The Schleitheim Articles in Light of the Revolution of the Common Man: Continuation or Departure?" *The Sixteenth Century Journal 16* (1985): 419-30.
_____. *Anabaptist History and Theology: An Introduction*. Kitchener, Ontario: Pandora Press, 1995.
_____. *From Anabaptist Seed: Exploring the Historical Center of Anabaptist Teachings and Practices*. Intercourse, PA: Good Books, 2007.
Snyder, C Arnold and Hecht, Linda A Huebert. Ed. *Profiles of Anabaptist Women: Sixteenth-Century Reforming Pioneers*. Waterloo, Ont.: Wilfrid Laurier Univ. Press, 1996.
Sobrino, Jon. *Jesus the Liberator: A Historical-Theological View*. Maryknoll, NY: Orbis Books, 1993.
_____. *The Principle of Mercy: Taking the Crucified People from the Cross*. Maryknoll, NY: Orbis Books, 1994.
Son, Yang-Rae. "A Hermeneutical Critique of Minjung Theology." *CTC Bulletin 15*, no. 1 (1998): 87-98.
Song, C. S. "Building a Theological Culture of People." In *An Emerging Theology in World Perspective: Commentary on Korean Minjung Theology*, edited by Jung Young, Lee, 119-34. Mystic,

CT: Twenty-Third Publications, 1988.

———. *Theology from the Womb of Asia*. Maryknoll, NY: Orbis Books, 1986.

———. *Jesus: The Crucified People*. New York: Crossroad Publishing Company, 1990.

Song, Gi-Deuk. "Recent Trends in the Minjung Theology of Prof. Dr. Byung-Mu Ahn: Critical Comments on Prof. Dr. Ahn's New Book, Story of the Minjung-Theology." *Theological Thought* 60 (1988): 127-65.

———. "The Identity of Minjung Theology." *Christian Thought* 33, no. 2 (1988).

Spinks, Bryan D. *Reformation and Modern Rituals and Theologies of Baptism: From Luther to Contemporary Practices*. Burlington, VT: Ashgate Publishing Company, 2006.

Spinoza, B. *The Road to Inner Freedom*. New York: Philosophical Library, 1957.

Stackhouse, Max L. "Public Theology and Ethical Judgment." *Theology Today* 54 (1997): 165-79.

Stalnaker, John C. "Towards a Social Interpretation of the German Peasant War." In *German Peasant War of 1525: New Viewpoint*, edited by Robert W. Scribner and Gerhard Benecke, 23-28. London: Allen & Unwin, 1979.

Stauffer, Ethelbert. "The Anabaptist Theology of Martyrdom." *MQR* 19, no. 3 (1945): 179-214.

Stayer, James, M. "Hans Hut's Doctrine of the Sword: An Attempted Solution." *MQR* 39 (1965): 181-91.

———. "The Münsterite Rationalization of Bernhard Rothmann." *Journal of the History of Ideas* 28, no. 2 (1967): 179-92.

———. "Thomas Müntzer's Theology and Revolution in Recent Non-Marxist Interpretation." *MQR* 43 (1969): 142-52.

———. "Melchior Hoffmann and the Sword." *MQR* 14, no. 3 (1971): 265-77.

———. *Anabaptists and the Sword*. Lawrence, Kansas: Coronado Press, 1972.

———. "Reublin and Brotli: The Revolutionary Beginnings of Swiss Anabaptism." In *The Origins and Characteristics of Anabaptism*, edited by Marc Lienhard, 83-102. The Hague:

Martinus Nijhoff, 1977.

―――. "Oldeklooster and Menno." *The Sixteenth Century Journal* (1978): 50-67.

―――. "Thomas Müntzer's Protestation and Imaginary Faith." *MQR* 55, no. 2 (1981): 99-130.

―――. "The Anabaptists." In *Reformation Europe: A Guide to Research*, edited by Steven Ozment, 135-59. St. Louis, MO: Center for Reformation Research, 1982.

―――. "Davidite vs. Mennonite." In *The Dutch Dissenters: A Critical Companion to Their History and Ideas*, edited by Irvin Buckwalter Horst, 143-59. Leiden: E.J. Brill, 1986.

―――. "Was Dr Kuehler's Conception of Early Dutch Anabaptism Historically Sound? Historical Discussion of Anabaptist Münster 450 Years Later." *MQR* 60, no. 3 (1986): 262-88.

―――. "Anabaptists and Future Anabaptists in the Peasants' War." *MQR* 62, no. 2 (1988): 99-139.

―――. *The German Peasants' War and Anabaptist Community of Goods*. Montreal: McGill-Queen's University Press, 1991.

―――. "Saxon Radicalism and Swiss Anabaptism: The Return of the Repressed." *MQR* 67, no. 1 (1993): 5-30.

―――. "The Radical Reformation." In *Handbook of European History 1400-1600: Late Middle Ages, Renaissance and Reformation*, edited by Heiko A. Oberman, James D. Tracy and Thomas A. Brady, 249-82. Leiden: E. J. Brill, 1995.

―――. "Anabaptists and the Sword Revisited: The Trend from Radicalism to Apoliticism" In *Pacifist Impulse in Historical Perspective*, edited by Harvey L. Dyck, 111-24. Toronto: University of Toronto Press, 1996.

―――. "The Passing of the Radical Moment in the Radical Reformation." *MQR* 71, no. 1 (1997): 147-52.

―――. "A New Paradigm in Anabaptist-Mennonite Historiography?" *MQR* 77 (2004): 297-307.

―――. "The Dream of a Just Society." In *People's History of Christianity: Reformation Christianity, Vol. 5*, edited by Peter Matheson, 191-211. Minneapolis: Fortress Press, 2007.

Stayer, James M, and Werner O. Packull. *The Anabaptists and Thomas Müntzer*. Dubuque, Iowa; Toronto: Kendall/Hunt Publishing Company, 1980.

Stayer, James, M., Werner O. Packull, and Klaus Deppermann. "From Monogenesis to Polygenesis: The Historical Discussion of Anabaptist Origins." *MQR* 59 (1975): 83-122.

Steinmetz, David C. *Luther in Context*. Grand Rapids, MI: Baker Academic, 1995.

Steinmetz, Max. "Über den Charakter der Reformation und des Bauernkrieges in Deutschland." *Wissenschaftliche Zeitschrift Der Karl-Marx-Universitat Leipzig. Gesellschafts und Sprachwissenschaftliche Reihe 14* (1965): 389-396.

_____. "Thomas Müntzer in Der Forschung Der Gegenwart." *Zeits Fur Geschichtswissenschaft 33* (1975): 666-85.

_____. "Theses on the Early Bourgeois Revolution in Germany, 1476-1535." In *The German Peasant War of 1525: New Viewpoints*, edited by Bob Scribner and Gerhard Benecke, 9-22. London: Unwin, 1979.

_____. "Thomas Müntzer in the Research of the Present." In *The Anabaptists and Thomas Müntzer*, edited by J. M. Stayer & W. O. Packull, 133-43. Dubuque, IA: Hunt Publishing Company, 1980.

Stephens, W. P. *The Theology of Huldrych Zwingli*. Oxford: Clarendon Press, 1986.

Stone, Alan. "The Korean Student Revolution: A Political Analysis." In *Occasional Papers on Korea*, edited by James, B. Palas, 132-43. Seattle: University of Washington, Center for Korean Studies, 1974.

Strauss, Gerald. *Luther's House of Learning: Indoctrination of the Young in the German Reformation*. Baltimore: Johns Hopkins University Press, 1978.

Stupperich, Robert. *Das Münsterische Taufertum*. Münster: Aschendorff, 1958.

_____. Ed. *Die Schriften der Münsterischen Taufer und Ihrer Gegner: Die Schriften Bernhard Rothmanns, Vol. 1*. Münster: Aschendorff, 1970.

Sugirtharajah, R.S. *Asian Faces of Jesus*. Maryknoll, NY: Orbis Books, 1993.
Suh, David Kwang-Sun. "Minjung and the Holy Spirit." In *The Minjung and Korean Theology*, edited by Committee of Theological Study KNCC, 302-16. Seoul: Korea Theological Study Institute, 1982.
———. "A Biographical Sketch of an Asian Theological Consultation." In *Minjung Theology: People as the Subjects of History*, edited by The Commission on Theological Concerns of the Christian Conference of Asia, 15-37. Maryknoll, NY: Orbis Books, 1983.
———. "Korean Theological Developments in the 1970s." In *Minjung Theology: People as the Subjects of History*, edited by Yong-Bock Kim, 38-46. Maryknoll, NY: Orbis Book, 1983.
———. *Theology, Ideology and Culture*. Kowloon, Hong Kong: World Student Christian Federation, Asia/Pacific Regional Office, 1983.
———. "'Called to Witness to the Gospel Today': Two Responses from Korea (the Priesthood of Han)." *The Reformation World* 39, no. 4 (1986): 597-607.
———. "Theology by Minjung." In *Reflections on Doing Theology in Community*, edited by Samuel Amirtham and John S. Pobee, , 65-77. Geneva: World Council of Churches, 1986.
———. *A Story of Han*. Seoul: The Borhee Press, 1988.
———. *The Korean Minjung in Christ*. Eugene: Wipf and Stock Publishers, 1991.
———. "Minjung Theology: The Politics and Spirituality of Korean Christianity." In *Perspectives on Christianity in Korea and Japan: The Gospel and Culture in East Asia*, edited by Mark R. Mullins and Richard Fox Yoimg, 143-62. Lewiston, NY: The Edwin Mellen Press, 1995.
———. "Minjung Theology." In *Dictionary of Third World Theologies*, edited by Virginia Fabella and R. S. Sugirtharajah, 143-44. Maryknoll, NY: Orbis Books, 2000.
———. "Foreword." In *A Protestant Theology of Passion: Korean Minjung Theology Revisited*, edited by Volker Küster, x-xviii. Leiden: Brill, 2010.

Suh, Jin-Han. "The Scientific Nature and the Grass-Root Nature of Minjung Theology of the 80s'." In *Korean Church in Travail*, 103-43. Seoul: Center for Studies of Problems in Christianity and Society, 1990.

⎯⎯⎯. "The Rise and Development of Minjung Theology." In *Introduction to Minjung Theology*, edited by The Institute of Minjung Theology, 9-27. Seoul: Hanul, 1995.

Suh, Kyung-Sok. "Crisis of Minjung Theology." *Theological Thought* 82, no. 9 (1993): 187-204.

Suh, Nam-Dong. *Theology at a Turning Point*. Seoul: KTSI, 1976.

⎯⎯⎯. "Historical References for a Theology of Minjung." in *Minjung Theology: People as the Subjects of History*, edited by Kim, Yong Bok, 155-82. Singapore: Commission on Theological Concerns, 1981.

⎯⎯⎯. "Confluence of Two Stories." In *Minjung and Korean Theology*, edited by Committee of Theological Study KNCC, 237-76. Seoul: KTSI, 1982.

⎯⎯⎯. *A Study of Minjung Theology*. Han-Gil-Sa, 1983.

⎯⎯⎯. "Towards a Theology of Han." In *Minjung Theology: People as the Subjects of History*, edited by Christian Conference of Asia Commission on Theological Concerns, 55-69. Maryknoll, NY: Orbis Books, 1983.

⎯⎯⎯. "Missio Dei and Two Stories in Coalescence." in *Asian Contextual Theology for the Third Millennium: A Theology of Minjung in Fourth-Eye Formation*, edited by Veli-Matti Kärkkäinen, Paul Chung, and Kim Kyoung-Jae, 51-68. Eugene: Pickwick Publications, 2007.

Sumner, William Graham. *What Social Classes Owe to Each Other*. New York and London: Harper and Brothers, 1883.

Sunshine, Glenn S. *The Reformation for Armchair Theologians*. Louisville, KY: Westminster John Knox Press, 2005.

Sye, In-Syek Paul. *The Cry of God: The Liberation of the Poor*. Waegwan: Benedict Press, 2001. Tabak, Mehmet. *Dialectics of Human Nature in Marx's Philosophy*. New York: Palgrave Macmillan, 2012.

Tagawa, K. A. *Guy Jesus*. Seoul: Han Gil Press, 1983.

_____. *A Phase of the Primitive Christian Church History.* Gwangju: Sa-Gye-Jul, 1983.
Tappert, Theodore G. Ed. *Selected Writings of Martin Luther: 1523-1526.* Philadelphia: Fortress Press, 1967.
Thiemann, Ronald F. *Constructing a Public Theology: The Church in a Pluralistic Culture.* Louisville: Westminster John Knox, 1991.
Thomas, Keith. *Religion and the Decline of Magic: Studies in Popular Beliefs in Sixteenth and Seventeenth Century England.* London: Weidenfeld and Nicolson, 1971.
Thomas, M. M. *Salvation and Humanisation.* Madras: Christian Literature Society, 1971.
Tinsley, Barbara Sher. *Pierre Bayle's Reformation: Conscience and Criticism on the Eve of the Enlightenment.* London: Associated University Press, 2001.
Tipler, Frank J. "Omega Point as Eschaton: Answers to Pannenberg's Questions for Scientists." *Journal of Religion & Science* 24, no. 2 (1989): 217-53.
Troeltsch, Ernst. *The Social Teaching of the Christian Churches.* New York: The Macmillan Company, 1931.
Vahanian, Gabriel. *Tillich and the New Religious Paradigm.* Colorado: The Davies Group Publisher, 2005.
Vedder, Henry Clay. *Balthasar Hubmaier: Leader of the Anabaptists.* New York: Knickerbocker, 1905.
Verduin, Leonard. "The Chambers of Rhetoric and Anabaptist Origins in the Low Countries." *MQR* 34 (1960): 192-96.
Verheyden, A. L. E. *Anabaptism in Flanders 1530-1650: A Century of Struggle.* Scottdale, PA.: Herald Press, 1961.
Verkuyl, J. *Contemporary Missiology.* Grand Rapids: Eerdmans Publishing Company, 1978.
Vidmar, John. *The Catholic Church through the Ages: A History.* New York: Paulist Press, 2005.
Vischer, Lukas. Ed. *Church History in an Ecumenical Perspective: Papers and Reports of an International Ecumenical Consultation held in Basel October 12-7, 1981.* Bern: Evangelische Arbeitsstelle Oekumene Switzerland, 1982.
Visser, Piet. "Under the Sign of Thau: The Bible and the Dutch Radial Reformation." In *Lay Bibles in Europe 1450-1800*, edited by M.

Lamberigts and A. A. Den Hollander, 97-118. Leuven: Leuven University Press, 2006.

Vogel, Ezra F. *The Four Little Dragons: The Spread of Industrialization in East Asia*. Cambridge, MA: Harvard University Press, 1991.

Vogel, Winfried. "The Eschatological Theology of Martin Luther, Pt 1: Luther's Basic Concepts." *Andrews University Seminary Studies* 24, no. 3 (1986): 249-64.

Vogler, Gunther. "Religion, Confession and Peasants Resistance in the German Territories in the Sixteenth to Eighteenth Century." In *Religion and Rural Revolt*, edited by Janos M. Bak and Gerhard Benecke, 173-87. Manchester: Manchester University Press, 1984.

_____. "The Anabaptist Kingdom of Münster in the Tension between Anabaptism and Imperial Policy." In *Radical Tendencies in the Reformation: Divergent Perspectives*, edited by Hans J. Hillerbrand, 99-116. Kirksville, MO: Sixteenth Century Journal Publishers, 1988.

Von der Lippe, George. *A History of the Münster Anabaptists: Inner Emigration and the Third Reich: A Critical Edition of Friedrich Reck-Malleczewn's Bockelson: A Tale of Mass Insanity*. Translated by Reck-Malleczewen. New York: Palgrave MacMillan, 2008.

Voolstra, Sjouke. *Meno Simmons: His Image and Message*. North Newton, KS: Bethel College, 1997.

Vos, Karel. "De Doopsgezinden Te Antwerpen in De Zestiende Eeuw." *Bulletin de la Commission Royale pour l' Histoire de Belgique* 84 (1920): 311-90.

_____. "Revolutionary Reformation." In *The Anabaptists and Thomas Müntzer*, edited by O Packull and James M. Stayer Werner, 85-91. Dubuque: Kendall, 1980.

Vosloo, R. "Quo Vadis Church History? Some Thesis on the Future of Church History as an Academic Theological Discipline." *Scriptura* 100 (2009): 54-64.

Wainstock, Dennis D. *Truman, Macarthur, and the Korean War*. Westport, CT: Greenwood Press, 1999.

Waite, Gary K. "Spiritualizing the Crusade: David Joris in the Context of the Early Reform and Anabaptist Movements in the

Netherlands, 1524-1543." Ph.D diss.: University of Waterloo, 1986.

———. "David Joris' Thought in the Context of the Early Melchiorite and Münsterite Movements in the Low Countries, 1534-1536." *MQR* 62, no. 3 (1988): 296-317.

———. "From Apocalyptic Crusaders to Anabaptist Terrorists: Anabaptist Radicalism after Münster, 1535-1544." *Archiv fur Reformationsgeschichte-Archive for Reformation History* 80, (1989):173-93.

———. *David Joris and Dutch Anabaptism, 1524-1543*. Waterloo: Wilfrid Laurier University Press, 1990.

———. "Popular Drama and Radical Religion: The Chambers of Rhetoric and Anabaptism in the Netherlands" *MQR* 65 (1991): 227-55.

———. "The Dutch Nobility and Anabaptism, 1535-1545." *The Sixteenth Century Journal* 23, no. 3 (1992): 458-85.

———. "Sixteenth-Century Religious Reform and the Witch-Hunts." In *The Oxford Handbook of Witchcraft in Early Modern Europe and Colonial America*, edited by Brian P. Levack, 485-506. Oxford: Oxford University Press, 2013.

Wallis, Roy. *The Road to Total Freedom: A Sociological Analysis of Scientology*. New York: Columbia University Press, 1977.

Wappler, Paul. *Die Tauferbewegung in Thuringen von 1526-1584*. Jena: Gustav Fischer, 1913.

———. *Thomas Müntzer in Zwickau und die "Zwickauer Propheten."* Gütersloh: Mohn, 1966.

Ware, Kalistos. *The Orthodox Church*. New York: Penguin, 1993.

Wartofsky, Marx W. *Feuerbach*. Cambridge: Cambridge University Press, 1977.

Watt, Jeffrey R. *The Long Reformation*. Boston, MA: Houghton Mifflin, 2006.

Weber, Max. *Economy and Society: An Outline of Interpretive Sociology*. CA: University of California Press, 1978.

Weems, Benjamin B. *Reform, Rebellion, and the Heavenly Way*. Tucson: University of Arizona Press, 1964.

Welch, John Dillenberger and Calude. *Protestant Christianity Interpreted through Its Development*. New York: Charles Scribner's Son, 1958.

Westerholm, S. *Jesus and Scribal Authority*. Coniectanea Biblica New Testament Series 10. Lund:CWK Gleerup, 1978.

White, Hayden. *Tropics of Discourse: Essays in Cultural Criticism*. Baltimore, MD: The Johns Hopkins University Press, 1978.

———. "'Figuring the Nature of the Times Deceased': Literary Theory and Historical Writing." In *The Future of Literary Theory*, edited by Ralph Cohen, 19-43. New York: Routledge, 1990.

Whitehead, Alfred North. *Process and Reality: An Essay in Cosmology*. Edited by David Ray Griffin and Donald W. Sherburne. New York: Free Press, 1978.

Whitford, David M. *Tyranny and Resistance: The Magdeburg Confession and the Lutheran Tradition*. St. Louis: Concordia, 2001.

———. *Luther: A Guide for the Perplexed*. New York, NY: Bloomsbury T&T Clark, 2011.

Wielenga, Bastiaan. "Liberation Theology in Asia." In *The Cambridge Companion to Liberation Theology*, edited by Christopher Rowland, 39-62. Cambridge: Cambridge University Press, 1999.

Wiesner-Hanks, Merry. "Traditional Orthodoxies and New Approaches: An Editor's Perspective on the Oxford Encyclopedia of the Reformation." *Church History* 67, no. 1 (1998): 107-13.

Williams, George Huntston. Ed. *Spiritual and Anabaptist Writers*. Philadelphia, PA: Westminster, 1957.

———. *The Radical Reformation*. London: Weidenfeld and Nicolson, 1962.

———. "German Mysticism in the Polarization of Ethical Behaviour in Luther and the Anabaptists." *MQR* 48 (1974): 275-304.

———. *The Radical Reformation*. 3rd ed. Kirksville, MO: Sixteenth Century Journal Publishers, 1992.

Williamson, Darrent T. "For the Honour of God and to Fulfil His Will: The Role of Polygamy in Anabaptist Münster." *Restoration Quarterly* 42 (2000): 27-38.

———. "Erasmus of Rotterdam's Influence Upon Anabaptism: The Case of Balthasar Hubmaier." Ph.D. diss.: Simon Fraser University, 2005.

Wilson, Edmund. *To the Finland Station: A Study in the Writing and Acting of History*. New York: Farrar, Straus & Giroux, 1972.

Wilson, Jonathan R. "Clarifying Vision, Empowering Witness." In *What Does It Mean to Be Saved? Broadening Evangelical Horizons of Salvation*, edited by John G. Stackhouse Jr., 185-94. Grand Rapids, MI: Baker Academic, 2002.

Woo, Jong-Seok. *Security Challenges and Military Politics in East Asia: From State Building to Post Democratization*. New York: Bloomsbury Academic, 2011.

Worth, Roland H. *Messianic Movements through 1899*. Jefferson, NC: McFarland & Company, Inc., 2005.

Wray, Frank J. "Bernhard Rothmann's Views on the Early Church." In *Reformation Studies: Essays in Honour of Roland H. Bainton*, edited by Franklin H. Littell, 229-38. Richmond, Virginia: John Knox Press, 1962.

Wriedt, Markus. "Luther's Concept of History and the Foundation of an Evangelical Identity." In *Protestant History and Identity in Sixteenth Century Europe*, edited by Bruce Gordon, 31-45. Aldershot: Scolar Press, 1996.

Wyman Jayson A. "Interpreting the History of the Workgroup on Constructive Theology." *Theology Today* (2017): 312-24.

Wyntjes, Sherrin Marshall. "Women in the Reformation Era." In *Becoming Visible: Women in European History*, edited by Renate Bridenthal and Claudia Koontz, 165-91. Boston: Houghton, 1977.

Yagi, Seiichi. "I in the Word of Jesus." In *The Myth of Christian Uniqueness: Toward a Pluralistic Theology of Religions*, edited by John Hick and Paul F. Knitter, 117-36. Eugene, OR: Wipf and Stock Publishers, 1987.

Yap, Kim Hao. Ed. *Asian Theological Reflections on Suffering and Hope*. Singapore: Christian Conference of Asia, 1977.

Yewangoe, Andreas Anagguru. *Theologia Crucis in Asia: Asian Christian Views on Suffering in the Face of Overwhelming Poverty and Multifaceted Religiosity in Asia.* Amsterdam: Rodopi, 1987.

Yi, Chi-Ho. *Korea: Its Land, People, and Culture of All Ages.* Seoul: Hakwon-sa, 1960.

Yi, Man-Yeol. *Korean Christianity and National Consciousness.* Seoul: Jisiksaneopsa, 2000.

Yim, Tae-Soo. *Minjung Theology for the Second Reformation.* Seoul: The Christian Literature Society of Korea, 2002.

———. "Reflection on Minjung Theology: Messianism and a New Understanding of Minjung-Messianism" In *Dalit and Minjung Theologies: A Dialogue,* edited by Samson Prabhakar and Jinkwan Kim, 135-47. Bangalore, India: BTESSC/SATHRI, 2006.

Yoder, John H. "The Turning Point in the Zwinglian Reformation." *MQR* 32 (1958): 128-40.

———. "A Summary of the Anabaptist Vision." In *An Introduction to Mennonite History: A Popular History of the Anabaptists and the Mennonites,* edited by Cornelius J. Dyck, 103-11. Scottdale, PA: Herald Press, 1967.

———. "Der Kristallisationspunkt Des Taufertums" *Mennonitische Geschichtsblätter* 29 (1972): 35-47.

———. *The Priestly Kingdom: Social Ethics as Gospel.* Notre Dame: University of Notre Dame Press, 1984.

Yoo, Boo-Woong. *Korean Pentecostalism: Its History and Theology.* New York: Peter Lang, 1988.

Yoo, Yani. "Han-Laden Women: Korean 'Comfort Women' and Women in Judges 19-21." *Semeia* 78 (1997): 37-46.

Young, Carl F. "Tonghak and Son Pyeong-Hui's Early Leadership, 1899-1904." *Review of Korean Studies* 5, no. 1 (2002): 63-83.

———. "The 1894 Tonghak Rebellion." In *Routledge Handbook of Modern Korean History,* edited by Michael J. Seth, 95-108. London: Routledge, 2016.

Yun, Kyong-No. *A Christian Understanding of Modern Korean History.* Seoul: Yokminsa, 1997.

Zeman, Z. K. *The Anabaptist and the Czech Brethren in Moravia 1526-1628: A Study of Origins and Contacts.* The Hague: Mouton Press, 1969.

———. Jarold Knox. "Anabaptism: A Replay of Medieval Themes or a Prelude to the Modern Age." *MQR* 50 (1976): 259-71.

Zietlow, Paul H. "Martin Luther's Arguments for Infant Baptism." *Concordia Journal* 20, no. 2 (1994): 147-71.

Zschabitz, Gerhard. Zur mitteldeutschen Wiedertäuferbewegung nach dem grossen Bauernkrieg. Berlin: VEB Rutten & Loenig, 1958.

www.ingramcontent.com/pod-product-compliance
Lightning Source LLC
Chambersburg PA
CBHW052111010526
44111CB00036B/1652